Heirs of Oppression

Studies in Social, Political, and Legal Philosophy

Series Editor: James P. Sterba, University of Notre Dame

This series analyzes and evaluates critically the major political, social, and legal ideals, institutions, and practices of our time. The analysis may be historical or problem-centered; the evaluation may focus on theoretical underpinnings or practical implications. Among the recent titles in the series are:

Gewirth: Critical Essays on Action, Rationality, and Community
    edited by Michael Boylan,
The Idea of a Political Liberalism: Essays on Rawls
    edited by Victoria Davion and Clark Wolf
Self-Management and the Crisis of Socialism: The Rose in the Fist of the Present
    by Michael W. Howard
Ecofeminist Philosophy: A Western Perspective on What It Is and Why It Matters
    by Karen J. Warren
Controversies in Feminism
    edited by James P. Sterba
Faces of Environmental Racism: Confronting Issues of Global Justice, Second Edition
    edited by Laura Westra and Bill Lawson
Theorizing Backlash: Philosophical Reflections on the Resistance to Feminism
    by Anita M. Superson and Ann E. Cudd
Just Ecological Integrity: The Ethics of Maintaining Planetary Life
    edited by Peter Miller and Laura Westra
*American Heat: Ethical Problems with the United States' Response
to Global Warming*
    by Donald A. Brown
Exploitation: What It Is and Why It's Wrong
    by Ruth J. Sample
Putting Humans First: Why We Are Nature's Favorite
    by Tibor R. Machan
Linking Visions: Feminist Bioethics, Human Rights, and the Developing World
    edited by Rosemarie Tong, Anne Donchin, and Susan Dodds
Moral Vision: How Everyday Life Shapes Ethical Thinking
    by Duane L. Cady
Ethics for Disaster
    by Naomi Zack
Heirs of Oppression
    by J. Angelo Corlett

Heirs of Oppression

J. Angelo Corlett

ROWMAN & LITTLEFIELD PUBLISHERS, INC.
Lanham • Boulder • New York • Toronto • Plymouth, UK

Published by Rowman & Littlefield Publishers, Inc.
A wholly owned subsidiary of The Rowman & Littlefield Publishing Group, Inc.
4501 Forbes Boulevard, Suite 200, Lanham, Maryland 20706
http://www.rowmanlittlefield.com

Estover Road, Plymouth PL6 7PY, United Kingdom

British Library Cataloguing in Publication Information Available

Library of Congress Cataloging-in-Publication Data

Corlett, J. Angelo, 1958–
  Heirs of oppression / J. Angelo Corlett.
    p.   cm.
  Includes bibliographical references (p.   ) and index.
  ISBN 978-1-4422-0814-8 (cloth : alk. paper)
  ISBN 978-1-4422-0815-5 (pbk. : alk. paper)
  ISBN 978-1-4422-0816-2 (electronic)
    1. African Americans—Reparations.   2. Indians of North America—Reparations.
  3. Reparations for historical injustices—United States.   4. Race discrimination—
  United States—History.   I. Title.
  E185.89.R45.C67   2010
  305.896'073—dc22

                                                                    2010028081

⊗ ™The paper used in this publication meets the minimum requirements of
American National Standard for Information Sciences—Permanence of Paper for
Printed Library Materials, ANSI/NISO Z39.48-1992.

Printed in the United States of America

For Howard McGary,
Brilliant mentor and true friend

Contents

Preface   ix

Introduction   1

  1 Reparations   19

Part I: Utilitarian Approaches to Reparations

  2 Cosmopolitanism and Compensatory Justice   35

  3 Utilitarianism and Historic Injustice   59

Part II: A Rights-Based Approach to Reparations

  4 Reparations as a Human Right   83

  5 Collective Responsibility and Reparations   113

  6 Reparations to American Indians   131

  7 Reparations to Blacks   161

  8 Reparations and Reconciliation   187

  9 Possible Reparations Policies   213

Part III: Challenges to Reparations

  10 Objections to Reparations, and Replies   249

Conclusion   293

Notes 299

Bibliography 349

Index 365

About the Author 371

Preface

Heirs of Oppression comprises a philosophical analysis of particular features of some of the most severe forms of oppression (genocide, slavery, and massive and violent land theft, for example) and the ethical problems that they pose for both its offenders (on the one hand) and victims (on the other). In oppressing others, oppressors not only vilify themselves, they often leave a legacy of collective retrospective liability responsibility for their heirs to provide rectification in the form of compensation (such as reparations) to the victims of their oppression. Yet the victims of the oppression are not just those who were directly massacred or enslaved. When collectives that are morally responsible for oppressing groups do not pay restitution for what they have done to wrongfully harm others, then that debt is sometimes passed on to the descendants of the original oppressors within the intergenerational group. And when unpaid debts stand, they become unpaid to the descendants of those directly oppressed. Thus the heirs of oppression are not only the oppressors and their descendants, but the victims and theirs. The heirs of oppression, then, comprise the legacies of both oppressors and their victims.

This book addresses a select number of cases in U.S. history wherein some groups have been severely harmed by agencies of the United States, whether it be the U.S. armed forces under the direction of their commander-in-chief, or whether it be wrongful decisions made by the U.S. Supreme Court (and other federal courts), or by the U.S. Congress. Or, in still other cases, it is state and local governments and their agencies that have caused the oppression. What makes these cases particularly important is that they remain unresolved after generations since the oppression took place, though it might be argued that if unrectified evil is evil still, then the oppression of such groups and the moral duties to rectify them remain.

The first case that will be covered is that of the American Indian.[1] It concerns the violent and often conniving taking of territories which are, taken together, now called the "United States." While history is clear that numerous attempts by Indians to gain back their land and receive justice for the human rights violations for the American holocaust[2] have been systematically denied by many U.S. courts, presidents, and the U.S. Congress, this in no way serves as a justification for denying current demands for reparations to Indians. Simply because an outlaw society[3] has the military and political power to deny justice to its victims of oppression in no way serves as a moral justification for the denial of justice for any society desiring to become even minimally just. This book shall examine carefully several concerns with the argument for reparations to Indians and conclude that none of them poses a tenable concern for those interested in justice and fairness.[4] In defending a program of reparations to Indians, it is undoubtedly important to understand that what is most vital to most Indians is their cultural heritage, including religious practices and the sacred lands that were taken from them by force and fraud. But the idea here is that monetary compensation can in some meaningful measure be used by Indians to purchase some of the lands and other means that might restore some of what Indians have had stolen from and denied them for generations. Like most any other case of criminal or tort compensation, reparations can serve as a meaningful means by which contemporary heirs of Indian oppression by the United States can attempt to restore Indian sovereignty and traditional ways of being prior to the harmful wrongdoings that devastated their lives. This is not to deny the significant involvement of other countries in the violent taking of the Americas. But this book limits itself to U.S. responsibility for American Indian oppression. What separates my analysis of reparations from most others is that it makes compensatory justice in the form of reparations a necessary condition for the United States' rectification of historic and severe harmful wrongdoings against Indians.

The second case of oppression considered in this book is that of the enslavement of Africans in the United States and the subsequent apartheid regime that oppressed newly "emancipated" slaves and their descendants under the regime of Jim Crow. While this feature of the book focuses on the oppression of the slave trade in the U.S. North and South, it recognizes that slavery also existed throughout the Americas (and certain other parts of the world) and included many Indians as victims (as a form of "punishment," many Indians were sold into foreign and domestic slavery). It also understands that the United States was not the sole party responsible for the peculiar institution. Among others, England, France, the Netherlands, Portugal, and Spain were also deeply involved. Indeed, even some African nations are blameworthy for the selling and trading of many of their own countrypersons into slavery, some of which have since offered official apologies for their involvement. These and some other countries and their respective governments are co-responsible for the transatlantic slave trade of Africans, and each bears a degree of liability for reparations to various blacks today. Of course, these are controversial claims, not pertaining to the history of the slavery, but regarding claims about who owes what to whom. So it is the burden of this book to explain why blacks today are owed reparations, and by whom, and why, relative to the United States. By "blacks" I mean those whose ancestry traces back to the enslavement of Africans in America, though the concern of this book is with blacks in the United States. This is in no way to deny the claims of other blacks throughout the Americas (or the world) to reparations for the harmful wrongdoings of slavery from various countries and agencies responsible for those evils should they still exist. Furthermore, while moral restoration between parties to oppression is sometimes admirable as a goal, it is hardly required for justice, and ought never to be imposed on a context because that will surely rob oppressed persons of their dignity and autonomy to live as they choose to live. Moreover, it will rob oppressed groups of their sovereignty. For as one philosopher puts it,

> The good of cultural self-determination, as suggested by slave experiences, consists in the construction and maintenance of cultural norms and mores by members of a particular ethnic group. It is also the creation and perpetuation of art forms, rituals, and traditions . . . that express and celebrate the group's unique histories and traditions. Cultural self-determination is thus the creation and preservation of an ethnic group's identity.[5]

Whatever else reparations require, they require the autonomy of oppressed individuals and the sovereignty of oppressed groups. And this autonomy and sovereignty implies freedom to not be reconciled or integrated with their oppressors if that is in fact what is desired by the victim heirs of oppression. The key here is that any adequate theory of reparations for oppression must make primary the right to oppressed persons and groups to freely choose with whom they desire to associate. I take this to be a human right, if indeed there are such rights. Whether or not there are human rights, it is a moral right, for example, a valid moral claim or interest possessed by oppressed persons and groups.

Millions of persons throughout the world believe that the United States is an evil empire. Now for most U.S. citizens, these words are quite disturbing, if not unthinkable. How in anyone's right mind can the United States, of all societies, be construed as being evil? When I state that the United States is evil, I am arguing that, *on balance*, the good things that it has contributed to the world are outweighed by the several unrectified acts of oppression for which it is responsible. So contemporary U.S. music, athletics, certain aspects of its higher educational system, the relative inclusion of women in various positive aspects of societal life, and so on, are clearly outweighed by the unmitigated evils of the greatest land theft in human history, which is part of the American holocaust (one of the worst genocides in human history), slavery of blacks and Jim Crow, and numerous other oppressive acts that have resulted in the unjust deaths in various Central and South American nations, just to name a few countries with which the United States has "meddled" often violently in the past century. Now there are the deaths of hundreds of thousands of innocent Iraqis and Afghanis, along with the torture of hundreds of Muslims without due process of law because they were deemed "terrorists" by the U.S. government and some of its recently adopted policies, human rights violations that count as some of the worst in recent history.[6] Indeed, to know U.S. history is to understand that the United States was founded on and continues to bolster itself by one oppressive human rights violation after another; to know the United States is to know evil. But even if the evil actions cease, they must be paid for by the United States. For unrectified evil is evil still, and no reasonably just society can exist without at least attempting in good faith to pay its debts of injustice no matter what the cost to itself. After all, perpetrators of oppression are in no moral position to refuse to pay what they owe in compensatory damages to others simply in order to save themselves or others complicit in their evils.

My rejection of the utilitarian-based approaches to restorative justice implies that justice by way of reparations is mostly concerned with justice to victims of oppression and their heirs as a matter of fairness under morally acceptable rules of law, including compensatory criminal and tort law. Assumed here is the fact that "victims of crime deserve to be compensated" and that "a central tenet of the modern penal revolution is the payment of restitution to victims for the crimes committed against them."[7] Should this make amends between heirs of oppression impossible because the debts are too great to pay or otherwise rectify in full, this hardly counts against my argument for reparations, any more than it would in other cases. For if a society finds that its payment of reparations to its oppressed groups makes extraordinary demands on its economy—even long-term ones—that is not to be taken as a fault with reparations or an excuse to not pay them. Valid moral principles cannot be made to succumb to the whims or perceived capabilities of outlaw societies, of which the United States is a salient case. Instead, justice, even compensatory justice, must be carried out, in Kantian fashion, as a matter of fairness. And outlaw societies such as the United States must come to learn, if they are indeed able to do so, that evils are truly unaffordable when compensatory rights of victims or victim-heirs are respected and justice reigns supreme.

Among other things, *Heirs of Oppression* exposes some of the key presuppositions of competing approaches to corrective justice, and demonstrates their inability to accommodate basic notions of rights and justice. It explains how ideological precommitments to extreme but vague notions of equality, fraternity, and paternalism, while well intentioned, undermine arguments for rights and justice for severely oppressed peoples. Furthermore, I point to an important distinction between reconciliation and rectification models of forgiveness which underlie corresponding reconciliation and rectification models of reparations. I shall argue that, given the current legal notion of compensatory justice, there are no moral or legal impediments to reparations to Indians and blacks by U.S. society. In so doing, I refute notions of equality, fraternity, and paternalism with ones such as reparations, autonomy, and sovereignty, and the rights and duties they imply relative to these cases of severe historic injustice. Rather than a utilitarian forward-looking model, my approach to reparations is both backward- and forward-looking. It takes its cue from Immanuel Kant's mixed theory of the justification of punishment as an institution and as a practice:

> Punishment can never be used merely as a means to promote some other good for the criminal himself or for civil society, but instead it must in all cases be imposed on him only on the grounds that he has committed a crime; for a human being may never be manipulated merely as a means to the purposes of someone else. . . . *He must first be found to be deserving of punishment before any consideration is given to the utility of his punishment for himself or for his fellow citizens.*[8]

So just as punishment finds its primary justification in terms of an offender's desert and its secondary justification in terms of considerations of social utility, reparations as group compensation is justified first and foremost in terms of what the oppressor deserves in light of her overall responsibility for the oppression, while secondarily matters of social utility may be taken into account in order to justify reparations. And this is true in terms of both the institution of reparations and particular implementations of it. My main argument is that this model of rectificatory justice in the form of compensatory reparations is the most morally promising one, all things considered. It fails to fall prey to objections to utility, paternalism, and fraternity, yet it respects and promotes the rights of oppressed individuals and groups to autonomy, sovereignty, self-respect, and compensation, among other things. For readers hoping for an anodyne analysis, *Heirs of Oppression* will surely disappoint. For interwoven throughout are arguments and analyses that make it somewhat of an animadversion among philosophical works on the topics of reparations for severe oppression.

Heirs of Oppression begins with a clarification of the nature and function of reparations. In part 1, significant attention is devoted to the statement and assessment of cosmopolitan liberalism and its rejection of reparative justice as a part of its program of global justice. This section of the book also assesses some most recent attempts to cast reparations in terms of reconciliation between the oppressor heirs of oppression and the victim heirs of oppression, rather than as compensation by the former groups to the latter ones. These approaches to reparations are found wanting in numerous respects, and the remainder of the book constitutes an argument in support of compensatory reparations by the U.S. government to the groups it has oppressed the most.

The general argument of part 2 of *Heirs of Oppression* runs as follows:

1. Those groups (governments, businesses, NGOs, social groups, etc.) responsible for severe harmful wrongdoings are oppressor heirs of

oppression that owe compensation in the form of reparations to the victim heirs of oppression in proportion to the harms wrongfully caused.

2. The U.S. government, some leading businesses, and/or some other nongovernmental agencies are co-responsible for the harmful wrongdoings
of either genocide or land theft against American Indians, the enslavement of Africans, or the establishment and enforcement of Jim Crow
laws which had their greatest deleterious effects on American Indians
and blacks.

3. Therefore, the U.S. government and some leading U.S.-based businesses
and/or NGOs owe reparations to the Indian and black heirs of oppression in the United States.

4. Once reparations are either paid or at least substantially under way in
payment for some years, reconciliation between the different heirs of
oppression may occur. But,

5. Reconciliation requires forgiveness.

6. Forgiveness of the offending groups requires an apology by them to the
victim heirs of oppression.

7. But an apology requires, among other things, rectification by them to the
victim heirs of oppression. Unless and until Indians and blacks receive
substantial reparations for the evils wrought on them by the U.S. government, then apologies are impossible, making forgiveness and reconciliation impossible also. Whether or not a genuine apology including
substantial reparations is forthcoming, it is the sole decision of the victim heirs of oppression to forgive and reconcile with the oppressor heirs
of oppression. So even if an apology obtains, it is always up to the victims to forgive. Yet both forgiveness and forgiving are required for reconciliation, and it is naïve to think that a genuine apology with rectification
and forgiving are not essential to reconciliation between heirs of oppression. Compensatory reparations are moral rights that belong to
oppressed groups. And if there are human rights, it is a human one as
well. If it is true that there can be no reconciliation with human rights
violations present or inadequately addressed, then there can be *no reconciliation without rectification*, including reparations.

8. In order to truly respect Indians and blacks, their rights must be
respected. This includes their rights to compensatory reparations.

Throughout this book, proper respect is paid to those whose seminal philosophical work has paved the way for any viable discussion of reparations,
especially for blacks. I refer here to the works of Bernard Boxill and Howard
McGary, respectively. It is a profound disappointment that many writers on
this topic in recent years have all but ignored the works of Boxill and McGary.
And this neglect is surely unacceptable. Whether such scholarly neglect is due
to racist motivations of disrespect or some other reason, it surely demonstrates
the limited quality of such work. For there is no question that Boxill's and
McGary's works serve as not only seminal, but among the very highest quality

of philosophical work on this vital topic. Thus they shall be accorded their proper place in this study.

While the philosophical content of this book addresses and is inspired by the respective reparations discussions of Boxill and McGary over the past few decades, it would be remiss if I did not at least mention the more general academic context in which this book arises. As a work in moral, social, political, and legal philosophy, this book, not unlike the works of Boxill and McGary, is based on mainstream work in analytical philosophy. Thus readers will find many a reference to the respective works of Joel Feinberg and John Rawls. However, since my arguments and analyses seek to account well for the factor of racist harmful wrongdoings in U.S. society, my work bears some resemblance to some important works in what might be broadly categorized as critical race theory. I have in mind here some of the works on reparations by Derrick Bell, Boris Bittker, Richard Delgado, Manning Marable, Mari Matsuda, Charles Ogletree, Robert Westley, and Patricia Williams. Part of what this book seeks to accomplish at its core is to explore the importance of oppression against a select number of the greatest cases of U.S. oppression and make the strongest cases possible for U.S. reparations to such oppressed groups without minimizing or ignoring the importance of the rights of the victim heirs of oppression, on the one hand, and the responsibility of the offender heirs of oppression, on the other.

Tremendous gratitude is owed to many for their varieties of assistance in this book. I thank Bernard Boxill and Howard McGary for their incisive comments on earlier drafts of the book. Also, I am grateful for the editorial expertise and support of James P. Sterba. Lorraine Corlett assisted with proofreading, and Marisa Diaz-Waian devised the index.

I am grateful for the use of "Forgiveness, Apology, and Retribution," *American Philosophical Quarterly* 43 (2006): 25–42, in part of chapter 8, for most of the contents of chapter 1, which is taken from "Reparations," in *Oxford Handbook of World Philosophy*, ed. Jay Garfield (Oxford: Oxford University Press, 2008). "Reparations and Human Rights" is a longer version of a paper with the same title presented at the John Jay College of Criminal Law Conference on Human Rights After 9/11, September 21, 2006, where I received helpful comments from George Andreopoulos, Gary Herbert, and Larry May. Chapter 6 contains a significant portion of "Ruminations on Reparations," in *Reparations*, ed. Howard McGary (Lanham, Md.: Rowman and Littlefield, forthcoming), which was presented both at the Conference on Collective Identity, Sovereignty, and Minority Rights, Santa Barbara City College, January 31, 2004, where it received helpful comments from both Richard Falk, Burleigh Wilkins, and other conference participants. Integrated into the book is "Evil," *Analysis* 64 (2004): 81–84 (Oxford University Press). Chapter 10 contains significant portions of "Race, Racism, and Reparations," *Journal of Social Philosophy* 36 (2005): 568–84 (Blackwell Publishers) and "Race, Ethnicity, and Public Policy," in *Race or Ethnicity? Black and Latino Identity*, ed. Jorge Gracia (Ithaca, N.Y.: Cornell University Press, 2007), 225–47.

Introduction

While John Rawls's theory of justice as fairness constitutes his attempt to construct a comprehensive theory of full compliance,[1] *Heirs of Oppression* is my attempt to address a limited number of problems in partial compliance theory pertaining to compensatory justice. And it is compensatory justice which serves as that imperfect means by which many violated rights are rectified, albeit approximately, including individual and group rights to life, liberty, and the pursuit of happiness. This book is devoted to a philosophical examination of the problems of compensatory reparations to a distinct set of most egregiously oppressed groups by the United States of America, where "compensatory reparations" includes but is not limited to monetary compensation.

In the twentieth century alone, numerous evils were perpetrated, so many that the January 2006 issue of *National Geographic* refers to it as the "Century of Death," where "death" means "mass murder."[2] Examples of such genocide or mass murder include the murder of about 30 million Chinese from 1950 to 1970, the murder of about 20 million Soviets between 1920 and 1960, the killing of about 11 million people by Nazi Germany between 1930 and 1950, the murders of about 10 million in Japan between 1930 and 1950, as well as over a million persons murdered in each of Turkey (1910–1930), India (1940–1950), Sudan (since 1950), Rwanda (in the early 1960s and in the mid-1990s), Indonesia (1960–2000), Nigeria (late 1960s), Pakistan (1970s), Uganda (1970–1990), Cambodia (1970s), and Afghanistan (1970–2000), as well as numerous other mass murders in countries and nations such as Namibia (1910), Algeria (early 1960s), Chile (mid-1970s), Zaire (between 1960 and 1980), South Vietnam (1960–1980), Iraq (since 1960), Equatorial Guinea (1960–1980), the Philippines (1970s), Burundi (since 1960), Angola (since 1970), Argentina (1970s), Ethiopia (late 1970s), Burma (late 1970s), Guatemala (1970–1990), El Salvador (1980s), Syria (early 1980s), Iran (1980–2000), Somalia (late 1980s), Sri Lanka (late 1980s), Bosnia (1990s), and Yugoslavia (late 1990s).[3] And while some acts of mass murder are more

evil than others due to kind, level, and degree of harmful wrongdoing, perhaps even constituting "pure" evil, even some allegedly purely evil acts are
often such that they are mixed with some degree of goodness, however minute
(for example, in the midst of a genocide, a soldier carrying out the genocide
willfully and knowingly assists a young child from danger).[4] I refer here not
only to the murderers themselves, but also to the governments and societies
responsible for them. For instance, a government of a country can engage in
evil actions, yet the country itself might well have some good features.

U.S. history is replete with examples of acts of evil perpetrated by the U.S.
federal, state, and local governments. I shall argue that based on its lengthy
train of rights abuses that date back to its inception until currently, the United
States is, on balance, evil. In fact, it is, on balance, so evil that it is astounding
that so many Christian theologians do not seem to admit or recognize in their
writings on the problem of evil that the United States stands as one of the
most obvious examples of the problem of nonnatural evil and that its oppression of Indians and blacks serve as apt examples of evil![5] Yet one would seem
to have to subscribe to a rather entrenched ahistoricism about the United
States in order to fashion a theology that would ignore the history of the
United States in addressing the problem of evil. Nonetheless, there are many
good people and things in and about the country, including much of its
music, athletics, advances in higher education and medicine, and some of its
charitable organizations. But on balance, all of these and other truly great contributions are outweighed by the facts of its history of unrectified evils that are
amongst the very worse in history. So, on balance, the United States is evil.
This is both a comparative and an on balance moral judgment. Compared to
other countries and societies throughout history, the entirety of rights violations by the United States seems to be the worst ever in cumulative magnitude
and duration, and even in light of its good features, the United States still
comes out evil on the balance of scales, all relevant things considered. For
most every U.S. citizen, this kind of judgment comes as a complete shock, and
even outlandish. For most U.S. citizens, the United States is clearly the greatest
country in the world. But in whatever sense this kind of statement could be
meant, it surely cannot reasonably be meant in a moral sense, that is, according to principles of a morally enlightened and historically informed conscience. My claim that the United States is, comparatively and on balance, evil
is meant as a moral assessment of its behavior over its lifetime. It is not meant
to be a judgment based solely on one or two acts of conduct indicative of its
general character.

Nor is the moral judgment that the United States is evil meant to suggest, in
referring to the unrectification of most of its worst evils, some instrumentalist
conception of compensatory justice that would suggest that should the United
States fully or adequately rectify its evils that it would somehow wipe the slate
clean between its victims and itself, realizing moral equality in the Aristotelian
sense. Rather, it is that the unrectified nature of some of the worst evils in

history adds greatly to how evil the United States is, and speaks directly to the moral character of the United States.

Throughout this book, "evil" and its cognates shall be used to connote what is less than purely evil, assuming that the category "pure evil" is not empty, but significantly greater than merely bad actions. And it is assumed that evil acts, like bad and good ones, do not somehow mysteriously lose their moral properties of evil, goodness, or badness with the mere passage of time—no matter what the length. Unrectified evil is evil still, where "evil" refers to extraordinarily bad or untoward outcomes of events, actions, or states of affairs.

As there are many bad events, actions, and states of affairs that fall under the general category of "evil," oppression is one of them. And racist oppression, like other forms of evil and badness, admits of degrees, levels, and kinds in terms of the harmfulness that it brings on its victims, both directly and indirectly. This study of racist oppression shall focus on a select number of severe racist evils that have and continue to oppress peoples today.

Although it is important to satisfy the requirements of distributive justice both domestically and globally, it is only by way of a viable process of rectification that even the mere hope of satisfaction and remedy can be realized for the oppressed.[6] Indeed, the failure or refusal to satisfy the requirements of compensatory justice to oppressed groups is itself a form of continued oppression. For oppression unrectified is oppression continued. Although oppression is often only one kind of evil, and there are many kinds of either oppression or evil, I shall use these terms interchangeably throughout this book. (At times I substitute the more sanitized phrase "severe harmful wrongdoing" or the like.) The key point to which I am drawing attention in my use of these terms is that the harmful wrongdoing referred to is that of the most severe quality and quantity, in terms of kind, level, degree, and duration.

Yet since this is a book about reparations to certain highly oppressed groups within and by the United States, it is incumbent on me to provide a sufficiently clear idea of the nature of oppression, and how it differs from evil as I have just construed evil for purposes of reparations for historic injustice.

Increasing numbers of philosophers have written on oppression. It seems that few have devoted to oppression the philosophical attention that it deserves. One who has devoted significant attention to the concept is Ann E. Cudd, who claims that

> feminists have long recognized the oppression of women but have had a hard time convincing others that women are oppressed. One of the main motivations for my work has been to construct a general theory of oppression to demonstrate that women are harmed unjustly in ways that are similar to the unjust treatment of other groups who are generally recognized as oppressed.[7]

Besides the disappointing fact that Cudd's book on oppression does not explicate in any interesting detail just how white women in the United States are oppressed in ways "similar" to, say, Indians and blacks in the United States, one reason why such feminists or womanists have had such a "hard time convincing others that women are oppressed" is precisely because of the problematic usage by such (though not all) feminists of "oppression" and its cognates in ways that end up inflating the adverse experiences of white women, and perhaps simultaneously even deflating the oppression of, say, Indians and blacks. Indeed, the above-quoted words exemplify exactly how badly some white feminists misunderstand oppression. They construe it in such simplistic terms that they implicitly use "women" which in the context really refers to white women as if it is meant to refer to women in general, thereby committing a kind of division fallacy in that not all ethnicities of women in the United States, for instance, are oppressed to the same extent, as Indian and black women have and continue to suffer oppression at rates unknown to white women, on average and as a class.[8] Thus what is often true of Indian and black women is hardly true of white women. So it is misleading or false to insist that "women" as a group are oppressed without clarification as to the various ways in which the oppression of women in the United States is experienced differentially between groups of women, say, based at least in part on ethnic considerations. But since the only manner in which the statement might be somewhat accurate is if "women" referred mainly to Indian and black women, or "women of color" more generally, the statement is quite misleading at best.

No reasonable person can deny that Indian and black women (and men) have been and are oppressed and greater than any other groups in U.S. history. But it is a very hard sell for one to be convinced that white women in the United States have been or are oppressed if what is meant by "oppression" is akin to what we mean when we say that "Indian and black women are oppressed" when the cumulative experiences of those respective groups is considered. Cudd's is an attempt to prove the historically and ethically improvable, namely, that white women rightly belong in the category of oppressed groups, without any consideration given to the complexity of the category in light of the variant circumstances of oppression from case to case. It appears to be a misguided attempt to secure white women's oppressed status in the minds of persons who are unsuspecting of logically fallacious reasoning, as just described. What is needed in analyzing the concept of oppression is a differentialist analysis that recognizes, among other things, the various degrees and kinds of oppression, thus implying a comparative analysis between different instances of it.

One wonders whether such feminists are unaware of U.S. history of Indians and blacks such that they do not know better than to think that white women are not oppressed in similar ways (except in insignificant ones) to Indians and blacks such that it constitutes a moral and perhaps even a racist insult to use "oppression" to refer to women's oppression generally or to implicitly lump white women's oppression into the group with Indian and black oppression, or at least to rather uncarefully mislead readers to think that it might be reasonable to compare Indian and black oppression with the experiences of white women in the United States. In fact, one might even go so far as to wonder whether or not certain white feminists are carrying on the age-old custom of many white women in the United States of narcissistically inflating their own wounds—however real in and of themselves—by any means necessary, even by misappropriating, intentionally or not, the experiences of those most oppressed in order to egoistically strive for the realization of their own agendas.[9]

In any case, it is false or misleading to use "oppression" without careful qualification to refer to experiences with such diverse realities. And one would think that Cudd would know better as she seems to agree that there can be mischaracterizations of oppression.[10] Indeed, her own admittedly general analysis of oppression fails to consider noninstitutional forms of oppression, levels of oppression, and kinds and degrees of it.[11] This is important in that her failure to address these matters serves the interests of certain white feminists in attempting to convince others that white women were and are oppressed in similar ways that Indians and blacks were and are oppressed, on average and as groups. This is particularly true of Cudd's statement that "even if one is a member of a privileged group, one need not oneself be an oppressor."[12] While this statement is true, Cudd makes no attempt to explore ways in which often those who might seem not to be oppressors in fact are oppressors in ways that make them co-responsible for oppression. While it is true that the experiences of Indians, blacks, and white women share a "set of features,"[13] it is far from obvious that this set of features justifies the use of "oppression" to implicitly refer to each such group equally, or unproblematically, as I have argued based on the levels, amounts, and kinds of oppressive harms experienced by the respective groups. Thus I concur with Cudd that "we need not fall prey to false consciousness or deformed desires, though these are understandable responses to oppression (or privilege)."[14] But while Cudd's claim is meant for enlightened leftist white feminists contemplating the concept of oppression, it indeed refers to her own understanding of what severe evil or tremendous harmful wrongdoing amounts to, and the confusion of her analysis of the nature of oppression insofar as it can and does conflate vastly differing degrees, kinds, levels, and durations of oppression.

While Cudd is correct to claim that "oppression, by definition, implies injustice,"[15] she has a simplistic notion of responsibility for oppression. She states that "oppressors bear full moral responsibility for their part in oppression."[16] However, this claim fails to recognize what moral responsibility theory recognizes, namely, that responsibility admits of degrees and there exist mitigating conditions that, when satisfied, mitigate responsibility and blameworthiness for one's actions, including oppressive ones.[17] It also does not recognize that oppressors, just as other harmful wrongdoers, can often share responsibility.[18] She also implicitly writes an agent's intent into the act of oppression as a necessary condition. That is, the oppressor "must be aware that he or she is acting unjustly and harming someone thereby."[19] Besides failing to understand that oppression involves not only harming another, but doing so wrongfully, Cudd's statement conveniently protects white women in their oppressive actions against Indians and blacks, among others. As privileged ones, most white women surely believed that they were superior to Indians and blacks, especially until most recently when the bulk of the oppression against those groups was greatest. White women believed that in treating Indians and blacks the way they did that they were not doing anything wrong. So in Cudd's view, it would follow that they did not oppress them. Yet on this theory, neither did white men oppress Indians and blacks because of all people, they surely thought they were right (and more often than not acting in the interest of the "negroes") in their white supremacist thinking and behavior. Intentional action is a requisite for responsibility for one's action. But Cudd owes us an independent, non-question-begging, and non-self-serving argument for the claim that intent to commit a harm against another is a necessary condition of oppression. Until such an argument is marshaled, her analysis of oppression is to be rejected because of its implausibility.

White women in the United States were and remain privileged, and their privilege was and still is the root of their oppression of Indians and blacks. Or, to quote Cudd's own words about privilege and oppression in general, "To be privileged is to be able to be blind to a system of oppression and the privileges it grants one."[20] These words apply to white women in the United States, on average and as a class. Of course, some white feminists will deny this fact. But then they must also deny the obvious, namely that the following words apply to them also: "being privileged and failing to see privilege commonly go together."[21] To deny this precisely is to be white and possess white privilege. And if Cudd is correct in her claim that "oppressors, on any reasonable moral theory, are morally required to desist and remedy past harm,"[22] then white women owe compensatory reparations to Indians and blacks, and surely do not deserve to continue to receive affirmative action benefits as the result of their own oppression of others, a point for which I shall argue in greater detail in chapter 10. This is the logical inference that must be drawn from the facts of history and Cudd's own words about responsibility for oppression:

> Some ignorance of oppression and privilege is morally blameworthy in itself. If a good case has been made that there is oppression, and that case is generally well known throughout society, then one is responsible for the knowledge of oppression, and hence also for doing one's part toward alleviating it. If one also can be held responsible for the knowledge of one's privilege, as would certainly be the case for whites, Americans, men, wealthy, and able-bodied persons with respect to at least some systems of oppression, then one is obligated to resist the oppression and renounce privilege where possible.[23]

I concur with Cudd's insightful remarks. But they condemn white women as co-oppressors for generations of abuse of Indians and blacks, and to a lesser degree, some other ethnic groups in the United States. Thus if anyone is co-responsible for the oppression of Indians and blacks, it is white women who enjoyed for centuries the privileged standing that only a white person could enjoy in the United States. Even today most white men and women alike are very much against compensatory reparations for Indians and blacks, and this is easily understood as their refusal to alleviate the oppression that continues in large part due to the failure of the United States to pay these reparations, thus continuing the cycles of poverty, unfreedom, and fourth-rate citizenship for millions of them. Affirmative action programs, from which white women have benefited more than any other targeted group, can never serve as an adequate substitute for the reparations that are owed Indians and blacks by compensatory right, monies that would provide vital resources for them to escape their oppressive states and live autonomous lives as individuals and sovereign lives as peoples. Of course, these claims require argumentative support, which is what the bulk of this book provides in the following chapters.

In the end, I agree with Cudd's claims of "the importance of generating general social knowledge of oppression" and that "information about oppression be prominently and convincingly presented so that it is undeniable and inescapable."[24] For this is precisely what I do, among other things, in chapter 10 where I reveal in plain and reasonable terms the extent of white women's co-responsibility for the oppression of Indians and blacks throughout U.S. history, oppression that is rooted in white privilege and for which they are co-responsible and blameworthy, and for which they along with other U.S. citizens owe reparations.[25] It is not the case, then, that white women ought to receive affirmative action benefits given the extent of their co-oppressor status. For no one ought to be permitted to benefit from their own (or another's) harmful wrongdoing.

But this is hardly Cudd's stance, as she concludes quite to the contrary that "the law must take the *oppressed group perspective* when it comes to crimes against women" and that "oppression ought to be recognized as a part of the crimes against women."[26] Since Cudd once again (as she does throughout her study) conflates the obvious differences between white women's and black and Indian women's experiences, I can only assume that Cudd is referring here to white women, among others. And given this fact, it is rather self-serving (of white women) and convenient for her overall argument about white women's oppression that she makes this inference about women's oppression. It is no wonder white women feminists have such a hard time convincing others of their own oppression!

What is needed is a more plausible analysis of the nature and function of oppression, specifically in terms of oppression of various ethnic and gender groups in the United States. In developing such an analysis, it is vital to bear in mind some of the desiderata of a plausible analysis of such oppression. First, a conception of oppression ought to recognize that oppression is experienced in degrees of harshness such that it is only appropriate to categorize oppressed persons and groups, however roughly, according to their degrees of oppression experienced. Otherwise, miscategorization of degrees of oppression experienced is likely to produce misleading statements, if not falsehoods, concerning this crucial problem, and equivocation is the likely result. Second, such an analysis ought to reflect various levels of oppression. Levels of oppression can be construed institutionally or noninstitutionally, as the case may be. At the highest levels of institutional oppression is often that oppression that issues from, say, the federal government, from either the executive, judicial or legislative branches. The Fugitive Slave Laws are just such an example, as are judicial decisions that support it. Levels of oppression also issue from state governments, such as legalized slavery, and constitute lower, but still powerful, levels of oppression. Still other levels of institutionalized oppression can be found in county or municipal governments, wherein Jim Crow laws serve as good examples. Yet not all oppression issues from governmental structures. Some oppression is the result of one group acting on its own to oppress others, as in the case of certain Ku Klux Klan (KKK) activities distinct from structural forces, or in cases where certain financial institutions refuse to provide essential services to certain groups out of a kind of racist exclusion.

Not only are there degrees and levels of oppression, there are kinds of oppression with which a plausible analysis of oppression ought to deal. Physical oppression wrongfully harms the body, or one's physical property. Murder, mayhem, rape are some such examples that can and often do result in oppression. But there is also psychological oppression, which includes the psychological damage that results from oppressive behavior. These kinds of oppression can lead to social oppression,[27] wherein one experiences serious ostracization from others as a result of something which may or may not be unjust. There is also economic oppression, which is the overt or unintended allocation of economic resources so that they harm certain people or peoples. There is religious oppression wherein certain persons or groups are persecuted for their religious practices or beliefs. And there is gender oppression wherein, for example, females are discriminated against or persecuted because they are females. Of course, some forms of oppression such as slavery often exhibit each of these kinds of oppression.

It is important to understand, as few philosophers seem to understand given the informational contents of their writings on oppression, that the degrees, the levels, and the kinds of oppression must be kept in mind in categorizing oppressions. It is misleading and sometimes even harmful to neglect this fact. Bearing in mind the degrees, levels, and kinds of oppression of groups enables us to better understand the experiences of such groups, and to better address matters of injustice toward them. Vague notions of group harms do little to service us here, except to bolster problematic claims to redress, or to deny plausible ones.

While this notion of oppression is incomplete as a general one, it is intended to serve as a corrective to Cudd's problematic notion of oppression and point us in the right direction by way of a more nuanced understanding of it, at least of the most severe kinds experienced in the United States. When oppression is considered in terms of its degrees of strength, its level of embeddedness in U.S. society, and its kinds, as well as its duration in time, a more accurate portrayal of oppression is able to emerge, one that can serve as the basis of our discussion of compensatory reparations for the oppression and the wrongful harms that result from it.

I assume that the historic occurrence and degree of harmful wrongdoing of racist oppression count as sufficient reasons to consider the cases of Indians and blacks to be of first priority among all cases of unrectified injustices in the United States. Other cases, though perhaps meritorious, shall await their turn in order of severity and importance. I have selected for discussion what I take to be the two most severe forms of unrectified oppressive evils that have taken place in the United States and for which, I shall argue, the United States is mostly, though not solely, responsible in the retrospective liability sense of "responsible." Thus a range of oppressions are included in this book: from genocidal land theft to enslavement and racial apartheid. What these cases share in common with each other is that the victims are owed reparations by the United States because they have experienced severe oppression by U.S. governments, businesses, and other nongovernmental organizations, and several individual citizens.

As stated in the preface, the heirs of oppression are members in one of at least two parties: as oppressor heirs or as victim heirs. For it is one thing to build a case for reparations to establish the fact of oppression of this or that group. One must also establish a "defendant" in the case to be charged with the payment of such reparations to the "plaintiffs." To be sure, other parties to evil acts and events include the societies in which such acts and events occur, and future generations or heirs of the first two parties in particular. Previous work on reparations or group compensatory justice focused mainly on the victims of oppression and directed attention to oppressors insofar as they owed a debt unpaid. But more needs to be said of oppressors, especially in terms of intergenerational justice where decades—even centuries—have passed and when justice is denied to victims and their heirs. I shall address this point by tackling the problems associated with collective (retrospective liability) responsibility for untoward events, intergenerationally speaking. The heirs of oppression, then, include at least two primary parties concerning the rectification of injustice: the victim heirs and those against whom they level, or are morally and legally entitled to level, charges against (the oppressors or their heirs).

But the case for reparations for oppression must also provide a link (or legally speaking, privity) between the victims of oppression, on the one hand, and the offending parties, on the other. In the case of my moral argument, this entails the establishing of a connection of liability responsibility between the two parties such that those who would be ordered by either legislation or the Court[28] to pay reparations are liable for the damages experienced by the original victims. In the case of historic injustices against Indians and blacks, this does not mean that the responsibility link is one of guilt or fault. As we shall see in chapter 5, there is no such thing as vicarious guilt or fault. Rather, the responsibility link is such that the offender heirs of oppression collectively "inherit" the unpaid debt of their forebears just as they might have inherited wealth from them. I write "inherit" because I do not mean by this a literal legal inheritance, but a morally principled one insofar as offender heirs are not morally entitled to all of what they possess insofar as they possess much of what they have in violation of the principle of morally just acquisitions and transfers[29] due to the genocidal theft of Indian lands, slavery, and Jim Crow. Just as in U.S. laws regarding inheritance, an estate must pay in full all valid claims against it by creditors. In the cases in question, the current generation of U.S. citizens and their government have inherited debts that amount to claims against the U.S. government by victim heirs of oppression, namely Indians and blacks.

In the cases of Indian and black oppression in and by the United States, a more challenging link between the victim heirs of oppression and the offender heirs of oppression must be established. I attempt this with my discussion of collective moral responsibility in chapter 5, along with my historical accounts of oppression by the U.S. governmental agencies and officials in chapters 6 and 7.[30] And since mine is a moral argument for reparations rather than a legal one (though my moral argument does seek to show that compensatory reparations in the cases discussed are legally viable), it poses a deep challenge to those who would think that the legal statute of limitations on most forms of injustice has, all things considered, an adequate moral foundation. Once these main obstacles to a legal case for reparations are satisfied, I identify damages based on a Feinbergian conception of harmful wrongdoing to establish what the United States owes to Indians and blacks. While unjust enrichment can function to strengthen the case for such reparations, it is not necessary to establish this factor in that mine is a harm-based and rights-based theory of reparations. This approach, then, evades the alleged problems of unjust enrichment due to problems of computing offsets of unjust gains posed by some detractors of reparations. My approach is one that can serve the interests of legal actions against the United States and various of its corporate oppressors as well as a basis of legislative action by the United States to provide adequate reparations to these groups as it has done, though not so adequately, for indigenous Hawai'ians, Alaskans, and certain Japanese Americans in recent years.

However, should the reparations case be made before, say, a U.S. federal court, it is noteworthy that my approach alone, replete with my genealogical analysis of ethnic group identification, can satisfy the court's "strict scrutiny" requirement that reparations, if awarded, meet a compelling state interest and that it is narrowly tailored.[31] While the compelling state interest would be justice and fairness and the strengthening of just democratic institutions by way of respecting the rights to compensatory reparations of oppressed peoples, the case for reparations is narrowly tailored insofar as it is only those who are genealogically tied to Indians and blacks in the requisite senses who qualify as beneficiaries of reparations remedies (see chapter 10 for a discussion of this issue). With this approach, the harms of Indian genocide, Indian and black slavery, and Jim Crow discrimination can be carefully, though approximately, calculated without references to inequalities and poverty in U.S. society. My theory of reparations is primarily (though not exclusively) about rectification, not inequality or poverty, though these factors are resultant from the oppression in question.

Seminal philosophical work by Bernard Boxill and Howard McGary (respectively) on reparations focuses on black reparations in the United States. Arguments guided by plausible moral principles were brought to bear in order to support the claim that reparations are owed to blacks in the United States for the damaging effects of the institution of slavery.[32] While the other philosophical works on reparations dealing with blacks in the United States that duly recognize this seminal work is sparse,[33] it is unfortunate that increasing numbers of those philosophers who write on the topic in recent years have all but ignored, or given very short shrift to, those works. Curious still is the fact that most of the writers on "reparations" who support justice for blacks argue not for reparations, but instead for a utilitarian-based notion of preferential treatment for blacks and "other minorities" and "women." And yet it is hardly the case that the full range of argumentation of Boxill and McGary on reparations and related issues is dealt with extensively so as to rule out the requirement of compensatory reparations. Thus entire arguments of Boxill's and McGary's are either handled quickly, dismissed, or entirely ignored. I believe that this is due to the precommitments to a degree of utilitarianism of many of those writing on the topic that is committed to some kind of (ill-defined) egalitarianism, though neither of these presuppositions is explicitly admitted by their authors.[34]

That such philosophers think that they support justice for blacks constitutes an embarrassment for their views in that utilitarianism has for generations been shown to falter because it cannot make adequate sense of rights and justice, which is precisely what compensatory reparations are about. Worst still is their commitment to some form of egalitarianism, though it is rather unreflective at best, unlike the more precise analyses set forth and defended by the likes of G. A. Cohen, Ronald Dworkin, Larry Temkin, among others. Thus the denial of compensatory reparations in favor of somewhat of a utilitarian-based egalitarianism prohibits these leftists, well-intentioned as they are, from supporting, or even grasping, the nature and implications of reparations. Once these errors in reasoning are exposed as they are in chapters 2 and 3, it will pave the way for a clarification of the nature and moral justification of a rights-based model of reparations to groups where the victims, oppressors, and their respective heirs are identifiable, and where the evidence for the severe harmful wrongdoings is clear.

I shall argue that the evidence for reparations satisfies each of the tests just mentioned in the cases of Indians and blacks. Each of these parties has a clear case for reparations for the evils that have been perpetrated against them. But by whom? And how much reparative justice is owed each of these parties? Each of these cases will be examined with great care to not argue in contradistinction to plausible moral and legal principles. Yet little place shall be given to utilitarian reasons, as they violate justice and rights and thus disqualify themselves from consideration regarding a topic that fundamentally concerns justice and rights. This does not mean that the manner by which cases of reparations ought to be examined is nonconsequentialist. For even Immanuel Kant placed some value on the consequences of an act regarding its moral justification, as I note in the preface. It is, rather, that an action's results cannot be the primary justification of moral actions. This assumes, of course, what others like Joel Feinberg have argued, namely, that no just society can obtain without a healthy respect for rights and justice.[35]

The previous paragraph contains some important meta-ethical pronouncements, but ones I believe are only controversial to those committed to a crass kind of utilitarianism, one that hardly deserves our serious attention. And until rule-utilitarianism can provide rules that are not already deontological in character and can separate itself conceptually from deontologism, it behooves us to argue from the most plausible moral principles to the most plausible conclusions, all relevant things considered, and this implies the rejection of consequentialism.[36]

Most major reparations studies mention but do not analyze the concept of racism.[37] However, it is essential that these two topics are treated together, as racism of substantial kinds serves as the basis of reparations in the cases of the United States' oppression of Indians and blacks. This can be understood in terms of the very nature of racism itself. Racism is considered to be morally wrong insofar as it constitutes a form of moral arbitrariness. It is morally arbitrary to treat someone or a group in this or that way for reasons that are morally irrelevant to her or its performance or characteristics that ought to be considered in judging the person or group.

However, not simply any instance of racism qualifies for reparations. Reparations as a form of compensatory justice to groups requires that the victims of racism be both substantially wronged and harmed. And while racism can always be considered a wrong, though not always a substantial one, it does not always eventuate in a substantial harm. This is especially the case if racism, properly construed, involves mere racist beliefs and not action, inaction, or attempted action, as the case may be, that results in a minor harm or even a mere offense. But on the assumption that racism involves prejudicial beliefs and discriminatory action,[38] not all racism is of the same seriousness in terms of harmfulness. Consider a black person's being called, with an accompanying mental state of hatred, resentment, and so on, a "nigger" by a white person. While typically this is a moral insult, it is hardly on par with a black person's being assassinated or otherwise lynched out of racist motives, as in the cases of Martin Luther King, Jr., Malcolm X, and Medgar Evers. Nor is it on par with Sojourner Truth's being disallowed to speak at the inaugural meeting of (white) women's rights advocates at Seneca Falls. Yet neither of these cases of racist harm even approximate the genocide of American Indians or the enslavement of Indians and blacks, or of life under Jim Crow for both groups. It is the more serious racist harmful wrongdoings that form the basis of any claim to reparations under considerations herein.

Now this raises the question of whether the racist element in the harmful wrongdoing adds anything to the charge that would rightly effect the punishment of a racist offender or her compensation to her victim. Consider James Chaney, the young black man murdered in Philadelphia, Mississippi, in 1964 for his participation in civil rights reform there. A team of KKK members, including law enforcement (the sheriff and a deputy), murdered Chaney and his two companion civil rights workers. Imagine that while he was being murdered, Chaney was hurled insults such as "Die, nigger, die!" Indeed, one who shot him in fact testified to saying (just prior to shooting and killing Chaney): "At least they left me a nigger." The question at hand is this: Does the fact that antiblack racism played a key role in the murder of Chaney imply that that racism in turn plays a legitimate role in the guilt *and* punishment of the crime against him? There is no question that what happened to Chaney is what is termed a "hate crime." And it was evil and should have been punished in proportion to the harm caused. But should the fact that it is a hate crime, a racist one, affect (increase) the sentencing of those criminals who so viciously killed him? Is there, in other words, an extra element in harming that the racism provides when it comes to the sentencing of racist hate criminals?

For those of us who categorize what happened to Chaney as a heinous hate crime, it is difficult indeed to see what it is that makes the racist element something for which the perpetrator ought to be punished. Why not simply argue that the measure of wrongfulness and harm are to function as the primary considerations in this evil act? The point is not that the racist element of this crime is irrelevant in the consideration of the full range of factors concerning the crime. Indeed, it seems to speak to the motive of the criminal. Rather, it is that there seems to be no discernible manner by which to factor in the racist element itself. What matters most is that Chaney was killed, and so brutally, and without justification. This alone and subsequent to due process is sufficient to execute those directly and substantially responsible for Chaney's murder, assuming no significant mitigation of responsibility on behalf of the offenders.[39] The fact that it was a *racist* hate crime seems to add nothing to the legitimate sentencing of his evildoers, though it normally affects the moral judgments of at least many criminals.

Now it might be argued that the case of Chaney represents a case of overdetermined guilt and responsibility for Chaney's murder such that capital punishment would be morally justified. But, it might be asked, what about cases of racist hate crimes wherein guilt and responsibility for harmful wrongdoing is not overdetermined? Might racism play a more meaningful role in the sentencing of criminals?

Insofar as racism is a motivation for racist hate crimes, it would appear that racism is a factor in judging the guilt and responsibility for them in such cases. But one must be careful here, as motivations can be seen as mitigating factors in guilt and responsibility attributions. And if the element of racism can enhance guilt and responsibility for racist hate crimes, it might also mitigate it. This is especially true in cases where racism was instilled in forcible fashion since childhood, or at least during formative years. In such cases, it is not that those guilty of racist hate crimes ought not to be punished or held accountable for their racist acts that wrongfully harm others. Rather, it is that their sentencing must and should be mitigated, based on the full range of relevant facts of each such case.

In light of these factors, I argue that the basic elements of a crime be used to determine guilt and responsibility, but that motivations like racism ought to be used to either mitigate or enhance ascriptions of guilt and responsibility, as the case may be. In some cases, the presence of racism might well enhance a criminal's sentence, yet in others it will mitigate it. Perhaps one salient issue here is the extent to which a racist criminal had sufficient opportunity to combat her racism as an adult, an issue that relies on the metaphysical facts of whether or not she was a moral agent both at the time of the racist crime and during those times prior to but most relevant to her committing it.

What, if anything, has this to do with reparative justice as a species of rectificatory justice? To the extent that racism plays a role in the genocide of Indians and theft of their lands and the institutionalized enslavement of blacks, the guilt and responsibility of those most responsible for these harmful wrongdoings will be enhanced so long as such racism is consistent with the fact of their genuine responsibility for the acts in question. An attempt to mitigate U.S. responsibility for these acts of continued and unrectified racist oppression seems to imply that the extent of the mitigation in turn implies the barbaric nature of the United States—from its inception until now. Chapter 10 will among other things consider an objection to reparations due to the barbaric nature of the United States.

Of course, the U.S. government is not the sole agent guilty and responsible for the atrocities mentioned. Various European governments, religious organizations, and businesses share responsibility for the harmful effects of the American holocaust and black slavery. Nonetheless, England, France, the Netherlands, Portugal, Spain, among some others, share guilt and responsibility in varying degrees for the evils of Indian genocide and African slavery. In fact, these and some other countries and nations, insofar as they contributed to the harmful wrongdoings of black slavery, also served as means by which the American holocaust of Indians could be effected. It seems plausible to think that without the slave labor of blacks, neither the British, the French, nor the Spanish prior to 1775 could have had the military might to conquer the Indian nations. For it was the free labor of black slaves that contributed substantially to the building of wealth which in turn made adequately powerful militaries possible at least in terms of the capital required to invest in, develop, and manufacture weapons of mass (gradual) destruction to overcome Indian revolts and other possible opposition to the emerging U.S. empire. So we see that there is a sense in which economic complicity in the "peculiar institution" also makes one co-responsible for the holocaust of Indians.

Reparations are quite complex. And this philosophical study is meant to demonstrate many of their complexities by comparing and juxtaposing the two cases mentioned. The cases for reparations for Indians and blacks involve historic injustices that raise the challenges of moral statutes of limitations and historical complexities involving collective moral responsibility, rights, and duties. While these cases of U.S. oppression share the commonalities of being cases of severe oppression, there are differences between them. First, while the U.S. military exacted genocide on Indians as a means to fulfill manifest destiny and the doctrine of discovery, state and local governments instilled and sustained slavery of blacks that was assisted by the federal courts and legislature by way of the Fugitive Slave Laws, and also winked at by the federal powers. Second, while slavery was, among other things, intended to "Christianize" blacks, westward expansion was intended to annihilate Indians of the plains and western coastal regions. (Even the use of Indian Boarding Schools was intended to achieve cultural annihilation of Indian children.) Third, while Indians and blacks were deemed only somewhat human by the white populace in the United States, curiously blacks were accorded no rights and Indians were seen as sufficiently human with whom to forge treaties.

Why consider only these two instances of oppression? To be sure, there are numerous other examples of U.S. oppressive imperialism alone that led to undue death and destruction. A short list of some of the evils of U.S. imperialism (absent the current invasions and occupations of Iraq and Afghanistan) is found in the following summary:

> But this would be a very long story. It would need to begin with the displacement of the Native Americans, which involved the extermination of about ten million of them. It would need to include the institution of slavery, which, besides all the other evils, probably involved the deaths of about another ten million human beings. This story would need to explain why in 1829 the South American hero Simon Bolivar said, "It seems to be the destiny of the United States to impoverish [the rest of] America." This story would need to deal with the theft of what is now the American Southwest from Mexico. It would need to deal with the increasing number of invasions after the American Civil War in countries such as Guatemala,

El Salvador, Chile, Brazil, and Venezuela. It would need to deal with the so-called Spanish-American Wars of 1898–1902, during which America took control of Cuba, Puerto Rico, the Philippines, Hawaii, and Guam. It would need to explain why the war to deny independence to the Filipinos led to the formation of the Anti-Imperialist League, with one of its members, William James, saying: "God damn the U.S. for its vile conduct in the Philippine Isles." This story of American imperialism would also need to tell of America's interventions further abroad—in Japan in 1854, China in 1900, Russia in 1918, and Hungary in 1919. Back in this hemisphere, this story would need to tell of America's theft of Panama from Colombia in 1903, then its repeated interventions in the Dominican Republic, Haiti, Nicaragua, Costa Rica, Guatemala, and El Salvador, with lengthy occupations in some of those countries. It would need to explain its imperial aims in Italy, Japan, Korea, and the Philippines, even though this meant turning against the Resistance movements, which had fought along side the Allies against the Fascist powers. This story would then need to explain, against deeply entrenched mythology, how the Cold War was far more the result of the imperial ambitions of the United States than those of the Soviet Union. It would also need to tell of the great number of countries in which the United States overthrew constitutional governments, such as Iran (1953), Guatemala (1954), Brazil (1961–64), the Dominican Republic (1965), Greece (1965 and 1967), Indonesia (1965–66), and Chile (1973), as well as its later interventions in Nicaragua and El Salvador. This story of U.S. imperialism would need to describe America's thirty-year effort to prevent the unification and independence of Vietnam, a process that also involved merciless bombings of Laos and Cambodia. It would then need to tell of the policies that have led to such hatred of America in the Arab and Muslim worlds. This story would need, furthermore, to tell of other dimensions of U.S. imperialism, such as the economic policies behind these interventions . . . and America's posture with regard to nuclear weapons.[40]

If even only the first half of what is listed in this statement of U.S. imperialism is true, it is hard to understand why anyone would deny my claim that, on balance, the United States is an evil empire, an outlaw society. And it is rather transparent and understandable why many millions refer to the United States as the "great satan" or the "evil empire." Indeed, given the factual bases of these combined acts of U.S. imperialist aggression and violence, the question seems not to be how anyone could dare bring themselves to think even for a moment that the United States is evil, but rather precisely how it is that any person with a minimal sense of justice and fairness and a fair-minded understanding of U.S. history could possibly deny it! That perhaps the entirety of the list—and then some—holds true, makes the United States perhaps the most evil country in today's world given that most if not all of the above atrocities remain unrectified. Yet this study is an attempt to provide an argument in favor of reparations by the United States to (for a start) two of its victim groups. And should the United States begin to adequately compensate these victim groups (American Indians and blacks), then it can truly be said that it is serious about becoming a society that is morally on track.[41] One moral principle in operation here is that, so long as cases for oppression and reparations are made on reasonably clear evidence, then those groups that were oppressed first and worst should be at the top of the list to receive reparations, as it seems unjust because unfair for those who were oppressed subsequent to and less than other groups to receive compensatory justice before the earlier oppressed groups.

Why focus on these two instances of oppression? One reason is because they represent arguably the harshest instances of U.S. oppression. Another reason is to illustrate the history of U.S. oppression as one of perhaps an unbroken chain from its inception to the present day, thereby illustrating in graphic detail the true nature of U.S. society, morally speaking. Yet another reason is to make clear the reasons why the United States must be brought to justice. And while many millions throughout the world want to achieve this end by way of violence, my method is to achieve justice for the heirs of the very worst U.S. oppression by way of compensatory reparations.

Moreover, why limit the analysis to U.S. evils when so many other countries owe so much for their atrocities committed over the generations? Of course, it is true that the United States is not the only oppressive and evil society. It has a few competitors for the dubious honor of "most evil." However, it is precisely because the United States is among the most evil countries that its oppression deserves our attention, especially in light of the fact that with the restructuring of the former Soviet Union in recent years, the United States is, even with its economic collapse, the dominant global empire. And with its seemingly instinctive desire to do evil throughout its history, the United States deserves our full attention insofar as ethical analysis and rectificatory justice are concerned. Moreover, with so many U.S. citizens who actually believe that the United States is the greatest country in the world, it behooves the serious student of history to put this widely held belief to the test, at least in light of moral considerations. For it is believed that one of the primary reasons why most U.S. citizens have never given serious thought to the provision of reparations to Indians and blacks is precisely because they believe that the United States is so great a country. Perhaps if even U.S. citizens can come to see that, morally and historically speaking, the United States is (on balance) evil, they might come to understand if only a bit just how unjust the United States is, and how much it owes to those whom it has wrongfully harmed most badly over the centuries. If the reparations arguments to Indians and blacks are plausible, then the recent economic meltdown of the United States becomes even deeper than the typical U.S. citizen realizes.

While a careful study of particular cases of compensatory reparations to severely oppressed groups is important in its own right, it has implications for full compliance theories of justice as well. For if historic injustices are both global and deep, then they may permeate political structures that make the very attempt to construct a full compliance theory of justice, while not futile, otiose in light of that fact that vast transfers of wealth required by the demands of compensatory justice in the form of reparations make the hopes of equality and fraternity relegated to the realm of unrealistic utopian theory.

1

Reparations

So, doing what is unjust is the second worst thing. Not paying what's due when one has done what's unjust is by its nature the first worst thing, the very worst of all.

—Socrates[1]

It is the increasing concern of many that certain historic injustices of serious proportions against groups be remedied by way of compensatory justice. For in the earnest attempt to construct and maintain a reasonably just society, we must understand that "justice can never grow on injustice."[2] Yet there are numerous philosophical and ethical questions that arise when considering such matters. This is particularly the case concerning the matter of compensatory justice to groups that have suffered from serious harmful wrongdoings such as genocide, enslavement, or other serious forms of undue violence, theft, and fraud. Reparations have been the main legal remedy for such injustices. Yet the problems of reparations stand in acute need of resolution for the sake of rectificatory justice.

THE PROBLEMS OF DEFINITION, VALUATION, AND JUSTIFICATION

Just as "there is no single 'problem of punishment,'"[3] there is no single problem of reparations. Among the problems of reparations are those of definition, valuation, and justification. The definition of "reparations" concerns the nature of reparations, which differs from the value of reparations, and its justification. While the nature of reparations involves the giving to a group its due, questions of valuation and justification are more complex. The reason for this is that reparations might have an economic, legal, political, or otherwise social or moral value, and the same might be said of their justification.

19

For example, the economic value of reparations is that groups that have been wrongfully and seriously harmed are restored (however approximately) to their previous economic status so as to suffer them no undue financial burden. The political value of reparations is that the wrongfully harmed group retains or justifiably enhances its political power within a larger society, which in turn can have an effect on how the law functions in that society. The social value of reparations is that it respects the compensatory rights of groups so that they suffer no further undue social disadvantage. And the moral value of reparations is that they support a system of rights that protects individual and collective autonomy, and allows groups and their respective members to be able to predict when they ought to suffer conflict with legal, social, or political authorities. In other words, reparations provides a means to effect peace between parties one of which has been unduly harmed by the other. In so doing, reparations can serve to support morally just political and legal institutions.

Just as with theories of punishment, theories of reparations and their justifications must assume a social, political, and legal context in which reparations can function. The justification of reparations might take an institutional or noninstitutional form. That is, reparations might be justified by law or morality, or both. When justified according to law, reparations satisfy a set of requirements deemed appropriate by the rules of a legal system. However, when reparations are morally justified they are justified according to a set of plausible moral principles and ones of a morally enlightened conscience. It is the balance of human reason that grounds such principles, rather than legal rules. This discussion of reparations, like most philosophical ones, focuses mainly on the matter of the moral justification of reparations, but one that is economically and legally feasible.

But whether institutional or not, reparations can be justified in at least two senses.[4] First, there is the justification of the institution of reparations. Then there is the justification of particular instantiations of it. An adequate theory of reparations must account for both such justifications, as it does little good to justify a particular awarding of reparations if the very institution of reparations is itself morally odious. Likewise, if the institution of reparations is justified, yet reparations cannot in practice be awarded justly, then reparations are inefficacious and thus problematic. Most of what follows is an attempt to address indirectly the problem of the general justification of reparations as an institution by way of an investigation of particular cases for reparations.

Failure to distinguish between questions of the nature, value, and justification of reparations will likely lead to confusion of reparations with other forms of justice. Reparations are forms of rectification that are typically made between groups, and are a species of compensatory justice between a harmful wrongdoer to its victim(s) regarding severe instances of injustice. Although there seems to be no conceptual barrier to thinking that reparations can be owed by or to individuals, they are typically paid by and to groups, whether countries, nations, organizations, corporations, companies, ethnic groups, and so on. Paradigmatic instances of historic cases of reparations include Germany's post–World War II reparations to Israel for Nazi Germany's genocide against European Jews, and the payment of reparations to some Japanese American families by the United States for the internment of those Japanese American families subsequent to Japan's military attack on Pearl Harbor on December 7, 1944. While these serve as examples of reparations paid by the offending governments within the same generation or two of the severe harmful wrongdoings, there is in U.S. law precedent for the compensation of the heirs of wronged and harmed parties by the government. As William O. Douglas confirms, with war against France imminent in 1798, the U.S. Congress enacted a series of Alien and Sedition Laws:

> One, which was approved July 14, 1798, made it a crime, among other things, to publish any "false, scandalous and malicious" writing against the government, the Congress or the President "with intent to defame them" or to bring them "into contempt or disrepute" or "to stir up sedition." The crime carried a penalty of $2,000 fine and 2 years in jail.[5]

John Adams sponsored the bill, while Thomas Jefferson opposed it. Kentucky and Virginia passed resolutions condemning the Alien and Sedition Acts as a protest against federal governmental usurpation of power. Most interestingly, for our purposes, is that for the next half-century the Congress passed several laws remitting the fines of those convicted under the Alien and Sedition Acts. More specifically, "in July 1840, it authorized the *repayment of the fine of Matthew Lyon with interest to his heirs* and in July 1850 payment to the heirs of Thomas Cooper of $400 plus interest for the fine he paid."[6] So there is precedent in U.S. law for intergenerational compensation with interest to heirs of those wrongfully accused, convicted of crimes, and sentenced to punishment and fines for their allegedly wrongful behavior. One question here is whether or not there is a sufficiently good reason to deny this same right to Indians and blacks in the form of reparations, assuming that race, ethnicity, or socio-economic class do not count as good reasons. For indeed, "the justice of modern law lies precisely in positive law's ostensible silences."[7] And we must consider the "possibilities of justice that lie in silence"[8] within the law. Moreover, it might be argued that if intergenerational reparations are justified, then how much more are same generational reparations? But prior to answering these questions, we must first answer in precise terms the query: Just what are reparations?

THE NATURE OF REPARATIONS

Reparations, according to the seventh edition of *Black's Law Dictionary*, involve "payment for an injury; redress for a wrong done." They are payments "made by one country to another for damages done during war." Reparations involve restitution, which is the "act of restoring . . . anything to its rightful owner; the act of making good or giving equivalent for any loss, damage or injury; and indemnification. . . . A person who has been unjustly enriched at the expense of another is required to make restitution to the other."[9] Reparations involve restitution, which is the act of restoring something to its rightful owner, the act of making good or giving equivalent for a loss, damage, or injury. One who is unjustly enriched at the expense of another owes reparations to the injured party. As Joel Feinberg states, "Reparations 'sets things straight' or 'gives satisfaction' . . . for redress or injury."[10] By this understanding of the nature of reparations, they might amount to monetary payments normally paid in one lump sum or over time by way of general tax revenues by the wrongful party,[11] or return or repair of property unjustly taken, acquired, or damaged to its rightful owner. In this way, reparations are a kind of compensation to victims of harmful wrongdoing, where the "harm" caused to another is the wrongful setting back of another's valid interest.[12] The harm-based account of reparations is that the harm inflicted on a group by an offender constitutes the violation of the victim group's rights and oftentimes its sovereignty and oversteps the bounds of the offender's own sovereignty (if the offender is a state).[13] Generally, "the aim of compensation is to create a certain sort of 'equality' (or 'equivalence')"[14] such that a harmed party is brought as close as possible to her level of well-being just prior to the harm.[15] As a form of compensatory justice to groups, reparations appear to constitute a species of what Aristotle, in the *Nicomachean Ethics*, refers to as "corrective justice."

Contrary to what increasing numbers of authors urge, reparations do not amount to efforts at "moral repair," or "making amends," or some form of "restorative justice,"[16] unless one understands "restorative justice" in terms that include as a necessary condition material compensation. Reparations do not make it their primary aim to reconcile offenders and victims of harmful wrongdoing. Reparations can be issued by court order or by legislation. In either case, they are not open to reconsideration any more than any other court order or legislative decree. Thus it is imperative that they be considered with all due care by all relevant parties. For in major cases of reparations, changing the terms of the decision could very well disrupt the lives of many people, and unjustly at that. Thus it is rather implausible to think that "both the performance and the content of reparative gestures must be open for assessment and reconsideration by and between injured parties and those who wish to make amends."[17] For that assumes wrongly that what is just in reparations ought to be a matter of the desires of those who owe them in cases of court-ordered reparations, or that a wrongdoer ought to be able to change her mind about what she owes to the victim(s). In either case, the problems implied by such a view loom large in legal contexts.

Although apologies, reconciliation, truth commissions, civil rights legislation and the like are neither necessary nor sufficient conditions of reparations for the most severe injustices, they may serve as meaningful features of an overall just reparations settlement or policy, as Howard McGary notes.[18] What is morally objectionable is the presumption that such measures in themselves serve as adequate rectification for severe harmful wrongdoing to groups as that would violate principles of proportional rectification for harmful wrongdoing. There is little or no question, however, that far lesser instances of harmful wrongdoing to groups may find justice in apologies, truth commissions, reconciliation, and truth commissions. What is crucial is that in cases of severe oppression of groups, reparations involve a full range of factors (including just monetary compensation), and that there is no presumption of forgiveness, reconciliation, or what they imply. For the full rights of victimized groups must always receive a fair measure of justice.

THE VALUE OF REPARATIONS

The value of reparations is that they serve to protect the rights of those groups that would suffer at the hands of harmful wrongdoers. In so doing, reparations have a complex expressive function that is similar to the expressive functions of punishment articulated by Feinberg.[19] Like punishment, reparations disavow the harmful wrongdoings committed and state that the harmful wrongdoers had no right to perform such wrongs. Moreover, they, like punishment, say publicly that such harmful wrongdoings do not represent society's highest aims and aspirations. In democratic societies, reparations speak in the name of the people against such harmful wrongdoings, upholding the genuine standards of law in the face of past failures of the legal system to carry out true justice. Furthermore, like punishment, reparations seek to separate a reasonably just society from its corrupt history, absolving it of at least some of its historic evils. Also, reparations "can express sympathy, benevolence, and concern, but, in addition, it is always the acknowledgement of a past wrong, a 'repayment of a debt,' and hence, like an apology, the redressing of the moral balance of the restoring of the *status quo ante culpum*."[20] More generally, the expressive function of reparations is to make public a society's or organization's own liability concerning the harmful wrongdoings it has wrought on a group. It is to offer an unqualified and unambiguous apology to the wronged parties (or their successors) without the presumption of forgiveness, mercy, or reconciliation. It is to acknowledge in a public way the moral wrongness of the act, along with its gravity. But it is also to remember the rights violation so as not to repeat it, as George Santayana might caution. Reparations send a message to all that justice and fairness are top priorities for a reasonably just society, or one seeking to become just. The value of reparations in a reasonably just society, then, is to protect and honor the rights of innocents. The expressive feature of reparations is articulated by Jeremy Waldron when he writes: "Quite apart from any attempt genuinely to compensate victims or off-set their losses, reparations may symbolize a society's understanding not to forget or deny that a particular injustice took place, and to respect and help sustain a dignified sense of identity-in-memory for the people affected."[21] Insofar as reparations have their expressive functions, they send messages to citizens (and noncitizens alike) which seek to build and strengthen social soli-darity toward justice and fairness within a society. In this way, the justification of reparations is forward-looking.[22]

But the protection of rights of innocents implies further and deeper values of reparations. In protecting the rights of innocents, reparations promote self-respect, respect for others, and self-worth. Feinberg notes these as features of rights more generally.[23] As a compensatory right, reparations (when respected by a viable legal system) send the message that innocents can depend on cer-tain valid claims or interests withstanding the test of violation, providing a certain level of personal and social security for those in a reasonably just soci-ety, or one that is attempting to be just. Charles J. Ogletree, Jr., notes of repara-tions or restitution that:

> It represents the moment at which we assert our independence, personal integrity, and humanity. By asserting our right to reparations, we assert the right to be respected as individuals and as equals, and treated accordingly. We assert the right to receive the compensation due to anyone who has suffered a deprivation, whether through crime or other wrongdoing.[24]

Furthermore, the result of a society's not respecting the right to reparations, or in its doing so sporadically or capriciously, is that justified resentment and distrust accrues between innocent victims of oppression or their heirs and those who benefited from the oppression. As Patricia Williams notes,

> In the law, rights are islands of empowerment. To be unrighted is to be disem-powered, and the line between rights and no-rights is most often the line between dominators and oppressed. Rights contain images of power, and manipulating those images, either visually or linguistically, is central in the making and mainte-nance of rights.[25]

The right to reparations as a species of the general right to compensation, then, is crucial for justice—especially for the less powerful in a society seeking to become or remain reasonably just. "Where one's experience is rooted not just in a sense of illegitimacy but in *being* illegitimate, in being raped, and in the fear of being murdered, then the black adherence to a scheme of both positive and negative rights—to the self, to the sanctity of one's own personal bound-aries—makes sense."[26] Furthermore, the payment of reparations when they are owed is a matter of being a good moral person, as being such a person means making reparations not just for one's harmful wrongdoings to those one has directly harmed wrongfully, but for the harmful wrongdoings against all of the groups one has harmed even indirectly, vicariously, "for the transgressions of all the groups to which one belongs."[27] The more comprehensive the injustice, the more comprehensive the required reparations to achieve justice for the oppressed.

THE JUSTIFICATION OF REPARATIONS

As with punishment, reparations involve an important distinction between the justification of the institution of reparations as a species of rectificatory justice, on the one hand, and the justification of particular awards or payments of reparations, on the other. And there are a number of possible ways to attempt to ground reparations, ethically speaking. First, one might attempt to provide a primarily forward-looking justification for both the institution of reparations and particular instances of them. Second, there might be an attempt to provide a primarily forward-looking justification for the institution of reparations while offering a primarily backward-looking justification for particular cases of reparations. Third, one might try to give a primarily backward-looking justification for the institution of reparations and yet provide a primarily forward-looking justification for the particular instances of them. Fourth, one may seek to provide a primarily backward-looking justification for both the institution of reparations and particular cases of them.

I shall argue for a version of the fourth approach. It is a backward-looking, rights-based one that seeks to base reparations on the wrongful harms groups and their members have experienced. It is further based on the notions of desert, responsibility, and proportionality: desert because only those who are responsible (though not necessarily guilty) ought to pay reparations, and only according to the harm(s) for which they are responsible.[28] Moreover, simply because both the institution of reparations and its particular cases are justified by way of backward-looking reasons does not rule out forward-looking considerations as secondary modes of justification. In practical terms, this means that, at least insofar as severe instances of historic injustice are concerned, monetary and other forms of compensation play a primary role in rectifying the harmful wrongdoing, while utilitarian considerations of reconciliation may play a secondary role. Otherwise, the rights of the victims or their heirs will go disrespected and injustice will ensue. With these important distinctions in mind, I proceed with an evaluation of the general approach to the justification of reparations.

Most of the discussion of reparations centers on whether they are morally justified or even morally required in a particular case. By this is meant whether or not the balance of human reason, informed by a morally enlightened conscience, supports reparations in a particular case. As noted earlier but stated first by Bernard Boxill, there are at least two general kinds of arguments: backward-looking and forward-looking.[29] In either case, reparations, in order to be morally just, must conform to principles of proportionality in compensation. In the case of forward-looking arguments for reparations, a utilitarian tack is usually taken, placing emphasis on social and economic programs that would benefit those individuals who themselves belong to groups that have been victimized by severe injustice. Thus forward-looking arguments for reparations take a distinctly conciliatory and integrationist approach vis-à-vis the oppressors and their respective victim groups. This can be construed as presumptuous by the victims themselves, as compensatory justice normally does not require either that the victims of injustice establish or continue to have social relationships with those who harm them, or that victims have to somehow earn (in the case of affirmative action programs of employment) their legislated or court-ordered "compensation."

Furthermore, those seeking to ground reparations in forward-looking utilitarian arguments face an even deeper problem. It is that such an emphasis is placed on the overall happiness of society that reparations is not taken as a compensatory *right* that can outweigh social utility considerations. This implies that considerations of social utility can and often do override valid moral claims to or interests in (i.e., or rights to) reparations, no matter how severe the injustice experienced by the victimized group. Yet a "right" that can be overridden by social utility considerations is no right at all,[30] and a more backward-looking justification for reparations is sought. Thus forward-looking arguments for reparations seem to not be arguments about reparations at all insofar as reparations are rights to *compensation*, but rather some form of distributive justice wherein the least advantaged are assisted for a variety of reasons, including the relief of poverty and the achievement of general equality. Indeed, the problem of reparations often distinguishes forward-looking utilitarians from backward-looking rights-based theorists. In light of these severe difficulties with forward-looking reasons for reparations, it might be concluded that, just as "if we care about justice, utilitarianism cannot be our theory of punishment,"[31] we must also conclude that if we are serious about compensatory justice, utilitarianism cannot be our underlying justification for reparative compensation to groups that are severely oppressed.

Backward-looking reasons theorists in favor of reparations construe reparations as a compensatory right that cannot be outweighed by considerations of social utility because they are based on valid moral claims or interests. A basic reparations argument runs as follows:

1. Instances of clear and substantial rights violations that result in harmful wrongdoings against groups ought to be compensated by way of reparations;
2. *X* has clearly committed substantial rights violations that resulted in harmful wrongdoings against *Y*;
3. Therefore, *X* ought to pay reparations to *Y*.

where "ought" implies that if the compensation is not paid, then there remains a moral duty unfulfilled and one is morally wrong for not fulfilling it. Thus the primarily backward-looking reasons approach to reparations favored by Boxill, Howard McGary, and myself construe reparations as a fundamental compensatory right just as other compensatory rights within a morally and reasonably just legal system. As such, reparations are part of the rights that support a group's self-respect and respect for others.

In particular cases of reparations, most of the discussion revolves around argument 2 of the above reparations argument. For even if it can be determined who *X* and *Y* are and that they are currently existing groups with reasonably identifiable members, and even if it is possible to identify a particular and serious harmful wrongdoing against *Y* that *X* is responsible for, it might still be asked *how X* violated *Y*'s right(s). This central point in reparations theory is answered by an appeal to moral principles. For example, in the case of indigenous peoples, the principle of morally just acquisitions and transfers is marshaled to ground the rights of indigenous groups to reparations for human rights violations, including genocide and land theft by colonizing countries: "Whatever is acquired or transferred by morally just means is itself morally just; whatever is acquired or transferred by morally unjust means is itself morally unjust."[32] This moral principle is based on Immanuel Kant's point that those who acquire stolen property have a responsibility to "investigate" the historical chain of acquisitions and transfers of the property, and if, unbeknownst to her, the property she deemed she purchased legitimately was the actual possession of another, then "nothing is left to the alleged new owner but to have enjoyed the use of it up to this moment as its possessor in good faith."[33] Such a principle reveals who *X* and *Y* are by way of thorough historical investigation, and in turn tells us who owes reparations to whom, and why. Similar moral principles can be devised in terms of unjust usurpation of a party's land, wages, or labor value as the result of, say, morally unjust enslavement.

Moreover, there are at least two sorts of arguments that might be given for reparations: end-state arguments and historical ones. A. John Simmons clarifies the difference between these kinds of reparations arguments:

> Historical arguments maintain that whether or not a holding or set of holdings is just (that is, whether or not we are entitled to or have a moral right to our holdings) depends on the moral character of the history that produced the holdings. We must see how holdings actually came about in order to know who has a right to what. End-state arguments maintain that the justice of holdings (and our rights to them) depends not on how they came about, but rather on the moral character of the structure (or pattern) of the set of holdings of which they are a part.[34]

Briefly, reparations can be supported on the ground that they truly respect the actions (and inactions, as the case may be) of history in the sense that they try to correct significant imbalances of power or fortune which result from undue force or intrusion, fraud, or other gross forms of wrongdoing. Moreover, reparations disrespect as being morally arbitrary any statute of limitations pertaining to the kinds of cases in question.[35] This is especially true where the extent of the facts of guilt, fault, harm, and identity of the perpetrators and victims are unambiguous. Whether it is a crime occurring forty or four hundred years ago, justice requires that significant harmful wrongdoings are compensated in manners that would do justice to the idea of proportional compensation for damages in cases where the perpetrator(s), victim(s), and damages are provable by current legal standards (beyond reasonable doubt, for example, in criminal cases, and by the preponderance of evidence in tort cases). With reparations, then, both the balance of human reason and history must be our twin and primary guides to the truth of whom (or what) owes what to whom (or what), and why. For my current purposes, it is assumed that the law ought to follow these guides. The argument for reparations to Indians insists that reparations ought to be made when a right has been infringed by way of significant injustice.[36] (In assessing the plausibility of precisely this sort of argument, David Lyons points out that it relies on the ideas of original acquisition and legitimate transfer of land.[37]) Thus the justification for reparations is essentially backward-looking, though it might involve secondary considerations that are forward-looking.

The foregoing also suggests the following about the above reparations argument: The basis for (1) in the above argument might be a desert-based (retributivist) one that insists that there is either a duty to rectify past injustices of a substantial nature. Or, to the extent that it is humanly possible to rectify substantial wrongs for which a wrongdoer is responsible, the offender ought to rectify the harmful wrongdoing.

However, there are numerous objections to the very idea of reparations, and these will vary depending on the case in question.[38] There are cases of historic injustice wherein questions about reparations can be raised, and there are also instances of current injustice. In regard to cases of historic injustice, the concern about a possible moral statute of limitations arises, wherein the contemporary cases do not involve this question. Related to this issue is the possible identification of offending and victim parties which is especially important for cases of historic injustice. Yet the identification of victims, especially for racist crimes, can be challenging. These and some other concerns with reparations are taken up in chapters 6 and 7 with the experiences of Indians and blacks, respectively.

It is important to note that the problem of a possible moral statute of limitations on historic injustice has been neutralized or defeated. First, those who argue in favor of a moral statute of limitations on historic injustice have the burden of argument in demonstrating that such a statute exists, or should exist.[39] Yet no successful arguments have been provided along these lines.[40]

Another general concern with reparations is the extent to which it is difficult to identify perpetrators and victims of injustice. This objection can take one of two forms. First, it might ask how ethnic groups and their members, for instance, might be identified. Second, it might ask how the complexities of history might render the awarding of reparations capricious. But the ethnic group identity matter is reasonably resolvable, as there are analyses of ethnicity based on existing models of identifying members of groups precisely for purposes of compensatory justice.[41] Moreover, no case of reparations is complete to the extent that it is overly complex, that is, where the evidence is weak. Only strong and convincing evidence should be taken as sufficient for awards of reparations.

Whether justified by way of purely backward-looking or a combination of backward- and forward-looking reasons, reparations are typically tied to the collective liability responsibility of the harmful wrongdoer, on the one hand, and the victim group, on the other.[42] As Feinberg argues, collective liability can obtain absent fault, or even guilt. Thus a society can owe damages to a group even though those who committed the harmful wrongdoings against it are no longer alive to pay restitution. But retrospective collective liability responsibility, like its individualist counterpart, admits of degrees, as not every member of a group is as co-responsible as another for harmful wrongdoings caused by the group.[43] Principles of proportional responsibility and compensation must be brought to bear in attempting to clarify more precisely collective responsibility for harmful wrongdoing. One effective manner by which to do this is to require that prior to forcing a collective itself to pay damages to a victim group, all reasonable efforts must be made to force those individuals within the group most directly responsible for the harmful wrongdoing to compensate the wronged group. Only after all such assets are expended and more is owed to the wronged group ought the collective owing reparations to be forced to pay them. The legal model of "piercing the corporate veil" in some criminal cases ought to be used in cases of group oppression in determining responsibility for such oppression that would issue in reparative justice for the oppressed.

How is it possible to identify a group that has wronged another group? How is it possible to identify groups at all? As a prelude to chapter 10 where this matter is addressed in greater detail, I offer the following preliminary observations. One such way is to find significant features of solidarity within an alleged group, for example, among its putative members.[44] Another is to identify aspects of alleged group members construing the goals one has with that of the putative group: "a cardinal feature of group identification is to take the goals of the group to be your goals."[45] This is because "a group is created by the mental processes of its occupants" and "the greater the disparity of existing interests in an aggregate of persons, relevant to current powers—the more competitive is the game the people find themselves in—the less likely it is that they innovatively identify as a group."[46] Thus group membership is a reflection of transformational group homogeneity among members of it. I would add that this construal of group identity seems to assume members' self-identifying as group members, and perhaps even their being identified as such by out-group members.

However, this notion of group identity, however interesting, still seems to beg important questions about whose goals are whose vis-à-vis a group and its members. In the end, I opt for a notion of ethnic group membership that is, for *purposes of positive public policy administration and the law*, genealogical. In other words, given that racial and ethnic groups are social constructions, those socially constructed notions of what ethnic groups are like serve as the basis for applying the genealogical criterion.[47] Thus the basis of racism, the social construction of ethnic or racial groups, becomes the means by which to compensate severe racist harmful wrongdoings. And this paradigm works well (though not perfectly) under the law to compensate groups for experienced oppression, certain legally defined conditions obtaining.

It is a grand confusion indeed to conflate reparations with affirmative action programs, as most forward-looking theorists seem to do. Affirmative action programs tend to justify "reparations" in terms of preferential treatment programs for "disadvantaged" groups in society, providing members of such target groups with education, job training, and employment opportunities.[48] Yet this construal of reparations mistakes reparations as a means of compensatory justice with social welfare programs. In no way is compensatory justice a matter of what one earns in employment, or in education or job training. Courts typically do and should award compensation based on the merits of a case, without regard to how the decision is to affect society as a whole in the ways noted. Stolen goods are not to be rectified by way of a court-ordered system of victims' working for the values of those goods stolen from them. Indeed, it is the thief who is to rectify her victim! The same holds true with a vengeance concerning the insidious notion that affirmative action is somehow a way of making up for genocide, slavery, and life under Jim Crow. Thus the confusion of reparations with affirmative action is a category mistake.

The category mistake of confusing reparations with affirmative action has in the United States led to unfortunate results in affirmative action whereby several groups targeted as "disadvantaged" include both ethnic and gender groups, each of which has experienced harmful wrongdoing at greatly varying kinds and degrees. Furthermore, this difficulty is complicated by the fact that some such groups have served as oppressors of others, yet they are all treated as legitimate targets of affirmative action, and for the betterment of society as a whole. This violates the legal principle that no one ought to be permitted to benefit from their own (or another's) wrongdoing. The most obvious case is that white women have benefited more by affirmative action than even the most oppressed groups combined, as evidenced by their respective social, political, and economic standings in the United States. This problem is explored in the closing chapter.

One further moral problem with this approach to reparations is that the principle(s) of proportional compensation is (are) ignored under such a provision, and often the most advantaged groups within the "disadvantaged" benefit most from affirmative action. So it is not just that those who benefit most from affirmative action programs are, historically and otherwise, oppressive of other groups within the group of "disadvantaged" ones, thereby violating the venerable legal principle that no one should be permitted to benefit from their own (or another's) harmful wrongdoing, it is also that they sometimes benefit more than the least well-off and most deeply oppressed by the most advantaged of the disadvantaged groups. Thus the forward-looking confusion of reparations with affirmative action programs has deleterious effects that, ironically, no self-respecting utilitarian could accept. So reparations must be grounded primarily in a backward-looking moral justification, though one that does not necessarily reject some forward-looking considerations after the backward-looking ones play their primary justificatory roles. This is likely, though not necessarily, to run afoul of some cherished principles of political egalitarians, at least regarding those whose egalitarianism is so crude that it would disallow for the awarding of compensatory justice that would eventuate in economically unequal groups. Yet to take such a line would disregard group rights to compensatory justice and the values thereof.

To the extent that reparations are morally justified in a given case of injustice, to what ought they amount? The answer to this question depends on the relevant facts of a given case. In the case of Indian genocide and gross land theft, reparations must include damages for both the land theft and the genocidal acts against them by the U.S. government. This might include awarding of damages, part of which would include the return of certain especially sacred lands and full mineral rights to Indian peoples. In the case of blacks in the United States whose ancestors were enslaved, land is not so much the issue as financial awards for unpaid wages and other rights abuses that are part and parcel of enslavement. In either case, it is important that possibilities of reconciliation be left primarily in the hands of the members of the victimized groups. For only this kind of policy would begin to accord to each group the sovereignty each deserves but has never experienced given their oppression by the U.S. federal, state, and local governments, as well as certain elements of the U.S. business sector.[49]

So other than cases such as the indigenous ones wherein both land and money are awarded to victimized groups by perpetrating ones, monetary compensation seems to be the principal manner by which reparations are awarded. But this does not rule out the sincerity of reparations being accompanied by official apologies issued by the leadership of the governments or organizations most responsible for the atrocities that justified the reparations in the first place, as argued by McGary.[50] While this is desirable, one must bear in mind that integrative reconciliation ought never to be presumed to be the legitimate aim of forgiveness, even though it requires forgiveness. But forgiveness requires genuine apology, which in turn requires rectification of past wrongs by the harmful wrongdoer.[51] Thus without rectification there can be neither apology, nor forgiveness, nor reconciliation. Reparations, then, serves as a necessary condition for reconciliation, both of which are in turn necessary for justice and peace. However, it is a mistake to think, on the one hand, that reparations are sufficient for reconciliation or forgiveness, or on the other hand that reparations are contingent on either for their moral justification. Just as compensatory justice in general is not contingent on reconciliation or forgiveness, neither reconciliation nor forgiveness constitute or are conditions of reparations. I see these points as being consistent with McGary's analysis.

These issues shall be given far more attention in the chapters that follow as they pertain to reparative justice to Indians and blacks. However, prior to addressing them directly from a rights-based perspective, it is important to assess some recent utilitarian approaches to reparations.

I

UTILITARIAN APPROACHES TO REPARATIONS

Whoever avoids paying his due for his wrongdoing, . . . is and deserves to be miserable beyond all other men, and that one who does what's unjust is always more miserable than the one who suffers it, and the one who avoids paying what's due always more miserable than the one who does pay it.

—Socrates, in Plato, *Gorgias*, 479e

2

Cosmopolitanism and Compensatory Justice

As one commentator puts it: "A lot is at stake in the current debate about the most desirable type of world order and this is why we need to examine carefully the arguments of those who assert that with the end of the bipolar world the opportunity now exists for the establishment of a cosmopolitan world order."[1] My discussion considers some of the arguments by leading cosmopolitan critics of John Rawls's Law of Peoples, and considers cosmopolitan liberalism on its own terms. But it does not highlight the various differences between cosmopolitan theories.[2] Rather, it seeks to concentrate on some ideas that most, if not all, cosmopolitan liberals share with each other, especially in terms of compensatory justice to oppressed peoples.

Among the various differences between cosmopolitanism and Rawls's Law of Peoples is that the former indexes the subjects of international justice to individual persons, while Rawls places the emphasis on justice between states. One of numerous examples of this view is found in the assertion that "we must come to see all humanity as tied together in a common moral network. . . . Since morality is universalistic, its primary focus must be on the individual, not the nation, race, or religious group."[3] One is struck, however, by the unreasonableness of being asked to choose between focusing concerns about global justice on either individuals or collectives, and one is left wondering precisely why this is a choice one *must* make, especially when it is not conceptually absurd to simultaneously affirm the need to *both* address concerns of justice between individuals and those between groups. This leads to a second difference between these theories, as cosmopolitan liberals often criticize Rawls's position for not being equipped to address questions of injustice within states since the point of Rawls's theory of international justice is justice between states. Thus, it is argued by cosmopolitan liberals, Rawls's Law of Peoples fails to address deeper injustices in the form of inequalities within states, and this will lead to toleration of states that mainstream injustices in the form of inequality.[4]

Of course, the cosmopolitan position here is often charged with a kind of cultural imperialism in the form of Bernard Boxill's objection from cultural diversity, or in legal terms, paternalism.[5] This point of criticism is latent in Rawls's own theory of domestic justice when he states that "the principle of fair opportunity can only be imperfectly carried out, at least as long as the institution of the family exists."[6] And Boxill extends Rawls's reasoning to the global context: so long as there are variations in how families raise their children, and analogously, as long as there are variations in how states behave culturally, the principle of fair equality of opportunity is limited in its application. If cultural ideals, for instance, interfere with the ideals favored by other cultures, this might well amount to a barrier to the implementation of the Rawlsian principle of fair equality of opportunity in global contexts. Indeed, Boxill argues, fair equality of opportunity might very well abolish cultural diversity![7] For it would be paternalistic and imperialistic (or, as Boxill argues, "invidious and presumptuous") to insist according to which values equality ought to be realized.[8] And there are degrees to which paternalism can manifest itself. While few would endorse hard paternalism wherein the state is justified in intervening into the affairs of citizens whenever it sees fit and despite the fact that the actions are voluntary because such an interference violates personal autonomy, others might endorse a softer version of it, wherein the state is sometimes justified in interfering into the affairs of its citizens only when it is to prevent serious harm to other citizens and where the actions of said citizens are voluntary. This Millian position is endorsed by, among others, Joel Feinberg and Gerald Dworkin, respectively.[9] And it is vital to see how Boxill's objection from cultural diversity serves as a challenge to cosmopolitan liberalism's reliance on a rather strong principle of global equality of opportunity.

Since the goal of this chapter is not to provide a comprehensive account of cosmopolitan liberal theories, but rather to juxtapose certain aspects of some of them to the Rawlsian account of international justice and relate this discussion to the problem of compensatory justice, I shall provide a set of cosmopolitan claims with which I believe most, if not all, cosmopolitan liberals concur:[10]

1. Various global structures (political, economic, cultural, etc.) eventuate, intentionally or not, in conditions that create and sustain injustice for millions of persons globally;
2. The injustices in (1) include, but are not limited to, inequalities of opportunity to realize basic and essential conditions of living;
3. The global structures in (1) are often, if not typically, those of the ruling and wealthiest countries in the world;
4. Those who cause the injustices in question have duties to address them systemically by way of humanitarian intervention;

5. Corresponding to the duties of those responsible for the injustices in (1) are rights that all persons in the world possess to equality of opportunities to realize the basic and essential conditions of living.

We must bear in mind that there may be some cosmopolitan liberal theorists who do not subscribe to all of these claims, as "there is no consensus among contemporary philosophers and theorists about how the precise content of a cosmopolitan position is to be understood."[11] Nonetheless, the above claims seem to capture a sufficiently robust version of what I shall refer to as "justice cosmopolitanism" that is helpful in our quest to assess some of its central tenets. As Samuel Scheffler notes in describing this version of cosmopolitanism:

> Cosmopolitanism about justice is opposed to any view that posits principled restrictions on the scope of an adequate conception of justice . . . it opposes any view which holds, as a matter of principle, that the norms of justice apply primarily within bounded groups comprising some subset of the global population. For example, this type of cosmopolitanism rejects communitarian and nationalistic arguments to the effect that the principles of distributive justice can properly be applied only within reasonably cohesive social groups . . . cosmopolitanism about justice is equally opposed to liberal theories which set out principles of justice that are to be applied in the first instance to a single society. . . . While remaining otherwise sympathetic to Rawls's ideas, these cosmopolitan critics have sought to defend the application of his principles of justice to the global population as a whole.[12]

In casting cosmopolitanism primarily in terms of considerations of justice, I am not ignoring "cultural cosmopolitanism," which normatively construes persons as citizens of the world instead of nationalistic ones. My discussion shall focus mainly on justice cosmopolitanism, though I shall delve into issues that raise concerns about culture. In fact, the issues I raise about cosmopolitan liberalism's apparent denial of the moral relevance of culture, ethnicity, and so on, amounts to a disrespecting of the rights to compensatory justice for various groups that were and are oppressed by certain states and those organizations and individuals supporting them.[13]

While it is admirable that cosmopolitan liberals seek a global order that will hold countries and nongovernmental organizations to duties of justice in making sure that those without have enough to make it in the world, it is unclear how such duties are to be well grounded so as to avoid a kind of "fuzzy innocence" against which Richard Falk cautions.[14] Just what is the duty in question? Is it a duty of assistance to relieve *poverty*, as Thomas Pogge and many other cosmopolitan liberals advocate? Or, is it a duty of assistance to address those truly in *need*? For as Larry Temkin argues, an individual or a group can be poor relative to others within their society, but be relatively wealthy, globally speaking. This suggests that poverty is a comparative notion, though the concept that seems to justify a duty of assistance seems to be one of need (another comparative concept), not poverty.[15]

COSMOPOLITANISM, EQUALITY, AND THE DUTY OF HUMANITARIAN ASSISTANCE

Once bases of need are determined, *can* they be realized in the way that cosmopolitan liberalism supposes they can? This question poses an "ought implies can" problem for global justice, as it might be argued that there are genetic differences between humans that prevent conditions of equality from obtaining even with significant efforts to equalize humans. It is noteworthy, however, that genetics does *not* support such a skepticism about global equality.[16] Moreover, precisely how ought these duties to be distributed? Just who or what has them? The moral duty to provide for those in need who are victims of natural disasters, I think, can be well grounded in the duty of assistance based on anti–bad Samaritan laws at the state level. And a corollary duty can be well grounded at the international level, though cosmopolitan liberals need to explain precisely the content of such an international duty along these lines and how it might be incorporated into international law. That much is relatively uncontroversial, so long as the duty is construed as an imperfect one, and the duty's fulfillment does not pose an unreasonable risk of harm to those carrying out the duty in good faith.[17]

But a number of difficulties arise here for the cosmopolitan liberal account of global justice and equality. G. A. Cohen points out that the Marxist notion of voluntary equality within a state assumes plenary abundance driven by capitalist modes of production. But Marxism is problematic in its insistence on equality in light of the lack of effectively limitless productive power.[18] This "pre-green" mentality has an interesting parallel to cosmopolitanism in that the global equality that cosmopolitan liberals advocate seems unrealistic in light of the realities of quite limited powers of production coupled with the lack of abundance of food, shelter, and clothing relative to the ever-increasing numbers of humans on earth. Thus it is unclear that the cosmopolitan ideal of wealthier states and nongovernment organizations assisting those in poverty can succeed in the long run, though with proper education, perhaps this problem can be dealt with in part by convincing all states and individuals to cease overpopulating the earth such that now dwindling natural resources will in fact sufficiently serve humans in the future. For just as it is "unrealistic to hope for voluntary equality in a society which is not rich,"[19] it is unrealistic to hope for global equality in a world wherein most individuals and societies continue, for whatever reasons, to overpopulate with reckless abandon, thereby threatening the viability of future generations with a significant lack of sufficient natural resources. Nonetheless, the cosmopolitan liberal may counter with a cautious optimism, "we may envisage a level of material plenty which falls short of the limitless conflicts-dissolving abundance projected by Marx, but which is abundant enough so that, although conflicts of interest persist, they can be resolved without the exercise of coercion."[20] So it is at least logically possible, and even practically so, to evade this pragmatic concern with cosmopolitan egalitarian distributive justice. How probable this prospect is in light of history is, of course, unclear.

Related to the problem of overpopulation of humans, however, is a difficulty confronting Marxists and equality, one that seems to also face cosmopolitanism insofar as it is committed to the latter. "Starving people," Cohen argues, "are not necessarily people who have produced what starving people need; and if what people produce belongs by right to them;[21] . . . then starving people who have *not* produced it have no claim on it."[22] Now as Cohen ingeniously explains, this

> forces a choice between the principle of a right to the product of one's labor embedded in the doctrine of exploitation and the principle of equality of benefits and burdens which negates the right to the product of one's labor and which is required to defend support for very needy people who are not producers and who are, *a fortiori*, not exploited.[23]
>
> When those who suffer dire need can be conceived as those coinciding with, or as a subset of, the exploited working class, then the socialist doctrine of exploitation does not cause much difficulty for the socialist principle of distribution according to need. But once the really needy and the exploited producers no longer coincide, then the inherited doctrine of exploitation is flagrantly incongruent with even the minimal principle of the welfare state.[24]

And what Cohen reveals about these Marxist principles, seemingly assumed or even adopted explicitly by cosmopolitan liberals, concerning states appears to apply globally. Given the environmental crises we have been facing for decades, it is far from obvious that material consumption will be matched by material production such that cosmopolitan ideals of global equality can be realized without posing serious problems for the well off. This poses the problem of good Samaritanism which states that there are duties of assistance to endangered strangers, but that such duties hold only to the point at which those assisting others are themselves placed at genuine risk of their own well-being. And it is an empirical question as to how much worse off the better off must become for the cosmopolitan ideal of global equality and redistributive justice to be deemed unreasonable. Cohen states the problem in cautionary terms:

> When aggregate wealth is increasing, the condition of those at the bottom of society, and in the world, can improve, even while the distance between them and the better off does not diminish, or even grows. Where such improvement occurs (and it has occurred, on a substantial scale, for many disadvantaged groups), egalitarian justice does not cease to demand equality, but that demand can seem

shrill, and even dangerous, if the worse off are steadily growing better off, even though they are not catching up with those above them. When, however, progress must give way to regress, when average material living standards must fall, then poor people and poor nations can no longer hope to approach the levels of amenity which are now enjoyed by the world's well off. Sharply falling average standards mean that settling for limitless improvement, instead of equality, ceases to be an option, and huge disparities of wealth become correspondingly more intolerable, from a moral point of view.[25]

There is a related problem for cosmopolitan liberalism, call it the "economic imperialism objection to global equality."[26] It is related to Boxill's objection from cultural diversity, and states that as cosmopolitan liberals are inclined to argue, poverty may prevent people from realizing many ideals, cultural and otherwise. But, this objection presses, if to eradicate such poverty means that Western values must be implemented, then economics dictates culture, which implies that Western values will control the values of Westerners and non-Westerners alike, thus threatening to destroy non-Western cultures and ways of being. The point of this objection is not to insist on the immutability of cultures, Western or otherwise. Rather, cosmopolitan liberals, if they want to demonstrate a genuine concern for cultural differences, must explain how combating and preventing global poverty will not pressure unnecessarily those in non-Western cultures to succumb to Western ideals when they would not otherwise desire to do so. The replication of any ideals— Western or not—ought always to be done voluntarily, not because one is economically coerced to do so in order to survive or to avoid dire poverty. This is especially the case where the consequences of poverty and need can be averted without cultural change. As Boxill exclaims, "We may not yet be in a position to confidently claim that poor countries must replicate the West to escape from poverty."[27]

Given the above considerations and what is at stake, it would appear that cosmopolitanism has an empirical burden of demonstrating how cultural diversity can be maintained in the midst of addressing the needy. For "if cultural diversity can thrive in a world without poverty, and if the distinct cultures can, while changing, yet retain distinct standards of success, global fair equality of opportunity may remain an unapproachable ideal."[28] Why is the preservation of cultural diversity important? This is where Boxill grounds the objection from cultural diversity in the objection from individual self-respect. As Boxill notes, cultural diversity lies at the heart of self-respect, which is, he implies, a necessary condition of justice.[29] There simply cannot be a just social order, domestically or globally, without those in it being respectful of themselves. And community life is essential to cultural elements that ground self-respect. After all, "By what reasoning do we know that desires for higher incomes will be satiated before pluralism is obliterated? And if they are not, why should we believe that any ideal will displace the sole and triumphant desire for wealth?"[30] The concern, of course, is to realize a world of autonomous, sovereign and culturally diverse states, each with its own sustaining power of growth within environmental limits.[31] Yet "a nation which is less affluent than others can still be autonomous. A nation which is the least-advantaged class of other nations is likely to lose its autonomy, and to have to order its affairs according to their dictates."[32] An example of this problem is the Westernization of Mexico and Latin American countries that see as their way out of poverty the adopting of Western values, values that to a certain extent can and often do endanger the family values that are so central to our way of life as Latinos/Hispanics. One way this occurs is when so many of us Latinos cross the U.S. border for employment, and end up adopting Western values that are incongruent with our original ones. It is unclear whether this happens as a natural process of acculturation in the meeting of peoples, or whether it is necessary in order to secure and maintain the employment so desperately needed to survive. In either case, it strongly suggests a caution that the equality that cosmopolitan liberals advocate must concern itself with safeguards against the threats to cultural and ethnic identity that lie at the foundation of self-respect.

It is dubious, then, that cosmopolitan liberalism's quest for global distributive justice is realizable in that of the problems that it seems to pose for diverse cultures which serve as bases of self-respect, which in turn is necessary for justice. Global poverty and need must be dealt with in ways that retain cultural diversity as much as practically possible, and when that is not possible, cultures ought not to be modified or changed by economic or other coercive means. Intuitively, it seems possible to address at least most needs of global peoples with no economic or cultural strings attached. But this sort of an approach to the needy tests the motives of those addressing the needs. And some of Rawls's principles for global justice are precisely intended to speak to this problem, delimiting the conditions under which it is justified to assist in the eradication of need.

But what about need and injustices that are caused, wrongfully, by humans? Do the victims of such harmful wrongdoings have *rights* that are global insofar as the duty-bearers of such rights are concerned? It would seem to distort plausible notions of collective responsibility to think that anyone but those who are significantly responsible for nonnatural harmful wrongdoings have duties *of compensation* to address the problems. But as Temkin states in terms of good Samaritanism and the pool lounger case:[33]

> After all, I *can* have a moral obligation to save a drowning child that someone else has thrown in a pool, or to drive a bleeding hit and run victim to the hospital. Of course, . . . my obligations towards others can be limited by the extent to which I can effectively aid them and the costs to me of my doing so, but the mere fact that another agent is responsible for someone's plight is not sufficient to automatically absolve me of obligations towards them.[34]

Thus there might be a duty to assist, either in a causally focused or a causally amorphous manner, those in need either by results of natural events beyond their control or due to the actions of others.[35] And while the former kinds of cases are relatively unproblematic in that most everyone believes that it is morally problematic to not assist those who are victimized by way of famines caused by, say, natural disasters beyond our control or predictability, the latter kinds of cases fall clearly within the purview of anti–bad Samaritan statutes and in no way excuse from responsibility those who could assist those in need without undue cost to themselves. But these are not duties of compensation, but of assistance. For duties of compensation pertain to those that are bound to make the injured parties as whole as they were prior to being injured. There are, rather, duties of assistance to those in need because of circumstances not of their own doing. In such cases, then, the well off cannot simply ignore the needy without being subject to serious moral criticism.[36]

COSMOPOLITANISM AND COMPENSATORY JUSTICE

But the problem of poverty or genuine need caused by harmful wrongdoing requires a more fine-grained analysis of who is and/or ought to be responsible for what. It is implausible to argue, as some cosmopolitan liberals do, that an entire country has a duty to assist in the eradication of global poverty and to address long-term issues of inequality if in fact only a certain, say, powerful elite in that country were indeed responsible for the problems in question, due to fraud, nepotism, and so forth. And this is true despite the fact that such responsible agents may have been elected by the people in some meaningfully democratic way. This is true not simply because of the widespread problem of the diffusion of responsibility in social contexts, but because of the fact that the citizens may not have (or could not reasonably be said to have) known about the workings of the primary responsible agents of the harms in question. Perhaps the most that can be said here is that, to the extent that the citizens of that country could and should have known about what their elected leaders did that might or would likely lead to harmful wrongdoings of others, that is the extent to which the citizens should be held liable and have a duty of addressing the problems adequately. But this is at best a secondary form of responsibility.

It would seem reasonable under the circumstances to adopt a differentialist model of addressing serious instances of nonnatural injustice. First, all primary responsible agents have duties of compensation toward those they have wrongfully harmed. Only subsequent to depleting all of their personal assets in addressing an injustice for which they are primary responsible agents would it be justified to hold citizens of the responsible country liable for compensatory damages, and this is largely because of the deeper pockets that groups have. This strategy makes sure that those who make the worse decisions and have them carried out are held accountable for what they do to wrongfully harm others. So if global need is caused by, say, a policy of the United States, then the first question to ask is who enacted and directly supported the policy and by way of commonsense reflection should have known the deleterious effects it might well or would have on others. Another key question is who, of secondary agents, knew or should have known about it. In many cases, holding primary agents compensatorily responsible for their harmful wrongdoings is sufficient to solve even problems of poverty. After all, if the primary agents are high-level government and corporate executives, there are plenty of personal assets for resolving, or almost resolving entire circumstances of need, at least in many cases. Only after all such personal assets are depleted in compensating for the damages incurred should any attempt be made to approach those indirectly responsible for their part in the wrongful harms. Assumed here, of course, is a plausible principle of proportional compensation according to which all wrongful harms should be compensated according to the levels or degrees of responsibility of those who are responsible (liable) for them. Thus most of the compensation should be paid, if possible given the situational factors of the case, by those most responsible for the creation of the injustice in the first place. This plan is not meant to address (or deny the importance of) the cosmopolitan liberals' concern with equality of opportunity. Rather, it is to address the harms themselves and those directly responsible for them.

Those wrongfully harmed have remedial rights to redress and compensation, while those primarily responsible for such harms have duties of compensation. And no theory of governmental or corporate limited liability carries sufficient moral weight to override these factors. In their incessant search for principles of global distributive justice, the cosmopolitan liberals seemed to have downplayed, if not given short-shrift to, principles of compensatory justice. An example of this is found in Pogge's attempt to address the "effects of a common and violent history":

> The present circumstances of the global poor are significantly shaped by a dramatic period of conquest and colonization, with severe oppression, enslavement, even genocide, through which the native institutions and cultures of four continents were destroyed or severely traumatized. This is not say (or deny) that affluent descendants of those who took part in these crimes bear some special restitutive responsibility toward impoverished descendants of those who were victims of these crimes. The thought is rather that we must not uphold extreme inequality in social starting positions when the allocation of these positions depends upon historical processes in which moral principles and legal rules were massively violated. A morally deeply tarnished history should not be allowed to result in *radical* inequality.[37]

One difficulty with this approach is that it wrongly construes the solution to the problem, not as one of reparative justice in terms of compensation as outlined above, but in terms of equal opportunities for those who are the least advantaged by historic injustice. In short, it implicitly subsumes any right to compensatory justice under the putative right to equality.

To see the absurdity of this position, one need only to think about it in terms of current U.S. law. Currently under the law in the United States those who wrongfully harm others can be held liable under certain circumstances for compensatory damages. And if my criticism of Rawls's theory of global justice holds true, then what is needed are remedial principles of compensatory justice to support the rights affirmed in his substantive principles of justice.[38] Indeed, there is no conceptual absurdity in this idea, nor is it a practical impossibility even at the level of international law—assuming that system of international justice is possible in the first place. But what Pogge seems to imply is that, instead of compensating those who are victimized by harmful wrongdoings, the perpetrators of the harmful wrongdoings are to pay no compensation whatsoever. His words, "This is not to say (or to deny) that affluent descendants of those who took part in these crimes bear some special restitutive responsibility," simply undermine the point of compensatory justice and reveal how seemingly unconcerned Pogge is with it. His real concern is with global distributive justice—apparently, even when history is clear as to the identity of the perpetrators of severe harmful wrongdoing! Moreover, Pogge's claim reveals that he does not understand that it is not only the wealthy descendants who would owe, but *any and all* such descendants of harmful wrongdoers, revealing once again his bias toward distributive justice and against compensatory justice. Furthermore, Pogge misunderstands the point of compensatory justice when he asserts that "a morally deeply tarnished history must not be allowed to result in *radical* inequality."[39] Apparently, the implication here is that such a history of "grievous wrongs" might be allowed to result in something other than "radical" inequality. And he goes on to argue that "this is the moral rationale behind Abraham Lincoln's 40-acres-and-a-mule promise of 1863."[40]

It is difficult to imagine a more distorted picture of U.S. history than Pogge's on what constitutes compensation. The U.S. government withdrew the suggestion of reparations to newly freed ex-slaves because it simply did not want to pay them in that it was too costly for those it deemed first-class citizens. Most whites thought they owed nothing to legally freed mostly Africans, many Indians, and some others. After all, many of them with great political and economic influence had just lost their investments due to the abolition of slavery, and if they paid reparations to newly freed blacks, then they would have to answer the repeated calls for reparations on behalf of generations of Indians, which was quite out of the question as it was not in line with the terms of manifest destiny. And it would have left most whites in dire poverty because of how much they would have owed to those whose relatives they murdered or had murdered by the U.S. Army in order to steal millions of acres of land, and to those who were forced to do their labors, unpaid. But if compensatory rights are to be taken seriously, such compensation is *deserved* for those whose rights are violated in such ways.

Rights to compensation have little or nothing to do with matters of inequality, normatively speaking. And it is this point that many cosmopolitan liberal philosophers cannot seem to fathom given their commitment to their particular ideology of social equality. This underscores my suspicions about both the agenda of many cosmopolitan liberals, namely, that they are inadequately concerned with compensatory justice. Hence they have no plans for or interest in reparations except insofar as they can (however mistakenly) construe them in terms of affirmative action programs, which has already been shown to be a category mistake.[41] They seem concerned about social equality instead of compensation and the true justice that compensation, when properly administered, can provide in terms of supporting autonomy and sovereignty rights. Indeed, my claim is that these liberals have at best articulated and defended half-truths about justice, for distributive justice without compensatory justice is grossly incomplete justice at best, as my argument is intended to make clear. For those who might construe this statement as hyperbole, consider the fact that continual denials of rights (valid claims) to compensation will always have the effect of withholding from right holders what is their due, which in turn is a significant injustice. I concur, then, with David Miller when he argues that cosmopolitanism does not err in making equality of central importance in dealing with world poverty. But it goes wrong in thinking that equality is all that is central to global justice.[42]

However, I would extend Miller's observation in the following way. Many cosmopolitan liberals seem to subscribe to a notion of equality that is too extreme for even many who have defended more reasonable and nuanced versions of egalitarianism. As Temkin argues quite apart from cosmopolitan liberalism,

> Moral responsibility matters to the egalitarian. On my view, this is because the concern for equality is ultimately a concern about comparative *fairness*, and it is not unfair if I am morally *responsible* for being worse off than you. This is why prior wrongdoing can matter. If I am worse off than you due to my own prior wrongdoing, the inequality between us need not be unfair, or in any other way morally objectionable.[43]

Thus it is not obvious that cosmopolitan liberals, whose theories of global (distributive) justice are grounded in some rather restrictive notion of egalitarianism, are working with a viable notion of equality. The cosmopolitan liberal notion of equality seems to be far to the extreme of many of those who have been analyzing the concept of equality before cosmopolitanism resurfaced in recent philosophical discussions. The cosmopolitan notion of global equality, it appears, is rather unmitigated and facile compared to the conceptions of equality of Richard J. Arneson,[44] John Broome,[45] G. A. Cohen,[46] Ronald Dworkin,[47] Rawls, John Roemer,[48] Samuel Scheffler,[49] Amartya Sen,[50] Peter Singer,[51]

Temkin,[52] Peter Unger,[53] Bernard Williams,[54] and others.[55] This lends credence to Charles R. Beitz's claim that "for the subject of political equality, the need for closer theoretical attention is especially acute."[56] And this places the burden of argument on cosmopolitan liberals to further clarify and defend their version of equality—especially one that either omits considerations of compensatory justice, or devalues them absent supportive argument.

Imagine being an American Indian or a descendant of African slaves in the United States and being informed by Pogge that what you really need is to be made "equal" to U.S. whites, many of whose forebears were significantly responsible for the genocide, enslavement, and part of the greatest land theft in human history that greatly affects your life situation and prospects even today. This means that many of such descendants benefited from such evils by the bequeathals of lands and other forms of wealth, unlike Indians and blacks. Also bear in mind that it is in part the "culture" of the United States that systematically and intentionally destroyed the cultures of the said people. To be fair, also imagine Pogge insisting that the United States has a duty to create a system of life that would provide you with equality. Would you not think that Pogge's plan would fall shy of what compensatory justice requires, not only in the genuine amounts of compensation owed, but also in terms of effectively forcing cultural integration with those who are descendants of the evil people who murdered, enslaved, and stole what is now the territory of the United States from your ancestors? It is here where the paternalistic cultural imperialism of Pogge's cosmopolitanism rears its ugly head. While Rawls simply neglects to include any principles of compensatory justice in his statement of principles of international justice,[57] Pogge implies that there is no room for any hearty ones in his theory of global justice. Pogge quite readily indexes equality to what the West regards to be minimally required for (distributive) justice. But such a notion neglects *compensatory and cultural opportunities* independent of Western dominance. Why would anyone desire to become a part of a global scheme of equality that denied rights to compensation and cultural freedom that would best ensure, if anything can ensure, liberation from the oppressive forces of at least parts of the West?

Pogge addresses the objection from Western imperialism:

> When human rights are understood as a standard for assessing only national institutional orders and governments, then it makes sense to envision a plurality of standards for societies that differ in their history, culture, population size and density, natural environment, geopolitical context and stage of economic and technological development. But when human rights are understood also as a standard for assessing the *global* institutional order, international diversity can no longer be accommodated in this way. There can be, at any given time, only *one* global order. If it is to be possible to justify this global order to persons in all parts of the world and also to reach agreement on how it should be adjusted and reformed in the light of new experience or changed circumstances, then we must aspire to a *single, universal* standard that all persons and peoples can accept as the

basis for moral judgments about the global order that constrains and conditions human life everywhere.[58]

But this reply to the anti-imperialism objection to cosmopolitan liberalism both misses the point and falls prey to Boxill's objection to a world government. What Pogge does in the above words is to essentially reassert the position of cosmopolitanism, rather than defend it from the stated objection. Where Pogge claims that what is needed is a "universal standard that all persons and peoples can accept," he seems to not understand that this is precisely the point of argument that is being challenged by the objection under consideration. And it will not do for him to state what he does if the charge is that the imperialism of cosmopolitan liberalism is precisely that which will hinder such agreement in the first place.

COSMOPOLITANISM AND HUMAN RIGHTS

Perhaps a clue to the cosmopolitan confusion lies with its rather vague conception of human rights, which are conceived as rights that all persons possess and are morally binding on others who have duties of compliance with the terms of such rights. Pogge avers: "Once human rights are understood as moral claims on our global order, there simply is no attractive, tolerant, and pluralistic alternative to conceiving them as valid universally." And, "Our global order cannot be designed so as to give all human beings the assurance that they will be able to meet their most basic needs *and* so as to give all governments maximal control over the lives and values of the peoples they rule *and* so as to ensure the fullest flourishing." Finally, he states:

> It is, for the future of humankind, the most important and most urgent task of our time to set the development of our global order upon an acceptable path. In order to do this together, peacefully, we need international agreement on a common moral standard for assessing the feasible alternatives. The best hope for such a common moral standard that is both plausible and is capable of wide international acceptance today is a conception of human rights. At the very least, the burden now is on those who reject the very idea of human rights to formulate and justify their own alternative standard for achieving a global order acceptable to all.[59]

Of course, "human rights as moral rights entail obligations on others."[60] In other words, there is in general a correlation of rights and duties such that if I have a right to something, then others have a duty to refrain from interfering in the exercise or enjoyment of my right if it is a negative duty, or to provide me with certain goods and/or services if it is a positive duty. In the former case, my right is said to be a positive one, and in the latter case it is said to be negative. The difficulty with Pogge's statements is that he merely asserts that certain egalitarian human rights exist, and that certain corresponding duties of others exist. Instead of taking his statements as a *reductio ad absurdum* of his own theory of global justice, he reasserts his own theory as if it is the only viable one. But if what Pogge argues is correct, then a global order of justice cannot exist in the way he envisions it insofar as a necessary condition of global justice is respect for compensatory rights. So it is false to claim as he does that the argumentative burden is on those who would deny cosmopolitan egalitarian justice.

To understand this point more clearly, consider the nature of a right—in particular, a human right. If it is true, as Pogge claims, that all persons have a right "to be able to meet their most basic needs," then there would correlate with that right a negative duty of others to not interfere with the exercise or enjoyment of that right. *That* is clearly what the human right in question, if it does exist, implies in the way of others' duties to the right holder. But what Pogge and other cosmopolitan liberals need to demonstrate is their much stronger claim that the positive duty of assistance is required by the human right in question. But why would such a positive duty of assistance hold? Perhaps it might hold in some cases of famine or other poverty caused by natural disasters. But as Joel Feinberg has argued, it cannot obtain where certain goods or services are in short supply (ought implies can).[61] But what about famine or poverty caused by human greed, selfishness, or fraud? Pogge has a partially plausible answer to this question. He states that "the primary moral responsibility for the realization of human rights must rest with those who shape and impose" the existing political and economic institutions, whether it be the International Monetary Fund, the World Bank, or other such global institutions.[62] This is an insightful claim. But it either draws its plausibility from some right of compensatory justice, as I have been advocating throughout this chapter, or it needs to explain why "the most powerful and affluent countries" are necessarily the ones who possess this positive duty. Again, if the duty at stake here is the negative one of noninterference, or of assisting an endangered stranger, few, if any, problems arise. But what if famine is eradicated, and a people is content to live the "simple life" and not one of equality construed in terms of Western ideals? Again, we are faced with Boxill's objection from cultural diversity that cosmopolitan liberals seem not to be able to adequately answer.

Perhaps this problem can be at least partially averted if the cosmopolitan liberal states that the positive duty of assistance is an imperfect one, only holding in cases where those in poverty communicate their desire to claim their right to or interest in equality of opportunity. But then how does this differ from arguing that the human right in question imposes only a negative duty of noninterference, in conjunction with the duty to assist endangered strangers so long as the fulfillment of that duty does not endanger oneself? As Miller writes, "The issue is how to identify one particular agent, or a group of agents, as having a particular responsibility to remedy the situation."[63] Unless and until cosmopolitan liberals can accomplish this, then in light of the general correlation of rights and duties, it would appear that they, in their incessant insistence on "human rights," might well be indulgent in what Onora O'Neill refers to as the "free-floating rhetoric of rights,"[64] or what has been referred to as the "proliferation of rights" talk.[65]

Indeed, some egalitarians who are not cosmopolitan liberals have argued that a plausible notion of equality need not, or ought not, to invoke the notion of rights at all. Temkin reasons accordingly:

> Telic egalitarians believe that equality, or inequality, is a feature that is relevant to the *goodness* of outcomes, such that, *ceteris paribus*, the worse a situation is regarding equality the worse the situation is. But it does not follow from this that "all persons have a general right, as against all other persons, *to be supplied with . . . some . . . good*, at the expense of all who have more of this good." Indeed, *rights* do not have to enter into the egalitarian's picture at all, and my understanding and characterization of equality does not invoke, or in any way rely on, the notion that the worse off have a *right* to equality, or a *right* against the better off to be made as well off as they.
>
> . . . The worse off may be improved through sheer good fortune, or the better off may be worsened—or "leveled down"—through sheer bad luck. *Either* event may bring about a *perfect* situation regarding equality. But, then, it obviously is not central to the egalitarian's view that the worse off should be made better off *at the expense* of those who are initially better off. . . . But then, *a fortiori*, it is not part of the egalitarian's view that the worse off must "be supplied with . . . some variable and some commensurable good," much less that the worse off have a *right* to be supplied with such a good.
>
> . . . Basically, egalitarians favor promoting equality between equally deserving people *whoever those people are*, regardless of race, gender, religion, nationality, sexual orientation, or any other characteristics or relationships of the people in question.[66]

Thus it is highly questionable whether cosmopolitan liberals are working with a conception of global equality that is not in need of independent argumentative support in light of the fact that what they regard as equality is quite stronger than what others who consider themselves egalitarians think it ought to be.

Furthermore, this problem of cosmopolitan liberals not being seriously interested in compensatory justice is found in other cosmopolitan liberal writers. In fact, some cosmopolitan liberals seem to have conflated compensatory justice with distributive justice. To see this, consider the following:

> If the remedy for imperialism were reparations for past injustices, the duty to correct the injustice would be fulfilled once the compensation for past injustices had been paid. There would be no guarantee that future economic relations would be to the maximum benefit of the least advantaged. Hence, on this account of remedying the injustice of imperialism may provide one-time relief for millions of disadvantaged people, but it would not secure long-term prospects for them in the way that institutions governed by democratic equality would.[67]

But these claims contain numerous problems. First, there seems to be an assumption and implication that reparative justice would take the form of "one-time" cash payments to beneficiaries. Yet it is clear that reparations can and would be institutionalized for efficiency and long-term value for the beneficiaries.[68] And let us not forget that reparations, properly construed and institutionalized, exert expressive functions that are vital to the kind of ethnic integration that cosmopolitan liberals desire.[69] Moreover, the conflation of compensatory justice with distributive justice is found in the further presumption that there is something wrong with even adequate and fair compensation for harmful wrongdoings. However, this view can only make sense according to an ethic that in effect subsumes rights under social utility considerations. But to take rights seriously is to disallow social utility to trump them, as Rawls argues. Otherwise, there are not rights at all, but in effect privileges at the whims of the perceived demands of social utility. What is so wrong with a world of adequately compensated harmful wrongdoings that cosmopolitan liberals seem to eschew them? The key to the presumption in question is found in the locution "There would be no guarantee that future economic relations . . ." But why ought compensatory justice be sacrificed for the sake of "future economic relations"? Even if we want to admit the unproven anti-compensatory rights stance concerning the importance of economic equality of opportunity, why should compensatory justice rights be jettisoned in favor of something that, contrary to the author's assertion, can very well make the victims some of the wealthiest people? To take my previous example, if adequate reparations were paid to Indians and blacks, there simply would not in the foreseeable future be any serious worry that they would even require distributive economic justice, thus making dubious the unsupported claim that democratic institutions would better ensure their long-term prospects.

Moreover, if someone becomes poor after becoming wealthy through reparations (not by direct cash disbursement, but indirectly by institutional compensatory measures), it would be folly to have any sympathy for them, and surely no moral duty to assist accrues to anyone on their behalf, that is, unless their poverty results from fraud or some other form of injustice beyond their control and for which they are not responsible. To not believe this would seem to imply that "there are very good reasons to believe that after a one-time compensatory payment, inequalities would continue to grow in the *lassiez-faire* global market."[70] But how is this an argument against the compensatory or remedial *right* to reparations? And how is reparations some kind of injustice? Reparations constitute a compensatory *right* that each person in a wrongfully harmed group possesses and that correlates with a duty of compensatory justice of her harmful wrongdoer, alienable only by the group harmed. Even if the group harmed wants to destroy all the monetary assets that compensation would pay it by law, it is its right and its alone to do so. And it is a kind of morally presumptuous paternalism that would even imply something one way or another about what might happen as a result of *her* realizing *her* compensatory benefits. It is the kind of view that subsumes rights under utility and compensatory justice under distributive justice as it conflates justice with equality without rights to compensation (where compensation is justified). From the standpoint of Indian and black experiences, furthermore, it is nothing short of morally insulting to desire a policy or system that would grant effectively forced integration and equality of opportunity to become, in essence, culturally Westernized, and deny what justice truly requires in terms of compensatory justice. If compensated according to just principles of proportionality, each Indian and black would become wealthy several times over, and very rapidly. Why would there be a need for future distributive justice in their cases?

There is no need for distributive justice that effectively brings forced integration of peoples that compensatory justice does not. It is a kind of Western liberal paternalism that seeks to replace the generations (in many cases) of calls for reparative justice with a Westernized notion of making everyone as equal as possible according to some middle-class notion of what cosmopolitan liberals desire for their seemingly unrealistic utopia. It is unrealistic in that many cosmopolitan liberals do not seem to understand that the world is replete with injustices that not only require compensation, but often create enemies between the harmful wrongdoers and their victims.[71]

Again, a Westernized notion of equality of opportunity is highly dubious in the world of harmful wrongdoers who deserve to be punished and forced to adequately compensate their victims. Nor should any form of reconciliation be required in such cases. Many cosmopolitan liberals claim that they seek justice in the world. But as Martha Nussbaum argues: "We must ask the questions, and we must know enough and imagine enough to give sensible answers."[72] But how "just" and "sensible" is it to spin theories of utopias where victims of harmful wrongdoings are uncompensated and then expected to integrate with those who harmed them (or their heirs)? Is that justice and sensibility, cosmopolitan style? If so, then cosmopolitanism must be exposed for the unjust utopianism that it is, ignoring the wrongfully harmed underclasses who have for generations sought compensation from those who have wrongfully harmed them, only to be given "equality" to live in ways of which the more economically privileged approve. To say that cosmopolitan liberals are in favor of human rights is somewhat of a misnomer in that they tend to misunderstand the nature of rights to imply duties for which they have not even proven exist for the wealthy. One cannot really be in favor of that of which one lacks sufficient knowledge.

In *Justice, Legitimacy, and Self-Determination*,[73] Allen E. Buchanan criticizes John Rawls's Law of Peoples in that it is overly minimalist in its list of human rights, and too tolerant of nonliberal societies that are not representative in their forms of government that, by Buchanan's lights, result in "extreme inequalities": "regardless of what Rawls thinks it implies, his standard for what

counts as a decent society allows extreme inequalities and indeed extreme inequalities that are morally arbitrary and indefensible."[74] Now this is a serious
charge, as it indicts the most influential analytical political philosopher of our
time on the charge of allowing what is morally indefensible and arbitrary,
despite Rawls's explicit attempts to avoid such problems. Buchanan continues,

> The fundamental flaw in Rawls' account of toleration can also be put this way:
> Rawls collapses respect for reason into an over-expansive conception of humility
> based on a subjectivistic view of what counts as a reasonable conception of public
> order, thereby sacrificing a commitment to equal consideration of persons to that
> flawed conception of reasonableness. . . .
>   Unless Rawls is willing to abandon the whole project of developing what he
> calls a political conception of justice—unless he is willing to rely on a compre-
> hensive conception of the good that elevates respect for reason to the highest
> moral principle, higher even than respect for persons themselves or equal consid-
> eration for their well-being—he must recognize that respect for persons' reasons
> is not the be all and end all of morality. He must recognize that respect for per-
> sons' reasons may sometimes have to be subordinated to the demands of a more
> comprehensive principle of equal consideration of persons, whether this is
> spelled out as equal respect for persons or equal concern for their well-being.[75]

There are several things that might be said in reply to this complex critique of
Rawls. The first is that its wording is a bit like a straw person, as it is unclear
that Rawls actually holds to a "subjectivistic view of what counts as a reasonable conception of public order." And it is highly questionable whether Rawls
thinks that respect for persons' reasons is the "be all and end all of morality."
And this is the case precisely because Rawls believes that "respect for persons'
reasons may sometimes have to be subordinated to the demands of a more
comprehensive principle of equal consideration of persons."

On a more generous reading of Rawls than Buchanan provides, Rawls is not
subjectivistic along these lines, but rather remains quite consistent with the
liberal pluralism articulated and defended in *Political Liberalism*.[76] In that
book, Rawls is hardly guilty of a kind of subjectivism, but rather of a reasonable tolerance of those whose views and lifestyles fall under a broad conception of "comprehensive" doctrines, though whose views or lifestyles are not
liberal in content. It is, Rawls insists, a liberally decent society that inculcates
and nurtures this kind of toleration. And in *The Law of Peoples*, Rawls elevates
liberal tolerance to the global level. There is no subjectivism here. In *Political
Liberalism*, Rawls neither grounds liberal tolerance in some subjectivistic idea
of what counts as reasonable within a liberal state, nor does he adopt a subjec-
tivist notion of what is reasonable and tolerable in the Society of Peoples. It is
not subjectivism that Rawls is engaged in as Buchanan asserts. It is, on a more
careful consideration of Rawls work, a deeper sense of liberal tolerance for
legitimate differences between peoples and a genuine respect for differential
decency between various peoples.

Repeatedly accusing Rawls's list of human rights as being "truncated," Buchanan charges Rawls with excessive minimalism along these lines.[77] At issue is which societies count as decent and which do not, the latter being the ones where, under certain conditions, humanitarian intervention is permitted, if not required. But here Buchanan would do well to study the most important sources in contemporary rights theory. On a Feinbergian account, a right is something that is a valid claim and/or interest, and there is a difference between one's having a right, one's claiming that right, and one's exercising it.[78] This distinction is important for Buchanan's criticism of Rawls's view of liberal tolerance and the possible duty of humanitarian intervention because Buchanan seems to distort what counts as a society that is not decent and in need of external reform.

Suppose that there is a people in Traditionsville that imbeds in its democratic constitution all of the same rights that would make it a liberal democracy, but wherein women of that society by and large do not choose to live what Westerners would deem a "liberated" life. Instead, citing the comforts of tradition, religious or otherwise, the women of this society by and large freely choose to bear children, raise their children, and not engage themselves in professional affairs outside their homes. They also freely choose to not bother themselves with the administration of their society, as they genuinely do not want to "waste" their lives with such "troublesome nonsense." These women, by and large, seek their own happiness and meaning in life in the nuclear family, rather than in politics and a career of hustle and bustle. They care about who represents them, demonstrated by the fact that they study candidates and vote conscientiously for who they want to represent them in governmental affairs of their state.

The point of the example of Traditionsville is that Rawls's Law of Peoples can accommodate it as a decent society in that the women of Traditionsville have rights and can exercise them at will should they want to, but Buchanan seems not to be able, or willing, to. Yet precisely what is it about Traditionsville that places it outside the realm of decency? For Buchanan, it would be that it fails to *conduct* itself as a liberal society. But is this really true? Each woman has every right that each man has, and each can claim that right at any time, without fear of reprisals of any kind. In fact, anybody—man or woman—in Traditionsville can even freely exercise his or her rights to this or that and the social structure is set up to accommodate this possibility. But Traditionsville is where women freely choose traditional women's roles over those of Westernized "liberated" ones. They simply choose to not exercise their rights to be the equals of men outside of the home.

Buchanan might complain that the traditions of Traditionsville brainwash women to accept rather than freely select their roles, and that no self-respecting woman would ever freely choose what subordinates them to men as Traditionsville does. But this is an answer based largely on Western bias as to what constitutes the "rightful" place of a man or a woman in a decent society. It

assumes that the ways of Traditionsville are flawed at the outset, with no consideration of the possibility that someone might really want to live in this or
that role within it. Consider what Buchanan writes in criticism of Rawls's
notion of a "consultation hierarchy" in certain hierarchical societies that are
to be tolerated as being reasonably just:

> Rights to basic education, to freedom of association and expression, and rights
> regarding employment and property ownership that provide opportunities for
> women to have some degree of economic independence if they do not conform
> to traditional roles—all of these rights may be necessary if women's basic interests
> are to be effectively represented in the consultation hierarchy.[79]

But the question for Buchanan is what constitutes a context in which these
necessary conditions for societal justice accrue? Is it that women *possess* these
as constitutional rights? If so, then the women of Traditionsville have such
rights and thereby live in a decent society. They can even *claim* their rights
openly, and without reprisals! But the fact that the women of Traditionsville
by and large do not *exercise* their rights to equality to men poses a particular
epistemic challenge to a position such as Buchanan's. How is it to be understood exactly what separates Traditionsville from a society that is truly unjust
toward women? Rawls's minimalist list of human rights in principle provides
an easier way to answer the question, as there are fewer standards of justice to
satisfy. But with Buchanan's less minimalist view containing a more robust list
of human rights, does this not pose a particular problem? Is it the freedom to
choose to exercise one's human rights that serves as the means by which to
discern decent societies from those that are not decent? Yet how is this standard of assessment to be known within the confines of a nonideal world that
Buchanan so stridently insists that we operate? It would appear that Buchanan
owes us a theory of how the influences of traditions can be separated from
citizens' free choices to live their lives in one way or another. Otherwise,
Buchanan's position seems to hedge on, if not exemplify, a rather blatant form
of strong paternalism, a view that he seems to not address or repudiate in his
criticism of Rawls's theory of international justice. To the extent that Buchanan's critique of Rawls's Law of Peoples charges Rawls with too much liberal
tolerance, Buchanan can perhaps learn something from those who exemplified many core liberal values far previous to the advent of cosmopolitan liberalism. As one American Indian elder expressed:

> You will forgive me if I tell you that my people were Americans for thousands of
> years before your people were. The question is not how you can Americanize us
> but how we can Americanize you. We have been working at that for a long time.
> Sometimes we are discouraged by the results, but we will keep trying.
>   And the first thing we want to teach you is that, in the American way of life,
> each man has respect for his brother's vision. Because each of us respected his

brother's dream, we enjoyed freedom here in America while you people were busy killing and enslaving each other across the water.

The relatives you left behind . . . are still trying to kill each other and enslave each other because they have not learned there that freedom is built on my respect for my brother's vision and his respect for mine. We have a hard trail ahead of us in trying to Americanize you and your white brothers. But we are not afraid of hard trails.[80]

In the end, verbiage about building egalitarian justice faces the same fact that all other systems of international law confront: Boxill's objection from national autonomy. At bottom, such issues must come to terms with the fact that questions of global justice are related quite directly to questions of the meaning of life, a question that is unnoticeable in the philosophical literature on global justice. And if this question is not adequately addressed, then paternalism is the likely result in that a certain standard of living is imposed on peoples which implies an acceptable meaning of life. For example, if the Diné nation found its cultural lifestyle quite fulfilling as it is, who is to say that it ought to partake of globally egalitarian lifestyles so its members can have an equal opportunity in life? The cosmopolitan liberal might argue that her theory does not force any nation to become equal to others and that it merely seeks a system of (distributive) justice that would provide individuals in the Diné nation an opportunity to have a certain kind of life. But precisely what is meant here by "kind of life"? In the many cases where compensatory justice retains that autonomy of ethnic groups and the individuals in them, cosmopolitan justice effectively coerces the Diné nation (or any member of it) to risk perverting its (or her) cultural lifestyle that it (she) so cherishes. Thus the meaningfulness of life changes, and in many cases it is, on balance, for the worse.

In short, cosmopolitan liberals must in the end explain either how their imperialism provides a more meaningful life for those in non-Western nations and their respective cultures than they would have if they did not receive adequate compensation from those who wrongfully harmed them, or it must explain how cosmopolitan justice is, all things considered (including the depth of one's culture), better than the baseline quality of life that the targets of cosmopolitan justice seek to assist, quite apart from compensatory justice considerations. It is one thing to relieve global poverty. That can be justified by way of the duty of assistance not only in Rawls's principles of international justice, but in obedience to anti–bad Samaritan statutes. But it is quite another to ignore or deny the legitimacy and importance of compensatory justice, especially when in so many cases the global poor are also the victims of historic and contemporary oppression that many existing countries simply fail to take responsibility for and compensate. These are two quite distinct moral and legal issues. I have argued for compensatory justice without denying the significance of the duty of assistance. But I have done so without embracing paternalism or in effect a crude kind of ethic that would ignore or deny the importance of compensatory rights.

In the end, cosmopolitan liberals, in their myopic concentration on a particularly narrow notion of global equality, confuse poverty with need, and confuse justice with a rather narrow conception of equality and make no significant room for compensatory justice that would best ensure the freedom and autonomy, and in many cases sovereignty, of oppressed peoples. They do not comprehend, it seems, the profound truth of the saying: "Justice cannot grow on injustice." Distributive justice is incomplete justice if it is meant to replace or ignore the importance of compensatory justice. Because cosmopolitan liberalism seems as a theory to denigrate compensatory justice considerations in favor of alleged rights to equality, I believe that Rawls's statist theory of international justice is more plausible than cosmopolitan liberalism.[81] As I argue in chapter 4 and elsewhere, Rawls can accommodate rights to compensation, while cosmopolitan liberalism is somewhat hostile toward anything that runs afoul of its Westernized version of equality of opportunity.[82] These points are missed by Samuel Scheffler's assessment of cosmopolitan liberalisms:

> Moderate cosmopolitanism about justice will be a compelling position only if it proves possible to devise human institutions, practices, and ways of life that take seriously the equal worth of persons without undermining people's capacity to sustain their special loyalties and attachments. And moderate cosmopolitanism about culture will be compelling only if two things turn out to be true. The first is that some people succeed in developing recognizably cosmopolitan ways of living that incorporate the sort of stable infrastructure of responsibility that more traditional ways of life have always made available to their adherents. The second is that other people succeed in preserving the integrity of their traditions without succumbing to the temptation to engage in the doomed and deadly pursuit of cultural purity.[83]

Unless by "responsibility" Scheffler means considerations of compensatory justice and the rights that must accrue therein, Scheffler's assessment of cosmopolitan liberalisms, though insightful in its own right, makes no mention of rights to compensatory justice for, say, crimes against humanity. Thus his assessment of cosmopolitan liberalism, though nuanced, is insufficiently complex to account for the hostility cosmopolitan liberalism seems to display—at least according to some of its adherents—toward rights to compensatory justice, rights that are often, I might add, affixed to the rights of ethnic groups and cultures to preserve their own ways of life.[84]

Thus it appears reasonable to think that oppressed groups have compensatory rights against their oppressors, that is, in a reasonably just society or in a reasonably just Society of Peoples. In chapter 4 I shall argue that if anything is a human right, rights to reparations as compensation to oppressed groups are human rights, and that for all the leading rights theorists argue about the nature and function of human rights, nothing seems to preclude reparations from qualifying as a human compensatory right. This poses quite an embarrassment, not so much for Rawls's list of human rights which is admittedly incomplete, but for cosmopolitan liberals and others who deny the legitimacy of the compensatory right to reparations in favor of some vague notions of equality and reconciliation between oppressors and the oppressed. And it is precisely this subsuming of compensatory rights under the value of social equality that is why I classify the general position of cosmopolitan liberalism as to some extent utilitarian. Even if it is problematic to categorize Pogge and some others as somewhat utilitarian on such matters, it is clear that they ignore or undervalue compensatory rights in the context of global justice.

3

Utilitarianism and Historic Injustice

Besides cosmopolitan liberalism, there are other more or less utilitarian-based denials of the right to reparative compensation as a means of realizing justice for oppressed groups. I shall focus on some views articulated in the recent philosophical literature.

In general, what these models of reparations share in common is the aim of "restorative justice." According to this approach to reparations, it is "making amends" between the victim and her perpetrator that is at issue, not the payment of compensatory damages by the offender and her victim. Moreover, restorative justice "involves the processes by which offender and victim meet to negotiate a disposition involving some kind of 'reparative' or 'restorative' task."[1]

REPARATIONS AS OBLIGATIONS OF EQUITY?

Janna Thompson argues for a general obligations-centered approach to reparations.[2] In her account, reparations require reconciliation between the oppressed and oppressors, entail considerations of equity, and involve programs designed to "repair" historic injustices. Reparations are based on "past-referring obligations" wherein those responsible (accountable in a duty sense) for keeping the promise or committing the wrongs on which reparations are based are not the ones who made the promise or committed the wrongs, but are their descendants or their successors. "Past-referring obligations" ground "transgenerational responsibilities" to honor valid treaties. And "transgenerational commitments create transgenerational obligations" wherein the latter are grounded in a "respect for nations" that ought to accrue between nations.[3] Failure to respect harmed or oppressed nations shows disrespect toward them by oppressive states. And such disrespect is immoral and wrong.[4] Those making reparative claims against oppressive states that owe them must make "reasonable" claims,[5] and there is a moral statute of limitations on claims to reparations for historic injustices.[6] Such a moral statute of limitations is based on common sense and pragmatic aspects of the complexities of human life. Reparations, then, entail the collective responsibility of those within countries from which reparations are owed.

But Thompson's justification for reparations raises serious concerns. First, no attempt is made by her to explain why certain groups, and not others, qualify for reparations. Moreover, she does not notice differences between arguments for and against reparations to American Indians and blacks, for instance, or those between Maoris and Aborigines. The fact that indigenous claims to reparations often involve both serious personal injury violations and theft of land, while reparations to the descendants of slaves in the Americas typically involve humans rights violations, seems to suggest that the bases for compensatory reparations in either case are important for the realization of reparative justice.

Secondly, Thompson reduces reparations to "justice as equity" which requires reconciliation, placing no *real* economic burdens on oppressive outlaw states like the United States.[7] While Bernard Boxill argues that reparations to blacks cannot be morally justified to the extent that it places the present white population in "danger of perishing," Thompson is quite unspecific regarding the extent to which those who are not awarded reparations might suffer when reparations are justified.[8] In any case, it is far from obvious that present day U.S. citizens, who of course are causally nonresponsible for the evils inflicted on, say, Indians, are somehow in a moral position to claim even an occupation right to the lands on which we reside. Short of a plausible argument in favor of a moral statute of limitations on injustice, no such right could make sense. Thus it would be rather prejudicial to think that reparative justice must keep a closer eye on the welfare of nonindigenous folk than it must on indigenous ones. The point here is not that considerations of social utility for nonindigenous peoples seem to count for nothing. Rather, it is that the first consideration of reparative justice is to rectify the wrongs for those whose forebears were wronged prior to making certain that those who reside illegitimately on what are in fact indigenous lands are not inconvenienced in their often opulent lifestyles.

Thirdly, Thompson's view of reconciliation places the moral "obligation" on the *victim*, not the perpetrator, to "accept reparation that they have reason to regard as just."[9] Although she states that "reconciliation makes sense only if there is a wrongdoer able and willing to engage in an act of reconciliation,"[10] what is the argument for the claim that reparations amount to or require reconciliation as opposed to construing reconciliation as a moral *prerogative* of the victims to accept reparations offers *without* reconciliation? Thompson appears to have not understood the nature of genuine reconciliation as forgiveness which in turn requires genuine apology of the wrongdoer to the victims, which entails a moral prerogative of the victims to forgive and reconcile with the perpetrators, as argued in chapter 8, below. Thompson's view of reparations as necessarily reconciliatory also implies that reparations are contingent on the reconciliation of oppressed with their oppressors: reparations cannot accrue unless and until the oppressed who are due reparations based on historic injustice agree to "accommodate" oppressors! This is counterintuitive if one takes rights seriously. Cannot reparations (especially compensatory reparations) accrue without reconciliation? How morally presumptuous it is to assume that it is a sign of moral virtue to always forgive one who has wronged you! How lacking in self-respect and self-esteem it is to forgive and reconcile with one's oppressor(s) without the time-consuming, tell-tale signs (and requirements) of a genuine apology for wrongdoing (as articulated in chapter 8)! Then again, Thompson is offering an obligations-based approach, not a rights-based approach, to reparations. And her restorative justice approach to reparations includes nothing akin to compensatory justice. Her position simply cannot make sense of forgiveness and reconciliation as a right, not a duty, of victims of oppression. In its concern to obligate even the oppressed to the dictates of social utility maximization, her approach makes no room for reparations as a right of the oppressed which is correlated with a duty of the oppressors to pay reparations to their victims as a necessary condition of a genuine apology. It would appear, then, that Thompson's obligations-based approach has matters in reverse vis-à-vis just where the duties lie in cases of severe oppression.

Furthermore, Thompson fails to give Robert Nozick's view of historical entitlement serious philosophical consideration, dismissive of it as "doomed to irrelevancy" when it fails to generate the conclusions that she deems "practical" or "common sense."[11] Practical or common sense for *whom*, and *why*? Of Nozick's historical entitlement view, Thompson writes:

> One of the problems with this account of how people acquire historical entitlements and obligations is that it does not cover all cases where we are assigned historical responsibilities. It does not have anything to say about reparative responsibilities for injustices that do not involve violations of right of possession. . . . Even if these titles exist, they may not justify a right to reparation for injustices that happened in previous generations.[12]

But the principle of morally just acquisitions and transfers[13] is based on Nozick's entitlement theory of rights (yet does not necessarily entail all of it) and it can and does justify reparations to American Indians to lands that were misacquired and wrongly transferred. However, Thompson's utilitarian and "pragmatic" presumption that it "cannot" do so because it violates considerations of "equity" (e.g., utility) holds that it does not justify such reparations.

She herself avers that "common sense suggests that temporal limitations have to be imposed on claims concerning historical injustices, but a theory of justice requires that this limitation not be arbitrary."[14] But where the evidence of historical records is plain as to which parties were wronged and which ones perpetrated evils on the victims, what kind of "common sense" would justify *not* imposing compensatory justice, except the self-serving intuitions of those whose "common sense" masks a utilitarian and anti-compensatory rights-based theory of "justice"? And where the historical evidence of generations of U.S. slavery are quite clear as to who or what some of the perpetrators (the U.S. government, in complicity with certain business enterprises, including but not limited to slave holders themselves) are most responsible for that crime against humanity, what except a kind of act-utilitarian ethic would dare deny justice to the descendants of the oppressed? As she herself points out concerning transgenerational commitments, "The burden of proof should fall on those who deny continuity of responsibility."[15] What Thompson refers to as a "right of reparation" seems to fail the true test of a right.

If Joel Feinberg is correct about the nature and value of rights, then surely the right of reparations is no exception in its being the kind of thing that provides authenticating empowerment to the oppressed who possess and seek to exercise it.[16] It must be a valid claim on which one can stand and demand, justifiably, her right to reparation over against any competing claims. And that includes claims to "equity" and any other consideration of social utility. It is not that claims and interests do not compete with one another. In the end, however, one claim or interest typically wins out over the others, all things and persons considered. Thompson's view of reparations fails to understand this point, and it, like its ethical underwriter (utilitarianism), fails to possess even the capacity to take rights seriously. Since this is true, then Thompson not only misleads perhaps even herself to think that she wants to take rights seriously, but she really has nothing to say about reparations of the legally acknowledged compensatory variety. For the *right* to reparations seems to be one that cannot possibly be guaranteed by a utilitarian ideology.

There is the growing sense in studying Thompson's view that she is concerned with reparations only to the extent that it does not overly and adversely affect those whose power and wealth would not be if not for the oppression that justifies the reparations in the first place. One also wonders if Thompson has an adequate appreciation for the kinds and degrees of oppression that the right to reparation is supposed to protect. Indeed, her "pragmatic" approach seems a bit protective of privileged power structures. This is especially clear when she has the unmitigated gall to reduce reparative justice to affirmative action programs! It is impossible to arrive at the conclusions arrived at by Thompson if one has a genuine and deep appreciation of the evils that Indians and African slaves experienced at the hands of European invaders and then whites in the United States, that is, if one takes seriously matters of proportional compensation and rights.

Perhaps equally problematic, it is difficult to know if Thompson's discussion of reparations relies on a plausible conception of collective responsibility since she provides or refers to no philosophical analysis of the concept of collective responsibility just where one ought to expect one in her argument—and this in light of the fact that there exist such philosophical analyses.[17] This prevents Thompson from delving deeply into the nuances of collective responsibilities of not only governments, but of their respective supportive businesses that "lobby" them in their complicity regarding historic injustices. Without a robust analysis of collective responsibility, there is unlikely to be a plausible account of reparations. It is no accident that Howard McGary's seminal discussion of reparations places collective responsibility at the forefront of the problem.[18] Perhaps this leads Thompson to draw a dubious distinction between reparative and retributive justice.[19] No explanation or argument is provided for this distinction. Nor is it grounded in the legal definition of "reparations." Yet it directly affects Thompson's notion that reparations entail considerations of equity and reconciliation, but not compensation. Indeed, it reveals the fact that her stipulative idea of reparations is based on a utilitarian conception of "justice," rather than on considerations of desert, proportionality of compensation, and historic and wrongful harms. The result is that Thompson confuses reparations with matters of distributive justice, amounting to a category mistake. One cannot, as she does, seek to alter by way of stipulation the understanding of the nature of reparations without sound reasoning for doing so. Yet this is precisely what Thompson attempts to do. Contrary to her, reparations precisely *are* matters of corrective justice from states and/or businesses to groups harmed by such states and/or businesses. So her confused notion of the nature of reparations leads her to a questionable notion of the function of reparations as requiring reconciliation and not inclusive of compensation.

Furthermore, Thompson provides no argument for her claim that there is a moral statute of limitations on injustice, and this despite the fact that in U.S. law there is no statute of limitations on murder, a crime committed by the U.S. Army against many Indians at the command of Andrew Jackson, among others. Her view ignores the fact that the *Laches* Defense (in U.S. law) does *not* apply to cases of Indian and black reparations, as each group has continually approached the U.S. government for rectification of past wrongs. The claims were simply refused. This vitiates against denials of compensatory reparations for such harms to the descendants of these groups based on the *Laches* Defense.

Thus Thompson's defense of reparations is problematic. Her account fails to take the right to compensatory reparations seriously enough to override the strength of her commitment to the welfare of some of the very same groups the forebears of which actually caused the oppression that justifies the reparations in the first place. In both cases, the commitment to considerations of "equity" directly imply the delimitation of reparations to mere social justice programs such as affirmative action in education and the workplace. But again, this is a category mistake as it confuses reparations which are means of monetary compensation rightfully deserved on the basis of harms suffered with affirmative action programs which are typically "benefits" earned by means of employment or educational training.

What I have hoped to demonstrate is that there is a wide gulf between what genuine justice and morality require in reparations based on a principle of proportional compensation, on the one hand, and reparations proposals which attempt to minimize what justice truly requires in favor of maintaining the very institutions in U.S. society some of which caused and maintained the various modes of racist oppression against Indians and blacks in the first place, on the other. We must forever keep in mind that without adequate justice, there can be no genuine peace between parties to reparative justice. Indeed, without such justice, there *should* be no peace! So it is vital that we strive toward articulating plausible conceptions of justice in regard to the correcting of severe forms of oppression. The victim heirs of oppression deserve no less than this.

REPARATIONS AS MORAL REPAIR?

Margaret Urban Walker provides her own account of "moral repair," which she at times calls "reparation." She seeks to make both victims and wrongdoers the dual focus of her account of reparations.[20] Although she contends that "people need to get what they deserve as victims, *and* to be called upon to do what they are obliged to do to make amends as wrongdoers,"[21] she also claims that "moral repair is the process of moving from the situation of loss and damage to a situation where some degree of stability in moral relations is regained."[22] On her view of reparations, "those most directly responsible for a wrong are also those with paramount and unique responsibilities for attempting to make amends for it" and "often it is in the gravest cases, . . . that wrongdoers are least inclined to accept responsibility" and she asks, "why should victims be left to the double jeopardy of injury and then the insult of wrongdoer's denial and refusal to repair?"[23] She even claims that "punishment, when proportionate and humane, is one indispensable response to wrongdoing."[24] However, before one makes the inference that Walker is some kind of a rights-based theorist of a retributivist bent who values justice in terms of desert and proportionality, one must think deeply about what she is arguing here. It is helpful to notice that Walker makes reparations contingent on the regaining of "some degree of stability in moral relations."[25] But why must this be so, unless one has subjected the right to reparative compensation to considerations of social utility? And so long as Walker intends her "discussion of moral repair to bear on the whole field of ways to address and redress wrongdoing," she faces a grave difficulty in not providing adequate emphasis on the right to reparations.[26] Walker sees this, and then claims that her account is "not exclusive of retribution," but that her account is superior to retributivism in some instances because it can provide outcomes for victims as well as for offenders.[27] She adds that "retributive responses are not the only way, and in isolation may not be a completely adequate way, for victims to achieve personal, but also public and socially shared, validation and vindication."[28]

Not unlike other restorative justice theorists, it appears that Walker has in mind a certain stereotypical rendition of retributivism, one that has long since been corrected and with great detail.[29] That is, Walker seems to construe retributivism and retribution as methods of addressing wrongdoing in ways that involve no consideration for matters of social utility, a view to which not even Immanuel Kant subscribes. As Kant indicates, retribution can consider as a justificatory aim matters of social utility subsequent to matters of desert.[30] Furthermore, Walker's assertion that "retribution in theory and practice centers on offenders and what they 'deserve,' without central attention to victims"[31] is a blatant misattribution to retributivism, which is the primary theory of punishment that employs conceptions of retribution precisely in part for the sake of the victim's right that has been violated. For the retributivist, retribution is justified to the extent that it proscribes hard treatment to those who deserve it in proportion to their full range of responsibility for their harmful wrongdoing against one or more victims. But it is also deeply concerned with providing victims their deserved measure of justice in punishing their offender(s), and/or in forcing her (them) to compensate the victim(s) in proportion to the damages wrought on the victim(s) by the offender(s).[32] These facts raise suspicions about Walker's attempt to juxtapose retribution to utilitarian justice, or to in some way dismiss the ability of a retributivist account of justice to be capable of providing a holistic approach to reparations. Indeed, chapter 9 provides details about precisely how a retributivist account of reparations seeks explicitly to provide monetary, psychological, and sociological reparations to victims of tremendous injustice. And chapter 8 discounts attempts without plausible argument to sneak into an adequate account of reparations or rectificatory justice requirements of forgiveness and reconciliation, concepts that are central to Walker's utilitarian approach to "moral repair."

It is the previous considerations that further reveal Walker's utilitarian approach to reparations. For her,

> moral repair is the task of restoring or stabilizing—and in some cases creating— the basic elements that sustain human beings in a recognizably moral relationship. By "moral relationship" I refer to a kind of relationship or mode of relating rather than to an order governed by a particular scale of values, set of imperatives, or system of role-bound obligations.[33]

But Walker's utilitarian perspective suffers from a fatal flaw in not providing an argument in favor of the claim that reparations morally requires a post-wrongdoing relationship between the wrongdoer and her victim(s), especially in cases like rape and child molestation. In fact, Walker's view is so extreme that it states the need for reconciliation even where there was no prior moral relationship between the oppressor and her victim(s). But why would any reasonable person think that a victim ought to either have her prior moral relationship reestablished with her offender, or that one ought to be created between the parties where one did not preexist? In chapter 8, I shall argue that such thinking is a disguised form of quasi-religious dogma that enjoys no plausible argumentative support. And no attempt by Walker to infuse the moral relationship with retributive emotions such as resentment and indignation will suffice here.[34] For while it is true that no wrongdoing can ever be adequately and proportionally righted or undone,[35] it hardly follows from this that essentially utilitarian standards for moral rightness ought to accrue in matters where the power of justice and rights are essential. Walker is incorrect, then, in subsuming the right of victims of oppression to compensatory reparations under the utilitarian concern to "set things right between people."[36]

Walker would reply that "neither compensatory justice nor retributive justice directly addresses the *moral quality of future relations* between those who have done or benefited from harm and those who have suffered it."[37] But it is unclear that this is true, as the remainder of this book demonstrates that crucial matters of individual autonomy and self-respect, as well as group sovereignty, are satisfied under a rights-based approach to reparations. Walker relies on rather unrefined notions of compensatory and retributive justice. Both can be and are at times quite concerned with both material and nonmaterial "amends," as she herself admits: "Reparation often includes restitution or compensation to make repair concrete and in some cases to give weight to other interpersonal gestures, such as apologies and expressions of sorrow, shame, guilt, or the wish to make amends."[38] Yet Walker still misunderstands the purpose of reparations of the material kind. It is not to "make things concrete," as she contends, but rather to compensate what was taken from victims by offenders *as a matter of right*, whether or not they "give weight to other interpersonal gestures."

The point here is not that there is no room for moral repair in many social relations. There certainly is. And Walker provides some helpful suggestions along these lines. However, to the extent that her analysis is meant to address even the most extreme forms of injustice, such as the degrees, levels, and kinds of oppression experienced by Indians and blacks in the United States, her approach fails to capture the aspects of compensatory rights that are, we shall see in the following chapters, basic to any rights-respecting society. And it is here where one notices the lack in Walker's analysis of "moral repair" of a *right* to compensatory justice.[39] Instead, what one finds are locutions of "responsibility" and "repair" that have much more to do with establishing or reestablishing "relations" between offenders and their victim(s) than with factors relevant to the self-respect and autonomy of oppressed individuals or the sovereignty of oppressed groups. It is, in short, much more about forgiveness and reconciliation than it is about rectificatory justice between victims and their offenders—even in cases of extreme oppression. And this is true even in light of Walker's attempt to explicate her analysis of moral repair in terms of three "ongoing tasks" that communities are claimed to have in creating and sustaining moral repair among their members,[40] ones that bear a rather close resemblance to some of Feinberg's expressive functions of punishment[41] and by extension, to the expressive functions of reparations as explicated in chapter 1, above, and elsewhere.[42] While I concur with Walker that "what must always be done is to acknowledge wrong and to make clear efforts at repair,"[43] what her account does not do is to respect the rights to compensation of groups victimized by especially some of the most horrendous degrees, levels, and kinds of oppression. In this respect, then, it is essentially utilitarian views such as her own that constitute, however unintentionally, moral insults[44] to the oppressed for really doing little if anything to address the compensatory aspects of oppression. To argue for the integrative reconciliation between the oppressed and their oppressors as a strong expectation, if not a moral requirement, is akin to arguing that black women who were raped by their slavers must or ought to reconcile and live with their rapists! There is scarcely a more morally counterintuitive implication than that.

Thus it is not that what Walker offers in terms of a theory of moral repair is irrelevant to reparations, properly construed. It is that it ignores the essential compensatory aspects of the right to reparations, especially for groups that have been severely oppressed. In so doing, Walker's view must explain why this particular right is disrespected while, presumably, certain other rights are to be respected in a reasonably just society, or one seeking to become reasonably just. Second, it makes forgiveness and reconciliation a necessary condition of reparations, which flies in the face of commonsense moral intuitions about justice and fairness. There is also the presumptuousness of requiring victims to have any relationship whatsoever with their offenders. This disempowers victims in subsuming their rights to autonomy under some utilitarian quest for social solidarity. In short, it denies the separateness of persons in society and undermines individual victims' autonomy to choose with whomever they want to associate. In effect, Walker's approach to reparations implies an expectation or a moral requirement of the oppressed that they reconcile with their oppressors, which in turn implies at least in many cases the integration of the two groups with each other. But this scenario implies the following coercive offer and threat to the oppressed and their heirs: Reconcile and integrate with your oppressors or their heirs (coercive offer), or you will receive no reparations (coercive threat).[45] And it is precisely such an implied threat that faces Indians and blacks on Walker's model of reparations as moral repair. Fundamentally, then, Walker's approach to reparations falters on these counts.

Assumed here of course is that respect for rights as valid claims or interests and respect for individual autonomy and group sovereignty are necessary conditions for a reasonably just society.

Walker provides a detailed account of forgiveness that serves as the basis for her claim that reconciliation is required for moral repair:

> First, forgiveness settles a wrong precisely as such in the past while releasing the future from its impact. Second, forgiveness overcomes or lets go of resentment or other "hard" feelings against the offending person. Third, forgiveness restores damaged or broken relations between those injured and their offenders, and perhaps relations among them and others.[46]

But even if forgiveness were a condition of reconciliation and even if reconciliation between victims and their offenders is morally required for a reasonably just society, it is unclear that Walker's notion of forgiveness is unproblematic. First, it ignores the crucial distinction between forgiveness and forgiving, one that is detailed in chapter 8, below. Throughout her discussion, Walker often conflates the two. In so doing, her analysis tends to confuse a victim's ability, for whatever reasons, to express her forgiveness toward her offender with the state of experiencing forgiveness, wherein a genuine apology is proffered by the offending party and willfully accepted by the victim, with there being no moral obligation of the victim to forgive her offender. Second, Walker's analysis fails to explain whether or not forgiving is a moral obligation victims have, and if so, why, and if not, why not. What if victims choose not to forgive their offenders? Are they morally wrong or weak for not doing so? If so, why? If not, then why ought one to forgive her offender, especially in cases of severe oppression? Should survivors of the Nazi genocide during World War II forgive their oppressors? Should Indians forgive the United States for violently stealing their lands and committing genocide against millions of Indians? Should African slaves have forgiven their masters here in the United States? Should blacks forgive the United States for slavery and Jim Crow?

Walker's answer is that while forgiving gives up the right of the victim to revenge, it hardly entails that victims are not entitled to moral repair or "satisfactory amends," or that offenders are not to be punished for their offenses.[47] She also states that for her own peace of mind, the victim ought to forgive her offender. (This is a point made by Howard McGary with regard to newly emancipated slaves in the United States during Reconstruction.[48]) But Walker's main reason for a victim's forgiving her offender is that it "restores relationships" or reconciles them in cases where there was a previous relationship between them, or can create a relationship between them where there was no preexisting one.[49] Take her assertions that "to understand the moral content of forgiveness, we need to understand the moral content of moral relations" and "forgiveness should restore, or return to a functioning state, the conditions of moral relationship" and that forgiveness is a "morally reparative process."[50] But these points just presuppose that reconciliation between oppressors and their victims is a desideratum of a reasonably just society. Yet what Walker offers as an argument here is the rather weak and unsupported claim that "we need to forgive the wrongdoer in serious cases."[51] Why? Presumably, as she asserts, because forgiveness can lead to reconciliation.[52] So Walker's claims about forgiveness and reconciliation seem to be as follows:

1. Reconciliation between victims and their offenders is desirable for a reasonably just society because it brings peace and tranquility to society and its members.
2. Reconciliation between victims and their offenders requires forgiveness on the part of the victims.

However, just what are we to make of these claims? They cannot provide us with a moral obligation to forgive others, that is, without delimiting human autonomy or group sovereignty in the process. And even if they could establish, by way of some hidden and plausible premise, that forgiveness is a moral duty of victims, Walker surely does not tell us what forgiveness entails in terms of an offender's apology. What she does state is that an apology is not a necessary or sufficient condition of forgiveness, and this is in part because that would, Walker claims, "hold the one injured hostage to the wrongdoer's willingness to take responsibility."[53] In other words, Walker is so deeply committed to her assumption that reconciliation is a good thing for a reasonably just society that she believes that everyone in that society—including victims of oppression—ought to want to reconcile with their oppressors and that nothing ought to prohibit this from happening, not even an offender's unwillingness to apologize for her oppression. Consider her statement that, according to "restorative justice," "all crime and wrong creates obligations on those responsible and able to repair harm and restore relationship."[54] Again, there is no argument given for the putative moral obligation of restorative justice. We are left to accept it as a quasi-religious dogma. Yet it is highly problematic.

Indeed, when one considers restorative justice more deeply, one finds that its implausibility becomes even more apparent. One of the "ideals" of "restorative justice," according to Walker, is that those responsible for "wrongs" can via "moral repair" be reintegrated into the society "without stigma" and "earn self-respect."[55] While in a utopian society of a certain kind this might be desirable, what about real-life atrocities such as the genocide of Indians by the United States and the enslavement of Africans in the United States and the Jim-Crowing of blacks in the United States? Is it even possible, cognitively, for Indians and blacks to not place stigmas on whites after centuries of oppression and then generations of neglect regarding reparations to them? And even if it is cognitively possible for them to not hold these matters against the United States and its non-Indian and nonblack citizens, *should* they not hold it against them in terms of stigma? If they do or should not, one wonders about the levels of self-esteem and self-respect that such folk might or might not possess.

So it is not clear that in the real world of oppression and failures and refusals to rectify oppression that some of Walker's ideals pertaining to restorative justice have but a damaging effect on the self-esteem and self-respect of the victims of oppression, or their heirs. As she herself admits, "It is not always possible, nor is it always desirable, to restore any relationship between those who have done harm and those who have suffered at their will or from their carelessness."[56] This is because, she states, "In cases of oppression, mass violence, and historic injustice, there may not be a morally acceptable status quo ante."[57]

Perhaps a key to understanding the limitations of Walker's viewpoint about moral repair lies in the fact that she presumes an integrationist standpoint about moral relations and harmful wrongdoings. And this is true despite the fact that she asserts, "It is not always possible or desirable to restore relations between victims and those who have hurt them, but it is always necessary to assist and support victims in repairing the moral fabric of their world."[58] The problem latent in Walker's claim here is in her locution "the moral fabric of their world." Reparations are primarily about compensatory justice, as noted in the definition of "reparations" in chapter 1. This implies that it is essential to reparations that, among other things, compensatory justice considerations are satisfied. To state that it is the moral fabric of a victim's world that is crucial in "moral repair" misses the point of what compensatory reparations can provide without coercing the integration of victims with their offenders. In the case of Indians and blacks, why would one think that the moral fabric of their worlds being "repaired" in white society is what justice requires, or even permits aside from the desire of Indians and blacks to live with whites? What this essentially utilitarian perspective requires is a sound argument in favor of the presumption of reconciliation between victims and their offenders, especially in cases of severe oppression.

Perhaps we can get an even better idea of Walker's viewpoint of "moral repair" by considering the following statement: "Looking at forgiveness through the lens of moral repair reveals that possibilities of forgiveness depend on the magnitude and severity of offense, the meaning of the wrong act and of the act that would forgive it in their contexts, and the situation of those who have done wrong and of those who would forgive them."[59] But nowhere in this assertion regarding the nature of moral repair, nor anywhere in her entire book, is there an explicit statement by Walker that an apology is required for forgiveness or reconciliation, or that compensatory justice is required.[60] For Walker's commitment to a utilitarian perspective is so deep that she has foresworn these matters altogether as being even merely necessary for justice in a decent society. Perhaps this is due to her commitment to the establishment of "a real or imagined community of moral understanding with others,"[61] which is difficult to understand apart from the idea of a utility maximizing-based utopian society. For it is precisely in such a society that "in forgiving one needs to humanize, rather than to idealize or demonize, the wrongdoer."[62] But it is very hard to understand how Walker's notion of "moral repair" is anything less than a utilitarian way of denying the rights to compensation, personal autonomy, and group sovereignty that most societies like the United States often seek to respect at least in principle if not completely in practice. The question is not, as Walker seems to think, whether forgiving can have a moral value. Rather, it is whether or not it is a moral requirement, and what are its moral conditions, and whether reconciliation is even morally justified absent the fully intentional, epistemic, and voluntary approval of the victims of oppression, or in the case of historic injustice, their heirs. Walker's sentiments about forgiveness are laid bare when she quotes with approval an author who asserts that "in forgiveness, the one *wronged* absorbs the cost" of that wrong.[63] Herein lies the problem with Walker's view of "moral repair." It is highly counterintuitive except to those with antiretributivist and anticompensatory rights biases to think that genuine forgiveness does not entail the offender's genuine apology, which in turn entails, among other things, rectification for her harmful wrongdoing. In fact, Walker dismisses such a "basic intuition" as being "tit for tat," as if ad hominem verbiage counts for sound argument.[64] Yet this seems to be all Walker has to offer along these lines, counterintuitive dismissiveness and ad hominem rhetoric.

In reply to utilitarian approaches to reparations such as Thompson's and Walker's, in chapter 8 I shall argue in favor of a retributivist analysis of forgiveness. Again, it is not that restoration, when victims desire it for good reasons, is never desirable in a reasonably just society. Rather, it is the problematic nature of the presumptuousness that underlies Walker's restorative approach to reparations as moral repair. Her restorative approach recognizes but fails to embrace the legal paradigm of justice in the form of "material compensation."[65] Yet she provides no reason for this position, as if to imply that material compensation by way of reparations is somehow irrelevant to what she calls "moral repair" or what in fact constitutes reparations (Walker's construal of reparations notwithstanding). Walker appears to work with a stipulative definition of "reparations" as "moral repair" which fails to account for its legal definition or venerable philosophical one as articulated in chapter 1, above.

In her mention of material compensatory reparations by the United States to Japanese Americans for the internment of many Asian (not all were Japanese!) during World War II, Walker states,

> The internment caused not only losses of income, investments and property, but also humiliation, physical and emotional hardship, and complex histories of concealment and shame within families affecting several generations. For this reason, measures other than money were needed to restore dignity, reputation, accurate historical understanding, and clear acknowledgment of the blamelessness of the victims.[66]

Walker's claim that repairing the victims of U.S. racist policies against certain Asian Americans during that period surely calls for more than material compensation is the closest she comes to acknowledging, but not explicating or making a main point of, compensatory reparations in "moral repair."[67]

Turning her attention to U.S. blacks and their history of oppression, Walker states that "restoring relationships" is of crucial importance. Out of generosity, I shall take her to be inclusive of the restoration of black-black relationships as well as the ones she really intends to mend, namely, those between blacks and whites. In other words, Walker is interested in the kind of moral repair that would bring reconciliation between the heirs of oppression. Instead of addressing the arguments for black reparations detailed in various philosophical writings by black philosophers like Boxill and McGary, among others,[68] Walker cites the works of a white philosopher and some social scientists on the matter. In any case, she wishes to "look instead at the task of repair and the question of responsibility as seen through a restorative justice lens."[69] It is here where she seeks to juxtapose restorative justice with reparative justice, the latter of which she understands in purely compensatory terms.

Walker claims that "restorative justice puts communities, and not only individual offenders, into the field of responsibility."[70] Of course, it bears pointing out that reparative justice as a species of corrective justice is analyzed in collectivist as well as individualist terms wherein both individuals and certain kinds of collectives (conglomerates, because they are decision-making bodies) can be held retroactively responsible in the liability sense for their harmful wrongdoings to others.[71] While she admits that "neither the retributive [n]or compensatory paths should be abandoned,"[72] it is hard to understand how this might be achieved if her overriding utilitarian ethic will decide when social utility is maximized and when it is not, when a claim to reparations is valid and a "right" and when it is not, and so forth. And in the end, Walker distances herself from this aim, as she reduces repair for blacks in the United States to the restoration of their relations with whites, including the resolution of issues related to black poverty in the United States.[73] So restorative justice, on Walker's account, is not so much concerned with the retributive aims of desert, responsibility, and rights as it is with social relations: Applied to black redress, "restorative justice insists that we focus on the distortion of relationship that is involved in American histories of race."[74] However, precisely why this ought to be so is hardly supported by argument.

In the end, Walker's view of redress for U.S. blacks amounts to the following:

> Reparations policies of monetary compensation or collective investment by the U.S. government might be an ultimate objective of black redress; but without the extended work of restoration, compensation is unlikely, and without restoration, the meaning of compensation, were some compensation achieved, might not be a respectable and reparative one.

> Material reparations might be welcome but would not magically instill interra-
> cial trust. . . . Hope is, after all, the most fundamental element that sustains moral
> relationship, and it is the only force powerful enough to revive it.[75]

The problems with this approach are numerous. First, it may be "unlikely" that compensatory reparations are forthcoming no matter what the practical realities, given U.S. attitudes about justice and fairness. But this has little to do with restoration between blacks and others (especially whites) in the United States. Why not? Because there has never been any relationship between blacks and others in the United States worthy to be restored! There has never been a time when healthy relations between blacks and others have been obtained. Thus Walker's notion of *restorative* justice is at best a misnomer. At worst, it is an ignorant view of U.S. history as it pertains to blacks, and, by extension of her view, to Indians also. Thus restoration of relationships between blacks and whites in the United States is perhaps Walker's ill-conceived fantasy of a uto-pia that never was. It is likely an example of what some of us "philosophers of color" refer to as "thinking whitely." The implied history of Walker's posi-tion on restorative justice between blacks and whites is badly in error, histori-cally speaking, an error that can be corrected by a careful study of chapters 6 and 7, below.

Second, even assuming that what Walker might have meant was a *creation* of a healthy relation between blacks and whites in the United States, and with other groups as well, there still exist problems with her statement that "with-out restoration, the meaning of compensation, were some compensation achieved, might not be a respectful and reparative one." This claim is prob-lematic because it assumes without supportive argument that massive com-pensatory reparations to blacks by the United States would have little or no meaning *for blacks* who are not enamored with the promise of integration with whites, when in fact little could mean more to them precisely because of con-siderations not only of compensatory and retributive justice, but of poverty and other underclass issues as well, as will be explained in chapter 9. The rea-son why Walker makes this assumption is because of her essentially utilitarian presuppositions, unexamined and undefended as they are, one of which seems to be that it is overall social utility maximization (including the sup-posed social peace and tranquility that are imagined to be involved in it) that matters instead of rights to compensation for harmful wrongdoing experi-enced. Why not assume that blacks are in no need of reconciliation with whites? Besides, for the same reason why there is no relationship healthy enough to restore between blacks and whites in the United States, there can be no reconciliation either. Who cares about bringing blacks into previously tainted and horribly unjust integration with whites? It has never worked gen-erally well for blacks previously. On what grounds does one think, besides white guilt or the belief that blacks are for some reason undeserving of true justice, including compensatory justice, that such integration—even enhanced in the ways that she herself supposes—between blacks and whites is good *for blacks*? As Claudia Card notes of reconciliation in general, "reconciliation may simply provide the offender easy opportunities to repeat the offense,"[76] or to wrong the victim again. And if it is not good for blacks, then is it not time for those who say they respect blacks to admit on balance the failure of black integration in U.S. society? Significant compensatory reparations of the amount that I defend in chapter 9 will likely suffice for black independence from white society, thus eliminating the need for Walker's hidden hard paternalism toward blacks. So her attempt at moral repair for blacks is dramatically insufficient to satisfy the demands of justice and rights. It must be rejected as yet another attempt to obscure what is really at stake for blacks with what white desires are vis-à-vis white guilt and perhaps white power and privilege. Moral repair as Walker describes it will not likely provide blacks with genuine hope, except the hope that they will once again be disrespected and have their rights denied by white society as they always have been throughout the duration of U.S. history—even until today with the denial of their right to compensatory reparations by leftists as well as rightists in the United States. Hope is personal autonomy and group sovereignty; hope is in the claiming and respecting of justice and rights, rather than in one's oppressors. This is what hope involves for realistic, nonutopian Indians and blacks in the United States.

What we have in Walker's utilitarian approach to "moral repair" is not an analysis of reparations as the term is normally understood, but rather a concern primarily with the restoration of human relationships in predominantly white society. It is simply false, as Card puts it, that "accepting reparations . . . is a way of renewing relations,"[77] any more than a plaintiff's court-ordered award of compensation is a way of renewing relations with her offender. Blacks, for instance, can accept compensatory reparations of the kind I detail in chapter 9 without as much as living in the same space as whites if they choose not to. For nothing about compensatory justice requires the integration of victims with their oppressors, nor of heirs of oppression with one another, contrary to Walker's restorative justice notion. There should be no strings attached to compensatory justice. By definition, "reparations" are a species of compensatory justice. So it is wrongheaded for those of the Thompson-Walker approach to reparations to attach as a necessary condition of reparations demands of "equity," forgiveness, reconciliation, and the like to their presumed goal of a social utility maximized society.

Indeed, Walker's perspective on moral repair is akin to the somewhat utilitarian ethic that underlies cosmopolitan liberalism assessed in the previous chapter. But it behooves one who is serious about the whole of justice to wonder whether her disregard for the victims of harmful wrongdoing in the form of disrespecting their obvious rights to compensatory justice is an indicator of a realistic and reasonably just society, or rather of an unrealistic utopian and ahistorical one. Moreover, one is left wondering if Feinberg's example of

"Nowheresville" is precisely what Walker has argued for, a society without compensatory (and perhaps other) rights being respected, yet one where duties and obligations are abundant. And we know where Nowheresville leads, morally speaking.[78]

In his review of *Race, Racism, and Reparations*, and after admitting the "powerful" and "plausible" nature of the arguments for Indian and black reparations therein, James P. Sterba writes,

> The question is how Corlett's arguments for reparations relate to an argument for distributive justice that says that each and every person living today is entitled to have his or her basic needs met—just the resources required for a decent life and nothing more. Part of the justification for this limitation on the use of resources is to make it possible for every person living today around the world to have sufficient resources for a decent life. . . .
>
> Assuming that this is what distributive justice requires of us, how should we weigh these requirements against the arguments for reparations that Corlett advances? Could it be that reparations would have to be met in a more symbolic way so as not to take away resources that are required to secure a decent life for both existing and future generations? Could it be that when defenders of reparations assume that large sums of money and resources should be transferred, making a new group of rich people and a new group of poor people, they are also assuming a much less demanding theory of distributive justice?[79]

These are important questions, as they juxtapose the demands of compensatory justice with those of distributive justice. And I have never denied the importance of distributive justice, either domestically or globally. In this respect I favor a Rawlsian approach to justice and fairness. However, unlike the cosmopolitan liberals we examined in the previous chapter who presumptuously assert the priority of their alleged cosmopolitan demands of distributive justice over the rights of compensation for harmful wrongdoings—even severe oppression—I assume with Rawlsians that whatever is done in terms of distributive justice cannot ignore the rights of compensatory justice. For if this happens, which is precisely what happens in the case of cosmopolitan liberalism and the other approaches examined in this chapter, the global poor would be fed and educated, housed, and clothed, but the cost of this would be that even the most oppressed folk in history will have their pleas for a fuller measure of justice go unheard. This would be the application of utilitarianism with a vengeance, an alleged theory of global justice that is so myopic about assisting the poor and needy that it apparently cares nothing about the rights to compensation of those who have been made destitute by its own unjust theory.

The probability is that if compensatory reparations are taken seriously, most of the global poor and needy will be among those groups compensated by the likes of the United States, Great Britain, Spain, France, Portugal, Italy, the

Catholic Church, among other states and nongovernmental colonial organizations that have enriched themselves by exploiting peoples who never invited them into their lives and onto their lands in the first place. And the amounts of such compensatory measures would, as we shall see in chapter 9, improve the lots of most of those targeted by cosmopolitan liberalism anyway. But the crucial difference is that in the case of reparative justice, paternalism is absent and rights are genuinely respected.

Sterba also argues that affirmative actions programs are more affordable than reparations awards and so can make room financially for the demands of global justice for the poor and needy. In light of this, "presently, it seems, affirmative action is the only political game in town."[80] While this is presently true, the same thing could be said of affirmative action in the early 1970s when it was seemingly not a viable option. Yet affirmative action was implemented just a few years later. The fact is that if leftists would consider the arguments for reparations and then, if they are plausible, support them politically, then they may well stand a good chance of meaningful implementation. After all, there has not yet been presented evidence that compensatory reparations to Indians and blacks and perhaps some other reparative measures for other groups persecuted or oppressed by the United States make the legitimate demands of global justice unaffordable. The remainder of this book seeks to make a case for the moral requirement and affordability of compensatory reparations to Indians and blacks as a first step toward a more general argument for the claim that other reparations are both affordable and required, though at lesser levels and degrees relative to U.S.-based oppression. In the end, we are morally required to assist those in need not of their own doing only to the extent that we can do so without placing ourselves in a genuinely self-endangering position, consistent with anti–bad Samaritanism.

My suggestion is that if we place the demands of global justice ahead of those of compensatory reparations, we place ourselves precisely in a poor moral position to assist others. For we have given up some of our most basic rights and duties in the process of assisting others. In effect, we have said that it is better to assist the poor and needy even though doing so ignores the requirements of compensatory justice! This means that we have sacrificed some basic remedial rights for considerations of social utility, and we have undermined the separateness of persons in the process. These are hardly novel points,[81] and I am continually surprised that so many cosmopolitan liberals do not even flinch at these implications of their view. Perhaps it is because their presumption of utilitarianism is too settled to care enough about its undermining of rights, justice, and personhood. If this is true, then what good does it do to "rescue" the global poor and needy if what they are offered is not a fuller measure of rights and justice, yet resources for a decent living, but with the constant fear of having their rights and valid claims for justice ignored when the next needy folk come along?

I take it that these are sufficient reasons to wonder if essentially utilitarian-based approaches to reparations even take seriously the demands of compensatory justice. As I have made plain, I have no reason to think they do. In light of this fact, one with an adequate sensitivity to race and racism might well wonder whether in general cosmopolitan liberalism and other such attempts to deny compensatory reparations to severely oppressed groups is a symptom of a deeper problem underlying most of contemporary political philosophy, for example, its "unacknowledged whiteness."[82] By this I mean that most political philosophers today do not seem to apply the same logical reasoning in cases of American Indian and black oppression and their possible rectification to matters of alleged "equality," "reconciliation," and "human rights" and related matters of global justice to individual or class-action suits in tort law as most of the latter cases are filed by whites who have the financial resources to file them, while most of the latter cases could very well involve indigenous and black peoples. Such hypocritical thinking might point toward a kind of white racism that seeks to continue global and domestic dominance of whites over the most oppressed peoples of the earth.

To deny Indians and blacks in the United States their compensatory reparations and instead stipulate reparations in terms of "moral repair" that includes the expectation or requirement of reconciliation between the heirs of oppression disrespects the moral autonomy of the victim heirs of oppression and treats them as mere means to the end of social utility maximization. In short, it denies the rights of victim heirs of oppression to compensatory reparations where they are owed, along with their right to exercise their autonomy to live with whom they please. It denies the moral rights of victim heirs of oppression along these and related lines. For a moral right is not only a valid moral claim or interest. As H. J. McCloskey argues, a moral right is

> a *moral entitlement* that gives rise to a moral authority to do what these individuals are entitled to have or to do, to be protected from interference, . . . moral rights are moral entitlements that confer moral liberties on their possessors to do, demand, enjoy, have, etc., depending on the nature and basis of the right; and they are moral entitlements that typically but not always impose moral constraints on others to abstain from various actions and activities, or to do, assist, provide services.[83]

Thus these utilitarian-based approaches to reparations deny the right of the oppressed and their heirs to compensatory reparations. Yet ironically it is the very notion of a moral right that they seem to think grounds their acceptance of the idea of human rights.

In the end, the utilitarian, restorative justice approaches to reparations face daunting substantive theoretical problems as noted. However, there are other difficulties that face them at the practical level of implanting restorative justice. As Andrew von Hirsch and Andrew Ashworth argue of restorative justice approaches in general, restorative justice "processes are said to 'restore' the bonds of community frayed through the offence, but it is not explained what kinds of bonds have been damaged or how this restoration is to take place."[84] Moreover, as I have intimated above, when, if ever, would monetary compensation be preferable or mandatory? If never, why never? Restorative justice theorists such as Thompson and Walker do not specify whether the demands of restorative justice should be discretionary or imposed. In either case, "having crimes dealt with through interaction between victim and offender has value only if it is possible to specify what goals such a procedure could accomplish."[85] Yet restorative justice theorists do not specify such procedures or goals:

> There should thus be some explicit principles suggesting what kind of dispositions might be appropriate, and what kind might not be. Leaving this purely to the discretion of particular participants is likely to lead to dispositions which, if capable of being rationalized at all, could be so on grounds having little or nothing to do with the making of amends.[86]

Moreover, a rights-based and retributivist approach to reparations involves a form of moral discourse, though not a negotiated one as found in restorative justice approaches. With restorative justice approaches,

> the procedure is a *negotiated* process between offender and victim, leading to a response that conveys acknowledgement of fault and the undertaking of a reparative task reflecting that acknowledgement . . . a way of showing concern for the victim's interests, on the part of a person (the offender) whose lack of respect and concern was expressed, precisely, in his act of wrongdoing.[87]

While both rights-based and restorative justice approaches can each concern themselves with backward-looking reasons (the fact of the oppression, for instance) for their respective models of reparations, rights-based approaches seek to honor proportional means to compensate and otherwise repair the damages suffered by victims of oppression, while restorative justice approaches do not. Although each approach involves an imposition on offenders, the imposition differs radically in kind. And plausible reasons must be adduced for why offenders ought to suffer one kind of imposition over another. I have argued why restorative justice approaches, in their myopic concentration on forgiveness and reconciliation, fail to adequately compensate victim heirs of oppression. In short, they fail to justify their radical departure from the current method of compensating victims of oppression by way of compensatory reparations, among other things.

One of the key lessons of part 1 of this book is how utilitarian-based approaches to reparations confuse questions of the nature of reparations with questions of their value. Utility-minded thinkers begin to address the question of reparations by unwittingly addressing the question of their value, and with all of the familiar forward-looking trappings that place the *right* to reparations under the dominion of considerations of social utility. This not only begs the justificatory question against rights-based approaches to reparations, it neglects the fact that part of the nature of reparations is that they constitute a *right* that oppressed groups possess, a right that is correlated with a duty of oppressors to pay reparations to those whom they oppress. As such, this right is not subject to the dominion of any utilitarian calculus, as Rawls eloquently argues in the first few pages of *A Theory of Justice*. I shall move forward with a rights-respecting approach to reparations, one that sees respect for rights as essential to any reasonably just society.

II

A RIGHTS-BASED APPROACH TO REPARATIONS

Each person possesses an inviolability founded on justice that even the welfare of society as a whole cannot override. For this reason justice denies that the loss of freedom for some is made right by a greater good shared by others. It does not allow that the sacrifices imposed on a few are outweighed by the larger sum of advantages enjoyed by many . . . *the rights secured by justice are not subject to political bargaining or to the calculus of social interests*. . . . Being first virtues of human activities, truth and justice are uncompromising.

—John Rawls, *A Theory of Justice*, rev. ed., 3–4 (emphasis provided)

4

Reparations as a Human Right

The limits of the possible are not given by the actual, for we can to a greater or lesser extent change political and social institutions and much else. Hence we have to rely on conjecture and speculation, arguing as best we can that the social world we envision is feasible and might actually exist, if not now then at some future time under happier circumstances.

—John Rawls[1]

To have a right is to have a claim against someone whose recognition as valid is called for by some set of governing rules or moral principles. To have a *claim* in turn, is to have a case meriting consideration, that is, to have reasons or grounds that put one in a position to engage in performative and propositional claiming. The activity of claiming, finally, as much as any other thing, makes for self-respect and respect for others, gives a sense to the notion of personal dignity, and distinguishes this otherwise morally flawed world from the even worse world of Nowheresville.

—Joel Feinberg[2]

The substance of human rights then resides in the formal conditions for the legal institutionalization of those discursive processes of opinion- and will-formation in which the sovereignty of the people assumes a binding character.

—Jürgen Habermas[3]

The question, "What are human rights?" is ambiguous. It might mean to ask what are the conditions both necessary and jointly sufficient such that, whether or not such conditions are satisfied, such conditions define who or what possesses or exercises the rights. Or, it might ask precisely which rights are declared to be "human" ones, say, in the United Nations Universal Declaration of Human Rights of 1948, or the European Covenant on Human

83

Rights. Alternatively, the question might ask what rights, assuming there are any in more than a conventional sense, are specifically human ones (whatever that is supposed to mean). While the third question seeks to uncover just what makes a right a *human* one, the answer to the second question is rather socio-historical, as what one must do is to look and see what the official declarations state about such rights, and to interpret them with reasonable care. Various kinds of answers have been given to the first version of the question. There are those who argue that human rights are merely conventional ones outlined in various declarations and other pronouncements, while most philosophers, it seems, consider human rights to be a species of moral or natural rights that accrue to humans *qua* humans regardless of what conventions and institutional structures admit.[4] I believe that this philosophical quarrel is misguided. If there are human rights, then they can be both conventional *and* nonconventional. In other words, human rights might turn out to be valid claims or interests that ought to be recognized by institutions of law and policies, and sometimes are. So we need not trouble ourselves with controversies over whether or not human rights, if they do exist, are merely conventional.[5]

The aim of this chapter is primarily normative. It argues that *if* there are human rights as species of moral rights that ought to accrue to humans *qua* humans, *then* there is one particular human right, namely, the group right to compensatory justice by means of reparations, that deserves attention in human rights discourse. It is among those human rights that ought not to be suspended during a national emergency. This right will be explored in a way that attempts to avoid providing a particularly Westernized conception of human rights,[6] or one that serves the interests of Western imperialism.[7] Issues of reducibility of the language of rights,[8] human or otherwise, will not occupy my attention, as reducibility of human rights talk certainly fails to prove the meaninglessness of human rights language. So unless a successful argument for the reductive eliminability of human rights talk is forthcoming, I shall proceed on the assumption that human rights talk is meaningful, or at least as meaningful as talk about rights in general, duties, and other related concepts. I also assume, along with Joel Feinberg, that rights are necessary for self-respect and human dignity and that rights are most important when they are backed by power to protect them.[9] I argue that this point can be extended to human rights should they exist in more than a conventional way. This chapter seeks to establish an oppressed group's right to reparative compensation.

It is a disappointing fact that most philosophers who have contributed to the proliferation of discussions of human rights during the decades subsequent to the UN Universal Declaration of Human Rights have not construed human rights as rights ought to be understood more generally. In other words, they do not understand the nature of human rights in terms of valid claims or interests.[10] I shall proceed along the lines of defining human rights as those rights that are based on valid moral claims or interests pertaining to individual or collective humans, with the balance of human reason as the determining factor of what counts as a human right in this or that circumstance.[11] What makes a moral right a human one is that it is globalized and places the emphasis on the fact that all humans possess such a right, however conditionally.[12] As Feinberg states: "A man has a moral right when he has a claim the recognition of which is called for—not (necessarily) by legal rules—but by moral principles, or the principles of an enlightened conscience."[13] My conception of human rights is based on Feinberg's notion of a right simplicitor.[14]

This Feinbergian conception of a human right implies that, in light of what the balance of human reason indicates about this or that circumstance where conflicting claims or interests obtain, a human claim or interest can be valid but not recognized by law or political conventions, and vice versa. This in turn implies that there can be a human right not recognized by law, political institutions, or declarations. On the other hand, something that is declared or pronounced to be a human right might not enjoy the support of the balance of human reason or the principles of an enlightened conscience.

As many philosophers are discovering by way of critiques of cosmopolitan justice,[15] it is one thing to pronounce something as a positive right that all humans ought to enjoy (say, equality), but it is quite another thing to demonstrate by way of careful philosophical argument and analysis that there is a corresponding duty of either individuals, businesses, states, or nongovernmental organizations (NGOs) to assist in the provision of that right for the global poor. For it might be that a particular individual, business, state, or NGO simply cannot fulfill that duty—even over some period of time. It might even be the case that all of them combined cannot fulfill the duty in question, and for a variety of reasons. As Feinberg argues: "It would be idle to claim that the right to enough food is an absolute, categorical right, exceptionless in every conceivable circumstance, because we cannot legislate over nature."[16] But it might also be the case that it is not their duty to fulfill, say, because of the fact that certain other individuals, businesses, NGOs, and states are significantly morally responsible (in the liability sense) for the plight of the global poor. Furthermore, perhaps those individuals, businesses, NGOs, and states are not in positions to fulfill their duties to those they have in large part made destitute. This does not mean that those who are responsible for wrongfully harming others do not have duties to compensate their victims. For a compensatory duty unfulfilled (in part or in whole) is nonetheless a duty, just as the right to be compensated as the result of being wrongfully harmed by another stands—even if not respected by the harmful wrongdoer. The point here is not that there are no duties to the distant poor. Rather, it is that "our obligations may be quite substantial. But we need to be clear about their basis and their limits."[17]

Human rights are understood by some philosophers as those prima facie valid moral claims that accrue to all humans[18] regardless of circumstance or era, subject to the "ought implies can" dictum. Furthermore, as Richard Wasserstrom notes, "they are *prima facie* rights in the sense that there may be cases in which overriding a human right would be less undesirable than protecting it."[19] Among other things, this raises the question of whether or not some or all human rights might be legitimately suspended, say, in times of national emergency, a point to which I shall return below. Others construe human rights as absolutely exceptionless ones not only within a limited scope but throughout a scope itself unlimited, accruing to all humans in all circumstances.[20] Among several others, A. John Simmons holds just such a view,[21] dubbed by Charles R. Beitz as the "orthodox conception" of human rights.[22]

But like rights in general, human rights are not absolute in this sense, as there seem to be counterexamples to any such absolutist claim to human rights. Even the alleged absolute human right to not be tortured, noted by Feinberg,[23] is nullified to the extent that proportional punishment (subsequent to genuine due process of law, of course) might permit the torturing of those who unduly torture others under conditions where responsibility for the crime is not excused or is unmitigated. Anything less than torture would in at least some cases be a punishment unbefitting of the crime, it might be argued. One cannot have it both ways, the argument might proceed: Either one must retain the fundamental moral principle of proportional punishment and retain torture as a rightful way to punish robustly culpable torturers, or they must give it up in favor of some absolute human right to not be tortured. Before many tempt themselves to jettison the idea of proportional punishment, however, they ought to think carefully, as to do so could then justify capital punishment, for instance, for minor offenses such as petty theft. After all, if proportional punishment is discarded in a reasonably consistent manner, then it is discarded not only in cases of torture, but in all cases of punishment, making the institution and practices of punishment unprincipled.[24] Thus the significance of proportional punishment reduces the putative right to not be tortured to a claim or interest, its validity to be determined by independent and plausible argument on a case by case basis in light of all relevant factors. Assumed here is the notion that *if* some human rights are absolute, then this also means they are nonconflictable such that if that human right conflicts with other rights, it must always win out over them, and no absolute human right is conflictable with another.

Feinberg also suggests that positive rights to goods that can never be in scarce supply (right to a fair trial, a package of negative and positive rights), equal protection under the law or equal consideration, the negative right not to be tortured, and perhaps the right to not be exploited or denigrated might qualify as human rights.[25] Of the latter he states that "rights in this category are probably the only ones that are human rights in the strongest sense: unalterable, 'absolute' (exceptionless and nonconflictable), and universally and *peculiarly* human."[26] And Feinberg provides the following caution to those who would construe human rights as absolute by definition:

> There is therefore no objection in principle to the idea of human rights that are absolute in the sense of being categorically exceptionless. It is another question as to whether there are such rights, and what they might be. The most plausible

candidates, like the right not to be tortured, will be passive negative rights, that is, rights not to be done to by others in certain ways. It is more difficult to think of active negative rights (rights not to be interfered with) or positive rights (rights to be done to in certain ways) as absolutely exceptionless. The positive rights to be given certain essentials—food, shelter, security, education—clearly depend upon the existence of an adequate supply, something that cannot be guaranteed categorically and universally.

If absoluteness in this strong sense is made part of the very meaning of the expression "human right," then it would seem that there is a lamentable paucity of human rights, if any at all. Clarity will be best served, I think, if we keep "absoluteness" out of the definition of "human right."[27]

Most philosophers believe that the rights to due process and freedom of expression comprise part of the core of such rights, though there are an increasing number of those who argue for the inclusion of welfare rights (social and economic rights) on the list of basic human rights.[28] Whatever the case, one must be careful to not, "in the manner of magicians, pull rights out of nowhere"[29] and unnecessarily proliferate rights (claims).[30] Perhaps one way to judge the reasonableness of a human rights claim or interest is to see if the same kind and strength of considerations in favor of it is used to justify already accepted (by convention or declaration) human rights, that is, ones deemed valid by many. If so, then by parity of reasoning either together such human rights claims or interests must be accepted or they must together be rejected. This is what I attempt to do herein, using the Feinbergian conception of rights.[31]

There is much discussion in recent years about "basic human rights." But it appears that few have the inclination to explain precisely what makes a human right basic. I offer the following in order to provide clarification on human rights discourse, assuming a Feinbergian notion of a right wherein there are no genuine conflicts of rights, but rather conflicts of claims or interests and wherein the all relevant things considered valid claim or interest grounds the right.[32] A nonbasic human right is one that is a part of a cluster of rights on which it depends for its validity. Human rights to due process would be examples of nonbasic rights because they are human rights to the extent that the entire group of them represent valid claims. A basic human right, on the other hand, is one that depends on no other valid claim or interest for its own validity. It stands alone in the spectrum of human rights, it is self-justificatory. But it might well serve to support other rights. Whether there exist such rights is a controversial notion. But those who make claims to basic human rights owe us an argument as to which rights would qualify as such, and why. I suggest that "basic" ought not to remain a part of human rights discourse until such rights are clarified. In the meantime, I shall treat human rights as a cluster of valid moral claims or interests that are to be taken with utmost seriousness and weightiness, with no human right trumping another absent other relevant considerations of weightiness. Thus I offer a coherentist, rather than a foundationalist, analysis of human rights.

There is a distinction between positivistic and moralistic views concerning human rights. Human rights positivists argue that human rights, whatever else they are, are only those recognized by legal rules or official declarations. And since what is in question are those rights that are to be recognized internationally or globally, such rights must be recognized by international law by way of legal rules or manifestos.[33] Human rights moralists, on the other hand, argue that human rights are fundamentally moral rights, noninstitutional in nature, and exist whether or not they are recognized by any legal system—global or otherwise. Indeed, if such rights do not find themselves supported by international law, they ought to. Just as a legal moralist might claim that "there ought to be a law to . . ." so too a human rights moralist might argue that "there ought to be a human right to . . ." to protect all humans from undue violations or conditions under certain circumstances. Thus according to the human rights moralist, human rights can be distinguished from international human rights, but human rights nonetheless do not depend for their bare existence on whether or not they are recognized and supported globally. While some such rights gain institutional support whenever they do, say, in the UN Declaration on Human Rights or the European Covenant on Human Rights, they are ultimately grounded in valid moral rules.[34] Fundamentally, however, human rights find their justification in "true morality," for they exist whether or not human institutions recognize them. Whether or not such institutional recognition of human rights obtains is a question concerning the support for such rights and those who possess and seek to enjoy them. But it is not a matter of whether such rights exist or are real.

In Rawlsian terms, we might say that human rights exist quite apart from whether or not they are recognized and respected by reasonable liberal peoples, decent peoples, outlaw states, societies burdened by unfavorable conditions, or benevolent absolutists, each of which can in principle make at least some room for some human rights.[35] While reasonable liberal peoples and decent (liberal or nonliberal) peoples, if they do exist, are significantly more likely to both make room for and respect human rights (or what they construe as human rights) because they are part of the Society of Peoples and follow the reasonably just Law of Peoples in their mutual relations,[36] such rights can still exist in any society, whether or not they are recognized or respected. This point has been made by Feinberg in defense of moral rights more generally,[37] and implies a vital distinction between the following questions concerning human rights as moral rights. First, there is the question of the nature of such rights, which involves the question of their existence conditions and whether or not they truly exist. Second, there is the question of the justification or grounding of human rights, assuming they exist at all. A third question concerns the value of human rights, which entails the question of their value in cases where they are not respected (whether or not they are recognized). A fourth question is what else might be needed for human rights to be fully effective, and the answer to this question will depend on the kind of society in which one lives. And as with rights in general, it is important that human right holders possess rights and know that they possess them,[38] but such persons must, for purposes of their having dignity and having it respected normally, know that they can claim their human rights and know how to do so effectively. For even if one knows that one has a human right, one might not know, for instance, that either the international legal "system" or moral principles confer on her the rightful claim to this or that protection or precisely how the claim might be made, and made effectively.[39]

It is noteworthy that the questions of the nature and value of human rights are intimately related to one another. For if the value of such rights is the Feinbergian notion that they are necessary for self-respect, respect for others and human dignity, then the content of their value will affect the content of the nature of human rights themselves. So it is not simply that a human right, if it exists, amounts to a valid moral claim or interest of a particularly human sort. Rather, it is that such a valid claim or interest must be of the sort that, when respected, provides the rightholder with a certain level of self-respect and dignity. This is not possible if human rights claims could then be overridden by social utility considerations, for example, because peoples' claims or interests can be overridden by whatever would maximize social utility. It is hard to imagine such a society wherein self-respect and human dignity would flourish. Since rights are matters of justice, then as Rawls states in the epigraph for part 2, justice cannot be overridden by the demands of social utility. This includes, I argue, the compensatory right to reparations. Hence my criticisms of utilitarian-based conceptions of reparations in part 1, above.

My argument will proceed from the Feinbergian assumption that human rights exist as valid moral claims or interests based on the balance of human reason, all relevant things considered. With most philosophers of rights, I also assume that generally there is a correlation of rights and duties, though the correlation is not perfect.[40] Moreover, Alan Gewirth notes of human rights that they are

> rights that are had by every human being simply insofar as he or she is human. But while the rights involve claims to the protection of individual interests, they also require of each person that she act with due regard for other persons' interests as well as her own. For, as human rights, they are not only had by all humans; they are also rights against all humans. In other words, each human being is both the subject or right-holder and the respondent or duty-bearer . . . every human has rights to freedom and well-being against all other humans, but every other human also has these rights against him, so that he has correlative duties toward them.[41]

Again, Gewirth argues, "The rights that are here in question are primarily claim-rights, that is, rights that entail correlative duties at least to refrain from interfering with persons' having the objects of their rights and, in certain circumstances, to help persons to have these objects."[42] Thus if I have a human claim right to X, then I have a valid moral claim to X as a human being. This in turn implies a correlative negative moral duty that everyone else has of noninterference with my exercise and enjoyment of my right. But it might also imply that everyone else has a correlative positive moral duty to provide me with the means by which to enjoy or experience X. While the first kind of rights-duties correlation is relatively unproblematic, the latter one is a contested point between political philosophies.

While much has been made of human rights by philosophers, there has been a glaring omission on the lists of those rights said to be possessed by all humans, absolutely or not. Whether or not the cause of such omission is ideological bias, such important omissions in human rights discourse serve as an embarrassing reminder of how far we are from an adequate conception of human rights.

My argument will take the form of a simple conditional: "If there are human rights as a species of moral rights beyond mere convention, then the right to compensatory reparations is a human right." For all that the leading philosophical analyses of human rights say, nothing on such accounts precludes an oppressed group's remedial right to compensatory reparations as being a human right. Thus either the right to compensatory reparations must be included in the list of human rights, or the analysis of human rights must be plausibly revised to exclude it in order to avoid confusion. My intention here is not to deny either the traditional liberal (narrow) conception of human rights as particularly freedom rights, or the cosmopolitan (wider) notion of human rights as those including a host of welfare rights.[43] Moreover, I shall not challenge the claim that there are human rights as a species of moral rights. Thus I shall argue that if human rights exist as valid moral claims or interests, then at least one additional right must be added to the list: the remedial right to compensatory reparations to groups that have experienced severe harmful wrongdoing. This right restores the self-respect of which inhumane treatment robs its victims, and the balance of justice that is one important source of human dignity.

I proceed according to the Rawlsian idea that "political philosophy is realistically utopian when it extends what are ordinarily thought of as the limits of practical political possibility,"[44] assuming that the notion of human rights ought to be construed as being realistically utopian. Of the essential aspect of a realistic utopia, Rawls states,

> The great evils of human history—unjust war and oppression, religious persecution and the denial of liberty of conscience, starvation and poverty, not to mention genocide and mass murder—follow from political injustice, . . . once the gravest forms of political injustice are eliminated by following just (or at least decent) social policies and establishing just (or at least decent) basic institutions, these great evils will eventually disappear. . . . I contend that this scenario is realistic—it could and may exist. I say it is also utopian and highly desirable because it joins reasonableness and justice with conditions enabling citizens to realize their fundamental interests.[45]

It should come as no surprise, then, that an argument would be made to include a certain cluster of remedial rights to group compensation under the category of human rights as part of what Rawls refers to as "just . . . social policies" and "just . . . basic institutions." This is especially the case if it is reasonable to argue that the human remedial right to reparations exists as a species of the human right to compensation. This right to reparations is a human right. For without its protection, there is little or no point to human rights that are of the freedom or welfare varieties. Indeed, as Rawls recognizes, it is often for the very sake of human rights protection that war (of which rebellion is one species) is engaged in by democratic societies.[46] Yet contemporary philosophers of human rights have paid no attention to this right.[47] Worst still, some actually deny the right of reparations, as noted in chapter 2.

Any theory or analysis of human rights, not unlike those of rights more generally, assumes a deeper moral, social, political, and legal theory. And so the plausibility of such analyses is contingent on the plausibility of their respective overarching or encompassing theories on which they depend. In arguing in favor of the inclusion of two particular and neglected rights in the category of "human rights," I shall explain the nature, justification, and purpose of such rights. Separating these questions is important so as to not cause confusion and needless complexity.

What about the human right to reparations of groups by businesses or governments that cause serious and wrongful harm to them? Rawls states that "people must recognize that they cannot make up for failing to regulate their numbers or to care for their land by conquest in war, or by migrating to another people's territory without their consent."[48] Of course, simply because some harmful wrongdoings cannot be fully rectified or compensated does not mean that such measures are not owed and ought not to be attempted in good faith. Yet countries such as the United States are precisely those that have committed several of these severely harmful wrongdoings, and have yet to rectify them, or to even take seriously such claims to remedy them. In so doing, the United States continues to deny or ignore remedial rights to reparations to the groups it has most seriously wronged. Just in the past half-century, the United States has engaged in economic colonialization, imperialism, and militarism in Guatamala, Iran, Lebanon, Haiti, Korea, Cuba, Laos, Thailand, Vietnam, the Congo, the Dominican Republic, Indonesia, Cambodia, Chile, Angola, Afghanistan, Lybia, Nicaragua, El Salvador, Grenada, Chad, Bolivia, Panama, Somalia, Yugoslavia, Macedonia, Bosnia, the Sudan, Yemen, the Philippines, Colombia, Liberia, among other countries. These are instances of the intent of the United States to shore up its empire globally by way of the "business of war" wherein the U.S. "military industrial complex" (as well as supportive congressional and executive branches) is to a large extent driven by some rather powerful business sectors and their respective interests.[49]

Rawls also argues that "so long as there are outlaw states . . . some nuclear weapons need to be retained to keep those states at bay and to make sure that they do not obtain and use those weapons against liberal and decent peoples."[50] This of course places the United States in a vulnerable moral position insofar as it has always seen itself as a liberal and decent society, and this in light of historical facts of its massive domestic and foreign rights abuses that would render it an outlaw state. It is not as if the United States had a morally sound beginning, but then departed from it in slight ways here and there. Instead, the United States was founded from the outset on a set of some the most evil acts in human history, most of which remain unrectified to this day. Insofar as domestic rights abuses are concerned, I refer here to the unjust establishment of the United States by the "American revolution" by way of a morally illegitimate secession from England,[51] which led to the continuance of American "Indian removal," and more generally, the "American holocaust,"[52] along with the continuance of the enslavement of Africans,[53] Jim Crow, and its involvement in some morally unjust wars, among various other instances of oppression, persecution, colonialism, and imperialism mentioned in the previous paragraph. This would seem to imply, from Rawls's words, that each and every liberal or decent society ought to obtain nuclear weapons in order to keep the *United States*, clearly an outlaw state, "at bay." For it is not only that the United States has committed a lengthy train of evils that it has never rectified, it does not even consider the rectification of such human rights abuses a legitimate topic of national conversation.[54] This would seem to render the United States an evil society, on balance, as clarified in the introduction.[55] For its positive contributions both to its own citizens and the world are outweighed by its generations of racist, classist, and sexist evils that cumulatively rival even the evils of Nazi Germany in terms of the duration of its oppression of Indians and blacks, in terms of the estimated numbers of Indians and blacks unjustly killed and enslaved, and in terms of land occupation rights violated by the United States, against hundreds of Indian nations.

The human right of groups to reparations for unrectified harmful wrongdoing is based on the valid moral claims to group compensation because such groups have experienced serious harmful wrongdoing at the hands of, say, an outlaw state (be it the United States, England, Nazi Germany, Stalinist USSR, etc.), perhaps in the form of genocide or slavery that one country has heaped evils on peoples that did not deserve them. On the basis of legal and moral principles of proportionality and responsibility, we would say that the victims of such evils deserve compensation in the form of reparations from the state(s) or other parties responsible for the evils in proportion, albeit approximate, to the harms wrongfully suffered.[56] And if it is true that unrectified evil is evil still,[57] then such states are transparent instances of outlaw states (in the Rawlsian sense) to the extent that they refuse to pay what they owe for such evils to those who have been harmed, or to their rightful heirs. Based on basic principles of desert which are essential to any plausible notions of responsibility and punishment, then if there are human rights, the individual right to be compensated for harmful wrongdoings suffered at the hands of another, and the group right to reparations from their harmful wrongdoers, are among such rights. To deny this claim would in turn seem to court the denial of the claim that fundamental rectificatory justice is a human right, that one who is wrongfully harmed is entitled to be made whole by the harmful wrongdoer. I take these statements to be problematic because they violate the Rawlsian idea that the prima facie moral duty to obey the law is properly grounded in legitimate expectations citizens share in knowing that the law will protect their rights and punish those who violate the rights of others and/or force oppressor parties to compensate their victims.[58] They are also problematic because they run afoul of the Feinbergian point that respect for rights builds self-respect, respect for others, and human dignity.[59] And it is difficult to imagine a society properly respecting people when it does not uphold rights to compensation, including a group's right to reparations when it is wrongfully harmed.

In sum, I have argued that if there are human rights as species of moral rights beyond mere convention, then among those rights is a group's remedial right to reparations from its harmful wrongdoer. Feinberg argues that "on many occasions we assert that someone has a right to something even though we know there are no regulations or laws conferring such a right. Such talk clearly makes sense, so any theory of the nature of rights that cannot account for it is radically defective."[60] The same is true of the human right to reparations. If it is not included in any system of legal rules, then it ought to be so included. It is a species of rights that already exist in U.S. law. The right to reparations is based on the idea of compensatory justice and rights and duties that accrue therein. In fact, the "equal protection" clause in Article 7 of the UN Universal Declaration of Human Rights, along with the "right to effective remedy" clause of Article 8, seem to ground or make room for the human right of groups to reparations.

Perhaps the right to reparations is a human right in what Feinberg calls the ideal and conscientious senses, respectively. An ideal right is one that, as stated above, *ought* to accrue, while a conscientious right is one that is called for by the principles of an enlightened conscience.[61] I shall combine and modify Feinberg's usage here to argue that the right to reparations is both an ideal and conscientious right. It is a right that all humans share *qua* humans insofar as they find themselves in circumstances such that they satisfy the conditions of their justified exercise should they decide to exercise them. This human right ought to accrue in a reasonably just legal system, whether or not it actually does. And it is confirmed by the principles of an enlightened moral conscience.

But most human rights theorists define "human rights" in terms of "generically moral rights of a fundamentally important kind held equally by all human beings, unconditionally and unalterably."[62] As I argued above, I am unsure whether there are such absolute rights. Rather, I believe that even the most important rights are conditional. Andrew Jackson and Adolf Hitler, if they were alive today, would have no moral rights to life or self-defense given their evil actions of genocide. Nor do those most responsible for the morally illicit invasions or wars have moral rights to life or self-defense. They have, in fact, no moral rights to life or self-defense once they violated the moral right to life of others the way they did. So not all humans possess valid human rights claims at all times and in all circumstances merely because they are humans.[63]

In his classic essay "The Nature and Value of Rights," Feinberg gives examples of Nowheresville and Nowheresville II to illustrate the value of rights as underlying self-respect, respect for others, and human dignity. In a recent article, I provide the example of Publicsville in order to underscore the importance of the right to privacy.[64] And in chapter 2, above, I provided the example of Traditionsville in order to refute a critique of Rawlsian liberal toleration between decent peoples under conditions of reasonable pluralism. Here I would like to argue for the importance of the human right to reparations with my example of Bullyville. Bullyville is a world without such rights, though its complex structure of international cooperation supports and touts human rights to basic equality of opportunity, including specific welfare rights for all humans throughout the world—regardless of ethnicity, creed, or political orientation. In Bullyville, strong efforts are made to combat world hunger, environmental injustices, and the like, within all states and societies. Several resources are spent by individuals, NGOs, and governments on providing education for all of the least well-off persons and societies. Indeed, hunger and ignorance are defeated in Bullyville! "Bullyville," it is proclaimed, is a "realistic utopia."

Now as utopian as Bullyville appears to be on the surface, there are problems at a deeper level. For it is impossible to have authentic peace without genuine justice. Nor is it desirable to attempt to achieve it. And although many individuals, businesses, NGOs, and governments give much to support the needy, and although many of the needy have improved their lives at least by Westernized standards, it would be a grand mistake to think that an adequate measure of peace and justice obtain in Bullyville. For many of the wealthiest and most powerful individuals and collectives in Bullyville rose to their positions by way of significant injustices against others. Whether by genocide, land theft, or enslavement, millions of persons, not just the most well-off and powerful, continue to benefit tremendously from some of the evils of the past. But these harmful wrongdoings remain unrectified. And so long as they do, those victimized by them (directly or indirectly, but nonetheless substantially) will always suffer unduly, and will never get what they deserve in terms of socioeconomic wealth and power. Bullyville ignores even the most horrendous of injustices so long as things can in the minds of Bullyvillians be forgiven and forgotten and so long as the worst-off can somehow be assisted in significant ways. For Bullyvillians it is the future rather than the past that is most important. Reconciliation, or at least perceived reconciliation, between oppressors and their victims is fundamental. And if the evils of the past must be ignored in favor of "building a better future" for the greatest number of people, then so be it.[65]

But Bullyville is an outlaw society, one that has a rather limited view of "equal rights." For any view of rights must include the right to compensation in even a realistic utopia. And, among other things, every person ought to have *this* right respected: Insofar as a person is wrongfully harmed, she has a moral right to compensation for the harmful wrongdoing and those who wrongfully harmed her must (e.g., have a moral duty to) compensate her in proportion to how badly they harmed her. And the same is true of groups, but in terms of reparations.[66] Any society—like Bullyville—that lacks an equal right to compensation for individuals and reparations to groups is not a society that can say that it truly respects persons and groups or protects their dignity. Reconciliation entails forgiveness; forgiveness entails apology; and apology entails the rectification of harmful wrongdoing by those primarily responsible for it.[67] But Bullyville fails to respect persons' and groups' rights to reasonable safety and ability to reasonably predict their safety by way of a system of rules that punishes those who violate the rights of others. Bullyville's ignoring past injustices effectively denies those who have been wronged in the past the moral standing to protest against the way they are treated by their oppressors. "But there are simply certain things, certain goods, that nobody ought to have to request of another. There are certain things that no one else ought to have the power to decide to refuse to grant."[68] And this includes reparations, and compensation more generally. But in Bullyville, there is no recourse to compensation or reparations, as to respect those rights might in some cases spell economic difficulties for Bullyville, something that the typical Bullyvillian cannot seem to accept. So Bullyville is a deeply unjust society, one that lacks fundamental justice insomuch as it disrespects compensatory rights such as reparations. It is not that Bullyville respects no rights to reparations. It might decide to "honor" some such rights, but not if doing so would place its majority constituents in a poor economic position relative to their current positions. Yet there are times when societies like Bullyville have accumulated so much unrectified harmful wrongdoing that the reparations owed by it are sufficient to doom it if the reparations were paid—even in installments and over generations.

Furthermore, Bullyville is morally flawed in yet another way. By refusing to remedy those groups wrongfully harmed by it, it in effect robs them of full participation in society. It says to them, "Various other rights will be respected in Bullyville. But if you are part of a group that is severely wronged, your claim to or interest in reparations shall not be respected unless it does not threaten the overall well-being of the majority of citizens." And when this circumstance involves ethnic groups that are wrongfully harmed, it is certain ethnic groups that are denied full participation in society because their rights to reparations are not recognized.[69] Indeed, respect for a group's remedial rights as valid claims or interests are part of what is minimally necessary for participation in a reasonably just Society of Peoples. Institutionalized remedial rights like reparations to wrongfully harmed groups not only enhance the legal quality of the human right, but create practical mechanisms to bring about such groups' enjoyment of the right as respected citizens having dignity.[70]

Under such conditions, one would think that those groups in Bullyville that have not had their severe harmful wrongdoings rectified by way of reparations would have a moral right to rebellion—perhaps even terrorism, to the extent that certain conditions are satisfied robustly—against those states and other agencies that were the primary causes of their undue suffering.[71] This is especially true in cases where the groups were victimized by genocide or race-based slavery, and over generations attempted nonviolently and in good faith to achieve rectification for their suffering but were met with repeated denials of their pleas for justice. However, I shall not pursue this point here as I have done so elsewhere.[72]

It might be objected that—even assuming the plausibility of the argument for remedial rights as human ones—the group right to reparations is not a human right. For human rights belong only to individual humans, not to collections of them.[73] But this objection reflects a kind of human rights individualism that requires justification. On what grounds are we to think that only individual humans possess human rights? Why cannot a collection of humans possess them, especially a group that has decision-making capacity and can form its own intentions, beliefs, and so forth? This point can force the problem of collective rights to a broader arena. For if human rights can be had only by individual humans, then why not rights in general? Human rights individualism is in need of a plausible non-question-begging argument as to why certain kinds of groups cannot possess and exercise them.[74] This reply has particularly strong force given that certain legal systems (including that of the United States) already recognize some group rights—even the right to group reparations.

Furthermore, while one might concur that the right to reparations is a human right, it might be argued that it is not one that cannot be overridden during a national emergency. Ought human rights to be "put on hold" or curtailed during national emergencies? Ronald Dworkin seems to imply a positive but qualified answer to this question.[75] I have already provided the basis of a Rawlsian and Feinbergian answer to this question. If a genuine right cannot be justifiably infringed because, all things considered, it is a valid moral claim or interest, then no national emergency can legitimately violate the right (though it may override a mere claim or interest). While it may be true that human rights may be waived in cases, say, where the rightholder perceives that it is morally objectionable to claim and exercise her right, it does not follow that all rights ought to be suspended by the state.[76] In Feinbergian terms, part of the value of such rights is that they provide one with the self-respect and dignity to stand up and claim what is their due with confidence—to be human in the robust sense. If this is true, then how can a society provide for its citizens even a modicum of self-respect, respect for others, and human dignity under conditions when rights are effectively infringed and reduced to claims or interests that are overridden by considerations of social utility?

Social utility maximization devalues humans as it devalues their rights,[77] while respect for rights tends to render considerations of social utility secondary in our moral deliberations. I infer from this that if human rights are to be valued at all, they must be valued as guarantors of certain essential elements of our lives. It is an important concession to hold that "human rights standards will provide substantial guidance in emergency situations only if they are specific about which rights can be infringed in emergencies and about what kinds of conditions can license infringements."[78] The European Convention on Human Rights, for example, recognizes the need for such a concession, though it is careful to make absolute the human right of life and rights against torture, degrading punishments, slavery, and retroactive criminal law. If it is true that these and perhaps other rights ought not to be suspended during times of national crises, I would argue that it seems to do no harm to a society experiencing emergency conditions to nonetheless uphold the right to reparations. This is especially true if the reparations in question involve a taxation of the government and its citizens to be paid to the group in question. If, say, reparations in the amount of 1 percent of every adult citizen's gross annual income is to be paid as reparations to a particular severely and wrongly harmed group, it is difficult to imagine how this would adversely effect the country in times of a genuine emergency. Emergencies, I assume, are temporary. Even if there is a suspension of the right to reparations in such a case because, say, the country must engage in a morally just war and requires all of the resources it can muster to succeed, there ought to be an understanding that the country will make up for the suspension of reparations payments as soon as the emergency ends, perhaps with interest and penalties accruing during the suspension of reparations due to the national emergency. After all, reparations are not a matter of charity, but of debts owed to those a government or social group or organization has wrongfully harmed. *Those who owe debts are in no moral position to refuse to pay them.* This is especially true in circumstances in which those who owe reparations are responsible for the situation in which they claim makes it overly difficult to afford to pay the reparations.

While it is true that in genuine national emergencies, not simply putative ones that are politically and economically expedient for those in power to declare as such, it is necessary for the government to reestablish basic services and provide special levels of security. This might involve arresting and detaining those who are deemed with adequate evidence to be severe threats to the national security of a morally legitimate regime. So rights to due process might need to be qualified, though not suspended, during such times.[79] However, as Article 6 of the European Convention on Human Rights states regarding the treatment of such detainees: There must be fair and public hearings within a reasonable period of time by an independent court or tribunal, that the detainees must be presumed innocent until proven guilty and informed of the charges against them, be given adequate time to prepare a defense and assistance in doing so, and be able to cross examine witnesses.

James Nickel argues that even "rights of freedom of speech and assembly might properly be suspended during a severe emergency, provided there were reason to believe that activities involving speech and assembly would do serious harm."[80] The problem with this statement is that the First Amendment to the U.S. Constitution already protects such speech, though it is delimited under certain conditions, according to various U.S. Supreme Court decisions over the years. There is no need or justification for such suspension of freedom of expression in emergency conditions. In fact, it is a misunderstanding of the meaning of that U.S. First Amendment right, as it protects all forms of expression except those that incite retaliatory violence or insurrection, for instance.[81] To suspend the right to freedom of expression—with its legally defined limitations—even in times of a genuine national emergency is to court a kind of tyranny that stifles criticism of those in power and how they handle the emergency. For the right itself, when respected by authority, stands precisely as a protection against abuses of governmental power, especially during real, contrived, or perceived emergencies.

Others might retort that, given the prima facie status of human rights, they may be legitimately suspended in times of national emergency. However, this claim poses several problems. First, the very notion of a prima facie right is not unproblematic. If we adopt the Feinbergian notion of a right as a protection of persons' self-respect, dignity, and confidence on which they ought to be able to stand and claim what is their due and have their valid claim respected, then this idea of a right easily lends itself to a person's claim being overridden by other considerations. For a right is an all relevant things considered valid moral claim or interest. But "not all claims put forward as valid really are valid; and only the valid ones can be acknowledged as rights."[82] So if one has a right (a valid, as opposed to a mere, claim or interest) in this sense, it is unclear that it is merely a prima facie one that can be overridden. Perhaps a better way to term matters here is that a party's claim to or interest in X is a prima facie one just in case it can be overridden by more powerful competing claims or interests. But this is different than saying that the claimant's prima facie right is overridden. On this account of rights, then, it is not that there can be a genuine conflict of rights in that rights do not differ in degree, one either has a right or one does not, but of claims to or interests such that, whichever ones are more compelling (all relevant things considered) ends up being the "real right."[83] Now if this line of reasoning is plausible, then a genuine human right cannot legitimately be suspended or denied even in emergency contexts and their various considerations. For that is precisely what it means to have a moral right, namely, that it overrides competing moral claims and interests. What ought to be asked is whether there are powerful but not valid moral claims or interests that might be overridden in times of national emergency.

Secondly, even if the notion of a prima facie human right being overridden makes sense, it is incumbent on those who would favor a suspension of human rights during a national emergency to provide plausible arguments as to which such rights are legitimately suspended in emergency contexts, and why. They must provide valid principled reasons why certain protections ought to be suspended. Yet it is unclear that even a context of war could serve as a sufficiently good reason to deny an oppressed group's right to reparations. A truly just society, or one that seeks to be reasonably just, is in no way justified in suspending rights, including the right to reparations.

Finally, what indeed *are* human rights if they do not serve as powerful protections against unwarranted harms and respectors of human dignity and self-respect? They are not much of anything, except often invitations to those who would seek to violate rights for their own ends. But if Feinberg is correct, "to claim that one has a right . . . is to *assert* in such a manner as to demand or insist that what is asserted be *recognized*"[84] and "a world without universal rights, would be one in which self-respect would be rare and difficult."[85] Moreover, he argues of rights in general:

> Having rights enables us to "stand up like men," to look others in the eye, and to feel in some fundamental way the equal of anyone. To think of oneself as the holder of rights is not to be unduly but properly proud, to have that minimal self-respect that is necessary to be worthy of the love and esteem of others. Indeed, respect for persons . . . may simply be respect for their rights. . . . To respect a person then, or to think of him as possessed of human dignity, simply *is* to think of him as a potential maker of claims . . . these are *facts* about the possession of rights that argue well their supreme moral importance.[86]

And what Feinberg argues about rights in general applies to human rights also. It is difficult to understand how the temporary suspension of human rights even during emergency conditions represents a society worthy of ultimate protection or worthy of our support. Neither Bullyville nor Nowheresville are preferable places to live compared to "*Rightsville*" in terms of respect for self and others, and in terms of promoting human dignity.

With this Feinbergian conception of the nature and function of moral and human rights in general, and of the plausibility of construing reparations as a human right, it is important to turn to some leading conceptions of human rights and consider precisely how plausible the idea of the human right to reparations is.

REPARATIONS AS A HUMAN RIGHT

In the remainder of this chapter, I shall argue that for all Rawls writes about human rights, there is conceptual room for the remedial right to compensation and of group reparations. Following this, I shall argue that Nickel's theory of human rights does not rule out such a right. Indeed, the remedial right to group reparations for harmful wrongdoings serves as a plausible way to strengthen their notions of what constitutes human rights. It also strengthens the case for group rights to reparations from their oppressors, a right which ought to be honored in any decent society or Society of Peoples. For as Rawls states so eloquently in the epigraph for part 2 and bears repeating,

> Each person possesses an inviolability founded on justice that even the welfare of society as a whole cannot override. For this reason justice denies that the loss of freedom for some is made right by a greater good shared by others. It does not allow that the sacrifices imposed on a few are outweighed by the larger sum of advantages enjoyed by many . . . the rights secured by justice are not subject to political bargaining or to the calculus of asocial interests. . . . Being first virtues of human activities, truth and justice are uncompromising.[87]

RAWLS'S LAW OF PEOPLES AND COMPENSATORY JUSTICE

In *The Law of Peoples*, Rawls sets forth and defends "principles and norms of international law and practice"[88] and "hopes to say how a world Society of liberal and decent Peoples might be possible."[89] His view is of one of a realistic utopia to the extent that "it extends what are ordinarily thought of as the limits of practical political philosophy"[90] and "because it joins reasonableness and justice with conditions enabling citizens to realize their fundamental interests."[91] In working toward his realistic utopia, Rawls employs a modified version of the original position employed in his earlier works.[92] However, his conception of the veil of ignorance is "properly adjusted" for the problems of international justice: the free and equal parties in the original position do not know the size of the territory or population or relative strength of the people whose basic interests they represent.[93] Although such parties know that reasonably favorable conditions possibly exist for the foundation of a constitutional democracy, they do not know the extent of their natural resources, the level of their economic development, and so on.[94] Moreover, Rawls states,

> Thus, the people's representatives are (1) reasonably and fairly situated as free and equal, and peoples are (2) modeled as rational. Also their representatives are (3) deliberating about the correct subject, in this case the content of the Law of Peoples. . . . Moreover, (4) their deliberations proceed in terms of the right reasons (as restricted by a veil of ignorance). Finally, the selection of principles for the Law of Peoples is based (5) on a people's fundamental interests, given in this case by a liberal conception of justice (already selected in the first original position).[95]

From this procedure, Rawls argues, the following "principles of justice among free and democratic peoples" will be selected:

1. Peoples are free and independent, and their freedom and independence are to be respected by other peoples.
2. Peoples are to observe treaties and undertakings.
3. Peoples are equal and are parties to the agreements that bind them.
4. Peoples are to observe a duty of nonintervention.
5. Peoples have the right of self-defense but no right to instigate war for reasons other than self-defense.
6. Peoples are to honor human rights.
7. Peoples are to observe certain specified restrictions in the conduct of war.
8. Peoples have a duty to assist other peoples living under unfavorable conditions that prevent their having a just or decent political or social regime.[96]

Various questions might be raised here, including one concerning the possible lexical ordering of such principles because such an ordering is essential to the proper application of such principles under conditions of uncertainty and rights conflicts.[97] But whether or not, and, if so, how the principles ought to be lexically ordered, this set of principles is importantly incomplete, especially in light of Rawls's repeated claim that "decent" peoples have rights to property, territory, and life. And consonant with Rawls's admission that "other principles need to be added,"[98] I offer a new international principle of justice that compliments Rawls's own list.

Rawls's eight principles of international justice seem to lack any mention or guarantee of compensatory justice between peoples. Yet without such a principle, there can hardly be a realistic global utopia as that which Rawls desires in that what helps to ensure social stability at the global level would be absent: remediation through compensation when certain rights are violated and harmful wrongdoing results. Insofar as Rawls's international principles of justice are to protect basic rights that would best ensure global stability, and insofar as rights to remediation are basic rights along with substantive rights,[99] then Rawls's principles lack what is essential to international justice in a realistic utopia. Liberal and decent peoples must compensate those whom they wrongfully harm. It is their duty correlated with the right of those they wrongfully harm to be compensated. And it will not do to argue in Rawls's defense that matters of compensatory justice are not the proper domain of Rawls's theory of international justice, as Rawls's principles reflect a concern for conditions of war and poverty and so imply the possibility of remedial rights. Thus it is an omission on Rawls's part—not to mention on the parts of various other philosophers who write on global justice—that there is no explicit mention of a basic principle of compensatory justice. This might appear to imply that reasonably just societies have no duties to compensate other societies they have severely and wrongfully harmed by way of, say, reparations. Because such injustices are so prevalent even in societies that Rawls believes are reasonably just, the issue of compensatory justice is especially important. Rawls seems to recognize (or at least leave room for) this idea in his claim (cited above) that just social policies and institutions are important for a "realistic" and reasonably just Society of Peoples.[100] Moreover, why would a party in the globalized original position select principles 1–8 above without some principle(s) of remedial rights that help(s) to guarantee them—either by their deterrent effect or by their granting the authority to an international agency of justice to award reparations or other appropriate compensation to seriously wrongfully harmed peoples by their offenders? It is reasonable and rational for those peoples in the original position to select not only Rawls's principles, but principles of compensatory justice that properly and fairly undergird them. But precisely what might some such principle be in the context of international justice?

Consider the following principle of compensation which I shall call the "principle of international compensatory justice" (PICJ) as it is intended to supplement Rawls's eight principles of international justice, though in such a way that it does not indicate a lexical ordering:

PICJ 1: To the extent that peoples wrongfully harm other peoples, they have a duty to compensate those they wrongfully harm in proportion to the harm caused them, all things considered.

Now this principle of international compensatory justice is phrased in terms of a *duty* of peoples to compensate others whom they wrongfully harm wherein the object of the duty has a corresponding right to the compensation in question. But it might also be couched in terms of a *right* that all peoples have to such compensation for experienced harmful wrongdoings wherein the object of the right has a duty to compensate the peoples they have wrongfully harmed:

PICJ 2: To the extent that peoples are wrongfully harmed, they have a right to be compensated in proportion to the harms suffered, all things considered.

Yet these principles of international compensatory justice are themselves vague, as they do not indicate precisely who ought to compensate whom. For it is open for someone to argue that even third parties have a duty of compensation toward those who have been wronged, whether or not the third parties have served as contributory causes of the harmful wrongdoing in question. Perhaps the precedent of anti–bad Samaritan legislation in certain jurisdictions of the United States and elsewhere, for example, might serve as grounds for such a claim. Thus clarification is in order if sense is to be made of the idea of international compensatory justice as a principle of international justice.

Consider this revised version of the duty of compensatory justice for the Law of Peoples:

PICJ 1': To the extent that peoples wrongfully harm other peoples, they have the primary duty to compensate those they wrongfully harm in proportion to the harm caused them, all relevant things considered.

According to our revised principle of international justice, peoples who wrongfully harm other peoples have a duty of compensation to them pursuant to our newly revised principle of international compensatory justice, and the corollary rights version of the principle of international compensatory justice seems likewise to hold:

PICJ 2': Peoples have a right to be compensated in proportion to the harms wrongfully suffered, all relevant things considered, by their primary offender(s).

One point of clarification here is that no third-party peoples have a duty to compensate what another people have a primary duty to compensate. Additionally, what Rawls himself refers to as "outlaw" states or societies are not to escape their compensatory duties toward those they have wrongfully harmed. And it is inconceivable that free and equal parties in the globalized original position would ignore compensatory justice considerations. For if they were to do so, then the Law of Peoples would lack a basic component to any legitimate and workable legal order. And recall that it is Rawls himself who seeks to articulate and defend principles of global justice that can be implemented with reasonable workability in a *realistic* utopia. Even in a realistic utopia rights are violated now and then, and require rectification if it is to remain a reasonably just social scenario. Nothing about Rawls's globalized original position excludes the possibility of the principle of international compensatory justice.

Moreover, this principle of international compensatory justice fits well into Rawls's list of eight principles. It supports principle 1 in that it provides a basic rule in cases wherein a peoples' rights to independence and freedom are disrespected by other peoples. Peoples wrongfully harming other peoples are to compensate those they harm to the extent of their harming them, all things considered. Furthermore, PICJs 1'–2' imply that Rawls's fourth and fifth rules can be broken by decent peoples in certain cases where the eighth rule is violated in a flagrant manner by an outlaw state. Indeed, third-party peoples might consider it their duty to confront the guilty peoples who refuse to adequately compensate the wronged party. In cases wherein an outlaw state refuses to compensate peoples it has wrongfully and severely harmed, Rawls's fifth principle must be supplemented by a corollary one stating that in defense of others war and certain other forms of political violence may be justified. I have in mind here cases where generations of race-based slavery (a case Rawls himself discusses) go uncompensated, or where indigenous peoples are victimized by genocide for the sake of societal expansion—again, without compensation. In such instances, it is clear that Rawls's fifth principle can be broken in light of his claim (a claim that he never recanted in print) that at times militancy is justified.[101] Indeed, it would appear that the principles of international compensatory justice uphold Rawls's sixth principle insofar as it is plausible to think that the first principle relies on such general rights being protected by compensatory rights. The principles of international compensatory justice further imply that, in the waging of war or other means of political violence, certain restrictions are to be obeyed in terms of going to war or engaging in political violence for the sake of enforcing laws of compensation and protecting compensatory rights. Finally, as mentioned earlier, PICJs 1'–2' are congruent with Rawls's eighth principle in that the former allows for the assistance of third-party peoples to involve themselves in the administration of compensatory justice in cases where offender peoples refuse to compensate those peoples whom they have wrongfully harmed, or where such compensation is forthcoming but grossly inadequate to return the compensated peoples to a decent level of living subsequent to the harms caused by the wrongful action of the offender peoples.

Thus a plausible set of principles of international compensatory justice is both necessary for the Rawlsian analysis of international justice, and congruent with many of the principles as stated. The revised version of the duty of compensatory justice should be added to Rawls's eight principles in order to better locate peoples in Rawls's realistic utopia. For if consistently respected, such principles would serve to maintain stability between peoples with good intentions regarding a reasonably just global order. So for all Rawls writes about human rights, he states nothing that rules out the compensatory right of reparations to severely and wrongfully harmed groups, a right that can be articulated in terms consonant with Rawls's overall view of human rights.

NICKEL ON HUMAN RIGHTS

In "Poverty and Rights," James W. Nickel defends economic and social rights as human ones and as a feasible manner by which to address world poverty.[102] My argument in this section shall take the following form. First, I shall concur with Nickel that economic and social rights as he and some other philosophers construe them are a feasible way to address poverty.[103] As controversial as it is to argue that economic and social rights are human ones, I shall not challenge this claim here. But in agreeing with Nickel on this point, I shall argue that, for all he claims about human rights, the right to reparations of seriously and wrongfully harmed groups stands as a human right ignored. As a result, the cluster of human rights Nickel defends is incomplete, as it is unable to fully guarantee self-respect, respect for others, and human dignity. If there are human rights, then the right of seriously and wrongfully harmed groups to compensatory reparations is among them. In arguing thusly, I shall analyze philosophically the nature and value of this human right. This is no mean addendum to a theory of human rights. For it continues to point to a glaring omission in human rights theory in general, a point that encourages philosophers to rethink the ethical underpinnings of their respective political philosophies that drive their conceptions of human rights.

Nickel argues that human rights are "concerned with ensuring the conditions, negative and positive, of a minimally good life."[104] Moreover, "they should attempt to address the worst problems and abuses in the economic area. Their focus should be on hunger, malnutrition, preventable disease, ignorance and exclusion from productive opportunities."[105] In short, Nickel endorses and defends the idea of human rights as minimal standards.[106] For he seeks to avoid the errors of offering "too minimal a conception of economic and social rights" (on the one hand), and "making them excessively grandiose" (on the other).[107] In short, Nickel defends a conception of human rights that includes the specific economic and social rights of survival, health, and education.[108]

Nickel employs a multijustificatory analysis of these human rights. He argues that "people have secure but abstract moral claims on others to have a life, to lead one's life, against severely cruel or degrading treatment, and against severely unfair treatment.[109] By "secure" he means that the rights do not depend on that person's ability to generate utility or other good consequences.[110] I shall assume that what he also means by this is that human rights as species of moral rights more generally are valid moral claims or interests, to put it in a way made explicit by Feinberg.[111] And these rights apply, argues Nickel, to individual persons, governmental officials, and corporate entities (collectives).[112] His is an interest-based conception of economic and social human rights, but deontological in the sense that "it starts with abstract rights and associated duties. The basic rights serve to orient the rights and duties."[113]

Furthermore, these basic human rights are "concerned with avoiding misery and ruinous injustice."[114] And among other things, they "address the standard threats in various areas to a decent or minimally good life."[115] Regarding the secure claim to have a life, Nickel argues that it is based on the "central human interest against actions of others that lead to death, destruction of health, or incapacitation."[116] It includes the duty to not use violence except in self-defense, including the claim to freedom and protection from unwarranted violence and harm, including positive duties to assist those threatened with violence.[117]

The secure claim to lead one's life yields moral claims to freedoms from slavery and the other uses of one's life without one's due consent.[118] This implies a secure claim to liberty that entails a claim to assistance in protecting one's liberty, "and for the creation and maintenance of social conditions in which the capacity for agency can be developed and exercised."[119]

One of Nickel's most central claims about the grounding of such human rights is that, "in deciding which liberties to include or exclude, the appropriate questions are whether a particular liberty is essential to our status as persons and agents, and whether the costs of respecting and protecting it are likely to be so high that it is not worth protecting."[120] And he goes on to write that "slavery is degrading because it treats the slave as if he lacks the agency needed to lead his own life" and "degradation may deprive a person of the respect of self and others. A secure claim against severe cruelty forbids these sorts of actions and requires individual and collective efforts to protect people against them."[121] Thus he implies the Feinbergian idea that a human right is one that guards and nourishes self-respect and respect for others.[122]

The secure claim against severely unfair treatment concerns forms of unfairness so severe that "they are matters of ruinous injustice."[123] As Nickel states: "The claim against severely unfair treatment is a claim to freedom from such treatment and a claim to individual and collective efforts to protect people against it."[124] And it is the aim of such human rights to protect aspects of human dignity: "We respect a person's dignity," argues Nickel, "when we protect his life and agency and when we prevent others from imposing treatment that is severely degrading or unfair."[125] In fact, the moral claims on others to have a life, to lead one's life, against severely cruel or degrading treatment, and against severely unfair treatment "should be thought of as requirements of human dignity, of ways to recognize and respond to the value or worth that is found in life as a person."[126]

Specifically, Nickel argues that "If people are to be the kind of rightholders who can effectively exercise, benefit from and protect their rights, the availability of subsistence, basic health care, and basic education must be secure."[127] His reasoning for the inclusion of these as human rights is that "without safe food and water, life and health are endangered, and serious illness and death are probable. The connection between the availability of food and basic health care and having a minimally good life is direct and obvious."[128] Furthermore, he states that

> Developing and exercising agency requires a functioning mind and body as well as options and opportunities. The availability of food and basic health care promotes and protects physical and mental functioning. And the availability of basic education promotes knowledge of social, economic and political options. Lack of access to educational opportunities typically limits (both absolutely and comparatively) people's abilities to participate fully and effectively in the political and economic life of their country.
>
> The secure claim against severely unfair treatment supports economic and social rights. It is severely and ruinously unfair to exclude some parts of the population (rural people, women, minorities) from access to education and economic opportunities. Basic economic and social rights protect against that kind of unfairness.[129]

However, even if one concurs with Nickel on the nature and justification of what he includes as economic and social human rights, his account omits other rights that satisfy the conditions he lays out for human rights. In particular, the right of wrongfully harmed groups to reparations by culpable governments and nongovernmental organizations (including corporations) is not mentioned in Nickel's analysis. Yet it is a crucial remedial right, the nonrecognition of which severely threatens a group's secure claims to *have* or to *lead* a life of its own against severely cruel and unfair treatment. In short, there is nothing in Nickel's analysis of human rights that would bar the inclusion of the right to reparations as a human right. The inclusion of reparations as a human right would seem to require a serious rethinking of what appears beyond the surface to be a utilitarian-based notion of human rights that would trump rights for the sake of a national emergency. Assuming that there are human rights, should reparations be included in the list of such rights?

As detailed in chapter 1, reparations are awarded to groups by states or other parties that have wrongfully and seriously harmed them. Reparations are the right of a group that has experienced serious harmful wrongdoing to receive rectification in the form of compensation from the party or parties responsible for harming it. It is the duty of the harmful wrongdoer to set things right with her victim. It is a species of compensatory justice that applies to individual agents.

My strategy is to argue that Nickel's conditions that make a right a human one are satisfied by the right of reparations. So that if there are any human rights, and Nickel's analysis of a human right is plausible, then groups wrongfully and seriously harmed have rights to reparations that hold against those states and other parties that wrongfully harm them.

As Nickel argues, human rights are "concerned with ensuring the conditions, negative and positive, of a minimally good life." But surely reparations to groups harmed by genocide or enslavement help to ensure the conditions of a minimally good life, especially when such compensation makes them more viable candidates to provide for their own life essentials. Assumed here is the truth of the claim that a minimally good life includes, among other things, the ability of members of groups to earn a fair wage and live on their own land without being disturbed, or even killed. A world without the human right to reparations being acknowledged and respected would be one in which, as I argued earlier in this chapter, bullies can threaten and even harm innocents, thus taking from the latter any sense of security of person they might otherwise possess in order to enable them to flourish.

Nickel claims that human rights "should attempt to address the worst problems and abuses in the economic area. Their focus should be on hunger, malnutrition, preventable disease, ignorance and exclusion from productive opportunities." I concur with him on this point as well. Yet reparations seek to address the worst human problems such as hunger and ignorance. But as history demonstrates, several states and other groups have grown well-off at the expense of others, and many of those injustices remain unrectified. Indeed, in many cases, the well-off were made so such that one effect of their becoming or remaining well-off was the impoverishment of others. Reparations seek to address this problem directly, so that the betterment of one state or group can never occur at the expense of another, thereby upholding the U.S. legal principle that no one ought to be allowed to benefit from their own wrongdoing. Fairness, not bullying, must rule human affairs. And reparations seek to provide compensation for groups that would in turn address problems of poverty and ignorance that were caused by the oppression that morally requires the reparative justice in the first place. In fact, without rights to reparations, there is no guarantee whatsoever that injustices will not recur, ones that will further exacerbate poverty and ignorance around the world. In this way, then, construing reparations as a human right best protects peoples' valid claim or interest in survival, health, and education, which is what Nickel believes a minimal conception of human rights ought to do. Yet how can human rights do this unless remedial rights to reparations are included among the list of human rights? After all, what is under discussion, I take it, is what Rawls refers to as a "realistic utopia."[130] So we must assume that there will always be either potential or actual threats to the very survival, health, and education of all groups, especially the ones least able to defend themselves against bully-states or other bully-parties.

Furthermore, Nickel argues that basic human rights are "concerned with avoiding misery and ruinous injustice." But so are rights to reparative justice. In the cases of American Indians and blacks, for instance, it is evident that ruinous lives have resulted from the genocide, massive land theft, and enslavement of countless of those peoples. Upholding the rights of these groups to reparations from the U.S. government and certain businesses that were responsible for these and other racist harms like the legislation and administration of Jim Crow would directly address the misery and ruinous injustice that millions of such persons experience today. This is true insofar as such reparations policies are implemented in creative and productive ways. Both of these groups experience to varying degrees constant struggles to survive, and much of this pertains to the effects of the serious harmful wrongdoings wrought against them for generations by quite powerful governmental and business interests some of which exist to this day.[131] So the heirs of oppression are identifiable for a legitimate and viable international system of justice to handle by way of legislation or other legal means.

Regarding the secure claim to have a life, Nickel argues that it is based on the "central human interest against actions of others that lead to death, destruction of health, or incapacitation." Yet the right to reparations helps to protect this interest. If wrongdoers are not forced to compensate those they harm, then on what basis are citizens—individuals or groups—able to rest assured that their lives are safe from threats to their lives and health? We do have duties to assist those in need. But why should this be limited to feeding the hungry and educating the ignorant? Thus the secure claim to have a life supports the human right to reparations by compensating victims of oppression so that they possess the means to provide for their own concerns related to health, deaths in the family, and the like.

The secure claim to lead one's life yields moral claims to freedoms from slavery and the other uses of one's life without one's due consent, as Nickel argues. This implies a secure claim to liberty that entails a claim to assistance in protecting one's liberty, "and for the creation and maintenance of social conditions in which the capacity for agency can be developed and exercised." But why should this not include the protection of such rights by way of, say, an international legal system's or agency's upholding the rights of wrongfully harmed groups to reparations from those parties that harmed them? Is this not what such groups deserve? And are they not capable in many cases of addressing the concern of defeating poverty and ignorance? As Nickel avers, we have positive duties to assist those threatened with violence. However, it might be argued that the rights to reparations of such groups ought to be upheld prior to any other group's involvement in assisting those in need. For in many cases, they are in need because others have done serious harm to them wrongly. Compensatory reparations provide critical resources for oppressed peoples to provide in turn for their own fundamental needs, as I shall explain further in chapter 9, below. So the secure claim to lead one's life supports the human right to reparations.

As quoted above, Nickel believes that a secure claim against severe cruelty forbids various sorts of violent actions and requires individual and collective efforts to protect people against them. Thus he implies the Feinbergian idea that a human right is one that guards and nourishes self-respect and respect for others. And he states that a human right is "essential to our status as persons and agents." But is this not precisely what the right to reparations does and amounts to? Does it not stand as a caution against those who would otherwise get away with severe cruelty toward others? Recall that a human right is a moral one, and if Feinberg is correct about the nature and value of moral rights, then a human right is a valid moral claim or interest that is supported by the balance of human reason and the principles of an enlightened conscience. The value of such rights is that they promote self-respect, respect for others, and human dignity (Feinberg). If this is true, and if as Nickel argues human rights are to have the same values of guarding and nourishing self-respect, respect for others, and human dignity, and if the moral right to reparations shares the same values, then why not include the right to reparations on the list of human rights? It would appear that the secure claim against severe cruelty does not rule out the human right to reparations. The right to reparations is, to use Nickel's own words, "essential to our status as persons and agents" insofar as it guards and nourishes self-respect, respect for others, and human dignity.

Recall also that, according to Nickel, the secure claim against severely unfair treatment concerns forms of unfairness so severe that "they are matters of ruinous injustice." As he states: "The claim against severely unfair treatment is a claim to freedom from such treatment and a claim to individual and collective efforts to protect people against it." And it is the aim of such human rights to protect aspects of human dignity: "We respect a person's dignity," argues Nickel, "when we protect his life and agency and when we prevent others from imposing treatment that is severely degrading or unfair." In fact, the moral claims on others to have a life, to lead one's life, against severely cruel or degrading treatment, and against severely unfair treatment "should be thought of as requirements of human dignity, of ways to recognize and respond to the value or worth that is found in life as a person." But reparations are precisely about addressing conditions of unrectified and ruinous injustice. And such a right recognized and protected as a human one helps to guard against or rectify precisely the problems Nickel has in mind here. In fact, given Nickel's words about respecting human dignity, one would think that it would include as a necessary condition respecting the right of reparations!

My point is not that there is no moral duty of most first-world peoples to assist in feeding the hungry and educating the ignorant, particularly in ways that do not sacrifice autonomy and sovereignty of the needy consonant with Bernard Boxill's concerns with cosmopolitanism discussed in chapter 2, above. But making the right of reparations a human right that is effectively upheld by suitable international legal venues is a keen way to serve compensatory justice and socioeconomic justice besides.

Furthermore, if reconciliation is what is desired among peoples, some of whom have been treated rather unjustly by others, then, as Howard McGary argues, it might plausibly be seen to require reparations.[132] For forgiveness is required for genuine reconciliation between the oppressed and their oppressors. But genuine forgiveness requires an apology, which in turn requires a sincere attempt to repair damages done to others by parties guilty of harmful wrongdoing.[133] So if it is global equality of opportunity and reconciliation that are desired, then reparations must play a pivotal role in achieving such ends. Without the human right to reparations to guard against or rectify violations of self-respect, respect for others, and human dignity, there appears to be no manner by which to reasonably ensure justice and fairness for the oppressed and their heirs.

The right to reparations (like Nickel's economic and social rights) exists "as justified international norms," "to be realized as far as and as soon as possible, whose lack of realization is an appropriate matter of regret."[134] As in the case of economic and social rights of which Nickel writes, the international communities ought to "require countries to be doing something, to be taking measurable steps" in compensating the victims of injustices that have for so long gone unaddressed.[135] But I would add that it is not simply states and their governments that ought to be held to this standard of rectification of injustice. It is also groups and agencies within states, including certain business sectors, that are responsible for them.[136]

In the present chapter, I have argued that, for all that Rawls states about the nature of human rights and principles of justice for a Society of Peoples, room can surely be made in Rawls's theory of global justice for reparations as a human compensatory right. In fact, the compensatory right to reparations satisfied Rawls's requirement that human rights are "necessary conditions of any system of social cooperation."[137] This being the case, reparations, when respected, fulfill "a necessary condition of the decency of a society's political institutions and of its legal order."[138] Whether or not reparations constitute a first-tier human right or a second-tier human right for the protection of some first-tier human rights is not my concern so long as the right to reparations is accorded its proper status among human rights, for the reasons given earlier.[139] Moreover, for all Nickel argues about the nature and grounding of the economic and social human rights, similar reasoning grounds the human right of wrongfully harmed groups to reparations. For all he argues, and given the nature and value of reparations, nothing rules out the right of reparations from being included as a human right. It satisfies the conditions that make something a human right, and what makes reparations valuable is also what makes a human right valuable. Yet nowhere in the philosophy literature on human rights is there an inclusion of the right of oppressed groups to reparations.

The implications of my argument for political philosophy are significant. Among them is the fact that many human rights theorists tend to assume a kind of rights-delimiting utilitarianism which is exposed when the genuine nature of a human right is revealed (at the very least) as a valid moral claim or interest. This conflict between rights and utility has a history in the philosophy of rights. But it has been mostly ignored in analyses of human rights, much to the detriment of what would lead otherwise brilliant minds to ideas that would change the world in ways that would respect what truly promotes self-respect, respect for others, and human dignity. Genuine justice ought not to be construed narrowly in order to rule out compensatory justice concerns and to effectively exempt states and businesses guilty of horrendous injustices toward others from paying what they truly owe to those they have wrongfully harmed. Instead, justice in its fullness will make those who deserve to pay indeed pay what they owe to those they have wrongfully harmed, and to the extent that they have harmed them. For once again, no one ought to be permitted to benefit from their own harmful wrongdoing.

Thus both Rawlsian and Nickelian models of human rights fail to rule out compensatory reparations as a human right. And the arguments I have provided both in this chapter and in the preceding two chapters serve as further considerations of why it is reasonable to understand group reparations as a human right or at least a remedial moral right, one that cannot legitimately be trumped merely by considerations of social utility, as Rawls's above quoted words in the epigraph for part 2 indicate.

5

Collective Responsibility
and Reparations

> We live in a world where we can no longer view ourselves as being detached from the actions of groups of which we are a part. We should be aware that efforts to achieve a morally good society for a time may bring about disharmony and social unrest. A morally decent society, in my judgment, is willing to pay these costs.
>
> —Howard McGary[1]

> Anyone who is prepared to accept the general idea of national responsibility ought also to accept the idea of responsibility for the national past.
>
> —David Miller[2]

David Miller argues for national responsibility for historic injustices. But he does so not by trying to demonstrate collective identity of the responsible nation over time, but rather because the oppressor heirs in his view do not deserve what they inherit and because they have a duty to make good the wrongful harms brought about by their predecessors.[3] But Bernard Boxill argues that even if reparations are owed to Indians and blacks, it is far from obvious that, for instance, the *current* U.S. government and citizenry rightly owe reparations to the *offspring* of the oppressed in question.[4] What needs to be shown, Boxill's concern implies, is that there is a collective retrospective moral liability responsibility (collective moral responsibility) of the current U.S. government, certain U.S.-based businesses, certain other institutions, and its citizens for the historical racist evils in question. Moreover, given that evil was perpetrated against American Indians, African slaves in the United States, and "emancipated" blacks by the U.S. government (among other parties both collective and individual), ought forgiveness and/or reconciliation to play any role whatsoever in matters of reparations to Indians and blacks? In this chapter, matters of collective responsibility are addressed. Forgiveness, reconciliation, and related concepts are taken up in chapter 8 after chapters 6 and 7 enumerate the cases for Indian and black reparations, respectively. What is collective moral responsibility? What kinds of collectives, if any, can rightly be held morally accountable for their collective harmful wrongdoing?

The previous line of reasoning is driven by the notion of collective moral responsibility.[5] For it is the concept of collective moral responsibility that makes possible the act of collective apology that would make possible collective forgiveness that would in turn make possible genuine reconciliation between oppressed groups and the larger oppressor societies to which they belong, that is, reconciliation that does not require, say, Indians and blacks to express some feeling of forgiveness out of either insufficient self-esteem or self-respect. And as Howard McGary points out, "The problem of collective liability . . . is to state and defend the conditions under which moral agents can be held morally liable for 'practices' that they themselves did not directly engage in."[6] While this is true, I would argue, collective moral responsibility can accrue to a group of agents each of whom is to some extent co-responsible and guilty of an untoward act, event, or state of affairs. This is a summativist model of collective moral responsibility. A nonsummativist model states that collective moral responsibility can accrue to a group not each of the members of which shares responsibility (causally) for the group's action, omission, or attempted action, as the case may be. Collective moral liability responsibility for the past is either nondistributive (in McGary's sense with regard to practices), or distributive, so long as certain conditions obtain relative to the group, its members, and an act, omission, attempted action, event, or state of affairs. In legal terms, what is being asked is whether or not it is possible to establish the concept of "unitary state liability" with regard to the United States and the oppression of Indians and blacks, respectively.[7] To what extent, if any, are the United States and certain U.S.-based business agencies liable for such massive harmful wrongdoings?

But just what is collective moral responsibility? In the sense used herein, it is an organized (decision-making) group's moral liability for what it has done, failed to do, or attempted to do in the past. It is a liability that admits of degrees of individual contributory liability within the group. But what are the conditions of collective moral liability?

A collective's decision-making capacity makes it a candidate for moral liability ascriptions. When I write that a collective makes decisions, I do not mean that everyone in it participates directly in that process, as a group can delegate certain decisions to certain subgroups and members. In U.S. society, certain kinds of decisions are delegated to the executive, judicial, and legislative branches of government, either federal, state, or local. And there are various other governmental agencies that decide and act "in the name of the people," whether or not "the people" as a whole are directly cognizant of such decisions made on their behalf. It is this sense in which the U.S. government decides and acts "for the people" of the United States, making the United States a collective moral agent. But is the United States a collectively responsible agent for the oppression of millions of Indians and blacks throughout its history?

COLLECTIVE MORAL RESPONSIBILITY[8]

In *Terrorism and Collective Responsibility*, Burleigh T. Wilkins argues that:

> I cannot provide a list of necessary and sufficient conditions for holding a collective responsible for the faulty actions of some of its members, but I can perhaps do some of the reflection, which would precede the creation of such a list.[9]

Wilkins goes on to argue that how a collective "responds" to events like the one for which it is being held accountable and whether or not it "took adequate precautions" to guard against such problems count toward whether or not the collective ought to be held liable for a certain wrongdoing. Also, he states that to the extent that a collective wrongdoing was the result of a group culture or "way of life" within the collective, then this may serve as a partially excusing condition of collective liability responsibility.[10]

But what does it mean to say that a system, group, or collective "responds" or "takes adequate precautions?" This would appear to imply some form of collective action on the part of the conglomerate that is responsible for something. If this is true, then collective moral agency is a necessary condition of collective moral responsibility. But what then does collective moral agency entail? It entails no less than what individual moral agency entails: collective intentionality, acting knowingly, acting freely, being "at fault," blameworthiness, and the required causal connection must exist between the faulty aspect of its conduct and the outcome. To explain and defend in full detail this theory of collective moral responsibility would indeed require more space than a chapter. However, I will develop the foundations of a theory of collective moral responsibility based on the concepts of collective intentionality, voluntariness, and knowledge that will serve as the starting point of a more full-blown analysis of collective moral responsibility. As a result, we will, I trust, better understand what qualifies as a morally liable collective.

Underlying the concept of collective responsibility is the idea of a collective. What *are* collectives? Stipulatively and generally speaking, collectives are either groups or conglomerates (or some admixture of both). While conglomerates (formal governments, corporations, organized revolutionary movements, etc.) can in principle and due to their structures act (as secondary agents) intentionally, voluntarily, and knowingly, groups (mobs or random collectives, etc.) cannot because they lack the essential structure that would enable them to act intentionally, voluntarily, and knowingly.

To be sure, there exist varying degrees of a collective's being a group or a conglomerate. And what might begin as a mob, for example, might develop or evolve into something akin to a conglomerate of some sort, especially if the mob engages in some kind of repetitive activity. I have in mind here the several lynchings of blacks in the United States by white mobs that were motivated by class consciousness or racism, or both. In such instances, the ongoing actions of such groups are more than mere mobs that do harm, say, on a one-time basis. Their repeated activities of harming blacks develop into something like a conglomerate (say, the nightriders of the KKK in some cases), even though there may be no formal collective decision-making structures. In these cases, the white lynchings of blacks amounted to what were commonly referred to by many whites as "nigger drives," the aim of which was often to force blacks from areas and steal their land. In several cases, it succeeded.

One reason for developing a plausible analysis of collective moral responsibility is that collectives of one kind or another are often the perpetrators or victims of oppression. And it is important to understand the extent to which a particular collective might be legitimately held liable for its wrongful harms to other individuals or groups of them. What is needed is an analysis of collective moral responsibility that might inform us of the extent to which, if any, members of a collective are indeed *collectively* responsible such that they qualify as morally legitimate targets of retributive sanctions.[11]

Thus it is crucial to explore what we ought to mean when we speak of a collective's being morally responsible or not for something. What are the conditions that would define collective moral (retrospective liability) responsibility for something that, let us say, causes such injustice that a collective responsible for the injustice is a justifiable target (i.e., deserving) of legal recourse?[12]

It does not make adequate sense to hold certain collectives morally accountable for untoward events. Random collectives or mobs, for example, would not qualify as morally responsible agents though some of their agents may. For they lack, in their randomness, collective moral agency. They neither act intentionally, voluntarily, nor knowingly. They are, rather, random in the sense that the members of such collectives act as individuals, having no significant explicit or implicit collective agreement or motivation(s). At best, their individual doings, inactions, aims, and motivations coincide *accidentally*. This claim is consistent with the statement that a random collective or mob might be *causally* responsible for an untoward event. For example, citizens conducting business in the Federal Building in Oklahoma City share *accidentally* the aim of conducting various transactions for or with the U.S. government. But their respective aims are not shared *because* of the fact that the others at the Federal Building have their aims. Collectives fitting this description, lacking a common goal, are aggregates. On the other hand, I shall refer to collectives, the constituent members of which share significant and explicitly common goals, officially or not, as "groups" or "conglomerates." And it is these goals that form the basis of the group's solidarity. On my analysis of collective moral liability responsibility, only conglomerates of this sort qualify as potentially morally responsible agents in the requisite sense.

It might be argued that some *aggregates*, not acting intentionally, might be morally responsible for an outcome.[13] For example, Virginia Held argues that "the requirements for moral responsibility appear to be such that they can be met by random collections only in special circumstances."[14] An aggregate can satisfy the conditions of moral responsibility, according to Held, "for not forming itself into an organized group capable of deciding which action to take."[15] Held provides one with an example of seven strangers on a subway car, where one of them is attacked by one of the others (a small person) without having a weapon. Although it is unlikely that any one of the aggregate could have successfully fended off the attacker, two or more of them could have (in all likelihood), and without seriously endangering themselves. If the group fails to act on the victim's behalf during this incident, it, as an aggregate, is morally responsible (to some extent) for its "failure to act as a group."[16]

But this objection confuses moral *causal* responsibility with moral *liability* responsibility. It might be true that the subway car aggregate failed to act. But this is responsibility only in the causal use of "responsibility." Thus if the aggregate is morally responsible for failing to act in warding off the attacker, then it is morally responsible (in the causal use of "responsibility") for failing to do so. However, this is not the same thing as the mob's being morally *liable* for doing (or not doing, as the case may be) the same. For moral liability responsibility requires intentional, voluntary, and epistemic action. It is not clear that any mob, as an aggregate, qualifies as a collective, which can act intentionally. It has no decision-making structure, much less a rule-defined one. And this seems to be one of the necessary conditions of a collective's acting intentionally. After all, as Held herself argues, for a collective to act, there must be some decision procedure within it. Otherwise, what it does is more like an accident than like an action.[17]

But even if one assumes, as Held does, that collectives *can* act and be held morally responsible for outcomes, her example does not prove its collective moral responsibility, and for the following reason. From the supposition that more than one member of the aggregate is required to subdue the attacker, it does not follow that the *aggregate* is morally responsible for stopping the attack, but only that each of the onlookers who did nothing is guilty of inaction.

Held argues that the aggregate is guilty for not acting as a group, "for not forming itself into an organized group capable of deciding which action to take."[18] But only certain *conglomerates*, not random collectives, have the power to make decisions. Thus Held is faulting the aggregate in the subway car for not *becoming a conglomerate*. Reason would tell us, however, that since the aggregate is not a conglomerate, which has a rule-governed, decision-making procedure (among other things) or a subgroup which does, it ought not to be held morally responsible for such inaction.

Furthermore, Held does not tell us for *what* the aggregate is responsible. Surely it is not responsible for the victim being attacked. Neither did the onlookers aid or abet in the attack. Other than its not becoming a conglomerate or *not attempting* to overcome the attackers, it is unclear precisely for *what* the aggregate is morally responsible in her example.

Finally, the moral responsibility of any collective seems to be contingent on at least the following (intentionality) conditions which do not obtain in Held's example. First, there must be an adequate degree of solidarity within a collective for it to be a morally responsible agent. Second, members of the collective must have an opportunity to control or power to effect significant change regarding the situation for which they are held morally responsible. It is unclear whether or not Held's aggregate in the subway car satisfies the condition of solidarity. Thus it is dubious that aggregates or random collectives qualify as being morally responsible. Should they somehow thwart an attack, it would constitute a morally supererogatory act.

Wilkins seeks to find a way in which collective moral responsibility attributions might be made morally palatable in light of some seemingly "insuperable" difficulties concerning the harming of innocent members of a group that is itself morally accountable for an untoward event or state of affairs.[19] Amending Joel Feinberg's analysis of collective legal liability responsibility, Wilkins argues plausibly that "although group liability is necessarily distributive, it is still up to us to decide who is still a member of a group and to determine how penalties are to be applied to a group."[20] With equal plausibility, Wilkins argues:

> Perhaps we could in some cases set a cut-off point and say that anyone who did not leave before that date would still be considered a member of a group. Also, we might be able to agree that anyone who joined after a certain date would not be counted as a member of the group, the ground for this exemption being that the wrongdoing in question had occurred prior to his joining.[21]

This argument is designed to minimize the likelihood those innocent members of a group who are responsible for a wrongdoing would suffer harm as the result of what guilty members of the group did. Wilkins's next "strategy" in determining collective responsibility is the following:

> My second strategy suggests that we try as far as possible to align penalties against a group with faulty performances by individuals in such a way as to have the least impact upon those who contributed the least, or did not contribute, to the wrongdoing in question. To the extent that we could predict the impact of the various penalties, we might be able to select just those which would best serve the purposes stated above.[22]

It is noteworthy that Wilkins's claim seems to be a special instance of the principle of proportional punishment and compensation, whereby wrongdoers are to be punished or forced to compensate others to the extent that they are liable, all things considered, for a wrongdoing. His point seems to extend the principle of proportional punishment and compensation to collectives, making punishments/penalties for crimes/torts apply to various members of a collective according to their respective roles in causing and being liable for a given wrongdoing that is attributed to the collective to which they belong.

Wilkins's two points can be restated in the following way. First, the lines of collective membership relative to a collective wrongdoing must be drawn carefully so as to avoid morally arbitrary ways in which members of the collective might be held accountable for that for which the collective is morally liable. Secondly, once the boundary lines of membership in a collective are drawn accurately relative to a collective wrongdoing, members of the collective should be assigned liability relative to their respective participatory accountability for the collective wrongdoing.

Wilkins has provided plausible means by which collective moral liability ascriptions can and should be made. However, collective moral liability ascriptions make little or no sense unless there exists some meaningful or significant degree of *collective* intentional action, collective voluntariness, and a collective's acting knowingly concerning a putative collective wrongdoing. Otherwise, how would we know the nature of the morally salient boundaries of membership in a particular collective for purposes of making collective liability attributions? Furthermore, how would we know with any reasonable degree of confidence how to assign liability to members in a collective so as to remain devoted to the principle of proportional punishment and compensation?

Thus I proffer an analysis of some conditions of Wilkins's account of collective moral liability. For lacking an analysis of what constitutes *collective* moral liability, Wilkins's claims about collective (distributive) liability might end up being little or no different from merely individual liability for wrongdoing.

What *are* the conditions of collective moral responsibility? Furthermore, does the United States in its oppression of American Indians and blacks satisfy these conditions? Consider the *Principle of Collective Moral Liability*: It is justified for one to ascribe to a conglomerate *moral liability* with respect to an outcome or a state of affairs *to the extent that*:

1. The conglomerate is an intentional agent concerning that outcome, i.e., that its action or inaction (say, in cases of negligence, where "negligence" is construed as the creation of an unreasonable risk of harm to others) is caused by its wants and beliefs (This condition entails the solidarity and power to effect significant change factors mentioned earlier in challenging Held's claim that random collectives sometimes qualify as being morally responsible.);
2. The conglomerate is a voluntary agent concerning that outcome;
3. The conglomerate is an epistemic agent concerning that outcome;
4. The responsible conglomerate did the harmful thing in question, or at least that its action or omission made a substantial causal contribution to it (i.e., that it is responsible for the harmful outcome in the causal sense);
5. The causally contributory conduct must have been in some way faulty (i.e., that it is responsible for the harmful outcome in the blame sense);[23] and

6. If the harmful outcome was truly the fault of the conglomerate, the required causal connection must exist between the faulty aspect of its conduct and the outcome.[24]

It is noteworthy that while McGary's analysis of collective liability concerns the practices of collectives, mine concerns actions, inactions, or attempted actions, as the case may be. As with individuals, we want to know whether or not conglomerates may be morally liable for their inactions (omissions) as well as for their actions as they are causes (of one kind or another) of outcomes or states of affairs.[25] I will try to solve a limited number of questions regarding 1–3 as I believe that, unlike 4–6, 1–3 are less understood by way of commonsense reflection. Among the most important matters here are whether or not a conglomerate *can* act or omit to act intentionally, voluntarily, and/or knowingly, and whether or not a conglomerate *does* act in such ways. Let us take on each of these important matters in turn.

Now it might be objected that the principle of collective moral liability wrongly construes collective moral responsibility in terms of what constitutes individual moral responsibility. For example, Held argues that "it is not clear . . . that the best way to decide about corporate responsibility is by adopting the criteria for individual personal responsibility to corporations. We might well need to analyze corporate responsibility on its own terms."[26] Perhaps, moreover, Held is correct in claiming that

> we cannot get by deduction from such judgments as "the corporation did *X*" or "corporation *C* is responsible for *X*," to judgments about individual responsibility. From judgments about collective entities, nothing follows logically about what any members of such a collective did or is responsible for. We have to know about the internal structure of the collectivity, and about the roles and activities of its individual members, to assign responsibility to individuals for what corporations do and are responsible for.[27]

Held's arguments for such a view about collective responsibility are the following. First, she argues that

> If it makes sense to say that the corporation "should have known" and hence can be "held responsible," perhaps we should conclude directly what this means for corporations, without the detour of analyzing what it means to say of individual persons that they "should have known," and then applying this to a corporation.[28]

She continues to argue that

> for the corporation to be responsible, we may have to suppose the outcome was such that the corporation "could have done other than it did" in some sense. But establishing this may be quite different for corporations than it is for individual persons.[29]

Moreover, Held claims that

> what to think about corporate intention is complex and difficult. Corporate inten-
> tion may well be very different from personal intention, and yet it may make per-
> fectly good sense to speak of a corporation intentionally doing something, or
> having an intention to do something.[30]

It is noteworthy, however, that in light of Held's three statements her own claim that "'responsibility' may be something which is quite different for corporations than it is for individual persons" is dubious.[31] For not only does Held not explicate precisely *how* collective and individual responsibility differ, analytically speaking, Held's own claims seem to *favor* an analysis that sees individual and collective liability by way of the *same* conditions. For Held's "should have known," "could have done other than it did," and "intentionally doing something" criteria are congruent with the fundamental analysis of collective knowledge, voluntariness, and intentionality, respectively. Thus it seems misleading, if not false, to argue that collective and individual responsibility ought to be analyzed differently. For how else ought collective responsibility to be analyzed if not in terms of intentional, voluntary, and epistemic action? And what is the reason for thinking that collective responsibility ought to be analyzed in terms significantly different than these?

Thus to the extent that a collective satisfies the conditions set forth in the principle of collective moral liability, then it is a plausible candidate for moral liability ascriptions. However, while it is possible for certain collectives (namely, highly organized conglomerates such as nations and corporations) to satisfy such conditions, I believe there are empirical factors which tend to undermine any claim to the effect that such collectives *do in fact* typically satisfy such conditions (at least in a strong sense). Consider three related problems with such a claim: the problem of collective intentional action, the problem of collective voluntariness, and the problem of collective knowledge. Each of these difficulties makes it problematic to justifiably say that a certain necessary condition for moral liability is satisfied by even the most highly organized collectives. Let us consider each of these problems in turn.

A collective (intentional) action is an action the subject of which is a collective intentional agent. A *collective behavior* is a doing or behavior which is the result of a collective, though not the result of its intentions. A *collective action* is caused by the beliefs and desires (wants) of the *collective* itself,[32] whether or not such beliefs and desires can be accounted for or explained in individualist terms. Although species of collective action include "shared cooperative activity" involving as few as two parties,[33] I am concerned with whether or not it is justified to ascribe intentional action to conglomerates of a numerically larger sort such as (large) countries and (large) corporations. If such conglomerates are not intentional agents, then they are not proper subjects of moral responsibility attributions.

Necessary, but perhaps insufficient, conditions of collective intentional action or omission include: official representatives of the collective engaging in a valid rule-governed, goal-oriented (putatively collective), decision-making procedure designed to "act" (or not act, as the case may be) for the conglomerate. This procedure should permit a conglomerate to admit and expel members at will according to its valid rule system. This affords the conglomerate the freedom to determine the boundaries of its own membership. Moreover, such a goal-oriented, decision-making procedure must be recognized by the official rule system of that conglomerate, be it a corporate or national charter, a legal system, and so forth. Thus if a conglomerate has a rule-defined, goal-oriented, decision-making procedure, then it can be said to have the capacity to do things or refrain from doing them.

But doing things and acting intentionally are quite different. For a conglomerate's doings to be plausibly construed as actions it is essential that that conglomerate act intentionally. So if the rule system of the conglomerate eventuates in a decision by official representatives of that conglomerate, and if that decision is an action which is caused by the wants and beliefs of that conglomerate (assuming the plausibility of the fundamentals of Alvin I. Goldman's theory of human action), then that conglomerate may justifiably be said to have acted (as a secondary agent) intentionally. Moreover, if the weight of moral reason supports that conglomerate's being held liable to sanctions as a result of the action or omission, then it is justified to ascribe moral liability to that conglomerate for that action or omission.

David Copp argues that a theory of collectives must be compatible with the claim that collectives *can and do* perform actions.[34] He goes on to argue that "collectives are moral agents" (a moral agent is an entity to which intentional agency can plausibly be ascribed, and where the content of one's action is moral).[35] I agree with Copp that certain collectives, namely conglomerates such as nations and corporations which have rule-governed and highly structured decision-making capacities, *can* be (restructured to qualify as) intentional agents. However, there are difficulties, which face any claim to the effect that such collectives commonly *do* act intentionally such that they might qualify as moral agents.

If one necessary condition of moral liability is that the party is an intentional agent, then it is important to ask whether or not conglomerates are plausible candidates for ascriptions of intentional agency, including omissions to act.

It might be thought that conglomerates do not act intentionally, and for two reasons. First, they do not act *intentionally* as individual humans often do. Instead, individual constituents of the conglomerate act on its behalf. And there are at least three ways in which a collective might be said to have an intention.[36] First, collectives might be said to have *future-directed intentions*, such as when I use the locution, "The United States intends to assassinate Fidel

Castro soon." Secondly, collectives might be said to have *present-directed intentions*, such as when I utter, "Exxon intends to remain economically competitive at all costs now, rather than to put profits behind environmental concerns." Thirdly, a collective is often said to *endeavor or will* something, as when I say, "The United States willed that the communist regime suffer great hardship so that it might feel better about its own persistent and severe difficulties."

Another reason why it might be thought that collectives do not act intentionally is that it is possible to reduce ascriptions of collective "agency" to ascriptions of individual agency in congruence with recognized rule systems[37]—without loss of cognitive meaning. This sort of reasoning would lead one to adopt some version of Moral Responsibility Individualism. For if ascriptions of collective "agency" are problematic, so are attributions of collective moral responsibility since moral liability requires intentional action by or on behalf of the morally liable agent.

It seems clear that aggregates and ethnic groups (*qua* ethnic groups) do not act intentionally because they do not function according to a recognized formal or informal rule system. Raimo Tuomela, however, argues that even crowds and rioters *can* properly be said to act:

> Crowds . . . can be said to act in virtue of their members' actions. . . . Thus in a riot the members of the collective typically perform their destructive actions *as members* of the collective without acting on its behalf. So we are here dealing with groups without much or any structure (and divisions of tasks and activities), . . . with respect to the goals and interests of the group.[38]

The difficulty with Tuomela's position is that rioters and aggregates such as crowds altogether lack common goals and interests, though their respective members can and do possess goals and interests. Rioters and crowds are aggregates, and aggregates are simply a loose collection of individual human persons lacking a decision-making structure. It seems, then, that such collectives are not plausible candidates for intentional action attributions.

But perhaps certain other sorts of collectives (namely, those of the conglomerate type) *can* act intentionally. In fact, nations and corporations act, though not in a primary way. They are secondary agents. A primary agent is one who has the capacity to act on her own, intentionally. A secondary agent, as I noted earlier, is one for whom another acts according to a legal or moral rule system, intentionally. In the case of secondary agency, both the one on behalf of whom the action is performed and the one performing the action "in her name" are intentional agents, but in different respects. The secondary agent, for whom the act is carried out, must have the capacity to have the action carried out according to her beliefs and desires. The one acting "in her name" must be capable of performing "her action" such that her own doings are caused by her wants and beliefs. For example, an attorney acts on behalf of (or "in the name of") her clients, and states, corporations, and even nations have attorneys. This makes at least some conglomerates secondary agents to the extent that there are those who properly represent their putative aims and purposes (according to official rule systems of those conglomerates).

Moreover, there seems to be no conceptual barrier to construing secondary agents as intentional ones. This means that if it is possible to reduce the language of collective action to that of individual action, this poses no logical problem for the justifiedness of collective agency ascriptions.[39]

In light of this consideration, it might be objected that to deny the very possibility of collective moral responsibility fails to take into account the fact that some conglomerates, such as corporations, *do* act intentionally *via* their respective corporate internal decision structures.[40] These structures are official regulations concerning the way in which the corporation should operate.[41]

Now to this line of argument it might be replied that there is no doubt that nations and corporations (and other highly organized collectives) often *behave* (without intention) according to official rules of their respective systems. But it is unclear that behavior resulting from such decision making is the result of the intentionality of the conglomerates themselves, or whether it is the consequence of the intentionality of certain powerful decision-makers in those collectives.[42] What the first objection needs is an independent argument adequately supporting the claim that such *collectives* do in fact exhibit intentional agency.

Against this reply it might be argued, as Copp does, that some collectives such as nations (in signing treaties) act "for a reason," which is sufficient for a collective's acting intentionally.[43] However, this counter does not suffice as an answer to the previous query. For what is questioned concerning collective intentionality also arises at the level of collective "reasons." That is, how does one know whether it is the collective itself which "acts for a reason," or whether it is merely a certain powerful individual representative or member of that collective (or group of them) who "acts for a reason"? Furthermore, the plausibility of this notion of what is sufficient for intentional action is contingent on the plausibility of G. E. M. Anscombe's theory of intentionality.[44] Thus it requires an independent defense of Anscombe's overall theory. However, if we assume as I do, that intentional action is that which is caused by the beliefs and desires of the agent,[45] then the Anscombian view of intentional agency (as acting for a reason) is not clearly warranted. This means that even if collectives such as nations and corporations can and do act "for a reason," it is not obvious that this is sufficient for collective intentional action.

Nor will it do to argue, as does Copp, that some collectives in fact act as secondary agents:[46] If a corporation's attorneys successfully defend that corporation against all suits brought against it for its alleged corporate wrongdoing, then it is not misleading to say that the *corporation* vindicated itself in the midst of such charges.

But even if Feinberg is incorrect in arguing that this line of argument *is* misleading,[47] and even if it does make some sense to say that the corporation vindicated itself from the said charges leveled against it, it does not necessarily follow from this that what the corporation did constitutes an *action*. At best it is a doing or a doing-related event. Actions entail intentionality, doings do not. And Copp's point, even if well-taken, requires an independent argument to show that what a conglomerate does amounts to an *action*, that is, what it does is caused by its *own* wants and beliefs, and not merely the wants and beliefs of certain powerful individuals of that conglomerate. For only then can such a collective hope to satisfy the conditions of being the subject of justified retrospective moral liability ascriptions.[48]

Another attempt to rescue the notion of actual collective intentional agency argues that collective intentional agency *supervenes* on individual intentional agency. The argument states: "actions by collectives supervene on the actions of the operative members of the collective."[49] This view may be construed as a response to my previous point requiring an argument for the claim that collectives have their own wants and desires requisite for intentional agency. Tuomela argues that "I accept that collectives may be said to have wants and beliefs and to act for a reason, the concepts for these mental states seem to acquire their meanings basically (or at least to a great extent) from the individual case."[50] Moreover, he argues, the actions of a collective supervene on the actions and joint actions performed by its members or representatives, and this involves two claims. First, whenever the collective does something, it does it *via* some actions of its members. Secondly, suitable actions by the members or representatives of the collective will (conventionally, legally, etc.) determine the collective's action. Tuomela intends his view to apply to both organized and unorganized collectives (or to what I refer to as "conglomerates" and "aggregates").[51] Thus, Tuomela argues, the properties of collectives—such as intention, belief, desire—are "embodied in" and "determined by" the properties of individual members or representatives of that collective.

However, Tuomela's position is problematic. For he begs a crucial question pertaining to the problem of collective agency: Do collectives act intentionally; do their own beliefs and wants cause their actions? As Tuomela himself admits, he *assumes* that collectives have the intentional properties of belief and desire. But the moral responsibility individualist demands that collective intentionality be proven by independent argumentation, and this requires the establishing of *collective* beliefs and desires which cause a collective's doings, forming a collective action. And this holds true whether or not collectives are construed as primary agents or as secondary agents. As Max Weber writes, "Social action is not identical either with the similar actions of many persons or with actions influenced by other persons."[52] Even as a secondary agent, a collective must have the capacity to believe and desire such that members or representatives may act for it, in its name.

Tuomela's argument for collective action is based on his analysis of "we-intentions."[53] But for his argument to succeed in showing that *collectives* act intentionally, it must be successfully argued that such collectives also have "we-beliefs"[54] and "we-wants" (or "we-desires"), which can and do somehow

causally generate a collective's doings and "convert" them into actions.[55] Thus
it is still unclear whether or not conglomerates as a class of entities commonly
act intentionally. In turn, it is not clear that they are (typically) legitimate candidates for moral liability ascriptions.[56]

But even if a solid case could be made for the claim that some conglomerates are commonly intentional agents, it is doubtful that the typical country or
corporation is a morally responsible agent. The reason for this is that collective
intentionality is at best only a necessary condition of collective moral responsibility. Significant levels of collective voluntariness and knowledge are also
needed.

If, as Harry G. Frankfurt argues of individual moral agents, having a higher-
order volition is sufficient for acting freely and for moral responsibility,[57] then
conglomerates that have the capacity for having such volitions are to be seen
as plausible candidates for moral liability attributions. And this holds true
even if conglomerates are viewed as secondary agents.

One might argue that the sometimes highly sophisticated and complex
goal-oriented decision-making structures of certain conglomerates like democratic countries and corporations are indicative of a kind of higher-order cognition. For in such processes, certain choices are weighed and balanced against
others, where in the end a higher-level decision is reached between competing
lower-level alternative desires. This implies that it is likely that some collectives do act freely and thus are morally responsible agents.

But this line of reasoning runs into the same trouble that arose in regard to
intentional agency. Is the putatively higher-order volition or metamental
ascent present in such conglomerates that of the conglomerates themselves,
or merely that of certain powerful individuals acting within the rules of the
conglomerates' decision-making structure? If the former is true, then it seems
justified to ascribe higher-order volitional action to some collectives. But if the
latter is true, then it is unclear to what extent, if any, collectives are volitional
agents. What is required by the moral responsibility collectivist is an independent argument rendering plausible the claim that conglomerates are volitional
agents in the requisite sense.

Thus there seem to be at least two skeptical concerns with the position that
random collectives (or even collectives in general) are indeed morally responsible agents. The first is that it is unclear that the intentionality present in conglomerate activities is the intentionality of the conglomerate itself (conceived
of in the "strange entity" sense). Second, it is difficult to understand how to
separate conglomerate voluntariness from the voluntariness of certain powerful decision-makers in the conglomerate, even if the conglomerate is solidary.

But even if collective intentionality and voluntariness obtained in a given
circumstance, collective moral responsibility would *not* accrue unless some
significant measure of *collective knowledge* also obtained therein. To the extent
that acting knowingly is a condition the satisfaction of which is crucial for
moral liability, it is unjustified, normally, to attribute moral liability to such

collectives. I say "normally" because there are cases where a moral agent's ignorance does *not* exculpate.[58] However, this point is not inconsistent with the fact that collectives are *not* clearly epistemic agents at all, at least in a sense which qualifies them as agents which act knowingly. To the extent that collectives are not clearly epistemic agents, they are not morally liable ones.

Concerning collective belief and truth (belief and truth are normally considered to be conditions of human knowledge), Margaret Gilbert writes that "there is no obvious reason to think that group beliefs in general have a high probability of truth, or that they are likely to be superior in this respect to the beliefs of individuals."[59] More specifically, there is the "problem of social epistemic reliability." This is a problem for collective knowledge attributions. There are at least three empirical problems with the claim that collectives such as conglomerates are plausible candidates for knowledge or belief acquisition based on collective decision-making, rendering problematic any collectivist account of social knowledge, which is based on the reliability of collective decision-making. Collectives can adversely affect the decisions of individual cognizers in at least three ways, which question the reliability of collective decision-making: by the group polarization effect, by pressure toward group consensus, or by deindividuation.[60] The problem of social epistemic reliability poses a difficulty not only for a conglomerate's satisfying the collective knowledge condition (3), it also poses a challenge to the collective intentionality condition (1) in that intentional action is caused (in part) by the agent's *beliefs.*

Thus there exist three widespread difficulties with any claim that group knowledge or justified belief arrived at on the basis of group decision-making is likely. For this reason, I argue that numerically large conglomerates such as countries and large corporations typically do not act as epistemic agents. This does not, however, deny the *possible* epistemic and responsibility status of some conglomerates or of certain subconglomerates or subagencies within these larger ones.

The upshot of the problem of social epistemic reliability is that there is good reason to doubt the plausibility of group beliefs being reliably produced (as collective beliefs) by a collective decision-making process. If collective knowledge depends in part on collective belief (and assuming, as many contemporary analytical epistemologists argue,[61] that belief or acceptance is a necessary condition of knowledge), and if justified collective responsibility ascriptions are contingent on there being collective knowledge, then collective responsibility attributions are dubious to the extent that collective knowledge and belief are doubtful. So even if Gilbert is correct in arguing that some attributions of *beliefs* to certain collectives as "plural subjects"[62] is justified or reasonable, it would not follow that such collectives are epistemic subjects in the requisite sense of their acting *knowingly.*

It is unclear, then, that it is justified to ascribe intentional action, voluntariness, and knowledge (and belief) to conglomerates such as countries and corporations. Again, I do not deny the *possible* epistemic status of conglomerates.

So it is not that conglomerates such as nations and corporations *cannot ever* satisfy the conditions of justified collective moral liability ascriptions. Rather, it is that, given a certain prevalence of a social cognitive nature, it is unclear that such conditions *do* (commonly) obtain when it comes to epistemic agency.

To the extent that certain conditions are satisfied (intentionality, knowledge, voluntariness, etc.), certain collectives are plausible candidates for liability attributions and thus may become *in some circumstances* legitimate targets of legal sanctions. Thus the principle of collective moral liability better enables us to discern the conditions under which the courts ought to supplement charges of individual criminal liability for acts of injustice and oppression, while it also helps to identify those collectives that oppress others.

In sum, I have argued that at least some of the ideal conditions that must be satisfied for justified collective moral responsibility attributions to obtain include intentionality, voluntariness, and knowledge. I further argued that in the actual world large conglomerates such as countries and large corporations do not typically satisfy those conditions (namely, the intentionality and epistemic conditions) robustly. Summatively speaking, conglomerates such as countries and corporations *can but sometimes do not* satisfy the conditions for being morally responsible (secondary) agents.[63] This point is significant in that previous philosophical theories of collective responsibility do not set forth conditions of collective responsibility (for actions[64]) in any straightforward way. Nor do they state whether or not existing collectives do or can satisfy such conditions.

Furthermore, as R. S. Downie states,

> The claim that individual persons and only such are morally responsible is a truth of the metaphysics of morality, but the claim that collective actions are not exhaustively analyzable into the actions of individual persons is a truth of the philosophy of law. We require a theory, which allows us to incorporate both truths without committing us to the existence of mystical entities.[65]

Finally, the principle of collective moral liability clarifies the extent to which collectives can be and are moral *agents*. It articulates an analysis of collective moral responsibility according to which we can better discern the plausibility of collective moral responsibility ascriptions. And this concept of collective moral responsibility better enables us to discern which collectives, *qua collectives*, are and which are not morally legitimate targets of legal sanctions.

But is the United States responsible in the requisite sense for the oppression of Indians and blacks? If not, a case for compensatory reparations cannot be made, as a necessary condition for such a case is the establishing of U.S. liability for the said oppressions. However, if a case can be made for U.S. responsibility for the oppressions in question, therein lies the heart of the case for reparations. The following two chapters examine each of these possibilities in that they argue by way of historical narrative that the *U.S. government* by way of its executive, judicial, or legislative decision-making branches repeatedly, intentionally, knowingly, and voluntarily oppressed Indians and blacks. This is true despite the fact that not all U.S. citizens or U.S.-based institutions supported such oppressive acts. And since, legally speaking, corporations and governments can and often do endure over time, to the extent that the U.S. federal, state, and local governments and certain businesses that endure today have oppressed Indians and blacks, they owe substantial reparations for such atrocities. This point is based on the age-old principle of corporate responsibility. It need not be shown that each and every official of the U.S. government or every U.S. citizen supported the oppression of Indians and blacks for collective liability to obtain regarding such evils. Rather, it must be shown that a significant degree of collective liability obtains concerning the federal, state, and local governments, and certain businesses or organizations insofar as their oppression of Indians and blacks is concerned. It is to this matter that I now turn my attention.

6

Reparations to American Indians

The fundamental factor that keeps Indians and non-Indians from commu-
nicating [with one another] . . . is that they are speaking about two entirely
different perceptions of the world.

—Vine Deloria, Jr.[1]

North American history is replete with accounts of atrocities being inflicted by
members of one collective on members of another. Some such examples
include: the violent seizure or fraudulent acquisition by the French, the British, the Spanish, and the Dutch (and later by the United States and Canadian
governments, respectively) governments of millions of acres of land inhabited
by American Indians; the genocide (or attempt therein) of various Indians by
the U.S. military at the order of, among others, former U.S. president Andrew
Jackson;[2] the enslavement of several Indians in the United States; the selling
of Indians into slavery outside the United States; the organization and direct-
ing of the infamous Indian Boarding Schools throughout the United states,
among others.[3] These and other evils have found little or no justice in the form
of reparations. This chapter seeks to clarify the nature of the U.S. oppression
of Indian nations and analyzes philosophically some key objections to reparations to Indians.[4]

In writing of Indian treatment by the United States and of Indian rights,
Felix Cohen notes that the U.S. Congress has treated Indians rather well, com-
paratively. But his description of U.S.-Indian history seems filled with excuses.
In referring to the acquisition of Indian lands, Cohen writes:

The purchase of more than two million square miles of land from the Indian
tribes represents what is probably the largest real estate transaction in the history
of the world. It would be miraculous, if, across a period of 150 years, negotiations
for the purchase and sale of these lands could be carried on without misunder-
standings and inequities.[5]

131

Cohen continues:

> We have often forgotten to make the payments that we promised, to respect the boundaries of lands that the Indians reserved for themselves, or to respect the privileges of tax exemption, or hunting or fishing, that were accorded to Indian tribes in exchange for the lands they granted us. But when Congress has been fairly apprised of any deviation from the plighted word of the United States, it has generally been willing to submit to court decision the claims of any injured Indian tribe. And it has been willing to make whatever restitution the facts supported for wrongs committed by blundering or unfaithful public servants. There is no nation on the face of the earth which has set for itself so high a standard of dealing with a native aboriginal people as the United States and no nation on earth that has been more self-critical in seeking to rectify its deviations from those high standards.[6]

Cohen's account contains historical inaccuracies far too numerous to correct here. But I shall briefly correct a few. While it might be thought that the United States had "forgotten" to make payments to Indians for the lands in question, that legally speaking constitutes theft by unlawful acquisition considering that there were incessant pleas for justice by Indian leaders throughout U.S. history to remind the United States what it owes to Indians, and why. How can such payments for the lands be merely the result of forgetfulness? That Indians "granted" land to the United States is misleading as it was often done by fraud or force, vitiating any putative claim that such lands were ceded knowingly (relative to understanding the contents and implications of the treaties) or voluntarily. Often, the United States fraudulently signed treaties with Indians who had no tribal authority to do so. Indeed, no Indian had the authority to sell land or to even give away sacred Indian lands, as it was against religious custom and was in some cases punishable by death. Moreover, the fact is that when Indian leaders several times approached Washington for justice, little or nothing was given, except the offers made by the United States that favored U.S. interests. Such offers ignored the fact that Indians do not believe that anyone else had rights to the lands in question except them, as they are its indigenous inhabitants, as Cohen admits. So Cohen's claim that the United States was willing to give Indians what the courts gave Indians is loaded with inherent problems, each one self-serving for the United States. Furthermore, that the U.S. government took most of the Indian lands by violent force is beyond question.

Cohen's absurd claim that the United States was always willing to provide "whatever restitution" the facts supported is hardly worthy of comment and constitutes an insult to the intelligence of those familiar with the bleak history of U.S.-Indian "relations." But since many U.S. citizens today still believe this shibboleth, it bears noting that most contemporary adult reservation Indians understand the historical facts of massive force and fraud that underlie what was part of the greatest land theft in history. And Cohen's apparent ignorance of the U.S. Indian removal campaigns to make available Indian lands in the westward expansion of the United States is irresponsible.[7] It is precisely these attitudes based on distorted notions of the history of U.S.-Indian relations that cries out for analysis of reparations for Indians. Indians did not cede their lands with the idea that whites could remain in territories indefinitely, and then for whites to commit one of the greatest genocides in human history against their indigenous hosts! In fact, the U.S. genocide of Indians would not have been "necessary" if the Indians were so accommodating throughout much of the process of manifest destiny. It was because Indians amounted to a serious obstacle to U.S. ownership and control of Indian lands that led to the conflicts of the American holocaust. As we shall see below, Indians believed and knew they had various rights to the land, and this is why so many of them who could fought to the death to retain it from violent and fraudulent white invasion.

It is an embarrassing fact that major Western political philosophies by and large ignore (or, at best, give short shrift to) the claims of Indians to property.[8] And given the importance of the concept of private property rights in historic and contemporary Western political philosophy,[9] it is vital to delve into problems that, among other things, question who has the overriding valid moral claim to or interest in, say, the lands on which entire countries and their respective citizens reside, such as with the United States. For the moral legitimacy of a country, it is assumed, is contingent on at least the extent to which that country acquires *justly* the land on which it and its citizens reside. The problem of reparations to Indians raises queries concerning the fundamental moral legitimacy of the United States and of the putative duty to obey its laws. For it challenges the moral basis of putative U.S. rights to lands which, it is assumed, are necessary for its economic and political existence and survival.

Briefly, reparations can be supported on the ground that they truly respect the actions (and inactions, as the case may be) of history in the sense that they attempt to correct significant imbalances of power or fortune which result from undue force or intrusion, fraud, or other gross forms of harmful wrongdoing. Moreover, reparations disrespect as being morally arbitrary any statute of limitations pertaining to the kinds of cases in question.[10] This is especially true where the extent of the facts of guilt, fault, harm, and identity of the perpetrators and victims are unclear. Whether it is a crime occurring forty or four hundred years ago, justice requires that significant harmful wrongdoings are compensated in manners that would do justice to the idea of proportional compensation for damages in cases where the perpetrator(s), victim(s), and damages are provable by current legal standards (beyond reasonable doubt, for example, in criminal cases, and by the preponderance of evidence in tort cases). With reparations, then, both the balance of human reason and history must be our twin and primary guides to the truth of who (or what) owes what to whom (or what), and why. For my current purposes, it is assumed that the law ought to follow these guides. The argument for reparations to Indians insists that reparations ought to be made when a right has been infringed by way of significant injustice.[11] (In assessing the plausibility of precisely this sort of argument, David Lyons points out that it relies on the ideas of original acquisition and legitimate transfer of land.[12]) Thus the justification for reparations is primarily backward-looking, though it may involve aspects of considerations that are forward-looking.

The foregoing suggests the following reparations argument concerning the oppression of Indians by the United States:

1. As much as is humanly possible, instances of clear and substantial historic rights violations ought to be rectified by way of reparations.
2. The U.S. government has clearly committed substantial historic rights violations against millions of Indians.[13]
3. Therefore, the historic rights violations of the U.S. government against Indians ought to be rectified by way of reparations, as much as humanly possible.

The basis for premise 1 might be a desert-based (retributivist) one that insists that there is a perfect duty to rectify past injustices of a substantial nature. Or, to the extent that it is humanly possible to rectify substantial wrongs for which a wrongdoer is responsible, the wrongdoer ought to rectify the wrongdoing. The locution "as much as humanly possible" in premises 1 and 3 is meant to capture the idea of the reparations being roughly proportional to the harms they are meant to rectify.

OBJECTIONS TO THE REPARATIONS ARGUMENT, AND REPLIES

If the reparations argument is plausible, then wherever there is significant injustice there is at least a prima facie reason to believe that such injustice deserves compensation as a means of rectification. Moreover, where the facts of the oppressor-collective's guilt, fault, voluntariness, intentionality, knowledge, harm, wrongfulness, and identity, along with the identity of their victims, and their respective heirs' identities are reasonably clear, reparations ought to be pursued for the sake of corrective justice.[14] Hence, there is a presumptive case in favor of reparations to Indians by the U.S. government, given the substantial wrongs many Indians have experienced at the hands of the United States.

Precisely what was the harm or cluster of harms wrongfully perpetrated against Indians by the United States? At the very least, it is the following. To the extent that Will Kymlicka is correct when he argues that cultural membership is crucial for self-respect,[15] and to the extent that a Rawlsian liberalism is correct in arguing that cultural membership is a primary good,[16] the *particular* cultural membership which is crucial to *their* self-respect was undermined for Indians by force and fraud. The campaigns against various Indian nations by the U.S. military serve as examples here. One specific instance of U.S. crimes against the Lakota Sioux was the massacre at Wounded Knee, which in turn culminated in the retaliatory violence against the U.S. military at Little Big Horn. Examples of U.S. torts against Indians are the fraudulent takings of lands, often followed by the U.S. government's refusal to honor its treaties made with various Indian nations, facts not mentioned in Cohen's account of U.S.-Indian relations. Yet for all of the several instances of unjustified violence and other crimes, torts, and contract violations committed by the United States against various Indians, few, if any, apologies or reparations have been issued by the U.S. government.[17] These are some reasons that form the presumptive case for reparations to Indians.[18] But such a presumption can be overridden if it can be shown that considerations against such reparations outweigh the strength of the prima facie case for them where the instances in question are not "hard cases."[19] Hence it is important to consider the plausibility of various of the strongest objections to reparations to Indians: the objection from historical complexity, the objection to collective responsibility, the no Indian conception of moral rights objection, the historical reparations objection, and the acquired rights trumping original land rights objection.[20] To the extent that such objections are defeasible, the presumptive case for such reparations gains strength, and the reparations argument gains plausibility.

THE OBJECTION FROM HISTORICAL COMPLEXITY

Given the above understanding of the nature of reparations, are reparations to Indians by the U.S. government morally required? Ought the U.S. government to provide reparations to Indians? A number of arguments can be marshaled against the imposition of reparations on the United States by the U.S. Congress, a U.S. federal court, or, say, the International Criminal Court, and they deserve close scrutiny. First, there is the *objection from historical complexity*. This objection avers that history contains far too many and complex situations of conflict such that it would be impossible to figure out all of the injustices that would putatively require reparations. Where the perpetrators of the evils are dead and cannot be punished for their horrors it would be sheer dogmatic idealism to think that respecting rights requires or even permits the kind of complex legal casework that would rectify all past wrongs. To award reparations to the wronged party or her descendants would end up forcing innocent parties (perhaps the descendants of the wrongdoer[s]) to pay for what they themselves did not do.[21] Among other things, the objection from historical complexity seems to assume that past injustices should not forever burden future putatively "innocent" generations.[22] The objection from historical complexity challenges premise 1 of the reparations argument, suggesting that there are some instances of historic injustice that ought *not* to be rectified by way of reparations.

In response to this objection to the reparations argument, it might be pointed out that the inability to figure out with precise accuracy *all there is to know* about *every case* that putatively involves reparations hardly prohibits either the U.S. Congress or a juridical system from awarding some measure of significant reparations where cases are clear (based on unambiguous historical records, for example). Even if it were true that a full-blown policy of reparations would involve reparations to Indians by not only the U.S. government, but by the governments of Spain, Portugal, England, France, the Netherlands, and so on, and even if it proved overly difficult to figure out the extent to which each such government contributed to harms against Indians, this would hardly show that clear cases of U.S. harms to Indians ought not to be compensated by the United States. Moreover, though the parties to a putative case of reparations would involve those who themselves did no harm to the victims in question, such "innocent" parties who currently reside on or "own" lands that were once resided on by Indians are in violation of the *principle of morally just acquisitions and transfers* (herein repeated from chapter 1):

> Whatever is acquired or transferred by morally just means is itself morally just; whatever is acquired or transferred by morally unjust means is itself morally unjust.[23]

The intended meaning of this principle is that to the extent that property is acquired or transferred in a morally justified way (i.e., without force, fraud, etc.), the acquisition or transfer of that property carries with it a genuine moral claim or entitlement to *occupy* it without interference from others. To the extent that the principle of morally just acquisitions and transfers is violated, there is no legitimate claim or entitlement to occupy the property being acquired or transferred. Thus the principle need not specify ownership rights to property. In this way, then, it is neutral concerning the matter of property rights of ownership between political liberals and Marxists. This point of clarification precludes a Marxist-style objection that reparations to Indians are not morally justified in that they are contingent on Indians having original land rights, which themselves are dubious on moral grounds. For the principle of morally just acquisitions and transfers does not support reparations to Indians by the United States because Indians had property *ownership* rights to the lands, but because Indians had property *sovereignty* or *occupancy* rights therein.[24]

Although the locutions "morally just" and "morally unjust" are somewhat vague, relatively clear cases of unjust acquisition or transfer, for instance, exist: when such acquisitions or transfers occur as the result of significant nonvoluntariness (the violent use or threat of force, for example) on the part of those relinquishing property;[25] when acquisitions or transfers involve fraud[26] or severe misunderstanding between principal parties.[27] In the case of Indian lands (then as currently a part of the United States) most of which were taken from them forcibly or violently by the U.S. military at the direction of Jackson and other U.S. officials (also, many of which lands were encroached upon illegally by U.S. citizens or civilians), there is no question who the wrongdoer was (the U.S. government, along with its citizen trespassers) and who the harmed parties were (Indians of various nations). In other cases, Indians were believed to have "given away" their land to invaders, interpreted as such, presumably, because of the general hospitality (or sometimes fear) of the Indian peoples toward the invaders. In such cases, the questions are not who is the guilty party and who was the victim, but precisely how ought the victims to be "reparated" for the wrongdoings. In still other instances, U.S. citizens have purchased in good faith lands from other non-Indian peoples to which the former did not in fact have an overriding moral right. That a person purchased in good faith a stolen item in no way entitles him to that item, as even the law stipulates. She who has a moral right to something is truly entitled to it, and that right must be respected by all who take seriously what "true" morality requires. Note that this argument is *not* contingent on the well-being of either the perpetrators or the victims of the evils inflicted that might require reparations. For reparations are morally required even if, say, the United States and its citizens were not well off and if Indians were indeed relatively better off. Reparative justice does not depend on the ability of perpetrators of wrongdoing to enrich their lives by inflicting wrongdoings on others. It is concerned primarily with rectifying past injustices regardless of whether or not perpetrators have been enriched by their wrongdoings. Thus the attempt of the objection from historical complexity to defeat premise 1 fails.

THE OBJECTION TO
COLLECTIVE RESPONSIBILITY

In the previous chapter, I outlined and expounded some of the conditions of collective responsibility. My analysis required that collectives such as countries or governments act intentionally, knowingly, and voluntarily in what they are to be rightly held accountable for. And such considerations are vital for an understanding of whether or not one country or its government is liable for the harms it caused to this or that group. Certain potential difficulties were discussed, and an analysis of collective retrospective liability responsibility emerged, one that forms the basis of the problem of collective responsibility.

The general problem of collective responsibility raises the issue of collective moral retrospective liability responsibility of, say, the U.S. government for severe wrongs committed in *its* name or on *its* behalf against Indians. The *objection to collective responsibility* challenges the morality of reparations to Indians on the grounds that it is problematic to hold the current U.S. government and its citizenry morally accountable for wrongs committed by previous generations of people who acted or failed to act, as the case may be, to harm Indians and on behalf of the U.S. government, its agencies, or on behalf of themselves as actual or putative U.S. citizens. Thus the objection to collective responsibility challenges premise 2 of the reparations argument insofar as premise 2 seeks to hold the U.S. *government* responsible for certain substantial wrongs against Indians.

However, the objection to collective responsibility falls prey to at least two weaknesses. First, the fundamental documents which form the basis of U.S. government operations and U.S. society are still those which govern the United States. Even though the atrocities committed against Indians generations ago were not the direct causal responsibility of today's U.S. citizens, the fact is that the U.S. government and its citizenry have persisted over time, and still exist. Furthermore, it is plausible to think that when the U.S. Army and the U.S. government acted in committing genocidal acts against various Indian nations that they did so in such ways that the United States (e.g., its governments, federal, state, and local, along with their respective executive, legislative, and judicial branches and many of their respective agencies) was to some meaningful degree collectively guilty, at fault, acted knowingly, intentionally, and voluntarily to such extents that *we* (since it is *our* government, acting on *our* behalves) *are* justified in inferring that they were both causally responsible and morally liable (culpable) for those harms committed by it against numerous Indian nations. Yet unrectified evil is evil still. And the unrectified evils of the United States against Indians of previous generations are our responsibility today.[28]

Just what is the story of U.S. oppression of Indians? Since this is a philosophy book and not a history one, a concise and partial story will have to suffice.[29] The aim of this brief account is to build a case for damages suffered by Indians at the hands of the U.S. government.[30] The importance of this concise account lies in the fact that most who consider these issues neglect to appreciate the gravity of Indian losses, and to see that it was not a brief accidental occurrence, but an ongoing, intentional, voluntary campaign over several generations that most every adult knew about and most every adult approved of and did little or nothing to combat. While I shall argue in terms of the United States' actions, inactions, and attempted actions being such that they make the United States responsible for the oppression of Indians over generations, Howard McGary would argue (as we saw in the previous chapter) that it is the social and political practices that make the United States guilty of such harmful wrongdoing.

Centuries prior to the European invasion of the Americas, including North America, hundreds of Indian nations lived and most thrived. Many such nations had extensive trading with others. Although some such nations engaged each other in war, sometimes over territorial disputes, most were peaceful. But in 1493, Pope Alexander VI urged Spanish *conquistadores* to secure the "New World" and convert all "savages" to Christianity. What followed was a lengthy process of violent conquest driven by the doctrine of discovery and with the "discovery" of North America by Europeans in the late fifteenth century came the beginning of the end of most Indian nations in North America by and large by Europeans who had unquenchable hungers for gold, silver, ore, and furs, among other things possessed in the lands occupied by Indians throughout North America. While the British Empire began early on to settle the mid to upper Atlantic coastal regions of what is now called the "United States," the French began to occupy northeastern coastal regions and near the Great Lakes. The Spanish explored the southeastern region in a rather marauding fashion.

While some such as John Locke argued for a "proviso" that required lands throughout the earth to be shared where there is more than is needed by the current occupants, it is far from clear that there was enough room for at most more than a few settlers in North America with hundreds of Indian nations thriving and growing as they were at that time. The Indian perspective on life was not akin to the European perspective. Indians do not see that there is so much permanent room for others as the quality of Indian life would be greatly diminished with European settlement, which we now know. With over 100 Indian nations and a combined Indian population of between 5 and 100 million in what we now call the United States area alone, what room was there for Europeans with their ambitious plans for "development"?[31] Also, the Lockean notion that there was sufficient space for Europeans in the region is prejudiced by the fact that Locke and others did not consider Indian peoples to be worthy of their own style of growth. So the Lockean proviso is prejudiced against the Indian perspective on human growth and flourishing, and is thus morally questionable. Beyond this, however, is the fact that while Indians first welcomed Europeans in Jamestown as trading partners, Europeans began their violent quest for what they thought of as divinely granted land. There is nothing even in Locke's proviso that would permit the violent or fraudulent taking of anything, much less lands that belong to others by at least occupation right.

If Indian nations are to be paid reparations, they are owed them by a cluster of nations such as Britain, France, and Spain, as each one had a major role in despoiling Indian nations for their own greedy aims, and for generations.[32] It is an interesting fact that before there were African slaves in North America, there were Indian ones. But my main concern and argument pertains to how Indians were treated by the United States. For it was the United States of course that won the wars and made the deals to procure what is now called the "United States." Cases of reparative justice to Indians in and by other countries can, and hopefully will, be taken up elsewhere.

From the outlawing of the ghost dance by the U.S. government in the late 1800s, to the driving the Indians into starvation by various U.S. policies that also destroyed Indian cultures and nations, if left to their own, Indians would have fared significantly better even after U.S. persecution. In 1890, Chief Big

Foot and his band of Souix were massacred at Wounded Knee by the Seventh
Cavalry of the U.S. Army just after Indians were surrendering around the flag
of truce. Those not killed immediately were ordered out of hiding and massacred as well. There were very few survivors. The wounded died shortly thereafter in (as reported by Thomas Tibbles, the surgeon on hand), "oppressive
silence." This was the last battle of the Indian wars, likely won in large part by
the invention and acquisition of the technology of the weapons of war, the
wealth of which to purchase such weapons was partly gained by slave labor
and stolen land.

The Pueblo Indians found by the European invaders had their roots in the
Anastasi who had lived throughout the Southwest. Their religious, cultural,
linguistic, and architectural lives find their roots in their predecessors.

Indians welcomed the British as potential trading partners and "gave" them
land on which to live. But they did not welcome their eminent invasion. By
1776 as the colonists' war of secession against the British began, the peaceful
confederacy between the Indian tribes of the Haudenosaune was forced to
civil war as the Oneida sided with colonists against the British and other
nations of the Haudenosaune sided with the British against the colonists.
Where peace was fashioned from war between nations prior to white contact,
white contact now brought death and destruction of the Indian confederacy
between Oneida, Cayuga, Onondaga, Seneca, and Mohawks.

The Indian confederacy tried to remain neutral in the war of secession
against the British, but when it could not, General George Washington
attacked the headquarters of the confederacy, and later sent Sullivan to destroy
it house by house, apple and peach tree every one where Seneca, Mohawk,
Cayuga, and Onondaga lived as they sided with the British. Many Indians were
coerced to side in the white war, Indian against Indian. Only two Haudenosaune villages were not attacked as colonial troops sought revenge against
Indians supportive of the British. But the ravages of the surrounding areas left
them to starve during the upcoming harsh winter. In retaliation, British troops
under Brandt attacked the Oneida villages because they sided with the colonists. Indians in either case were forced to play as pawns in the white war of
secession, to which neither of the white collectives had a territorial right, as a
necessary condition of morally justified secession is that the seceding group
have a moral right to possess the land it claims as its own, something that the
colonists and other invaders clearly lacked. Ironically, the British did not even
have the right to prevent the secession as they had no right to be in the territories in the first place! Each party violated the "territoriality thesis," a principle
accepted by most all secessionist theorists.[33] In gratitude to the Oneida support for colonist troops during their secession from Britain, just after the successful war the United States seized Haudenosaune lands, though in 1790 the
Haudenosaune forced concessions from the United States that permitted them
to remain on their homelands.[34] By 1783, Haudenosaune nations were

reduced by white expansion protected by the U.S. Army to mere reservations not even 10 percent of the size of their former territories.

The U.S. government, then bankrupt by the secession war, paid former soldiers with land grants in various of the Indian territories, leading to the westward expansion. In the Ohio Valley during 1782 to 1808, the Shawnee and Miami territories were thickly inhabited by white settlers. The white settlers were armed themselves, and many being former soldiers, did not hesitate to secure their land grants by force against Indian resistance. The U.S. Army regularly fought and killed Indians who sought to defend their old territories against the white invasion of the Ohio Valley lands. For twenty years, the United States seized lands from Indians. By 1795, the United States forcibly seized most of the Great Lakes region. Indian treaties with whites were powerless to thwart westward expansion. Manifest destiny was under way with full force now that there was no longer European competition for Indian lands in the region.

The record of U.S. genocide of Indians includes the massacres or attacks of civilian Indian populations at Blue River in 1854, Bear River in 1863, Sand Creek in 1864, Washita River in 1868, Sappa Creek in 1875, Camp Robinson in 1878, and Wounded Knee in 1890, among dozens of others.[35] But the U.S. genocide of Indians included more than the military campaigns against mostly civilian populations. It included the dispossession of Indians from their lands by deliberate opportunism when it came to the realization that Indians did not share Western values concerning land ownership. This was accomplished by way of the U.S. Supreme Court's ignoring Indian occupation rights to their lands (*Johnson v. M'Intosh*), the diminishing of Indian sovereignty (*Cherokee Nation v. Georgia*) in 1831 by declaring Indian nations as "domestic independent" ones, by declaring the U.S. Congress to have final authority over Indian affairs (*Worcester v. Georgia*), which was backed by U.S. military intervention to squelch Indian opposition, as well as congressionally approved allotment of Indian lands to non-Indians and Supreme Court support of allotment policies.[36] As William C. Bradford notes, "In sum, the synergy of discovery, the trust doctrine, and plenary power perfected the legal theft of Indian land. Despite infrequent restitution and compensation, the Constitution affords no protection to Indian tribes, and what remains of their land continues under siege."[37]

Not only did the military force of the U.S. Army drive the Indians from their homelands, but the acculturation of Indian values was undermined by Christian missionaries who vigorously sought to convert them to their own particular brand of puritanical faith which was diametrically opposed to Indian values in almost every conceivable respect. There was legislative intent, knowledge, and voluntariness exhibited in the late nineteenth-century congressional funding of Indian oppression by the founding of the infamous Indian Boarding Schools, the primary purpose of which was to forcibly change young Indians, stripped from their families, into "good white folk." Indian Boarding

Schools like the Carlisle Indian School, the Sherman Indian School, as well as others staffed by Christian missionaries sought to thoroughly acculturate young Indians in one or another heretical form of the Christian religion while deprogramming Indian children of their indigenous-based religious faith. Across the United States, Indian children as young as four years old were often stolen or otherwise taken by force from their Indian parents and families and tribes and acculturated in these schools where children were stripped of all Indianness and punished harshly for speaking Indian languages. Their Indian belongings were destroyed. Long hair, a sign of Indian pride, was cut off. They were fed distorted images of "evil" Indians. Forced to eat white food and wear white clothes, these children were reprogrammed to be white. Students slept on cots and drilled in military regimen to assist in the breaking of their Indian ways. Priests whipped "disobedient" Indian children. Photos and memories of Indian family members and life were not permitted. It is perhaps the worst case of sustained and ordained child abuse in the history of the United States, at least roughly comparable to the horrific experiences of black slave adults and children in the United States who were forcibly "converted" from their African religions to one or another perverse version of Christianity. This had the effect of cultural genocide of Indians, especially when tribal religions were banned even on reservations. The enactment of American Indian Religious Freedom Act in 1978 came too late to address the deep harm done by the United States to Indian culture, as even today some aspects of Indian religion are not protected by the act. There was also the overall suppression of Indian sovereignty by way of "disintegrating tribal institutions and supplanting them with European American forms of governance."[38] In short, a kind of legal imperialism occurred wherein the United States granted to states ultimate authority over Indian legal disputes. Along with forced assimilation and relocation of Indians, the cultural genocide of Indians by the United States was realized. So with military attacks and famine and disease also came acculturation for those who survived.[39] It is no wonder, then, that utilitarian approaches to reparations to Indians involving forgiveness and reconciliation bring back haunting nightmares of coerced integration with whites wherein whites ultimately control Indian lives. Without the power of rights, social utility will always reduce Indians to whatever whites decide to do with them in the United States, as history clearly demonstrates.

Thus what military force could not kill or otherwise destroy of the Indian, perverse religion would ruin of Indian culture and identity. Forced religion on the Indian sought to liquidate them as a "final solution" to the "Indian problem." Many fail to understand that the very same "Christian" evangelical forces alive in current U.S. society grew out of the evangelic missionary movements during the time of Indian removal.[40] Many of their histories are tainted with Indian genocide of one kind or another.

Because white settlers stealing their lands and forcing them to become as whites demoralized Indians across the continent that was once theirs in relative peace, many Indians took to alcohol and their tribes, families, and lives were ruined. As is well known, this problem persists until this very day on reservations throughout the United States. It is just one of the several legacies of U.S. oppression of Indian nations.

But there is much more to the story of U.S.-Indian relations than this. Backing up to the early nineteenth century, Prophetstown on the Wabash River gained a political and military following from which Tecumseh (Shawnee) arose as the powerful Indian leader of that time. He reasserted former Indian rights to lands and sought to unite Indians on this theme. W. H. Harrison, then-governor of the Indiana territory, saw this as a threat to white security. In 1809 at a treaty conference, Harrison convinced the Miami and some other Indian nations to sell 3,000,000 acres of land in Indiana and Illinois territories. This was against Indian custom and belief: No one has a right to sell land to anyone, not even to another Indian! Tecumseh threatened to defend the lands anyway against white settlement. For a morally unjust treaty is no treaty at all.

In 1811, Tecumseh sought to bring the Choctaw, Creek, and Chickasaw into alliance against whites. But many southern Indian leaders became acculturated to white ways, and encouraged their followers to do the same as many saw military conflict with the United States as futile because it was deemed suicidal due to U.S. military power. Thus Tecumseh's effort to unite southern Indians failed. In 1812, Prophetstown was destroyed and people dispersed by Harrison and the U.S. Army while Tecumseh was away attempting to garner Indian alliances in the region. Later Harrison became president when U.S. citizens voted for him in significant part because of his "successes" over Indians.

While there were some Indian uprisings and military defeats against the United States, such as Tecumseh's 1813 forced surrender of the United States at Frenchtown, such victories were eventually met with defeat. The United States always seemed to have what the Indians never had: superior weaponry. The technology of war was to provide the United States with certain victory over almost all foes even until this day, a superiority, again, made possible in significant part due to the wealth created and sustained by stolen Indian lands and the enslavement of Indians and Africans.

Thomas Jefferson and some others advocated intermarriage between Indians and whites, financial incentives, and religious conversion to acculturate Indians. Traditional Indians were eliminated in the South by these and other means as the Cherokee, Creek, Chickasaw, Choctaw, and Seminole became the Five "Civilized" Tribes.

The Cherokee made their home in Echota, Tennessee. In 1817, John Ross replaced the Cherokee government with a U.S.-style one in New Echota, Georgia. The cotton industry's demand for land in the South meant that even more Indian lands were lost to whites and overall white social utility considerations. In 1828, Andrew Jackson won the U.S. presidency largely on his platform to eradicate Indian nations, and gold was discovered in Georgia on Cherokee land. Jackson, himself a land speculator, sought to remove the Cherokee for

white gold prospecting on their lands. This led to the Long Walk of the Cherokee and some other Indian nations in the region. It was primarily the discovery of gold in Indian territories of that region in 1830 that led to Jackson's
supporting of the passage of the Indian Removal Act by the U.S. Congress that
same year.[41] The resultant Trail of Tears moved the Cherokee and neighboring
nations to the Oklahoma territory.

The Choctaw were first to be expelled between 1831 and 1832. Thirteen
thousand Choctaw were removed, two thousand died on the way west. The
Creek surrendered at gunpoint; one-third of the Creek died on their westward
march. Then came the Cherokee. Ross tried to forestall removal consistently
from 1830 to 1838, but with no success. He even sued in the U.S. Supreme
Court! The executive and judicial branches failed to do justice, except when
the Supreme Court ruled that the Cherokee were a sovereign nation and not
subject to Georgia jurisdiction. But Jackson belittled the power of the Court
and disregarded the ruling. His position was that the political will of whites
will override court rulings when the latter disregarded white demands. Georgia then held lotteries for Cherokee lands and Indians were escorted from
their lands by military. The Trail of Tears, one of history's most horrendous
evils, was carried out by the U.S. military at the direction of the U.S. government by the will of most of the U.S. citizenry primarily for land and the gold
therein. Once again Indian rights were disregarded in favor of white social
utility maximization.

So where whites of the United States did not wrongly gain their legal titles
to land from the British, French, or Spanish, they took it from Indians by force
and fraud. When Indians fought back, they were accused of being dangerous
savages and killed. But this view only makes "moral" sense if one does not
accord to Indians the same rights to self-defense and defense of property that
every other human is supposed to possess by moral right—perhaps even by
human right. So the fact that such a double standard was so often used against
Indians exposes a kind of racism against them that explains why they were
oppressed in the manners they were by U.S. whites. It explains well, though
not completely, why there were massive violations of the principle of morally
just acquisitions and transfers by whites against Indians.

Ridge (Cherokee), without authorization from the Cherokee Council, pri-
vately signed a treaty with the United States to cede Cherokee lands. The
United States was all too glad to sign the treaty as it had done in similar cases
with other Indian nations. But very few, if any, of such Indians had the proper
Indian authorization. Just because one or two or an otherwise small group of
Indians sign a treaty does not mean either that they do so voluntarily and
without significant U.S. coercion or that they have proper authorization by the
Indian nations they putatively represent. But they cannot have such authoriza-
tion because, to repeat, it is a deeply held Indian belief that land is sacred
("Our Mother") and given to Indians by the creator and never to be sold to
anyone for any reason. So while an Indian with proper tribal authority can

permit others to occupy lands for this or that amount of time, they cannot sell it. And they would surely not give it away. But Ridge sold the Georgia Cherokee lands for $5,000,000 and removal assistance. While Ridge believed that the forced treaty conditions were the only path to Cherokee survival in light of manifest destiny attitudes of whites, his attempt to garner Cherokee support for his treaty with the federal government was met with hostile rejection by the National Cherokee Council. But he signed the treaty anyway. It was not a legal treaty, as Ridge, his son, and some others did not have the authority to make it. Cherokee law in particular, incidentally, calls for the death of anyone who sells Cherokee lands to anyone. Just as Thomas Aquinas believed that an unjust law is no law at all, so did Indians believe that an unjust treaty is no treaty at all. And treaties could be unjust in a variety of ways. One was where the United States coerced by various means the signing of the document. Another is where an Indian without proper authorization signed the treaty. In neither case does it have binding power for Indians, nor in a just legal context.

In 1836, the U.S. Senate ratified the treaty and Cherokees were given two years to move west to the Oklahoma territory. The result is that massive acreage is stolen by whites from Indians. General Scott was sent to Georgia to remove the Cherokee. When Cherokees refused to move, they were placed in stockades and removed at gunpoint by the U.S. Army. They were not allowed to take anything but what they could wear, as they were prisoners. In all, 16,000 Cherokees were herded west like cattle. About 4,000 died en route to Oklahoma in the infamous Trail of Tears. Hundreds of Cherokees evaded U.S. troops and escaped to the Smokey Mountains, but were recovered by the military. Their freedom was eventually negotiated and those Cherokee form the basis of current ones in Cherokee, North Carolina. Ridge and others who signed the treaty of removal of the bulk of the Cherokees were assassinated in Oklahoma, a confirmation of the deeply held Indian belief that no one has a right to sell Indian lands to anyone for any reason. The Trail of Tears resulted in Indian deaths and removal for social utility maximization for *whites* in light of *white* goals. And we saw in chapters 2 and 3 that a general utilitarian approach to reparations cannot seem to make room for rights that would help to restore the oppressed to a position of roughly where they were prior to the oppression. This is true, at least, in the case of the Indians.

Then there was the far westward expansion of whites into California wherein 300,000 Indians lived at the time of contact with Europeans. The Indians there cumulatively spoke eighty languages and were highly structured. By 1772, the Chumash nation included priests, government leaders, astrologers, and basket- and canoe-makers. They lived near the mid-coast region, located in what is now called Santa Barbara County and the surrounding areas. The Chumash were the center of California economy. But during that same year, Spanish missionaries led by Serra arrived in Chumash territory, and sought to convert Indians to their own brand of Christianity, often kidnapping Indians to convert them by physical force. The Santa Barbara mission was a center for such abuses. Indians were forced to live and work in the missions as slaves, and were beaten as slaves. Escaped slaves were often beaten badly. This treatment lasted for fifty years, making Indian lives in the missions both miserable and short. Despite what the docents inform tourists in the Santa Barbara Mission to this day, the *Indians* built the missions from their own forced slave labor by the priests. Indeed, on the grounds of the Santa Barbara mission alone there are over 4,000 Chumash names on registry and their bodies are buried on mission grounds (without proper burial rites, of course). Other California missions were similar in their oppression of Indians. To this day, the mission docents fail to inform visitors of these important mission facts, often claiming that the "priests built the mission."

In 1821, the control of California was transferred to the United States of Mexico after it won its independence from Spain. Missions were secularized, and Indians were free to leave them akin to the way in which black slaves were "emancipated." But fifty years of slavery and acculturation ruined them (again, not unlike newly freed black slaves) and Mexicans stole their homelands. Mission Indians were forced to become peasant workers on ranches on lands that they themselves used to own.

But when California became a U.S. territory at the advent of the California Gold rush in 1848, there was indiscriminate killing of Indians. Miners raped Indian women, vigilantes wiped out Indian villages, and it was open season on Indians. Indian men were killed and women and children taken as slaves or peasant workers, sometimes shipped overseas as slave labor. A pattern had repeated itself. As with the Cherokee and other Indians of the Georgia region, the white hunger for gold spelled the further demise of Indians.

Just when things seemed that they could not get any worse for Indians, the 1850s demand for agricultural labor led to *legalization of Indian slavery* as farmworkers! Governor of California Dole signed the bill that meant that the murder of Indian men could mean the enslavement of their families. Only 30,000 Indians survived the California gold rush era. Only 10 percent of the previously most densely Indian populated area north of Mexico remained. The slaughter made white life a permanent reality. During this time, moreover, the Ventura Indians were decimated.

In 1680, the Spanish were driven out of the Southern Plains areas by Indians. Horses and such were left behind for the Plains Indians (Arapaho, Souix, Cheyenne, Crown, Blackfeet, Kiowa, Pawnee, and Comanche) to use, which they did. The Plains Indians flourished until gold was discovered by whites at Pike's Peak, Colorado, in 1858. This was followed by the 1862 Homestead Act which sparked a tremendous white invasion of the region—100,000 in one year alone! U.S. Army forts were erected throughout areas of the plains to protect white settlers and to confine Indians to reservations. Indians were forced to give in to white settlement of their lands, or to fight the U.S. Army for them which by that time was indeed futile given the superior weaponry of the United States.

Many Indian leaders saw little hope in challenging the U.S. military weaponry, such as Black Kettle and White Antelope, because they had many elderly, women, and children in their tribes. So in 1861 they ceded by treaty vast lands to the United States. They were promised food and money to replace their lost hunting lands. They met with President Abraham Lincoln to seal the agreement. But the promises of provisions in exchange for Indian lands were rarely delivered.

Fear of Indian revolts caused lawmakers in plains areas to encourage white settlers to take up arms against Indians. Black Kettle and White Antelope went to Denver to make peace with whites and the governor of Colorado. They did not want to be mistaken by whites as being violent Indians. They were promised safety if they settled near Fort Lyon in southern Colorado. So Indians settled in Sand Creek. But Colonel Chivington hated Indians and believed that deceiving and killing Indians presented no moral problems. And in 1864 the Indians encamped there were massacred, even under protection of treaty and the U.S. flag, by Chivington's volunteer army. Black Kettle's people were unarmed and presented themselves peacefully at first, they only fought back when attacked. But it was too late. Most (over 500) Indians were killed. Several of those found wounded were killed.[42] White Antelope, wearing the peace medal presented to him by Lincoln, was shot dead, unarmed, in front of his own lodge by one of Chivington's troops. Black Kettle's wife was shot nine times, though he himself was able to escape. Chivington returned with over 100 Cheyenne scalps.[43] In 1868, Black Kettle was encamped on another reservation. At dawn, the U.S. Army under Custer attacked the sleeping Indians. Over 100 Indians were killed in another unprovoked massacre. So the Cheyenne quest for peace ended in yet another U.S. massacre of Indians contributing to the overall genocide.

In 1871, both treaties and the U.S. Army pushed the Kiowa to a reservation in the Great Plains, where there was some armed resistance to U.S. military and settlers. Money, food, and supplies promised by "treaty" with the United States for lands ceded did not arrive. The United States then ordered the killing of all plains buffalo by hunters to drive Indians to reservations because Indians of the plains depended on buffalo to survive. It worked. Thousands of buffalo were killed every day; most of their carcasses left to waste. Some of the Southern Plains Indians went to war with the United States to regain their lands, attacking a buffalo hunter camp in Texas. But they were no match for the hunters with such powerful guns. The result was that the Indians were forced back onto reservations in the plains.

In order to make certain that there could be no further Indian revolts in the plains areas, the U.S. Army rounded up 10,000 Indian horses, shot and killed most, and sold the rest to whites. As a result, Indians had no viable weapons against the U.S. Army, and they had no horses. They simply could not resist with success, and were finally defeated.

In 1876, several thousands of Souix Indians joined Sitting Bull and Crazy Horse at Little Big Horn. Custer (known as "woman-killer" to Indians) advanced on Sitting Bull's camp in a surprise attack. The U.S. Army was soundly defeated in perhaps the greatest Indian victory ever over the United States. All 260 troops of the Seventh Cavalry were killed in battle, even though whites referred to it as a "massacre." Of course, in a colloquial sense it was a massacre as Custer and his men were beaten soundly. But the whites started the battle, while Indians just finished it. This begs the following question: Is a massacre something that happens only to your own people, even if they begin the fight, unprovoked, as in the case of Little Big Horn and the vast majority of confrontations between the U.S. Army and Indian nations? Or it is what happened to Indians at Sand Creek and elsewhere throughout the Indian removal campaigns where Indians were provoked to defend their own lives and defend lands being taken from them by whites?

Perhaps the example of Little Big Horn exemplifies that if Indians would have rallied to kill whites back on the East Coast centuries previous, the United States and all of its evils throughout its history would have never transpired. It is hard to fathom that life on these Indian lands would be, on balance, anywhere akin to as awful as it has been and continues to be under white domination.

In any case, U.S. citizens called for revenge for Little Big Horn; the U.S. Army was commanded to hunt down Indians at full force. Finally, the United States made peace with Crazy Horse in 1877, when Crazy Horse led the surrender for promises of food and other provisions for the Apache. But instead of sending the provisions promised, Crazy Horse was killed (stabbed in the back by a soldier's bayonet) when he refused to be jailed. He was buried at Wounded Knee. This was just one example of the several times that the United States believed that lying to Indians was like lying to an animal; it was simply not a moral issue because Indians were not fully human.[44] By 1880, the number of Indians had been reduced largely by Indian contact with European diseases introduced to the Indians by whites, massacre of Indians by the U.S. Army and white settlers or Indian hunters, and enslavement of Indians by whites, often by Catholic or Protestant missionaries or churches.[45]

But the United States was not finished conquering Indians just yet. White settlers coveted Nez Perce lands in the Pacific Northwest, and the U.S. government supported the white settlement. This meant, of course, that Indian removal was on again for purposes of white settlement. Chief Joseph relinquished his homeland. In retaliation for some white settlers who committed atrocities against Nez Perce, a few Nez Perce killed them. In response, the U.S. military was sent to war against the Nez Perce. Their arrival on the edge of Nez Perce territory was met by a peace delegation by the Nez Perce. But this was met by Colonel Howard's attacking the Nez Perce. Chief Joseph and others fled to Canada to meet Sitting Bull who was waiting there for them. They reached Bear Paw in Montana, but were attacked by surprise. Days of fighting ensued between the Nez Perce and the U.S. Army. General Miles called for peace talks under a truce flag. But the United States did not honor Chief Joseph's terms of truce and he was taken into custody. He devoted the rest of his life to struggle for his people. He even traveled to Washington to approach President Hayes about justice for his people, and in 1885 won the right to return to the Northwest, but not to his homeland. Chief Joseph was eventually taken to a reservation in Washington where he died. So in the end, there was no significant justice (compensatory or otherwise) from whites, but instead massive land theft and squalor for Chief Joseph and the Nez Perce.

Indians in the United States were no longer free: (a) to worship as they pleased; (b) to their own education; (c) to hunt as they pleased; (d) to eat as they pleased; (e) to work as they pleased; (f) to enjoy their own culture, dance, and ritual, as most of these things were outlawed by federal, state, or local laws because whites were so fearful of the "savages" and coveted their lands and the rich natural resources on them. Most Indians who returned to their homelands found whites settled there who actually thought it was theirs by right. Indian life as they knew it prior to white contact was now over; whites with their superior weapons of war finally secured the continent. It was then, and is now, the "land of the free, the home of the brave." At least, this is what most U.S. citizens think even to this day.

The Apache defended their lands in the desert Southwest against Spanish and Mexican invaders. But Apache accommodated whites for some time, until whites increased in numbers by 1861. The U.S. Army sought out Apaches to kill men and capture women and children on false pretenses that Cochise harmed a white child. And in 1876, the United States ordered the Apache to the barren San Carlos reservation in Arizona. Two-thirds of the Apache refused to go to the reservation and fought for freedom. They did not want to face slavery or imprisonment. Geronimo was among them. In 1886, thousands of U.S. and Mexican troops hunted Geronimo's band of warriors. His family, unarmed, was murdered by U.S. Army and Mexican army while he was away from camp. Eventually, with only just over a dozen warriors left, Geronimo surrendered to Miles with the stipulation that they would be reunited with the other Apaches on the San Carlos reservation. Miles lied, and after accepting Geronimo's surrender, shipped them to Indian prisons in Florida instead after a couple of years of holding. Geronimo died after twenty-three years as a prisoner of war in U.S. custody.

If the military attacks on Indians secured the physical genocidal dimensions of Indian contact with the United States, reservation life secured the poverty of Indians and the U.S. attack on Indian cultures secured the cultural genocide of Indians. By the 1870s, many Indian reservations had become U.S. Army–guarded concentration camps with no game or capability to grow crops, desert lands fit only for rattlesnakes and rocks. Provisions promised by treaty from the U.S. government in return for Indian lands to over 200,000 Indians was corrupted by government agents and their partners, a practice known as the

"Indian ring." This constant and thoroughgoing theft of what was promised to Indian nations of already meager subsidies left Indians in abject poverty and starvation. Many whites capitalized on the fraud. As trains and wagons finally arrived with the sparse provisions, whites would steal most of them, leaving the worst for the Indians. Indians were given meat scraps and various left-over rations. And there was no punishment for those involved in the Indian ring even though it was a widely known practice among whites and the U.S. government.

To make matters even worse for Indians, the 1887 General Allotment Act disallowed communal land ownership and forced Indians to live like individual white farmers instead. Supported by an alliance of eastern reformers and western speculators, the Allotment Act attacked Indian sovereignty and communal ownership of land, making it extremely difficult for Indians to remain communal and maintain what little remained of their cultures. The allotment system declared small Indian children and animals as those who were allotted lands, but since they could not legally own them the lands were seized and given to whites who adopted the Indian children, leaving Indians with even less land than before as remaining reservation lands were sold to whites because Indians as individual families were given only a certain portion of reservation lands, not all of it as promised by treaties. During the allotment era, Indians lost two-thirds of the land that remained in their hands after reservation life. White greed for Indian lands knew no bounds, and treaties with Indians were simply ignored to accommodate white greed. Manifest destiny was a doctrine that most whites believed must be fulfilled to secure white supremacy or what many referred to as "God's will."

Then came the infamous land rushes in Oklahoma where Indians such as the Creek and Cherokee (that is, the Trail of Tears Indians!) of that region lost even more of their lands to whites. These, like the reservation lands, were promised by U.S. treaties to Indians as "unassailable" but not unlike other Indian lands of the past now in U.S. control, were lost forever to numerous white settlers and businesses. And it is very important to understand that U.S. businesses profited much from the great land grabs from Indians. Just as white wealth and U.S. wealth over the generations was built with the unpaid wages of African slaves, it was also built with the violent theft of Indian lands. Without Indian lands and unpaid slave wages of both Indians and blacks, it is highly improbable that there could have been wealth in the United States sufficient to support its growing economic strength throughout the years. Indeed, without the American holocaust there would be no United States as there would not have been an economic base sufficient to found and develop it.

As this brief history shows, Indians hardly ceded lands to whites and the United States voluntarily. They fought it mostly when they thought they could win. Moreover, it was the United States that coveted what was the Indian's by moral right, and the wealth gained largely through land possession and slave labor of Indians assisted greatly in the affordability of newly invented weapons of war in order to defeat Indians from coast to coast, as well as competing militaries such as the British and Mexican armies. It was a concerted effort of many U.S. citizens and their governmental leaders to eliminate Indians through a variety of means. The genocide was completed enough for the United States to become a military and industrial power in the twentieth century.[46] The U.S. citizens elected officials who devised and implemented policies of Indian genocide, removal, and land theft throughout generations. The genocide of the Indians by the United States was no accident, nor was it inevitable according to divine dictates, but the carefully crafted plan of white greed and avarice that eventually gained whites supremacy over much of a continent and enabled it to create and build wealth so great that today the United States stands as the most powerful country in the world—even despite its economic problems. There is, then, between most U.S. citizens, businesses and the political structure a collusion of sorts against the Indians, one that makes the United States collectively responsible for the genocidal land theft of the indigenous nations. It happened with the leadership of the three branches of government, supported by the business sectors and political victories of Jackson and others supported by most voters.

Although legally speaking it is not required that a guilty party apologize to the victim(s) of its wrongdoing(s), the extent of the harms committed by the U.S. government against various Indian nations would seem to suggest one. If this is true, then it would appear that both U.S. governmental (collective) feelings and expressions of guilt and remorse are suggested. That is, we would expect that the U.S. government would, in some official manner, express its genuine feelings of guilt and remorse to Indians, publicly denouncing its history of racially motivated oppression and holocaust against Indians and vowing that it never occur again. Of course, a clear record of governmental policies should reflect a support for such genuine feelings of guilt and remorse. But this is largely absent from U.S. history.

In light of this very concise history of U.S. oppression of Indians, it is reasonable, then, to hold *it* (the U.S. government) accountable for *its* past wrongdoings, pending some adequate argumentation in support of the morality of a statute of limitations on trying and punishing/compensating such crimes.[47] If it was just "discovered" that a corporation committed a gross wrongdoing (including murders) in 1900, would not justice dictate that the courts seek rectification in such a case, especially if that corporation is still in operation? The reasoning behind this might be either that the putatively guilty corporation is simply deserving of being forced to compensate some parties for the wrongdoing in question (a retributivist rationale) or that the corporation has gained an unfair advantage in committing such acts (a nonretributivist rationale). In either case, where matters are clear, past wrongs of such magnitude as what happened to many Indians require that justice be realized and there appears to be no adequate reason why past wrongs against Indians by U.S.

governmental representatives should not be treated in a similar manner as those in which we treat gross corporate wrongdoings that result from corporate representatives' actions or inactions.[48] As for the individuals or aggregate mobs of whites who committed theft, and violent crimes against Indians, in some cases some criminals' transfers of assets/fortunes can be traced to current U.S. citizens or institutions, thereby providing a possible source of reparations. Of course, one who inherits what has been acquired or transferred to her hardly deserves what she inherits if possession of it is in violation of the principle of morally just acquisitions and transfers and reparations are in order if the evidence of harmful wrongdoing is clear and there is an identifiable plaintiff to rightly receive the reparations from an identifiable perpetrator. One burden of argument, then, seems to be on those who would suggest that there is a moral statute of limitations on injustice. Furthermore, this burden of argument must be satisfied absent question-begging and/or self-serving reasoning.

A second problem with the objection to collective responsibility for U.S. reparations to Indians is that the principle of morally just acquisitions and transfers renders irrelevant the issue of whether or not the current U.S. government and its citizenry can legitimately be held accountable for the past injustices committed against Indians. In other words, the principle of morally just acquisitions and transfers renders otiose the objection to collective responsibility. And the principle does this in the following way: *If, say, most or all of the lands currently occupied by the U.S. government and its citizens are in fact occupied in violation of the principle, then it matters not whether current occupants of those lands are actually guilty of the illegitimate transfer of the lands. What truly matters here is whether or not the lands in question have indeed been transferred legitimately. Since most or all of them have not been legitimately transferred to current non-Indian occupants, then no such occupants can have legitimate and overriding moral claims to the lands they occupy.* The problem of collective responsibility simply does not affect this fact. It is a red herring given the plausibility of the principle of morally just acquisitions and transfers. This rebuttal to the objection to collective responsibility relies on a "weak" form of compensation.[49]

The significance of these replies to the objection to collective responsibility is that one provides a link between the U.S. government and many of the serious wrongs committed against Indians, satisfying the legal criteria of privity, standing, and nexus, each of which is necessary to establish a legal case for reparations. The second reply renders the objection to collective responsibility impotent insofar as Indians' moral rights to the lands in question are concerned. Thus the objection to collective responsibility fails to defeat premise 2 of the reparations argument, unless, of course, it can be shown by way of independent argument that there is a moral statute of limitations on injustice. In either case, the objection to collective responsibility fails to defeat the argument that today's U.S. government owes reparations to today's Indian heirs of oppression.

THE NO INDIAN CONCEPT OF
MORAL RIGHTS OBJECTION

Yet another objection to reparations, especially in the cases of Indian nations, is that the Indians had no conception of rights as entitlements to the lands in question. As Locke argues, Indians lived in a state of nature and had no government that would adjudicate rights claims to land and other property.[50] I shall refer to this as the *no Indian conception of moral rights objection*. It follows, according to this argument, that reparations to Indians are not required because lands were acquired from those who did not even believe in rights, not to mention land rights. Moreover, the objection continues, invaders acquired moral rights to at least some of the lands, though such rights may not have justified the violent and evil ways in which such lands were taken. (This part of the objection is developed elsewhere in the "acquired rights trumping original land rights objection."[51]) The no Indian conception of moral rights objection is a complex one, and is aimed at specific kinds of cases of putative reparations, such as those said to accrue to Indians.

In reply to this objection, it must be pointed out that it is a fallacy of reason to think that simply because someone does not believe that they possess X that they in fact do not have X. Many persons who do not enjoy the moral right, say, to a good education often do not understand that they have such a right. But it is hardly true that such persons do not have such rights, morally speaking. For they might simply be ignorant or fearful of claiming such rights, especially in the face of coercive force, propaganda, and so on. Thus the argument that Indians should not be awarded reparations for past injustices due to the claim that Indians had no notion of rights is beside the point. The real issue here is whether or not the balance of human reason requires that reparations be awarded to Indians.

But even if it were true that the moral requirement of reparations to Indians is contingent on Indians, many of whom held some concept of rights, one must ask which rights concept is required? Given that philosophers have not themselves settled on a singular notion of rights (indeed, many doubt the very sense of rights talk itself![52]), it can hardly be argued that reparations to Indians are required only if there is a singular notion of rights among Indians.[53] So it appears that the question here is whether or not Indians, or at least many of them, had some working idea of rights, especially rights to the lands on which they resided and that which in most cases was subsequently and forcibly taken from them. On this score, E. Pauline Johnson, a Mohawkan poet, writes:

> Starved with a hollow hunger, we owe to you and your race.
> What have you left to us of land, what have you left of game,
> What have you brought but evil, and curses since you came?
> How have you paid us for *our* game? how paid us for *our* land? . . .
> You say the cattle are not ours, your meat is not our meat;

When *you* pay for the land you live in, *we'll* pay for the meat we eat.
Give back *our* land and *our* country, give back *our* herds of game;
Give back the furs and the forests that were *ours* before you came; . . .[54]
But they forget we Indians *owned* the land
From ocean unto ocean; that they stand
Upon a soil that centuries agone
Was *our* sole kingdom and *our right alone*. . . .
By *right*, by birth we Indians *own* these lands, . . .[55]

Other Indians expressed notions of rights, in particular, rights held against invaders of their lands. Sitting Bull states that "What treaty that the whites have kept has the red man broken? Not one. What treaty that the white man ever made with us have they kept? Not one. Where are *our* lands? Where are *our* waters? Who owns them now? Is it wrong for me to love my own?"[56] Old Tassel, in a letter to the South Carolina governor (1776) stated that "We are the first people that ever lived on this land; it is ours."[57] In a letter to John Ross, Aitooweyah, The Stud, and Knock Down wrote: "We the great mass of the people think only of the love of our land . . . where we were brought up . . . for we say to you that our father who sits in Heaven gave it to us."[58] In 1860, Ross advised the Cherokee council that "our duty is to stand by *our rights*" and he wrote to Ben McCulloch that "our country and our institutions are our own. . . . They are sacred and valuable to us as are those of your own . . . I am determined to do no act that shall furnish any pretext to either of the contending parties to overrun *our country* and destroy *our rights*."[59] Isaac Warrior of the Seneca once said, "Then we always thought . . . when we ran away we did nothing, and *always consider the land we have as ours yet*, and we want to stand there yet."[60] Ten Bears of the Comanche once said, "I want no blood upon *my land* to stain the grass. I want it clear and pure, and I want it so that all who go through among my people may find peace when they come in and leave it when they go out."[61] Satanta added: "A long time ago *this land belonged to our fathers*; but when I go up the [Arkansas] river I see camps of soldiers on its banks. These soldiers cut down *my timber*; they kill *my buffalo*; and when I see that it feels as if my heart would burst with sorrow."[62] Towaconie Jim of the Wichita once said, "We have always thought *our lands would remain ours*, and never be divided in severalty, and *it can never be done with our consent*. The Government treats us as if we had no *rights*, but we have always lived at our present place, and that is *our home*."[63] Certainly these words contain at least a prereflective notion of rights as entitlements to sovereignty over natural resources, for those, that is, who acquire them legitimately and care for them responsibly. So it is simply false, and perhaps even unusually insulting, to think that rights are indicative of a civilized society and that Indians were too barbaric to have and understand some notion of rights which would be recognizable today.

Moreover, as James Tully insightfully points out, various Indian nations indeed had governments which recognized equality and trust in negotiations and treaties between parties, and European invaders themselves (at least many colonists) recognized Indians as being sovereign nations with whom treaties could and should be negotiated and signed.[64] Hence the baselessness of Locke's rather naive analysis of Indian peoples as having no governments that articulate and protect property rights, including land rights.

It is false, then, to claim that the moral requirement of reparations is contingent on the wronged party having a sense or conception of rights which would ground the reparations, and it is also false of many Indians in particular that they had nothing akin to a contemporary notion of rights, broadly construed. One wonders why the constant cries for Indian rights to be respected were ignored by the majority of the European invaders and especially by the U.S. government and its citizenry each of whom proclaimed to respect the rights of all humans. One plausible answer is that the treatment of Indians by most European invaders was nothing short of racist in their construing and treating them as "savages," a racism motivated perhaps by fear, ignorance, a sense of self-superiority European invaders obtained from, among other things, certain religious beliefs.

THE HISTORICAL REPARATIONS OBJECTION

Yet another objection to reparations to Indians is that reparations have already been paid to Indian nations in the past for wrongs committed by the U.S. government. I shall refer to this objection as the *historical reparations objection*. In the case of those awarded to Indians by the United States, there are the examples of Georgia's restoration of many Cherokee landmarks and a newspaper plant and other buildings in New Echota, and Georgia's repealing of its repressive anti-Indian laws of 1830. (It took until 1962 for this to occur, however.) Moreover, in 1956 the Pawnees were awarded over $1,000,000 in a suit they brought before the Indian Claims Commission for land taken from them in Iowa, Kansas, and Missouri. In 1881, the Poncas were compensated by the U.S. Congress for their ill-treatment by the Court of Omaha, Kansas. For the illegal seizure of the Black Hills in 1876, then occupied by the Sioux, compensation was offered. In 1927, the Shoshonis were paid over $6,000,000 for land illegally seized from them (the amount was for the appraised value of *half* of their land, however). More recently, in 1971 the U.S. Congress passed the Alaska Native Claims Settlement Act which provided Indians in that state $962,500,000 and 44,000,000 acres of land.[65] And in 1995, the State of Hawai'i settled *Ka'ai'ai v. Drake* in what is referred to as the Hawai'ian Trust Lands, where indigenous Hawai'ians were awarded $600,000,000 for the mismanagement of the Hawai'ian Homelands Trust.[66] There are a few other instances of reparations to certain Indian nations.[67]

However, the historical reparations objection is based on evidence of reparations to a few Indian nations for property rights violations. There is a multi-
fold difficulty here. First, such reparations were hardly sufficient to serve as
anywhere close to adequate compensations for the property, "maltransfers,"
damages, and other matters in question. Furthermore, the objection ignores
completely the question of reparations for undeserved violence in the form of
human rights violations against Indians in the cases of reparations to main-
land U.S. Indians; much of such violence was inflicted on various Indians by
the U.S. military in genocidal or holocaust proportions. And as for Alaskan
and Hawai'ian Indians, the reparations cannot possibly suffice for the destruction of those cultures. Finally, it ignores the fact that the vast majority of property rights violations and civil rights violations against Indians in general are
as of yet *un*compensated. Recall that there were over 100 such nations most
of which were thriving at the time of European contact and even until the
point of the founding of the United States. That there have been a few cases
of Indian reparations, however inadequate, hardly shows that Indians as a
whole have been reparated. The historical reparations objection, then, seems
to be more of a non sequitur than a genuine concern.[68] Indeed, it actually
serves as a precedent for a far more comprehensive reparations policy for
Indians.

THE ACQUIRED RIGHTS TRUMPING ORIGINAL
LAND RIGHTS OBJECTION

Some would argue that certain rights can be acquired where previously there
were no such rights. In particular, some would object to the moral requirement of reparations to Indians on the grounds that the U.S. descendants of
the European invaders are not themselves morally accountable for the evils
inflicted on earlier Indians peoples in America, thus escaping the pale of moral
retrospective liability responsibility on which such reparations are said to be
based. Those who currently reside on putatively U.S. soil and who are not
Indians did not secure the land illicitly. Furthermore, it is argued, recent generations of U.S. citizens have actually acquired moral rights to the lands on
which they reside.[69] What grounds such rights? To be sure, many U.S. citizens
have mixed their labor with the land in the forms of building/purchasing
homes, working the land, and so on.[70] This Lockean point regarding what one
has a right to is said to ground the moral rights of contemporary U.S. citizens
to "their" land. In addition, one might argue that what the supporters of reparations to Indians neglect to see is that there is more to this matter than mere
original land acquisition rights. There are also the issues of merit and desert.
Arguments for reparations to Indians based on original land acquisition are
implausible given that they ignore the fact that current non-Indians peoples
have since acquired rights to the lands based on their acquiring such lands

legitimately. Because property (including land) rights change over time, argues David Lyons, today's Indians would probably not have rights to their ancestors' lands even had they not been often forcibly stolen from them by the U.S. government. Thus reparations to Indians by the U.S. government for the past injustices are unwarranted.[71] I shall refer to this as the *acquired rights trumping original land rights objection.*

But the acquired rights trumping original land rights objection is flawed, and for several reasons. First, reparations do *not* require that those who pay them are morally accountable for the wrongdoing that justifies—or even requires—them. This point was addressed when answering the objection from historical complexity and the objection to collective responsibility. Suffice it to add that, as Joel Feinberg argues, there are cases of collective liability where there is no fault distributed among members of a collective.[72] Even apart from collectives, however, "a person may incur legal liability even though they were not in any sense responsible for the event that triggered the liability. Restitutionary liability of an innocent, passive recipient of a mistaken payment or beneficiary of fraud is a good example. There may . . . be both responsibility without legal liability, and legal liability without responsibility."[73] Secondly, a ruthless invader can steal land and then mix her labor with it and thereby, according to the Lockean argument, gain rights to the stolen land. This might serve well the purposes of invaders seeking to establish their own putative democracy. Yet this is hardly morally justified. Furthermore, that invader's selling her ill-gotten land to an "innocent" party is a clear violation of the principle of morally just acquisitions and transfers. In a similar way, then, the mixing of one's labor with the land is insufficient to ground a moral right had by U.S. citizens to the lands in question. Furthermore, as Waldron argues,

> The Lockean image of labor (whether it is individual or cooperative) being literally embedded or mixed in an object is incoherent. . . . For it would be impossible to explain how property rights thus acquired could be alienable—how they could be transferred, through sale or gift, from one person to another—without offense to the personality of the original acquirer.[74]

So something else must be true to make plausible the claim that current U.S. citizens have overriding moral rights to the lands on which they reside. But what would that be, except that one must inherit or acquire land *without* it being the case that the principle of morally just acquisitions and transfers is violated? One cannot legitimately inherit or deserve what has been acquired or transferred by way of immorality or injustice. As Christine M. Korsgaard argues, "If a theft or swindle succeeds, we do not take it that the new distribution of property is legitimate."[75] Finally, if some U.S. citizens have moral rights to "their" lands by "just" inheritance, then why would we not think that original land rights of Indian peoples in turn accrue to current Indians?[76] This would mean that the real question of which set of moral rights claims/interests "trumps" another's boils down to, among other things, whether or not there was a violation of the principle of morally just acquisitions and transfers concerning what is now deemed U.S. territory.

It might be argued, perhaps instead of there being a moral statute of limitations on injustice, that there is a justified limitation of time placed on rights claims, and that the limitation on the claim of a right to reparations has expired for Indians to justly claim their rights to the lands. In U.S. law, this is referred to as the "*Laches* doctrine": If there is a significant amount of time that passes without a wronged parties attempting to claim its right to something, then the claimant loses her right to that thing. Or, at the very least, the right "fades" over time.[77]

But this line of reasoning neglects the historical reality that at several points in time various Indian nations have publicly claimed their land rights—even to the U.S. government! That such claims were made repeatedly and not respected is a matter of historical fact, and that the claims of many Indians were not respected fails to count as evidence for the claim that the opportunity to claim the right to reparations has truly expired.[78] For many Indians satisfied the condition in question. But their pleas were simply ignored or turned away. We must bear in mind that an unjust legal system's failure to uphold Indian claims to lands (and compensation for crimes constituting violence to persons, among other things) hardly serves as a rational foundation for a moral (or even a legal) statute of limitations on Indian claims concerning what they deserve as compensation for wrongdoings. Reparations to Indians in the United States are either morally required or they are not, regardless of the fact that morally corrupted legislative and judicial systems were put in place to (among other things) bias decisions against Indian claims, thus supporting the idea of the expiration of the statute of limitations on Indian land claims. Furthermore, that contemporary U.S. citizens are not causally responsible for the past wrongs committed against Indians in no way nullifies the fact that today's lands are, in the main, occupied by those who have acquired them through a chain of possessions which is in clear violation of the principle of morally just acquisitions and transfers. For as was pointed out in the refutation of the objection to collective responsibility, that one has not wronged Indians in some direct way hardly justifies one being in the possession of stolen or ill-gotten property. Thus there needs to be a reason other than the one provided by the moral statute of limitations advocates that would ground the acquisition of moral rights to lands now occupied by U.S. citizens.

Some might argue, along the lines noted in the historical section of this chapter, that the Lockean proviso grounds the rights of current U.S. citizens to the lands on which they reside in that Indians in the distant past had more land than they could use, and that the Indians had no right to deprive European "invaders" of their settlement of North American lands that were not in use by Indians. However, this line of reasoning is problematic for the following reasons. First, most of the land acquired by the European invaders (including the U.S. government) was by way of force and fraud against Indians. So even if Indians had an obligation (based on the Lockean proviso) to share some of the North American lands with others, it does not follow that the lands had to be shared with those who dealt Indians injustices of the harshest orders. This holds whether the invaders were conquering "explorers" or "mere settlers." The possible difference between these two groups in terms of their putative collective moral liability for harms against Indians does not diminish the fact that each group played an important role in the unjust acquisitions and transfers of lands that were inhabited by Indians.

Secondly, the Lockean proviso states that one has a right to X to the extent that there is enough and as good of X for others.[79] However, U.S. history is replete with examples of Indians *welcoming with open arms* European invaders, under the assumption, no doubt, that something like the principle of morally just acquisitions and transfers would not be violated in the course of the latter groups' settling the lands. So Indians, by and large and from the outset of the invasion of the Americas, acted in congruence with the Lockean proviso both in terms of their dealings with non-Indians and in terms of their dealings with most other Indians. Yet history tells the complicated and dismal stories of injustices Indians experienced in losing their lands oftentimes violently to European invaders, hardly a moral foundation for current U.S. claims to North American lands.[80]

Moreover, it is unclear whether the Lockean proviso was violated by Indians on other grounds. Considering that there were hundreds of such nations in North America, and that many of them were nomadic, it is not at all certain that there was sufficient land and resources for them to share with Europeans.[81] This is especially plausible if one accords to Indians the same moral and legal right to have families, and to meet the needs of expanding families (including the need for additional land). Thus it is difficult to see how original rights of Indians to the lands and resources in question are trumped by subsequent European putative rights to the same lands and resources for reasons of the Lockean proviso.

It should be acknowledged that various of the nations that constitute Indians as a broad set of ethnic groups have varying degrees of experiences with oppression at the hands of the European invaders, and that a principle of proportionality must be used to distinguish variant levels of reparations to different Indian nations, that is, where history is clear about the differences in evil experienced by them. In general, however, whether it be the Navajos, the Cherokees, the Mohawks, the Senecas, or other Indian nations, sufficient evils have been perpetrated against them by the U.S. government that would require some form of compensatory reparations of a significant measure.[82] One obvious reason for this is noted by George Sher: "In the case of . . . Indians, . . . we may indeed have enough information to suggest that most current group members are worse off than they would be in the absence of some initial wrong."[83] Yet it is unnecessary to impose a standard of strict proportionality that the law cannot uphold even in much easier cases. After all, one possible strategy is to argue that even if compensating for such wrongs would not restore full justice to Indians, it would at least bring Indians substantially closer to justice than they currently stand.

If the objections to reparations to Indians in the United States are defeasible for the reasons given herein, then the presumptive case in favor of reparations to Indians gains strength. Barring further argumentation that would render morally problematic such reparations, then, a case for such reparations has been made along the following lines.[84] To the extent that history is unambiguous concerning the extent of guilt, fault, wrongdoing, and the identities of perpetrators and victims of historic injustices, policies of reparations to Indians should be enacted according to some fundamentally sound principle of proportional compensation.

If the foregoing analysis is sound, then one hope that the United States has of dragging itself out of the mire of its own perpetration of historic injustices against Indians is for it to institute adequate policies of reparations to them. Even so, such policies must receive far more commitment by the U.S. government than the treaties made by the U.S. government with Indian nations had received in the past. What is also needed is a national sense of shame-based guilt[85] and collective remorse[86] for the roles that the U.S. government and its citizenry played in founding the United States. Yet if such shame requires a higher-level self-consciousness,[87] this might well be precisely what U.S. society lacks, providing its critics with ammunition for claims of the fundamental immorality of the United States in general. For a society that is based on unrectified injustice is itself unjust. But a society that simply refuses to admit its unjust history toward others not only remains unjust on balance, but serves as a stark reminder of the unabashed arrogance of its unspeakable badness.

If the objections to reparations to Indians are specious for at least the reasons noted, and if the principle of morally just acquisitions and transfers is plausible and applicable to the Indian experiences, then the balance of reason suggests at least the prima facie plausibility of some U.S. policy of reparations to Indians. Moreover, it is incumbent on the supporter of such reparations to devise a plausible policy of reparations. Although a full-fledged theory and policy of reparations to Indians is beyond the scope of this book, chapter 9 is devoted to this issue.

7

Reparations to Blacks

Having in the previous chapter argued in favor of the reparations argument as it applies to the case of American Indians, I shall now consider to what extent a slightly modified version of the same argument might ground the case of compensatory reparations to blacks.[1] But prior to engaging this problem, it is important to explore some preliminary matters of significance, including some ways in which the problem of reparations to blacks differs from the problem of Indian reparations. First, as noted in chapter 1, it is crucial to separate the question of whether or not reparations to blacks is morally justified (or even required) from the question of which policies of reparations would be justified (or even required) if it turns out that such reparations are justified in the first place. The reason why this is an important distinction is that there are certain objections to reparations to blacks which seem to conflate the two questions, unwarrantedly assuming, for instance, given the problem of how to exact reparative justice, that it somehow follows that reparations to blacks are unjustified. Such an inference would follow, it might be assumed, from "ought implies can." But even if it were the case that no proposed reparations policy to date is plausible for whatever reasons, it would not follow logically that blacks are not owed *reparations of a just nature*. To think otherwise would be to fallaciously infer that our supposed inability to work through the problem of how to award reparations logically implies something about what blacks deserve, in this case, as a matter of corrective justice through compensation. For this reason, we must not confuse the question of the moral justification and requirement of reparations to blacks with the question of how, if such reparations are indeed justified and required (the question of moral justification relative to reparations), they ought to be awarded (the question of policy relative to reparations). The former is a question of deserved compensation based on injustices experienced by blacks and their forebears, the latter is a question of how such reparations, assuming they are deserved, are to be awarded to blacks. The same conceptual point holds just as well in the case of reparations to Indians, as discussed in the previous chapter. In this chapter, I discuss the question of justification, while I postpone until chapter 9 the question of policy.

One obvious difference between the experiences of Indians and blacks is that, while Indians experienced both gross rights violations (including genocide and slavery) and massive land theft at the hands of both the United States government and several of its citizenry, blacks for the most part experienced human rights violations (but not the latter) by way of the slave trade. In fact, there is a real sense in which the human rights violations of black slavery were somewhat less severe than those suffered by Indians. Not only were several Indians enslaved as were (by definition, all) blacks' ancestors, and not only were both groups the victims of brutal forms of acculturation (for the former it took the form of acculturating Indian children in the ways of whiteness in Indian Boarding Schools, for instance, for the latter it took the form of infesting African slaves with various forms of insidious "Christian" religion, however well-intentioned, in the guise of missionary work with "savages"[2]), but as a general rule African slaves were not the subjects of genocide as were Indians. Instead, they were treated as the valuable "property" they were by southern slave masters, slave traders, and slave transporters each of whom, among others, saw slaves as mere commodities. So there is a sense in which reparations to Indians, if based on a principle of proportionality of reparations to harms inflicted, ought to be greater than reparations granted to blacks. For not only did Indians as a group suffer the loss of an entire continent of land and natural minerals and other resources to the United States (as well as to Canada, Mexico, Brasil, Colombia, England, Spain, Portugal, etc.), but the loss of lives and other forms of human sufferings experienced by them are not even rivaled by the horrendous evils of U.S. slavery. Nonetheless, it might be argued with some plausibility that the enslavement of blacks entailed an array of evils that are thought to be such that, if experienced, one is better off dead.[3] With this understanding, it is nonetheless helpful to investigate philosophically the plausibility of claims to black reparations for slavery of Africans in the United States. For it is quite clear that the evils experienced respectively by Indians and blacks together stand in a class by themselves relative to whatever wrongdoings experienced by other groups at the hands of the U.S. government.[4]

Another difference between the cases of Indian and black oppression is that the Indian experiences often, but not always, involved treaties and their being broken by the U.S. government, while U.S. enslavement of Africans involved no such treaties. This is easily explained by the fact that treaties are made between governing bodies, and African slaves in the United States did not constitute a governing body. Nor were they considered by most U.S. citizens as sufficiently human with whom to forge treaties. Perhaps this is one reason why blacks posed less of a threat to "manifest destiny" than did Indians, as suggested elsewhere.[5] As I pointed out in the previous chapter, without Indian and black slavery in the United States, it is difficult to imagine how the U.S.

empire would have even come about. For it provided much of the capital necessary to, among other things, garner weapons of mass, though not immediate, destruction in order to subdue entire Indian and European nations.

Nonetheless, it is vital to make sure that we have at least an adequate grasp of what blacks experienced at the hands of their U.S. oppressors.[6] It is not only the physical brutality of enslavement itself, but the fact is that it was race-based slavery wherein the slavemasters and slave traders actually believed in the (at best) partial humanity of blacks, quite apart from slavery. This means that in virtually every aspect of U.S. culture there were reminders of antiblack racism that rooted slavery. The beatings, rapings, kidnappings, familial separations, and acculturation were certainly part of the ongoing lives of slaves. But we must not forget about the constant violent and nonviolent threats to well-being that blacks encountered incessantly even during and post-Reconstruction. If slavery kept blacks from exercising their right to work as they pleased (e.g., in whatever area of work they desired and were capable), Jim Crow masterfully continued this severe rights violation. To add insult to injury, black slaves were not even paid a minimum wage for their work (they were unpaid, of course). And all of this in "exchange" for miserable living conditions of the typical slave quarters! Thus blacks, males and females, worked as either "house niggers" or "field niggers" for whites, and more often than not most of the day and even into the night, at the beck and call of white men and white women.

But there is much more to this story of white on black oppression. The previous paragraph noted some of the direct effects of slavery on black lives. But there are indirect effects as well. While white society had all of the rights and privileges that came with first-class citizenship, blacks were prohibited, for generations under U.S. rule, from earning wages so that they could purchase property, invest income, become well educated in good schools so that they could then attend and graduate from the best universities. Most of them could not then afford to start their own businesses, and when a few did, many were met with threats or violence that drove them out of business so that whites could continue their dominance in "their" society. Blacks could not, then, bequeath their assets and wealth to their heirs as whites could theirs and did for generations until blacks could then do so. But more than that, the theft of unpaid black wages by whites infused itself so deeply into U.S. economic and social and political structures that there is scarcely today an area of the U.S. economy that has not been infected with the blood money of black slave labor. Generations of theft of the labor value of slaves has a way of infiltrating virtually every aspect of an economy. Consider, for instance, the fact that black slave labor made it easy for slavers to garner and develop wealth, and to the extent that slavery formed part of the basis of the economy for other whites to afford products and services, thereby enabling each party to build wealth—white wealth—to bequeath, among other things and for the most part, to white heirs. So while blacks could not pass on their wealth to their heirs because it was appropriated by whites in the form of unpaid slave labor, whites enjoyed the possibility (and for many, the reality) of bequeathing their wealth to their heirs. As Malcolm X states of blacks in the United States,

> The greatest contribution to this country was that which was contributed by the black man. . . . Now, when you see this, and then you stop and consider the wages that were kept back from millions of black people, not for one year but for 310 years, you'll see how this country got so rich so fast. And what the economy as strong as it is today. And all that, and all that slave labor that was amassed in unpaid wages, is due someone today. And you're not giving us anything when we say that it's time to collect.[7]

Indeed, white oppression of blacks succeeded in making it possible for many whites to become well-off at the expense of black slave labor. Again, the legacies of slavery were solidified by Jim Crow, even after the Civil Rights Act of 1875.[8] Indeed, black slavery was a "human rights crime without parallel in the modern world," whether or not it was "far and away the most heinous human rights crime visited upon any group of people in the world over the last five hundred years."[9]

This oppression of blacks by whites poses at least two ethical problems. One is the unjust enrichment problem, another is the harm-based problem. It is important to separate these two matters, as one can violate another's rights by way of wrongfully harming them, but without enriching oneself in the process. But in the case of U.S. slavery, in one significant way or another, whites unjustly enriched themselves (at least, in a short-term sense) at the expense of blacks. This is true of poor whites as well as well-off ones, as each enjoyed white privileges such as "first hired, last fired" that blacks (and Indians) did not. And this unjust enrichment is part of the reason why the United States gained the economic and political power that enabled it to become the empire it is today. Moreover, it is how so many whites became so well-off (in a long-term sense), as they were able to legally inherit wealth that blacks (and Indians) could not, and it was the blacks (and Indians) from whom much of the white wealth was gotten. So not only were the initial theft of Indian lands and unpaid slave wages of Indians and blacks ill-gotten gains that led many whites to wealth or at the very least reasonable sustenance, but they were able to pass on their economic well-being to their white heirs. Moreover, the U.S. economy more generally benefited greatly from these unpaid wages of slavery.

However, even absent the ill-gotten gains from black slavery, whites still wrongfully harmed blacks. If, as Joel Feinberg argues, to harm another is to unwarrantedly set back their legitimate interest,[10] then various harms were wrought on blacks as the result of slavery. First, there was the loss of their valid interest in their own personal autonomy, including their freedom to pursue life, liberty, and happiness. Second, there was the setting back of their valid interest in personal safety and equal protection under the law. Third, there was the setting back of their valid interest in receiving a fair wage for the value of their labor. Fourth, there was the setting back of their valid interest in religious and cultural freedom. These are some of the fundamental harms experienced by blacks as the result of their enslavement in the United States. So the problem of black reparations finds solid grounding in either unjust enrichment, harmful wrongdoing against blacks, or both.

Recall the reparations argument from the previous chapter concerning the oppression of Indians by the United States herein modified for the case of U.S. blacks:

1. As much as is humanly possible, instances of clear and substantial historic rights violations ought to be rectified by way of reparations.
2. The U.S. government has committed substantial historic rights violations against millions of U.S. blacks.[11]
3. Therefore, the historic rights violations of the U.S. government against U.S. blacks ought to be rectified by way of reparations, as much as humanly possible.

Like the argument for Indian reparations, this one focuses on the U.S. government as the primary perpetrator of oppression against blacks that would justify and require reparations to blacks, though it is also the case that state and local governments as well as various businesses and nongovernmental organizations (NGOs) also severely harmed blacks and benefited unjustly from black oppression. As with the argument for reparations focusing on Indians, there are challenges that might be raised to the move from 2 to 3 in the above argument. I shall consider the objection from historical complexity and the objection to collective responsibility.[12]

It is interesting to note that these objections, unlike the objections to Indian reparations, do *not* include objections involving land claims by blacks. Nor does it involve claims to national sovereignty. Thus there is a sense in which the reparations argument pertaining to the black experience is simpler (not simple, but simpl*er*) than the case of Indian reparations. For in the case of Indian reparations, it would seem that any reparations settlement which did not involve a substantial return of land to them is grossly unjust, especially in light of the plausibility of the principle of morally just acquisitions and transfers (discussed in the previous chapter), and the importance of land to Indians' philosophies and religions. Yet in the case of blacks, reparations might well be made in the form of a policy the details of which are discussed in chapter 9.

An important similarity between Indian and black reparations cases is that each group would appear to have a case not only against the U.S. government, but also against other colonial governments and powers such as Portugal, Spain, England, the Netherlands, France, the Roman Catholic Church, various Southern Baptist and certain other Protestant churches, and a number of other extant countries, businesses, and NGOs which played substantial roles in the transatlantic slave trade and/or the colonization of the Americas, especially North America. So if the respective cases for Indians and black reparations go through as they target the United States, then they might well also succeed if they target those other collectives co-responsible for such antiblack racist oppression. One can only wonder and estimate if such countries and organizations would be as well-off as they are today if not for the tremendous assistance of free land, natural resources, and free labor which were acquired by violent force or fraud against Indians, enslaved Africans, and blacks under Jim Crow.[13]

The main question before us in this chapter is whether or not the United States in particular owes reparations to blacks for the brutality of slavery in the United States. However, it is not only the physical and psychological brutality of slavery that is at issue, but the wrongful gain by way of coerced free labor power and the value that it brings illicitly to slaveholders in particular, and to an entire U.S. economy more generally, and the incessant refusal over generations of the U.S. government to rectify its injustices against blacks by way of slavery. I refer to this argument as a "Marxist" one in that it is based primarily, though not exclusively, on the illicit (because forced) labor power of Africans and the illicit (because forced) extraction of labor value from their labor power, which then illicitly (because forced from the slaves) enriched not only slaveholders, but the southern and U.S. economies more generally.[14] But as I shall argue, this Marxist argument hardly depends on whether or not anyone—slaveholder or not—benefited (in the sense of profited, on balance) from the forced labor power of Africans.

It is important, moreover, to point out that it is not only the injustice of black slavery (e.g., slavery of Africans in the United States) that is at issue, but also Jim Crow and all of the significant ramifications of segregation throughout the entire United States for generations subsequent to slavery. In the words of one author, my theory would be "thick," as a "thin" theory of reparations to blacks would base the positive reparations argument on the institutional racism against blacks post-slavery.[15]

THE HISTORICAL REPARATIONS
OBJECTION TO BLACK REPARATIONS

It might be thought that blacks have already received a certain measure of reparations from the United States, thereby rendering otiose my argument to the contrary. So it is important to investigate briefly the history of what might be thought to amount to reparations to blacks and see if the objection is plausible as a challenge to the reparations argument above.

There is important precedent for reparations to blacks in the United States. In 1781, Quock Walker, a Massachusetts slave, sued his owner for freedom as he claimed he was unjustly enslaved. He won his suit and was freed, though there is no indication that he was compensated.[16] Walker's was but one of a few such cases of wrongfully enslaved blacks who won their freedom through the courts (see *Negro Peter v. Steel* [Pennsylvania, 1801]; *Thompson v. Wilmost* [Kentucky, 1809]).[17] However, though such suits won freedom for the wrongfully (legally speaking) enslaved blacks, there seems to be only one case on record where a black person who sued for (legally) wrongful enslavement issued in monetary compensation for the ex-slave: "One Missouri court even awarded compensation to a former slave who was wrongfully held in bondage."[18] However, these seem to be the extent of the "successes" of reparations to blacks in the United States. Other forms of redress were attempted. Abraham Lincoln's Emancipation Proclamation in 1862 was seen by many as a form of redress, though the Lincoln address said nothing about compensation for blacks for the injustices of slavery. And even though in 1865 General William Tecumsa Sherman set aside hundreds of thousands of acres of land on the Georgia coast for ex-slaves (each ex-slave's family was to receive forty acres and a military-loaned mule, from which the saying, "forty acres and a mule" is derived), Andrew Johnson revoked the order and used the military instead to evict blacks from the area.[19] Although the Freedman's Bureau was established in 1865 to transition ex-slaves into emancipation during Reconstruction, its sometimes successful efforts were often undermined by policies enacted by other governmental agencies or officials. "Black codes" were enforced by local governments and their respective law enforcement agencies, and they were provided tremendous strength when in 1876 the U.S. Supreme Court limited the Enforcement Act of 1870 such that the U.S. Congress had no authority to punish local crimes (*U.S. v. Cruickshank*). Numerous ex-slaves ended up working for their former owners, and for wages that were the lowest in the economic system. Thus even the best that the United States had to offer in terms of "reparations" for black slavery did not amount to very much, unless one counts various civil rights acts and court decisions that sought to provide blacks equal opportunities in education, employment, and housing, and unless one counts various apologia offered by U.S. presidents.[20] The equal opportunity legislation targeted the disadvantaged as a whole, not just blacks. Thus to think of these measures as means of reparations to blacks is to stretch beyond credulity the meaning of "reparations." Ironically, significant reparations for slavery were awarded not to ex-slaves or their heirs, but to some former slaveholders for the economic losses sustained by them as the result of changes in U.S. policies regarding slavery! One example is the 1864 congressional compensation to slaveholders who remained loyal to the Union wherein $3,000 was paid to each such slaveholder in Washington, D.C., for each slave "lost" to emancipation. Thus the evidence for the claim that blacks have already been awarded reparations for slavery or Jim Crow is very weak at best. In this way, black reparations by the United States are somewhat different from Indian reparations by the United States.

Perhaps what is meant by the objection under consideration is that blacks have received a fair amount of reparations by way of affirmative action programs. But as we saw in chapter 1, it is a category mistake to construe reparations in terms of affirmative action. So it is unclear just how this objection to reparations to blacks counts as worthy of further consideration.

BLACK REPARATIONS AND COLLECTIVE MORAL RESPONSIBILITY

I concur with Bernard R. Boxill and Howard McGary that what is relevant to the case for black reparations by the U.S. government is a plausible case for collective moral responsibility, along with the historical fact of human rights violations. However, each of these points must lead to the conclusion that the current U.S. government owes reparations to contemporary blacks for the said atrocities of the distant and more recent past. The conditions necessary and sufficient for collective moral responsibility have been articulated and defended in chapter 5. However, even assuming the plausibility of the notion of collective responsibility, it simply will not suffice to show that there were indeed evils that were perpetrated against blacks, even by the U.S. government, without also linking the normative case for reparations to the present day.

So even if it is true, as Boxill argues of black slavery, that

> the slaves had an indisputable moral right to the product of their labor; these products were stolen from them by the slave masters who ultimately passed them on to their descendants; the slaves presumably have conferred their rights of ownership to their descendants; thus, the descendants of slave masters are in possession of wealth to which the descendants of slaves have rights; hence, the descendants of slave masters must return this wealth to the descendants of slaves with a concession that they were not rightfully in possession of it,[21]

McGary is correct in claiming of Boxill's argument that

> it fails to show how whites who are not the descendants of slave masters owe a debt of justice to black Americans. In order to argue that the total white community owes the total black community reparations, we must present an argument that shows how all whites, even recent immigrants benefited from slavery and how all blacks felts [sic] its damaging effects.[22]

Although I find the cumulative effect of both Boxill's and McGary's arguments convincing, I shall argue that their unjust enrichment argument, though insightful, is not necessary for establishing the case for black reparations. For even if no slave master (or a descendant of one) ever benefited (in the profiting sense of "benefited") from the enslavement of Africans or the racist treatment of their descendants in the United States, reparations might nonetheless be owed to blacks today. But how might this be the case? And precisely by whom or what ought the reparations to be paid, and to whom, and what kind and how much reparations ought to be awarded?

Prior to examining in depth some other objections to black reparations, it is important to gain a perspective on the implications of a certain line of reasoning regarding the matter. Consider the *objection from intergenerational justice* which states that justice between generations is problematic because those who pay reparations at time t_{n+1} for significant injustices at t_n must be the ones directly guilty and at fault for the wrongs done to the reparated group. Intergenerational justice is problematic because it violates precisely this rule, making allegedly innocent parties pay for what other guilty parties did in wrongfully harming others. It is clear how this objection underlies a concern about collective moral responsibility. Indeed, the objection from intergenerational justice seems to be the foundation of the objection to collective responsibility.

It is important to understand, however, that if the objection from intergenerational justice counts against reparations to blacks, then by parity of reasoning it also counts to a significant degree against reparations to Israel by Germany prior to the attempted genocide of Jewish persons by the Nazi regime during the World War II era. Not only does it count in some significant measure against the case for reparations to Israel by Germany, but it also counts against the case for reparations to certain Japanese Americans by the United States for the internment of many Japanese and other Asian Americans during the same era. The reason that the objection from intergenerational justice counts in some significant measure against these historic acts of reparations is that—even though many German and U.S. citizens who bore the fiscal brunt of such reparations were actually alive as adults during the oppression of Jewish persons during the Nazi attempt to extinguish them and during the U.S. oppression of Japanese Americans—millions of "innocent" German and U.S. citizens ended up paying the reparations in each case, citizens who themselves were children, or not even born at the time of the atrocities in question. Thus there is a violation of the principle that forms the bedrock of the objection from intergenerational justice, namely, *that those who are innocent must not suffer harm or be forced to compensate for wrongful harms they did not cause.* There is indeed a regress argument at work here, one which attempts to render problematic any attempt to justify reparations to Israel and Japanese Americans in that some allegedly innocent parties end up paying the fiscal brunt of the reparations payments, persons who in some cases could not have had anything whatsoever to do with the oppressive events in question.

With this point made, is it true that "we must present an argument that shows how all whites, even recent immigrants benefited from slavery and how all blacks felts [*sic*] its damaging effects" as McGary argues? Not only do we not *need* to present such an argument, but I argue that we *ought* not to, and for the following reason. It is entirely possible that there are significant numbers of folk who benefited *accidentally* from the enslavement of Africans in the United States. Yet if someone benefited in such a manner—even from an evil such as race-based slavery—it is unclear whether or not the persons benefiting from it are guilty or even at fault and ought therefore to pay reparations for slavery. Would it not be more sensible, morally speaking, to hold accountable only those who, according to the general line of the unjust enrichment argument, benefit nonaccidentally from the atrocity? I believe that this is what McGary has in mind with his words, however, so I do not see that this point refutes, but rather clarifies and supports, his general line of argument. It narrows the focus of responsibility for the oppression of blacks in and by the United States, rather than diffusing it so that it might become meaningless in legal contexts.

There is another reason, however well-intentioned, why the unjust enrichment argument is problematic. It is that persons might owe reparations to a group even if the persons did not benefit in a long-term sense from a particular injustice which forms the basis of the group's receiving reparations. An example of this sort of case would be, say, a white slave master whose "empire" ended up, largely and ironically due to slavery, ruining him forever. Perhaps the having of others do forced labor for his family and such was far outweighed by his mismanagement of his slaves, increasing and significant social and political pressures against slavery at the time of his having slaves, and so forth. Yet simply because this slave master, perhaps due to his own incompetence as a master of slaves, did not benefit from his having slaves hardly means that he is not morally responsible for his having of slaves. Or, consider the example of a civil disobedient to U.S. slavery, one who not only refuses to support with her taxes the United States or even state or local governments, but who also lives a holistic lifestyle of protest of the "peculiar institution." This citizen hardly benefits from U.S. slavery of Africans, but is rather in protest opting out of whatever significant ways in which she might benefit. Thus we need not demonstrate that those responsible for providing reparations to blacks were those who benefited from the wrongs against blacks that would justify such reparations. For an incompetent slave master's not benefiting from slavery hardly exempts him from what he owes based on Boxill's argument that he has deprived slaves of the value of their labor, unforced, and one who protests incessantly and holistically U.S. slavery of Africans benefits, it seems, in no interesting way from it. Yet each owes reparations for slavery due to the fact that each is, with the slavers, collectively to some degree responsible for it, though not necessarily guilty or at fault for it, as Feinberg argues concerning collective responsibility in more general terms. Those who are collectively responsible for a harmful wrongdoing "sport the same uniform" of those more directly responsible, provided that a certain degree of intentionality, knowledge, and voluntariness obtains in their cases as well. Otherwise, the unjust enrichment argument would seem to imply that those who benefited most from U.S. slavery ought to be held most accountable for paying their fair share of reparations, for example, more of the reparations amount than those who benefited significantly less than they. Moreover, when all is said and done, the amount of reparations owed according to this scheme would only be as much as the amount of fiscal benefit to those guilty and at fault for slavery. Yet this amount might not reflect the amount of reparations owed based on the amount of labor value stolen from the slaves. In turn, this scheme of reparations would make black reparations contingent on the successes and failures of the market of slave holdings, rather than on the value of the labor stolen from the slaves. Since it seems more intuitively plausible to award reparations on the basis of labor value stolen from slaves and other wrongful harms wrought on enslaved Africans in the United States, the amount of reparations ought to reflect these facts. Yet this would seem to imply that we need not demonstrate the plausibility of the unjust enrichment argument, at least, in a way that ignores meaningful collective responsibility for the harms of slavery.

But what precisely would establish, on moral grounds, the plausibility of the reparations argument concerning blacks? I argue that it is, as Boxill implies and as I am attempting to make more explicit, the illicit taking by force and/ or fraud of the labor power of the slaves and all that factors into that oppressive state of affairs. It is at this point of argument that the principle of morally just acquisitions and transfers plays a fundamental role in the reparations argument for blacks as it did in the case of Indians. *For whatever is acquired or transferred by just means is itself just, and whatever is acquired or transferred by unjust means is itself unjust.* Yet forced labor power and the extraction of value from it is clearly unjust as it violates the principle just restated from the previous chapter. Since slaveholders and the U.S. government permitted slavery to go unchecked for generations and even supported the institution of slavery of Africans, slaveholders, certain businesses, and the U.S. government are responsible for the harmful effects of slavery and are liable to pay reparations to descendants of the slaves should such descendants exist or have trusts in their names. Further harms to blacks accrued as the federal and various state and local governments institutionalized racism against generations of blacks. This much can serve as the locus of agreement, however, between supporters of black reparations and their detractors. For detractors might concur that the stealing of the labor power and hence value of the slaves entitles reparations to slaves, but to no one else. Thus an argument is needed which establishes on moral grounds reparations to contemporary U.S. blacks, not simply to their forebears who were enslaved or who were victims of Jim Crow.

Boxill provides the basis of such an argument when he states that "the slaves presumably have conferred their rights of ownership to the products of their labor to their descendants." Yet it is precisely at this point where objections to the reparations argument might be challenged as it pertains to contemporary U.S. blacks. It might be argued, with John Rawls, that the very idea of inheritance is morally arbitrary and has no basis in a morally sound system of social living. Be this as it may, it seems that Boxill's point is made in light of the way the legal system works in the United States: *given that inheritance is recognized in U.S. law,* it would seem to follow that the stolen value of the slaves' labor power ought to be recognized, naturally, as inherited by the heirs of slaves, who would by (my) definition be contemporary U.S. blacks. I too shall share Boxill's assumption and shall not here take on the task of challenging the morality of inheritance systems under the law. Yet it is important to recognize that should such systems in the end fail on moral grounds, Boxill's argument runs aground on such problems (as does my own argument here). But then so would the legal practice of inheritance more generally, wreaking significant havoc in U.S. society should it be legally abolished.

However, my argument for reparations to blacks does not simply depend for its overall plausibility on matters of inheriting certain rights to compensation from one's benefactors. The primary focus of my argument is that to the extent that slavery and Jim Crow led to widespread injustices to African slaves in the United States and their descendants, reparations are owed blacks on moral grounds because the *same governmental systems that harmed African slaves enacted and enforced Jim Crow, and exist today as those that have yet to pay reparations even though formal and informal democratic demands for reparations have been made since Reconstruction.* Reparations to blacks, not unlike those to Indians, are debts unpaid by an *existing perpetrator,* namely and primarily (though not exclusively), the U.S. government. In short, the black heirs of oppression by the United States are owed reparations by the non-Indian and nonblack oppressor heirs in the United States.

It will not do, morally speaking, for one to argue that reparations are not owed in that today's U.S. citizenry is "innocent" of any act of slavery or oppression against blacks. For this line of argument wrongly assumes that a government that for generations simply ignores demands of justice is legitimate in then not paying what it owes to those against whom it has committed atrocities such as slavery and Jim Crow. Ever since Reconstruction there have been demands for justice by blacks, often in the form of reparations arguments in the halls of the U.S. Congress. So the same governments that harmed African slaves and even their descendants via Jim Crow stand to pay what they owe to blacks. Here I mean by such governments those of the southern states as "slavery was almost exclusively a creature of state law,"[23] and even the U.S. government to the extent that it aided and abetted in the oppression of slaves and blacks after slavery.

If the foregoing is correct, then it seems that reparations to blacks are grounded in the historical fact that reparations for black slavery were requested but never paid during and subsequent to Reconstruction, and that Jim Crow was not only oppressive of blacks living in the southern states, but that such oppression was aided and abetted by the U.S. government in significant ways.[24] One among many ways in which the U.S. government aided and abetted to the enslavement of Africans in the United States was by way of its enacting and enforcing the Fugitive Slave Laws whereby a southern slave master could recapture and reenslave his fugitive "property" by way of the federal court system.[25] As one commentator puts it, "The infamous federal Fugitive Slave Act of 1850 deprived blacks of some of the most basic fair-trial rights: confrontation, cross-examination, and an unbiased decision maker, to name just three."[26] To add insult to injury, the U.S. government sat idly by as for generations Jim Crow was used to further solidify the oppression of blacks. The U.S. government was indeed a bad Samaritan in that it was grossly negligent as for generations it stood by and permitted southern states to flourish not only under slavery, but under Jim Crow.[27] (It is assumed here that slavery was hardly the main reason for the Civil War on the part of the northern states.) Recall also that it took the federal government about a century subsequent to the Civil War to pass (and eventually enforce) civil rights legislation, primarily to combat Jim Crow and other forms of racist segregation throughout the United States. That the U.S. government was a bad Samaritan along these lines is important, as such bad Samaritanism serves as part of the moral basis for reparations owed by the same government responsible, in one way or another, for both the evils of slavery and of Jim Crow, and how much reparations are owed. Assumed here, of course, are the ideas that governments have duties to respect and protect the rights of their respective citizens, and that individuals and governments have duties to assist those in need insofar as such assistance does not pose a serious threat to their own well-being. Concerning the case at hand, it is implausible to think that the U.S. government was not a bad Samaritan as it very well could have acted in various ways to provide adequate justice to former slaves, and to blacks for the effects of Jim Crow, and to hold accountable states that failed to comply with civil rights legislation that should have been enacted and enforced immediately subsequent to slavery in the United States. After all, the U.S. government has the military might to ensure its results anywhere within "its own territory." No coalition of Southern states could begin to challenge the U.S. military, especially after the devastating loss (by the South) of the Civil War. This placed the federal government in a particularly powerful position vis-à-vis the South. It is clear that there were reasons why it took so long to pass and enforce civil rights legislation. That such reasons are adequate, morally speaking, is quite unclear. Assumed here is the plausibility of the claim that massive and significant human rights violations ought to be handled adequately as soon as humanly possible, implying that the timing of the federal government's handling of severe rights violations against African slaves and blacks was nothing less than morally inept.

Now each of the conditions of collective moral responsibility discussed in chapter 5 obtain in the racist oppression of Indians and African slaves by the U.S. government and its citizens, historically speaking. Most U.S. citizens strongly supported their federal, state, and local governments in the intentional, knowing, and voluntary oppression of blacks by way of, among other things, legislation that delimited the rights of blacks. Even though the newly founded United States inherited from the colonies a race-based system of slavery, those representative legislators of the new country intentionally, knowingly, and voluntarily chose to not abolish slavery despite the fact that abolitionist views were significant by 1787 and were around at least since the early eighteenth century. In fact, as Lyons points out: "By the time of the constitutional convention, three northern states had abolished slavery, three had enacted gradual emancipation statutes, and others were about to follow, as would three of the states that were soon to be carved out of the Northwest Territory."[28] These facts, coupled with the fact that there was fierce debate over the peculiar institution during the convention, points strongly to the idea that there was a collective intention, knowingly and voluntarily formed, by the new legislature of the United States, to retain slavery. This is perhaps no more greatly exemplified than by the fugitive slave clause adopted by the convention. In short, "If Northern delegates had actually represented antislavery sentiment, the slave states might have actually agreed to a constitution that tolerated but did not so vigorously support slavery. The federal government instead became committed in law and policy to that institution."[29] The U.S. Congress also failed to deliver on reparations to newly emancipated blacks, which kept them among the poorest people in U.S. society. While Thaddeus Stevens's proposal for the taking and redistribution of Southern lands to blacks lacks a moral foundation because the lands were forcibly or fraudulently acquired from Indian nations and thus belonged to Indians by moral right, as we saw in chapter 5, no form of compensatory reparations succeeded or was even taken seriously by more than a few U.S. citizens. Blacks were left to fend for themselves among people in the South, most of whom resented blacks because they were no longer slaves and posed a new threat to their economic welfare, and Northerners, most of whom resented blacks because of their perception that so many white lives were lost for blacks during the Civil War. All of this provides support, moreover, for McGary's point that certain practices make the United States liable for the oppression of blacks.

Furthermore, during the next few decades the federal government refused to uphold the amended Constitution during times when blacks were terrorized by many whites throughout the states. In this way, the federal government assisted state and local ones in securing white supremacy over blacks, the apex of which is perhaps the U.S. Supreme Court ruling in *Plessey v. Ferguson* in 1896. Thus the 1875 Civil Rights Act was not duly enforced for blacks. And almost a century later when the federal government enacted the Civil Rights Act of 1965, which many refer to as the "Second Reconstruction," it did not take long for subsequent members of the executive, judicial, and legislative branches of the federal government to erode what the second civil rights act attempted to solidify in terms of equal opportunities in employment, housing, education, and the like for blacks. All the while, the federal, state, and local governments for the most part stood idly by as another generation of blacks became heirs of oppression. In fact, "In the Jim Crow South, blacks who violated the etiquette of segregation were routinely subjected to violence at the hands of the white citizenry. On many occasions this violence was facilitated by the action or inaction of the state."[30] Thus it is hardly the case that the enslavement and Jim-Crowing of blacks was not intentional, knowing, and voluntary, as those who had the desire to oppress blacks did so, and they knew what they were doing in doing so. And it is implausible to think that whites, with all their power, were coerced to do so, say, by economic factors and the like. In short, whites as a group in their positions of citizen or governmental power were responsible either directly or indirectly for the oppression of blacks, a responsibility that makes it such that there were moral debts created, accrued, but never paid to blacks. Again, these factors serve as evidence of what McGary would term as individual and collective practices that oppressed blacks.

Nor is there serious question as to whether or not the current U.S. government and its citizenry constitute collectives that are morally accountable for what they do as decision-making bodies. On average and as a group, they acted knowingly, intentionally, and voluntarily in committing or supporting the enslavement, as well as in establishing and maintaining Jim Crow. Slavery and Jim Crow were neither unintentional nor accidental. Rather, they were legal institutions and policies voluntarily and knowingly intended to ensure white supremacy.

One question many raise is whether or not there exists collective identity over time between the U.S. government of today and the U.S. government of the past, and between the U.S. citizens of today and those of the past. If there is no argument that can succeed in identifying significantly either of these two sets of collective agents, then arguments for reparations to Indians and blacks seem to falter. For such an argument is needed in order to provide a sufficient reason to think that such collectives have a moral duty to provide reparations to the heirs of historic U.S. racist oppression. The age-old personal identity problem in philosophy of mind confronts the ethics of reparations to Indians and blacks in the form of the problem of collective identity. For collective identity is essential for collective responsibility; for there to be a responsible oppressor of blacks, there must an identifiable agent responsible for the oppression of Indians and blacks that can pay reparations today.

And it is not just the problem of the collective identity of the U.S. government and citizenry over time—from the perpetration of historic injustices against Indians and blacks until presently—but also the problem of being able to identify the members of "Indians" and "blacks." The heirs of oppression, then, must be identifiable in order for there to be a viable case for reparations in these cases. Why should today's U.S. government and citizens pay reparations for debts incurred by the U.S. government and citizenry of the distant past? And even if this question can be answered in favor of reparative justice to Indians and blacks, precisely to whom should such reparations be paid?

These are core questions of collective retrospective liability responsibility relative to these heirs of oppression and compensatory justice.

Elsewhere I have argued that the current U.S. government is *sufficiently similar* to the historic U.S. government that oppressed Indians and the slave forebears of blacks that the former can and ought to be held morally liable for such evils it perpetrated intentionally, knowingly, and voluntarily in proportion (roughly) to the wrongs it perpetrated on others (in this case, Indians and blacks as the descendants of those who were oppressed by the U.S. government).[31] That argument rests on the idea that the fundamentally governing documents containing the governing moral and legal rules and principles of the United States are essentially the same today as they were since the commencement of the "American experiment": namely, the U.S. Constitution (and its amendments) and Declaration of Independence.[32] Of the U.S. Constitution, Joseph Raz writes: "It is still the constitution adopted two hundred years ago, just as a person who lives in an eighteenth-century house lives in a house built two hundred years ago. His house has been repaired, added to, and changed many times since. But it is still the same house and so is the constitution."[33] Moreover, the basic structure of U.S. society and its political checks and balances remain the same, however problematically implemented. In fact, even the same two-party political system has been in place since the very beginning of the country.[34] Perhaps of equal significance here is the fact that the U.S. Supreme Court seeks to interpret cases it chooses to hear in light of both extra-legal principles as well as the U.S. Constitution. The fact of the matter is that the Constitution serves today as the most defining document of U.S. life just as it did when it was adopted. Witness to this fact are the numerous and ongoing debates in U.S. society concerning free speech, hate speech, handgun control, affirmative action, matters of legal due process, and the like, each of which is based on this or that interpretation of this or that right allegedly based in the U.S. Constitution.

Furthermore, if Ronald Dworkin is correct, then U.S. Fugitive Slave Laws were misinterpreted by some judges who ignored extra-legal principles that would have led them to see such laws as unconstitutional.[35] Even if Dworkin were incorrect about this point, the fact is that judges who upheld Fugitive Slave Laws did so because they construed them as being constitutional. Not only did the U.S. Constitution serve as the primary document according to which U.S. law is to be understood during the enslavement of Africans in the United States, but it remains today as the primary defining document against which societal conduct and conflict is to be judged. Indeed, to think that today's U.S. government and society is not essentially the same as the U.S. government of yesteryear borders on disingenuousness. This suggests that the U.S. Supreme Court, the U.S. Congress, and the executive branch are seemingly united from years past to the present insofar as a web of purposive actions, inactions, and attempted actions are concerned, including the oppression of Indians and blacks—though the individual agents have changed. This in turn suggests that there is a collective identity relation over time between the branches of the U.S. government past and present, linking the actions of the U.S. government of the past to the governmental branches of the present. And if it is true that where there are rights inherited by present-day U.S. citizens and officials, then it is plausible to think that responsibilities are inherited as well. Reparations for past evils perpetrated by the U.S. government against Indians and blacks are responsibilities inherited by present-day citizens and officials from the very same government from which present-day rights are inherited. In short, reparations are inherited duties of current U.S. citizens and their government owed to those who were denied their due from the same U.S. government that still exists today which seeks to ignore or further deny such duties it has. Note that this inheritance argument is one in which the U.S. government and its citizenry inherit moral duties of reparations to Indians and blacks. And as Boxill reminds us, it is not just that blacks have a claim to reparations based on the enslavement of their ancestors. Rather, the argument is that blacks "have a claim to collect the compensation that was owed to their ancestors but was never paid."[36] In my view, then, it is the U.S. government, certain culpable U.S.-based businesses and other institutions, and its citizenry that inherit the obligation to rectify the past evils against Indians and African slaves in the United States. I shall focus on the culpability of the U.S. government as well as its most relevant policy- and decision-makers, as they have the greatest responsibility and deep pockets for purposes of compensatory reparations.

Now it might be argued that if it is reasonable to think that the current U.S. government is the same one that oppressed and supported the oppression of Indians and African slaves in the United States, then it seems that the current U.S. government can and ought to, *for purposes of positive public policy administration*, offer genuine apology to the offspring of the oppressed in question. Such an apology would include, pursuant to condition 3 of the analysis of an apology in chapter 8, the provision of adequate compensatory reparations by the U.S. government to such groups, reparations that are approximately proportional to the magnitude and duration of rights violations wrought against such groups in the past. This position does not rule out that private companies or corporations and some of their executives that contributed to the oppression of Indians and African slaves owe reparations to current members of such groups. Certain railroad companies, telegraph companies, textile and tobacco companies, insurance companies, and so on, come to mind here, as some exist to this day either in the same name or as derivative business enterprises. It also does not rule out the extent to which certain other institutions or organizations might owe reparations as well: the KKK, various churches, municipalities, and other social groups that oppressed blacks.

The legacy of the DeWolf family in the transatlantic slave trade serves as a dramatic example of the responsibility for reparations of oppressor heirs to their victim heirs. According to Katrina Brown, who is a descendant of Mark

Anthony DeWolf, and her testimony on the KPBS Point of View 2008 program, "The Trade Triangle," there are currently hundreds of descendants of
Mark Anthony DeWolf, infamous slave trader and then one of the wealthiest
persons in the United States, whose businesses not only were designed to
secure his stronghold in the business of trading slaves, but were also strongly
supported by way of recruited stockholding (stockholders of slave trading
expected about a 25 percent return on their investments in the slave trade voy-
ages) by what is arguably the center and most complicit locale of the slave
trade in the United States: Bristol, Rhode Island. That entire community supported the slave trade, and serves as a microcosm of how the U.S. citizenry
generally supported it. It was the insurance companies that insured slaves,
many banks that supplied loans to slave trade businesses, the ironworkers
who produced the shackles of slavery, the coopers who manufactured the rum
barrels, and the distillers who made the molasses into rum which was the primary currency of purchasing slaves in Africa (though food and clothing were
also used). Let us not forget that it was slaves who produced the sugar and
molasses to make the rum. And it was not just Bristol that was involved in
slavery in this deeply interconnected manner. Boston, Salem, New London,
New Haven, and many rural areas surrounding these towns were also deeply
supportive of and involved in the slave trade. The DeWolf slave trade business
was so large and successful that it established many sugar and molasses slave
plantations in Cuba. DeWolf became so wealthy from the selling of slaves that
he sold several millions of dollars worth of them. In today's currency values,
it would equal billions or trillions of dollars in sales. And during most of the
time that the DeWolfs practiced in the slave trade, *it was illegal in the United
States.* But political favors were cashed in by the congressman with Thomas
Jefferson who supported what his fellow privileged politico was doing by
appointing DeWolf's brother-in-law as Bristol's customs official, who turned a
blind eye to DeWolf's shipping and cargo.

In point of fact, the citizens of Bristol, through their economic support of
the DeWolfs' slavery enterprise, made it the largest slave trading operation in
U.S. history, bringing over 10,000 Africans to the Americas as slaves. (It is estimated that more than 500,000 of the descendants of such slaves could be alive
today.) But it was not only Mark Anthony DeWolf who was a successful slave
trader, but George DeWolf and John Jay DeWolf as well. Indeed, there were at
least three generations of DeWolfs who traded in slaves to secure the family
name as the most infamous in U.S. slave trading history. Indeed, the slave
trade was no mistake of a particular generation or by a few people. It was a
calculated and intentional act of generations of businessmen, supported
rather strongly by their community members both North and South.

However, the slave trade was not just about misappropriating the value of
slave labor power, as Boxill emphasizes. It was about the physical brutality
that was often involved. One such example is in Bristol, Rhode Island, where
one local businessman requested that the slave whipping post be removed

from the front of his building because of the blood splatterings on the windows. The violence against slaves was acute and often, something unappreciated by most of us who think about it today.

The infamous legacy of the DeWolf family in the transatlantic slave trade serves as a paradigmatic case of the responsibility of the oppressor heirs to victim heirs vis-à-vis reparations. As mentioned, there are currently hundreds of descendants of at least three generations of the DeWolf family that were heavily involved in the slave trade and supported (then) by the town of Bristol, Rhode Island, which is arguably the U.S. business center for the slave trade during much of that era. With the DeWolf family are those who to one degree or another benefit unjustly from the bequeathal of wealth passed on to them in one form or another. The "rum for slaves" operations lasted generations in the DeWolf family, wreaking havoc on the lives of thousands of blacks from Ghana to Cuba, and in turn, the United States.[37]

Of course, most U.S. citizens would object to this line of reasoning in that if the U.S. government has a moral obligation to pay such reparations, it does so at the real expense of the citizens of the United States. But it will be objected that the U.S. citizens are not causally linked to the horrors of the past, and should therefore be immune from being burdened with the costs of rectifying past evils.[38]

However, this objection fails to consider some important matters. One factor is that just as current U.S. citizens inherit benefits, so too they inherit the burdens that accompany the benefits. It would be morally one-sided to think that only benefits, but not burdens, can be justifiably inherited. This is especially true considering that many of the benefits inherited by most U.S. citizens are made possible at the expense of the burdens that have been experienced by the forebears of blacks! One such example of this point is understood in terms of the principle of morally just acquisitions and transfers as it relates to the violent and continual (legacy of) theft of Indian lands by pre-citizens of the U.S. government, and by citizens of the U.S. government, as noted in the previous chapter.[39] But another instance is the evils of the enslavement of Africans in the United States, which amounted to the theft of labor power and surplus labor value of the slaves, monetary values never returned to them by the United States. Yet another factor is that of Jim Crow legislation which directly oppressed such groups (in ways that no other groups in U.S. history have experienced, except Indians). So just as U.S. law permits the inheritance of benefits, it ought to be made to judiciously enforce reparations in proportion to the harms unduly wrought as the inheritance of burdens that can reasonably be tied to the benefits wrongly inherited by the U.S. populace through its governments: federal, state, and local.

To this line of reasoning it might be argued that it misses the point entirely because current U.S. citizens cannot be held morally liable for the evils of past generations of U.S. citizens. Perhaps the arguments face a dialectical stalemate relative to one another regarding the matter of whether or not reparations are owed by the U.S. government for the enslavement of Africans and for the oppression of Indians. But this counter-reply misses the point of collective moral responsibility in that it fails to take into account that Jim Crow legislation oppressed millions of blacks who are *still alive*, not to mention those who lived and died during the very same era of wrongdoings that, on Boxill's account, justify reparations to Japanese Americans because of their oppression by the United States during WWII, and to Jews because of the Nazi holocaust of the Jews. So why is it that the United States simply refuses to pay reparations to blacks for the evils of oppression wrought *in recent times* on such groups? Within the past few decades or so, certainly since the internment of many Japanese Americans, Jim Crow ensured that not only Indians but blacks were not to receive full treatment as citizens in deep and lasting ways. Surely reparations are owed for these more recent forms of injustice, and there is no time lag suggesting that today's U.S. citizens are not responsible (causally) for the oppression in question. It is a simple refusal to provide justice for those for whom you have no genuine respect and concern. It is racism, plain and simple.[40] So even if Boxill's argument staved off attempts to ground reparations to blacks as the reparations argument attempts to do (for more distant harms), it certainly cannot succeed in explaining why reparations are not owed to blacks for the more recent evils of Jim Crow. Millions of U.S. citizens and government officials alive today were contributors to Jim Crow in various and sundry ways, and surely *they* bear primary or secondary responsibility—even in Boxill's mere causal sense—for the oppression caused by Jim Crow. And such harms would be rectified on grounds of proportional punishment and compensatory reparations.

Boxill raises a rather strong objection to my general line of argument from collective responsibility:

> We can have duties that we do not take on deliberately and are unaware that we have, if such duties are required by Natural Law. The U.S. Government at the time of slavery was complicit in the crime of slavery, and therefore had a duty required by Natural Law to make reparation to the slaves. . . . It is sufficient that the government assisted the slave holders and did so culpably. None of this supports the claim that the present U.S. Government owes present day African Americans the reparation an earlier U.S. Government owed their ancestors but never paid. Since present day U.S. citizens were not complicit in the crime of slavery that claim can only be based on the morally repugnant idea that individuals can be burdened with the duties that other people incurred. Present day U.S. citizens were not even born when the transgressions involved in slavery were being committed. They could not possibly have committed these transgressions, or consented to them. . . . Further, the Natural Law does not require them to pay for the damages their ancestors' transgressions caused.[41]

Boxill's concern here is that something akin to my attempt (above) to ground reparations in a collective moral responsibility of U.S. citizens and their government runs afoul of forcing folk to pay for the crimes of "other" people.

But Boxill's line of reasoning raises several concerns. First, it is excessively individualistic in that it does not acknowledge that groups can be responsible such that an identity relation can be seen to exist over time between, say, the "old" U.S. government that oppressed blacks and the current one. This form of methodological individualism "inherited" by Boxill from John Locke requires the careful argumentative support that it has never yet received in philosophy. It is an assumption that has been made over the generations of philosophers who construe matters of collective identities and responsibilities and duties to be overly complex, and indeed intellectually unpalatable. But that a concept is difficult hardly means that it is implausible, as we saw in chapter 5. That collectives of the conglomerate sort do not always satisfy the conditions of liability does not imply that they never can, or never do. I have provided a historical account that, however concise, adduces evidence in favor of the claim that the U.S. government and certain businesses oppressed several Africans as slaves and blacks under Jim Crow. Such evidence forms a bridge between the identity of the original perpetrators of the oppression in question and today's U.S. government. A similar point can be made concerning certain state and local governments, and even certain businesses or their individual or familial constituent heirs.

Secondly, Boxill's line of reasoning seems to suggest that duties cannot be inherited by agents who were not causally responsible for (or guilty of) serious and wrongful harms. But if causal responsibility is a necessary condition of the inheriting of moral duties, then is it not also a necessary condition of the inheritance of moral rights and benefits? Perhaps the rights guaranteed by the U.S. Constitution and its amendments, and Declaration of Independence ought not to accrue to anyone in U.S. society because, after all, they did not choose to live here as naturalized citizens. Moreover, those were rights articulated and fought for by previous generations of U.S. citizens, not current ones. Indeed, present-day U.S. citizens hardly know or understand what such rights are. So just as it is "morally repugnant" to think that duties can be inherited, so too by parity of reasoning it is morally repugnant to think that rights are. However, this does not mean that today's U.S. citizens have no constitutional rights. It is to argue by parity of Boxill's reasoning that such rights could not accrue on the basis of the most officially defining documents of the United States, however ironically. But both certain rights and duties, both benefits and burdens, both wealth and debt, are "inherited" by U.S. citizens by virtue of their U.S. citizenship.

Thirdly, Boxill's Lockean view seems to not acknowledge some of the implications of his reasoning about reparations. The only kind of instance in which Boxill's Lockean conception of justified reparations could obtain is where such reparations are paid within the very generation in which the oppression took place. Otherwise, Boxill's Lockean concern that individuals would be burdened with the duties that other people incurred would be violated. This implies that the reparations paid by Germany to Israel are wrong, just as the reparations paid to some Japanese Americans by the U.S. government were. Why? Because in each case there were those who had nothing whatsoever to do with the oppressions in question (some had not even been born when the evils were enacted, as Boxill and some others would note) yet they helped pay reparations by way of taxes to their government years subsequent to the oppressive wrongs in question. Like it or not, even these cases of reparations were wrong given Boxill's Lockean position about protecting the sacredness of individualism at all costs (it would appear): only those German citizens who were causally responsible for the persecution of Jews and other "undesirables" should have to pay the reparations to Israel. But why *Israel*? Are there not Jews in Israel who were unaffected (directly) by the Nazi persecution? And why did, say, I as a taxpayer in the United States have to pay for what the U.S. government did to some Japanese Americans generations previous to my birth? Boxill's Lockean reasoning suggests that only those reparations that are paid by causally responsible parties are truly owed, nothing else. While this is a morally admirable position to take as it honors the idea that only the guilty should be punished or forced to compensate for their wrongs (a fundamental principle of retributivisms), it seems to disallow for the plausibility of modes of responsibility that are not delimited by the biased individualist approach. In particular, it seems to beg a certain kind of regress argument that individualism faces pertaining to collective identities such as the U.S. citizenry and its government.

If Boxill is correct in arguing that the U.S. government cannot be responsible for what was done to African slaves in the United States, then he seems to imply that it is because there is a discontinuity of collective identity between what are, on his view, two different entities. In other words, there are really two different governments, not just one as I have argued above. But if this is true, then we are owed an argument as to why there are not several different "U.S." governments, perhaps one with each new administration, over time. In fact, what we have here is the old problem of personal identity applied to a collective entity. But the regress problem is the same. Just as we would not deny that Boxill is the same brilliant philosopher today as he was several years ago due to the fact that there is sufficient continuity between the person of his past and who he is today, parity of reasoning would inform us that the U.S. government today is the same entity that it was in years past, as I argued above using the most fundamentally defining documents of the country. That the continuity is imperfect or somewhat problematic on metaphysical grounds hardly prohibits us from making the requisite identity relations for positive purposes of public policy administration. But Boxill's Lockean argument seems to insist that the U.S. government today is not the same perpetrator of evils to African slaves, which implies a discontinuity of identity on the part of the U.S. government. In light of my argument to the contrary, we are owed a non-question-begging reason (in favor of individualism and against the general Humean view of identity) as to why such continuity cannot or does not accrue. Short of an individualist bias, it is hard to imagine what that argument might look like without making nonsense of the notions of personal identity and collective identity.

A final problem with Boxill's Lockean position on reparations is his claim that reparations cannot be justified if they "would put the present white population in danger of perishing."[42] While this concern is to be taken seriously, we must note that this line of thought delimits retributive or deserved justice and compensatory rights to reparations to the social utility of a majority group, contrary to the words of John Rawls in the epigraph for part 2. As such, it is akin to the argument from social utility that is debunked in *Race, Racism, and Reparations*. Another reason why this utilitarian argument is problematic is that it seeks to index social utility to a current group of majority folk without understanding that the rights which were violated and in need of rectification were those of majority group in the past. So in order for Boxill's utilitarian argument to succeed, it must be shown by independent and non-question-begging argument why social utility ought to be indexed to the current majority of white U.S. citizens, rather than to the compensatory rights of the heirs of oppression. At least, this holds for the case of Indian reparations. In the case of black reparations, it might be argued that the social utility of the general U.S. citizenry hardly outweighs the moral and civil rights that were violated by the very government representing such citizens, say, under Jim Crow. And there are times when a society "wrongs itself off the face of the earth" when it commits evils such that it cannot possibly pay for them. The United States is precisely such a case, and it is morally presumptuous to think that the United States deserves to continue to exist in light of its incessant and unrectified evils. If current U.S. citizens are to place the moral blame for U.S.-owed reparations anywhere, it should be on the same leaders after whom they themselves often name post offices, federal buildings and highways, and parks and monuments, many of whom are directly responsible (in Boxill's narrowly causal sense) for unspeakable acts of evil which together rival even the Nazi holocaust of millions of Jews, homosexuals, and gypsies. *That* is where the blame lies if the United States seeks to exist because it cannot pay in full measure its debts of injustice. The justice of reparations must never be diminished in light of what is convenient for an oppressor government and/or society. Rather, the costs of oppression must be borne to the fullest extent deserved in light of the evils committed and harms unduly wrought on others. Nonetheless, in chapter 9 I shall detail a policy of U.S. reparations to blacks that is affordable for whites, and does not "put the present white population in danger of perishing." This should satisfy Boxill's concern rather well.

I have set forth and defended a rights-based theory of compensatory reparations that assumes neither that reconciliation is a necessary condition of reparative justice, nor that victims of evil are required to forgive their perpetrators in the name of social utility maximization and social tranquility. It requires perpetrators of injustice to apologize for their wrongful acts, omissions, or attempts that harm others severely, and this includes, among other things, making adequate means of compensatory rectification to victims of their oppression. Reparations to Indians, as with indigenous peoples everywhere, are morally justified and required to the extent that they have a valid moral claim to and/or interest in the lands from which they were dispossessed, violently or otherwise, in violation of the principle of morally just acquisitions and transfers and because of several rights violations resulting in genocide. Reparations to blacks are morally justified and required to the extent that the U.S., state, and local governments and certain existing business enterprises each acted, failed to act or attempted to act separately or in collusion to instigate, maintain, and strengthen the "peculiar institution" of slavery of Africans, and to the extent that they instituted Jim Crow legislation subsequent to slavery in order to oppress blacks, depriving African slaves of their rights to both their labor power and the full value of their labor, and depriving blacks of many of the basic civil rights guaranteed under the U.S. Constitution.

Unless there is a sound argument in favor of a moral statute of limitations on historic injustice, and given that unrectified evil is evil still, then such circumstances leave the U.S. government and nongovernmental organizational perpetrators of the evil open to morally legitimate responses to their unrectified evils, including acts of terrorism.[43] Hopefully, matters will not reach that juncture. But unrectified evils do not vanish into the convenient air of denied guilt of governments and citizenries that simply refuse to pay for their evils. Nor is a government or its citizenry in a moral position to deny the moral rightness of harsh acts wrought on them so long as its past includes unrectified evils.

Yet with all of this said and done, there is a rather nagging curiosity concerning the issue of why reparations to blacks is so greatly resisted in the United States. For even if it were conceded, contrary to the previous line of argumentation, that the enslavement of Africans on U.S. soil did not justify reparations to the descendants of such slaves today, there remains a series of queries which tend to suggest the fundamental racism that U.S. citizens have toward blacks. For might it not very well be much more plausible on moral grounds to ground reparations to blacks given the depths and almost permanent racist effects of generations of segregation throughout the United States? And is it not true that many millions of blacks who have experienced the heavy hand (fist?) of such oppression are still alive? And would it not also be true that what Japanese Americans experienced at the hands of the U.S. government was not nearly as harmful as what blacks experience(d), both in terms of the very kinds of racist oppression and in terms of the duration of them? And would not such facts suggest that, just as the United States willingly apologized and provided reparations to certain Japanese Americans, so too ought the United States to do so to blacks?[44] Moreover, should not the amount of reparations to blacks be substantially larger than that which has been provided to certain Japanese Americans? This would follow from both the kinds of racist oppression and the duration of it to an entire ethnic group, as well as plausible principles of proportional compensation.

One concern here is that my argument fails to consider that U.S. reparations to *certain* Japanese Americans were just that, for example, reparations to only those Japanese Americans who actually suffered in the internment camps during WWII. However, my argument for black reparations can accommodate this concern. For what might be done is that the U.S. government award reparations to only those blacks who have suffered significant harm under Jim Crow. Even today, this amounts to a substantial number of those who were forced to live under conditions of a much larger concentration camp: U.S. segregationist society (north, south, east, and west). And the amount of deserved and owed reparations would be substantial.

Perhaps it is this final point that makes most U.S. citizens recoil at the very idea of reparations to blacks. But this simply exposes the racism at work in U.S. society, especially in light of the arguments, the facts underlying them, and how a lesser but important case of racist harm against some Japanese Americans was handled compared to the utter refusal of U.S. society to even take seriously reparations to even some blacks. The inference to the best explanation here seems to emerge as insidious racism, a racism which seeks to cloak itself in the guise of sophisticated philosophical argumentation, argumentation that is not, by the way, applied to the Jewish and Japanese cases by parity of reasoning. It is obvious that U.S. citizens on average and as a class do not believe that blacks deserve reparations, and for at least the reason which amounts to the objection from intergenerational justice. Holding to the plausibility of this objection is not in itself constitutive of racism against blacks. However, holding this view as a reason against providing reparations to blacks for the harms of Jim Crow experienced by contemporary blacks who experienced Jim Crow while simultaneously supporting reparations to many Japanese Americans for much lesser oppressive harms seems to demand an explanation as to why such a view is not racist toward blacks. Sociologically speaking, perhaps it is a case of a society of evildoers supporting the injustice they can *afford* to compensate, rather than supporting the full range of what is owed due to their government's evil actions. But it also seems to be a blatant instance of simply expressing respect for those for whom you have it, while denying it to those you disrespect.[45]

The previous line of reasoning addresses straightforwardly the objection from intergenerational justice which underlies the objection to collective responsibility. But in answer to the objection from historical complexity, it might be replied that, though U.S. history is complex as regards to the enslavement of Africans and Jim Crow oppression of blacks, there is nonetheless extraordinary historical evidence of the fact of U.S. oppression of both groups, along with continual pleas for reparative justice ever since the "forty acres and a mule" suggestion was declined during Reconstruction. That every detail of every case of African and black oppression is unavailable to us because of lost records and the complexities of U.S. history is hardly a good reason for the U.S. government to deny reparations to blacks. The libraries of volumes of critical U.S. history serve as a resounding reminder of the fact of U.S. oppression of these groups. So the argument from historical complexity, not unlike the objection to collective responsibility, is as implausible in the case of reparations to blacks as it is in the case of reparations to Indians.

In this chapter I have articulated the reparations argument for blacks. Then I considered some objections to the argument. Along the way, some similarities and differences between the cases for reparations to African and Indians were noted. In the end, it was concluded that not only are reparations owed to Indians, but to blacks also.

Perhaps motivated by some complex array of self-serving biases that in turn lead U.S. citizens and their government to repeatedly deny reparations for some of the most horrendous evils in the history of the world, reparations have not been paid to blacks. This is no surprise, even though so many U.S. citizens and governmental leaders declare that the United States is the best country in the world. But once again, if unrectified evil is evil still, and if the United States is responsible for the oppression of blacks and their forebears, then the United States owes it to blacks to adequately rectify the evils, however approximately and tardily. Time may heal old wounds, as goes the old saying. But it hardly erases injustice! And the United States cannot by any stretch of the imagination continue to claim to be a morally legitimate country unless and until it rectifies adequately its worst evils. For the evils of one's past do not in any way wither with the passing of time. Rather, they cling to one's being with incessant fury until that moment when the flight from one's evil ways has ended with evil catching up with one, only to terrorize the evildoer with a frightful vengeance.

8

Reparations and Reconciliation

There can be no future without forgiveness.

—Nelson Mandela[1]

Reconciliation is a spiritual process, but . . . it must also deal with economics and justice.

—Winona LaDuke[2]

The United States must fulfill its obligations and right all the injustices that they visited on the original people here before we can collectively move on to the next step that is regeneration and a fruitful future.

—Chief Oren Lyons[3]

Much has been written in recent years about the moral duty to reconcile matters between surviving victims of oppression and their oppressors. In chapters 2 and 3, various such approaches were explored and found wanting on various counts. Chapters 4 and 5 established both the human right to compensatory reparations and the conditions under which an oppressor-collective qualifies as a liable agent. Chapters 6 and 7 made the cases for reparations for American Indians and blacks. The U.S. government, among certain other agencies or groups, owes such reparations. However, many believe that bygones ought to be bygones, and that compensatory reparations ought not to be paid. Instead, what matters most is harmonious living conditions between the heirs of oppression (both victim heirs and oppressor heirs) in the United States and elsewhere. Forgiving, rather than reparations, is what is required in order to bring genuine peace and tranquility between the heirs of oppression.

But not much, if anything, has been articulated in terms of exactly what is required for reconciliation to occur, or even if it is a good thing for all individuals, groups, or society as a whole. What is reconciliation, and what are the conditions under which it is morally required, or even justified?

FORGIVENESS, RECONCILIATION,
AND REPARATIONS

The philosophical literature on forgiveness reflects at least two general stand-points on social relations. The dominant view of forgiveness is what I shall call a "reconciliation model" according to which the healing of broken relations between a harmful wrongdoer and her victim is the chief goal. According to the "rectification model" of forgiveness, while reconciliation might, at the vic-tim's choosing, be a by-product of the process of forgiveness, it need not be. On this model, the very possibility of forgiveness is contingent, among other things, on the offender's providing a genuine apology, which in turn is contin-gent on her offering, among other things, adequate rectification (including compensation) for her harmful wrongdoing.

A recent proponent of the reconciliation model of forgiveness is Charles Griswold. He argues that the "reasons" for forgiveness consist in (1) "the wrong-doer's demonstration that she no longer wishes to stand by herself as the author of those wrongs"; (2) "she must repudiate her deeds"; (3) "the wrong-doer must experience and express *regret* at having caused that particular injury to that particular person"; (4) "the offender must commit to becoming the sort of person who does not inflict injury"; and (5) "the offender must show that she understands, from the injured person's perspective, the damage done by the injury."[4] In other words, a "genuine apology" amounts to: "the taking of responsibility, recognition that the act was wrong, a change of heart sufficient to disavow the action and to say so to the victim . . . and implicitly the commitment not to repeat the offense."[5] To the extent that these condi-tions are satisfied, the victim of harmful wrongdoing can declare that "forgive-ness is granted."[6]

Griswold is careful to clarify that his analysis of forgiveness assumes that the nature of the harmful wrongdoing is forgivable in the first place. His notion of political forgiveness is appropriate for the discussion of the heirs of oppres-sion and reparative justice, and it is intended to explain the conditions under which opposing parties to evil states of affairs may be reconciled in political contexts. But Griswold situates his conception of forgiveness squarely within the reconciliation model when he states that "the logic of *forgiveness* does not require compensation and rectification; but this is perfectly compatible with the view that *justice* requires them."[7] Indeed, it is a primary purpose of forgive-ness to reconcile offenders and their victims.

However, there are problems with Griswold's reconciliation model of for-giveness. While he does not make the mistake of thinking that forgiveness implies mercy, it is unclear why a political conception of forgiveness such as his is *not* justice-centered especially in the compensatory sense.[8] This is another way of raising the question as to why the reconciliation model of for-giveness proffered by Griswold does not make adequate rectification a neces-sary (or any) condition of an apology, which in turn would make such rectification a necessary condition of forgiveness. But from the perspective of the reconciliation model there are no good answers to this question. From the standpoint of the rectification model of forgiveness, to not make adequate rectification a necessary condition of an apology and forgiveness is tantamount to making forgiveness and apology nearly "all about words," a view that Griswold himself rightly eschews.

Another difficulty facing the reconciliation model of forgiveness is that it fails to adequately explain why reconciliation between offenders and their victims is always a good thing, that is, *from the perspective of the victims*. There is little doubt that reconciliation between such parties is sometimes good, especially for the offenders. One such kind of case is where both such parties had a previous positive relationship and desire to continue it post-atrocity or oppression of one group against the other, absent coercion or fraud. But what about instances where no such prior relationship between the parties exists, or where such a prior relationship did exist but where the victims of oppression understandably no longer desire to remain in contact with their oppressors? Under these conditions, why is reconciliation even a desideratum? In fact, might it not under certain circumstances amount to a means of further oppressing an already oppressed group—especially if, as on Griswold's account, rectification is *not* required for forgiveness and reconciliation? By not making rectification a necessary condition of forgiveness and apology under such circumstances, the reconciliation model of forgiveness runs the serious risk of placing putatively reconciled groups who were oppressed in a context of economic and political disadvantage beyond repair. In other words, the reconciliation model of forgiveness, unlike the rectification model, does not guard against the continued oppression of groups post "reconciliation" due to "forgiving" and "apologizing," and the absence of compensation.

In reply, Griswold (not unlike other reconciliation theorists) opposes retributive motivations in favor of a notion of "common humanity."[9] On this view, offenders are "due" forgiveness under the conditions stipulated, and because they are "members of the moral community."[10] But this begs important questions concerning the reconciliation model itself. If it is true that oppressors, for instance, knowingly, intentionally, and voluntarily oppress others, then why does their status as human beings make it such that those whom they oppress ought to forgive them, especially absent rectification? And how can this reconciliation model of forgiveness insist that such forswearing of resentment and other retributive emotions toward the oppressors by the oppressed is a moral virtue? All in all, Griswold and other reconciliation model theorists seem to implicitly or explicitly rely on a quasi-religious notion of forgiveness as a moral virtue for a common humanity. Yet it is precisely this notion that requires independent argumentative support, especially in light of the fact that the world's evils do not point to a common humanity, but rather to a warring and deeply troubled one.

In contrast, I shall set forth a rectification model of forgiveness that is based on a properly construed retributivist theory of corrective justice, one that in turn rescues forgiveness and its related concepts from the mire of quasi-religious presumptions. Moreover, just as there is a distinction between reconciliation and rectification models of forgiveness, there are reconciliation and rectification models of reparations. In chapters 2 and 3, it was argued that reconciliation models of reparations are problematic for a variety of reasons. This chapter intends to provide a rationale for a rectification model of reparations given that in the previous few chapters and elsewhere objections to the basic reparations arguments for American Indians and blacks are defeated.[11]

Reparations ought not to presuppose anything like reconciliation or social integration between the perpetrators of evil and their victims, or even between the respective offspring of either group. Moreover, it is presumptuous to think that the offspring of oppressed groups ought morally to desire to live with the offspring of oppressors. Should Indians and blacks want to reconcile and remain integrated with the rest of the ethnic groups in the United States, so be it, and they ought to be treated with the dignity and respect they so richly deserve, no matter what their decisions along these and related lines. But only an unthinking ideology of forgiveness would entail that there is a moral duty of Indians and blacks to "forgive and forget" the evils perpetrated against their forebears by the U.S. government, certain U.S.-based business and institutions, and the U.S. citizenry. Reparations are required in such cases, as was argued in the preceding few chapters.

According to a rectificatory model of forgiveness, forgiveness is always morally supererogatory, and cannot accrue until and unless there is a genuine apology made from the perpetrator of the wrongdoing to those she harms wrongly.[12] Forgiveness requires a genuine apology, and a genuine apology requires that a wrongdoer: (1) communicate effectively to the victim *what* she did that was wrong; (2) communicate effectively to the victim *why* what she did to the victim was wrong; (3) communicate effectively to the victim *that and in what particular ways* she is *actively committed* to rectifying the wrong; and (4) offer to the victim *good reasons* why she will not harm the victim again.[13] Only victims of harms suffered by a perpetrator are in moral positions to forgive the perpetrator, no one else is—not even the state, nor even the closest of relatives or loved ones of the victims. *Strictly speaking, there is no vicarious forgiveness.* Moreover, though I can "forgive in my heart" another for harming me to my heart's content, genuine forgiveness is impossible without the above conditions of genuine apology obtaining. Under such conditions, reconciliation is impossible to the extent that it requires forgiveness. What, then, is forgiveness in criminal justice contexts? And how might the concepts of forgiveness and reconciliation relate to the problem of reparations for the oppression of Indians and blacks by the United States?

FORGIVENESS, APOLOGY, AND COMPENSATORY JUSTICE[14]

While a number of contemporary philosophers have analyzed the concept of forgiveness, most, however, do not link it to a notion of an apology. Even those very few who do link the concepts of forgiveness and apology to one another fail to say much, if anything, about the nature of an apology. But if the ideas of forgiveness and apology are intimately connected, then it behooves philosophers to explore the nature of an apology and its relation to forgiveness. Subsequent to assessing some leading conceptions of forgiveness, I articulate and defend a new analysis, one that construes an apology as a necessary condition of forgiveness. In so doing, I draw distinctions between forgiving and apologizing on the one hand, and forgiveness and apology on the other. Crucial to my analysis of forgiveness are the conditions necessary for an apology. However, even if such conditions obtain in a given case, the one receiving the genuine apology is under no moral duty to forgive. Assumed throughout my discussion is the claim that those offenders who are the objects of forgiveness have not committed their harmful wrongdoings under conditions of excuse or significant mitigation. In other words, they are assumed to be for the most part responsible for their wrongfully harmful acts, failures to act, and attempted actions.

Perhaps a discussion of forgiveness and apology in criminal justice contexts is in order as it might illuminate what might be plausibly said in terms of the role forgiveness and apology might have concerning the heirs of oppression and reparations possibly due them. Some philosophers have made the suggestion that forgiveness and mercy play meaningful roles in the sentencing of criminals. But what precisely *is* forgiveness in retributivist punishment contexts? There are variant analyses of the nature and function of forgiveness.[15] Subsequent to providing descriptions and assessments of some views of the nature and function of forgiveness, I will provide my own analysis of forgiveness in the context of "crimes against humanity." Along the way, I shall discuss the nature and possible role of an apology in a reasonably just legal system.

One reason why I delimit my discussion to forgiveness and apology in criminal justice contexts is because it is not entirely clear to me whether or not my analysis applies straightaway to some or all personal and familial ones. One obvious difference between the two contexts is that, while forgiveness of criminals typically involves parties who do not know each other, forgiveness in personal or familial contexts is most often quite different in this regard. And while in the latter kinds of contexts it might be safely assumed, generally, that the preservation of a relationship, while not necessarily creating a duty to forgive those who have wrongfully harmed me, nonetheless often makes forgiveness a condition of sustaining the relationship between my offender and me, the creation or preservation of a relationship is usually irrelevant in circumstances of criminal justice. Thus my discussion concerns only the moral status of forgiveness and apology in criminal justice contexts where criminals and their victims do not have a prior relationship that would make pertinent significant personal or familial factors.

I also seek to undermine the popular idea among philosophers and other academicians that no version of retributivism can make sense of the concept of forgiveness and that this is a telling objection to retributivisms because they cannot accommodate the (implied) duties to at least sometimes forgive and show mercy on criminals. Although it is not my aim in this chapter to defend my own or any other version of retributivism, it is important to know whether or not retributivism can have anything plausible to say about forgiveness, and what is plausible, if my account is right, for any theory of punishment to hold concerning forgiveness and criminals. In other words, if there is no moral duty to forgive criminal offenders, then there is no requirement of the state to have mercy on them, and the popular "forgiveness and mercy objection" to retributivism flounders. By extension, if there is no moral duty to forgive one's oppressor, then Indians and blacks are under no moral obligation to forgive the United States for oppressing them.

Is there room in retributivism, especially genuinely Kantian retributivism, for forgiveness and mercy? Assuming that pardoning is at least a species of mercy that entails forgiveness, then even Immanuel Kant, with all that he makes of the state's right and perfect duty to punish offenders, seems to make room by way of implication (in his mention of the sovereign's right to pardon) for forgiveness and mercy of some kind or another. Elsewhere, I pointed out that the logical problem this poses for Kant's idea of the right and duty of the state to punish offenders.[16] As I argued therein, a retributivist such as Kant who argues for both the state's right and perfect duty to punish offenders cannot, without pain of contradiction, argue for the pardoning of any criminals. This is why I argue that the state has a right, but not a perfect duty, to punish offenders. This leaves open the state's prerogative to not punish some offenders, not out of forgiveness or mercy, but rather out of a sense that certain minor offences are, practically speaking, overly troublesome to prosecute. It seems to me, then, that retributivism ought *not* to espouse the notion of pardon or forgiveness, unless, perhaps, for practical considerations such as the offence is "not worth punishing." There seems to be no non–ad hoc means by which to make it a requirement given retributivism's commitment to the concepts of desert, responsibility, and proportional punishment.

Mercy might be construed as compassion or forbearance shown to an offender, a forbearance to punish even when justice demands it. So too with forgiveness. "Like forgiveness, mercy is a *gift* to which the wrongdoer never has a right."[17] It is *"the suspension or mitigation of a punishment that would otherwise be deserved as retribution, and which is granted out of pity and compassion for the wrongdoer."*[18] This makes forgiveness and mercy moral prerogatives, not duties.

And this holds true even if offenders sincerely apologize for their wrongs and become fully rehabilitated. Retributivism of the sort defended by me has no room for forgiveness and mercy as duties, as they thwart justice and fairness.[19] They fail to respect humanity's sense of moral responsibility (in the duty and liability senses). Aside from rather minor cases, forgiveness and mercy by the state are morally unjustified. If forgiveness and mercy make any sense at all, they make some limited (perhaps personal, psychological, or religious) sense between a victim and the offender(s) of crimes against her. But neither the state nor anyone else ought to presume to have the right to forgive the criminal "for the victim."

FORGIVING

In light of the foregoing, I shall now set forth and defend my own analysis of forgiveness. Forgiveness is to be contrasted with forgiving. Although forgiveness entails forgiving, forgiving does not entail forgiveness. *Forgiving* is related to what Peter Strawson refers to as "reactive attitudes" such as hatred or resentment.[20] Forgiving someone, either oneself or another, involves adopting a certain attitude toward them. It is the ceasing of resentment or hatred toward another because of what the other did to them wrongly.[21] As Joel Feinberg notes, "To resent someone . . . is not merely to dislike him, but to have a negative feeling toward him in virtue of something he has done."[22] Of course, the person to be forgiven must have wrongfully harmed me in that their merely harming me, say justifiably, would not call for forgiving. This construal of the nature of forgiving is consistent with Jeffrie G. Murphy's definition of "forgiveness,"[23] though I shall distinguish two kinds of forgiving.

ATTITUDE FORGIVING AND ACTION FORGIVING

Forgiving may be of one or more of the following kinds: attitude forgiving or action forgiving. *Attitude forgiving* is the change of *attitude* that a person has when one no longer harbors resentment or hatred toward a person who has harmed one unjustifiably.[24] Here I might, for the sake of my own mental health or for social or religious reasons, adopt a forgiving attitude toward the person who has harmed me, while at the same time still want her to be punished properly for her wrongdoing. This seems to be what Murphy has in mind when he states:

> To forgive a wrongdoer involves a change in heart toward that person (the overcoming of resentment toward him), but this is not necessarily a change in one's view on how that wrongdoer is to be treated. Because I have ceased to hate the person who has wronged me it does not follow that I act inconsistently if I still

advocate his being forced to undergo punishment for his wrongdoing—that he, in short, gets his just deserts.[25]

Action forgiving, on the other hand, accrues when I change my hateful or resentful *action* toward another who has harmed me wrongly. Here I might harbor resentment toward the person who has harmed me, but nonetheless not want her punished because I am not convinced that she will be punished fairly, or because of religious reasons I hold against harsh treatment of any kind. Action forgiving might be seen as a species of mercy, wherein what underlies mercy is attitude forgiving. Of course, forgiving might be both attitudinal and action-oriented.

Whether attitude or action forgiving (or both), it is possible that I can forgive another without that person being genuinely forgiven. In other words, there can be forgiving without forgiveness. This is because the attitude or action of forgiving might not "take." One reason why it might not take or become real is that the person being forgiven might not have committed an act such that they qualify as being in need of forgiveness, that is, they might not have wrongfully harmed anyone. If I forgive Bonnie for her being a racist, yet Bonnie is not a racist, Bonnie is the recipient of my attitude and/or action forgiving, yet forgive*ness* does not necessarily accrue to her. Perhaps the only sense in which this kind of forgiving is helpful is for the person forgiving, though it is hard to imagine that forgiving someone for something for which they are not guilty is helpful to anyone. Nonetheless, it could make the forgiver feel better in some way or another. Another reason why forgiving might not truly occur is that, though Bonnie knowingly committed a harmful wrongdoing toward another, Bonnie failed to apologize to her. In this kind of case, Bonnie is a racist of, say, the worst kind. But for whatever reason(s) (denial, lack of moral character, etc.) she refuses to apologize, or fails to apologize adequately. Her victim can forgive Bonnie to her own heart's content; but as I argue below, unless and until Bonnie offers a genuine apology to her victim, *forgiveness* cannot accrue to her. That is, though Bonnie is (rightly or wrongly) forgiven, she is not one to whom "forgiveness" properly applies in this situation. Thus it is clear that there can be forgiving without forgiveness. This renders dubious the assertion that "forgiveness is *unilateral*. The wrongdoer need not be involved in any way for forgiveness to occur."[26] What this statement really describes is forgiving, not forgiveness.

FORGIVENESS

So there is a logic to forgiveness. Part of that logic is that it is necessary that if I forgive you, I must have been wrongfully harmed by you.[27] Forgiveness "presupposes an affront, injury, transgression, trespassing or offence committed by one person against the other and consequently the other's readiness or refusal to 'forgive' him."[28] But there is more to the logic of forgiveness than this. It is unfortunate that many philosophical accounts of forgiveness seem to write about it as if the focus of forgiveness ought to be on the one who, on their accounts, is required to forgive. Take, for example, the following statement:

> Forgiveness requires that a wrong not be disregarded or overlooked, but it also requires that the wrong not be allowed permanently to damage and distort one's personal relations. We are required to accept back into our heart a person who is responsible for having hurt and damaged us. If I am to forgive I must risk extending my trust and affection, with no guarantee that they will not be flung back in my face or forfeited again in the future. One might even say that forgiveness is an unconditional response to the wrongdoer, for there is something *un*forgiving in the demand for guarantees.[29]

Indeed, it is said that forgiveness is possible "even in the absence of repentance."[30]

What is astounding about some of these statements is how counterintuitive they are. Let us begin with the claim that "we are required to accept back into our heart a person who is responsible for having hurt and damaged us." On what rational basis are we to think that this statement is plausible, especially in criminal justice contexts? Does the statement really mean to suggest that women victimized by rape, for example, are "required" to forgive their rapists? On precisely what grounds would this claim rest? On the basis of what non-question-begging principle would we be required to forgive others who wrongfully harm us? It seems to rest on the question-begging assumption that forgiving is a moral virtue and that the unwillingness to forgive is a moral vice.[31] Indeed, it is asserted without supportive argument that "forgiveness is a high virtue, and also a hard one."[32] Yet this virtue ethics standpoint on forgiving is questionable. Assuming a roughly Aristotelian view of the moral virtues, a moral virtue is that moral property that is a mean between two extremes. In the case of forgiving, it is the moral virtue between the deficiency of never forgiving on the one hand, and always forgiving on the other. This implies that unconditional forgiving, for example, a kind of forgiving that does not place any conditions on forgiving, is problematic from such a virtue ethics perspective.[33] Unconditional forgiving cannot be a moral virtue if what it means is that one ought to forgive no matter what the circumstance. There is, then, no moral duty to forgive unconditionally. And this assumes for the sake of what I shall refer to as the "argument for forgiveness as a moral virtue" that forgiveness is a moral virtue in the first place.

Furthermore, if there is no absolute moral duty to forgive, one must be ever cautious to not make ad hominem assertions like the following regarding the forgiving of others who have wrongfully harmed us: "It is indicative of the honour in which we hold the virtue that our criticism of people who cannot forgive those who have harmed them tends to be rather muted; we think of them not as falling short of some minimally acceptable standard of behaviour but as failing to rise to a superior, quasi-godlike, level."[34] I take this as paradigmatic of the victim-centered view of forgiving in that it places the primary moral burden on the victim of harmful wrongdoing to forgive, rather than placing that burden on the offender to perform some virtuous action. Moreover, some philosophers believe that those who choose to not forgive those who have wrongfully harmed them harbor resentment, even vengeance, toward the wrongdoer(s). But neither of these points is always true. One can refuse to forgive someone and yet hold nothing against them simply out of respect for justice and fairness and a sense of having persons held responsible by the law for their harmful wrongdoings. There need be no emotive content one way or another regarding the refusal to forgive. Yet so many philosophers cannot rid themselves of the quasi-religious dogmas that in part motivate them to attempt to persuade us that forgiving, though not always the right thing to do, is in general the morally virtuous thing. And so they tend to deliver ad hominems about those who do not forgive others rather than plausible arguments for why they are morally wrong for not doing so. One thing seems clear: "Forgiveness must always be freely chosen and should never be understood as obligatory."[35]

Moreover, the statement (quoted above) that "If I am to forgive I must risk extending my trust and affection, with no guarantee that they will not be flung back in my face or forfeited again in the future" is problematic in that, while it is true that forgiveness might in some cases involve psychological risk for the one forgiving a wrongdoer, it certainly need not, as one who forgives need not be concerned with whether or not the wrongdoer becomes a recidivist. Also, it is dubious for such a claim to assume that forgiveness does not require at least the sincere promise not to harm the victim again.

Is it, furthermore, true that "forgiveness is an *unconditional* response to the wrongdoer, for there is something *un*forgiving in the demand for guarantees"? Certainly blind or naive forgiv*ing* would satisfy this description. But forgive-*ness* unbound to such ideological dogma need not be. Why should not for-giv*eness* be conceptually tied to a genuine apology of the wrongdoer? Would not the failure to do this result in a kind of cheapening of both the wrong done to the victim, but also in a devaluing of wrongdoing itself? Would it not also lead one to think that forgiveness is granted and effective automatically, regardless of the wrongdoer's desire to apologize? Do not these factors give us pause in thinking about the real nature of forgiveness and apology? It would appear that she who forgives her rapist without at least sincerely expressed guarantees from the wrongdoer that he will not harm her (or another) again amounts to some sort of lack of the victim's self-esteem and self-respect. Indeed, genuine forgiveness would seem to require a genuine apology. For as Murphy argues, "Acceptable grounds for forgiveness must be compatible with self-respect."[36] It would seem that a victim's self-respect would require a genu-ine apology on behalf of the offender for his wrongfully harming her.

The previous point leads to the matter of whether or not forgiv*eness* requires an apology. As noted, some argue that forgiveness does not require it. Others simply stop short of arguing that apology is a necessary condition of forgive-ness.[37] However, it is unclear precisely what is meant by "forgiveness" if it does not require an apology, unless, of course, all that is meant is that the forgiver simply places herself in a psychological state of not hating or harboring ill-will toward the wrongdoer. If this is all that is meant, then this sort of forgiving is innocuous. Yet it is difficult to understand how this psychological notion of forgiveness (i.e., forgiving) as one's attempt to preserve her own mental sanity from consuming hatred has a legitimate place in criminal justice contexts. For whether or not an offender ought to be punished by the state is a function of the extent to which the criminal is responsible for the harmful wrongdoing. That the victim or anyone else desires or decides to distance herself psycholog-ically from, say, hating the offender is irrelevant to what the criminal deserves for what she did. Thus some other kind of "forgiveness" (indeed, forgiving) must be meant in criminal justice contexts. And the confusion about the nature of forgiveness suggests that some clarity needs to be achieved along these lines. Hence my distinction between forgiving and forgiveness: While forgiveness requires both the harmful wrongdoer's apology to the victim and the victim's forgiving her, forgiving (as we saw) does not require an apology from her harmful wrongdoer. Yet neither forgiveness nor forgiving, properly construed, place the moral burden on victims of harmful wrongdoing vis-à-vis their offenders.

The foregoing discussion of recent views of the nature of forgiveness points to a fundamental flaw in previous philosophical accounts of forgiveness. They are victim-centered in the sense that they place the moral burden on victims of those whom they have the alleged duty to forgive. Consider, for example, Jean Hampton's understanding of the nature of forgiveness as that which involves a changing of the heart which does not amount to mere condoning of the wrongful act, and which is accompanied by an "offer of reconciliation."[38] Hampton goes on to claim that "reconciliation need not be made in words (we have a variety of ways of welcoming someone back). Forgiveness, on her view, can also take place without reconciliation: an offer may be impossible (e.g., if the wrongdoer has died) . . . and yet forgiveness of the wrongdoing can still occur."[39] But this seems counterintuitive. Notice the victim-centeredness of Hampton's model of forgiveness. It is the *victim* who bears the moral burden of forgiveness and reconciliation. It is the *victim* who is to make room in *her* heart for the wrongdoer and/or her harmful act. (In fact, it is, given Hampton's account, the *victim's* death that makes reconciliation impossible! Even more counterintuitive is her idea that forgiveness of the wrongdoing can nonethe-less occur.) We find no arguments for these claims in Hampton's otherwise interesting work on forgiveness. Her distinction between wrongdoers (as responsible agents) and performers of wrongs (those who commit wrongs but who are not, for one reason or another, responsible for them[40]) will not help here, as the criminal law already makes the distinction between those who bear responsibility for their harmful wrongdoings and those who do not, based on the conditions of responsibility.[41] As Hampton herself states, forgiveness pertains to resentment or hatred in regard to culpable wrongdoings, "demeaning actions for which their agents can be not only held responsible but also blamed."[42] But why place the moral burden of forgiveness on the victim? Why not place it on the harmful wrongdoer? After all, it is the rapist, for instance, who ought to humbly ask for forgiveness of the woman he rapes. To place the moral burden on the victim to forgive her rapist would be tantamount to arguing that supererogatory actions (like forgiving) are morally required. It is to fail to understand that wrongdoers have moral duties to apologize and that their victims never have moral duties to forgive their offenders.

In studying several accounts of "forgiveness," it seems that many scholars mistake quasi-religious notions of the category for philosophical and ethical ones. In many instances, they unwarrantedly either intentionally or unintentionally sneak into the definition of "forgiveness" some quasi-religious conceptual underpinning, often noted in terms of reconciliation or peace of mind or the like, rather than simply analyzing the term. For instance, one philosopher asserts that "the teleology of forgiveness is reconciliation."[43] But quasi-religious articles of faith can never replace the need for rigorous philosophical argument and analysis. And underlying ideas of reconciliation and peace of mind are in just as much need of justification as any other; they enjoy no privileged status in philosophical discussions.

This implies that the previous (unconditional) account of "forgiveness" is a category mistake, as it conflates what is supererogatory for moral virtue with what is required for it. Indeed, there are entire accounts of "forgiveness" that hardly, if at all, mention the apology of the wrongdoer, much less do they insist on the necessity of a genuine apology by the wrongdoer.[44] Even when some philosophers do recognize some extent to which an apology by the wrongdoer is important to forgiveness, the moral burden is still placed on the victim to forgive the apologetic wrongdoer.[45] Consider the following assertion made by H. J. N. Horsbrugh: "I share with Professor Downie, [the view] that one ought always to forgive one's injurers so far as this lies in one's power."[46] This appears to amount to the claim that we have an absolute moral duty to forgive those who have wrongfully harmed us. Yet this position is vulnerable to considerations noted above, such as when there is no authentic apology forthcoming from the wrongdoer.

Moreover, to discuss the concept of forgiveness without understanding that it is tied essentially to the notion of apology is to distort significantly the nature of forgiveness. It is, in essence, to conflate it with forgiving which can obtain absent an apology (as noted earlier). And this conflation amounts at least in some cases to an error of equivocation between "forgiveness" and "forgiving." Furthermore, other philosophers argue in favor of a conception of the nature of forgiveness that makes apology essential to it, and amounts to an activation or reactivation of a relationship.[47] Indeed, it is claimed that "the moral apology implies a request for forgiveness and is an initiative toward reconciliation."[48] Again, the concept of reconciliation enjoys no privileged position in ethics and is in need of philosophical justification. It is not a self-justified "basic" belief. It should never be presumed in contexts of criminal justice, including those of racist oppression. For it is problematic in cases wherein criminals harm victims whom they do not know or those with whom they want or have no meaningful and positive relationships such as in the cases of American Indians and blacks in the United States. And if it is insisted that such victims and their offenders ought to want to reconcile with one another, either out of moral principle, the good of society, or moral virtue, then such a claim must be supported by sound argument. After all, moral intuitions are hardly in accord on this matter. And a utilitarian ethic with its several deep ethical problems cannot simply be assumed to be plausible to make room for the notion of reconciliation between victims and their offenders.

Concerning "repentance" or apology, Hampton has little, if anything, to write, except that it "of course provides excellent evidence of the decency of the wrongdoer."[49] But there seems to be no indication from Hampton as to what a wrongdoer ought to do or what she needs to do in order that a victim of wrongdoing might have a perfect or imperfect duty to forgive her. In other words, Hampton provides no meaningful content to the notion of an apology that might provide "excellent evidence of the decency of the wrongdoer" and make forgiveness meaningful. As such, the informational content of her concept of forgiveness seems lacking in a crucial respect. Moreover, insofar as Hampton's notion of forgiveness asks us to distinguish the wrongdoer from the wrongful action itself,[50] and insofar as she rejects the moral hatred of the wrongdoer in favor of the act except in instances where the wrongdoer "thoroughly identifies himself with that cause,"[51] she seems to advocate a distinctly utilitarian model of punishment, or even a moral education model of "punishment."[52] For her, forgiveness is not inconsistent with the expression of the value of the wrongdoer's victim, with deterrence and with moral education.[53] However, what Hampton's conception of forgiveness fails to capture is the consistency of a plausible conception of forgiveness according to which wrongdoers are held responsible for their actions, at least to the extent that they satisfy the conditions of responsibility. In other words, Hampton's notion of forgiveness appears to reveal her underlying antiretributive bias, one that, for all she has written, ignores (if Robert Nozick[54] and Feinberg[55] are correct) the distinction between retribution and vengeance.[56] Yet, as I shall now argue, the concept of forgiveness itself entails an apology on behalf of the wrongdoer. But what exactly might it mean to genuinely apologize for a wrongdoing? And precisely to whom must a wrongdoer apologize in order for the apology to be legitimate, morally speaking?

On my conception, another distinction between forgiveness and forgiving is that the latter does not require an apology from the wrongdoer in order for forgiving to be effective. One of several examples of a conception of forgiving that is mistakenly cast in terms of forgiveness is found in the following claim: "in some instances merely saying, 'I forgive you,' *does* constitute forgiveness. . . . It is a mistake to imagine that there is some specific and definable activity, which activity and no other constitutes forgiveness."[57] According to this view an apology is not a necessary condition of forgiveness, making the performative of forgiving sufficient by itself for forgiveness. On my analysis, such a notion really describes forgiving, which requires no apology. It is a performative utterance that expresses the injured party's harboring no resentment toward the wrongdoer. But forgiveness is not a mere performative. It is a relational state that occurs between a victim and her offender under particular circumstances.[58] What most philosophers of "forgiveness" confuse is the subjective recognition of a person's being the recipient of a forgiving expression with the relational state of forgiveness, which requires an apology.

APOLOGY AND APOLOGIZING

Forgiveness, then, is the ceasing of the harboring of reactive attitudes or actions toward one who has wrongfully harmed her typically (but not always) by way of the performative act of forgiving which requires the offender's genuine apology.[59] But what precisely is an apology such that it might effect forgiveness? Further, is forgiveness (forgiving and an apology and the relational state that they imply between the victim and her offender) a moral duty of a victim of harmful wrongdoing? If so, what kind of moral duty is it, and why?

The first distinction to be drawn concerning the concept of an apology is similar to the distinction made between forgiveness and forgiving. It is common knowledge that anyone can "apologize" if by this is meant that one simply utters (or otherwise communicates) words that seem to indicate by their mere content that one is sorry for what they said or did to another. But when such "apologizing" is offered without sincerity, we ought to refer to it as mere "apologizing." So we must be ever mindful of the distinction between genuine and pseudo apologies: "Asking to be forgiven is sometimes expressed by apologizing to an injured person. But, of course, apologising and genuinely asking for forgiveness cannot always be safely equated."[60] I shall distinguish this notion of apologizing from the much more robust one of an apology. It is not apologizing that is required for forgiveness, but an apology.[61]

Forgiveness requires an apology,[62] which is the sincere and genuine admission of one's own harmful wrongdoing and regret for having committed it because it was harmful and wrongful. The sincerity of an apology has to do with its being serious and honest. And it requires communication between a harmful wrongdoer and her victim(s),[63] that is, should the latter still be alive for the communication to occur. A genuine apology requires that a harmful wrong-doer: (1) communicate effectively to the victim *what* she did that was wrong; (2) communicate effectively to the victim *why* what she did to the victim was wrong; (3) communicate effectively to the victim *that and in what particular ways* she is *actively committed* to rectifying the wrong;[64] and (4) offer to the victim *good reasons* why she will not harm the victim again.

Condition 1 requires that the wrongdoer admit *to the victim* that what she did was indeed wrong and requires an apology. Assumed here is the notion that a genuine apology cannot obtain to the extent that the one offering it understands and admits that her harmful wrongdoing requires an admission of both guilt and wrongfulness of the crime.

Condition 2 requires that the offender explain *to the victim* why what she did to her was wrong. This is not the same as the wrongdoer's rationalizing her actions, or trying to "explain away" their significance regarding the perpetration of the wrongdoing and the harm it caused the victim. The idea here is that the offender of the harmful wrongdoing needs to effectively communicate to her victim(s) the reasons why the harmful act was wrong, thereby demonstrating that the offender understands the extent of her harmful wrongdoing.

Condition 3 requires that the wrongdoer outline *to the victim* specific ways in which she will make things as right as they can be made right for the victim, without minimizing the harmfulness caused or providing lame excuses. It is the expression of the criminal's rectificatory responsibility for the harmful wrongdoing in question. This is the sort of explanation that is not likely to occur soon after the crime has taken place. For it takes some time to map out an intelligent and workable strategy for rectification, even if it is not the one imposed by law. Most important of all, this condition of an apology requires *action* on behalf of the apologetic one in her making as right as possible the harm wrongfully done to the victim. As Charles J. Ogletree, Jr., states: "Taking responsibility for one's acts, especially in the criminal context, often involves some kind of affirmative act to the detriment of the criminal . . . This often includes . . . paying some form of restitution."[65] It is vital to understand that *condition 3 makes adequate rectification a necessary condition of a genuine apology. And since a genuine apology is a necessary condition of forgiveness, it would follow that adequate rectification is a necessary condition of forgiveness. Genuine forgiveness cannot obtain without a genuine apology and adequate rectification,* though *forgiving* may rightly occur where such reconciliation is in process. This suggests that there is normally a process to forgiveness as rectification can require some time to complete. It is noteworthy that this element of an apology is absent from leading accounts of the nature of an apology, such as one found in Martha Minow's account.[66] Yet Minow states that "any diversion from accepting responsibility is not an apology," and "full acceptance of responsibility by the wrongdoer is the hallmark of an apology."[67] Perhaps part of the difficulty with

Minow's view is that she sees an apology as a major aspect of reparations,[68] which in her view do not require (and often eschew) compensatory measures in favor of "humble acts" of symbolic reparations that transform relationships between victims and their wrongdoers.[69] In contrast, I argue that it is the converse: a genuine apology requires compensatory reparations, among other things that constitute reparations in this or that context. For without this kind of justice, the peace requisite for the reconciliation that Minow and others so badly desire cannot be possible for those who want to retain their self-respect and dignity.

Condition 4 serves as the criminal's word, whatever good it is, to her victim that she will refrain from ever harming her again in the way she did. This involves expression of practical ways in which the criminal will not engage in recidivistic behavior toward the victim. It may or may not include a more general promise of antirecidivism. It is transparent that my analysis of a genuine apology is offender-centered, thereby making my analysis of forgiveness offender-centered. Moreover, conditions 1–4 also require sufficient expressions backed by actions to make the offender's apology as genuine as can reasonably be assured. This in turn tends to make it more likely that forgiveness can accrue based on the self-respect of the victim in forgiving her offender. Why? Because at the very least, it is required for forgiveness that the offender demonstrate, among other things, that she knows and admits why her harmful wrongdoing was both harmful and wrongful, and that she is by word and deed already committed to rectifying her harmful wrongdoing. And so long as her victim knows these facts about her offender, it is unlikely, if not impossible, for her to engage in forgiving behavior out of a lack of self-respect. What is implausible is an analysis of an apology that omits sincere deeds as well as a changed attitude on the part of the harmful wrongdoer in that such an omission would not ensure that the offender properly respects the rights of her victim she wrongfully harmed. Thus a genuine apology on behalf of the offender serves as the reasonable basis of both the offender's respect for the victim's rights that she violated and the victim's self-respect should she in the end choose to forgive her offender or not.

Note that my analysis of an apology does not list in lexical or some other prioritized order the conditions thereof. This stands in sharp contrast to those who assert (without supportive argument) that "the most important part of an apology" is "the acknowledgement of the offense."[70] It is precisely this kind of thinking that leaves open the possibility of insincere apologizing, for example, those offering to their victims no deeds of rectification. By contrast, my analysis holds that each of the above four conditions is equally necessary for a genuine apology, making rectification just as essential to all other aspects of an apology. On my analysis, then, it is impossible to have a genuine apology without, among other things, adequate rectification by the offender to her victim(s). This implies that in the case of the United States' oppression of Indians and blacks, it is impossible for there to be genuine reconciliation and peace between these groups and others in the United States absent genuine forgiveness. But it is also impossible for forgiveness to accrue between these groups and the oppressor heirs in the United States without the latter groups providing a genuine apology to the victim heirs (Indians and blacks). But a genuine apology requires, as we have seen, adequate rectification by the oppressor-heirs to the victim heirs, between the United States on the one hand, and Indians and blacks on the other. This implies that reparations are required of the United States to Indians and blacks if there is to be genuine peace and reconciliation between them. And this holds true no matter how much many Indians and blacks engage in forgiving behavior toward the United States, and no matter how much the United States engages in apologizing behavior toward Indians and blacks.

My analysis places no moral duty on victims to forgive their offenders, or on the state to forgive "its" offenders. It is also implied here that harmful wrongdoers who do not satisfy conditions 1–4 lack the moral standing either to be eligible for forgiveness or to have forgiveness accrue to them because it would be a morally unjustified forgiveness or one that lacks proper moral standing. Thus it is clear that my analysis of forgiveness differs from the others discussed above in requiring an apology that is designed to promote self-respect in the victim and the harmful wrongdoer's respect for the rights of the person whose rights she violated.

The locution "to the extent that" indicates that there are degrees to which apologies can be offered by harmful wrongdoers. In particular, there are degrees to which an offender might comprehend her harmful wrongdoing. This in turn will affect the extent to which she can effectively communicate to her victim what she did that was wrong and harmful and why it was wrong and harmful. Furthermore, note that "communicate" includes not only verbal but nonverbal expressions. Thus apologies—even genuine ones—need not always be made in words, though they must be made in ways understood by and acceptable to the victim. In sum, apologies are genuine to the extent that conditions 1–4 are satisfied.

This analysis of the nature of forgiveness (and an apology) is similar to the one found in Joanna North. In her account, there are nine "stages" of an apology from the wrongdoer's perspective. One stage involves the "cognitive recognition on the part of the wrongdoer of the harm he has done" which entails a full understanding by him of the consequences of his action. Stage two is the wrongdoer's remorse for committing the harm.[71] Stage three involves the wrongdoer's resolving never to commit such an act again, but also to become a better person. Stage four involves a consciousness of "some measure of self-improvement and development of self-respect." Stage five is the offender's desire to be forgiven. Stage six involves his plea to his victim to be forgiven. Stage seven entails the wrongdoer's self-forgiveness. Stage eight involves his acceptance of the victim's forgiveness. And at stage nine "the wrongdoer and the injured party are reconciled."[72]

North's first stage of forgiveness is captured more or less by conditions 1 and 2 of my analysis of an apology. But insofar as remorse is an emotional mental state, it is unnecessary for an apology on my account, and hence unnecessary for forgiveness since a genuine apology is all that is necessary for forgiveness. However, if I. Thalberg is correct in stating that "genuine remorse must include a disposition to mend one's ways,"[73] then remorse is consistent with conditions 3 and 4 of my analysis of the concept of an apology insofar as a disposition leads one to action since remorse is directed at the results of one's actions.[74] That the wrongdoer is resolved never to harm the victim again is captured in condition 4, though I see no reason to require for an apology that an offender commit herself to otherwise becoming a better person. The apology is directed at the act for which the wrongdoer seeks to be forgiven, not for future things that have yet to occur.[75] This implies that the wrongdoer's awareness of self-improvement and development of self-respect is also unnecessary for an apology. That a wrongdoer desires to be forgiven seems to be implied by conditions 1–4, as does his actual plea to be forgiven by her victim and her acceptance of the victim's forgiving her. But what does the wrongdoer's self-forgiving have to do with forgiveness, except to suggest that "ideal" or complete forgiveness (e.g., beyond the criminal justice context) entails not only the proper forgiving of the wrongdoer by the victim, but also the proper forgiving of the wrongdoer by herself? Finally, that victim and offender be reconciled is in no way a requirement for an apology, or for forgiveness, for the reasons stated above. It is rather suspect that so many thinkers are rather presumptuous along these lines.[76] Yet a moment's reflection would inform the careful philosopher that to require reconciliation for forgiveness places the moral burden on the victim to forgive her offender. In other words, the implication of the "forgiveness for the sake of reconciliation" notion is that victims must be morally virtuous and at least in most cases forgive those who harm them wrongfully, lest society have a host of unreconciled persons. Yet we find no independent argument in support of such a claim. It is presumption, perhaps based on some form of religion or humanism (or both) which holds that no human is beyond the pale of forgiveness and reconciliation with others. But this seems to amount to a viciously circular argument: we ought to forgive because we ought to reconcile ourselves to one another when there are breaches of decent conduct that would alienate us one from another; we ought to reconcile ourselves to one another because we ought to forgive!

My analysis of forgiveness and apology also bears some resemblance to the following one:

> A person who apologizes and asks for forgiveness acknowledges by so doing that he was wrong. In this admission, he is seeking, in effect, to separate his character and future actions from his past wrongs. If he sincerely apologizes, he is indicating that he is sorry for the wrongdoing, is committed not to repeat it, and wishes to be understood as a person so committed.[77]

That the wrongdoer is committed not to repeat her harmful wrongdoing is captured by condition 4 of my analysis of an apology. And perhaps conditions 1–4 imply that the wrongdoer should feel a true sense of sorrow for her action, inaction, or attempt that wrongfully harmed her victim. However, the above conception of an apology does not require that the wrongdoer communicate anything *to the victim*. Yet it is the wrongdoer's apology to the victim that is necessary for the wrongdoer to experience forgiveness. Moreover, nothing in this view of an apology seems to capture the following consequences of conditions 1–3: that what she did was wrong; that it was wrong for such and such reasons; and that the offender *will do* all that she can to rectify (including compensate) the harm done to the victim. It is difficult to understand how anything short of what is contained in conditions 1–4 can constitute a genuine apology. Yet until this moral fact is understood by those analyzing forgiveness, then crucial questions about this important concept will remain begged here and there, often in subtle ways.

Another argument in favor of the moral duty to forgive unconditionally those who have wrongfully harmed us is that if causal determinism is true, then there is no freedom of action and no moral responsibility for our actions, inactions, or attempted actions, as the case may be. Thus it is quite in order to forgive wrongdoers because (if causal determinism is true) wrongdoers are not to be blamed for their harms to others. Neither are they legitimate subjects of punishment or forced compensation. In reply to this argument, it must be pointed out that if causal determinism is true in the hard deterministic sense, then there is no sense to be made of normative ethics and moral responsibility, and not even moral practices such as forgiving others make much, if any, sense. For we only forgive those who are blameworthy for wrongful behavior, not those who could not have done otherwise than what they in fact did. So forgiving such "persons" (if "persons" is not too flattering a term for them in a completely deterministic world) seems to make little or no sense. Moreover, reconciliation as a goal or even as a prerequisite for forgiveness also makes little or no sense. Why ought we to be concerned with reconciling those who are causally determined in a strict sense to do whatever they do? And how might our attempts at reconciliation via forgiving them make a difference in the deterministic sequence of life? The general moral skepticism resulting from hard determinism also infects moral concepts and practices of forgiving and reconciliation. Thus the argument for forgiveness and reconciliation cannot plausibly be based on the idea of hard determinism.

IS THERE A MORAL OBLIGATION TO FORGIVE?

One thing seems clear if the forgoing analysis is plausible: There is no moral obligation to forgive under any circumstance. This point has been made previously.[78] Some have argued that the reason for this is that one might be unconvinced of the sincerity of the apologetic harmful wrongdoer.[79] However, this view makes a harmful wrongdoer's reform sufficient for forgiveness. But why should we think this is so? Why ought whether or not one has an obligation to forgive another be contingent on whether or not the wrongdoer is reformed either attitudinally or behaviorally—or both?

There are those, like Claudia Card, who argue that "although forgiveness cannot be compelled, one can be at fault in failing to offer it to those who deserve it or refusing to grant it when asked by those who have done all they can to atone."[80] But to deny that there is no obligation to forgive is to misunderstand the nature of forgiveness itself. Among other things, forgiveness is an act of grace by the victim in response to her harmful wrongdoer's genuine apology. It is always the victim's, and the victim's alone, moral prerogative. It is never an obligation of any kind, perfect or imperfect. Although it might make for good quasi-religious dogma to insist that agents are required to forgive those who wrongfully harm them, it is nothing that enjoys philosophical support. Forgiveness is an agent's moral prerogative under any circumstance; it is not a moral obligation. Indeed, it would constitute a queer and cruel irony of justice (not to mention, counterintuitive) to think that a victim has an obligation to forgive even the most apologetic of harmful wrongdoers! When all is said and done, the victim of the harmful wrongdoer's action (or failure to act or attempt to harm) is not necessarily in the wrong for not forgiving. It is completely up to the victim, and the victim alone, to decide whether or not to forgive. In no way is she necessarily morally or otherwise defective or unjustified for not forgiving her harmful wrongdoer.[81] While it is probably prudent to forgive minor offences against oneself or others, it is surely not obligatory. Moreover, it can sometimes be a sign of a significant lack of self-respect or respect for others to become overly forgiving of more serious wrongs, as Murphy argues.[82]

For example, while I might find it not worth my while to harbor resentment toward a colleague for his unintentional racist actions toward me, I might find it more difficult to forgive his trying to (actively and over time) sabotage my career. But I would not be morally wrong if I did not forgive him for the racism. Likewise, I might find it easier to forgive my spouse for being inconsiderate once in a while in ways that are not overly serious. However, I might find it more difficult over time to forgive consistent and seriously inconsiderate acts or words on her part. Although it might be true that forgiveness can in some instances be the first step toward healthy reconciliation between parties alienated by the wrongful acts of another, nevertheless hasty forgiveness, or forgiveness where it ought not to be granted, can in some cases be a step in the direction of permissiveness that is sometimes a sign of diminished self-respect and respect for others.

Note that each of the four conditions of an apology that I set forth (1–4) requires that the offender communicate in some way *to the victim*. Of course, there are many cases where this would be impossible in a full sense, for example, where victims have been murdered, are comatose, etc. The implication of the above analysis of forgiveness is that where conditions 1–4 of an apology are not satisfied, forgiveness is impossible, except in third-party cases. I might, if I so choose for whatever reasons (good or bad) forgive the murderer of my brother for the harm caused to *me* by my brother's being murdered, but this in no way serves as a proper substitute for my murdered *brother's* forgiving the murderer (in the case where my brother's murderer is alive to be forgiven). I surely cannot forgive, *for my brother*, the murderer for her murdering my brother. Only my brother can do that, should he be alive (but he is dead, and so he cannot forgive her!). All that I can do, should I choose to do so if my brother's murderer truly apologizes for the murder of my brother, is to forgive her for the harm that she caused *me* in her murdering my brother. This too is part of the logic of forgiveness. The scope of forgiveness is agent-relative. One can forgive only those who have harmed one and then only for the harms caused to oneself. This is because, as Murphy argues, I do not myself have the moral standing to forgive you unless I have myself been the victim of your wrongdoing.[83] *There is no such thing as vicarious forgiveness*, philosophically and morally speaking. As J. D. Mabbott avers, "No one has any right to forgive me except the person I have injured."[84] All of this renders dubious that idea that there can be "unilateral cases of forgiveness."[85]

One important question here concerns the matter of third-party forgiving. It is morally problematic for the state to so much as consider third-party forgiving as sufficient for the state's forgiveness of any criminal for any serious crime. While some citizens, even members of the surviving family of murder victims, might forgive the murderer, say for religious or psychological reasons, this might affect attitude forgiveness. But in no way ought it to influence the state's meting out justice.[86] After all, the unexcused murderer has in effect eliminated the only party who can effect forgiveness on her. Hence the seriousness of murder without excuses. As we know, Kant argues that murderers must be put to death. Where there are no excusing or significant mitigating factors, murderers must receive capital punishment. What is consistent with Kant's view here is that there is no manner in which forgiveness can accrue to the murderer,[87] since the only person(s) to whom she can truly apologize cannot receive her apology. And since a genuine apology is a necessary condition for forgiveness, and in turn forgiveness a necessary condition of mercy, forgiveness cannot possibly accrue to murderers. For if the victim is dead, one philosopher writes, "and if the offender is sincere in his repentance, then the offender must endure the burden of knowing that he can never be fully forgiven."[88] Third parties may engage in attitude forgiving to their heart's content, but this ought in no way whatsoever change the fact that the murderer in such cases has robbed herself of any opportunity to experience the forgiveness necessary to save her from the same treatment that she enacted intentionally, voluntarily, and knowingly on her victim.[89] Pseudo-forgiveness is not the same as genuine forgiveness. One can be forgiven yet not have forgiveness accrue to her, as I noted earlier.

Moreover, if the concept of forgiveness just discussed is to be applied to the state and its citizenry, it seems not to lend itself to a widening of application from individual to state. For in individual cases of wrongful harms and forgiveness, it is relatively clear who the victim is and who the offender is, and who needs to apologize if there is any hope, not demand or obligation, of forgiveness. But with the state and its punishment of offenders, things are more complicated. There are wide differences of moral intuition concerning whether or not forgiveness ought to play any role at all in a criminal justice system. Although it is clear who is to apologize if forgiveness of offenders is to be forthcoming, it is not clear who ought to do the forgiving. Is it the victim herself? Is it the state? It would seem that a system of punishment and compensation cannot rely on the whims of individuals and their variant abilities and willingness to forgive, nor of a majority of citizens. Because the laws of the state need to be public and predictably and otherwise fairly enforced in relevantly similar circumstances, the state must be the agency that employs forgiveness, if it is ever justified in the first place.

In personal life, forgiveness surely has its place, especially when interpersonal relationships are at stake. Indeed, to err is to be human, but to forgive is just as human. Indeed, as Murphy states, "The person who cannot forgive is the person who cannot have friends or lovers."[90] But is it justified for the state to forgive and show mercy on duly convicted criminals? If crimes are offences against not only victims but the state, then a question arises as to whether or not the state ought to have a right to forgive a criminal for what she has done to harm another citizen. This is especially important in cases where the victim has no intention to forgive her offender. On what grounds might the state forgive the criminal? On utilitarian grounds because to forgive provides for social stability in some cases? This would sacrifice, among other things, a citizen's right to peace and tranquility. On retributivist grounds, say, because the criminal does not deserve to be punished? But if a criminal does not deserve to be punished, then she is not a candidate for punishment in the first place, and forgiveness is not appropriate. Furthermore, how many citizens must want to forgive an offender before the state can rightly forgive her? A majority? If so, how large a majority? And what if the crime in question is a racist hate crime? Is it a numerical majority of the general population that would be required for forgiveness and mercy toward the criminals? Or, would a numerical majority of those within the victim's ethnic group be required to justify forgiveness and mercy? Or both? Forgiveness and mercy in rectificatory justice contexts is quite problematic, though these practices have room in personal life as Murphy's above statement about forgiveness, friends, and lovers makes plain.

From the forgoing it follows that contemporary Indians and blacks have no moral authority to forgive anyone or anything who or that oppressed their respective ancestors. So those evils are forever unforgiven and unforgiveable. But it hardly follows from this that a debt of compensatory justice in the form of reparations is not owed by the oppressor heirs of those acts of violence. The most that today's Indians and blacks can do, if they choose to, is to forgive the oppressor of their ancestors' oppression of Indians and blacks *insofar as such oppression impacts themselves as contemporary Indians and blacks.* While it is far too late for the United States to experience genuine forgiveness for its historic evils committed against Indians and blacks, it is not too late for it to experience true forgiveness from contemporary heirs of the oppression. But that requires, among other things, a genuine apology, which entails compensatory reparations to the victim heirs of the oppression.

My primary aim in this chapter was to expose some of the weaknesses in the concept of forgiveness as some philosophers have attempted to apply it to criminal justice contexts often to seek to undermine some version of retributivism in that, it is argued or assumed, retributivism cannot make sense of the (implied) duties of forgiveness and mercy due to its demand for retribution for harmful wrongdoings. Forgiveness has, perhaps, significant sentimental value in such contexts. But it is hardly morally required. One way in which previous forgiveness theories have erred is to have placed the moral burden of forgiveness on the victim of wrongdoing, rather than on the offender.

What was argued concerning crimes against persons and punishment of such crimes might well be argued regarding compensation for harms, whether to individuals or groups. So the putative role of forgiveness in a criminal justice system as it pertains to punishment might well be the same as it would be in a juridical system as regards matters of compensation, including reparations.

If the forgoing analysis of apology and forgiveness and the line of reasoning based on them is plausible, then the following seems reasonable to accept. If genuine reconciliation requires self-esteem and self-respect on the parts of oppressed victims and their heirs sufficient to require in turn forgiveness and apology, then in the cases of Indians and blacks whose ancestors were brutally oppressed by the U.S. government, certain U.S.-based businesses and other institutions, and many U.S. citizens, no one today can either apologize for or forgive anyone or anything regarding the evils of oppression experienced in the past. For both perpetrators and victims are dead and there is no such thing as vicarious forgiveness. Note that what is not being argued here is that no one can adopt an *attitude* of apology or of forgiveness. In fact, for purposes of coexisting in even an approximately stable and peaceful society, it is likely that such attitudes of apology and forgiveness are necessary. Indeed, Howard McGary argues that "reparations, when properly conceived, involve reassessment. The reassessment requires the alleged victims to examine their victimization, the alleged wrongdoers to come to grips with what they have done, and the victims and the wrongdoers to explore their relationship with one another" showing "that there is an appreciation for the consequences of their wrongdoing."[91] But it hardly follows from McGary's plausible articulation of forgiveness, based on even genuine apologies by current U.S. citizens, that apology and forgiveness actually accrue in ways sufficient and relevant to apply genuinely to the cases in question.

So if genuine reconciliation between the U.S. citizenry in general and Indians and blacks in particular requires genuine forgiveness on the parts of Indians and Africans oppressed by the U.S. government, certain U.S.-based businesses and other institutions, and its general citizenry,[92] such forgiveness is, strictly speaking, impossible in that current Indians and blacks are in no moral positions to forgive anyone or anything for historic oppression. Nor is the current U.S. citizenry in a moral position to apologize for the past evils in question. If this is true, then the notion that reconciliation, genuine reconciliation (e.g., beyond mere attitude), is impossible and ought to be discarded as a goal in U.S. social relations. Yet contemporary Indians and blacks have been tremendously disadvantaged as the results of the evils perpetrated on Indians and Africans during previous generations. Thus there is good reason, granting the self-esteem of the members of both disadvantaged groups, to think that Indians and blacks have been dealt indirect forms of oppression due to the unrectified evils of the U.S. government, a government under which each group lives to the present day. So even if it is correct to argue that present-day whites (and some others) do not owe to Indians and blacks reparations because they themselves are not (causally) responsible for the evils in question,[93] it is wrong to infer that the U.S. government does not owe reparations to such groups for the indirect oppression caused by the primary oppression of the forebears of these peoples. For this fails to take sufficiently seriously the ramifications and complexities of collective moral responsibility discussed in chapter 5.[94]

If this line of argumentation makes one feel uncomfortable, it is perhaps in part because one believes that it makes good sense to hold that reconciliation is a good thing, especially for purposes of rectifying historic evils of racial oppression such as those experienced by Indians and blacks at the hands of the U.S. government, certain U.S.-based businesses and other institutions, and its supportive citizenry. Furthermore, many also believe that it makes good sense to hold that forgiveness by victims of such evils of governments and societies that genuinely apologize for such evils, pursuant to the conditions of apology quoted above, is dutiful. And this holds true, most would think, regardless of whether those making the genuine apology and those extending the forgiveness are the ones who on the one hand perpetrated the evils, or on the other hand were those who directly experienced them as victims. But this line of thought cannot, because of its disallowing present-day U.S. whites the inheritance of moral duties to pay reparations for the evils perpetrated on Indians and African slaves by the U.S. government in that present-day citizens did not cause the harms, place anyone in a legitimate moral position to either apologize or forgive unless she is an agent in the circumstance of evil in question. So it would follow in that view that genuine reconciliation is impossible, and certainly not a viable goal as "ought implies can." Contrary to Margaret Urban Walker and Janna Thompson, among many others whose theories of reparations were rendered dubious in chapters 2 and 3, if there is no genuine apology, there can be no true forgiveness; and if there is no forgiveness, there can be no reconciliation! And this is true even if reconciliation is, contrary to fact, a desired goal in a reasonably just society, or one seeking to become reasonably just. For no such society can renounce rights to compensatory justice and be adequately just.

It would appear, then, that in order for there to be anything remotely akin to genuine reconciliation between the U.S. government, certain of its businesses and other institutions, and its general citizenry on the one hand, and Indians and blacks on the other hand, there must be some allowance for extenuating circumstances of positive public policy administration such that current members of the U.S. government and its general citizenry can offer an apology to current Indians and blacks for the racist oppression experienced at the hands of the U.S. government and its citizens of the past, *an apology sufficient for purposes of positive public policy administration.* Moreover, such circumstances of positive public policy administration would make room for the possibility (not the moral requirement or obligation) of Indians and blacks to express forgiveness to the U.S. government and its general citizenry for the racist oppression of the past. Surely this would be the hope of many U.S. citizens, at least of those who genuinely appreciate the horrors and realities of the historic oppression of Indians and blacks in and by the U.S. government and many of its citizens.

Thus in order for the positive goal of reconciliation to accrue, there must be forgiveness, as McGary holds. But forgiveness requires a genuine apology. The only way in which these can occur is if we allow, *for purposes of extenuating circumstances of positive public policy administration,* for the notion of vicarious apology *expression* by the offender heirs of oppression and the U.S. government and the moral prerogative of vicarious forgiveness *expression* by the victim heirs of oppression. Without this conventional allowance, there can and ought to be no hope whatsoever for reconciliation between blacks and Indians on the one hand, and the U.S. government and its general citizenry on the other. For factors of self-esteem would and ought to prohibit blacks and Indians from even thinking about forgiving the U.S. government and its general citizenry for what are among the worst evils in human history unless and until an apology sufficient for positive public policy administration accrues. To disagree with this point is morally disingenuous toward both the victims and the victims' offspring of some of the most evil acts humans have *ever* perpetrated on other humans. We must recall that *unrectified evil is evil still: Neither the evils nor the deserved punishments and compensations owed by the perpetrators to their victims or victims' families fade over time, barring some sound argument for a moral statute of limitations on historic injustice.* The burden of argument lies with those who support a moral statute of limitations on injustice or that considerations of social utility override rights to compensatory justice in the form of reparations.

All of this assumes that genuine apology, forgiveness, and reconciliation are desirable under the circumstances of tremendous injustice under discussion. However, even in their absence, there is no reason to think that reparations are not owed as a matter of compensatory justice, as was argued in the previous few chapters. Forgiveness and reconciliation are morally supererogatory actions on behalf of victims. In order to respect the autonomy of individual victims of oppression and the sovereignty of the groups to which they belong, reconciliation between heirs of oppression must be left to the victims, not the heirs of oppressors as so many presume absent non-question-begging utilitarian, rights-disrespecting, and supporting argument.

In light of my previous arguments in favor of compensatory reparations and the rebutting or neutralizing of the many key objections to them, the remaining issue seems to pertain to whether or not a plausible case can be made for a particular policy of reparative justice for Indians and blacks by the United States. It is to this matter that I now turn.

9

Possible Reparations Policies

The people might get mad but freedom got a high price. You got to pay.
No matter what it cost. You got to pay.

—August Wilson[1]

It is one thing to present plausible arguments in favor of reparations in cases
such as the historic injustices against American Indians and blacks. And it is
one thing to rebut all manner of objections to the reparations arguments,[2]
showing that on balance, the preponderance of argumentation favors compensatory reparations to these groups. However, it is another thing to be able
to demonstrate with some meaningful degree of accuracy the viability of such
reparations given the complex realities of contemporary economic and political life. And there are at least two ways in which the viability must be demonstrated. First, it must be shown that a country as politically, economically, and
militarily powerful as the United States can be "brought to justice," for example, that it can be forced to pay reparative compensation should it follow its
history in mostly not wanting to hold itself legislatively responsible for its
own oppressive harmful wrongdoings, whether domestic or foreign. My plan
for reparations to these oppressed peoples is primarily legislative,[3] though if
the United States fails to hold itself responsible (subsequent to a meaningful
and lengthy national discussion of the issues of reparations to these groups)
for its oppression of them and pay adequate reparations roughly as I describe,
then a case must be brought to the International Criminal Court in order to
try the United States for crimes against humanity.[4] And should the United
States ignore such an indictment, or refuse to pay the reparations imposed on
it by the ICC should that body make such a ruling, then an international coalition of countries can and should impose diplomatic and, if necessary, nondip-
lomatic measures against the United States for as long as it takes to bring the
United States to justice. In the end, I concur with Boris Bittker when he writes

that this inquiry into reparations "presupposes a society that is prepared to respond to the meritorious of these claims, rather than dismissing all of them as man's ineluctable fate."[5]

Furthermore, to object to my arguments for reparations to Indians and blacks solely on the ground that it is very unlikely that the United States could be successfully coerced to pay them is to ignore the essential normative import of my moral argument. The possibility that the United States may never pay what it owes to these groups does nothing to discount the normative plausibility of my arguments in favor of the claim that Indians and blacks deserve and are owed reparations from the United States. Instead, it would point to the possible recalcitrant nature of a country that has never been serious about doing justice with regard to what are among history's worst atrocities for which it is primarily co-responsible.

Second, even if it can be shown that the first problem can be addressed in such a way as to provide good reason for thinking that the United States can be forced to pay reparations should it express an unwillingness to do so through congressional legislation, the problem of "ought implies can" raises its head in another way: even though it has been explained that the party who owes the reparations and the parties to whom reparations are owed can be identified, precisely what is owed by the United States and can the United States possibly pay, even during disastrous economic times? This is a particular problem in light of the fact that it has already been shown in chapter 1 that affirmative action programs are not, strictly speaking, forms of reparative compensatory justice. Can the United States afford to pay what it owes in reparations to Indians and blacks? Precisely how might such reparations be effected?

We must understand that, as in most any legislative matters or a case that would be brought to court, it is approximate justice, not exact justice, that is the practical goal. To think that reparations are somehow unjustified because exact justice cannot be achieved is like arguing, by parity of reasoning, that no punishment for murder, rape, or any other crime or tort that cannot be rectified with exact precision is justified. For it is a rare case indeed that can satisfy that strict standard of justice! Thus it will do no good to retort that complexities abound in these cases of reparations, and that it is impossible to provide reparations for all of the modes of oppression experienced by Indians and blacks. Instead, we must strive, as we ought to do in any other case, for the closest we can achieve to proportional compensatory justice, realizing that compensatory justice, like punishment, is more of an art than a science. This is not intended to be an excuse for inexactitude, but rather a recognition of the practical complexities involved in solving even many of the simplest cases of injustice.

As for the first difficulty noted above, and as I noted in chapter 4, John Rawls provides the best answer for cases in which a powerful outlaw regime refuses to do the right thing. In *The Law of Peoples*, Rawls argues that a carefully crafted coalition of countries might well be able to stand up to and coerce the outlaw state into complying with the demands of justice, in this case, the demands of compensatory justice, both domestically and globally. The United States gains little, if anything, by standing against a coalition of countries such as Canada, China, Cuba, India, Mexico, North Korea, Russia, and most Middle Eastern, Central and South American, and African countries that refused to join the "coalition of the willing." Not only is this true economically, but militarily as well. Economically, the United States' recent successes at capitalist globalization in turn and perhaps unwittingly make the U.S. economy contingent for its stability and overall success on the very cheap labor provided by China, India, and Mexico, among some other nations and countries. Without such affordable labor, U.S. citizens would surely not be able to afford their comfortable standards of living and the goods and services therein. And without the U.S. citizens spending their money on this or that, the U.S. economy stumbles (as it has), and can eventually collapse. Furthermore, the U.S. military threat of noncompliance means little or nothing in such a context, as it cannot short of enslavement coerce the compliance of cheap labor—not even with the most powerful of weaponry. No matter how poor, those whom the United States has then turned into enemies would not likely provide labor to create and sustain U.S. wealth. This is particularly true if the coalition countries currently providing the cheap labor are made aware of the power of their labor to bring the United States to its knees and in light of the likelihood that the United States has over the years provided most or all such countries and nations with ample reason to desire to work against the United States.

Additionally, "jawboning," or criticism and condemnation of other states that are not accompanied by various diplomatic sanctions such as disassociation with the United States by the coalition states, closing their U.S. embassies and calling home their own ambassadors, and breaking off formal diplomatic relations, might be employed before these more drastic measures, however, in order to pressure an unwilling United States to rectify its oppression of Indians and blacks.[6] In short, these and other similar efforts might amount to "an international system of public shame"[7] or an adverse publicity sanction[8] of the United States for noncompliance with an ICC order to pay (preferably, by way of its own federal legislation) reparations to whom the United States owes them.

So the United States can be made by a carefully crafted coalition of countries to understand the following coercive offer: either the United States submits to the demands of compensatory justice concerning Indians and blacks, or it faces the likely doom of its economy, which in turn will lead to the demise of its political clout globally and its society in general. Now it is certainly possible that such a move would not result in the noted results, perhaps because the United States might be able to provide economic incentives or military threats sufficient to block the imagined coalition. But the very serious attempt to form the coalition for the reasons mentioned (as well as others) would surely deal the United States a serious blow insofar as its self-perception is concerned. And what is at stake is not a zero-sum game. To the extent that such a coalition is formed, the United States will likely suffer significantly in political and economic terms. Whether this is sufficient to coerce justice in these or other related cases is uncertain. But it is far from obvious that the formation of coalition countries to confront outlaw states such as the United States is not possible, or even to some meaningful extent effective. And to the extent that it is successful, either on the first or subsequent attempts, the U.S. citizenry is faced with the dilemma of whether it is worth it for it to remain globally despised and protect its corrupted leadership and ill-gotten gains, or to follow the demands of justice and fairness and to enjoy the fruits of more harmony with the rest of the world. It is, of course, a deeply ethical problem, and it assumes what I have denied elsewhere, namely, that the U.S. citizenry has a certain minimal and decent level of moral character. It also assumes, of course, that countries such as England, France, Spain, and others that were also complicit or at least co-responsible in the American holocaust, or the transcontinental trade of Africans as slaves are coerced into providing their fair share of reparations owed to the victim heirs of their oppressive acts. Indeed, as sort of a plea bargain agreement, such countries and nations might be encouraged to join the reparations coalition to in certain ways mitigate what they themselves owe in reparations to the plaintiffs in question.

However, it must be borne in mind that many nongovernmental agencies and businesses were responsible for the oppression of Indians or blacks, some of which still exist today. Railroad, stagecoach, telegraph, and many other companies owned and operated by U.S. citizens could not have existed and thrived without the wrongful taking of Indian lands from coast to coast, for example, and they assisted in the payment of military services to secure those territories for the United States. Moreover, thanks to the California legislature, from 2000 to 2002 there was a mandate for all insurance companies in California to disclose details of insurance policies on slaves' lives, though the act imposes no penalties for nondisclosure or for companies that were in fact involved in the slave trade. It was about this same time that Aetna Insurance Company apologized for insuring slaves' lives and in this way promoting significantly the slave trade in the United States. Furthermore, between 2002 and 2004 the city councils of Chicago, Detroit, and Los Angeles each mandated the disclosure of companies complicit in U.S. slavery.[9] Even some universities have begun to admit their involvement in or ties to slavery in the United Staets. In 2004, the University of Alabama apologized for its use of slave labor, and Brown University admitted that some of its campus buildings were built in part from slave labor, and Nicholas Brown of the Brown family after whom the university is named, profited from the slave trade.[10] One wonders how many more historic colleges and universities in the United States would find themselves in similar positions should they decide to order investigations into their possible histories of collusion with Indian and black oppression. As we understand from the previous chapter, however, such apologies are not the same as such institutions offering a genuine apology for their roles in the slave trade. For that would require, among other things, restitution in the form of reparations.

Prior to exacting reparations from the United States, U.S.-based corporations, companies, and other businesses that are responsible in significant measure for such oppression should be made (by legislation) to pay to Indians and blacks what they owe in proportion to their shared responsibility for the oppression. Only subsequent to this step should U.S. citizens be levied a reparations tax for what their predecessors have done to oppress these groups.

Now assuming the practical possibility of some meaningful and effective level and degree of coalition countries that would serve as a means to encourage and even coerce the United States into compliance with the demands of justice and fairness, and assuming the plausibility of my arguments in favor of reparations to these two oppressed groups, approximately what is owed to Indians and blacks by the United States? This is a most complicated matter, as "the costs of a meaningful program of reparations—will be colossal."[11] In the case of Indians and blacks, even the most detailed study of history cannot possibly provide sufficient information to factor in all of the details that compensation must address. Nevertheless, I shall attempt as best I can to provide a rather *conservative* but fairly precise estimate of what is owed to each of these groups, providing reasons for my estimates.[12] For reparations, if carefully and fairly devised, can resolve in meaningful (though incomplete) ways the chasms that alienate victim heirs and offender heirs of oppression from one another and prevent them from genuine reconciliation that would bring authentic peace and tranquility to a society. For as Bittker writes: "Should no wrongs be corrected unless all can be?"[13]

There is one more set of problems that must be addressed prior to outlining my proposal for U.S. reparations to Indians and blacks. It is an issue raised by Bittker concerning whether or not reparative compensation ought to be made to these groups as wholes, or to their constituent members.[14] The problem as it is typically conceived is this: On the one hand, if reparations are paid to individual Indians or blacks, then the compensation will be spent or handled in ways that each such individual sees fit which tends to not address the group values and harms that require rectification; on the other hand, to award such damages to the two groups in question is to ignore personal autonomy that seems deserved for each such victim heir of oppression. While Bittker and most other scholars opt for the group compensation plan, I shall argue in favor of a reparations proposal that respects both individual autonomy and group sovereignty of the victim heirs of oppression. Following the approach that the U.S. government has used for generations in dealing with Indians (and recognizing its problems), my proposal is rooted in the plan for group-based reparations. However, unlike alternative plans which assume that the U.S. government would decide on the disbursement of such reparations, my plan requires that each group select its own representatives of Indian or black people, as the case may be, to serve on a plebiscite reparations committee that would serve the best and varied interests of its people by the establishing of widespread and well-subsidized housing, healthcare, and education for members of their groups, including the payments of monthly or annual sums of individual or familial cash payments of an amount determined by the committee members.

And while it is correct that the Indian model "cannot be automatically transferred to black-white relations," this is why I propose that each group select by democratic vote the membership of its own reparations committee (perhaps constituting, say, twenty to twenty-four members, along with an unavoidable bureaucratic structure of support staff to assist in the recording and disbursement of various benefits). In this way, the United States has no influence concerning the expenditures of the reparations it owes. Nor should it.

Those adults who qualify as being members of each of these groups by way of my genealogical analysis of ethnicity[15] would then select the membership of the respective reparations committees, terms that can be stipulated to last for, say, two to four years, renewable upon vote. This addresses the problem that Bittker notes facing a situation wherein the U.S. government would "have" to select such committee members.[16] As he notes, such a system would "stir up justified resentment among those who were not selected for official recognition, and expose those who were selected to the charge of being official spokesmen despite their alleged representative character."[17] My proposed model would also address the concern that those Indians and blacks skeptical of U.S. intrusion into the reparations committees' business or of more general concerns with institutionalized structures, as even such persons would have votes to attempt to secure their interests on the committees. Moreover, the fact that the committees would more likely than not (because most individual members of these groups would want to receive some cash payment of reparations) satisfy the individual members of their groups and would maximize the likelihood that individuals would receive at least some meaningful, if not substantial, individual benefit from the reparations. This would in turn address to some meaningful extent the wrongful harms suffered by some victim heirs of oppression over others.[18]

Furthermore, it might be objected that my genealogical analysis of ethnic identification "would put pressure on millions of persons of mixed blood to make an official declaration of their racial origin, instead of allowing their allegiance to remain private, ambiguous, submerged, neglected, or changeable."[19] But this concern faces numerous difficulties other than the obvious one that no one is not of "mixed blood." First, there is no requirement for anyone to declare ethnicity and receive reparations. Should one not desire to do so, the choice is theirs. But they are then hardly in a moral position to complain about their not receiving reparations benefits. There must be some manner by which to determine who the rightful beneficiaries are, and even a privacy-respecting method of DNA analysis via health care providers cannot guarantee complete privacy concerning such matters. Secondly, most of those who receive reparations will be made so much wealthier than they currently are that they really ought to have no serious concerns about anyone else's knowing their ethnicity. It is not as if they would then need to depend so much on others for their livelihoods that revelations of such matters would adversely affect them in ways they do currently. Thirdly, that one's ethnicity ought to remain "submerged" or "neglected" is a sign of lack of ethnic pride, and should hardly serve as a good reason why there should not be a determinable ethnic identification requirement for reparations payments. Finally, ethnicity, for purposes of public policy considerations, is not mutable as the concern assumes without supportive argument.[20] After all, as Bittker admits, "There is undoubtedly a bitter irony in arguing that a country that used racial classifications for many years should be wary of preserving or reviving them in a program of reparations."[21] And to those Indians and blacks who for other reasons would resent reparations being contingent on their being reclassified as "Indians" or "blacks," perhaps those Indians or blacks can take refuge in the fact that such reparations would constitute such great amounts of money that they would no longer be dependent on the United States for anything should they desire that kind of lifestyle. Moreover, they might take refuge in the further possibility that my reparations proposal is so comprehensive that it truly brings a meaningful measure of justice to the lives of the descendants of millions of murdered Indians, the hundreds of millions of acres of land stolen from Indians, unpaid Indian and African slave labor, and unjust treatment of such persons, and Indians and blacks who suffered under Jim Crow.

Perhaps the reparations can be construed by such victim heirs of oppression as their taking responsibility for the receiving of rectification for those and other past injustices. In the end, Bittker accepts as "not irrational" the idea of a "racial code" based on "the individual's percentage of" blood quantum[22]—a genealogical tie to Indians or blacks. But he raises the question as to whether the amount of genealogical tie to these groups ought to determine the amount of reparations benefits one receives. My model of reparations, insofar as it in part concerns the individual cash payments to Indians and blacks, stipulates an equal percentage of cash payments to all who truly qualify as Indians and then an equal percentage to those who qualify as blacks as it is more often than not far too difficult to establish the varying degrees of oppression experienced by each Indian and black family. And while it is strictly speaking true that "a program of reparations treating all beneficiaries alike would be flawed because all beneficiaries are not alike"[23] and are due differential benefits because of the plausibility of the principle of proportional compensation, it is also true that the compensation amounts and kinds of reparations received would recognize the practical limitations of exactitude of such awards and distinguish the victim heirs of oppression from others, which at least satisfies in a meaningful way a broad requirement of proportional compensation. It would, moreover, provide a wide range of benefits to a set of diversely oppressed groups and their constituent members each of whom faces her unique cluster of challenges due to the oppression in question. My model of reparations, then, stands in sharp contrast to those discussed in chapters 2 and 3, and to others who argue against any monetary payments to the victim heirs of oppression.[24]

The real problem looming over my approach is the same one facing any such policy program, namely, that of selecting a fair and just percentage of genealogical tie required for membership in a relevant group for reparations. This is an important problem because it affects not only the eligibility to vote for members of a reparations committee, but possible membership on such a committee, and eligibility to receive reparations benefits. I have already admitted this problem, though it is hardly a reason to deny reparations to oppressed peoples. Nor is it a problem unique to my model of reparations. Nonetheless, the case of Indian identification might be used as a relatively successful and unproblematic way of determining group membership. Perhaps a DNA certified blood quantum of 1/8 or 1/16 or 1/32 might work, though this question ought to be open to discussion among some highly uncontested members of these groups and perhaps subject to revision over time if the members of each group believe that the membership of the group should be enlarged because it appears to disallow those who are clearly members of the group. The idea is to set a minimal requirement that would capture as many of those who appear to be and have been Indians or blacks without including those of us who clearly do not share a sufficiently significant DNA tie to these groups. More will be said about this in the next chapter. Initially, this DNA analysis can select a starting point as to what constitutes membership in each group, though discussion of reparations policies ought to be open and respectful of diversity of viewpoints on all matters. Thus the selection of reparations committee members and even the determination of who counts as members of reparated groups are not dictated by the U.S. government, but decided by members of the groups themselves, thereby securing a meaningful degree of group sovereignty and individual autonomy. In turn, the control of reparations more generally is in the hands of those who most deserve them, and not in the hands of the perpetrator(s) or their heirs. Individual autonomy and group sovereignty of the victim heirs of oppression is largely preserved, unlike in competing approaches to reparations.

Thus compensatory reparations do not need to be restricted to either individuals or groups as most scholars think. Rather, they can be structured to address the needs and desert factors of both. As we shall see, various nonmonetary programs as well as individual or family cash payments can be administered by reparations committees, none of which are required to serve the interests of anyone but themselves and their constituents. This implies that Bittker is wrong when he states that "Congress or some other public body, rather than its unofficial advisers, will have to decide in the end whether a program of reparations should consist of individual or group payments, specific nonmonetary programs, or some combination of these."[25] On the contrary, the U.S. Congress must decide whether it wants to pay such reparations to these groups. If it does decide to pay them, it ought to decide on fair and just amounts to each of these groups, a topic that I shall address in the following sections of this chapter. Should Congress decide on fair and just amounts of reparations to these groups, it must instruct the proper agencies of the government and whichever U.S.-based businesses owe them to pay them and establish accountability and severe penalties for nonpayment. That is the extent of the authority of the Congress regarding such reparations, morally speaking. Congress is not to decide in any way the shape that such reparations ought to take, as that is the task of the duly elected members of the reparations committees. If Bittker's proposal is taken seriously, then one of the principal human rights offenders of Indians and blacks would be in a position to dictate how reparations function to such groups, which is absurd. Contrary to Bittker, no one has a right to determine how reparative compensation to Indians and blacks is spent except Indians and blacks themselves. For only they have the *rights* to such reparations and they are not bound by considerations of social utility (e.g., the greater good of the United States) regarding the manner in which they handle them.

It is crucial to understand that these concerns, though important and relevant to the payment by the reparations committees of reparations to individual members of these groups, do not in any way undermine the plausibility of the claim that reparations are owed to these groups by the U.S. government and some of its businesses. Nonetheless, having addressed them I shall move on to outline my model of reparations to Indians and blacks respectively, leaving further concerns to be addressed in part 3.

REPARATIONS TO AMERICAN INDIANS

As I have argued in *Race, Racism, and Reparations*, the case of compensatory justice to Indians must take into consideration the facts that genocide (part of the "American holocaust") was committed against a host of Indian nations by the U.S. Army at the direction of the executive and legislative branches of the federal government, not to mention at the request of many state and local governments, and with tremendous popular support, but also that perhaps the greatest theft of land ever occurred in the process. Indeed, most concur that it was the aims of manifest destiny and the doctrine of discovery that provided the primary motivation for the genocidal acts against Indians for over a century by the United States, and prior to that by the Spanish, British, and French governments for centuries.

As I argued in that book, strict justice would require that the lands stolen by force and fraud from Indian nations by the United States be returned to them. In the words of one legal theorist,

> There are many good reasons for requiring me to return to you what I have taken. One is that while you may have no right in justice to all that you own, it does not follow that I do, or that I have a right to take it. Thus, requiring me to return the property to you is a way of recognizing that I had no right to take it from you in the first place.
>
> If I have no right to take your property, then justice might require that I give up my unjust enrichment.[26]

Why is this so? Because, "According to corrective justice, individuals have a duty to repair the wrongful losses for which they are responsible."[27] And I would add that this principle of corrective justice applies to compensatory justice between groups. Moreover, I would add that it is not just that the loss results from wrongdoing, but from harmful wrongdoing, as not all wrongful acts result in harms to others. Furthermore, not all harmful wrongdoings result in compensable damages. Additionally, compensable harmful wrongdoings are those that result from the doings of a responsible agent, one that, as we found in chapter 5, commits a harmful wrongdoing intentionally, knowingly and voluntarily. And in this case we want to know about harmful wrongdoings that amount to oppression. Certainly the genocidal theft of Indian lands qualify as most oppressive, especially given how central land is to Indian cultures. So the dispossession of such lands from Indians clearly constitutes oppression of a fundamental sort. Reparations, then, are a compensatory means of rectifying the theft of resources that result from other forms of harmful wrongdoing.[28]

Now if we consider as a matter of contemporary precedent that Catholic dioceses across the United States are currently awarding in legal settlements an average of about US$1,000,000 per victim of priestly sexual abuse, we must then figure on some amount of what a human life is worth, especially ones taken so violently and with such evil motives. And all the while, we must, as do the courts, tie ourselves closely to principles of proportionality, lest moral and legal arbitrariness run rampant in our thinking about these matters.

If a victim of Catholic priestly sexual abuse rightly receives in settlement about $1,000,000, then the families of genocide ought to receive at least $10,000,000 per victim.[29] This figure, as conservative and approximate as it is, is meant to reflect the fact that while victims of child molestation are indeed harmed and wrongly so, victims of genocide are killed[30] and can no longer enjoy life or pursue their projects. No amount of psychological therapy can assist them to live a decent life, because they are dead. And as the previous chapter made plain, death (at least in these cases) is an evil thing, as it provides the victims, in the case of Indians, including children, no manner by which to even have a life much beyond birth. The genocide also wiped out entire cultures and civilizations, as well as any earning power and assets they might have had and could have passed on to their heirs. None of this, and so much more (such as the centuries of duration of the severe rights violations against Indians), is true of cases of child sexual abuse. It really does seem as though what happened to millions of Indians is worth (individually) at the very *least* ten times more than the current average individual settlement of child sexual abuse by the various priests and leadership of the Catholic Church. But again, I am figuring matters rather conservatively in order to make my case for the amount of Indian reparations as strong as possible, avoiding the objection that the amount I end up with is inflated or in some other way incorrect via overestimation. Indeed, the figure I suggest in the end will be insultingly low from an Indian standpoint, and for that I truly apologize to Indians past, present, and future. However, I offer the following reasoning for the sake of policy implementation.

Now, if it is true that the estimates of illicit Indian deaths from 1492 to 1900 during the years of European empire expansion and manifest destiny in the United States is about 10,000,000,[31] the total estimated compensation just for the U.S. genocide of Indians can be set at $10,000,000 per Indian murdered multiplied by 10,000,000 Indians killed by the United States and its citizens = $100,000,000,000,000, an ominous figure indeed! I have not figured in compounded interest as I simply took current figures of what such a human life is worth in economic terms given and compared to current court settlements of child sexual abuse victims.

But to this figure of $100,000,000,000,000 must be added the value of the lands taken either by violent force or otherwise by fraud, land that is sacred to Indian cultures and indeed the basis of their lives! It would surely be incorrect to figure today's fair market value for the lands in question, because U.S. citizens, corporations, businesses, and so forth, have "increased" the value of the lands in some ways, but grossly and irreparably ruined it in others. Only some of the lands remain in about the same condition as they were when seized from Indians long ago. How ought reparations for the lands in question to be computed? There is no simple or uncontroversial way to accomplish this. However, I believe that given that current market values are impossible absent the taking of the lands in the first place, perhaps a percentage of the fair market value of the land ought to be given to Indians by way of a reparations tax, computed with the figure we have for millions of genocided and enslaved lives. Again, I shall suggest very conservative figures here, ones quite insulting to those who are seriously concerned about justice to Indians. But again this is because my strategy is to argue for a figure so conservative that its denial would reveal a significant level of disingenuousness. So I aim to appeal to whatever sense of justice the typical U.S. citizen might possible have, and rationally pressure and embarrass them into grasping that such reparative amounts are easily affordable and justified in light of the facts of the case.

Given the fact that those U.S. citizens with home mortgages and rental payments on average pay about 30 to 40 percent of their gross annual incomes
on mortgage or rent, I shall suggest the extremely conservative amount of 3
percent of all working adults' gross annual incomes in perpetuity, no matter
what their poverty or wealth level. This is a rather insulting percentage given
that without the theft of the lands in the first place, the market values of the
lands and their property on them would not even exist. However, what I am
after is an affordable amount that can satisfy the "ought implies can" dictum.
Besides, even though, as we saw from the argument of chapter 6, the typical
U.S. citizen is not morally entitled to that which was obtained unjustly, is she
not entitled to the fruits of her labor/investments above and beyond the basic
value of the unjust inheritance or acquisition or transfer of Indian lands to
them?[32] Perhaps strict justice would mean that most or all U.S. occupied lands
would be transferred to Indian nations, and that Indians would, as a coalition,
become a sort of "landlord" over those who currently reside on the lands.[33]
But I am not advocating such a position, as it is not feasible under the circumstances. Thus I am suggesting a more practically feasible but highly principled
manner by which Indian reparations can and should accrue, one which seeks
to maximize both Indian sovereignty and autonomy rights.

Now according to the 2000 U.S. Census, there are about 100,000,000
employed taxpayers (this might or might not be made to include currently
undocumented people who might be granted legal taxpayer status) in the
United States, and the current average annual gross income is approximately
$30,000, then the current figure of 3 percent of the gross annual incomes of
taxpayers is about $900 multiplied by 100,000,000 = $90,000,000,000.
Again, this is a very low figure indeed for the entire land mass of the United
States! And I once again beg the forgiveness of all Indians for suggesting such
an insultingly low amount. Surely the value of the lands in question is greater
than this figure, and it is against Indian custom to think of land in such terms.
Yet we are facing anything but a realistic utopia here, and we are not engaged
in full compliance theory. In light of these considerations, I am after a conservative figure with which any reasonable person with a minimal amount of
moral character can concur given the facts of the case.

However, when the extremely conservative reparations figures for genocide
and land theft are added together, we arrive at the very conservative sum of
$100,000,000,000,000 (genocide and slavery debt for 10,000,000 Indians
wrongfully killed or enslaved at $10,000,000 per Indian) + $90,000,000,000
(land theft debt) = *$100,090,000,000,000*, a rather staggering figure indeed!
But this figure is to be paid to Indians by several governments, so long as the
same kinds of arguments can establish the collective identity and responsibility of, say, England and Spain, among other offender countries. But since the
United States purchased the Louisiana Territory from France in a "fair deal"
between those two parties this would seem to leave the United States with the
primary burden of what is owed for that territory, though it hardly relieves

France from its share of genocidal reparations. One tremendous irony here is that the U.S. empire fought so hard to gain, retain, and expand its borders, now only to have to pay the bulk of the reparations owed for the lands and genocide. But it is clear that most of the genocidal activities in what is not called the "United States" was done by the United States, subsequent to the morally unjustified secession of the United States from England.[34] A fair-minded study of U.S. history would seem to reveal that the bulk of the reparations owed to Indians is by the United States.

So the United States owes the bulk of these reparations to Indians because the United States caused most of the damages to Indians by way of severe rights violations. The United States, then, owes at least *$100,090,000,000,000 to Indians*, and recall that this is in many ways a conservative figure. The number of Indians wrongfully killed, tortured, enslaved, or otherwise severely oppressed by the United States has been estimated to be much higher, and the actual value of U.S. stolen lands could easily rise into the trillions of dollars— even in modest real estate values in an economic downturn. If the United States has the unmitigated gall to approach the ICC in efforts to have the court force England, France, Spain, among others, to pay their fair shares of these reparations, it is its own responsibility to secure these outcomes through the ICC. But if that route is taken by the United States, then perhaps figures more closely resembling accurate compensatory justice will be used, and the U.S. attempt to evade its own responsibility for these human rights abuses would not be worth the effort and costs, or would indeed backfire because it may very well be that what the United States is ordered to pay according to more exact and less conservative figures far exceeding most of the figures with which I am working.

What should one think about this figure? We have not yet considered what the United States owes to blacks. Yet it appears that the United States cannot possibly pay an amount anywhere akin to $100,090,000,000,000, not even on credit! For if each adult U.S. income is taxed at a rate of only 3 percent of her gross annual income, given current demographic figures it would take the United States generations, perhaps even centuries, to pay the debt, and this does not even figure interest from the current date (I am ignoring interest and penalties for the unpaid debt owed to Indians until the reparations payments commence) until the debt is paid generations or centuries later. This is especially true in light of the current economic crises in the United States and in light of its future cyclical economic crises. So in yet another effort to suggest an extremely viable but fair amount of reparations to Indians, I suggest that every adult U.S. citizen be taxed *in perpetuity* according to what I shall call the *"Indian reparations tax" at the rate of only 5 percent of her gross annual income.*[35] Given the above statistical figures from the 2000 U.S. census, 5 percent of $30,000 × 100,000,000 = *$150,000,000,000*, which would be transferred to the committee on Indian reparations annually, in perpetuity. The amounts will be extracted from each income check by the Internal Revenue Service, the work of which shall be overseen by a leading accounting and auditing firm paid by the United States but hired by the committee on Indian reparations in order to best ensure accuracy and minimize governmental or citizen fraud against Indians. No Indian shall pay this tax, nor any other tax, to the United States or any other state or local government in U.S. territory as a means to settle matters between Indians and their oppressors. Any taxes paid by Indians in the past shall not be refunded to them by the IRS with interest and penalties in order to once again further ensure the conservative nature of my estimate of reparations to Indians, and an official written apology shall be issued by the U.S. government for all of its evils against Indians, listing them in kind, signed by the current U.S. president, vice president, and a majority of current members of the U.S. Congress. Of course, the United States, or its citizenry, is in no moral position to complain about such a tax given that it is a rather conservative figure. And any U.S. citizen who cannot live on 5 percent less than what they currently live on is simply incompetent and not in a position to blame anyone else for their lack of minimal ability to live a decent life in such a materialistic country. Compared to much of the rest of the world population, even the poor in the United States would fare well.

The payment of the Indian reparations tax would be made by the IRS directly to the committee on Indian reparations, which would constitute duly elected (only by Indians) Indians who would serve in, say, two- to four-year terms and would be remunerated for their service but not supervised by the federal government as an additional penalty for its primary role in the American holocaust. It is believed that many traditional elders and formally educated Indians, especially those who are expert at finances and economics and investments, would serve in such a capacity and decide on the disbursement and investment of such funds. One obvious result of this committee would be to bring every Indian out of poverty immediately, with provisions of housing, education (Indian, as well as any other kind of education Indians deem important to themselves, including training in Indian languages and cultures), food, healthcare, including massive purchases of lands to be held in trust throughout North America. This should not be difficult given that today there are, thanks to the U.S. genocide of Indians, only about 2,000,000 Indians in United States. And though it is perhaps controversial whether monetary reparations paid to individual Indians ought to be *the primary* means of compensation or rectification, it is surely uncontroversial, given my arguments in preceding chapters, that such compensatory reparations ought to be a primary means of reparations should individual Indians desire to access such funds to which they have a compensatory right. It is likely that so much money would accrue to Indians that they would be able to purchase and place in legal trusts many of their lands from non-Indians within a few generations. And the irony of the Indians hiring their own accounting and auditing firm to audit the IRS (at the expense of the U.S. government) is so astounding that it requires no comment for those of us aware of the lengthy history of Indians being harassed by the IRS. Moreover, Indian gaming would no longer be necessary, though ironically the state and local governments of U.S. citizens might well see gaming as a needed source of non-Indian employment in order to survive economically. Perhaps most important of all is the restoration of Indian national sovereignty that such reparations can to a significant extent enable through economic and political power.

However, this Indian reparations tax accounts only for the harmful wrong-doings of the U.S. federal, state, and local governments against Indians. It does not account for the harmful wrongdoings against Indians by U.S.-based businesses. Even though various existing businesses contributed greatly to the U.S. economy in a variety of ways, including the provision of numerous jobs for whites and other non-Indians, I shall ignore this factor in my estimating the reparations owed to Indians as yet another way to multiply ensure the conservative nature of my reparations estimate of 5 percent of each gross annual income in the United States in perpetuity. Surely, then, what is owed to Indians is far, far greater than what I estimate herein.

Whereas pleas for reconciliation between Indians and the United States leaves Indians without sovereignty, reparations as I construe them provide Indian nations with the wherewithal to regain as much of their former lands and sovereignty as possible, including cultural practices, in peace and freedom apart from U.S. intrusion. If Indians are paid reasonably adequate reparations as I outline, their in perpetuity payments received will best ensure that they gain and retain the economic and political power to reestablish their lives apart from the destructive forces of U.S. cultural, including religious, values. As centuries of integration of Indians with U.S. whites has shown, a clear balance of damaging influences have accrued to Indians in that process. This data of history can be used to justify the segregational protection of Indians from the United States, except, of course, where Indians desire integration perhaps for purposes of business (recall that it was for trading purposes that Indians first welcomed whites onto the eastern shores of Indian territory centuries ago). A question here, however, is whether Indians as groups would heed George Santayana's caution to remember the errors of the past so as not to repeat them. Ironically, what morality seems to require is that severely oppressed but reparated groups such as what might develop as the Coalition of American Indian Nations have the prerogative to use the same tool of ethnic segregation that oppressed them to liberate themselves from their oppressors, or their oppressor heirs.

REPARATIONS TO BLACKS

Having in chapter 7 argued in favor of reparations to blacks, it is helpful to explore some ways in which such reparations might accrue. And just as with U.S. reparations to Indians, we must separate the questions of moral desert from those of implementation. Whereas previous chapters have established the deservedness of reparations to Indians and blacks based on U.S. oppression of these groups, the questions now focus not on whether such reparations are deserved, but on who or what owes what to whom and how much is owed. This implies that it is not a sufficiently good reason to deny reparations to these groups solely on the ground that the matter of proper payment of the reparations is complex.

It is noteworthy that many have argued in favor of affirmative action or preferential treatment as a legitimate form of reparations to blacks.[36] However, as I have argued, to construe affirmative action or preferential treatment as a form of reparations is a category mistake since affirmative action in many forms amounts to programs of preferential treatment the benefits of which are *earned* by recipients in the form of employment wages, whereas this is not true of reparations. Compensation is not for "awarded" monetary damages earned by victims (or their heirs) via their working for such "reparations," but paid because it is deserved as the result of the harmful wrongdoing that they or their forebears suffered. It is a grand confusion indeed to suppose, as most do, that descendants of U.S. slavery who deserve reparations for their ancestors' human rights being violated (in millions of instances, for the durations of their entire lives!) are to be adequately compensated by *earning* their salaries by way of positions awarded them by way of preferential treatment.

Unlike possible policies of reparations to Indians that ought to consider ways in which substantial acres of land as well as monetary damages be awarded to Indians, reparations to blacks ought not to involve U.S. territory since the moral entitlement to such territory belongs by and large to Indians. So in this regard, reparations to blacks are comparatively simple as they involve some amount of monetary compensation as in the cases of Germany's reparations to Israel and the United States' reparations to certain Japanese Americans each for WWII-era atrocities.

To argue, as some do, that programs of social welfare might be considered as reparations to blacks not only runs the risk of the category mistake just mentioned, but also presumes that blacks ought to or must integrate or remain integrated into the very society the government of which has served as their most ardent oppressor for generations. Surely justice cannot require—or even presume—that victims of racist evils ought even to desire to coexist alongside those whose government has oppressed them so badly, especially without compensation after centuries of brutal rights violations. This being the case, reparations to blacks ought not to assume an integrationist posture. And given that the amount of reparations owed to blacks would be the amount owed for the estimated costs of labor power and value stolen by coercion from the millions of African slaves in the United States, all human rights violations at the hands of the U.S. government and various state governments, it is plausible to think that blacks would have sufficient funds to successfully segregate themselves from their U.S. oppressors once and for all. There is no question that thousands, perhaps millions, would do precisely that.[37]

Strict justice, it would appear, might well require that the U.S. government pay to blacks as a group (by way of the committee on black reparations) the approximate monies owed blacks for the evils of slavery and of Jim Crow.[38] However, as in the case of American Indian reparations, "ought implies can," and such payments could not, without bankrupting the U.S. economy, be made in a lump sum anytime in the foreseeable future. So some sort of annual "tax" would need to be assessed. The overall amount of reparations owed might be calculated and then paid over, say, 100 years, including compounded interest, penalties for previous nonpayment and inflationary factors, and so on. It might be argued that in perpetuity payments of reparations to Indians and blacks run the danger of such ethnic groups being diluted over time (relative to whatever percentage of ethnicity is required for public policy purposes) such that members of the oppressed groups in question receive lesser percentages of reparations payments. It might be suggested that an adequate amount of reparations be paid to blacks within a century so that more of those who experienced some of the historic evils can benefit from reparations. On the other hand, if reparations payments end up being inadequate in sum, then it would seem fair to make such payments accrue in perpetuity as in the case of reparations to Indians. Yet given the limited durations of all empires, the U.S. empire is not likely to last long enough for the ethnicity of blacks to be so diluted that it would have tremendously adverse effects on their general population. Thus, I favor reparations to blacks in perpetuity, assuming that the United States survives long enough to pay at least most of what it owes to blacks, and Indians also. Admittedly, as in the case of Indian reparations, no amount of reparations will suffice for the evils wrought on these oppressed peoples. But this is hardly a good reason for not making an honest effort to do the right thing. Concerns about the possible corruption of blacks actually distributing the reparations monies need not concern us any more than German citizens have a legitimate concern about how Israel ought to distribute reparations payments received from Germany. The same can be said in the case of U.S. reparations to Indians.

There is no question that should the United States finally own up to what it truly owes in reparations to blacks (and to Indians), the United States could no longer survive as it now does. But as we saw, considerations of social utility neither negate the reparations argument in the Indian case, nor in the case of blacks. Whatever suffering accrues to the United States as the result of its paying fair reparations to Indians and blacks might be seen rightly as the moral and economic costs of constructing a society by murdering and otherwise oppressing millions of Indians and blacks and refusing for centuries to pay its *grand debts*. If such suffering spells the demise of the United States as we know it, then perhaps the costs would serve as a reminder to the remainder of the world as to how *not* to build a society. It must be borne in mind that the United States as a perpetrator of severe evils on these groups is not in a moral position to complain about whatever hardships it is forced to endure as the result of its paying adequate reparations to Indians and blacks. Indeed, reparations seem to be the moral cost of the United States to attempt to redeem itself from the dredges of immorality in which it alone has placed itself, generation after generation, by refusing to pay what it owes to those whom it has murdered, enslaved, and otherwise oppressed, or to the heirs of its oppressed victims en route to the establishment of the U.S. empire.

The circumstances of black reparations are similar to those of Indian reparations in that the general cases of oppression stand in a class by themselves in world history in terms of both harshness and duration of the evils inflicted on them. And both cases of oppression are experienced primarily by the United States and its citizenry, but also by some foreign countries, as mentioned above. Yet there are some important differences. One such difference is that while Indian reparations must figure both the genocide of millions of Indians by the United States as well as the theft of what is now called the "U.S. territory," black reparations involves chiefly the unpaid labor of slaves over generations, monies that were usurped by force by slavemasters, slave catchers, slave traders, as well as insurance companies, tobacco and cotton companies, and so on, as well as violent oppression experienced under Jim Crow. Indeed, it is no exaggeration to note that much of the entire foundation of the U.S. economy and state economies both North and South were highly dependent (directly or indirectly) on slave labor (as well as their theft of Indian lands). So it is only fitting that what was kept from slaves and passed on to many white heirs now be returned to blacks in the form of reparations to the heirs of U.S. oppression against blacks. And while it is true that Jim Crow applied to all "colored" folk from Reconstruction until the 1960s or 1970s depending on which states complied with federal laws against segregationism, Jim Crow most directly targeted and affected blacks. So while there is not much property or land in question for reparative justice to blacks in the United States, the main issues pertain to generations of unpaid wages and the physical, psychological, and sociological brutality of that peculiar institution and post-slavery legal systems that further oppressed blacks.

Considering first the physical, psychological, and sociological harms of black slavery, it is important to see that aside from early death, such slavery was accompanied by its abundant share of beatings and rapes, constant psychological abuse, and being torn asunder from one's family and culture all so that one could be forced to serve white society which then, hypocritically and ironically, declares that "niggers are lazy"! While the first generation of Africans who survived the voyage from the African continent spent the remainder of their lives as slaves, subsequent blacks for generations until Emancipation spent their entire lives under the yoke of slavery. They were not merely sexually abused now and then as children as in the cases of contemporary victims of Catholic priestly child abuse. Nor were they merely raped now and then as in the cases of the raping of white women in U.S. society. Nor were they merely prohibited from voting and choosing a spouse, or from becoming first-class citizens as white women experienced. It was all of this, and much, much more that blacks experienced for their entire lives! And we know who the perpetrator is (the slavers and the U.S. legal systems that supported slavery) and who the victims are as a class. We know who should pay whom. But precisely what form ought the reparations to take?

Roy L. Brooks distinguishes between compensatory reparations and rehabilitative reparations. While compensatory approaches state that victims of oppression as individuals ought to receive monetary damages, among other things, from their oppressors, rehabilitative approaches seek to address the victims as a group to aid in group self-empowerment and the reconciliation between parties and cultural and social transformation.[39] Brooks opts for the latter approach. But prior to assessing it, I would like to point out that a compensatory approach to reparations such as mine can easily accommodate the interests of groups. For that is the primary goal of my compensatory approach, as we shall see.

Brooks's "atonement model" of rehabilitative reparations has as its primary purpose of slave redress racial reconciliation between whites and blacks in the United States.[40] Although it involves an apology on behalf of the United States, that apology requires no compensation.[41] For Brooks, such an apology can be vicarious on behalf of contemporary blacks for enslaved ones, but an apology can still be valid if no qualified person (victim) is alive to receive it,[42] contrary to what I argued in the previous chapter. Brooks rejects the retributive notion of an apology for two reasons. First, it stymies racial reconciliation, and second, "in the interest of urgent social, political, or moral considerations."[43] These constitute perhaps the most straightforwardly utilitarian reasons for nonretributive reparations that have been provided. Brooks is commended for his intellectual honesty. But it is this honesty that reveals the fundamental weakness in his thinking about reparations, a weakness it shares with the utilitarian approaches to reparations covered and refuted in part 1.

In practical terms, Brooks favors an atonement model of reparations for blacks that constitutes two main elements: "The two rehabilitative reparations I favor most are a museum of slavery and an atonement trust fund. The former would be a memorial to the slaves, and the latter would be a governmental response to some of the capital deficiencies today's blacks have inherited from their ancestors."[44] He describes the aim of the trust fund thusly: "The purpose of the trust fund is to provide a core group of blacks with one of the most important resources slavery and Jim Crow denied them—financial capital, family resources, or an estate, handed down from generation to generation."[45] The trust fund would function as follows, on Brooks's view:

> A board of commissioners, consisting of reputable citizens selected by blacks, would oversee fund operations in their respective regions of the country. Commissioners and their staff would, for example, help fund recipients make the right choices in schools and business opportunities. All payments from the trust fund would be by electronic transfer. Recipients would never really see or handle the funds.

Money accumulated in the atonement trust fund would only be spent for education or to start or invest in a business. . . . Finally, wealthy black families would
be excluded from the program.[46]

In the end, Brooks notes, this twin set of programs "present easy burdens for
our government."[47]

However well-intentioned Brooks's approach of slavery redress is, it is
fraught with major problems. First, that Brooks actually sees the United States
as "our" government in no way speaks for millions of blacks who hold no
such view of the relationship between that oppressor state and blacks. Second,
compensatory justice for oppression of the magnitude of black slavery and
Jim Crow, if it is at all adequate, ought never to be "easy burdens." What
makes Brooks think that the U.S. government ought to get off in so easy a
fashion for committing some of the most evil acts in human history? Third,
why ought wealthy blacks to be excluded from reparative justice? The fact that
Oprah Winfrey is extremely wealthy and would never think of receiving such
monies is hardly a good reason to prohibit her from her right to enjoy her fair
share of them. After all, she has experienced a great deal of racism throughout
her life under Jim Crow, and beyond. That is precisely what it means to say
that Winfrey has a *right* to compensatory justice from her oppressor! Brooks's
approach essentially denies the rights of all blacks to fair compensation for
their oppression by the United States. It effectively denies to the black heirs of
oppression what is owed them in favor of the utility of white society. Moreover, what if blacks neither want to invest in business nor want to be educated? Are they not entitled by right to receive at least some measure of the
compensation owed them and do with it as they please? Brooks echoes what
so many antireparationists state when they desire to control what belongs only
to blacks by compensatory right. This is so absurd it deserves no comment, as
no one, especially Brooks I take it, would deny, say, Donald Trump's right to
do what he pleases with whatever compensatory monies he receives, say, due
to theft or fraud against him or his grandparents should a successful legal case
be made along these lines. So why then are blacks being told what to do with
their compensation, if "compensation" is not too flattering a term for what
Brooks's atonement trust fund provides?

Furthermore, Brooks's view seeks to draw a problematic division between
compensatory and rehabilitative approaches to reparations, as the welfare of
blacks as a group can be accommodated by the compensatory model. His
rehabilitative model of reparations seeks as a primary goal the reconciliation
of blacks and whites in the United States, which effectively coerces blacks to
remain integrated with whites, thus minimizing black autonomy (especially
from their white oppressors). Moreover, Brooks's approach to reparations for
blacks is not generalizeable to other cases of U.S. oppression, such as Indians.
For it would constitute a serious lack of self-respect for either of these groups
to want to reconcile or integrate with U.S. whites after all that mostly whites
did to destroy the entire civilization of the former groups. One wonders just

how blacks would retain a modicum of self-respect if they are forced by the atonement model to integrate with their oppressor heirs. Additionally, Brooks naively assumes that white racism will cease enough to make reconciliation between blacks and whites possible, or that white racism can even lead to such reconciliation in the first place. What makes Brooks so sure that there is even a remote possibility that enough U.S. whites would even entertain the idea of respecting blacks in whatever ways Brooks believes are adequate for genuine reconciliation? He seems to not understand the human cognitive architecture of racism, and how practically impossible it is to rid it from most U.S. whites in order to effect the kind of utopian dream he envisions between whites and blacks.[48]

But the worst problem Brooks's approach to reparations faces is precisely that which I attacked in part 1, above. It suffers from the destructive malady of a compensatory-rights-disrespecting, compensatory-justice-disrespecting version of utilitarianism in that it essentially denies black compensatory rights to reparations with considerations of social utility maximization, which in this case amounts mostly to white utility maximization. Assumed here, and argued in part 1, is the idea that no analysis of reparations is adequate unless it adequately accounts for rights (in particular compensatory rights) and justice. And Brooks's model of reparations fails precisely in the ways that the views of cosmopolitan liberalism, Janna Thompson, and Margaret Urban Walker fail. They simply do not give sufficiently serious weight to the remedial rights of the oppressed. For as utilitarians they are more concerned with matters of distributive justice than they are with the compensatory justice and in this case the rights of U.S. blacks. And Brooks's utilitarian rehabilitative reparations fail to do justice to the magnitude of the oppression blacks experienced at the hands of whites in the United States, thereby violating any plausible principle of proportional compensation. Is Brooks serious about a slavery museum and an atonement trust fund for some worse-off blacks? Is this his idea of justice and proportional compensation? The fact is that Brooks is not concerned with compensatory justice that seeks to compensate blacks to the extent of their suffering, however approximate. If he were, then he would have used what he stated as his entire and favorite approach as the mere start of a much more robust and deeply compensatory approach, one that provides blacks with a meaningful measure of justice, returned wealth, sovereignty, and autonomy. For these are some of the very things that slavery and Jim Crow robbed from blacks for so many generations.

To be sure, U.S. whites seeking a "good deal" and a way out of paying what they truly owe to blacks will find Brooks's suggested settlement quite congenial. For all of these reasons, I solidly reject Brooks's proposal though much of what he argues about forgiveness and apology is quite in line with my own view as I articulated it in chapter 7. And it is for these reasons, then, that Brooks's very modest atonement plan of slavery redress must be rejected in favor of an approach that respects black people the way they deserve to be respected. Brooks's following words must be rejected outright:

But if the federal government atones for slavery and Jim Crow, we must fully commit ourselves to a process of racial reconciliation. If the federal government's apology and reparations are substantial, then there is no reason for us to withhold forgiveness. My argument, then, comes down to this: meaningful reparations render the apology believable and produce a redemptive effect; and meaningful reparations induce civic forgiveness and make racial reconciliation possible. Atonement (apology plus reparations) and forgiveness foster racial reconciliation.[49]

While most whites in the United States would gladly concur with Brooks's words here, they are highly problematic. First, while Brooks does not believe that there is a moral obligation for victims of oppression to forgive their oppressors, he does believe, without supportive argument, that victims of oppression have an "unconditional civic obligation" to forgive their oppressors in participation in the process of racial reconciliation.[50] What is to be done if the U.S. government fails to atone for slavery and Jim Crow? Brooks provides no answer. Yet it is clear that if there is one country that has refused to adequately compensate its victims of oppression it is the United States! That it chose to provide small amounts of reparations to Japanese Americans in recent years for their WWII-era internment, and that the United States has in very inadequate ways "compensated" Indians for a few of their injustices hardly makes the United States a willing participant in the atonement of its harmful wrongdoings throughout its evil history.

But let us assume for the sake of Brooks's argument that the United States completely atones for its oppression of blacks. Of course, what this really means for Brooks is what he stipulates: an atonement trust fund for some worst-off blacks and a slavery museum. Does it follow that even if the United States totally committed itself to funding these projects that blacks ought to "fully commit" themselves without loss of self-respect to a process of racial reconciliation, as Brooks states? Does it follow that even under such conditions that "there is no reason for" blacks "to withhold forgiveness"?

I shall of course leave it to each U.S. black person to answer these and related questions for herself. But few blacks today would be even remotely satisfied with Brooks's proposal, and for the reasons I noted. Brooks cannot be correct that his version of atonement and forgiveness can possibly foster reconciliation between the heirs of oppression. For it is at the cost of fundamental justice to blacks. After all, genuine reconciliation is not possible without true justice, including for example, fair, proportional *compensatory* justice. And would we not think that after centuries of justice denied that blacks deserve a great deal more respect than to propagate a theory of how blacks ought to forgive whites for centuries of oppression? In short, Brooks's approach, while well-intentioned, is naïve regarding the possibility of reconciliation with U.S. whites most of whom disrespect blacks so very badly, and does a fundamental injustice to blacks in denying them what is their due according to basic precepts of proportional compensatory justice.

It is time to respect blacks so that we proffer only approaches to remedies that truly seek to provide blacks their due as the result of U.S. oppression. Hopefully, the refusal to continue to placate whites and their interests in favor of justice and fairness is not too much for even many bourgeois blacks to handle. Brooks's approach to "justice" for blacks is essentially one that mirrors the attitude of the "house negro" who is so concerned about his white master that he would do anything reasonable to protect those interests—even sacrifice greatly his own remedial rights and those of other blacks. What I shall offer is an approach to reparations for blacks that is much more akin to the attitude of a "field negro" who cares little or nothing about those who oppress him. Of field and house "negroes," Malcolm X said:

To understand this, you have to go back to what the young brother here referred to as the house Negro and the field Negro back during slavery. There were two kinds of slaves, the house Negro and the field Negro. The house Negroes—they lived in the house with the master, they dressed pretty good, they ate good because they ate his food—what he left. They lived in the attic or the basement, but still they lived near the master; and they loved the master more than the master loved himself. They would give their life to save the master's house—quicker than the master would. If the master said, "We got a good house here," the house Negro would say, "Yeah, we got a good house here." Whenever the master said "we," he said "we." That's how you can tell a house Negro.

If the master's house caught on fire, the house Negro would fight harder to put the blaze out than the master would. If the master got sick, the house Negro would say, "What's the matter, boss, *we* sick?" *We* sick! He identified himself with his master, more than the master identified with himself. And if you came to the house Negro and said, "Let's run away, let's escape, let's separate," the house Negro would look at you and say, "Man, you crazy. What you mean, separate? Where is there a better house than this? Where can I wear better clothes than this? Where can I eat better food than this?" That was that house Negro. In those days he was called a "house nigger." And that's what we call them today, because we've still got some house niggers running around here.

This modern house Negro loves his master. He wants to live near him. He'll pay three times as much as the house is worth just to live near his master, and then brag about "I'm the only Negro out here." "I'm the only one on my job." "I'm the only one in this school." You're nothing but a house Negro. And if someone comes to you right now and says, "Let's separate," you say the same thing that the house Negro said on the plantation. "What you mean, separate? From America, this good white man? Where you going to get a better job than you get here?" I mean, this is what you say. "I ain't left nothing in Africa," that's what you say. Why, you left your mind in Africa.

On that same plantation, there was the field Negro. The field Negroes—those were the masses. There were always more Negroes in the field than there were Negroes in the house. The Negro in the field caught hell. He ate leftovers. In the house they ate high up on the hog. The Negro in the field didn't get anything but what was left on the insides of the hog. They call it "chit'lings" nowadays. In those

days they called them what they were—guts. That's what you were—gut-eaters.
And some of you still are gut-eaters.

The field Negro was beaten from morning to night; he lived in a shack, in a
hut; he wore old, castoff clothes. He hated his master. I say he hated his master.
He was intelligent. That house Negro loved his master, but that field Negro—
remember, they were in the majority, and they hated the master. When the house
caught on fire, he didn't try to put it out; that field Negro prayed for a wind, for a
breeze. When the master got sick, the field Negro prayed that he'd die. If someone
came to the field and said, "Let's separate, let's run," he didn't say "Where we
going?" He'd say, "Any place is better than here." You've got field Negroes in
America today. I'm a field Negro. The masses are the field Negroes. When they
see this man's house on fire, you don't hear the little Negroes talking about "*our*
government is in trouble." They say, "*The* government is in trouble." Imagine a
Negro: "*Our* government"! I even heard one say "*our* astronauts." They won't even
let him near the plant—and "*our* astronauts"! "*Our* Navy"—that's a Negro that is
out of his mind, a Negro that is out of his mind.

Just as the slavemaster of that day used Tom, the house Negro, to keep the field
Negroes in check, the same old slavemaster today has Negroes who are nothing
but modern Uncle Toms, twentieth-century Uncle Toms, to keep you and me in
check, to keep us under control, keep us passive and peaceful and nonviolent.[51]

Indeed, if what justice requires does great harm to an oppressor, one surely
need not regret it so long as the harm is proportional to the harm of one's
oppression experienced by the oppressor in question. In any case, adequate
reparations to blacks, like those to Indians, require compensation sufficient to
enable both Indians and blacks to live autonomously and in peace, with or
without whites should segregation from whites be what these heirs of oppression desire.[52] And just as one can be optimistic that there is an authentic
Indian life possibly to be had for Indians even in what is left of what used to
be their homeland, I concur not only with Malcolm X, but with Derrick Bell
that "there is something real out there in America for black people. It is not,
however, the romantic love of integration."[53] This is especially wise advice in
light of Santayana's statement that those who do not remember the wrongs of
the past are doomed to repeat them. Blacks, not unlike Indians, know all too
well what integration with most U.S. whites so often brings.

In light of the highly problematic ethical nature of Brooks's rehabilitative
approach to reparations, I argue in favor of a compensatory approach, one
that is not meant to deny that there might be some significant rehabilitative
results that issue from compensatory justice toward blacks. For instance, given
the amount of compensatory reparations I shall argue are owed to blacks as a
group, there is little question that blacks will as a group experience various
kinds of rehabilitation, whether psychological, in education, medicine, etc.
But my primary concern, unlike Brooks's, lies not with the welfare of the
oppressor group and its heirs, but rather with the victims of oppression and
their heirs. Thus the scope of rehabilitation as the result of compensatory reparations is limited, and rightly so, under my compensatory reparations

approach. Justice is its true and only concern, justice to blacks as the primary victims of white oppression.

So what shall be the amount of black reparations owed, first, for the unpaid wages, and second, for the brutality of slavery and for the oppression under Jim Crow? It is estimated that millions of Africans died en route to the Americas in the slave ships, yet another mode of torture. And it is estimated that about 10,000,000 Africans died in slavery in the Americas.[54] Very conservatively, let us suppose that only 1,000,000 Africans were enslaved in the United States, and that whomever was responsible for the shipping of the slaves is primarily responsible for the millions of African deaths en route to their enslavement in the Americas. Perhaps that would include shippers from England, France, the Netherlands, Portugal, Spain, among others, including some businesses some of which might remain under the cover of different names today. So I will use the figure of only 1,000,000 African slaves in the United States, including all of their immediate offspring! This makes the figure so immensely conservative that it is insulting to blacks, to whom I very sincerely apologize. However, what I am after here is a workable figure of reparations that no reasonable person can deny (as in the case of American Indian reparations). The figure I end up with for black reparations is conservative.

If there were only 1,000,000 slaves working for only minimum wage for their entire working lives (no health care, no other benefits as was typical in U.S. workplaces until unionization in the middle of the twentieth century, and not including pay increases of any kind), and using current figures for the value of minimum wage to simplify matters in favor of the United States and what it owes blacks, it is estimated that the United States owes about the following:

1,000,000 (conservative number of blacks enslaved in the United States)
$7.00 hr. (U.S. federal minimum wage in current dollars, less 25 cents)
62,400 (average hours worked by slaves who did not live until fifty years of age, figuring no greater than fifty-two forty-hour work weeks for only thirty years of slave work)
= US$436,800,000,000.00

And this fails to include interest accrued on what is owed over generations! At a conservative annual rate of only 10 percent interest over 230 years *non-*compounded, it would appear that the interest accrued on $436,800,000,000 would amount to about **$10,046,400,000,000**. So this is at *least* what the United States owes, especially because the unpaid slave wages have by now infused and embedded themselves into virtually every aspect of the U.S. economy. This figure is likely to be more accurate at a triple or quadruple rate, factoring in penalties and fluctuating interest on the U.S. dollar, the fact that many blacks could have much higher wages and salaries and other incomes than what is figured here, adjusted for inflation. Moreover, most blacks pre-Reconstruction were forced into slavery at young ages such that they would likely have worked for longer than the thirty years calculated here. And of course there may have been well in excess of 1,000,000 Africans brought to the United States to serve as slaves. Counting their enslaved offspring also, 1,000,000 seems like a rather low estimate indeed.

Yet there is still the matter of the violent and nonviolent severe rights abuses of enslavement of blacks by the United States and Jim Crow legislation and policies that were used to keep blacks down at the bottom of the socioeconomic scale in the United States, and the federal government's and courts' winking at such institutional racism. As pointed out in previous chapters, there are millions of blacks still alive in the United States who experienced firsthand the awful racism of Jim Crow: the unrectified lynchings of thousands of black men and women, the racist nonemployment of millions of blacks throughout generations and the cycle of poverty that ensued, the poor education of blacks, the constant fear of being violated in a myriad of ways, and the like. What are they owed? Let us remember that currently the going rate for a Catholic priestly child molestation is $1,000,000 per victim, on average. It would appear that, minus the unpaid wages which have just been estimated, the conservative figure of 1,000,000 slaves ought to at least amount to an award of $10,000,000 each in today's dollars. Thus 1,000,000 multiplied by $10,000,000 = **$1,000,000,000,000**! Of course, this hardly includes any figure that would account for the amount of unpaid slave labor prior to 1775 within the thirteen colonies alone that might well have transferred itself to enrich the newly formed colonial regime after 1775. So the total conservative estimate of U.S. reparations to blacks for the unpaid wages of slavery and for its brutality is at approximately $10,046,400,000,000 + $1,000,000,000,000 = **$11,046,400,000,000.**

Now in light of the fact that working U.S. citizens already owe, conservatively, a 5 percent in perpetuity Indian reparation tax, it is unlikely that the United States can afford to pay off blacks what is owed them in the near future. So installments, with interest, are required as in the case of Indian reparations. In light of the interest on the amount owed, and the amount of time it would take the U.S. to pay it, I suggest a *"black reparations tax" of 3 percent of each adult U.S. citizen's annual income, in perpetuity*. If the average U.S. income is about $30,000, and there are about 100,000,000 workers on average per year, then 3 percent of $3,000,000,000,000 would be given in reparations to blacks. This would figure at about *$90,000,000,000* that would accrue and be transferred to the committee on black reparations as the annual U.S. reparations tax to blacks, in perpetuity.

Like the Indian case, this money would be diverted from each paycheck by the IRS into an account controlled completely by the committee on black reparations, a black-only elected committee of a couple of dozen or so black-elected professionals and community folk, and there is no shortage of such persons who would do well to administer and supervise the investment and distribution of such reparations. From the 500 black businesspersons in Chicago, to a host of other black business leaders, economists, investors, educators, community leaders, attorneys, and so forth, they could serve two- to four-year terms, and serve again with a supportive black vote. Just as with Indians, the IRS's collection and diversion of the reparations tax would be audited by a reputable firm of the committee's choosing for which the United States would pay. The monies collected at the rate estimated would little doubt be spent in precisely the same sorts of ways in which the committee on Indian reparations would spend its funds, with the exception of the purchase of U.S. lands as they belong by moral right to Indians. And like the Indian reparations committee, the black reparations committee would not only likely invest much of the funds and allot much of the remainder into educational, health care, housing provisions for blacks of all economic conditions, but it would disperse a certain amount of compensatory reparations to individual blacks contingent on funds available as in the case of Indian reparations. At some stages in the future the committee, like the committee on Indian reparations, might choose to allot more funding for individual payments of funds, while at other stages of history it might choose to allot more funds for investments, or for black health care, education, and housing. The history of blacks in the United States suggests that a balanced approach to this matter is likely to accrue, with W. E. B. Du Bois's "talented tenth" leading the way through the complex decision-making process facing the committee.[55]

The United States owes a combination of a total of 8 percent of each working citizen's annual gross income to Indians and blacks. This is still quite affordable for most unless one is incompetent at personal finances. Even so, since when did one's alleged inability to pay a fine or tax amount to an excuse for not paying it? U.S. citizens of all kinds except Indians and blacks will have to become accustomed to a different standard of living. For it is time to pay all debts owed, beginning with the most longstanding and serious ones.

FURTHER CONSIDERATIONS ABOUT REPARATIONS

Now thus far my reparations analysis has focused on monetary rectification by the U.S. government to Indians and blacks in rather substantial amounts in perpetuity. And I do so by way of what might be termed "gain-based" and "harm-based" reasons. In other words, my arguments focus both on the ill-gotten gains of oppression as well as the wrongful harms to the oppressed. The first strategy is based on the common law doctrine of unjust enrichment, while the latter is grounded in the legal concept of negative rights and duties (i.e., that I have a negative right that you not harm me unduly, and you have a duty to not harm me unduly).

But Bernard Boxill and Howard McGary have each argued that reparations ought also to address the psychic and social dimensions of the harms of genocide, land theft, acculturation, slavery, and Jim Crow. As we saw, Brooks argues in favor of an "atonement model"[56] of reparations, one that includes a genuine reconciliation between the heirs of oppression in the United States. I concur with Boxill and McGary that whatever else reparations do, they must also address matters of self-respect that result from oppression. But, contrary to Brooks, Thompson, Walker, and others, this need not involve anything to do with reconciliation between oppressed with their oppressors, or between the heirs of oppression as Brooks's atonement model of "reparations" suggests. Reconciliation, I have argued, is neither a necessary nor sufficient condition of reparations, properly conceived. To think otherwise is to disregard the analysis of forgiveness, reconciliation, and apology addressed in chapter 8, above. It is also to disregard how U.S. law functions in cases of compensatory justice.

Brooks points out that the tort model of reparations faces some serious procedural difficulties. I concede this. But my model of reparations seeks primarily legislative remedies from the United States.[57] And it might well be too much to expect perhaps the oppressor of all oppressors to legislate itself into such debt, especially when the results would make those it most disrespects wealthier than most whites in the United States. So it is unlikely to occur in these ways. This is why I believe that such reparations must then issue from the ICC, backed by credible coalition diplomacy, and, if necessary, threats of force (and, if necessary, force itself) for U.S. noncompliance.

Reparations, at least in severe cases such as the ones examined here, require more than just monetary compensation to the victims of oppression. This is especially the case when the amount of reparations, though quite substantial, is estimated conservatively. For this reason I support more programmatic reparations in the forms of the United States' apology for its evils to these groups and all that that entails (see chapter 8), as well as a holistic revision of its national myths, monuments, lores, symbols, iconography, legends, and publicly funded arts to accurately reflect the contributions and sensibilities of Indians and blacks. For instance, this means the destruction of Mount Rushmore because it honors those who committed evil acts of oppression, the renaming of various public buildings, public parks, institutions, libraries, post offices, streets and other roadways, and so on, currently named after such evildoers as Andrew Jackson, George Wallace, Eugene "Bull" Connor, Thomas Jefferson, George Washington, and anyone else whose efforts have served the oppression of Indians or blacks. It would mean that the likenesses of those who appear on U.S. legal tender ought not to include oppressors such as Andrew Jackson. It would also mean the destruction of public monuments dedicated to such people, just as the statue of Saddam Hussein was destroyed at his fall, and Stalin's statute was destroyed at the fall of the former Soviet

Union, and so forth. Even more importantly, the false histories that are propagated by miseducated docents of historical sites must be taught to propagate truths about U.S. history, rather than the legends that make most U.S. folk feel so good about themselves and often negatively toward certain others. If privately funded organizations want to attempt to instill falsehoods about the United States and its oppression of peoples, that would appear to enjoy First Amendment protection. But no publicly funded organizations should be permitted to continue to propagate the falsehoods that have plagued U.S. society from its inception and have miseducated millions of folk about what really happened in this or that era of U.S. history. The publicly funded institutions ought not to be permitted to continue to instill in unsuspecting people falsehoods about U.S. history. For "Western history is a running commentary on the efforts of the powerful to impose a conception of reality on those they would rule."[58] And it is part and parcel of any adequate reparations program to Indians and blacks that U.S. propaganda about these groups cease and desist immediately insofar as publicly funded aspects of society are concerned. This is a feature of reparative justice that is essential for a reasonably just society, or one seeking to become reasonably just. These kinds of changes are matters of justice and fairness, and ought to be made regardless of whether or not Indians and blacks choose to continue to live with whites in the United States during reparations. The likelihood is very high that many such folk will choose to remain integrated with whites, making the suggested changes all the more important from a practical standpoint of reconciliation should Indians and blacks desire it.

Even more important than the revision of U.S. myths about itself and many of its leaders is what McGary refers to as the damaging psychological and sociological effects of oppression on victims of oppression:

> If the injustice deprives them of their just deserts in terms of goods and services, then they certainly will and should resent it. But if the injustice cuts at their very right to be treated as bona fide members of the moral and legal communities, then this creates an even deeper resentment. When this resentment is allowed to fester it can lead to psychopathology or to a disrespect for the institutions and persons that caused or failed to prevent the injustice which led to the resentment.
>
> Individuals who have been systematically denied full membership within our moral and legal communities for long periods of time because of characteristics like their race or sex will feel this deep resentment. All too often when we focus on the victims of this type of unjust discrimination, we tend to focus only on the material consequences of being treated unjustly. When we do this we fail to address the emotional damage that results from a prolonged systematic denial of basic moral and legal rights. To merely halt the unjust practice and to enhance the economic well-being of the victims is not enough to remove this rightful feeling of resentment.[59]

McGary's point is well taken, and I concur with it. It grows out of W. E. B. Du Bois's "ethical paradox" of blacks in the United States, each of whom face a dual psychological tendency to resent U.S. whites and segregate from them and retain dignity and self-respect in the face of tremendous injustice, or to forgive and reconcile with them and thus face denial of oppression and their own self-respect in facing that denial.[60] I think, however, that it would be, practically speaking, too much to think that the psychological and sociological damage done to Indians and blacks by way of their oppression in the United States can be achieved without monetary reparations, coupled with the respected right of Indians and blacks to choose for themselves whether or not they wish to live with whites. McGary does not deny this. For it is the monetary reparations that can and will provide black (and Indian) communities the resources to educate the hundreds and perhaps thousands of black (and Indian) psychotherapists who can assist in exactly the kind of healing that McGary notes so profoundly.

My rights-based approach to reparations has the virtue of providing U.S. Indians and blacks with the individual autonomy and in the case of Indians, group sovereignty, required for Indians and blacks to face the dilemmas of ethnic integration in the United States constructively and without jettisoning self-respect and the demands of remedial justice. Unlike the anti-compensatory rights-based approaches discussed in chapters 2 and 3, mine also lacks the hard paternalism that impedes genuine Indian and black progress along these and related lines already noted. Like McGary, then, I concur with Du Bois when he writes to U.S. blacks: "We shall never secure emancipation from the tyranny of the white oppressor until we have achieved it in our own souls."[61] And the same idea applies to Indians.

Furthermore, McGary's point about the resentment that oppressed persons and peoples will and should experience toward those who oppress them is consonant with Peter Strawson's explication of the retributivist emotions that are justified when one is seriously wronged.[62] It is also consonant with John Rawls's point that resentment is a natural response to one's offender being unjustly enriched at one's expense, though Rawls adds that punishment can serve to partly give offenders what they deserve in such cases, nullifying in part their unjust gains.[63] However, it is important to understand that such feelings of resentment, so long as they do not develop into a psychological disorder, as McGary notes they can, are the appropriate response to injustice, as Joel Feinberg notes in his discussion of rights.[64] For the response of a moral rightholder to a serious violation of her rights, such as the oppressive events under discussion, is not one of humble apology or excuse-making by the victims of oppression, but rather righteous indignation at the oppressors who violate their rights. Indeed, it is part and parcel of the having of rights that they endow rightholders with an appropriate sense of entitlement the serious violation of which calls for condemnation, not cowering. McGary's point must be accommodated by any approach to reparations, then, to remind us that it is not all about transfers of wealth, but that part of what should be done with the wealth that accompanies reparations is that Indians and blacks allocate resources for the training of many Indians and blacks to serve as ongoing sources of psychological strength and development vis-à-vis the multifarious damaging effects of their oppression. However, what this hardly means is that reparations are not about adequate compensation, contrary to the reconciliation theorists refuted in chapters 2 and 3. Nor are reparations to be confused with affirmative action programs that essentially permit Indians and blacks to "work off"[65] their oppression by way of preferential employment opporunities.

Furthermore, a comprehensive rights-based and rectificatory approach to reparations to Indians will entail a full-scale return of all Indian remains (including "art") from museums, colleges and universities, archives, and so on, where they have been stored subsequent to being harvested by archeologists and anthropologists for over a century: "American law criminalizes grave plundering, but for more than a century Native Americans were denied this protection."[66] This is, it might be argued, a violation of the equal protection clause of the Fourteenth Amendment to the U.S. Constitution. And because of this blatant and long-term breach of law, each institution or organization that engaged in this behavior should be forced to pay monetary compensation in the form of reparations to Indian nations above and beyond the Indian reparations tax. Perhaps a cost of $1,000,000 per complete or nearly complete set of human remains is reasonable, as is $10,000 per human remain part, not to mention bearing the costs of the proper transportation and reburial of such remains according to each distinct tribal custom where the custom is known. With these kinds of compensatory measures in place, perhaps such "scientists" (it is hard to think of grave robbing as a science) will think harder (in moral terms) before violating the rights of others, before, that is, using others as a mere means to their own ends. For the multimillion-dollar endowment reserves of many museums, colleges, and universities will then pay a heavy and deserved price for their grave-robbing years of fundamental disrespect of Indian rights. Since the human remains are overly difficult in many cases to identify by nation of origin, and because "few tribes are organized to deal with these new cultural possibilities and responsibilities,"[67] the monetary reparations can be paid in such cases to the committee on Indian reparations. Perhaps these compensatory reparations can be used for the protection and preservation of Indian sacred sites throughout the United States consonant with the 1990 Native American Graves Protection and Repatriation Act which, among other things, grants the right of Indians (including Hawai'ians) to determine the final disposition of their human remains.[68]

And for the few decades repatriation of Indian remains has been under way, there is no indication of either suits for compensatory damages for graverobbing institutions, nor of punishment for grave-robbing "scientists" and their assistants, many of whom have since become "scientists" themselves in U.S. colleges and universities.[69] The latter, of course, is a state charge left to the decisions of prosecutors. But what besides racial bias can account for the fact that no such charges have been brought against so many criminals? It could not be that the identification of perpetrators is a problem, as such "scientists" have likely made known their exploits in articles in leading academic journals and published in books and monographs. And what about the lack of criminal prosecution for those museologists or museum acquisitions personnel who intentionally, knowingly, and voluntarily accepted Indian remains? Why have they not been charged with aiding or abetting grave robbers? These issues are made even more acute in light of the moral right to not have one's own remains disturbed post mortem, a right that is said to accrue to all humans. As Feinberg argues, "Most persons while still alive have certain desires about what is to happen to their bodies, their property, or their reputations after they are dead,"[70] and honoring such desires, when reasonable and when they do not infringe the rights of others, is to keep "faith with the dead."[71] These are valid interests that survive one's death, "constituting claims against us that persist beyond the life of the claimant."[72] Thus "we have an interest while alive that other interests of ours will continue to be recognized and served after we are dead."[73] So "conceptual sense then can be made of talk about dead men's rights."[74] Feinberg's arguments for the existence of our valid moral interests grounding our moral right to the disposition of our remains after we die serves as the moral underpinning of our "death rights," rights that all Indians have but have in many cases been carelessly and flagrantly violated by those who apparently do not believe that legal prohibitions against grave robbing protect Indians. It also bears noting that the same rights apply to blacks that would protect slave remains from "scientific discovery" by means of grave robbing.

Currently there exist thousands of people throughout the United States who are primarily or secondarily responsible for the racist oppression of Indians and blacks during Jim Crow, and even thereafter. Hundreds of thousands of blacks alive today have been the victims of Jim Crow, and yet nothing has been done to track down the perpetrators of these abuses: whether active members in the night riders of the KKK, or those who violently attacked free-dom riders in the mid-1960s; judges, jurors, or attorneys who acting wrongly in the decisions of courts (in either wrongfully convicting black defendants innocent of charges or improperly sentencing them, or acquitting white defen-dants obviously guilty of the charges against them, or unfairly mitigating their sentences), or those who are responsible for the murders and lynchings of so many blacks until about 1968.[75] There is no statute of limitations on murder in the United States. So there is no good reason to not properly investigate these and other related sorts of harmful wrongdoings (the cost of which can itself be construed as part of the overall reparations project) wherein the per-petrators of the injustices are still alive. As one author puts it, "From a retribu-tive justice standpoint, there are outstanding crimes of the Jim Crow and civil rights periods that can still be prosecuted, and a continuing need to document and prosecute racially motivated illegal discrimination and violence."[76] Such persons, now old and perhaps feeble, should not be permitted to live in peace.

Depending on the extent of their harmful wrongdoings, they must be investigated, and if due process duly convicts, they must be sentenced to imprisonment or death according to their kinds and levels of responsibility, as the case may be. As matters currently stand, every living criminal who was not properly convicted and sentenced for their serious crimes against Indians or blacks stands as an affront to justice. Just as there are those who hunt former Nazis in order to bring them to justice for their responsibility for "crimes against humanity," so too must the United States, if it is truly serious about its belief that it is the greatest country in the world, hunt down every living oppressor of Indians or blacks and bring them to justice.

Justice requires that what is owed is paid as fully and as soon as possible, first by those most directly responsible by attaching their personal assets in full, and then by attaching corporate assets until the debt is paid as fully as possible. This very same retributivist attitude must be employed with respect to Indians and blacks regarding their respective claims to reparations. In the cases of Indians and blacks, the federal government must through its taxpaying citizens pay reparations taxes for the historic injustices experienced by these groups. However, with respect to the more recent injustices, those individuals (for example, night riders of the KKK who were widely known to commit all manner of violent acts against blacks) who are most directly responsible for unprosecuted violent crimes against blacks and who are alive today must be targets of an extensive manhunt (assuming that klanswomen were not involved in such violence) in order to track them down and bring them to justice wherein in the cases of murder and other serious crimes, they are forced to compensate their victims or their heirs with their complete assets before they are severely punished—even by death as the case may be. And if as the case sometimes is that the offender's personal assets were recently transferred to someone, those assets will be seized in order to compensate their victims or their heirs. Justice must be served wherein the evidence of oppression is sufficiently clear and compelling to justify conviction of such rights abuses. And one true measure of the ethical character and integrity of a reasonably just society is that such cases are handled expeditiously, and without apology to the harmful wrongdoers.

So my model of reparations not only addresses adequate amounts of monies paid to victims of oppression and their heirs, but it also addresses sociopsychological issues among the oppressed, and the punishment (hard treatment) of deserving criminal oppressors still alive. This salubrious (for the recipients of the reparations) approach to reparative justice combines compensatory and punitive elements of justice, and is the most comprehensive philosophical and ethical account articulated to date. For the providing of monetary reparations alone might ignore the addressing of sociopsychological ramifications of experienced oppression, as well as the fact that so many thousands of oppressors continue to go unpunished. But the provision of sociopsychological assistance for the oppressed and even the punishment of those (still living) who oppressed them most does little or nothing to address some of the worst rights violations in history. Monetary compensation, though in itself insufficient, is required to even begin to address these problems.

The punishment of living oppressors serves the expressive reparative function, noted in the chapter 1, of society's disavowing what these oppressors did, and it also speaks in the name of the people against it. It also vindicates the law, as a system that has often failed Indians and blacks throughout U.S. history. There is perhaps no better way to univocally condemn the oppression of Indians and blacks than to provide holistic and in perpetuity reparations to them as a constant reminder of what should have never happened, and what should never happen again. And since reparations is a compensatory right that Indians and blacks have, their appropriate response to their receipt of them is not gratitude, for gratitude is not an appropriate response to the receipt of something that is yours by right.[77]

My estimate of Indian and black reparations taxes amounting to a combined total of 8 percent of each annual U.S. citizen's income exempts Indians and blacks, as it is unfair and unjust to force Indians and blacks to pay taxes toward their own reparations, as argued earlier. On balance, Indians owe the United States nothing, all relevant things considered, and should be forced to pay no U.S. taxes whatsoever, in perpetuity. All in all, these reparations taxes would serve as a constant reminder to current and future generations of U.S. citizens, as well as to the rest of the world, that the United States has finally become serious about the rectification of its most serious evils, that it is apologizing for them publicly and genuinely.

What I have provided in this chapter is the most comprehensive account of the nature of reparations from a philosophical perspective. It distinguishes nuanced differences between the Indian and black experiences of oppression, and seeks an amount of reparations that not only respects the differences in wrongful harms experienced by each group at the hands of the United States, but is also reasonably affordable for U.S. citizens to pay, in perpetuity. It requires more than monetary payments to the respective committees on reparations. It requires the noncompensatory reparations of rewriting and teaching history so that it reflects truth rather than fictions designed to justify the oppressive manner in which the U.S. empire was established. And it involves programs dealing with the psychic effects of Indian and black oppressions. Indeed, mine is a holistic approach to reparations, serving as a constant reminder to generation after generation of U.S. citizens that to oppress is too costly a thing to do, as the economic and day-to-day sacrifices one then has to make to become and continue as a decent society are grand indeed. Of course, for those with more of a morally astute mindset, it is simply the right thing to do what is morally required.

III

CHALLENGES TO REPARATIONS

10

Objections to Reparations, and Replies

Having in previous chapters rendered problematic reconciliation models of forgiveness and reparations, and having articulated my own position vis-à-vis American Indians and blacks for their oppression at the hands of the United States and many aspects of its business sector, it is important to consider several concerns that might be raised about my account.

THE DECREASING VALUE OF THE TRANSFERABILITY OF ENTITLEMENTS OBJECTION

George Sher objects that:

> if the transferability of entitlements from rectified worlds does decrease with every generation, then over the course of very many generations, any such transferability can be expected to become vanishingly small. Where the initial wrong was done many hundreds of years ago, almost all of the difference between the victim's entitlements in the actual world and his entitlements in a rectified world can be expected to stem from the actions of various intervening agents in the two alternative worlds. Little or none of it will be the automatic effect of the initial wrong act itself. Since compensation is warranted only for disparities in entitlements which *are* the automatic effect of the initial wrong act, this means that there will be little or nothing left to compensate for.[1]

Sher's objection constitutes a direct challenge to part of the heart of my argument for reparations as it challenges my claim that the wealth inherited by whites as the result of unpaid slave wages amounts to ill-gotten gains and (all of) those unpaid wages must be paid to the heirs of black oppression because they were used throughout the U.S. economy for centuries to build white wealth.

But the error of Sher's reasoning is that it assumes that what is at issue is whatever *assets or wealth* would have been bequeathed or otherwise passed down to blacks by slaves or freed ones. However, this is not only impossible to calculate, as Sher and others have argued given the historical distance from the oppression, but it neglects the fact that slave labor deprived several millions of blacks the wages off of which to live and sustain themselves from year to year. Those wages are unaccounted for by Sher's argument. Those unpaid wages are the moral entitlement of the slaves, and since they were never paid, the unjust enrichment that the United States experienced as a result of them must now be settled by way of the moral and legal principle of unjust enrichment. My argument does not depend on how much black slaves might have been able to accumulate and bequeath to the heirs of their oppression, but rather on the fact of the unpaid black slave wages themselves. In light of this fact, Sher's contention that "a proper appreciation of the entitlements upon which claims to compensation are based suggests that these claims must fade with time" is dubious.[2] Just as unrectified evil is evil still, unpaid slave wages are still owed. No mere passage of time discounts their worth and due. Furthermore, Sher's argument fails to consider the value of the oppression of black slavery itself, quite apart from the unpaid slave wages. This is of course even more important than the unpaid wages. It is difficult to see how the value of such oppression can fade over time, as Sher's "transferability of entitlements" premise assumes.

When applied to the case of Indians, Sher's argument is even less plausible in light of the principle of morally just acquisitions and transfers. His misunderstanding of what the Lockean proviso implies leads him to think that whites had rights to be in the Americas, already well populated by Indians of hundreds of nations. But when one considers the rights that Indians have to flourish in peace, unencumbered by white settlement and expansion, the conditions of the Lockean proviso remain unsatisfied by whites in the Indian world.

Thus Sher's important cluster of concerns is rebutted, and the arguments for reparations I have offered in previous chapters remains plausible. The moral claims of the heirs of oppression do not fade over time as Sher suggests once one understands the problematic assumptions of Sher's challenge.

THE INDETERMINACY OF ETHNICITY OBJECTION[3]

Another concern is that my analysis of reparations fails the test of racial or ethnic identification. Unless victims of racist injustice can be identified as belonging to a victimized group, then even if a case can be made for the oppression, precisely who ought to receive the reparations? As Jacques Novikow writes: "no one has ever been able to say which features set the characteristics of a race."[4] Of course, since Novikow's incisive claim, some contemporary philosophers have provided analytical substance to it.[5] What, then, are we to use as a means by which to categorize members of wrongly harmed groups? Here the words of Alcides Arguedas on *mestizos* come to mind: "an individual's ethnic quality [race] is determined here only by how society regards him."[6] It is noteworthy that he invokes a kind of social constructionist theory of group member identity here: "determined only by how society regards him." It is this criterion that most philosophers of race and ethnicity use in identifying members of racial or ethnic groups.

In saying that race is fundamentally a social construct, I am not disagreeing with the intended meaning of José Martí's claim that "there is no racial hatred, because there are no races."[7] Rather, it is to deny that there is some metaphysical truth to racial claims such as "I am a member of the Negroid race." The truth of the matter about races is that they do not exist apart from their social constructions, they have no genomic basis, and they face a myriad of philosophical problems that remain unanswered.[8] But this does not mean that, unfortunately, there is no racial hatred. Perhaps it is best termed "ethnic hatred." In any case, there exists hatred of races by many millions of persons throughout history, and even today. The fallacy of racial hatred is that the metaphysical or ontological content of the concept of human races is empty, without sense or reference. It is without basis in reality, except in the minds of those who still think there are races.

RACE AND ETHNICITY

In *Race, Racism, and Reparations*, I argued, first, that the concept of race is highly problematic and a poor means by which to identify people for purposes of positive public policy administration, and second, that we instead ought to follow sound social science in adopting the more nuanced ethnic categories. Unlike race, ethnic categories can and do recognize the importance of culture, language, names, self-identification, and out-group and in-group identification, among other things, in describing who and what we are. Moreover, ethnic categories, numbering well over one hundred, do not face the problem that the few race (excluding mixed race) categories do in not being able to find room for us Latinos, certain indigenous peoples, and the like. In short, the concept of ethnicity is much more nuanced than that of race, and perhaps ethnicity has done less damage to promote racism than race has, at least in the United States. Besides being able to best, though not unproblematically, categorize us into ethnic groups for purposes of positive public policy administration, genealogically based ethnic categories when properly construed can serve as proper sources of ethnic pride as well as the basis of

certain ethnically based medical research such as sickle cell anemia and osteo-
porosis.

Some have pointed out, however, that the retention of race talk has an
important value. At the very least, even this metaphysically empty concept can
play a crucial role in helping to describe the problem of the color line in U.S.
society. I concur with this observation, and have no intention of downplaying
it. However, I would caution that race is still an incoherent concept, for reasons that Anthony Appiah, Jorge J. E. Gracia, Naomi Zack, myself, and others
have argued at some length, and with significant plausibility.[9]

That the concept of race is helpful in explaining the current state of racism
in the United States and perhaps elsewhere in no way implies that race is a
metaphysically sound notion. After all, myths can serve a positive function in
life, so long as we do not think that there is an ontological essence to them.
And if the myth is relatively harmless, then there is no problem. But if the
concept in question prohibits us from adequately categorizing us for positive
and worthwhile purposes, then there is sufficient reason to replace the concept
with a better one *for that purpose*. It is for these reasons that I reject race categories in favor of ethnic ones.

We cannot use race as a way to adequately categorize people into groups for
purposes of positive public policy administration. "Black" will not suffice to
identify the groups of persons who deserve reparations based on the U.S. slave
trade, for example. For this category would include those who are not blacks
who by my definition are all of those whose genealogical roots trace to U.S.
slavery, excluding many Indians who were not also Africans but were nonetheless enslaved. It would include those with black or dark skin, whether or
not their roots trace to U.S. slavery. And it might, on some accounts, exclude
those of lighter skin color yet whose ancestry indeed traces back to U.S. slavery. The first group would pose serious difficulties for anyone who is interested
in reparations for U.S. slavery. Just as in a legitimate class action lawsuit one
cannot include as plaintiffs those who have not been harmed by the defendant's harmful wrongdoings, inactions, or attempted actions, one cannot
rightfully include as plaintiffs blacks whose ancestry does not trace back to
U.S. slavery, though such folk might well be included in a legal action against
the United States or other countries on different charges. Blacks whose ethnic
roots do not trace back to slavery in the United States would pose a problem
of a different sort, namely, that of arbitrarily discriminating against a subgroup of blacks in the pursuit of reparations for the enslavement of their forebears. In short, the concept of race is highly problematic in public policy
contexts. Moreover, it is too crude to include such major categories as Latinos,
the various indigenous Americans, and certain other groups as they are neither
Negroid, nor Caucasoid, nor Mongoloid. And race cannot serve well to categorize people for purposes of positive public policy administration.

Race, Racism, and Reparations analyzes ethnicity in terms of Latino identity and argues for a conception of how we ought to categorize ourselves for purposes of positive public policy administration, while recognizing that the discussion of these issues relies on social constructs. After clarifying the nature of primitive race theories in chapter 1 of *Race, Racism, and Reparations*, I argue for the replacement of such theories with a way to plausibly categorize us into groups for purposes of positive public policy administration, especially reparations. I follow sound contemporary social anthropology here in adopting the more nuanced categories of ethnicity as they make room for a wider array of nonmorphological factors that make us who we are *for purposes of positive public policy administration*. I use as my example "Latino/a" and argue that knowledge, use, and respect of a particular language is neither necessary nor sufficient for ethnic group membership. Arguments are also adduced in order to defeat the claims that knowledge, participation in, and respect for a particular culture is either necessary or sufficient for ethnic group membership. The same holds for the possession of a certain kind of name, self-, in- and out-group identification. None of these proposed conditions of ethnic group membership are either necessary or sufficient for ethnic group membership. Not even the combination of them is either necessary or sufficient. What is left is what I refer to as the "genealogical" conception which indexes ethnicity to whatever ethnicities of one's parents and grandparents, and so on, and there are both kinds and degrees of ethnic identities.[10]

My genealogical analysis of ethnicity is a conception that evades certain problems of pan-ethnicity. For it might be argued concerning Indians that "the economic, cultural, and religious circumstances of various tribes differ dramatically. From the relative sovereign and cohesive Indians of the Southwest, to the largely extinct tribes in the East and Midwest, to the poor unrecognized tribes all over the country, the Native American spectrum is wide and diverse."[11] Now from this it might be argued that the genuine diversity of Indian nations poses a problem for Indianness or Indian identification for purposes of reparations.

However, this is a pseudo-problem in that "Indian" identity can be and has for generations been determined (insofar as it is determined by Indians themselves rather than the U.S. government[12]) by way of tribal membership or descent, which amounts to an application, however imperfectly, of my genealogical conception of ethnicity. And this stands as the most viable manner by which to identify members of severely oppressed groups for purposes of reparations. As I have pointed out previously, whichever percentage of bloodline quantum is selected as most reasonable by the oppressed groups is going to be somewhat arbitrary.[13] But this need not cripple sincere attempts at rectificatory justice any more than imperfect compensatory justice should in any other case. Thus my ethnic identity analysis does not get in the way of justice for Indians or blacks in terms of their deserving reparations from the United

States. To the contrary, my analysis encourages such reasoning as no competing analysis of ethnic identification does.

CIRCULARITY AND THE GENEALOGICAL
CONCEPTION OF ETHNICITY

Now Gracia has already pointed out the circularity of this sort of analysis.[14] It
might be objected that I have said nothing to expound on the notion that
some circular arguments are more virtuous than others in that the latter provide a more informative account of reality than the former. And if sense cannot be made of this notion, then there is good reason to reject my analysis.
Let me answer by pointing out that every argument can be traced to its "first
principles" or assumptions, which themselves afford no argumentative support. In this sense, most every, if not every, argument will be circular. Still,
Alvin I. Goldman, following William P. Alston, has noted that, epistemically
speaking, some circular accounts are more virtuous than others.[15] Consider
the well-known example of a viciously and unvirtuously circular argument:
"The Bible is the word of God because God wrote it." But, insofar as epistemic
coherence is a necessary though insufficient condition of knowledge, and
insofar as coherence is contingent at least in part on how informative the philosophical account provided is, then it seems reasonable to infer that an analysis of ethnicity or race that provides the most informative account of who we
are is, other relevant things being equal, the better analysis.

If this were all that can be said to answer the charge of circularity, there
would appear to be a kind of dialectical standoff between my genealogical
analysis and its critics. Fortunately, there is more that can be said to quell the
concern of circularity. American Indian nations and tribes in the United States
more often than not employ a genealogical standard in order to determine
membership in their respective groups. By this it is meant lineal descendancy
from someone named on the nation's or tribe's base roll. (A "base roll" is the
original list of members as designated in a tribal constitution or other document specifying enrollment criteria.) This method of categorizing ethnic
group membership is quite consistent with my analysis (or, more accurately,
my analysis is consistent with the way Indians most typically categorize themselves as Indians). Insofar as base rolls are employed to form the standard
against which to judge Indianness from Indian nation to Indian nation, it
serves as a social construction as to the baseline of Indian categorization. But
then the charge of circularity is mitigated because *relative to each Indian nation's
base roll*, this or that person is either accepted of rejected as counting as an
Indian, and genealogically so. And while it may be argued that this sort of
reasoning trades the problem of circularity for one of a regress in how to justify the legitimacy of the base roll, that becomes a historical question in determining the accuracy of the base roll. But so long as the vast majority of Indians

in this or that Indian nation accept the informational contents of the base roll (i.e., who is listed thereon), then the regress problem is mitigated. Why? Because ethnicities are social constructs, and it is up to each ethnic group to decide for itself by way of social convention what constitutes membership in the group. Thus both circularity and regress problems are mitigated by the genealogical analysis of Latino identity and ethnicity more generally, especially in light of the primary purpose(s) of the analysis in question.

With this in mind, I have argued at length in various venues the following: knowing, speaking, and respecting a Spanish language or dialect is neither necessary nor sufficient for Latino/a identity; having a traditional Latino name is neither necessary nor sufficient; participating in and respecting a Latino culture is neither necessary nor sufficient; and self-, in-, or out-group identification are neither necessary nor sufficient. This reasoning provides a *via negativa* account of Latino identity. And it goes a long way, perhaps further than any competing positive account, in explaining Latino identity.

Additionally, I have argued that genealogy is both necessary and sufficient for Latino identity as the analysis is indexed precisely to public policy contexts. This means that I am, for instance, a Latino to the extent that my parents, grandparents, and great-grandparents, say, are Latinos. I have already conceded that this is in the end circular, but again I am not confident that such circularity can be avoided in either this or any other philosophical context. Still, perhaps the notion of the social construction of ethnic concepts may further rescue it from the charge of vicious circularity. For when I say that I am a Latino, I mean to convey that I am a Latino according to what a major segment of society has, rightly or wrongly, named Latinos. More precisely, what I mean to express is that I sufficiently satisfy the description of what groups refer to as Latinos, especially others who refer to themselves and certain others as Latinos. As history progresses, the social notion of what a Latino is evolves, but also crystallizes into a notion with which increasing numbers of people concur. Some agree with the notion of what a Latino or Latina is for purposes of racist domination or exclusion, whereas others make use of this social construct for purposes of ethnic pride and the like. So when I refer to myself as a Latino, I am adopting for the most part what societies have constructed over time as the identity of those of us with Iberian ancestry.[16] Now if it turns out that this social notion, like other ethnic concepts, is a myth without ontological basis, then so be it. But this fact hardly discounts the influence of this concept on people's lives. In short, my coherentist analysis is hardly a *viciously* circular account of ethnic concepts, even though it is, like any other analysis or argument, circular. In this way it contrasts with the well-demonstrated unvirtuously circular traditional analysis of race, or what I refer to as "primitive race theories."[17]

I concur with Goldman and Alston that all conceptual analyses are in some manner circular. But it is an accepted matter of contemporary epistemology that, though all analyses are circular, some conceptual circles are more virtuous and informative than others depending on the overall value of the accounts they offer (including the extent to which they are based on and reflect facts of the external world). My genealogical conception not only tells us precisely what does not count for ethnic identification and why, but it also enjoys the support of the primary method of generations of Indian self-identification in dealing with the U.S. government. And while no analysis of race or ethnicity will likely escape the problem of circularity, it hardly follows from this that a plausible and workable analysis cannot be devised for purposes of positive public policy administration.

Thus while I am a skeptic about the metaphysics of race and ethnicity, I am a realist concerning the ethics of ethnicity. My view, unlike its competitors, can accommodate valid claims to the right to compensatory reparations. To simply deny that there is any workable conception of human categorization along these lines is a sure defeat for either reparations or affirmative action programs as they fall prey to legitimate charges of morally arbitrary implementation insofar as the identification of beneficiaries of these programs is concerned. Perhaps equally vital is that such metaphysical accounts of race run counter to common sense. For purposes of positive public policy administration, genealogy is what matters in classifying us properly and fairly into this or that ethnic group. But genealogy indicates only what my parentage consists of. It is a matter of social construction that there are ever-evolving conceptions of various ethnic groups. Thus genealogy and social construction are different sides of the same coin of ethnic identity. Genealogy finds its proper use in establishing ethnic identities for use in positive public policy domains, while it is still true that, metaphysically speaking, ethnic groups are matters of social construction. Thus when Gracia criticizes my position in that "membership in a descent line presupposes the line" and that "the identity of the line has to be assumed"[18] and concludes that it is viciously circular, my reply is that his criticism is too hasty. For it is not that the descent line in its entirety is presupposed on my view, it is that the *origin* of the line of descent is assumed. And it is assumed according to what social constructions of the ethnic group tell us what the origin is. For purposes of positive public policy administration, such an origin is assumed because that is how certain groups were identified by way of social construction and often persecuted because of their perceived ethnicities. Now public policy can use the socially constructed "origins" of ethnic groups to award them compensation insofar as they are racially oppressed in light of relevant facts and as the case may be. Insofar as the administration of public policy is concerned, primitive race theories must be replaced by a genealogical conception of identification of the rightful beneficiaries of reparations. So one question is how positively useful my analysis of ethnic identification is, while another is how much it actually reflects the reality of ethnic group membership. I believe that the answers to each of these questions reveals the superiority of my analysis over competing ones.

Moreover, Gracia objects that "genealogy is as imprecise, in the social context, as most of the other markers used to identify members of ethnic groups."[19] While there is some measure of imprecision in my genealogical conception of ethnicity, one ought not to lose sight of how well, though not unproblematically, genealogy has functioned in terms of identifying Indian beneficiaries and the awarding of certain "benefits" to Indians by the U.S. government, and for generations. And it is the particular Indian nation or group that determines the blood quantum necessary and/or sufficient for membership in the nation or group.[20] Moreover, with the recent advent of human genome research and DNA research, it is actually more precise to measure ethnicity in genealogical terms than in any other way, contrary to Gracia's claim. So long as we remember that in my view, the origins of ethnic groups are socially constructed, science can with meaningful precision use those constructions to identify members of those groups who were persecuted by oppressors, for purposes of positive public policy administration. By this I do not mean that current DNA analysis the way it is practiced by most "ancestry" businesses is adequate, as they face some ethical and scientific challenges.[21] I mean that DNA analysis has the capacity to develop into a science that can overcome such concerns in providing a meaningful and adequate means of ethnic identification. Thus Gracia's first worry about my view concerning its alleged vicious circularity is neutralized.

Gracia's second concern about my genealogical analysis of ethnic identity is that

> descent appears to be both too narrow and too broad as a criterion of membership in an ethnos such as Latinos. It is too broad because there are people classified as Latinos who have no genetic link to other Latinos (e.g., children of Welsh immigrants to Argentina who have settled in the United States). And descent is too broad because it would have to include far-removed descendents of Latinos who have not lived in a Latino country, have not associated with other Latinos, and do not share with them any perceptible traits.[22]

Gracia concludes that "Corlett's criterion of descent, then, taken by itself, is ineffective for the very purpose he has devised for it, namely, as a sufficient condition of being Latino for social policy implementation."[23]

In reply to Gracia's important concern, I must point out that this line of thinking is baldly question-begging against my analysis. It simply denies, rather than refutes, my analysis insofar as it asserts that "there are people classified as Latinos who have no genetic link to other Latinos." My view is that if society has categorized *X* to be a Latino, then we go as far back as we can to find socially categorized Latinos and then construct a genealogy for them. Whoever fits on that branch of the tree of descent is a Latino, not metaphysically, but for purposes of positive public policy administration. If one has no such link, then one is not a Latino for these purposes. And it does nothing to refute my analysis to simply assert that there are Latinos who are not thusly linked to other Latinos. Rather, it begs the question against my analysis. The same thing can be said of Gracia's reason for thinking that my analysis is "too broad" in that it would include Latinos who are "far-removed" descendants of Latinos, both geographically and culturally. This also begs the question as to what constitutes a Latino. Why cannot a Latino remain a Latino while living for years as a hermit, apart from other Latinos?

One of the strengths of my analysis is that it grants Latinos and others the personal autonomy to live as they choose without "losing" their ethnic heritage. Gracia's view, on the other hand, forces Latinos to "remain" Latinos in traditionally proscribed ways insofar as morphology, surname, and so on, are used to measure Latinohood, forgetting that the entire group categorization schema originates from social constructions and not metaphysical ones. A consequence of my analysis of ethnicity is precisely that an American Indian, for example, can leave her reservation and live integrated, even acculturated, with whites who despise Indians (as many do), *and still remain an Indian!* This exposes the manner in which Gracia's account fails to accord persons proper levels of autonomy, whereas my analysis implies that persons in ethnic groups can live as they may and yet they retain their ethnicity *no matter what.* One ought to be rather suspicious of any analysis of ethnicity that denies the autonomy of persons and the sovereignty of groups, ethnically speaking. Gracia's requirement that "the genealogy criterion needs to be more specific; we must be told where it begins and where it stops,"[24] when applied to my analysis, is a problematic statement, as in my analysis where the boundary lines of an ethnic group cease is where the genealogical tie fails to exist. Thus we are "told" "where it stops." And I have already explained where it begins—at its social construction and at whatever percentage of blood quantum is properly deemed appropriate to be a member of this or that ethnic group. Thus Gracia's second round of concerns with my analysis are found wanting.

Another objection to my analysis of ethnic identity is whether genealogy is a necessary condition of it. This argument insists that a child of white ancestry who is raised in, say, the United Mexican States (*los Estados Unidos Mexicanos*) for the entirety of her childhood and who has adopted the Mexican culture as her own, is indeed a Latina. Yet my account denies this. Part of my reply to this concern is that my analysis is not a metaphysical one, but ethically oriented for purposes of positive public policy administration. I concur with observations that lead to a kind of metaphysical skepticism about racial and ethnic identities. I have made this clear elsewhere.[25] But I also make it clear that I am, insofar as the *ethics of ethnicity* is concerned, a realist. I do not believe that the white child in the example is (read: ought to be construed as) anything but white. The reason is that public policy cannot handle well such a convoluted practice of ethnic identification. Fraud would abound and the basic reasons for ethnic-oriented public policies would be defeated. I still believe that my reasoning here is correct, and to deny it would court disaster for affirmative action and other ethnically based public policies.

It is genealogy that places us into this *or* that ethnic group, or into this *and* that ethnic group, as the case may be. But if it is true that, *after* genealogy, what distinguishes ethnic groups from one another is their diverse *experiences* in the world, then this surely becomes a focal point of differentiating between groups insofar as what they deserve in the administration of public policy.

Gracia proposes what he takes to be counterexamples to my analysis. The first is his claim that those who become Jews through conversion count against my requirement of genealogy.[26] But this is hardly a successful counterexample, as what happens in such cases is that persons *who are not ethnically Jewish to begin with become religiously Jewish.* Thus this alleged counterexample amounts to an equivocation on "Jewish" and its cognates, as it conflates Jewish ethnicity with religious Judaism (after all, one can be ethnically Jewish without being a religious Jew, and vice versa). But in no way does this show that Jewish ethnicity is wholly a matter of choice or convention as becoming a religious Jew is. My analysis requires genealogical ties to an ethnic group in order for one to be an authentic member of that group to one degree or another. This is, by the way, the folk understanding of ethnicity. That a certain religion like Judaism allows conversion into its membership is not an example of an *ethnic* group wherein membership is gained without genealogical ties. As Gracia knows, the Christian religion not only allows, but actually beckons, nonbelievers to join its ranks. Yet this is hardly a sign of *ethnic* conversion, despite the fact that ethnic acculturation often occurs in religious conversion. The fact is that, given my understanding of my own ethnic heritage, I can no more become a member of, say, an Asian ethnic group than I can become a dog or a cat, a koi or a rat. I simply lack the genealogical tie requisite for membership in such honorable groups. Now if there were no social constructions of ethnicity wherein we could index our origins of them for whatever aim, things would be such that we would all be humans, which we are, and that would be that. But the fact is that ethnicity has emerged by way of racism in many cases and in many societies, and we can, genetically speaking, identify through genealogy who belongs to which socially constructed groups.[27] As Henry Louis Gates, Jr., has made known to the public in his PBS television program *African American Lives*, mitochondrial DNA studies, for instance, can effectively link contemporary blacks to their respective homelands in Africa. And the same can be done for any other ethnic group, provided sufficient scientific resources are available. Hence, this concern of Gracia's is defeated.

The second supposed counterexample Gracia offers to my analysis is one of adoption. This is actually a version of the objection that I consider in my book, *Race, Racism, and Reparations* when I assess the proposal that cultural participation is either a necessary or sufficient condition of ethnic group membership. It is also a rendition of the above example of the white child raised in Mexico. The proposal is rejected in both respects. Gracia's argument amounts to the assertion that it is sufficient for ethnic group membership that one's becoming a member of a family of an ethnic group is enough to make one a member of that ethnic group. It is really the same argument as the Jewish conversion argument which conflated religious conversion with ethnic "conversion," and deserves a similar reply.

There is no question that in typical cases of adoption, a child reared by parents of a certain ethnic group is likely to experience the culturally and socially transmitted characteristics of that group. But as I have argued at great length elsewhere, cultural or social characteristics are neither necessary nor sufficient for ethnic group membership, at the very least in public policy–related contexts.[28] Gracia's concern would count against my analysis if it were one attempting to address the question of the metaphysical or ontological essence of ethnic groups, of which I too am skeptical, as I have made plain elsewhere for the very same reasons Gracia himself notes in various of his works on this subject. But it hardly counts against my public policy or ethically based analysis of ethnicity.

Thus Gracia's concerns with my genealogical analysis of ethnic group identity are rebutted, and my analysis remains undefeated. *While it is possible to simply deny by way of question-begging objections certain aspects of my analysis, these attempts fail to refute my analysis on grounds that are philosophically neutral.* Thus my analysis of ethnic identity is an internally coherent one, conceptually speaking. Moreover, it is what underlies generations of legal relations between Indians and the U.S. government, which speaks to the practical viability of such an analysis. It provides philosophical underpinnings for how Indians have chosen to self-identify for purposes of public policy relations with the U.S. government. While I do not claim that it is unproblematic, it seems to work reasonably well for the purposes of the implementation of reparations policies. Furthermore, the science of DNA measurement for ethnicity can, with significant improvements in the current ways in which it is conducted, accurately identify persons as belonging to this or that region of the world in terms of ethnicity.

Thus my analysis of ethnic group identification escapes the clutches of Gracia's concerns. But I will now turn my attention to explaining why my analysis is the best available option by explaining why Gracia's own model of ethnic group identification is problematic. Gracia's proposed model is what he refers to as the "familial-historical" model of ethnic identification. Coincidentally, it is the Wittgensteinian "family-resemblance" model that I pondered when I first began to think about matters of ethnicity in a philosophical vein over a decade ago, and as a direct result of Gracia's seminal article on Latino identity.[29] Here I will register my reservations with such a view which will in turn explain why I did not adopt it or even articulate it philosophically for publication.

Gracia begins by stating that ethnic groups belong to larger family groups. But "a family does not have a single feature, let alone a set of them, that is shared by all of its members."[30] So where my analysis states that a genealogical tie to an ethnic group is necessary and sufficient, and the only thing that is necessary or sufficient, for ethnicity, Gracia's model denies this claim in favor of the Wittgensteinian denial that family members share only crisscrossing similarities, some members with some other members, but not with all other members: "A family resemblance does not entail that all members of a family share the same features, but that every one of them shares some feature with at least some other member of the family."[31] This is precisely Ludwig Wittgenstein's notion of family resemblance as outlined in his *Philosophical Investigations*,[32] among some of his other writings,[33] one that has been much discussed in Western analytic philosophy, especially between 1960 and 1980.

As is well known, Wittgenstein developed the notion of family resemblance in terms of games: "Instead of producing something common to all that we call language, I am saying that these phenomena have no one thing in common which makes us use the same word for all,—but that they are *related* to one another in many different ways. And it is because of this relationship, or these relationships, that we call them all 'language.'"[34] Gracia applies it straightaway to ethnic identity.

The manner in which Gracia applies Wittgenstein's notion of family resemblance to ethnicity is essentially by taking each of the features that I deny is either necessary or sufficient for ethnicity and arguing that, while each such feature is neither necessary nor sufficient for ethnicity, each can be seen as one feature that is possessed by members of an ethnic group, though none is possessed by all such members. He writes: "A family does not get its unity from common features among its members, but rather from the particular historical relations that tie its individual members, which in turn produce features common to some of those members."[35] And he adds, "Yet families are distinct entities based on the concrete historical relations that tie their members, also separating them from the members of other families. And families are distinguishable based on the features that those relations have generated."[36] Just what are these properties that family members possess in ethnic groups? Gracia tells us: "In some cases, the members of the family are distinguishable because of the shape of their noses, in others because of their big eyes, in others because of their last name, in others because they speak Spanish, and so on."[37] However, Gracia denies that such properties can include self-identification or out-group identification in terms of ethnic group membership.[38] But he also denies that ethnicity is a matter of social construction. For him, ethnicity is a matter of changing historical relations rather than social construction. And the difference is crucial. For it is one thing to say that such groups can be the mere constructions of, say, dominant groups in a class struggle to oppress other groups for their own gain. But it is quite another to think, for instance, that the evolution of historical interactions between ethnic groups and within such groups creates and sustains their respective identities.

In assessing Gracia's Wittgensteinian model of ethnicity, it is helpful to point out that, first, it need not be denied either that the evolution of historical interactions between ethnic groups and within such groups creates and sustains their respective identities, or that such groups can be the constructions of, say, dominant groups in a class struggle to oppress other groups for their own gain. There is no conceptual absurdity in accepting both of these propositions. In fact, the acceptance of both seems to me an accurate account of what often occurs. Thus Gracia's familial-historical model need not reject the idea of the social construction of ethnicity, and Gracia has provided insufficient reason to do so.

Secondly, that Gracia's inclusion of morphological features as one of the properties that makes one a member of an ethnic family is problematic in that it would rule out or minimize as a black person, for instance, one who shares no noticeable morphological features with other blacks, but who is the offspring of a black couple, and yet shares no other features listed by Gracia as being ones possessed by ethnic family members, such as the use of recognizably "black" pronunciations, perhaps having a name such as Kimberly Feinstein, not participating in events of black culture or even knowing anything about black history, or having very light skin color. Yet she has a clear genealogical tie to black folk. Does this not pose a difficulty for Gracia's model, as it would have to preclude membership in the ethnic group, black, to this person? Gracia can assert that "families are not coherent wholes composed of homogeneous elements; they include members that differ substantially from each other and may clash in various ways."[39] But this does not refute my analysis which argues that for purposes of positive public policy administration genealogy is both necessary and sufficient for ethnic group membership. Both the folk conception of ethnicity and commonsense intuition would confirm that Kimberly Feinstein is black. And it is precisely because the folk conception of ethnicity and commonsense intuition concurs with my genealogical analysis that genealogical ties are what matter for ethnicity. But my analysis clarifies that it is because of public policy considerations that we often do and ought to think this way. It is not a matter of the ontology or metaphysics of ethnicity. It is, rather, a matter of the ethics of ethnicity.

Furthermore, my genealogical analysis of ethnicity also holds that there can be and typically is significant diversity within ethnic groups, contrary to Gracia's misattribution to me of the view that "ethnic categories must have clear and distinct boundaries, so that their membership is never in doubt."[40] Recall that it is my analysis that prohibits the infusion of political or morphological elements into the defining of ethnicity precisely to preserve diversity within such groups. What unites members of ethnic groups, then, is that they share a common genealogical origin (even if that origin is at least in part a matter of social construction). But within such groups exist and thrive a variety of morphological characteristics, language usage, cultural and social relations, lifestyles, and so on. However, my analysis concurs with Gracia that "there are no features that can be shown to be necessarily common to all members of ethnic groups at all times and in all places."[41] But this does not logically preclude the idea that ethnic group genealogy is both necessary and sufficient for ethnic group membership. Why not? Because ethnic group genealogy is not a feature like the other ones mentioned by Gracia and myself, but relative to the social construction of ethnicities a biological and evolutionary fact about each of us. It is not a feature in the same way as morphological properties are, or my use of language, or participation in culture, and so on. Unlike these features, I cannot change my genealogy no matter what I do. Yet I can alter in various ways each of these other features about myself. Just as my genealogy is unchangeable in terms of my being a member of the human race, it is also immutable in terms of my being a member of the group, Latino, and whatever other ethnic groups to which I belong. But I can change my morphological features, my usage of languages, my cultural practices, my social practices, and my names, among other things. For example, Michael Jackson, despite his morphological alterations and some changes in his social and cultural practices relative to his upbringing, was nonetheless black as he himself reiterated when many doubted his ethnicity, or his perception of his own ethnicity. So Gracia's claim is misleading in this way as it misconstrues all of our properties (mentioned in terms of ethnicity) as being similar ethnic identifiers when they are not.

However, where my genealogical analysis of ethnicity preserves what is good about Gracia's familial-historical model, it does not suffer from the fatal flaw of not being implementable in public policy or ethnically based medical research. Perhaps these are not Gracia's concerns as his discussions never address such matters. But it is a stark fact about his view that it provides the law, medicine, and public policy absolutely no manner by which to categorize persons into ethnic groups. And in case this matters not to Gracia in his preoccupation with the metaphysics of ethnicity, consider the facts that it is not only public policies such as affirmative action or reparations that are adversely affected here, but ethnically based medical research. How, in Gracia's model, are members of ethnic groups to be identified for purposes of ethnically based medical research (such as sickle cell anemia) if not genealogically? Are research physicians to simply look at the morphological features of their subjects in determining their ethnic statuses? Or, perhaps equally absurd, are they to consider their surnames, or their abilities to speak this or that language? Or, even more absurdly, are they to simply consider the geographical location where they were raised, hoping that the patients in question were not raised in a multiplicity of cultures and contexts? The plain fact is that Gracia's Wittgensteinian account of ethnicity provides no way for research physicians to conduct viable ethnicity-based research in, say, sickle-cell anemia or the like, because in such cases the research cannot be conducted properly without a means by which to properly categorize members of certain ethnic groups. My genealogical analysis of ethnicity handles this problem with precisely the kind of answer medical researchers need, one that can be established by way of the examination of DNA samples.

Thus there exist several deep problems with Gracia's Wittgensteinian familial-historical model of ethnicity, ranging from the identifiability of certain problematic cases of ethnic group membership illustrated by the Kimberly Feinstein example, to public policy considerations such as the identification of targets of affirmative action and reparations and the viability of ethnicity-related medical research. For these reasons, then, Gracia's model of ethnicity must be rejected. Moreover, Gracia's and other concerns with my analysis have been met, or at least neutralized. And if it is true that Gracia's and my own respective accounts of ethnicity are the most plausible philosophical ones being offered thus far, it would appear that mine succeeds thus far in being the most plausible for the stated aims.

Positive public policy administration motivates my analysis. Social constructions of race have often led to racist atrocities, and it is many of those very racist acts, omissions, and attempts that justify compensatory remedies to the descendants of those victimized by racist oppression in the distant past.

But it is not enough to establish a practical way to identify victims of racist harmful wrongdoing. What is crucial in those cases is that there is an identifiable and existing perpetrator of the gross forms of injustice, identifiable and existing groups that experienced the evils, and credible evidence of the harmful wrongdoing that serves as the basis for such judgments. In the end, I claim to have demonstrated that the best way to classify Latinos for purposes of reparations and affirmative action, for instance, is by way of genealogy, following the way various Indians have classified themselves for generations for purposes of public policy administration in dealing with the U.S. government. What makes me a Latino is that I am, genealogically speaking, predominantly a Latino. And this just means that to some meaningful extent my parents were predominantly Latinos, as were my grandparents, and so on. The reason why this is somewhat circular, though it remains to be seen whether or not it is viciously circular, as opposed to virtuously so, is because what it means to say that my parents and grandparents are Latinos is contingent on the evolution of the social construction of that ethnic category over time. Once again, I am not confident that we can escape circularity regarding this matter.

Now if leftists genuinely believe in reparations and affirmative action for racial injustice, then given the problem of identifying accurately and fairly ethnic group members they seem to have no alternative but to adopt something like my genealogical conception of how people are to be classified, ethnically speaking. Still, it will be true that the philosophically dubious concept of race can assist public policy in understanding *how* the racism that leads us to the need for public policy programs and awards of reparations originates. Race assists ethnicity in terms of public policy administration, turning Jim Crow upside down. Race best enables us to understand the racism that warrants and requires compensation, whereas genealogically based ethnic categories best assist us in identifying those who ought to be compensated, and to what degree.

However true it is that genealogical considerations place us predominantly in a particular group for purposes of positive public policy administration, it is also true that existential considerations play a role, not in actually "placing" us into the group, but rather in understanding the *depth to which* we belong to it.[42] The result is that we can not only understand the depth to which one is, say, black versus a Latino (or both), but also the ways in which it is completely reasonable to classify blacks and Latinos differentially in terms of how much each group has (on balance) experienced harmful wrongdoing in and by U.S. society. This in turn makes it possible to develop or revise public policies that can better address historic racist injustices within the bounds of fairness. Thus my genealogical conception of ethnicity assists in providing a practical and viable means by which to identify Indians and blacks for purposes of reparations.

What does it mean to be black in the United States? What does it mean to be a Latino or a Latina? In terms of public policy administration, it means that one has a predominant genealogical tie to members in that group as that group has been socially understood. If I have a Brazilian grandfather and an Argentinean grandmother each on my mother's side, and great-grandparents also from those countries, and so forth, then I am predominantly (at least 50 percent) Latino to the extent that they are Latinos. As noted above, recent breakthroughs in genetic research demonstrate it to be possible to verify or falsify ethnic claims by way of DNA examination. Indeed, much can be done to trace one's genealogy by scientific investigation.[43] Howard McGary, for instance, is black to the extent that his parents and grandparents are of African or black descent and trace back to the enslavement of Africans in the United States. To be sure, there is some incongruity here, as I have defined "Latino" in terms of genealogy, while I have defined "black" in terms of genealogically based historic injustice, namely U.S. slavery. But this need not overly concern us now, as the point simply reemphasizes the role that genealogy plays in positive public policy administration.

Furthermore, no amount of ideological politicization ought to affect how we categorize ourselves and others in terms of public policy administration. Whether or not McGary is a rightist or a leftist on social issues, he is what he is (ethnically speaking) in terms of *his genealogical ties* to the enslavement of Africans in the United States. Whether or not I am a moral or social/political leftist, I am a Latino in terms of my genealogical ties to my parents and grandparents who are Latinos of this or that kind. Metaphysically, race and ethnicity are problematic concepts. On this much Gracia and I concur with one another. But insofar as positive public policy administration is concerned, my genealogical conception of ethnic identification serves as a reasonable and plausible philosophical analysis of the very conception of ethnicity at work in the identification of, say, Indians for purposes of dealing with the U.S. government, a conception that has been at work for generations and with reasonable success.

Charles W. Mills's two major concerns with my analysis of race and ethnicity are: (a) that I do not engage the philosophical defenses of social constructivism concerning the concept of race; and (b) that I do not consider certain objections to the replacement of race talk with the language of ethnicity.[44] Although he is correct in pointing out that any treatment of the concept of race that does not address such a view is incomplete, it was not my aim to set out a full account of the concept of race. Rather, my goal was to introduce readers to what I call "primitive race theories," a cluster of theories that affirms what some refer to as "classical race theory."

I agree with Mills that my not addressing social constructivist accounts of race leads me to not address conceptions of race that are not primitivistic. So even if my arguments against primitive race theories are correct, it might nevertheless be possible to devise and defend a conception of race that evades the difficulties I pose for *primitive* race theories. I suppose that my more general aim of *Race, Racism, and Reparations* focused my arguments against those conceptions of race that typically led to racism of the kind that the chapters on reparations are intended to address. I would have thought that my specific characterization of primitive race theories, along with my admission that race and ethnicity are social constructs, would imply that mine was not a comprehensive rejection of any possible conceptions of race. When I argue that the concept of race ought to be replaced by a plausible notion of ethnicity, I mean that we ought to reject primitive race theories as I describe them and for at least the reasons I provide. Thus the narrower goal of that chapter is accomplished, as one set of rather implausible views of race is undermined. Nonetheless, I believe that what I refer to as "primitive race theories" are incoherent for the reasons I provide in chapter 1 of *Race, Racism, and Reparations*.

Now it might be argued that my admission along these lines does not in itself entitle me to adopt as I do a revisionist conception of ethnicity to replace the concept of race. However, it must be noted that strictly speaking, chapters 2 and 3 of *Race, Racism, and Reparations* on ethnicity are meant to articulate and defend a conception of ethnicity that evades the problems confronting primitive race theories and can therefore be considered to be more adequate than *they* and hence replace *them*. However, if Mills is indeed correct that a social constructivist conception of race not only evades the concerns I raise about primitive race theories, but ought to replace primitive race theories, then it would appear that I have ignored such social constructivist accounts and perhaps have leaped prematurely to an adoption of a genealogical conception of ethnicity. After all, social constructivist accounts of race might then amount to competitors with my genealogical conception of ethnicity insofar as the adequate identification of folk into groups is concerned.

Unless an effort *succeeds* in categorizing racial groups much more inclusively and nonarbitrarily than do primitive race theories, it appears that they are too crude to include the dozens of human groups that ethnic categories can and do embrace. As a result, primitive (and perhaps other) race theories, for all that is said in their favor, seem to be incapable of serving as guides to the administration of positive public policy. As metaphysical theories, primitive race theories are impotent to assist the leftist along these lines. So the challenge for leftist race theorists is to devise a plausible race theory that can properly and fairly categorize us into groups for such purposes. Not only, then, does my analysis of race and ethnicity evade various misplaced concerns with my assessment of race more generally, but it poses a serious challenge to leftists who claim to support affirmative action programs or reparations to seriously and wrongfully harmed groups.

My genealogical conception of ethnic identity admits of no pure ethnicity or race: Each of us belongs to *more than one* ethnic group, more or less to one, *and* more or less to another, as our particular genealogies indicate. This is more true to fact and intuitively plausible than some view that seeks to categorize people into this race *or* that one, without understanding the facts of group membership and how in nuanced ways they evolve over time. Although it is true that for purposes of positive public policy administration it might well be necessary for us to categorize ourselves as "predominantly" Latino or Jewish or such, my analysis rather shows how each one of us is, all things considered, *predominantly* this *or* that, but also this *and* that, ethnically speaking. As Linda Alcoff states of my view, "The largest percentage of an individual's parentage needs to be Latino in order for a person to count as a Latino."[45] Although for purposes of public policy, that "largest percentage" ought to satisfy some basic minimum in order for one to be counted among Latinos/as.[46] To repeat: the primary purpose of my genealogical conception of ethnicity is to provide a fair manner by which we can classify ourselves for purposes of positive public policy administration. Other aims include positive (not racist) ethnic pride and ethnic categorization for purposes of ethnicity-based medical research.

What I mean when I state that I am a *metaphysical antirealist* as pertains to race and ethnicity is that there are no racial or ethnic natural kinds, as some primitive race theories presume. Thus there are no natural races or ethnicities; they are social constructs often devised by those groups seeking power in various forms over others, often inspiring such evils as the American holocaust of hundreds of Indian nations, the enslavement of millions of Africans in the United States, and the "Jim-Crowing" of blacks, Indians, Latinos/as, and some others. However, I am an *ethical realist* when it comes to ethnicity (or, I now add, when it comes to a much more sophisticated conception of race than I have considered *if* one truly exists) insofar as a reasonably just legal system requires such categorization for purposes of adequate and fair reparations. And perhaps this is where social constructivists of race may have become a bit shortsighted. For most every one of us in philosophy who devotes herself to the analysis of racial categories is one who also supports some sort of leftist-type solutions to racist harmful wrongdoing. But I remain unconvinced that broad categories of race as they have been construed historically are sufficiently nuanced to be used by a reasonably just legal system to redress historic evils such as those against Indians, enslaved Africans, and blacks in the United States.

So I have provided a genealogical conception of ethnicity that not only includes largely, if not wholly, socially constructed ethnic identities, but has a principled criterion for distinguishing ethnic group members for purposes of, say, reparations and affirmative action. To the extent that I have a Latino genealogical tie is the extent to which I am a Latino—for purposes of positive public policy administration like affirmative action programs. The law *can* and sometimes does handle such cases in a reasonably fair way. In fact, my analysis of ethnic identification is directly inspired by and seeks to mimic how Indian nations even today demarcate members of their respective groups for purposes of U.S. government subsidies and programs.

Thus there are replies that neutralize or defeat the main concerns with my analysis of ethnicity. Moreover, there are some very good reasons why my genealogical conception of ethnicity fares far better than others in terms of positive public policy administration.

But what role would the genealogical conception of ethnicity play in determining, for purposes of positive public policy administration, a differentialist or proportional conception of reparations? Malcolm X once said concerning matters of justice that history is our most important teacher. I would add that philosophy, especially normative ethics, must be our guides along with history. Nonetheless, the role of history in assessing who we are and what we deserve can hardly be exaggerated.

THE AFFIRMATIVE ACTION OBJECTION

As mentioned in previous chapters, it has been argued that affirmative action ought to be used as the means of reparations, despite my argument to the contrary. It might be argued that affirmative action can and ought to be a way to provide some measure of practical justice for oppressed groups in the United States, including Indians and blacks. I have argued and continue to argue that it is a category mistake to conflate affirmative action with reparations, especially compensatory reparations. While reparations are by definition a kind of compensatory right a group has that has been wrongfully harmed, affirmative action is typically justified, whenever it is justified, by way of considerations of distributive justice, rather than by way of a right to compensation. Thus while affirmative action, say, in employment requires beneficiaries to work for their wage or salary, it is wrongheaded to think that recipients of reparations owe work for their compensation. For while there might be something to the idea that affirmative action might constitute a right of distributive justice, it surely is incorrect to mistake it for the reparative (remedial) right to compensation. Thus it is a category mistake to confuse affirmative action with reparations.

Nonetheless, let us proceed with the common idea among many that affirmative action programs can bring a modicum of meaningful justice to underrepresented groups in society, and that it might be a good way to level the playing fields between groups having historically unequal opportunities in life. Even with this assumption, is affirmative action in the United States a good thing if it turns out that it is the only realistic way to bring some measure of equal opportunity to Indians and blacks?

Assuming that affirmative action programs are morally justified, there are several kinds of theories of affirmative action, based on competing notions of what justifies such programs on moral grounds. As Bernard Boxill makes clear, backward-looking approaches seek to justify affirmative action based on the need to rectify historic racist harmful wrongdoings, while forward-looking approaches justify it based on considerations of distributive justice and fairness.[47] Perhaps a synthesis of these views is more plausible, using both backward- and forward-looking reasons to ground affirmative action. Whichever of these views of affirmative action one adopts, it might employ either an inclusionistic or a differentialist strategy insofar as the identification of affirmative action beneficiaries is concerned. An inclusionistic view is most common in the literature, and it holds that there is one conglomeration of groups that for backward-, forward-, or backward- and forward-looking reasons ought to be the recipients of affirmative action programs.[48] Accordingly, "blacks and women" are included in the same category for affirmative action purposes. A differentialist view holds that, insofar as affirmative action programs are at least in part a collective response to racist harmful wrongdoings in the past and present, and insofar as groups experience such racist harmful wrongdoings to varying degrees,[49] then each group ought to receive affirmative action benefits to the extent that it has experienced racist harmful wrongdoing, all relevant things considered. This implies that, based on U.S. history[50] there must be a ranking of the severity of experienced racist harmful wrongdoings, and that this ranking ought to determine which groups receive which benefits and in what amounts. Groups and their respective harms ought to be differentiated from one another based on a plausible principle of proportional compensation already at work in U.S. law.

The differentialist conception of positive public policy administration rests on notions of kinds and degrees of experienced harmful wrongdoings by members of ethnic groups, along with the *principle of proportional compensation wherein each compensated party is to receive remedial benefits in albeit rough proportion to the harms they have experienced wrongfully.* The implication of this principle for affirmative action programs and their beneficiaries is that groups such as Indians and blacks ought to receive far greater affirmative action benefits than any other groups in U.S. society based on the history and current harmful wrongdoings experienced by them, while far fewer and much lower levels of affirmative action benefits ought to be made available to Latinas, Latinos, Asians, and certain other discriminated groups residing in the United States, based on the kinds and levels of actual harmful wrongdoings experienced by members of these groups. Since *no one, on balance, ought to be permitted to benefit from her own wrongdoing,* quite surprising (to some) results follow from this line of thought. It follows, for example, that white women, being a group currently counted in the collective that constitutes legally legitimate targets of affirmative action benefits, ought to be removed from this group of beneficiaries. It does not follow, however, that well-qualified white women ought not to be hired in the workplace, any more than it would follow that their well-qualified white male counterparts ought not to be hired when it comes to employment matters. The implication of this line of thought for employment, educational, and other affirmative action contexts is that whatever monies are set aside for such programs ought always to be reserved for the most deserving, rather than for those who are least deserving. This is especially the case in light of the inadequacy of the resources available for affirmative action programs.

However, even if affirmative action programs are seen as a way to "compensate" the past harmful wrongdoings against groups, it surely amounts to a moral insult to Indians and blacks whose oppression in and by the United States towers in comparison to all other wronged groups combined. A consideration of the conservative figures of what is owed to Indians and blacks by the United States as calculated in the previous chapter shows that affirmative action programs, even if significantly improved over the current programs in place, amounts to a proverbial drop in the bucket compared to what these groups are owed. And to lump these groups in with all manner of other "minorities" and "women" for purposes of affirmative action programming adds insult to injury, as I shall now explain. This is especially true if we discuss affirmative action on the assumption that no reparations policies for Indians and blacks exist.[51]

THE WHITEWASHING OF AFFIRMATIVE ACTION

There exist some deep problems with affirmative action programs as they currently function in the United States. I shall focus on one such difficulty: the whitewashing of affirmative action. This is the vague and ambiguous declaring of various groups "of color" and (mostly white) "women" as "oppressed" and the inclusion of them under the category of legitimate and equal affirmative action beneficiaries. The primary justification for this belief is forward-looking, and declares affirmative action to be a kind of egalitarian justice that seeks to maximize overall social utility by way of equal opportunity in education and employment.

But this view is precisely what has perniciously influenced social justice thinking for decades in the United States. One reason for this is that current affirmative action programs seem to imply a kind of ethnic integration that is presumed to be a good thing. But why in the name of the Lakota massacred at Wounded Knee would we think that Indians ought to be *presumed* to *desire* to become harmonious with the offspring of evil invaders, slaveowners, and Jim Crowers, especially those contemporary whites who in most cases are indeed racists against them? Why in the name of Sojourner Truth should we think that blacks ought to even *desire* to integrate with a society of mostly those who have *yet* to seriously address with *punishment* the several KKK terrorists most responsible for the murders and other kinds of terrorist acts against so many blacks? Why in the name of Red Cloud, Sitting Bull, Chief Joseph, and Geronimo would we dare insist that Indians, those relatively few who still exist as nations, ought to *want* to live alongside the descendants of those who intentionally attempted to commit against them perhaps the worst genocide in human history and what that meant to the devastation of their cultures? It is another way to, albeit for the most part perhaps unintentionally, violate Indians' and blacks' rights to fair treatment under the law and public policy. What the American holocaust and U.S. slavery did to violate fundamental rights of Indians and blacks, a utilitarian-based, compensatory rights-denying policy does also, but less conspicuously as it cloaks itself in the guise of doing well by Indians and blacks. What Indians and blacks need and deserve is no more rights denials, but respect for their rights, including those of compensatory justice that are due them.

Under normal circumstances of U.S. criminal or tort law, compensation is *not* awarded with the proviso that the victim and the perpetrator share in the compensatory benefits, that is, that the compensatory award benefit "all" or both parties. Underlying this brand of leftism is an insidious kind of utilitarian rights-*dis*respecting humanism which seems to ignore the fact that life includes enemies of justice and rightness, and they should *not* be perceived as being on the side of goodness and virtue, but rather *punished* and/or forced to compensate others to the extent of their culpable and harmful wrongdoing. On the contrary, evildoers should whenever possible get what they deserve, and what they deserve, roughly, is the extent of the harm they inflict on others wrongfully, intentionally, knowing, and voluntarily.

Reparations are *not* about social harmony. To think that they are continues to confuse reparations with affirmative action instead of understanding what reparations in these two cases *really* mean. As noted in chapter 1, reparations are matters of what compensation victims of harmful wrongdoing *deserve* because their rights have been wrongfully violated. They are matters of adequately rectifying past evils. As Joel Feinberg states: "Reparation 'sets things straight' or 'gives satisfaction.'"[52] Several examples throughout U.S. history alone exist to illustrate this point. But suffice it to say that after being convicted and sentenced to pay hundreds of dollars in fines for violating the Alien and Sedition Acts that were passed within two generations of the ratification of the U.S. Constitution, both Matthew Lyon and Thomas Cooper, white men, found their fines (with interest to their heirs) remitted by 1850 acts of the U.S.

Congress. There was simple reparation without any expectation that their rights to compensation be diminished or take a form other than cash settlements in light of social utility considerations, or that Lyon and Cooper be expected to live with others in U.S. society. Nor should reparations be different with regard to Indians and blacks. The United States must, to even hope to become a morally legitimate state, provide sufficient reparations to both Indians and blacks so that their individual autonomy and group sovereignty, once alienated from them by violence by mostly U.S. whites and their government, can be restored. Reparations to Indians and blacks should be made in ways that are consistent with their autonomy and sovereignty as persons and groups. Reparations programs ought not to be contingent on factors that would exacerbate such frustration and despair against the wills of those compensated. In short, there should be no double standards in the awarding of legal compensation for harmful wrongdoing.

So it is important to expose this utilitarian move to unintentionally but nonetheless further oppress Indians and blacks by presumptuously insisting that they remain or become integrated with the offspring of their most ardent oppressors by the imposition of effectively coercive integrationist public policy programs instead of respectfully paying them the genuine reparations they deserve based on the kinds and degrees of oppression they experienced. Compensatory justice in no way forces the recipient of it to integrate into the larger society. It is primarily about providing redress for significant forms of experienced injustice. But a utilitarian-based scheme of public policy administration is more concerned about social utility maximization than it is about compensation for rights violations.

This form of utilitarianism is precisely the kind of leftist thinking that both identifies affirmative action with reparations and actually supports, for example, the inclusion of white women into the pool of U.S. affirmative action beneficiaries *as equally deserving of affirmative action benefits* relative to folk of color (even Indians and blacks!), a scheme which has played into the hands of not-so-well-meaning whites when it comes to things like the awarding of government contracts only to those companies that satisfy affirmative action guidelines. After all, under current guidelines, some of the most exclusionary racist companies can satisfy affirmative action requirements by insisting that they employ white women at some of the highest ranking positions in their companies. So here we have cases that exclude even companies of color from winning government contracts—largely because some of the other ones, often having governmental connections, can claim to have satisfied the affirmative action requirements by hiring white women as executives. And this is part of what explains largely why white women have benefited more *than any other group* in the United States from affirmative action programs.[53] Yet they are among the least deserving of affirmative action benefits based on historical facts of harmful wrongdoings suffered in the United States, which includes the

bad Samaritanism of most white women which makes most of them complici-
tors, at the very least, in the racism that oppressed so many millions throughout U.S. history. As Margaret Urban Walker points out: "There are situations
in which the same people who are victims of wrong in one respect are responsible for wrongs to others in another."[54] I take this as a moral datum, based
on a fair-minded reading of U.S. history. After all, most white women have
been a part of the racist ruling classes (wealthy, middle classes, and poor) that
oppressed Indians and blacks often with *impunity* and for generations! Recall
that the KKK's membership, which with violent impunity not experienced by
U.S. white women, had oppressed blacks with the support of Jim Crow,
included white men and women from various socioeconomic classes. Moreover, as Alcoff observes, "white women are often the first line of offense. . . .
White women can benefit economically and politically from white dominance."[55] I would add that it is not just white dominance, but the white privilege[56] made possible and sustained by white dominance from which most
white women benefit, as most white women are part of who has fought to
preserve it over time. This is in general terms what I mean when I write that
white women in the United States are among the greatest oppressors of Indians and blacks, and discriminate against other folk of color in the United
States. I shall make more of this point below.

So let us begin by recognizing the true distinction between reparations and
affirmative action, as the laws must do in attempting to respect justice and
fairness. Then we must understand that reparations presuppose no principle
of equality except the Aristotelian point that similar cases must be treated sim-
ilarly and that dissimilar ones must be treated dissimilarly. Reparations presuppose, among other things, that harmful wrongdoers get what they deserve,
or pay what they deserve to pay, to those who qualify as recipients of the reparations. And no vague, overly inclusive conception of races or the disadvantaged (or of "oppression," as we saw in the introduction) seems to be of any
use in determinations of who qualifies as members of reparated groups. We
need as much precision as tough philosophy and workable public policy will
permit, which is itself a Herculean task, to determine the boundaries of group
membership concerning groups that have experienced evil by an identifiable
and existing perpetrator.

One need not worry that I "seriously" underestimate the "oppression" of
women in general.[57] Given that women of color collectively constitute a
majority of women in the world and perhaps even in the United States, my
accounts of reparations and affirmative action recognize more than any other
philosophical account just how genuinely oppressed the majority of women
(of color) were and are. However, I hope that we can see that U.S. white
women in general (as a class and on average) were *not* and are *not* oppressed,
if by "oppressed" we mean to delineate the truly *severe* injustices experienced
by some groups from the less severe injustices experienced by others. I believe
that it amounts to nothing short of a moral insult and is extremely misleading,

simplistic, and even equivocal to use the same term ("oppression") to refer to the American holocaust of Indians, the enslavement of Africans in the United States, and the Jim-Crowing primarily of blacks, while using that same word without careful qualification to describe injustices toward most white women (even the poorest of them![58]) in the United States, both historically and today. This kind of equivocal error (call it the "error of 'oppression'") occurs too often in white feminist writings, as we saw in the introduction.

Thus even if affirmative action were an unproblematic way to mete out reparations, it is fraught with difficulties. This is why I focus my attention on reparations to the most oppressed groups in U.S. history. Fortunately, the oppressor and oppressed are generally identifiable, either in terms of themselves (the U.S., state, and local governments, and contemporary Indians and blacks who have experienced oppression directly, perhaps as the result of Jim Crow) or their heirs.

In my account of reparations, I go so far as to argue, based on principles of desert, responsibility, and proportionality, that Indian and black women deserve greater reparations than their male counterparts due to the facts of racism and sexism experienced by the former. If this does not take seriously sexism's role in life, I do not know what does. But we must omit white women from this part of the discussion, as we do not want to do to reparations what we have wrongly done to affirmative action.[59] By conflating more severe with less severe forms of injustice, we exaggerate the inequality of white women to white men in U.S. society, thereby denigrating the genuine oppression wrought on Indians and black women and men in the United States. We need a more complex analysis here. And that is precisely what I provide. But mine does not, nor will it ever, conflate the historic injustices against white women in the United States with the oppression of Indians and black women and men. As a class and on average, white women in the United States have never been oppressed if by "oppressed" we mean something akin to what Indians and black women and men experienced historically in the United States and even today. We must begin to respect Indian and black women and admit that whatever happened and happens to white women in the United States in their quest for full freedoms was and is experienced in much worse terms (quantitatively and qualitatively) by the average Indian or black woman—both by the racist U.S. society at large and sometimes by their own spouses, families, and so forth. So no matter how badly off some white women were and are, their collective plight does *not* amount to much compared to the *severe* oppression experienced by Indian and black women and men.[60]

Just one of several general examples that can be extracted from U.S. history wherein white women were consistently accorded not only civil but political rights that no Indian or black enjoyed is the following:

> Consider the key nineteenth-century distinction between political rights and civil rights. The former were rights of members of the polity—call them First-Class Citizens—whereas the latter belonged to all (free) members of the larger society.

Alien men and single white women circa 1800 typically could speak, print, worship, enter into contracts, hold personal property in their own name, sue and be sued, and exercise sundry other civil rights, but typically could not vote, hold public office, or serve on juries. These last three were political rights, reserved for First-Class Citizens.[61]

While white women in the United States on average and as a class were busy enjoying second-class citizenship and all that it provided, Indian and black men and women (as well as the African slaves, of course) enjoyed *nothing of the sort!* White women were by and large discriminated against, but experienced *nothing* of the horrific oppressions of genocide, slavery, massive land theft, cultural holocaust, and so on, much, if not most, of which was the result of the pervasive influence of the doctrine of discovery that few, if any, white women in the United States rejected or protested in a meaningful and consistent manner. Nor did they protest, as many white women did for their own advancement from second-class to first-class citizenship, the congressional passage of the Indian Appropriations Act of 1871, or the Dawes Act a few years later, each of which resulted in the loss of millions of acres of Indian lands to white men and white women alike, and the consequences of such legislation were enjoyed by both in relatively congenial support of one another. And let us not forget how white women, along with their white male counterparts, benefited from the Slave Powers Act, the Fugitive Slave Laws, the Mann Act, *Plessy v. Furguson,* and a host of other legal decisions truly oppressive of African slaves and blacks that white women on average and as a class did not experience. In light of U.S. history, then, it is apparent that to continue as most do to equivocate in the use of "oppression" in applying it to both Indians and blacks on the one hand, and to white women on the other, is to fail to understand both a commonsense and more nuanced study of U.S. history.

Several well-meaning leftists have for decades supported what turns out to be a conspicuously flagrant violation of justice and fairness as it pertains to the administration of affirmative action programs. Lumping all ethnic groups together (except whites) into what many (and at times myself) refer to as "people of color," and deeming them "oppressed," they affirm a blanket support for them. But this leads to the categorization of white women as oppressed. This has the adverse effect of minimizing the oppression of, say, Indians and blacks and simultaneously inflating the levels of oppression of white women. Indeed, it ignores Kimberlé Crenshaw's insight that "black women," for example, "can experience discrimination in ways that are both similar to and different from those experienced by white women and Black men," in fact, she argues, and often experience "double-discrimination."[62] Moreover, she argues that white feminism often "overlooks the role of race. Feminists thus ignore how their own race functions to mitigate some aspects of sexism, and, moreover, how it often privileges them over and contributes to the domination of other women."[63] I would add that it is also true that white women on average, on balance, and as a class have served as oppressive forces against Indians and black men in particular. This is true both in terms of their overt acts of racist oppression, but also in terms of their moral negligence in failing to do the right things when the most oppressed needed their support.[64] But it is also true of white women's racist attitudes against others, especially Indians and blacks. For example, as Clarence Darrow points out: "A black woman, no matter how black, may sit all day in a Pullman car if she is holding a white child on her lap; nobody objects to that, but if the white child was not there nobody could possibly stand it to be anywhere near that black woman."[65] Are we to think that most white women did not share precisely this attitude? The fact is that on average and as a class white women were oppressive toward Indians, blacks, and a host of others who did not share their coveted position of white privilege. While matters of white women's racism might not be as blatant today as they were in yesteryear, it is yet a story to be told whether or not they will explicitly acknowledge their roles as oppressors of others on their road to white female power and glory in the United States.

Now the reason for affirmative action programs for white women is typically construed as assisting the least advantaged group in order to improve the condition of society as a whole. But this "whitewashing of affirmative action" has deleterious effects on society, and more importantly, on the compensatory rights of the most wronged persons in society to receive what is their due according to morally justified *backward-looking* considerations. Moreover, by ignoring such *compensatory rights* it harms society as it says, in effect, that certain rights can and should be trumped for the greater good, which effectively nullifies the very notion of a right to begin with, as the Rawlsian epigraph for part 2 makes clear.[66]

A plausible ethic must take seriously what people *deserve* both in terms of considerations of distributive justice and compensatory justice. Furthermore, if it is true that backward-looking considerations are among the most important in a reasonably just society, then it would seem that we must adopt a differentialist policy of affirmative action according to which those groups that have experienced the greatest amounts and kinds of harmful wrongdoings ought to receive the greatest kinds and amounts of benefits either directly or indirectly from those who have harmed them wrongfully, whereas those groups that have experienced lesser amounts and kinds of harmful wrongdoings ought to receive lesser amounts and kinds of benefits from those who have harmed them wrongfully. I use the locution "indirectly" in that governmental policies sometimes for the sake of expediency employ notions of collective or vicarious responsibility (with or without fault) in order to effect such programs.[67] This implies that the current policy of affirmative action, while well-intentioned, is in violation of crucial considerations of justice and fairness. It implies, moreover, that the forward-looking underpinning of the current program which ignores backward-looking considerations of differentialist

historic evils experienced by various groups must be replaced by a more complex policy which does not place such a high premium on forward-looking
considerations of social harmony while failing to take compensatory rights
seriously. After all, how can genuine social harmony accrue if affirmative
action programs ignore the historic oppression that presumably motivates the
concern for affirmative action in the first place?

Implied in my revision of affirmative action policies is a restructuring of
beneficiaries according to principles of compensatory justice currently at work
in U.S. law. As noted, one such principle is that *one ought, on balance, never to
be permitted to profit from her own wrongdoing*. Another is that *those who have
experienced wrongful harms ought to be compensated in albeit rough proportion to the
harms they have experienced from others*. If we take these two principles as necessary for any just public policy's implementation, then any violation of them
is indicative of a public policy gone wrong and in need of revision.

These principles imply that current programs of affirmative action must be
revised in favor of a differentialist awarding of benefits. Assuming that there is
no adequate and substantial policy of reparations for Indians and blacks in
the United States, I shall now address in general terms a differentialist allotment of resources that would and should comprise an *appropriate* affirmative
action policy administration budget in the United States. Using a fair-minded
and commonsense reading of U.S. history as our guide, it is unquestionable
that Indian and black women and men should be placed at the top of the
list of beneficiaries in terms of both the *amounts* of affirmative action benefits
received and the *kinds* of such benefits received. Given the horrendous evils
and levels of oppression experienced by these groups, it would be reasonable
to think that all available kinds and the very highest levels of benefits should
be reserved for members of these groups, taking sexist oppression into account
as well as racist oppression. By taking sexist experiences of harmful wrongdoing into account, I mean to suggest that Indian and black women ought to
receive qualitatively and quantitatively more affirmative action benefits than
even their male counterparts. Following this, certain Latino and Asian women
and men, and perhaps some other ethnic groups ought to be included, though
to far lesser degrees than Indians and blacks. A fair-minded and commonsense
reading of U.S. history justifies this differentialist strategy in light of the moral
and legal principles noted. My aim here is to make meaningful progress in
the discourse concerning racist oppression and affirmative action programs: to
repeat, "we need to think clearly about oppression" and "not all oppressive
structures are equally harmful, and they should not all be regarded with the
same degree of concern."[68] However, if adequate and fair reparations are provided to Indians and blacks, then there is no longer a need to consider these
particular groups as targets of affirmative action programs. Perhaps Latinos
would then be the group most targeted by affirmative action programs, assuming that we Latinos too do not qualify for substantial reparations (assuming
we qualify for reparations at all). But if adequate and fair reparations are not

paid to Indians and blacks, it is obvious that they stand together as the most deserving of most of the affirmative action benefits.

But just as it is appropriate to exclude white men from this list, it is also clear that white women ought to be excluded from it as well. The whitewashing of current affirmative action programs has led to an unfortunate result, to repeat, that white women (and many white men) have benefited by way of affirmative action more than *all* nonwhite folk combined.[69] Yet *they* are the ones who previously benefited from *their oppression of various folk of color* in either their own ways or in their aiding and abetting their white male counterparts. As Gloria Watkins makes painfully plain regarding the racism of white women and their experiences of injustice, "The hierarchical pattern of race and sex relationships already established in American society merely took a different form under 'feminism': the form of women being classed as an oppressed group under affirmative action programs further perpetuating the myth that the social status of all women in America is the same."[70] The truth of these words from Watkins serves to underscore the racist oppression perpetrated in part by most white women on others from the beginning of U.S. society, and which continues perhaps in different forms and manifestations, until today. It would take more conniving gall than that of Meletus to insist that white women are on average, on balance, and as a group anything less than oppressors of "colored" folk. And it would take even more nerve to continue to insist, in light of my argument, that white women ought to be granted continuance *as beneficiaries* of affirmative action programs—especially at the same levels of benefits as Indians and blacks. After all, to continue to refuse reparations to Indians and blacks in light of the plausibility of the evidence for such reparations counts as a stark refusal to pay what is owed a denial of compensatory rights that is a form of continued oppression. As Gerda Lerner argues, "Historians of women have long ago come to see that 'women' cannot be treated as a unified category any more than 'men-as-a-group' can. Women differ by class, race, ethnic and regional affiliation, religion, and any number of other categories. . . . If one ignores 'differences' one distorts reality. If one ignores the power relations built on differences one reinforces them in the interest of those holding power."[71]

History and affirmative action have proven to be the greatest bedmates of most white women, for these women have oppressed various of us folk of color and yet have benefited from affirmative action programs from the start. And where are most of these white women today? Many of them insist on their own affirmative action rights being respected prior to, and often instead of, those others who deserve them more, such as Indians and blacks. White female racism against Indian men and black men is joined to their racism against women from those groups.[72] The very inclusion of white women in the group of affirmative action beneficiaries today is a form of injustice that they perpetrate on those more deserving folk of color.

Still one may wish to argue that white women *on average, on balance, and as a class* were and are themselves *oppressed* and that this entitles them to affirmative action benefits as the others. But it hardly follows from the problematic supposition that white women are oppressed that they deserve affirmative action benefits. Remember the legal and moral principle that no one ought to be permitted to benefit from her own wrongdoing. Even if white women were and are oppressed, their experience of oppression would hardly compare, qualitatively or quantitatively, to the harsh experiences that accompanied genocide, slavery, and the massive land theft that were experienced by Indians and blacks.[73] Moreover, even if it were true that somehow white women do rightly qualify as being on the list of genuine affirmative action beneficiaries because they are themselves oppressed, it would hardly follow that what they ought to receive is much more than the bare *minimum* of kinds and amounts of affirmative action benefits.[74] The differentialist approach to affirmative action benefits does not permit any group to benefit more than it deserves, as it cannot plausibly violate the legal and moral principle of proportional compensation.

Did the general injustices experienced by white women occur at the hands of Indians or black women? No. Nor did they occur at the hands of Indians or black men. Were white women abused by other men of color? Perhaps to some extent and in relatively few cases. But in general these injustices are clearly outweighed by the oppression of nonwhites by white women themselves. So even if it were true that white women as a class and on balance were and are oppressed,[75] they were oppressed mostly by white men. The correct picture of white women in the United States (on average and as a class) is that they are at worst *perhaps* mildly oppressed (definitely treated unjustly), but are themselves oppressive of others. This makes them poor candidates, on balance, for *any* kind of affirmative action, assuming of course that the moral justification of affirmative action is largely if not wholly backward-looking. By and large, the case for the harmful wrongdoing of white women is against white men, not in the main against men of color. But white women should not be allowed to benefit from their own oppression of others, and not to benefit *out of proportion* to the balance of harmful wrongdoing experienced by them.

Yet this is a far cry from what white women have and continue to receive from affirmative action programs today. So even if the principle that no one ought to be permitted to benefit from their own wrongdoing is disregarded, certainly the principle of proportional compensation and benefits applies. The very best that white women could possibly deserve in affirmative action benefits are the very lowest levels of support. For it is not only white men who are responsible for the greatest forms of racist evil in the history of the United States, but also white women, though perhaps they are so to a lesser degree in light of their own treatment by white men. And there might well be very good reason to think that on average and on balance the experience of injustice by white women is outweighed by the oppression they have wrought on others. And if this were true, then surely white women deserve *nothing at all* by way of compensation and ought to be excluded from affirmative action programs altogether.

Still, it might be objected that only privileged white women oppressed non-whites and that white women of lower socioeconomic classes were not in positions to oppress them. Hence unprivileged white women ought to be included among legitimate affirmative action beneficiaries. This objection tries to undermine my differentialist strategy by pointing out that it is insufficiently sensitive to the many ways in which white women have suffered socioeconomic class-based injustices and in which they deserve affirmative action benefits.

In reply, let me admit that socioeconomic status is relevant to this discussion of oppression. But I would remind those unfamiliar with U.S. history that it is false that even unprivileged white women experienced anything akin to the kinds and degrees of oppression that were wrought on colored folk (especially Indians and blacks). White women, privileged or not, were *not* enslaved, no matter how much some (certainly not black feminists or other black progressives, for instance) would have us think to the contrary. White women, privileged or not, were *not* victims of genocide. Nor were they victims of perhaps the largest land theft in history, an evil act from which *most all* white women benefited and to which they contributed by their support of white men. Injecting socioeconomic class into the discussion of racism and affirmative action mostly obfuscates matters and ignores the fact that there are degrees of oppression, just as there as degrees of racist harmful wrongdoing. No appeal to "unprivileged" white women can obscure the fact that white women on average, on balance, and as a class participated in and greatly benefited from, for instance, the westward expansion that led to "Indian removal." Let us also remain mindful of the evil acts of many white women who helped direct the Indian Boarding Schools which effectively deprogrammed Indian children taken from their families and reprogrammed them with some insidious version of Christianity. Furthermore, were white women, wealthy or poor, victims of the dangers and indignities of slave patrols and Fugitive Slave Laws? No, but it is a fact that many white women enjoyed various of the economic benefits of the peculiar institution. Nor can one dissuade reasonable people of the historical fact that so many "unprivileged" (relative to white men, but certainly not relative to Indians and blacks) white women did also serve in the racist oppression of blacks, especially during Reconstruction and under Jim Crow. Recall that the *KKK was formed in large part to make sure that unprivileged white men and white women would not fall below the socioeconomic status of then newly freed slaves.* Thousands of white women throughout the United States were members of the KKK, even though thousands were not. Yet implying that even the often-poor white women who were not KKK members did not share responsibility for the racist oppression of blacks by the KKK is quite like arguing that the spouses of terrorist mobsters are not co-responsible in some significant measure for the harmful wrongdoings of the mobsters themselves when they very well not only knew basically what their mobster spouses did for a living, but themselves knowingly benefited from the injustices of their spouse mobsters. It is to take a rather simplistic stance on moral responsibility for acts of racist oppression. It is, moreover, to assume that very bad Samaritanism is an excuse for not doing the right things by working to eradicate the racist oppression from which they as white women surely benefited. It is also to ignore how many white feminists have attempted to divert the issues of white women's racist oppression of others by adopting the language of their own oppression.[76] It may be true that privileged white women benefited from the racist oppression of Indians and blacks more than underprivileged white women, historically speaking. But it would be implausible to hold that even the poorest Angla of Appalachia did not both support and benefit significantly from the outright genocide and land theft and enslavement of the peoples in question. After all, those poorest of white women surely would not even be in the United States if not for the theft of those very hills in which they reside. And it is *all* white women today in the United States who *continue in one way or another to benefit unjustly* from the past racist evils in question.

Let us become and remain ever mindful that white women as a group demanded (and being backed by laws that they themselves supported and never as a class protested) that blacks step off the sidewalks as they walked by, sit at the back of the buses while white women sat in the front, never be seated and served in "white" sections of restaurants, and had to enter from the kitchens. Moreover, blacks, famous or not, were disallowed from staying at white hotels where white women enjoyed their privileged lifestyle. One is reminded of cases of Martin Luther King, Jr., who with his entourage of civil rights workers, could not stay in white hotels but were instead forced to secure rooms at "colored only" ones, which were typically not the finest ones in any town or city. And let us not forget the cases of black athletes such as the Harlem Globetrotters and Negro Baseball League players who experienced the same treatment. And recall that Josephine Baker, who was good enough for so many white folk to see perform in various cities throughout the United States, was not served in many a white restaurant. Time and time again, there are cases too several to recount of blacks being relegated to a status far below one that white women enjoyed thoroughly. Yet how many white women cried out for reform of Jim Crow? Certainly, as some white feminists remind us, many women (read: white women) were and are raped (in most cases, by white men). But so many more black women have been and are raped and quite often by white men, though with far less public sympathy, media attention, or legal recourse. Indeed, as Patricia Williams reminds us: "Few will believe a black woman who has been raped by a white man."[77] Yet when was the last time a white man was *lynched* simply because a *black woman accused* him of *looking* at her, much less raping her? Yet thousands of black men have been lynched simply because a white woman accused them (or some generic black man, as "any will do") of somehow violating her precious womanhood (as in the case of Rosewood, Florida), mostly with no legal repercussions for either the members of the lynch mobs or the white women accusers themselves for, in many cases, obstructing justice.[78] The depth of such evils is recognized by Clarence Darrow, who writes:

> I do not believe in hanging anybody, much less do I believe in burning anybody, but above all things else I believe in equality between all people, no hypocrisy; treat everybody alike, and if the southern gentlemen, or the northern gentlemen, believe it is necessary to build bonfires to burn colored men for assaulting white women, well and good, but let them also build bonfires to burn white men for assaulting colored women; treat them all alike.[79]

And one might add to Darrow's stinging words that fires might be burned to lynch white women who falsely accuse black men of wrongs against them as an exercise of white privilege, power, and domination over black men and the women to whom they are related. Undeniably, white women on average and as a class served as a strident force of racist oppression against the entire black family in these and other ways.

Furthermore, while the mere accusation by a white woman that a black man looked at her sexually or insulted her prideful womanhood could easily result in a black man's being lynched, rarely, if ever, were adequate punishments meted out for white women who falsely accused blacks of these or other "crimes" against white womanhood. And where were the white women in protest of these tremendous injustices against all blacks? Did white women do much to end such Jim Crow–related abuses? What we do know is that the Mann Act was enacted precisely to protect white women. So while several merely alleged sexual crimes of black men against white women were punished (or "telished," as John Rawls would describe it[80]) by death in the name of protecting white womanhood, many actual sexual crimes of white men against black women were not only not considered crimes but were considered white male rights, or at least liberties.[81] And as Crenshaw observes, "Rape statutes generally do not reflect *male* control over *female* sexuality, but *white* male regulation of *white* female sexuality. Historically, there has been absolutely no institutional effort to regulate black female chastity."[82] The "erasure" by many of the black woman's experience of rape at the hands of white men is further articulated by Crenshaw in no uncertain terms:

> The singular focus on rape as a manifestation of male power over female sexuality tends to eclipse the use of rape as a weapon of racial terror. When Black women were raped by white males, they were being raped not as women generally, but as Black women specifically: Their femaleness made them sexually vulnerable to racist domination, while their Blackness effectively denied them any protection. This

white power was reinforced by a judicial system in which the successful conviction of a white man for raping a Black woman was virtually unthinkable.[83]

More generally, when was the last time any law was passed in the United
States to explicitly and uniquely protect *Indians or blacks*, especially from the
white men and white women who oppressed and continue to oppress *them?*
Consider the words of Lerner on the attempt by many to conflate the experiences of oppression of white women in the Old South by white men with the
oppression of black women by white men and white women, among others:

> Although neither group controlled their sexuality or their reproduction, the differ-
> ences between them were substantial. White women, regardless of class, owed
> sexual and reproductive services to the men to whom they were married. Black
> women, in addition to the labor extracted from them, owed sexual and reproduc-
> tive services to their white masters and to the black men their white masters had
> selected for them. Since the white master of black women could as well be a white
> woman, it is clear that racism was for black women and men the decisive factor
> which structured them into society and controlled their lives. Conversely, white
> women could offset whatever economic and social disadvantages they suffered by
> sexism by the racist advantages they had over both black men and women. Practi-
> cally speaking, this meant that white women benefited from racism economically,
> insofar as they owned slaves; that they could relieve themselves of child-rearing
> (and at times even childbearing) responsibilities by using the enforced services of
> their female slaves; that they were relieved of doing unpaid domestic labor by
> using slave labor.[84]

Nor will it close the tremendous gap between the levels and degrees of oppression between Indians and blacks on the one hand, and white women on the
other, to note the unfortunate reality of domestic violence against women.

The reason for this excursion into some of the history of white antiblack
racism in the United States is because it is believed that only a proper understanding and appreciation of such history can correct the confused rhetoric of
many who conflate the treatment of white women with that of, say, Indians
and blacks. Yet it is these historical facts of racism in the United States that
ground the differentialist approach to affirmative action. No one who has a
proper grasp of the horrors of the oppression of Indians and blacks can seriously believe that white women are oppressed in anything akin to the ways in
which Indians and blacks were (and still are, as many would argue). Once we
begin to see that history reveals this truth, the way is paved for the infusion of
moral principles to be brought to bear on the matter concerning affirmative
action.

The fact is that *there is no significant mode of harmful wrongdoing that white
women experienced that Indians and black women have not experienced. But there
are several kinds and degrees of oppression that Indians and black women and men
experienced (sometimes at the hands of white women) that white women on average*

and as a class never experienced. Thus to say that white women were oppressed without careful qualification is quite misleading as it makes it seem as though white women's oppression is comparable to Indians' and blacks' oppression.

As intimated above, there is a real sense in which it might well constitute a fallacy of equivocation to say that white women were/are oppressed if "oppressed" is also supposed to describe absent careful qualification the evil horrors of the Indian and black experiences partly at the hands of white women. To accept without careful qualification the claim that white women are on balance oppressed in anything like the ways in which those they helped to oppress were and are oppressed is to ignore the past and the manners in which the past influence significantly the present state of affairs in the United States, ethnically and socioeconomically speaking. It is to accept by implication the claim that white women on average, on balance, and as a class are not co-responsible for the very evils that made it possible to found and sustain the United States.[85] As Lerner concludes of white women, "it is their class privilege which helps them offset any disadvantages arising from their subordinate status as women."[86] To ignore the vast differences in the extent of the oppression between white women and folk of color in the United States (especially Indians and black women and men) tends to erase the significance of the worse forms of oppression, and conveniently much that was wrought on them by white women themselves![87] It is this, Lerner and Watkins argue, that amounts to a form of continued racist oppression of folk of color by white women. Practically speaking, white women exemplify this racist oppression today by willingly accepting what is not theirs by moral right. Instead of removing themselves from the list of affirmative action beneficiaries based on my principled arguments herein, they continue to accept what they do not deserve, effectively robbing from Indians and blacks valuable resources that are in general not only far more deserved, but can be used to address socioeconomic problems that exist in these communities that are greater than any problems white women have experienced in North America. Apparently, the "Indian ring" abuses mentioned in chapter 6 continue, but in more subtle forms.

Moreover, it might be objected that there exist mitigating factors concerning white women's racist oppression of nonwhites in the United States. Both historically and currently, to some extent white women in many cases would likely be threatened with physical violence or institutional threats of loss of employment and such if they did or do resist the oppression of nonwhites in the United States. In light of these factors, our judgments of white women's racist oppression ought to be mitigated.[88]

However true it is that there existed and do exist today various and sometimes complicated mitigating factors that undergird white women's racism, certain factors must be borne in mind. First, several white women of old and even today seem to have had little difficulty in risking their own freedom or security when it came (comes) to pressing for their own rights, suggesting that they were bad Samaritans pertaining to the drive toward freedom for non-whites. To argue that white women on average, on balance, and as a class were so oppressed that they feared violent reprisals from white men if white women stood up for what was right ignores the fact that so many white women were not that afraid of white men to stand up to them in burning some of their undergarments and walking openly in the streets to proudly and bravely demand their own freedoms. Second, even if it were true that white women deserve only our mitigated moral condemnation, it hardly follows that they are deserving recipients of affirmative action benefits based on the fact that they ought not to be allowed to benefit from their own racist oppression of others and because they on balance do not deserve such benefits in light of the oppression they on average, on balance, and as a class have wrought on others that clearly outweigh the injustices they as white women experience(d). Given a commonsense and fair-minded reading of U.S. history, the burden of argument lies clearly with those who would think that white women deserve to benefit from affirmative action because their experienced injustice outweighs the oppression that they brought on others.

In most cases, white women on average, on balance, and as a class could have at least raised some form of resistance to the oppression of nonwhites, but they rarely, if ever, did and even rarely do today. Even when white women had no alternative but to support the oppression of nonwhites as indicated, it hardly follows that they did not have a higher-order volition to do so in order to enjoy the grand and varied benefits of being privileged more than colored folk, both yesteryear and today. Both individually and collectively, most white women are surely guilty of racist oppression as they rarely, if ever, cared or care about the true plight of racist oppression. Remember the above wisdom from Crenshaw, Lerner, and Watkins: U.S. feminism was and is racist, and seems to demonstrate no tremendous signs of change.[89] And if the most progressive of all white women were racists, then on what grounds are we justified in believing that the rank and file white women (hardly progressives in the United States) were not racists? Of course, one way to signal a significant change would be to refuse to accept affirmative action benefits and work politically toward the revising of such programs in order to steer such programs and benefits toward those who most deserve and need them. History will show whether or not most white women in the United States possess the level of moral character and integrity to decide that this is something they will support.

Thus I have argued that based on a fair-minded and accurate reading of facts of U.S. history, generally and as a class white women have not suffered oppression nearly to the extent that Indians and black women and men have. This is a comparative judgment, one that clarifies greatly the extent to which white women have committed fraud on our system of affirmative action. But I also made the noncomparative judgment that there is reason to think that, on balance, white women do *not* deserve affirmative action because of their own incessant acts of racist oppression against others that clearly outweigh the injustices they have experienced by white men. White women's sheer power has awarded white folk in general the de facto largest amount of affirmative action benefits, and they whitewashed affirmative action from the standpoint of white privilege. And their oppressive political power enabled this to happen. Furthermore, they have many leftists affirming white women's role as *"oppressed"* persons who presumably *deserve* affirmative action. White women have once again secured their own desires at the cost of others who are far more deserving and in need. And they have accomplished this in part by way of an equivocation on "oppressed" and its cognates.

Finally, it might be argued that, given past and current factors of supply and demand pertaining to the availability of sufficient numbers of Indians and blacks, Latinos, among others, that it is morally justified to hire white women in their places for purposes of affirmative action. There are not enough non-whites interested in or qualified for positions in, for instance, philosophy and certain other academic areas to fill the increasing demands placed on colleges and universities in light of growing student enrollments. Thus white women assist along these lines in filling these positions that would otherwise lie vacant.

In reply to this concern, it must be stated that while it is certainly true that there has never been a time in U.S. educational history—including the present era—in which there were sufficient numbers of qualified (degreed) blacks, Indians, Latinos, and certain others to "fill" affirmative action hiring demands at all U.S. colleges and universities, this is no good reason to substitute for such would-be deserving hires those who, as we have already seen, are hardly deserving of affirmative action benefits. Valuable and already shrinking affirmative action resources have for decades been effectively transferred to non–affirmative action resources by the hiring of white women who do not deserve affirmative action benefits (or, they do not deserve them nearly to the extent that they have received them over the years). And it lessens the import of my argument in no way to point out that administrators are to blame for hiring white women instead of those deserving of affirmative action, as that simply emphasizes the significance of my argument. Policies of affirmative action must be revised so that this sort of fraud cannot occur again, and if it does it would be punished severely.

Moreover, leftist white women would have a meaningful opportunity to step aside of affirmative action self-benefits and support—not just talk the talk—programs that would train Indians, blacks, Latinos, and certain others for careers in philosophy and certain other academic areas where they are underrepresented. Again, if Indians and blacks are paid adequate and fair reparations, then there is no longer a good reason to target them as affirmative action beneficiaries, making room perhaps for Latinos and Asians as the main targets for such programs. In either case, white women should not remain beneficiaries of such programs for the reasons provided, and the budgetary funding saved on affirmative action programs by no longer funding Indians, blacks, and white women can be used to benefit Latinos, Asians, and certain other groups suffering discrimination.

Having clarified a plausible differentialist strategy for affirmative action programs, I argued that well-intentioned policies of the past were ruined in large part by race and gender categories that were so crude and imprecise that they did not allow the differentialist thinking that could have prevented the oppressive wrongdoing of allowing white women to wrongfully benefit from their own oppression of others more than the folk who should have been the primary beneficiaries of such programs in the first place.

Will white women consider the principles that undergird my argument to be essential to the implementation of justice and fairness? If so, then they would have to decline further benefits from affirmative action programs on grounds that they most assuredly do *not* deserve them. Or, will many white women continue on with business as usual approaches with recantations of the racist mantra of "equal opportunity" as the primary goal of affirmative action, thus sustaining their own ill-gotten gains from such a wrongheaded policy?

It is time to do the right thing by way of affirmative action. Doing the right thing often requires the relinquishing of wrongfully acquired power and wealth by those who have devastated others with their greed and avarice. The whitewashing of affirmative action must cease if leftists want to retain an important sense of moral decency in their support of affirmative action.

If it is true that what distinguishes many as members of ethnic groups is, among other things, their disparate experiences of racist harms, then what differentiates—indeed, alienates—those nonwhites from white women is that such classes of ethnic groups have experienced directly and indirectly *white women's* racist oppression of *us*, while they have been racist oppressors who on average, on balance, and as a class (even many of the leftists among them!) fail to realize or admit the depth and perseverance of their racist oppression of others.

And if it is objected that affirmative action would never have become a reality in the first place without the support of white women, my reply to this political point is that if white women begin to on average and as a class develop a genuine sense of ethical sensitivity and justice as expressed above, then their relinquishing their benefits vis-à-vis affirmative action and supporting much more deserving nonwhites would seem to constitute just as much (or perhaps even more) support for affirmative action as there is in the current situation. So the difference in political terms is whether or not white women possess the moral character and integrity to admit that what is argued herein is plausible, and to step aside and support wholeheartedly the fact that only certain folk of color should receive affirmative action benefits based albeit on a differentialist programmatic structure.

THE OBJECTION FROM IMMIGRATION

Furthermore, it might be argued that with regard to the proposed policy concerning reparations to Indians (5 percent of each U.S. citizen's gross annual
income in perpetuity) and blacks (3 percent of each U.S. citizen's gross annual
income in perpetuity), a quandary emerges vis-à-vis currently undocumented
immigrant workers in the United States. On the one hand, it would seem that
they ought to pay their reparations taxes like everyone else (e.g., non-Indians
and nonblacks) in the United States as they are using the economy, land,
wealth infused with unpaid slave labor, and so on to earn livings for themselves. But in order to effect such reparations, it would appear that legal citizenship (or at least some other legal status) would need to be granted to such
workers so that the Internal Revenue Service can effectively excise reparations
taxes from such workers' incomes. While this is a pleasant prospect for those
who strive for the rights of such immigrants, it might pose difficulties for those
who argue that immigrants (legal or not) are continually securing increasingly
desirable employment that would otherwise be open to U.S. citizens, whatever
their ethnicity. This, it is argued, poses an increasingly serious difficulty as the
U.S. and global economies struggle and the perceived demand by employers
for more affordable employees increases. One consequence of the legalization
of such migrant workers is the greater unemployment rate for U.S. citizens
who might well have access to the positions "filled" by the newer immigrants.
In turn, it is argued, economic and social strife will ensue. So, it is argued, the
proposed reparation policy, while adding to the pockets of those reparated,
has adverse socioeconomic implications for the United States. On the other
hand, to not tax the illegal immigrant workers is transparently unjust because
it is unfair both to the Indians and blacks and to those U.S. citizens bearing
the primary burden of those taxes. This practical puzzle seems insoluable, and
stands, it is argued, as a good enough reason to not pay reparations unless
they can be paid justly and fairly.

In reply to this concern, it might be argued that the Indian and black heirs
of oppression can waive their rights to compensatory reparations from such
undocumented migrant workers, thus not requiring that the legal status quo of
their citizenship and taxable statuses be altered. This protects certain obvious
economic benefits for the U.S. economy. However, this gesture by the heirs of
U.S. oppression does not address the unemployment problems that are likely
to worsen as the reserve army of new immigrant labor increases. Perhaps a
more productive way to address the difficulty is for the United States to legal-
ize a certain number of immigrant workers without prejudice as to country of
origin. This way adequate documentation can lead to the collection of reparations taxes and lessen the reparative burden of other U.S. citizens. If the U.S.
economic structure is sufficiently strong, it should be able to handle the problems of unemployment that ensue from this strategy.

THE OBJECTION THAT THE U.S. CIVIL WAR
HAS ALREADY PAID THE "BLOOD SACRIFICE"
FOR SLAVERY

It might be objected that my arguments for reparations to blacks due to their enslavement is problematic because it "invites the retort that America has already paid for the wrong of slavery, not with money but with the blood shed in the Civil War."[90] Thus any argument for reparations for blacks by the United States ought not to make reference to slavery, but to other forms of oppression blacks experienced in the United States. While this represents a concern with reparations for the enslavement of blacks and not for injustices suffered by blacks under Jim Crow, it serves as a challenge to my overall argument for reparations to blacks.

This objection is hardly a new one, as it can be traced at least as far back as Abraham Lincoln's statement about the Civil War from his Second Inaugural Address that "there flowed a drop of white blood upon the battlefield as an atonement for the enormous crime that had been committed against an innocent people."[91] However, the plausibility of this objection is nullified by the following factors. First, there were several thousand blacks who fought on either side of the Civil War, as Lincoln himself admits when he states in that same address that "but there came a day of reckoning and for every drop of sweat and blood that the humble black slaves poured upon the soil of the cotton fields."[92] It was not only whites who shed blood in the war, as the objection seems to assume. Second, the black Civil War soldiers, unlike the white ones, were poorly provided for and were paid far less than their white "colleagues." Thus even as colleagues in war, they were unequal in fundamental ways, which casts doubt on the genuine reason(s) for the war. If it really was for the liberation and equal rights of blacks, then why did the union army segregate their soldiers by ethnicity, white and black, and why did the blacks receive far worse provisions and remuneration for their services as soldiers? Third, the objection wrongly assumes that northern whites fought in the Civil War primarily (or at all) for the abolition of slavery and to emancipate blacks and make them equal to whites. But contrary to fact, northern whites were motivated by economic factors as much as anything else. The north was rather concerned about the economic successes in the southern states as the result of slavery. The emancipation of slaves because slavery was immoral does not seem to be a real motive for the war by northerners, as Reconstruction hardly resulted in black freedom, but instead the horrors of Jim Crow, often violently enforced while the northern states sat idly by for decades. Fourth, it was the wealth created by slave labor that helped to provide the instruments of war. So not only did so many blacks serve in the war, they actually financed it in significant part with their own unpaid labor. In light of these factors, the very idea that the United States has already paid a blood sacrifice for black slavery is problematic. This is especially true given the fact that during Reconstruction federal, state, and local governments both North and South did more to intentionally, knowingly, and voluntarily halt black (and Indian) progress than to enable it.[93] All in all, one must not forget that when it comes to the oppression of Indians and blacks in the United States, W. E. B. Du Bois referred to slavery as the "arch-crime."[94] Far from being anything akin to an adequate "blood sacrifice" of whites for Indian and black freedom, the Civil War represents the very depth of white greed wherein whites will kill each other to, among other things, retain oppressive control over those they deem (for many, on religious grounds!) as being less than fully human. The historical facts of Indian and black slavery in the United States must count as part of the core of any plausible reparations argument pertaining to these groups. Finally, neither Indians nor blacks requested of whites that they go to war with one another. I imagine that if they were approached by Indians or blacks along these lines, each would have denied the request, as it is hard to see what good it would do to end the oppression of these groups themselves. As history reveals, the Civil War did little to end either Indian or black oppression. I strongly suspect that if whites would have respected Indians or blacks enough to ask them what they would have wanted from whites, the answer would have been rather different than to fight in a civil war. It would have included at least the genuine and holistic recognition of these groups as fully human and worthy of all the rights of every white person in U.S. society, and all that this brings with it. In the end, the idea that the Civil War was a blood sacrifice of whites for Indians and blacks and that it itself served as a form of reparations to these groups is paternalistic at best, and a rather queer and grossly inappropriate form of compensatory justice at worst.

THE OBJECTION FROM NONRESPONSIBILITY

It might be objected that the individual and collective perpetrators of the original acts of omissions of injustice against Indians and blacks, respectively, were not responsible for their harmful wrongdoings because they failed to satisfy the conditions necessary and sufficient for moral responsibility as discussed in chapter 5. Thus their oppression of these peoples is either excused or mitigated. Political, economic, religious, and other factors combined to coerce the United States and its citizens into committing such atrocities, and whatever compensation is owed must be mitigated at best, or even excused altogether in light of the circumstances.

However, such a supposition, while far-fetched in light of the historical data of the oppressions by the United States, might tend to mitigate U.S. responsibility for the evils. But even if such acts of oppression are mitigated, it hardly means that they are not deserved, as argued. The fact that my estimated reparations taxes are based on rather conservative factors takes this possibility into account. But it must be noted that the plausibility of this concern is only as strong as the historical evidence adduced to support it.

THE OBJECTION THAT REPARATIONS ARE CONFRONTATIONAL

One of the main reasons why most detractors of compensatory reparations reject them as a form of redress for oppression is because it is perceived by many that demands for such reparations are confrontational and as a strategy for redress this is mistaken and should be replaced with a "conversational" tone of redress that does not alienate many potential allies in the quest for justice for past oppression.[95] Indeed, this is a rather popular response by most U.S. whites to the demand for compensatory reparations and of those who often opt for a utilitarian-based, reconciliatory approach to redress.

But while the confrontational approach to reparations alienates many potential allies, genuine allies are those who have no psychological aversion to the pains of conflict expressed legitimately by the victim heirs of oppression. Instead, the potential allies of concern are those who possess at least a modicum of respect for the rights of peoples to their due, especially when their rights are so badly violated. Those who are psychologically averse to pain and confrontation and what amount to the contents of reparations "victim impact statements" or testimonials of how oppression affects them are in no moral positions to condemn such expressions. In fact, those who say they are in favor of truth commissions are hypocritical if they then express a disdain for confrontation. For it is precisely such truth commissions that ought to embody confrontation, that is, if they are concerned with truth and the pain that the truth always brings with it under circumstances of severe injustice. I assume here that truth commissions entail claims for the rectification of injustice as well as merely truth assertions about the facts of the injustice. In this way, perhaps they are better termed "truth and justice commissions" instead of "truth and reconciliation commissions."

Furthermore, why should we think that the offender heirs of oppression ought *not* to hear the testimonial anger, resentment, and other retributive emotions of the victim heirs of oppression? Would this not be a sign of true respect for them as peoples, instead of offender heirs of oppression attempting to shelter themselves from the expressed pain of others' oppression? The rectification of oppression requires confrontation as a part of the overall process of forgiveness and apology as noted in chapter 8. Just as the proper response to having one's rights respected is not one of gratitude, but of expectations of justice, and just as the proper attitude regarding the violation of one's rights is one of moral indignation of sometimes the strongest degree, so too a proper attitude toward a group's being oppressed and having its oppression rectified

is confrontation. And if the offender heirs of oppression truly desire reconciliation and peace with, say, Indians and blacks, then an important factor of
such reconciliation is the understanding of the terrible pain suffered by these
groups at the hands of the United States. Otherwise, the depth of the harmful
wrongdoing will not be adequately understood by the offender heirs of
oppression. And absent this kind of expression and learning, the cherished
goal of reconciliation with oppressed peoples that so many whites worldwide
say they desire is unlikely, if not impossible. There is no easy way out of the
road to reconciliation that so many leftists desire. The road to reconciliation,
genuine reconciliation, is paved with painful memories of experiences that
respect for the oppressed requires being heard in even the most confrontational ways. It is difficult to understand how those who say they desire moral
repair (see chapters 2 and 3, above) really want it while at the same time they
shun the very idea of confrontation expressed for some of the worst evils committed in world history.

Assuming, then, that these are the main and most plausible concerns with
my arguments about reparations to Indians and blacks, it is safe to conclude
that the general reparations argument succeeds in establishing a moral right
to compensatory reparations to these groups by the U.S. government by way
of reparations taxes that accrue to all adult U.S. wage earners.

Conclusion

The general argument of this book is that the U.S. government, some of its businesses and social groups, and some of their leaders are co-responsible for racist harmful wrongdoing and constitute offender heirs of oppression and thus owe compensatory reparations to the victim heirs of oppression in proportion to the harms caused by the oppression. Such reparations are a necessary condition of an apology by the responsible, though not necessarily guilty, parties. And since an apology is a necessary condition of forgiveness, this makes reparations in this case necessary for forgiveness, which in turn is necessary for the possibility of genuine reconciliation between the respective heirs of oppression. Reparations are a remedial right that can be waived not by those obsessed with reconciliation at almost all costs. Rather they are able to be waived only by the victim heirs of oppression. To genuinely respect someone is to give them justice. And this applies to American Indians and blacks as much as in any case. And no form of redefined "reparations" absent compensation will disguise the moral and legal facts that compensation is due, given the plausibility of the arguments herein.

The U.S. claim to moral greatness is nullified until it has begun to pay substantial reparations for its evils against but not limited to Indians and blacks. Of course, some other countries, nations, and groups stand in line for their fair share of reparations claims against the United States. I do not mean to imply that the United States is the only country that owes reparations to these groups: some other countries also owe reparations to Indians and blacks, but unless the United States can diplomatically persuade those other countries to enact policies of payment, it is suggested that the United States file suits against them with the ICC, ironically, a court the United States consistently refuses to recognize.

If the arguments presented in this book are plausible, then several things follow. One is that the United States and most of its citizens who proudly and loudly proclaim the United States to be the greatest country in the world are sadly mistaken insofar as morality (not morals) has anything significant to do with the truth-value of such an assertion. Given its history of unrectified oppression, the United States qualifies as one of the most evil countries the world has ever known. This holds even in light of the fact that some of its citizens are morally outstanding persons. This historical and moral datum about the United States being (on balance) evil is hardly an a priori necessary truth. Rather, the United States can mitigate its evil history. And I have provided a means for achieving precisely such an end. By way of fair and adequate reparations to these groups, the United States can begin to pull itself out of the mire of its own evils and become a much better country than it currently is, morally speaking. Exactly how great the United States can become is really a function of its own decisions and actions. But moral greatness costs plenty, and history will tell whether or not the United States has what it takes morally to rectify its past evils and cease committing new ones.

Not only is it the burden of those who would deny reparations to American Indians and blacks to provide a plausible argument in favor of the claim that there is a moral statute of limitations on historic injustice, there is yet no plausible argument provided in favor of a moral statute of limitations on historic injustice that would vitiate reparations owed by the United States to Indians and blacks. More interesting still is the fact that arguments from collective responsibility, the principle of morally just acquisitions and transfers, and the principle of unjust gains, coupled with there being no plausible argument in favor of a moral statute of limitations on historic injustice, support reparations to Indians and blacks by the federal, state, and local governments. The case for such reparations as described in the preceding chapters is more plausible than ever, and calls on those serious about justice to do all they can to bring genuine justice to these most oppressed peoples.

We must be careful to avoid confusion here. Most who begin to think about matters of responsibility for historic injustice fail to understand precisely what is meant when we say that the United States is (both yesteryear and today) liable for the atrocities against Indians and blacks. What is not meant is that today's U.S. citizenry is guilty of those evils, or that it is at fault for them, or that it caused them, or is blameworthy for them. Collective moral responsibility of the liability variety does not mean that guilt, blame, causation, or fault are transferred from one party or generation to another, in this case from the historic U.S. society which is guilty of the evils to today's U.S. society which is not. As Joel Feinberg argues, "It is only the liability that can be passed from one party to another . . . *there can be no such thing as vicarious guilt.*"[1] Moreover, he states: "Liability can transfer, but not agency, causation, or fault . . . , and certainly not guilt."[2] In Feinberg's view, collective liability responsibility without fault among each of its members requires group solidarity and organization, factors discussed in a previous chapter. By "solidarity," he means that there exists "a large *community of sentiment* among all the members," "associated with the bonds of sentiment directed toward common objects, or of reciprocal affection between the parties," such that the group members "share a common lot, the extent to which their goods and harms are necessarily collective and indivisible."[3] Group solidarity, he notes, is best indicated by the presence of "vicarious pride and shame."[4]

There is little question that the United States and its branches of government and agencies constituted an organized group with patriotic solidarity, and it remains as such today. There is little question that the United States is solidary. While some of its hundreds of millions of citizens do not concur with much of what the majority desires and does, the vast majority of U.S. citizens agree with what the United States did and did *not* do to the Indians and blacks. As for the few of us who despise what the United States has done to these groups and continues to do to them, we too are responsible for the evils wrought against them, though not directly but vicariously. Just as in the U.S. South during the downfall of Jim Crow "collective responsibility . . . might be ascribed to all those whites who were not outcasts, taking respectability and material comfort as evidence that a given person did not qualify for the exemption,"[5] today there is the vast majority of U.S. citizens who concur with the leadership in what it does and in what its predecessors did to Indians and blacks, and while they are vicariously liable in a more direct sense than the citizen detractors of those past evils, each of the U.S. citizens bears some responsibility for these acts of evil.

There are those who would argue, even quoting Feinberg, that "if the conditions of justifiable collective liability—group solidarity, prior notice, opportunity for control, and so on—are not satisfied, group liability would seem unjustified."[6] And if Feinberg is correct on this point, they might argue, then collective responsibility in the liability sense does not accrue to current U.S. citizens or their governments for the historic injustices against Indians and blacks.

However, this line of thinking is flawed. As I have argued, the United States acted intentionally, knowingly, voluntarily, and in solidarity in oppressing Indians and blacks.[7] The evidence for this claim, crucial for my argument for reparations to these groups, is found in the orders of U.S. presidents past and present, as well as numerous decisions of the U.S. Congress and Supreme Court past and present, as well as the decisions of state and local governments. The fact that there was very little resistance from U.S. citizens in the past and in the present against such evils before they happened, while they happened, and subsequently to them speaks loudly to the fact that most every U.S. citizen supported them in one way or another, by act or by omission. And it matters not that at the times of these evils that most in the United States believed them to be the morally right things to do.

The issue here is one of responsibility of the United States for these evils based on the fact that the far majority of its leaders and citizens agreed with them. Even when current U.S. citizens are confronted with the facts of Indian genocide and Indian and black slavery, most every U.S. citizen reasons that things would not be so good for us today (in fact, we would not even be here) if not for those evils, and that the ends justified the means, however "regrettable" the means. The primary issue here is whether today's U.S. citizen will begin to take seriously the oppressions of the past and present, and take seriously the Indian and black victim heirs of oppression such that they are sufficiently respected to pay them their genuine due in the form of reparations. And then a question arises as to whether the United States, should a moral miracle occur and it pays reparations to these groups, will cease and desist in committing further acts of evil both domestically and globally. Or, will its "patriotic" citizens sit idly by and not raise serious questions about domestic or foreign policies that *ceterus paribus* justify certain acts of violence against it?

It is genuinely disappointing today to find so many well-intentioned leftist philosophers and other scholars taking great pains to argue in support of effectively coerced integrationism for the heirs of perhaps the most evil acts of oppression in human history. Precisely what will it take to persuade many that, as John Rawls points out, the demands of rights and justice should not succumb to a contrived sense of peace and tranquility made to appear as though what is sought is a maximization of genuine social utility. And it is ironic that many U.S. leftists support calls for global justice to better the poor. But when it comes to domestic justice for the victim heirs of oppression, nothing better than the crumbs of coerced integration, motivated by an entrenched hard paternalism, is what they support vis-à-vis Indians and blacks. And if this is all that can be fathomed by well-intentioned leftists, it is perhaps unthinkable that rightists would support what justice truly requires in the cases discussed herein.

On the utilitarian-based analysis of reparations, what is essential is that the heirs of oppression are brought together under the umbrella of "peace," "fraternity," and "equity" accorded by putative forgiveness and reconciliation. In contrast, my analysis of reparations is both backward and forward-looking and requires that the definitional aspects of "reparations" to obtain: Fair and adequate compensation is a necessary condition of reparations, though non-compensatory means of restitution are often helpful in achieving justice for the oppressed. What my analysis requires for reparations is precisely what competing analyses deny. Yet given the legal definition of "reparations" in chapter 1, one wonders whether the detractors of the rights-based and rectificatory approach are simply confused about what reparations essentially are, or whether they simply deny their legitimacy by way of a redefinition of "reparations," or both.

In the end, the call for reparations to Indians and blacks, along with the supportive argumentation, is nothing short of a call for monetary compensation and the individual autonomy and group national sovereignty that the monetary compensation enables these groups to achieve without presumptions of integration, apology, forgiveness, and reconciliation. While it is true that my model of reparations, based on the rights-based ones of Bernard Boxill and Howard McGary, might be thought unrealistic because it calls on the United States to legislatively or by way of the federal court system provide adequate and deserved justice to Indians and blacks and that its failure to do so would possibly result in an ICC verdict and subsequent possible coalition of countries and nations prepared to coerce, in gradual but effective fashion, U.S. compliance, competing models of reparations fare much worse in terms of conceptualization and feasibility. And if the arguments I have provided in this book are plausible, then anti-compensatory reparations positions pertaining to Indians and blacks are nonstarters. The idea of reparations as restitution ought to involve, in these cases, the United States (on the one hand) and Indians and blacks (on the other hand) to voluntarily negotiate the terms of reparations smacks of idealistic utopianism[8]—especially when the history of U.S. "relations" with these peoples is concerned. After all, if the United States has committed such heinous acts of inhumanity against these peoples and has yet to express a desire to holistically and adequately compensate them after generations of peaceful pleas for justice, on what grounds is it reasonable to think that the United States will do so now, much less in good faith and with genuine justice for its victims in mind? If it is a choice between utopian dreams of "peaceful negotiation" between grossly unequal parties, on the one hand, and compensatory justice come what may between a quite possibly recalcitrant United States and much of the rest of the world, on the other, the oppressed are far better off with demands for real reparations instead of the morally and economically diluted substitute which in the final analysis continues the oppression of the United States over these peoples with only cosmetic changes to the status quo. In either case, the demands for rights-respecting justice will not likely be respected by the United States. And while the demands for reparations may be made dispassionately, they amount to demands nonetheless, and should never be reduced to mere requests by bargaining away their moral powers.

The demand for reparations is a demand to respect the violated rights of the oppressed that resulted in the severe harmful wrongdoings of Indians and blacks. And as I have argued previously, where there is no justice, there can be no genuine peace among oppressors and the oppressed. Nor should there be.

Notes

PREFACE

1. By "American Indian," I mean those peoples who are most indigenous to the territories currently and collectively referred to as the "United States of (North) America."

2. This term is borrowed from David Stannard, *American Holocaust* (Oxford: Oxford University Press, 1992).

3. This term is borrowed from John Rawls, *The Law of Peoples* (Cambridge, Mass.: Harvard University Press, 1999).

4. Other such concerns are addressed in J. Angelo Corlett, *Race, Racism, and Reparations* (Ithaca, N.Y.: Cornell University Press, 2003), chap. 8.

5. Nancy Snow, "Virtue and the Oppression of African Americans," *Public Affairs Quarterly* 18 (2004): 69.

6. For a defense of the claim that the United States owes reparations to Iraq for its unjust invasion and occupation of that sovereign nation, see J. Angelo Corlett, "U.S. Reparations to Iraq" (forthcoming).

7. Charles J. Ogletree, Jr., "The Current Reparations Debate," *U.C. Davis Law Review* 36 (2003): 1058.

8. Immanuel Kant, *The Metaphysical Elements of Justice*, trans. John Ladd (London: Macmillan, 1965), 100, emphasis provided.

INTRODUCTION

1. John Rawls, *A Theory of Justice*, rev. ed. (Cambridge, Mass.: Harvard University Press, 1999), 8.

2. Lewis M. Simons, "Genocide and the Science of Proof," *National Geographic*, January 2006, 30.

3. Simons, "Genocide and the Science of Proof," 30.

4. In Joel Feinberg, *Problems at the Roots of Law* (Oxford: Oxford University Press, 2003), 144, we find an analysis of the nature of pure evil as one requiring, among

other things, that the evil act creates puzzlement in those who come to know of it. Contrary to Joel Feinberg, I argue that such evil may in fact be quite explicable in terms of a variety of motives or reasons for action on behalf of the evildoer. Not unlike Feinberg's own example of the Nazi holocaust of Jews and other "undesirables," the pure evil of the United States against American Indians during the American holocaust is explicable in terms of the U.S. government's and citizenry's desire to fulfill manifest destiny. Thus evil of the purest and harshest kinds have reasons or motives if we search sufficiently deeply for them. They are hardly, if ever, puzzling. Indeed, the more deeply we search for and discover such reasons or motives, the more accurate we are in categorizing such actions as being evil, pure evil! (See J. Angelo Corlett, "On Evil," *Analysis* 64 [2004]: 81–84.)

5. One notable example of this neglect is found in M. M. Adams, *Horrendous Evils and the Goodness of God* (Ithaca, N.Y.: Cornell University Press, 1999).

6. Although chapter 2 contains a critique of cosmopolitan liberalism's conception of equality and human rights in support of its conception of global distributive justice, it is also a mitigated defense and expansion of the Rawlsian conception of global justice and human rights. Thus my theory of compensatory reparations does not discount the importance of global justice. Unlike many cosmopolitan liberals, however, my view respects all rights as untrumped by social utility considerations. And the main right at the forefront of this book is the group right to compensatory reparations for severely oppressed groups relative to the U.S. oppression of certain groups.

7. Ann E. Cudd, *Analyzing Oppression* (Oxford: Oxford University Press, 2006), ix.

8. Ada María Isasi-Díaz, *Mujerista Theology* (Maryknoll, N.Y.: Orbis Books, 2002), 109: "Certainly there is no moral primacy among the causes or factors or elements of oppression: there is no one kind of oppression that is worse than another, no one face of oppression that is more oppressive than another." It is this kind of simplistic thinking that fails to grasp the obvious differences in kind and degree between the oppressions of American Indian genocide and black slavery, on the one hand, and whatever white feminists claim that white women in the United States have experienced, on the other. The differences, however, are made plain in chapter 10, below.

9. More will be argued concerning this issue in chapter 10.

10. Cudd, *Analyzing Oppression*, 3.

11. Cudd, *Analyzing Oppression*, 20ff.

12. Cudd, *Analyzing Oppression*, 25.

13. Cudd, *Analyzing Oppression*, 26.

14. Cudd, *Analyzing Oppression*, 188.

15. Cudd, *Analyzing Oppression*, 195.

16. Cudd, *Analyzing Oppression*, 195.

17. J. Angelo Corlett, *Responsibility and Punishment*, 3rd ed., Library of Ethics and Applied Philosophy (Dordrecht, Netherlands: Springer, 2006), chaps. 1 and 7.

18. Larry May, *Sharing Responsibility* (Chicago: University of Chicago Press, 1992).

19. Cudd, *Analyzing Oppression*, 195.

20. Cudd, *Analyzing Oppression*, 196.

21. Cudd, *Analyzing Oppression*, 196.

22. Cudd, *Analyzing Oppression*, 196.

23. Cudd, *Analyzing Oppression*, 196–97.

24. Cudd, *Analyzing Oppression*, 197. It is noteworthy that nowhere in Cudd's discussion of resistance to oppression (201ff.) does she even mention compensatory reparations for anyone, much less Indians and blacks. Hers is a reformatory strategy rather

than a rights-based one that respects Indian and black rights to compensatory reparations for clearly documented cases of massive oppression. Not only, then, do such non-
rights-based approaches to reparations inflate milder forms of oppression, they tend to
deflate the horrors and values of the harshest forms of oppression as all oppressions
are melded into one large group so that social utility can be maximized and egalitarian
considerations are not too badly threatened. In these senses, then, Cudd's analysis of
oppression is so broad that it does not appreciate the intricate differences between
multitudinous kinds and degrees of oppression.

25. When I write that white women are "co-responsible" for the oppression of
Indians and blacks, I mean they share some significant degree of such responsibility
with white men, though the degree of their shared responsibility is likely less than that
of white men given the historical relations between white men and white women in
the United States.

26. Cudd, *Analyzing Oppression*, 215.

27. J. Harvey, *Civilized Oppression* (Lanham, Md.: Rowman and Littlefield, 1999).

28. Whether compensatory reparations to Indians and blacks should take the legislative or court-ordered path is discussed later in the book.

29. This principle is stated and discussed in chapters 6 and 7, below.

30. As Boris L. Bittker and Roy L. Brooks state: "Because such discrimination can
occur years, even decades, prior to the crafting of the remedy, the beneficiary and the
victim need not be, and often are not, the same person" (Boris L. Bittker and Roy L.
Brooks, "The Constitutionality of Black Reparations," in *Redress for Historical Injustices
in the United States*, ed. Michael T. Martin and Marilyn Yaquinto [Durham, N.C.: Duke
University Press, 2007], 155.)

31. While Roy L. Brooks argues that "the strict scrutiny test is nowhere to be found
in the Constitution or in its legislative history. It is a legal doctrine made up entirely
by judges" (Bittker and Brooks, "The Constitutionality of Black Reparations," 151), it
is important to bear in mind that such a point assumes a kind of constitutional origi-
nalism that is problematic (J. Angelo Corlett, *Race, Rights, and Justice*, Law and Philosophy Library 85 [Dordrecht, Netherlands: Springer, 2009], chaps. 1–2). Whether the
idea of strict scrutiny is plausible as a legal doctrine is independent of whether or not
it can find its roots in the U.S. Constitution, as judges often must interpret the meaning
of the Constitution by way of extralegal principles. The rules of logical reasoning, for
instance, are not found in the Constitution either, but judges use them each time they
interpret the Constitution. And we are all the better for their doing so, that is, instead
of what might result if they did not use logical laws and principles.

32. Bernard Boxill, "The Morality of Reparation," *Social Theory and Practice* 2 (1972):
113–22; "The Morality of Reparations II," in *A Companion to African-American Philosophy*,
ed. Tommy Lee Lott and John P. Pittman (Malden, Mass.: Blackwell, 2003), 134–47;
Howard McGary, *Race and Social Justice* (London: Blackwell, 1999), chaps. 5–7.

33. Examples include J. Angelo Corlett, *Race, Racism, and Reparations* (Ithaca, N.Y.:
Cornell University Press, 2003), chap. 9; Rodney C. Roberts, "The Morality of a Moral
Statute of Limitations on Injustice," *The Journal of Ethics* 7 (2003): 115–38.

34. It might also be due to racist disregard by some white philosophers of Boxill's
and McGary's works in this area, as implied in Bernard Boxill, "Power and Persuasion,"
Journal of Social Philosophy 32 (2001): 382–85.

35. Joel Feinberg, *Rights, Justice, and the Bounds of Liberty* (Princeton, N.J.: Princeton
University Press, 1980), and *Freedom and Fulfillment* (Princeton, N.J.: Princeton University Press, 1992), chaps. 8–10; Corlett, *Race, Rights and Justice*, chaps. 5–6. For an

assessment of rights in general, and one at least partly critical of the Feinbergian analysis of rights, see F. M. Kamm, *Intricate Ethics* (Oxford: Oxford University Press, 2007), chap. 2.

36. Samuel Scheffler, *The Rejection of Consequentialism* (Oxford: Clarendon, 1982); Samuel Scheffler, ed., *Consequentialism and Its Critics* (Oxford: Oxford University Press, 1988).

37. Notable exceptions are Bernard Boxill, *Blacks and Social Justice* (Totowa, N.J.: Rowman and Allanheld, 1984); Corlett, *Race, Racism, and Reparations*; McGary, *Race and Social Justice.*

38. Corlett, *Race, Racism, and Reparations*, chap. 4.

39. Of course, those most directly responsible for the violation of Cheney's civil rights (not murder) were not executed, but sentenced to a couple of decades in prison at most. Unfortunately, it took until 1997 for the first KKK member to be executed for the murder of a black person in the United States.

40. David Ray Griffin, "America's Non-accidental, Non-benign Empire," in *The American Empire and the Commonwealth of God*, ed. David Ray Griffin, John Cobb, Jr., Richard Falk, and Catherine Keller (Louisville, Ky.: Westminster John Knox Press, 2006), 4–5. With regard specifically to U.S. imperialistic economic policies, see John Cobb, Jr., "Imperialism in American Economic Policy," in *The American Empire and the Commonwealth of God*, ed. David Ray Griffin, John Cobb, Jr., Richard Falk, and Catherine Keller (Louisville, Ky.: Westminster John Knox Press, 2006), 23–43.

41. That is, of course, so long as the United States then seeks to provide adequate reparations to its other oppressed groups, mentioned above, as well as still others.

CHAPTER 1

1. Plato, *Gorgias*, trans. Donald J. Zeyl, 479d, in *Plato: Complete Works*, ed. John M. Cooper and D. S. Hutchinson (Indianapolis: Hackett, 1997).

2. Clarence Darrow, *Verdicts Out of Court* (Chicago: Quadrangle Books, 1963), 144.

3. John Kleinig, "Punishment and Moral Seriousness," *Israel Law Review* 25 (1991): 401.

4. This distinction is borrowed from a similar distinction about punishment found in Anthony M. Quinton, "Punishment," *Analysis* 14 (1954): 133–42; John Rawls, "Two Concepts of Rules," *The Philosophical Review* 64 (1955): 3–13; and echoed in E. Stanley Benn, "An Approach to the Problems of Punishment," *Philosophy* 33 (1958): 325–41.

5. William O. Douglas, *An Almanac of Liberty* (Garden City, N.Y.: Doubleday, 1964), 12.

6. Douglas, *An Almanac of Liberty*, 14. Emphasis provided.

7. Marianne Constable, *Just Silences* (Princeton, N.J.: Princeton University Press, 2005), 8.

8. Constable, *Just Silences*, 8.

9. Note that nothing in this conception of reparations requires that the reparations be "paid" or rendered by the perpetrators of wrongdoing only. (Compare the conception of reparations set forth in D. N. MacCormick, "The Obligation of Reparations," *Proceedings of the Aristotelian Society* 78 [1977–1978]: 175.) Contrast this notion

of reparations with one articulated by Bernard Boxill: "Part of what is involved in rectifying an injustice is an acknowledgement on the part of the transgressor that what he
is doing is required of him because of his prior error" (Bernard Boxill, "The Morality
of Reparations," in *Reverse Discrimination*, ed. Barry R. Gross [New York: Prometheus,
1977] 274).

10. Joel Feinberg, *Doing and Deserving* (Princeton, N.J.: Princeton University Press,
1970), 74–75.

11. Sanford Levinson, "Responsibility for Crimes of War," *Philosophy and Public
Affairs* 2 (1973): 250.

12. For this analysis of the nature of harm, see Joel Feinberg, *Harm to Others*
(Oxford: Oxford University Press, 1984).

13. W. Sadurski, "Social Justice and the Problem of Punishment," *Israel Law Review*
25 (1991): 311.

14. Sadurski, "Social Justice and the Problem of Punishment," 308.

15. Feinberg, *Doing and Deserving*, 93.

16. See chapter 3 for an assessment of these understandings of reparations. Also
see Martha Minow, *Between Vengeance and Forgiveness* (Boston: Beacon, 1998), chap. 5.
Minow's conception of reparations represents a common confusion between questions
of the nature and value of reparations, as will also be demonstrated in consideration
of views of reparations in chapter 3. For a collection of essays that also run afoul of
this error, see E. Barkan and A. Karn, eds., *Taking Wrongs Seriously* (Stanford, Calif.:
Stanford University Press, 2006).

17. Margaret Urban Walker, *Moral Repair* (Oxford: Oxford University Press, 2006),
198.

18. Howard McGary, *Race and Social Justice* (London: Blackwell, 1999).

19. Feinberg, *Doing and Deserving*, chap. 5.

20. Feinberg, *Doing and Deserving*, 76.

21. Jeremy Waldron, "Superseding Historic Injustice," *Ethics* 103 (1992): 6.

22. That reparations also recognize the personhood of victims is argued in Mari
Matsuda, "Looking to the Bottom: Critical Legal Studies and Reparations," in *Critical
Race Theory*, ed. Kimberlé Crenshaw, Neil Gotanda, Gary Peller, and Kendall Thomas
(New York: New Press, 1995), 74.

23. Joel Feinberg, *Social Philosophy* (Englewood Cliffs, N.J.: Prentice-Hall, 1973);
Rights, Justice, and the Bounds of Liberty (Princeton, N.J.: Princeton University Press,
1980); *Freedom and Fulfillment* (Princeton, N.J.: Princeton University Press, 1992),
chaps. 8–10.

24. Ogletree, "The Current Reparations Debate," 1059.

25. Patricia J. Williams, *The Alchemy of Race and Rights* (Cambridge, Mass.: Harvard
University Press, 1991), 233–34.

26. Williams, *The Alchemy of Race and Rights*, 154.

27. C. Fred Alford, *Psychology and the Natural Law of Reparation* (Cambridge: Cambridge University Press, 2006), 116.

28. I discuss some of the nuances of these concepts in part 2.

29. Bernard Boxill, "The Morality of Reparation," *Social Theory and Practice* 2
(1972): 113–22. More recently, see Alfred L. Brophy, *Reparations* (Oxford: Oxford University Press, 2006), 9: "We might think of reparations, then as *programs that are justified
on the basis of past harm and that are also designed to assess and correct that harm and/or
improve the lives of victims into the future.*" The vagueness of this statement is an example

of why it is important to bear in mind the distinctions between the justification of the institution of reparations and the justification of its particular instances.

30. John Rawls, *A Theory of Justice*, rev. ed. (Cambridge, Mass.: Harvard University Press, 1999), 3–4.

31. Igor Primoratz, "Utilitarianism, Justice and Punishment," *Israel Law Review* 25 (1991): 396. Also see Igor Primoratz, *Justifying Legal Punishment* (London: Humanities Press International, 1989), chap. 3.

32. J. Angelo Corlett, *Race, Racism, and Reparations* (Ithaca, N.Y.: Cornell University Press, 2003), 155. This principle is a modification of one found in Robert Nozick, *Anarchy, State, and Utopia* (New York: Basic Books, 1974), 150.

33. Immanuel Kant, *The Metaphysical Elements of Justice*, 302, in *The Metaphysics of Morals*, trans. and ed. Mary Gregor (Cambridge: Cambridge University Press, 1996), 82.

34. A. John Simmons, "Historical Rights and Fair Shares," *Law and Philosophy* 14 (1995): 150–51.

35. Of course, this claim is unproblematic in cases involving murder, as the United States itself recognizes no legal statute of limitations in murder cases. For a refutation of a variety of arguments in favor of a moral statute of limitations on injustice, see Rodney C. Roberts, "The Morality of a Moral Statute of Limitations on Injustice," *The Journal of Ethics* 7 (2003): 115–38.

36. MacCormick, "The Obligation of Reparations," 179.

37. David Lyons, "The New Indian Claims and Original Rights to Land," *Social Theory and Practice* 6 (1977): 252. Indeed, it is a historical, rather than an end-state, argument for reparative justice.

38. Corlett, *Race, Racism, and Reparations*, chaps. 8–9.

39. For a negative argument against such a claim, see Corlett, *Race, Racism, and Reparations*, 152, 214.

40. For positive arguments against the proposal, see Rodney C. Roberts, "The Morality of a Moral Statute of Limitations on Injustice," and "More on the Morality of a Moral Statute of Limitations on Injustice," *The Journal of Ethics* 11 (2007): 177–92.

41. See chapter 10. Also see Corlett, *Race, Racism, and Reparations*, chaps. 2–3.

42. Corlett, *Race, Racism, and Reparations*, 157–60, 197–213; McGary, *Race and Social Justice*, chap. 5.

43. For a philosophical analysis of the concept of collective moral responsibility, see Corlett, *Responsibility and Punishment*, chap. 7.

44. Michael Hechter, *Principles of Group Solidarity* (Berkeley: University of California Press, 1987).

45. Michael Bacharach, *Beyond Individual Choice*, ed. Natalie Gold and Robert Sugden (Princeton, N.J.: Princeton University Press, 2006), 75.

46. Bacharach, *Beyond Individual Choice*, 74–75.

47. "I think: my raciality is socially constructed, and I experience it as such" (Williams, *The Alchemy of Race and Rights*, 168). Patricia Williams also notes that her "racial ambiguity" is "society's constant reminder" of her blackness. For an argument for the notion that race is both biological and a social construct, see P. Kitcher, "Does 'Race' Have a Future?" *Philosophy and Public Affairs* 35 (2007): 293–317; "Race, Ethnicity, Biology, Culture," in *Racism*, ed. Leonard Harris (Amherst, N.Y.: Humanity Books, 1999), 87–117. Also see Michael O. Hardimon, "The Ordinary Concept of Race," *The Journal of Philosophy* 100 (2003): 437–55.

48. An example of this mistake in found in Albert Mosley, "Affirmative Action as a Form of Reparations," *University of Memphis Law Review* 33 (2003): 353.

49. Compensatory reparations can also be owed for war crimes, including the declaring and commencing of an unjust war. Indeed, some of the genocidal acts against American Indians would qualify as war crimes. For an analysis of war crimes, just and unjust wars, see Michael Walzer, *Just and Unjust Wars*, 3rd ed. (New York: Basic Books, 2000).

50. McGary, *Race and Social Justice*, chap. 12.

51. Corlett, *Responsibility and Punishment*, chap. 6.

CHAPTER 2

1. Chantel Mouffe, *On the Political* (London: Routledge, 2005), 90.

2. Samuel Scheffler, "Conceptions of Cosmopolitanism," *Utilitas* 11 (1999): 255–76; reprinted in Samuel Scheffler, *Boundaries and Allegiances* (Oxford: Oxford University Press, 2001), chap. 7.

3. Louis P. Pojman, "The Moral Response to Terrorism and Cosmopolitanism," in *Terrorism and International Justice*, ed. James Sterba (Oxford: Oxford University Press, 2003), 146.

4. It is important, however, to understand that it is quite possible that the difference between Rawlsian statism and cosmopolitan liberalism on the basic structure of international law might well turn out to be less than well-grounded. As Allen Buchanan points out,

> Once we take the idea of bundling sovereignty seriously we must consider the possibility that the contrast between a "state-centered" and a "world-state" system will become blurry. The more political differentiation there comes to be within states . . . and the stronger international legal structures become, the more difficult it will be to draw a sharp contrast between a state-centered and a world-state system. (Allen Buchanan, *Justice, Legitimacy, and Self-Determination* [Oxford: Oxford University Press, 2005], 57)

5. Bernard Boxill, "Global Equality of Opportunity and National Integrity," *Social Philosophy and Policy* 5 (1987): 148ff. Basically, the objection is that "the world is made up of different societies with different cultures and different standards of success" and that these pose insurmountable roadblocks before the cosmopolitan liberal attempt to successfully apply the Rawlsian principle of fair equality of opportunity.

6. John Rawls, *A Theory of Justice* (Cambridge, Mass.: Harvard University Press, 1971), 73.

7. Boxill, "Global Equality of Opportunity and National Integrity," 150.

8. Boxill, "Global Equality of Opportunity and National Integrity," 148.

9. On paternalism, see John Stuart Mill, *On Liberty* (Indianapolis: Hackett, 1978); Joel Feinberg, *Rights, Justice, and the Bounds of Liberty* (Princeton, N.J.: Princeton University Press, 1980), chap. 5; Gerald Dworkin, "Paternalism," in *Philosophy of Law*, 5th ed., ed. Joel Feinberg and Hyman Gross (Belmont, Calif.: Wadsworth, 1995), 208–19; Gerald Dworkin, "Paternalism: Some Second Thoughts" in *Philosophy of Law*, 5th ed., ed. Joel Feinberg and Hyman Gross (Belmont, Calif.: Wadsworth, 1995), 219–23. Also see Patrick Devlin, *The Enforcement of Morals* (Oxford: Oxford University Press, 1965), chap. 6.

10. Some of the philosophical proponents of some version or another of cosmopolitan liberalism include: Brian Barry, *Liberty and Justice* (Oxford: Oxford University Press, 1989); Charles Beitz, *Political Theory and International Relations* (Princeton, N.J.: Princeton University Press, 1979); Buchanan, *Justice, Legitimacy, and Self-Determination*; Onora O'Neill, *Towards Justice and Virtue* (Cambridge: Cambridge University Press, 1996); Thomas Pogge, *World Poverty and Human Rights* (London: Polity, 2002); Fernando Tesón, *A Philosophy of International Law* (Boulder: Westview, 1998).

11. Scheffler, *Boundaries and Allegiances*, 111.

12. Scheffler, *Boundaries and Allegiances*, 112.

13. Consider Martha Nussbaum's assertion that "to count people as moral equals is to treat nationality, ethnicity, religion, class, race, and gender as 'morally irrelevant'—as irrelevant to that of equal standing" (Martha Nussbaum, "Reply," in *For Love of Country*, ed. Joshua Cohen and Martha Nussbaum [Boston: Beacon, 1996], 133).

14. Richard Falk, "Revisioning Cosmopolitanism," in *For Love of Country*, ed. Joshua Cohen and Martha Nussbaum (Boston: Beacon, 1996), 57.

15. Larry Temkin, "Thinking about the Needy," *The Journal of Ethics* 8 (2004): 412–13. For discussions of global poverty and need, see *The Journal of Ethics* 8, no. 4 (2004); Garrett Cullity, *The Moral Demands of Affluence* (Oxford: Oxford University Press, 2004); Paulette Dieterlen, *Poverty* (Amsterdam: Rodopi, 2005).

16. Theodosius Dobzhansky, *Genetic Diversity and Human Equality* (New York: Basic Books, 1973).

17. For an analysis of the concept of harm, see Joel Feinberg, *Harm to Others* (Oxford: Oxford University Press, 1984).

18. G. A. Cohen, *Self-Ownership, Freedom, and Equality* (Cambridge: Cambridge University Press, 1995), 127. See also G. A. Cohen, *If You're an Egalitarian, How Come You're So Rich?* (Cambridge, Mass.: Harvard University Press, 2000), 114.

19. Cohen, *Self-Ownership, Freedom, and Equality*, 129.

20. Cohen, *Self-Ownership, Freedom, and Equality*, 131.

21. "The great cry of world Justice today is that the fruit of toil go to the Laborer who produces it" (W. E. B. Du Bois, *An ABC of Color* [New York: International Publishers, 1963], 109).

22. Cohen, *If You're an Egalitarian, How Come You're So Rich?* 106.

23. Cohen, *If You're an Egalitarian, How Come You're So Rich?* 108.

24. Cohen, *If You're an Egalitarian, How Come You're So Rich?* 110–11.

25. Cohen, *If You're an Egalitarian, How Come You're So Rich?* 113–14.

26. The idea behind this objection is borrowed from Boxill, "Global Equality of Opportunity and National Integrity," 150–51.

27. Boxill, "Global Equality of Opportunity and National Integrity," 152.

28. Boxill, "Global Equality of Opportunity and National Integrity," 152.

29. Boxill, "Global Equality of Opportunity and National Integrity," 154.

30. Boxill, "Global Equality of Opportunity and National Integrity," 155.

31. Boxill, "Global Equality of Opportunity and National Integrity," 168.

32. Boxill, "Global Equality of Opportunity and National Integrity," 158.

33. For discussion of anti–bad Samaritanism, see Joel Feinberg, *Freedom and Fulfillment* (Princeton, N.J.: Princeton University Press, 1992), chap. 7; John Kleinig, "Good Samaritanism," *Philosophy and Public Affairs* 5 (1975): 382–407.

34. Temkin, "Thinking about the Needy," 421–22.

35. This distinction is borrowed from Peter Unger, *Living High and Letting Die* (Oxford: Oxford University Press, 1996), 48.

36. Temkin, "Thinking about the Needy."

37. Thomas Pogge, *World Poverty and Human Rights* (London: Polity, 2002), 203.

38. J. Angelo Corlett, *Race, Rights, and Justice*, Law and Philosophy Library 88 (Dordrecht, Netherlands: Springer, 2009), 88–92.

39. Pogge, *World Poverty and Human Rights*, 203.

40. Thomas Pogge, "Real World Justice," *The Journal of Ethics* 9 (2005): 38–39.

41. J. Angelo Corlett, *Race, Racism, and Reparations* (Ithaca, N.Y.: Cornell University Press, 2003), 164–65. Also see the introduction, above.

42. David Miller, "Against Global Egalitarianism," *The Journal of Ethics* 9 (2005): 55–79.

43. Temkin, "Thinking about the Needy," 431.

44. Richard J. Arneson, "Egalitarian Justice versus the Right to Privacy," *Social Philosophy and Policy* 17 (2000): 91–119; "Equality and Responsibility," *The Journal of Ethics* 3 (1999): 225–47; "Luck and Equality," *Proceedings of the Aristotelian Society* 75 (2001): 73–90.

45. John Broome, *Weighing Goods* (Oxford: Oxford University Press, 1991), and *Weighing Lives* (Oxford: Oxford University Press, 2004).

46. Cohen, *If You're an Egalitarian, How Come You're So Rich?*; Cohen, *Self-Ownership, Freedom, and Equality*. For discussions on the latter book, see *The Journal of Ethics* 2 (1998).

47. Ronald Dworkin, "What Is Equality? Part 1," *Philosophy and Public Affairs* 10 (1981): 185–246; "What Is Equality? Part 2," *Philosophy and Public Affairs* 10 (1981): 283–345; "What Is Equality? Part 3," *Iowa Law Review* 73 (1987): 1–54; "What Is Equality? Part 4," in *Philosophy and Democracy*, ed. Thomas Christiano (Oxford: Oxford University Press, 2003), 116–37.

48. John Roemer, *Equality of Opportunity* (Cambridge, Mass.: Harvard University Press, 1998), and *Theories of Distributive Justice* (Cambridge, Mass.: Harvard University Press, 1996), chaps. 7–8.

49. Samuel Scheffler, "What Is Egalitarianism?" *Philosophy and Public Affairs* 31 (2003): 5–39.

50. Amartya Sen, *On Economic Inequality*, exp. ed. (Oxford: Oxford University Press, 1978), and *Inequality Reexamined* (Cambridge, Mass.: Harvard University Press, 1992).

51. Peter Singer, "Famine, Affluence, and Morality," *Philosophy and Public Affairs* 1 (1972).

52. Larry S. Temkin, *Inequality* (Oxford: Oxford University Press, 1993).

53. Unger, *Living High and Letting Die*. See especially pp. 8–10 for an argument for the incompleteness of Singer's argument for assisting those in need.

54. Bernard Williams, *In the Beginning Was the Deed*, ed. Geoffrey Hawthorn (Princeton, N.J.: Princeton University Press, 2005), chap. 8.

55. Christopher Lake, *Equality and Responsibility* (Oxford: Oxford University Press, 2001); Michael Otsuka, *Libertarianism Without Inequality* (Oxford: Oxford University Press, 2003); Hillel Steiner, "How Equality Matters," *Social Philosophy and Policy* 19 (2002): 342–56. The notion of equality of opportunity is criticized in Matt Cavanaugh, *Against Equality of Opportunity* (Oxford: Oxford University Press, 2002). Also see Andrew Levine, *Rethinking Liberal Equality* (Ithaca, N.Y.: Cornell University Press,

1998), for a critical assessment of some theories of equality. For a historical account of recent egalitarian reforms in the United States, see J. R. Pole, *The Pursuit of Equality in American History* (Berkeley: University of California Press, 1978).

56. Charles Beitz, *Political Equality* (Princeton, N.J.: Princeton University Press, 1989), ix.

57. See Corlett, *Race, Rights, and Justice*, 88–92.

58. Thomas Pogge, "Human Rights and Human Responsibilities," in *Global Responsibilities*, ed. Andrew Kuper (London: Routledge, 2005), 24.

59. Pogge, "Human Rights and Human Responsibilities," 26. Slightly less vague is the description of human rights found in Thomas Pogge, "The International Significance of Human Rights," *The Journal of Ethics* 4 (2000): 46.

60. Larry Alexander, *Is There a Right of Freedom of Expression?* (Cambridge: Cambridge University Press, 2005), 4.

61. Joel Feinberg, *Social Philosophy* (Englewood Cliffs, N.J.: Prentice-Hall, 1973), 87.

62. Pogge, "Human Rights and Human Responsibilities," 31.

63. David Miller, "Distributing Responsibilities," in *Global Responsibilities*, ed. Andrew Kuper (London: Routledge, 2005), 95.

64. Onora O'Neill, "Agents of Justice," in *Global Responsibilities*, ed. Andrew Kuper (London: Routledge, 2005), 42.

65. Carl Wellman, *The Proliferation of Rights* (Boulder, Colo.: Westview, 1999).

66. Temkin, "Thinking about the Needy," 431–33.

67. Moellendorf, *Cosmopolitan Justice*, 91.

68. In the United States, there seems to be insufficient toleration for cash payouts for those who, by their lights, should not even be accorded affirmative action of any kind.

69. Corlett, *Race, Racism, and Reparations*, chaps. 8–9. See also chapter 1, above.

70. D. Moellendorf, *Cosmopolitan Justice* (Boulder, Colo.: Westview, 2002), 91.

71. This is ironically interesting in light of the fact that some cosmopolitan liberals fancy themselves as propounding theories of "real world justice" (Pogge, "Real World Justice").

72. Martha Nussbaum, "Reply," in *For Love of Country*, ed. Joshua Cohen and Martha Nussbaum (Boston: Beacon Press, 1996), 137.

73. Buchanan, *Justice, Legitimacy, and Self-Determination*.

74. Buchanan, *Justice, Legitimacy, and Self-Determination*, 165. Also see pp. 165ff.

75. Buchanan, *Justice, Legitimacy, and Self-Determination*, 173–74.

76. John Rawls, *Political Liberalism* (New York: Columbia University Press, 1993).

77. Buchanan, *Justice, Legitimacy, and Self-Determination*, 164ff.

78. Feinberg, *Social Philosophy*; Feinberg, *Rights, Justice, and the Bounds of Liberty*; Feinberg, *Freedom and Fulfillment*, chaps. 8–10.

79. Buchanan, *Justice, Legitimacy, and Self-Determination*, 170.

80. Quoted in Robert A. Williams, Jr., "The Algebra of Federal Indian Law," in *Jurisprudence Classical and Contemporary*, 2nd ed., ed. Robert L. Hayman, Jr., Nancy Levit, and Richard Delgado (St. Paul, Minn.: West Group, 2002), 639.

81. By "statist" I mean no disrespect to Rawls's theory. Rather, I mean to convey what many cosmopolitan liberal critics of Rawls refer to his theory as. Indeed, no theorist today would dare be a statist in some strong sense of thinking that the only legitimate subjects of international law and global justice are and ought to be states. For this

would imply that it would be wrong for international law to place on trial individual war criminals or such, which would be absurd. So the old legal positivist doctrine that only states can be the legitimate subjects of international law must be discarded as a view no one holds. As one legal commentator puts it: "Like various other tenets of the positivist creed, the doctrine that only states are subjects of international law is unable to stand the test of actual practice" (H. Lauterpacht, *International Law and Human Rights* [Hamden, Conn.: Archon Books, 1968], 9).

82. Corlett, *Race, Rights, and Justice*, 88–92.

83. Scheffler, *Boundaries and Allegiances*, 129–30.

84. Furthermore, if one philosopher has it right, then cosmopolitan liberalism, in its focus on radical equality, seems also to ignore totally the rights that nonhumans might possess that would imply duties we have toward them. If sound, this criticism reveals the deeply speciesist nature of cosmopolitanism, but I would add, of Rawls's theory of international justice as well (James P. Sterba, "Global Justice for Humans or for All Living Beings and What Difference It Makes," *The Journal of Ethics* 9 [2005]: 283–300).

CHAPTER 3

1. Andrew von Hirsch and Andrew Ashworth, *Proportionate Sentencing* (Oxford: Oxford University Press, 2005), 110.

2. Janna Thompson, *Taking Responsibility for the Past* (Cambridge: Polity, 2002). For an alternative discussion of Thompson's position, see David Miller, *National Responsibility and Global Justice* (Oxford: Oxford University Press, 2007), 143–47.

3. Thompson, *Taking Responsibility for the Past*, 27.

4. Thompson, *Taking Responsibility for the Past*, 30–37.

5. Thompson, *Taking Responsibility for the Past*, chap. 6.

6. Thompson, *Taking Responsibility for the Past*, 10. See note 40 in chapter 1, above, for sources that refute several arguments for a moral statute of limitations on injustice.

7. Thompson, *Taking Responsibility for the Past*, 47–53, 83–86, 91, 140–41.

8. Boxill writes of the right to reparations to blacks: "It fails to hold or is outweighed when allowing it to hold would make innocent people destitute, or create large inequalities that are likely to lead to exploitation and domination" (Bernard Boxill, "A Lockean Argument for Black Reparations," *The Journal of Ethics* 7 [2003]: 80).

9. Thompson, *Taking Responsibility for the Past*, 51.

10. Thompson, *Taking Responsibility for the Past*, 48.

11. Thompson, *Taking Responsibility for the Past*, 57.

12. Thompson, *Taking Responsibility for the Past*, xiii.

13. See chapters 6 and 7, below, for explications of this principle. Also, see J. Angelo Corlett, *Race, Racism, and Reparations* (Ithaca, N.Y.: Cornell University Press, 2003), chaps. 8–9.

14. Thompson, *Taking Responsibility for the Past*, xvii.

15. Thompson, *Taking Responsibility for the Past*, 74.

16. Feinberg, "The Nature and Value of Rights," *Journal of Value Inquiry* 4 (1970): 243–57.

17. Thompson, *Taking Responsibility for the Past*, 8–11, 44–46.

18. Howard McGary, *Race and Social Justice* (London: Blackwell, 1999), chap. 5.

19. Thompson, *Taking Responsibility for the Past*, xi, 45.

20. Margaret Urban Walker, *Moral Repair* (Cambridge: Cambridge University Press, 2006), 6–7.

21. Walker, *Moral Repair*, 7.

22. Walker, *Moral Repair*, 6.

23. Walker, *Moral Repair*, 7–8.

24. Walker, *Moral Repair*, 9.

25. Also see p. 15 where she states: "Restorative justice embodies a view of crime of violence as a violation of people and relationships that entails an obligation to set things right, repairing victims and communities, and ideally humanizing and *reintegrating offenders*" (emphasis provided). By why, one might ask, ought the well-being of offenders be a consideration at all in the process of reparations? In posing this question, I assume that by "reintegration" Walker means something like reconciliation, or a social process that would involve it.

26. Walker, *Moral Repair*, 10.

27. Walker, *Moral Repair*, 15.

28. Walker, *Moral Repair*, 16.

29. J. Angelo Corlett, *Responsibility and Punishment*, 3rd ed., Library of Ethics and Applied Philosophy 9 (Dordrecht, Netherlands: Springer, 2006), chap. 4; Joel Feinberg, *Doing and Deserving* (Princeton, N.J.: Princeton University Press, 1970); Andrew von Hirsch, *Censure and Sanctions* (Oxford: Clarendon, 1993); Andrew von Hirsch, *Doing Justice* (Boston: Northeastern University Press, 1986); Andrew von Hirsch, *Past or Future Crimes* (New Brunswick, N.J.: Rutgers University Press, 1987); Andrew von Hirsch and Andrew Ashworth, eds., *Principled Sentencing* (Boston: Northeastern University Press, 1992); Von Hirsch and Ashworth, *Proportionate Sentencing*; John Kleinig, *Punishment and Desert* (The Hague: Martinus Nijhoff, 1973).

30. Corlett, *Responsibility and Punishment*, chap. 3. Also see chapter 1 of this book, above.

31. Walker, *Moral Repair*, 210.

32. See note 29.

33. Walker, *Moral Repair*, 23.

34. Walker, *Moral Repair*, 24.

35. Walker, *Moral Repair*, 7.

36. Walker, *Moral Repair*, 210–11.

37. Walker, *Moral Repair*, 211.

38. Walker, *Moral Repair*, 211.

39. Walker, *Moral Repair*, 28.

40. Walker, *Moral Repair*, 30–32.

41. Feinberg, *Doing and Deserving*, chap. 5.

42. Corlett, *Race, Racism, and Reparations*, 150–52.

43. Walker, *Moral Repair*, 39.

44. This is ironic given Walker's own claim that "moral repair" is better than the "insult of doing nothing" (Walker, *Moral Repair*, 39).

45. For a philosophical analysis of coercive offers and threats, see Joel Feinberg, *Harm to Self* (Oxford: Oxford University Press, 1986).

46. Walker, *Moral Repair*, 154.

47. Walker, *Moral Repair*, 156.

48. Howard McGary explains that there were psychological and sociological reasons why many emancipated blacks forgave their former slavers: to clear one's mind of the clutter of unforgiven sins against oneself, as well as to attempt to cope in a dangerous Reconstruction world in which former slavers and many other whites existed as more powerful than blacks. But this is not meant as a normative thesis about whether or not such blacks ought to have forgiven their ex-slavemasters, or whether or not other persecuted blacks ought to forgive their oppressors (Howard McGary and Bill E. Lawson, *Between Slavery and Freedom* [Bloomington: Indiana University Press, 1992], chap. 6).

49. Walker, *Moral Repair*, 158ff.

50. Walker, *Moral Repair*, 162.

51. Walker, *Moral Repair*, 163.

52. Walker, *Moral Repair*, 164ff.

53. Walker, *Moral Repair*, 165.

54. Walker, *Moral Repair*, 207.

55. Walker, *Moral Repair*, 209.

56. Walker, *Moral Repair*, 209.

57. Walker, *Moral Repair*, 209.

58. Walker, *Moral Repair*, 210.

59. Walker, *Moral Repair*, 167.

60. Walker states, "It is perfectly possible to retaliate against someone for wrong, and *then* forgive them once they have paid *that* particular price" (Walker, *Moral Repair*, 178). But in the context of Walker's several other statements, it seems to stretch her meaning to think that "paid *that* particular price" means anything like compensatory reparations as that phrase is typically understood in legal contexts.

61. Walker, *Moral Repair*, 166.

62. Walker, *Moral Repair*, 168.

63. Walker, *Moral Repair*, 181.

64. Walker, *Moral Repair*, 182.

65. Walker, *Moral Repair*, 183.

66. Walker, *Moral Repair*, 183.

67. Also see her admission that "material" "costs" of a wrongdoing can affect a victim's judgment about forgiving her offender (Walker, *Moral Repair*, 184).

68. See the works of Boxill, McGary, and Roberts in the bibliography, below.

69. Walker, *Moral Repair*, 221.

70. Walker, *Moral Repair*, 221.

71. Corlett, *Responsibility and Punishment*, chaps. 1, 7–9. Also see Feinberg, *Doing and Deserving*.

72. Walker, *Moral Repair*, 225.

73. Walker, *Moral Repair*, 226–27.

74. Walker, *Moral Repair*, 227.

75. Walker, *Moral Repair*, 228.

76. Claudia Card, *The Atrocity Paradigm* (Oxford: Oxford University Press, 2002), 179.

77. Card, *The Atrocity Paradigm*, 181.

78. Joel Feinberg, *Rights, Justice, and the Bounds of Liberty* (Princeton, N.J.: Princeton University Press, 1980), chap. 7; J. Angelo Corlett, *Race, Rights, and Justice*, Law and Philosophy Library 88 (Dordrecht, Netherlands: Springer, 2009), chaps. 5–6.

79. James Sterba, "Review of Corlett, *Race, Racism, and Reparations*," *Mind* 114 (2005): 408–9.

80. Sterba, "Review of Corlett, *Race, Racism, and Reparations*," 408.

81. The separateness of persons concern is found in John Rawls, *A Theory of Justice*, rev. ed. (Cambridge, Mass.: Harvard University Press, 1999); R. G. Frey, ed., *Utility and Rights* (Minneapolis: University of Minnesota Press, 1984).

82. Charles W. Mills, "Contract of Breach," in *Reparations for African Americans*, ed. Howard McGary (Lanham, Md.: Rowman and Littlefield, forthcoming).

83. H. J. McCloskey, "Respect for Human Moral Rights versus Maximizing Good," in *Utility and Rights*, ed. R. G. Frey (Minneapolis: University of Minnesota Press, 1984), 125.

84. Von Hirsch and Ashworth, *Proportionate Sentencing*, 111.

85. Von Hirsch and Ashworth, *Proportionate Sentencing*, 113.

86. Von Hirsch and Ashworth, *Proportionate Sentencing*, 116–17.

87. Von Hirsch and Ashworth, *Proportionate Sentencing*, 115. These authors also note that restorative justice approaches tend to face other practical problems as well, including those of uncooperative offenders and routinization in the restoration process (Von Hirsch and Ashworth, *Proportionate Sentencing*, 125–26).

CHAPTER 4

1. John Rawls, *The Law of Peoples* (Cambridge, Mass.: Harvard University Press, 1999), 12.

2. Joel Feinberg, *Rights, Justice, and the Bounds of Liberty* (Princeton, N.J.: Princeton University Press, 1980), 155.

3. Jürgen Habermas, "Private and Public Autonomy, Human Rights and Popular Sovereignty," in *The Politics of Human Rights*, ed. Obrad Savić (London: Verso, 1999), 64.

4. As Richard Wasserstrom argues, "If there are any human rights, these constitute the strongest of all moral claims that all men can assert" (Richard Wasserstrom, "Rights, Human Rights, and Racial Discrimination," in *Rights*, ed. David Lyons [Belmont, Calif.: Wadsworth, 1979], 50).

5. For a helpful historical account of philosophical views on rights in general, see Gary B. Herbert, *A Philosophical History of Rights* (New Brunswick, N.J.: Transaction, 2002), and "Postscript to *A Philosophical History of Rights*," *Human Rights Review*, 2002, 3–29.

6. This kind of concern is registered in R. Panikkar, "Is the Notion of Human Rights a Western Concept?" *Diogenes* 120 (1982): 75–102; Charles Taylor, "Conditions on an Unforced Consensus on Human Rights," in *The Politics of Human Rights*, ed. Obrad Savić (London: Verso, 1999), 101–19.

7. This particular concern is raised rather poignantly in *New Left Review*, 1999.

8. The reducibility of the language of group (human) rights to the language of individual (human) rights is discussed most recently in James Griffin, *On Human Rights* (Oxford: Oxford University Press, 2008), chap. 15.

9. Joel Feinberg, *Freedom and Fulfillment* (Princeton, N.J.: Princeton University Press, 1992), 241–42.

10. For an analysis of collective rights in terms of valid claims or interests, see J. Angelo Corlett, "The Problem of Collective Moral Rights," *Canadian Journal of Law and Jurisprudence* 7 (1994): 237–59; J. Angelo Corlett, *Race, Rights, and Justice*, Law and Philosophy Library 85 (Dordrecht, Netherlands: Springer, 2009), chap. 6.

11. Note that this definition does not preclude the possibility of some human rights being shared by certain other beings or entities. Thus I do not construe human rights as being *possessed* exclusively by humans, though it might be argued that only humans can effectively *claim* them.

12. In the end, there may be no substantive difference between moral and human rights.

13. Feinberg, *Rights, Justice, and the Bounds of Liberty*, 154.

14. Joel Feinberg, *Social Philosophy* (Englewood Cliffs, N.J.: Prentice-Hall, 1973); Feinberg, *Rights, Justice, and the Bounds of Liberty*; Feinberg, *Freedom and Fulfillment*, chaps. 8–10; Joel Feinberg, *Problems at the Roots of Law* (Oxford: Oxford University Press, 2003), chap. 2. An alternative account is found in James Griffin, *On Human Rights* (Oxford: Oxford University Press, 2008).

15. See chapter 2, above. Also see David Miller, "Against Global Egalitarianism," *The Journal of Ethics* 9, nos. 1–2 (2005): 55–79; "National Responsibility and International Justice," in *The Ethics of Assistance*, ed. Deen Chatterjee (Cambridge: Cambridge University Press, 2004), 123–43; Onora O'Neill, "Global Justice" in *The Ethics of Assistance*, ed. Deen Chatterjee (Cambridge: Cambridge University Press, 2004), 242–59; Rawls, *The Law of Peoples*; Amartya Sen, "Elements of a Theory of Human Rights," *Philosophy and Public Affairs* 32 (2004): 315–57.

16. Feinberg, *Social Philosophy*, 87.

17. Miller, "National Responsibility and International Justice," 124.

18. James Nickel, *Making Sense of Human Rights* (Berkeley: University of California Press, 1987).

19. Wasserstrom, "Rights, Human Rights, and Racial Discrimination," 50.

20. This definition of "absolute rights" is found in Feinberg, *Social Philosophy*, 86.

21. See A. John Simmons, *Justification and Legitimacy* (Cambridge: Cambridge University Press, 2001), 185; Maurice Cranston, "Human Rights, Real and Supposed," in *Political Theory and the Rights of Man*, ed. D. D. Raphael (Bloomington: Indiana University Press, 1967), 49.

22. Charles Beitz, "Human Rights and the Law of Peoples," in *The Ethics of Assistance*, ed. Deen Chatterjee (Cambridge: Cambridge University Press, 2004), 196ff.

23. Feinberg, *Social Philosophy*, 87. For some philosophical and legal studies of torture, see Sanford Levinson, ed., *Torture* (Oxford: Oxford University Press, 2004).

24. This is one reason why the problem of proportional punishment stands as a challenge for all positive and plausible theories of punishment. J. Angelo Corlett, *Responsibility and Punishment*, 3rd ed., Library of Ethics and Applied Philosophy 9 (Dordrecht, Netherlands: Springer, 2006), introduction and chap. 4. See this source also for a defense of a cluster of principles of proportional punishment, ones that evade numerous concerns with proportional punishment. For a discussion of some of the philosophical challenges to proportionalism in punishment, see Jesper Ryberg, *The Ethics of Proportionate Punishment*, Library of Ethics and Applied Philosophy 16 (Dordrecht, Netherlands: Kluwer, 2004).

25. Feinberg, *Social Philosophy*, 96.

26. Feinberg, *Social Philosophy*, 97.

27. Feinberg, *Social Philosophy*, 88.

28. Allen Buchanan, *Justice, Legitimacy, and Self-Determination* (Oxford: Oxford University Press, 2005); Norman Daniels, *Am I My Brother's Keeper?* (Oxford: Oxford University Press, 1988); James Nickel, "Poverty and Rights," *The Philosophical Quarterly* 55 (2005): 385–402; Thomas Pogge, *World Poverty and Human Rights* (London: Polity, 2002).

29. James Griffin, "First Steps in an Account of Human Rights," *European Journal of Philosophy* 9 (2001): 306.

30. This caution is found in Carl Wellman, *The Proliferation of Rights* (Boulder, Colo.: Westview, 1999).

31. Later on in this chapter I shall argue that for all John Rawls writes about human rights, nothing precludes reparations from being a human right, and that for all James Nickel argues about human rights, nothing precludes reparations from correctly being classified as a human one.

32. For an alternative conception of rights and their possible confictability, see H. J. McCloskey, "Respect for Human Moral Rights versus Maximizing Good," in *Utility and Rights*, ed. R. G. Frey (Minneapolis: University of Minnesota Press, 1984), 121–36.

33. An example of this position is found in Philip Alston, "Conjuring Up Human Rights," *The American Journal of International Law* 78 (1984): 607–21.

34. Feinberg, *Freedom and Fulfillment*, chap. 8.

35. Rawls, *The Law of Peoples*, 4.

36. Rawls, *The Law of Peoples*, 5.

37. Feinberg, *Freedom and Fulfillment*, chaps. 8–10; *Problems at the Roots of Law*, chap. 2.

38. As Feinberg admits, "It is not enough to have the rights; one must know that one has the rights" (Feinberg, *Rights, Justice, and the Bounds of Liberty*, 156).

39. J. Angelo Corlett, "The Philosophy of Joel Feinberg," *The Journal of Ethics* 10 (2006): 138.

40. D. Braybrooke, "The Firm but Untidy Correlativity of Rights and Obligations," *Canadian Journal of Philosophy* 1 (1972): 351–63; Feinberg, *Rights, Justice, and the Bounds of Liberty*, 143; David Lyons, "The Correlativity of Rights and Duties," *Nous* 4 (1970): 45–55; Bernard Mayo, "What Are Human Rights?" in *Political Theory and the Rights of Man*, ed. D. D. Raphael (Bloomington: Indiana University Press, 1967), 72ff.; McCloskey, "Respect for Human Rights Versus Maximizing Good"; D. D. Raphael, "Human Rights, Old and New," in *Political Theory and the Rights of Man*, ed. D. D. Raphael (Bloomington: Indiana University Press, 1967), 54–67.

41. Alan Gewirth, *The Community of Rights* (Chicago: University of Chicago Press, 1995), 6. For discussions of Gewirth's notion of human rights, see Ari Kohen, "The Possibility of Secular Human Rights," *Human Rights Review* 7 (2005): 49–75; Richard B. Friedman, "The Basics of Human Rights," in *Human Rights*, ed. J. R. Pennock and J. W. Chapman (New York: New York University Press, 1981), 148–57.

42. Gewirth, *The Community of Rights*, 8.

43. This issue is addressed in chapter 2.

44. Rawls, *The Law of Peoples*, 6.

45. Rawls, *The Law of Peoples*, 7.

46. Rawls, *The Law of Peoples*, 8.

47. Some of many such examples are found in Nickel, "Poverty and Rights"; Martha Nussbaum, "Capabilities and Human Rights," in *Global Justice and Transnational Politics*, ed. Pablo De Greiff and Ciaran Cronin (Cambridge: MIT Press, 2002), 117–49;

Sen, "Elements of a Theory of Human Rights." The only example of which I am aware of a philosophical account of human rights that mentions the right to reparations (compensation to groups) is that of Miller, "National Responsibility and International Justice," 132.

48. Rawls, *The Law of Peoples*, 8.

49. This was one of former U.S. president Dwight D. Eisenhower's specific cautions to the U.S. citizenry in his farewell speech in 1961.

50. Rawls, *The Law of Peoples*, 9.

51. The colonists' secession from England was morally unjustified to the extent that it violated the "Territoriality Thesis," widely considered to be a moral requirement of justified secession (Allen Buchanan, *Secession* [Boulder, Colo.: Westview, 1990]); J. Angelo Corlett, *Terrorism*, Philosophical Studies Series 101 (Dordrecht, Netherlands: Kluwer, 2003), chap. 4. What makes the colonists' secession a violation of this important moral principle is that they had no moral right to the land they claimed as their own against England. The American Indians possessed that moral claim.

52. David Stannard, *American Holocaust* (Oxford: Oxford University Press, 1992).

53. For philosophical discussions of issues pertaining to the enslavement of blacks in the United States, see Howard McGary and Bill E. Lawson, *Between Slavery and Freedom* (Bloomington: Indiana University Press, 1992).

54. In recent years, various calls for reparations have been made to rectify certain historic and substantial harmful wrongdoings to certain groups. Perhaps the most recent one regarding blacks in the United States is that of the U.S. House of Representatives Resolution 194 (29 July 2008), which includes the following statement: that it "expresses its commitment to *rectify* the lingering consequences of the misdeeds committed against African Americans under slavery and Jim Crow and to stop the occurrence of human rights violations in the future." Clearly the matter of reparations for historic and substantial harmful wrongdoings lingers in the minds of many U.S. blacks, as well as several American Indians. But it is hardly the case that the call for such reparations has ever been a matter of serious national discussion.

55. For philosophical discussions of the concept of evil, see Feinberg, *Problems at the Roots of Law*, chap. 5; J. Angelo Corlett, "On Evil," *Analysis* 64 (2004): 81–84.

56. For philosophical discussions and analyses of the concepts of desert, proportionality, and responsibility, see Corlett, *Responsibility and Punishment*, chaps. 1, 4.

57. J. Angelo Corlett, *Race, Racism, and Reparations* (Ithaca, N.Y.: Cornell University Press, 2003), chaps. 8–9.

58. John Rawls, *Collected Papers*, ed. Samuel Freeman (Cambridge, Mass.: Harvard University Press, 1999), 117–29.

59. Feinberg, *Rights, Justice, and the Bounds of Liberty*, chap. 7.

60. Feinberg, *Social Philosophy*, 84.

61. Feinberg, *Social Philosophy*, 84–85.

62. This definition is found in Feinberg, *Social Philosophy*, 85. It is important to note that Feinberg does not necessarily think there are such rights as defined herein: "Of course, it is also an open question whether there *are* any human rights and, if so, just what those rights are." But this does not mean that he denies the existence or importance of human rights.

63. Moreover, as Feinberg points out, human rights might sometimes accrue to nonhumans (Feinberg, *Social Philosophy*, 85). If the right to life is a human right, conditionally or otherwise, it is also a valid interest of nonhuman animals or a valid claim made on behalf of them by some humans in a valid moral position to do so.

64. Corlett, "The Philosophy of Joel Feinberg," 139–40.

65. The general point that human rights can be sacrificed in a utilitarian theory and that this counts against the plausibility of utilitarianism is found in E. M. Adams, "The Ground of Human Rights," *American Philosophical Quarterly* 19 (1982): 191. For a defense of a utilitarian theory of rights, see David Lyons, "Human Rights and the General Welfare," in *Rights*, ed. David Lyons (Belmont, Calif.: Wadsworth, 1979), 174–86; *Rights, Welfare, and Mill's Moral Theory* (Oxford: Oxford University Press, 1994).

66. That reparations amount to group compensation from a government or business or some other group is found in Corlett, *Race, Racism, and Reparations*, 149.

67. For a philosophical analysis and argument concerning forgiveness and apology in punishment contexts, see Corlett, *Responsibility and Punishment*, chap. 6. Also see chapter 9 of this book, below.

68. Wasserstrom, "Rights, Human Rights, and Racial Discrimination," 57.

69. A similar point is made concerning reparations to blacks in the United States. See Howard McGary, *Race and Social Justice* (London: Blackwell, 1999), chap. 7.

70. A general point about remedies in global contexts is found in Louis Henkin, "International Human Rights as 'Rights,'" in *Human Rights*, ed. J. R. Pennock and J. W. Chapman (New York: New York University Press, 1981), 271.

71. This position is set out and defended in J. Angelo Corlett, "Was 9/11 Morally Justified?" *Journal of Global Ethics* 3 (2007): 107–23. The position that terrorism can be morally justified in self-defense is found in Burleigh Wilkins, *Terrorism and Collective Responsibility* (London: Routledge, 1992).

72. Corlett, *Terrorism*.

73. This point is found in Carl Wellman, *A Theory of Rights* (Totowa, N.J.: Rowman and Allenheld, 1985), 184. However, collective human rights against genocide, for instance, are recognized as "third-generation" human rights in Wellman, *The Proliferation of Rights*, 29ff. The right of groups to reparations, I argue, would follow as a protection against or a remedy for genocide, for example.

74. Corlett, *Race, Rights, and Justice*, chap. 6. See also Larry May, *The Morality of Groups* (Notre Dame, Ind.: University of Notre Dame Press, 1987), chap. 7.

75. Ronald Dworkin, *Taking Rights Seriously* (Cambridge, Mass.: Harvard University Press, 1978), 191.

76. A caution that "there is many a moral slip between having a right and being morally justified in its exercise" is stated in A. I. Melden, *Rights and Right Conduct* (Oxford: Basil Blackwell, 1959), 18.

77. Again, see John Rawls, *A Theory of Justice*, rev. ed. (Cambridge, Mass.: Harvard University Press, 1999), 3–4.

78. Nickel, *Making Sense of Human Rights*, 131.

79. Nickel, *Making Sense if Human Rights*, 143.

80. Nickel, *Making Sense of Human Rights*, 145.

81. For a more comprehensive philosophical account of the limits to freedom of expression under the First Amendment to the U.S. Constitution, see Feinberg, *Freedom and Fulfillment*, chap. 5.

82. Feinberg, *Rights, Justice, and the Bounds of Liberty*, 152.

83. Feinberg, *Rights, Justice, and the Bounds of Liberty*, chap. 7. For a contrary position, see Richard B. Brandt, "The Concept of a Moral Right and Its Function," *The Journal of Philosophy* 80 (1983): 35–36.

84. Feinberg, *Rights, Justice, and the Bounds of Liberty*, 141.

85. Feinberg, *Rights, Justice, and the Bounds of Liberty*, 142.

86. Feinberg, *Rights, Justice, and the Bounds of Liberty*, 151.

87. Rawls, *A Theory of Justice*, 3–4.

88. John Rawls, *The Law of Peoples* (Cambridge, Mass.: Harvard University Press, 1999), 3.

89. Rawls, *The Law of Peoples*, 6.

90. Rawls, *The Law of Peoples*, 6.

91. Rawls, *The Law of Peoples*, 7. See Rawls, *The Law of Peoples*, 11–23, for his elaboration of the nature of a realistic utopia.

92. See, for example, John Rawls, *A Theory of Justice* (Cambridge, Mass.: Harvard University Press, 1971); John Rawls, *Political Liberalism* (New York: Columbia University Press, 1993).

93. Rawls, *The Law of Peoples*, 32.

94. Rawls, *The Law of Peoples*, 33.

95. Rawls, *The Law of Peoples*, 33.

96. Rawls, *The Law of Peoples*, 37.

97. Burleigh T. Wilkins, "Principles for the Law of Peoples," *The Journal of Ethics* 11 (2007): 161–75.

98. Rawls, *The Law of Peoples*, 37.

99. Hence the old legal adage: "Absence of remedy is absence of right."

100. Rawls, *The Law of Peoples*, 7.

101. Rawls, *A Theory of Justice*, 368: "Now in certain circumstances militant action and other kinds of resistance are surely justified."

102. James W. Nickel, "Poverty and Rights," *The Philosophical Quarterly* 55 (2005): 385–402.

103. Roughly, this position is argued in Allen Buchanan, *Justice, Legitimacy, and Self-Determination* (Oxford: Oxford University Press, 2005); Thomas Pogge, *World Poverty and Human Rights* (London: Polity, 1999).

104. Nickel, "Poverty and Rights," 386.

105. Nickel, "Poverty and Rights," 386.

106. Nickel, "Poverty and Rights," 387.

107. Nickel, "Poverty and Rights," 387.

108. Nickel, "Poverty and Rights," 387. Also see Nickel, *Making Sense of Human Rights*.

109. Nickel, "Poverty and Rights," 391.

110. Nickel, "Poverty and Rights," 391.

111. That moral rights in general serve to protect self-respect, respect for others and human dignity is argued in Feinberg, *Social Philosophy*; Feinberg, *Rights, Justice, and the Bounds of Liberty*; Feinberg, *Freedom and Fulfillment*, chaps. 8–10; Joel Feinberg, *Problems at the Roots of Law* (Oxford: Oxford University Press, 2003), chap. 2.

112. Nickel, "Poverty and Rights," 391.

113. Nickel, "Poverty and Rights," 391.

114. Nickel, "Poverty and Rights," 392.

115. Nickel, "Poverty and Rights," 392.

116. Nickel, "Poverty and Rights," 392.

117. Nickel, "Poverty and Rights," 392.

118. Nickel, "Poverty and Rights," 393.

119. Nickel, "Poverty and Rights," 393.
120. Nickel, "Poverty and Rights," 393.
121. Nickel, "Poverty and Rights," 394.
122. See note 111, above.
123. Nickel, "Poverty and Rights," 394,
124. Nickel, "Poverty and Rights," 394.
125. Nickel, "Poverty and Rights," 394.
126. Nickel, "Poverty and Rights," 394.
127. Nickel, "Poverty and Rights," 395.
128. Nickel, "Poverty and Rights," 396.
129. Nickel, "Poverty and Rights," 397.
130. Rawls, *The Law of Peoples*.
131. These points are addressed more fully in chapters 6 and 7.
132. Howard McGary, "Achieving Democratic Equality: Forgiveness, Reconciliation, and Reparations," *The Journal of Ethics* 7 (2003): 93–113.
133. That a genuine apology entails, among other things, rectificatory action on behalf of the harmful wrongdoer toward her victim(s), and that forgiveness requires an apology and is simultaneously a necessary condition for genuine reconciliation is found in J. Angelo Corlett, "Forgiveness, Apology, and Retributive Punishment," *American Philosophical Quarterly* 43 (2006): 25–42; J. Angelo Corlett, *Responsibility and Punishment*, 3rd ed., Library of Ethics and Applied Philosophy 9 (Dordrecht, Netherlands: Springer, 2006), chap. 5.
134. Nickel, "Poverty and Rights," 400.
135. Nickel, "Poverty and Rights," 401.
136. Several additional questions might be raised about whether or not reparations are justified or required in this or that circumstance, all relevant things considered. Such questions have been addressed in Bernard Boxill, "The Morality of Reparations," *Social Theory and Practice* 2 (1972): 113–22; Bernard Boxill, "A Lockean Argument for Black Reparations," *The Journal of Ethics* 7 (2003): 63–91; Corlett, *Race, Racism, and Reparations*, chaps. 8–9; Howard McGary, *Race and Social Justice* (London: Blackwell, 1999); James Nickel, "Should Reparations Be to Individuals or to Groups?" *Analysis* 34 (1974): 154–60; Rodney C. Roberts, "The Morality of a Moral Statute of Limitations on Injustice," *The Journal of Ethics* 7 (2003): 115–38; Rodney C. Roberts, "More on the Morality of a Moral Statute of Limitations on Injustice," *The Journal of Ethics* 11 (2007): 177–92. Also see Rodney C. Roberts, ed., *Injustice and Rectification* (New York: Peter Lang, 2002).
137. Rawls, *The Law of Peoples*, 68.
138. Rawls, *The Law of Peoples*, 80.
139. I borrow the notion of first and second-tier human rights from James Nickel, "Are Human Rights Mainly Implemented by Intervention?" in *Rawls's Law of Peoples*, ed. R. Martin and David Reidy (London: Blackwell, 2006), 274–75.

CHAPTER 5

1. Howard McGary, *Race and Social Justice* (London: Blackwell, 1999), 91.
2. David Miller, *National Responsibility and Global Justice* (Oxford: Oxford University Press, 2007), 161.

3. Miller, *National Responsibility and Global Justice*, 150–51.

4. Bernard Boxill, "A Lockean Argument for Black Reparations," *The Journal of Ethics* 7 (2003): 63–91.

5. The first philosophical analysis of the concept of collective moral responsibility aimed specifically at the problem of reparations to blacks is found in McGary, *Race and Social Justice*, chap. 5, originally published as "Morality and Collective Liability," *The Journal of Value Inquiry* 20 (1986): 157–65. The seminal work on collective responsibility in legal contexts is found in Joel Feinberg, *Doing and Deserving* (Princeton, N.J.: Princeton University Press, 1970), chap. 9. It was originally published as "Collective Responsibility," *The Journal of Philosophy* 65 (1968): 674–88.

6. McGary, *Race and Social Justice*, 83.

7. For a discussion of this term in relation to U.S. reparations to blacks, see Boris Bittker, *The Case for Black Reparations* (New York: Random House, 1973), 65.

8. The analysis will be congruent with, for the most part, the views set forth in J. Angelo Corlett, "Corporate Punishment and Responsibility," *Journal of Social Philosophy* 28 (1997): 96–100; J. Angelo Corlett, "Collective Punishment," in *Encyclopedic Dictionary of Business Ethics*, ed. Patricia Werhane and R. Edward Freeman (London: Blackwell, 1997), 117–20, 120–25; J. Angelo Corlett, "Collective Responsibility," in *Encyclopedic Dictionary of Business Ethics*, ed. Patricia Werhane and R. Edward Freeman (London: Blackwell, 1997), 120–25; J. Angelo Corlett, "Corporate Responsibility for Environmental Damage," *Environmental Ethics* 18 (1996): 195–207; J. Angelo Corlett, "Collective Punishment and Public Policy," *Journal of Business Ethics* 11 (1992): 207–16; J. Angelo Corlett, "Corporate Responsibility and Punishment," *Public Affairs Quarterly* 2 (1988): 1–16. This section of the chapter is a revised version of J. Angelo Corlett, "Collective Moral Responsibility," *Journal of Social Philosophy* 32 (2001): 573–84.

9. Burleigh T. Wilkins, *Terrorism and Collective Responsibility* (London: Routledge, 1992), 97.

10. Wilkins, *Terrorism and Collective Responsibility*, 102.

11. For a discussion of the concept of desert, see George Sher, *Desert* (Princeton, N.J.: Princeton University Press, 1987). Also see J. Angelo Corlett, *Responsibility and Punishment*, 3rd ed., Library of Ethics and Applied Philosophy 9 (Dordrecht, Netherlands: Springer, 2006), chap. 4.

12. For analyses of various kinds of responsibility, including "retrospective responsibility," see Joel Feinberg, "Responsibility *Tout Court*," *Philosophy Research Archives* 14 (1988–1989): 73–92; Joel Feinberg, "Responsibility for the Future," *Philosophy Research Archives* 14 (1988–1989): 93–113.

13. Virginia Held, "Moral Responsibility and Collective Action" in *Individual and Collective Responsibility*, ed. Peter A. French (New York: Schenkman, 1972), 110–11. Also see Virginia Held, "Can a Random Collection of Individuals Be Morally Responsible?" *The Journal of Philosophy* 67 (1970): 471–81.

14. Held, "Moral Responsibility and Collective Action," 110.

15. Held, "Moral Responsibility and Collective Action," 111.

16. Note that this example is similar to Feinberg's Jesse James train robbery example in Feinberg, *Doing and Deserving*, 248. Thus my reply here counts against Feinberg's notion of collective responsibility where contributory group fault is collective, but not distributive. It also renders dubious Wilkins's reliance on Feinberg's notion of collective (legal) responsibility for his own view of collective (moral) responsibility and terrorism (Wilkins, *Terrorism and Collective Responsibility*, chap. 7).

17. Virginia Held, "Corporations, Persons, and Responsibility" in *Shame, Responsibility and the Corporation*, ed. Hugh Curtler (New York: Haven, 1986), 165.

18. Of course, Joel Feinberg makes this very same point with his example for the Jesse James train robbery (Feinberg, *Doing and Deserving*, 248).

19. Wilkins, *Terrorism and Collective Responsibility*, 128–29.

20. Wilkins, *Terrorism and Collective Responsibility*, 129.

21. Wilkins, *Terrorism and Collective Responsibility*, 129.

22. Wilkins, *Terrorism and Collective Responsibility*, 130.

23. This condition is related to the notion of collective feelings of guilt based on collective wrongdoing. For an incisive discussion of collective guilt, see Margaret Gilbert, "Group Wrongs and Guilt Feelings," *The Journal of Ethics* 1 (1997): 65–84.

24. This notion of collective fault (4–6) is borrowed from Feinberg's notion of individual liability. See Feinberg, *Doing and Deserving*, 222.

25. For an incisive discussion of shared moral responsibility for inaction, see Larry May, "Collective Inaction and Shared Responsibility," *Nous* 24 (1990): 269–78; Larry May, *Sharing Responsibility* (Chicago: University of Chicago Press, 1992); David Copp, "Responsibility for Collective Inaction," *American Philosophical Association* (Central Division, Chicago, 1990); and Gregory Mellema, "Shared Responsibility and Ethical Dilutionism," *Australasian Journal of Philosophy* 63 (1985): 177–87.

26. Held, "Corporations, Persons, and Responsibility," 164.

27. Held, "Corporations, Persons, and Responsibility," 164.

28. Held, "Corporations, Persons, and Responsibility," 165.

29. Held, "Corporations, Persons, and Responsibility," 166–67.

30. Held, "Corporations, Persons, and Responsibility," 166.

31. Held, "Corporations, Persons, and Responsibility," 161.

32. This is a Goldmanian account of collective action based on the analysis of human (individual) action of Alvin I. Goldman. For suggestive remarks about whether or not collectives are intentional agents, see Alvin I. Goldman, *A Theory of Human Action* (Princeton, N.J.: Princeton University Press, 1970), 226. For a helpful discussion of the plausibility of collective beliefs, desires and intentionality in light of Daniel Dennett's "intentional stance," see Austen Clark, "Beliefs and Desires Incorporated," *The Journal of Philosophy* 91 (1994): 404–25.

33. Michael Bratman, "Shared Cooperative Activity," *The Philosophical Review* 101 (1992): 327–41; "Shared Intention," *Ethics* 104 (1993): 97–113; "Responsibility and Planning," *The Journal of Ethics* 1 (1997): 27–43.

34. David Copp, "What Collectives Are," *Dialogue* 23 (1984): 250.

35. Copp, "What Collectives Are," 268.

36. Raimo Tuomela, "Intentional Single and Joint Action," *Philosophical Studies* 62 (1991): 237.

37. Such collective rule systems may be enacted formally, as in a national or corporate charter, or informally, as when the, say, behavioral rules of the system are unwritten but understood and abided by members of the collective (as in the case of an academic association or society such as the American Philosophical Association).

38. Raimo Tuomela, "Actions by Collectives," *Philosophical Perspectives* 3 (1989): 476.

39. Copp writes,

A collective, one might say, could not have any "immediate impact" on the world, but can only have impact "through" the actions of persons. Alleged actions of collectives can always be explained ultimately in terms of the actions of persons. The question here, of course, is why should we regard this as showing that collectives do not act, rather than merely as showing how their actions can ultimately be explained? (See David Copp, "Collective Actions and Secondary Actions," *American Philosophical Quarterly* 16 [1978]: 178)

40. Larry May, *The Morality of Groups* (Notre Dame, Ind.: Notre Dame University Press, 1987), 65ff.

41. Peter A. French, *Collective and Corporate Responsibility* (New York: Columbia University Press, 1984), chap. 4.

42. This point against French's argument for the moral responsibility of some corporations is found in Corlett, "Corporate Responsibility and Punishment," 4. (For a more recent assessment of French's theory of collective responsibility, see Corlett, "Corporate Punishment and Responsibility," 86–100). This argument counts also against Larry May's argument for a version of moral responsibility collectivism, where he asserts that the key to corporate intentionality lies in the redescriptions of actions of corporate-individuals into acts of corporations themselves (see May, *The Morality of Groups*, 65ff.).

43. Copp, "Collective Actions and Secondary Actions," 178.

44. G. E. M. Anscombe, *Intention* (Ithaca, N.Y.: Cornell University Press, 1969). For a critical assessment of Anscombe's idea of intention, see Cora Diamond and Jenny Teichman, eds., *Intention and Intentionality* (Ithaca, N.Y.: Cornell University Press, 1979).

45. Goldman, *A Theory of Human Action*, 71.

46. Copp, "Collective Actions and Secondary Actions," 178.

47. Feinberg, *Doing and Deserving*, 227.

48. John Ladd argues that there is a "logical" way to distinguish collective actions from those of its constituents, especially in highly organized collectives. See John Ladd, "Morality and the Ideal of Rationality in Formal Organizations," *The Monist* 54 (1970): 488–516. However, this logical distinction is blurred in the actual world of collective decision-making, where it is often difficult to distinguish between a conglomerate and its constituents as intentional or as teleological (goal-oriented) agents. To the extent that this is true, the notions of collective intentional action or teleological agency are problematic as a foundation for ascribing moral responsibility to certain collectives, that is, where such a view pertains to a collective's *actually being* an intentional and morally responsible agent.

49. Tuomela, "Actions by Collectives," 494.

50. Raimo Tuomela, "Collective Action, Supervenience, and Constitution," *Synthese* 80 (1989): 243.

51. Tuomela, "Collective Action, Supervenience, and Constitution," 254–55.

52. Max Weber, *The Theory of Social and Economic Organizations*, trans. A. M. Henderson and Talcott Parsons (New York: Free Press, 1947), 113.

53. Raimo Tuomela, "We Will Do It: An Analysis of Group-Intentions," *Philosophy and Phenomenological Research* 60 (1991): 249–77.

54. The plausibility of collective belief attributions is considered below.

55. It is assumed, of course, that the Goldmanian notion of human action is an adequate model for collective intentional action.

56. It might be argued that collectives themselves need not act intentionally for collective intentional action ascriptions to be justified. Instead, one might argue, collectives are intentional agents to the extent that their members share an intention. However, this point assumes the plausibility of the idea of the intersubjectivity of intentions, a notion which is itself problematic. See Wilfred Sellars, *Science and Metaphysics* (London: Routledge and Kegan Paul, 1968), 217ff.

57. Harry G. Frankfurt, *The Importance of What We Care About* (Cambridge: Cambridge University Press, 1988). See Keith Lehrer, *Metamind* (Oxford: Oxford University Press, 1990), and "Freedom, Preference, and Autonomy," *The Journal of Ethics* 1 (1997): 3–25, for a competing higher-order or "metamental" compatibilist theory of freedom. For discussions of freedom and moral responsibility, see John Martin Fischer, ed., *Moral Responsibility* (Ithaca, N.Y.: Cornell University Press, 1986); John Martin Fischer, *The Metaphysics of Free Will* (London: Blackwell, 1994); John Martin Fischer and Mark Ravizza, *Responsibility and Control* (Cambridge: Cambridge University Press, 1998); John Martin Fischer, *My Way* (Oxford: Oxford University Press, 2006); John Martin Fischer, "Responsibility, Control, and Omissions," *The Journal of Ethics* 1 (1997): 45–64; John Martin Fischer and Mark Ravizza, eds., *Perspective on Moral Responsibility* (Ithaca, N.Y.: Cornell University Press, 1993).

58. Holly Smith, "Culpable Ignorance," *The Philosophical Review* 92 (1983): 543–71.

59. Margaret Gilbert, "Modelling Collective Belief," *Synthese* 73 (1987): 198.

60. For an account of the difficulties of collective knowledge see J. Angelo Corlett, *Analyzing Social Knowledge* (Lanham, Md.: Rowman and Littlefield, 1996), 33ff.

61. For example, see Roderick Chisholm, *Theory of Knowledge*, 3rd ed. (Englewood Cliffs, N.J.: Prentice-Hall, 1989); Alvin I. Goldman, *Epistemology and Cognition* (Cambridge, Mass.: Harvard University Press, 1986); Keith Lehrer, *Theory of Knowledge* (Boulder, Colo.: Westview, 1990); John Pollock, *Contemporary Theories of Knowledge* (Totowa, N.J.: Rowman and Allenheld, 1986).

62. Margaret Gilbert, *On Social Facts* (Princeton, N.J.: Princeton University Press, 1989).

63. This is not to deny Weber's claim that some properties such as solidarity often accrue to "profit-making organizations where the participants personally conduct the business" (see Weber, *The Theory of Social and Economic Organizations*, 145).

64. It should be noted that sufficient conditions for collective liability for practices is found in McGary, *Race and Social Justice*, 88.

65. Richard S. Downie, "Responsibility and Social Roles," in *Individual and Collective Responsibility*, ed. Peter A. French (New York: Schenkman, 1972), 69–70.

CHAPTER 6

1. Vine Deloria, cited in Phil Cousineau, ed., *A Seat at the Table* (Berkeley: University of California Press, 2006), xviii.

2. Similar points might well apply to Indians in Central and South America. Indeed, Indians in (former) island nations of the Americas, for example, the Hawai'ian islands were victimized (accompanied in the end by threat of military force) by unjust takings by the United States and others. See Michael Dougherty, *To Steal a Kingdom*

(Waimanalo, Hawaii: Island Style Press, 1992). That Hawai'ian culture was significantly affected by the intrusion of Europeans is noted in Martha Beckwith, *Hawaiian Mythology* (Honolulu: University of Hawaii Press, 1976).

3. William L. Anderson, ed., *Cherokee Removal* (Athens: University of Georgia Press, 1991); Garrick Bailey and Roberta Glenn Bailey, *A History of the Navajos* (Santa Fe, N.M.: School of American Research Press, 1986); Robert Berkhofer, Jr., *Salvation and the Savage* (New York: Atheneum, 1965); Dee Brown, *Bury My Heart at Wounded Knee* (New York: Henry Holt, 1970); Angie Debo, *A History of the Indians of the United States* (Norman: University of Oklahoma Press, 1970); Angie Debo, *And Still the Waters Run* (Norman: University of Oklahoma Press, 1989); John Ehle, *Trail of Tears* (New York: Anchor, 1988); Grant Foreman, *Indian Removal* (Norman: University of Oklahoma Press, 1932); Michael D. Green, *The Politics of Indian Removal* (Lincoln: University of Nebraska Press, 1982); Robert V. Remini, *The Legacy of Andrew Jackson* (Baton Rouge: Louisiana State University Press, 1988); David E. Stannard, *American Holocaust* (Oxford: Oxford University Press, 1992); Ian K. Steele, *Warpaths* (Oxford: Oxford University Press, 1994); Clifford E. Trafzer, *The Kit Carsen Campaign* (Norman: University of Oklahoma Press, 1982); Peter H. Wood, Gregory A. Waselkov, and M. Thomas Hatley, eds., *Powhatan's Mantle* (Lincoln: University of Nebraska Press, 1989); Grace Steele Woodward, *The Cherokees* (Norman: University of Oklahoma Press, 1963).

4. The main philosophical works that focus on reparations to Indians include: J. Angelo Corlett, "Reparations to Native Americans?" in *War Crimes and Collective Wrong Doing*, ed. Aleksandar Jokic (London: Blackwell, 2000): 236–69; David Lyons, "The New Indian Claims and Original Rights to Land," *Social Theory and Practice* 6 (1977): 249–72. Other philosophers have written on the problem of reparations to Aboriginals in Australia. See John Bigelow, Robert Pargetter, and Robert Young, "Land, Well-Being and Compensation," *Australasian Journal of Philosophy* 68 (1990): 330–46; Robert Goodin, "Waitangi Tales," *Australasian Journal of Philosophy* 78 (2000): 309–33; Roy W. Perrett, "Indigenous Language Rights and Political Theory," *Australasian Journal of Philosophy* 78 (2000): 405–17; Robert Sparrow, "History and Collective Responsibility," *Australasian Journal of Philosophy* 78 (2000): 346–59; Janna Thompson, "Historical Injustice and Reparation," *Ethics* 112 (2001): 114–35; Janna Thompson, "Historical Obligations," *Australasian Journal of Philosophy* 78 (2000): 334–45; Janna Thompson, "Land Rights and Aboriginal Sovereignty," *Australasian Journal of Philosophy* 68 (1990): 313–29.

5. Felix Cohen, *The Legal Conscience* (New Haven, Conn.: Yale University Press, 1960), 287.

6. Cohen, *The Legal Conscience*, 288.

7. See also Cohen, *The Legal Conscience*, 256ff., 286ff. Perhaps Cohen's attitude toward Indians can be best understood by his own words where he characterizes Indians as a "minority" having the same rights as other minorities: "The rights of each of us in a democracy can be no stronger than the rights of our weakest minority" and "only insofar as we realize that the struggle for Indian rights is simply one sector in a worldwide struggle for human rights, can we see our own efforts in proper perspective" (257). But if we take Cohen seriously on these points, then we can see that it is his ignorance of historical relations that prohibits him from seeing what the United States owes to Indians, and exactly the wide and deep ranges of their human rights claims against the United States, as opposed to the legal relation Cohen sees which is quite paternalistic (254–55). In short, Cohen already presupposes that the United States has

rights to the territories in question, without seriously considering the deeper historical facts behind the acquisitions and transfers of such lands.

8. James Tully, "Aboriginal Property and Western Theory," *Social Philosophy and Policy* 11 (1994): 153. I assume that Indians are indigenous peoples to North America, and that even if they are not so indigenous, that they acquired the lands on which they resided in North America in ways that did not violate the principle of morally just acquisitions and transfers, discussed below.

9. Jules L. Coleman, "Corrective Justice and Property Rights," *Social Philosophy and Policy* 11 (1994): 124–38; Gary Lawson, "Proving Ownership," *Social Philosophy and Policy* 11 (1994): 139–52; A. John Simmons, "Makers' Rights," *The Journal of Ethics* 2 (1998): 197–218; A. John Simmons, "Original Acquisition Justifications of Private Property," *Social Philosophy and Policy* 11 (1994): 63–84. It is assumed herein that the concept of property rights is itself an important part of a plausible political philosophy.

10. Of course, this claim is unproblematic in cases involving murder, as the United States itself recognizes no legal statute of limitations in murder cases. For a refutation of a variety of arguments in favor of a moral statute of limitations on injustice, see Rodney C. Roberts, "The Morality of a Moral Statute of Limitations on Injustice," *The Journal of Ethics* 7 (2003): 115–38.

11. D. N. MacCormick, "The Obligation of Reparations," *Proceedings of the Aristotelian Society* 78 (1977–1978): 179.

12. Lyons, "The New Indian Claims and Original Rights to Land," 252. Indeed, it is a historical, rather than an end-state, argument for reparative justice.

13. These acts amount to a series of intentional actions that were crimes, torts, and/or contract violations.

14. For a discussion of the concept of corrective justice that is helpful in the context of reparations, see Jules L. Coleman, "Corrective Justice and Wrongful Gain," *Journal of Legal Studies* 11 (1982): 421–40.

15. Will Kymlicka, *Liberalism, Community, and Culture* (Oxford: Oxford University Press, 1989), 165. Discussions of Kymlicka's argument are found in John Tomasi, "Kymlicka, Liberalism, and Respect for Cultural Minorities," *Ethics* 105 (1995): 580–603; Robert Murray, "Liberalism, Culture, Aboriginal Rights," *Canadian Journal of Philosophy* 29 (1999): 109–38.

16. John R. Danley, "Liberalism, Aboriginal Rights, and Cultural Minorities," *Philosophy and Public Affairs* 20 (1991): 172.

17. Even the reparations that have been offered by the U.S. government have been inadequate.

18. Another reason might concern factors of distributive justice: the continual failure or refusal of a government to recognize in the form of compensation its harms against some of its constituents often results in the social alienation and violence that erupt in society as a result (at least in part) of such nonrecognition. For such nonrecognition of a government's harms leads many to believe that the government supports the status quo of what happened to the victims.

19. For a discussion of hard cases in the context of law, see Ronald Dworkin, *Taking Rights Seriously* (Cambridge, Mass.: Harvard University Press, 1978), chap. 4.

20. Several additional objections to reparations to American Indians are treated in J. Angelo Corlett, *Race, Racism, and Reparations* (Ithaca, N.Y.: Cornell University Press, 2003), chap. 8.

21. A version of the argument from historical complexity seems to be articulated by Loren Lomasky when he writes: "It is undeniably the case that virtually all current holdings of property descend from a historical chain involving the usurpation of rights. It does not follow that those holdings are thereby rendered illegitimate, morally null and void" (Loren Lomasky, *Persons, Rights, and the Moral Community* [Oxford: Oxford University Press, 1987], 145). A similar view is articulated, but not endorsed, in A. John Simmons, "Original Acquisition Justifications of Property," *Social Philosophy and Policy* 11 (1994): 74–75.

22. This assumption will be taken up in discussing the objection to collective responsibility, below.

23. This principle bears a keen resemblance to the principle of just acquisitions, transfers, and rectification found in Robert Nozick, *Anarchy, State, and Utopia* (New York: Basic Books, 1974), 150. However, the principle of morally just acquisitions and transfers makes no particular theoretical commitments to Nozick's entitlement theory or its implications.

Writing on the recovery or repossession of stolen or lost property, Immanuel Kant argues that those who acquire such property have a responsibility to "investigate" the historical chain of acquisitions and transfers of the property, and if, unbeknownst to her, the property she deemed she purchased legitimately was the actual possession of another, then "nothing is left to the alleged new owner but to have enjoyed the use of it up to this moment as its possessor in good faith" (Immanuel Kant, *The Metaphysical Elements of Justice*, 302, in Immanuel Kant, *The Metaphysics of Morals*, ed. and trans. Mary Gregor [Cambridge: Cambridge University Press, 1996], 82).

24. Note that the matter of property *ownership* is not at issue here. Rather, *sovereignty* over land, a notion consistent with Indian worldviews, is at issue.

25. For descriptions of examples of the taking of Indian lands by force and violence, see Debo, *A History of the Indians of the United States*, 47, 87, 96, 118, 297, 304–5, 317, and 320.

26. For descriptions of examples of the taking of Indian lands by fraud, see Debo, *A History of the Indians of the United States*, 89, 106, 118, 207, 261, 320–21, and 379.

27. For descriptions of examples of the taking of Indian lands by misunderstanding, deliberate or otherwise, see Debo, *A History of the Indians of the United States*, 76, 190–91.

28. Joel Feinberg argues that there is a kind of collective responsibility, namely vicarious responsibility, which derives from the process of authorization. See Joel Feinberg, *Doing and Deserving* (Princeton, N.J.: Princeton University Press, 1970), 226. Thus when former U.S. president Andrew Jackson, duly elected by the U.S. citizenry, commands the U.S. Army to conduct the policy of "Indian removal" even by violent force, vicarious responsibility accrues to the United States and its citizens. Presumably, such responsibility, insofar as it entails culpability, would accrue at least until adequate reparations are made to the various Indian nations that were victimized by the said policy and others akin to it.

29. See note 2 for a select list of sources on U.S.-Indian history and a more in-depth account of the same.

30. My account consists of a condensing and synthesis of various sources consulted in note 2, including the PBS documentary, *500 Nations* (1995).

31. This Indian population range is found in William C. Bradford, "Beyond Reparations," *Human Rights Review* 6 (2005): 7.

32. The Spanish were notorious for enslaving Indians who were left after Spanish attacks on villages and after they appropriated the Indian lands. But this does not detail the levels of Spanish cruelty toward Indians. In 1539, DeSoto and his army invaded the Florida coast and killed their way here and there among Indian peoples. They plundered villages one by one and many Indians were enslaved. Several Indian women were raped. The few who revolted against the Spanish army were defeated and most of the few Indians who survived were enslaved. Indian towns were burned and looted by Spanish soldiers, often killing up to thousands of Indians in a single Indian town (such as the Mobile Indians where 11,000 Indians were killed in 1540). Eventually, Desoto died in 1542 and his military was forced out of the Gulf of Mexico by Nachi Indians with whom they had fought and attempted to conquer for some years.

But one of the weapons used against the Indians was European germ warfare wherein several entire towns and nations of Indians were decimated by smallpox and other European diseases administered to Indians often intentionally. Just one example of this was in 1560 and the Cusa nation in Moundville, Alabama, were there were very few Indians left because of disease left by DeSoto's army years earlier. Indians knew no such diseases until whites came. So it killed thousands very quickly. It took only twenty years to take down several Indian nations in this manner.

33. These points are argued in J. Angelo Corlett, *Terrorism: A Philosophical Analysis*, Philosophical Studies Series 101 (Dordrecht, Netherlands: Kluwer, 2003), chap. 4.

34. The Great Law and Grand Council of this Indian confederacy were able to rebuild as a sovereign confederacy for some time even until today when they travel the world with their own passports.

35. Bradford, "Beyond Reparations," 8.

36. Bradford, "Beyond Reparations," 11.

37. Bradford, "Beyond Reparations," 11.

38. Bradford, "Beyond Reparations," 13.

39. Robert Berkhofer, Jr., *Salvation and the Savage* (New York: Atheneum, 1976).

40. See Sydney Ahlstrom, *A Religious History of the American People*, 2 vols. (New York: Image Books, 1975); Catherine C. Cleveland, *The Great Revival in the West* (Gloucestor, Mass.: Peter Smith, 1959).

41. How quickly a president and Congress can act when white greed is at stake!

42. Perhaps their being killed was an improvement over the slavery that awaited so many Indians captured by the U.S. military in previous times and places.

43. This author is not aware of any punishment of Chivington and his men subsequent to Lincoln and other U.S. leaders hearing of these facts.

44. For an examination of whites' attitudes of Indians, see Robert Berkhofer, Jr., *White Man's Indian* (New York: Alfred A. Knopf, 1978).

45. Bradford, "Beyond Reparations," 7.

46. H. Wayne Morgan, *America's Road to Empire* (New York: Wiley, 1965).

47. Such arguments are examined and found unwarranted in Roberts, "The Morality of a Moral Statute of Limitations on Injustice."

48. For discussions of corporate responsibility, see J. Angelo Corlett, *Responsibility and Punishment*, 3rd ed., Library of Ethics and Applied Philosophy 9 (Dordrecht, Netherlands: Springer, 2006), chap. 8.

49. For a distinction between weak and strong forms of compensation, see Bigelow, Pargetter, and Young, "Land, Well-Being, and Compensation," 336–37.

Bigelow, Pargetter, and Young argue for compensation in a strong sense as a reply to the objection to collective responsibility.

50. John Locke, *The Second Treatise of Government* (Indianapolis: Bobbs-Merrill, 1952), secs. 14, 28, 30, 34, 36, 37, 41–43, 48–49, 108–9. For a helpful assessment of Locke's views on the political status of Indians, see Tully, "Aboriginal Property and Western Theory," 158ff.

51. Corlett, *Race, Racism, and Reparations,* chap. 8.

52. J. Waldron, *Nonsense Upon Stilts* (London: Methuen, 1987), 44.

53. For a sample of some of the leading contemporary thinking about the nature, value, and function of rights, see Joel Feinberg, *Social Philosophy* (Englewood Cliffs, N.J.: Prentice-Hall, 1973); Joel Feinberg, *Freedom and Fulfillment* (Princeton, N.J.: Princeton University Press, 1992), chaps. 8–10; Will Kymlicka, ed., *The Rights of Minority Cultures* (Oxford: Oxford University Press, 1995); Loren Lomasky, *Persons, Rights, and the Moral Community* (Oxford; Oxford University Press, 1987); L. W. Sumner, *The Moral Foundations of Rights* (Oxford: Oxford University Press, 1987); Judith J. Thomson, *The Realm of Rights* (Cambridge, Mass.: Harvard University Press, 1990); Carl Wellman, *A Theory of Rights* (Totowa, N.J.: Rowman and Allenheld, 1985); Carl Wellman, *The Proliferation of Rights* (Boulder, Colo.: Westview, 1999).

54. From "The Cattle Thief" in E. Pauline Johnson, *Flint and Feather* (Ontario: PaperJacks, 1972), 13–14. Emphasis provided on the use of "our" and "ours."

55. From "A Cry from an Indian Wife," in Johnson, *Flint and Feather,* 15–17. Emphasis provided.

56. Quoted in J. Angelo Corlett, "Moral Compatibilism" (Ph.D. diss., Department of Philosophy, University of Arizona, 1992), 224, emphasis provided.

57. Debo, *A History of the Indians of the United States,* 86.

58. Debo, *A History of the Indians of the United States,* 124.

59. Debo, *A History of the Indians of the United States,* 171.

60. Debo, *A History of the Indians of the United States,* 181.

61. Debo, *A History of the Indians of the United States,* 219.

62. Debo, *A History of the Indians of the United States,* 220.

63. Debo, *A History of the Indians of the United States,* 302.

64. Tully, "Aboriginal Property and Western Theory," 169–79.

65. Alfred Brophy, *Reparations* (Oxford: Oxford University Press), 30.

66. Eric Yamamoto, "Race Theory and Political Lawyering in Post–Civil Rights America," *Michigan Law Review* 95 (1997): 821.

67. Debo, *A History of the Indians of the United States.*

68. In chapter 9, an estimate shall be devised for reparations to Indian nations in and by the United States.

69. This argument is set forth and defended in Lyons, "The New Indian Claims and Original Rights to Land," 252ff.

70. See Locke, *The Second Treatise of Government.* For a helpful discussion of Locke's positions on rights and other political concepts, see A. John Simmons, *The Lockean Theory of Rights* (Princeton, N.J.: Princeton University Press, 1992), and A. John Simmons, *The Edge of Anarchy* (Princeton, N.J.: Princeton University Press, 1993). Locke's line of reasoning has been plausibly refuted in Robert Nozick, "Distributive Justice," *Philosophy and Public Affairs* 3 (1973): 70ff. See also Jeremy Waldron, *The Right to Private Property* (Oxford: Oxford University Press, 1988), chaps. 6–7; "Two Worries about Mixing One's Labor," *The Philosophical Quarterly* 33 (1983): 37–44.

71. Lyons, "The New Indian Claims and Original Rights to Land," 254ff. Lyons argues, astonishingly, that the genuinely compensable wrongs against Indians by the U.S. government might be more recent acts of discrimination against them, rather than the historic injustices of murders and illegitimate takings of their lands (Lyons, "The New Indian Claims and Original Rights to Land," 268–71).

72. Feinberg, *Doing and Deserving*, 248ff. Or as noted in the previous chapter, as Howard McGary argues, there are instances of collective liability absent guilt among the members of the collective.

73. Peter Cane, *Responsibility in Law and Morality* (Oxford: Hart, 2002), 1.

74. Jeremy Waldron, "Superseding Historic Injustice," *Ethics* 103 (1992): 17.

75. Christine M. Korsgaard, "Taking the Law into Our Own Hands: Kant on the Right to Revolution," in *Reclaiming the History of Ethics*, ed. Andrews Reath, Barbara Herman, and Christine M. Korsgaard (Cambridge: Cambridge University Press, 1997), 307.

76. That inheritance is justly and fairly delimited by principles of justice is argued in John Rawls, *A Theory of Justice* (Cambridge, Mass.: Harvard University Press, 1971), 277ff., and *Collected Papers*, ed. Samuel Freeman (Cambridge, Mass.: Harvard University Press, 1999), 142ff.

77. A similar point is found in Waldron, "Superseding Historic Injustice," 15.

78. As noted above, U.S. law recognizes no statute of limitations in cases of murder. Thus neither the moral statute of limitations objection to reparations to Indians (rejected earlier) nor the *Laches* doctrine in U.S. law count against reparations to Indians in instances where murders of Indians were perpetrated by the U.S. government and representatives of its agencies in the fulfilling of their duties as official representatives of the U.S. government.

79. See Locke, *Second Treatise on Government*, sec. 27; Nozick, *Anarchy, State and Utopia*, 175–82; Simmons, *The Lockean Theory of Rights*, 278ff.

80. Furthermore, it has been argued that it is reasonable to hold that the Iroquois indeed acquired rights to some North American lands, and on a Lockean basis! See John D. Bishop, "Locke's Theory of Original Appropriation and the Right of Settlement in Iroquois Territory," *Canadian Journal of Philosophy* 27 (1997): 311–38. See also Naomi Zack, "Lockean Money, Indigenism, and Globalism," *Canadian Journal of Philosophy*, Suppl. no. 25 (1999): 32ff.

81. See Thompson, "Historical Obligations," 320–21.

82. This is not to deny that certain corporate or other business parties played roles in the American holocaust of Indians. The development of railroads, telegraph and certain other industries did play such roles.

83. George Sher, *Approximate Justice* (Lanham, Md.: Rowman and Littlefield, 1997), 15.

84. A number of other objections to reparations for historic injustices to groups such as Indians and blacks are considered and rebutted in Corlett, *Race, Racism, and Reparations*, chaps. 8–9, including those proffered by J. Waldron. Since they have been disposed of therein, they shall not be given attention here.

85. For an account of collective feelings of guilt, see Margaret Gilbert, "Group Wrongs and Guilt Feelings," *The Journal of Ethics* 1 (1997): 65–84. For a more recent account of the concept of collective guilt, see Margaret Gilbert, *Sociality and Responsibility* (Lanham, Md.: Rowman and Littlefield, 2000), chap. 8.

86. For an account of collective remorse, see Margaret Gilbert, "Collective Remorse," in *War Crimes and Collective Wrongdoing*, ed. Aleksandar Jokic (Malden, Mass.: Blackwell, 2001); Gilbert, *Sociality and Responsibility*, chap. 7.

87. Gabrielle Taylor, *Pride, Shame, and Guilt* (Oxford: Oxford University Press, 1985), 67.

CHAPTER 7

1. By "blacks," I mean those of African descent whose ancestors were enslaved in the United States, though for purposes beyond the scope of this project an extended use of the category might include, among others, all such persons whose African ancestors were enslaved throughout the Americas: North, Central, and South.

2. Robert Berkhofer, Jr., *Salvation and the Savage* (New York: Atheneum, 1965).

3. For a more in-depth comparison between and contrast of the Indian and black experiences in the United States, see J. Angelo Corlett, *Race, Racism, and Reparations* (Ithaca, N.Y.: Cornell University Press, 2003), chap. 5. James P. Sterba, "Understanding Evil," *Ethics* 106 (1996): 424–48.

4. This is not to suggest that Indians and blacks are the only groups worthy of consideration for reparations from the U.S. government. Rather, it is to suggest that a fair-minded reading of U.S. history seems to place these two groups in a category apart from all others relative to evils experienced by the U.S. government.

5. Corlett, *Race, Racism, and Reparations*, chap. 5.

6. A select list of some of the numerous works on the oppression of African slaves and blacks in the United States includes: Mortimer Adler, ed., *The Negro in American History*, 3 vols. (Encyclopedia Britannica Educational Corporation, 1969); Ira Berlin, Marc Favreau, and Steven F. Miller, eds., *Remembering Slavery* (New York: New Press, 1998); Alfred L. Brophy, *Reparations* (Oxford: Oxford University Press, 2006), chap. 2; Clayborne Carson, consultant, *Civil Rights Chronicle* (Lincolnwood, Ill.: Legacy, 2003); Stanley M. Elkins, *Slavery* (Chicago: University of Chicago Press, 1968); Leslie H. Fishel, Jr., and Benjamin Quarles, eds., *The Black American* (Glenview, Ill.: Scott Foresman, 1970); John Hope Franklin, *From Slavery to Freedom*, 3rd ed. (New York: Knopf, 1967); *Reconstruction* (Chicago: University of Chicago Press, 1961); Leon F. Litwack, *North of Slavery* (Chicago: University of Chicago Press, 1961); Oscar Handlin, *Race and Nationality in American Life* (Garden City, N.Y.: Doubleday Anchor, 1957); Hugh Hawkins, ed., *The Abolitionists*, 2nd ed. (London: D. C. Heath, 1972); Thomas Holt, *Black Over White* (Urbana: University of Illinois Press, 1977); *The Problem of Race in the 21st Century* (Cambridge, Mass.: Harvard University Press, 2000); Harriet A. Jacobs, *Incidents in the Life of a Slave Girl*, ed. J. F. Yellin (Cambridge, Mass.: Harvard University Press, 2000); Winthrop D. Jordan, *White Over Black* (Baltimore: Penguin, 1968); Martin Luther King, Jr., *Stride Toward Freedom* (New York: Ballantine, 1958); August Meier and Elliot M. Rudwick, eds., *From Plantation to Ghetto* (New York: Hill and Wang, 1966); *The Making of Black America* (New York: Atheneum, 1969); Gerald W. Mullin, *Flight and Rebellion* (Oxford: Oxford University Press, 1972); William H. Pleas and Jane H. Pleas, eds., *The Antislavery Argument* (Indianapolis: Bobbs-Merrill, 1965); Allan Peskin, ed., *North into Freedom* (Kent, Ohio: Kent State University Press, 1988); Alphonso Pinkney, *Black Americans* (Englewood Cliffs, N.J.: Prentice-Hall, 1969); Benjamin Quarles, *Black*

Abolitionists (Oxford: Oxford University Press, 1969); Benjamin Quarles, *The Negro in the Making of America* (New York: Collier Books, 1964); Saunders Redding, *On Being Negro in America* (New York: Bantam, 1951); Richard C. Wade, *Slavery in the Cities* (Oxford: Oxford University Press, 1964); Booker T. Washington, *Up from Slavery* (Garden City, N.Y.: Doubleday Page, 1924); C. Vann Woodward, *The Strange Career of Jim Crow*, 2nd rev. ed. (Oxford: Oxford University Press, 1966).

7. Bruce Perry, ed., *Malcolm X: The Last Speeches* (New York: Pathfinder, 1989), 50–51.

8. For additional descriptions of black oppression in the United States, see Howard McGary and Bill E. Lawson, *Between Slavery and Freedom* (Bloomington: Indiana University Press, 1992), chap. 1; Randall Robinson, *The Debt* (New York: Dutton, 2000).

9. Both quotations are found in Robinson, *The Debt*, 216.

10. Joel Feinberg, *Harm to Others* (Oxford: Oxford University Press, 1984).

11. These acts amount to a series of intentional actions that were crimes, torts, and/or contract violations.

12. Several objections to reparations not covered here are discussed in Corlett, *Race, Racism, and Reparations*, chap. 9.

13. Not that they are each well-off given some objective measurement, but in comparison to how badly off or worse-off each would be had each not benefited from African slavery in particular.

14. Those familiar with Karl Marx's criticism of capitalism recognize this point as derivative of his claim that capitalism illicitly extracts labor value from forced labor power of workers. For discussion of Marx's critique of capitalism in that it forces workers to sell their labor power, see G. A. Cohen, *History, Labour, and Freedom* (Oxford: Oxford University Press, 1988), part 3.

15. Robert Fullinwider, "The Case for Reparations," *Institute for Philosophy and Public Policy* 20 (2000): 1-11.

16. Brophy, *Reparations*, 20.

17. Brophy, *Reparations*, 20. There is also the case of Bridget "Biddy" Mason, who was awarded her freedom and that of her daughters by Judge Benjamin Hayes in Los Angeles, California in 1856.

18. Brophy, *Reparations*, 23.

19. Brophy, *Reparations*, 24–25. Contrast this account to the historically dubious one claimed by Thomas Pogge in part 1, above.

20. In 1998, U.S. president William Clinton *apologized* to the descendants of slaves, and in 2003 George W. Bush offered the same. Neither act of apologizing was accompanied by compensatory reparations, causing some to doubt their veracity. In fact, given the analysis of the nature and function of an apology in chapter 8, neither one of these acts counts as a genuine apology.

21. Bernard Boxill, "The Morality of Reparations," *Social Theory and Practice* 2 (1972): 117.

22. Howard McGary, "Justice and Reparations," *The Philosophical Forum* 9 (1977–1978): 253. Also see Howard McGary, *Race and Social Justice* (London: Blackwell, 1999), 96.

23. Akhil Reed Amar, *The Bill of Rights* (New Haven, Conn.: Yale University Press, 1998), 160.

24. Derrick Bell, *And We Are Not Saved* (New York: Basic Books, 1987), part 1. For a historical argument for the claim that the United States intentionally and collectively oppressed blacks during slavery and Jim Crow, see David Lyons, "Racial Injustices in the U.S. and Their Legacy," in *Redress for Historical Injustices in the United States*, ed. Michael T. Martin and Marilyn Yaquinto (Durham, N.C.: Duke University Press, 2007), 33–54. Lyons also notes how "hypersegregationism" in the U.S. real estate industry created black ghettos and largely helps to sustain them to this day (46–48). Also see David Lyons, "Corrective Justice, Equal Opportunity, and the Legacy of Slavery and Jim Crow," *Boston University Law Review* 84 (2004): 1375–1404.

25. For a discussion of how the federal courts decided such cases, see Robert Cover, *Justice Accused* (New Haven, Conn.: Yale University Press, 1975); Ronald Dworkin, "Review of Robert Cover, *Justice Accused*," *Times Literary Supplement*, December 5, 1975.

26. Amar, *The Bill of Rights*, 278–79.

27. For discussions of bad Samaritanism, see Joel Feinberg, *Freedom and Fulfillment* (Princeton, N.J.: Princeton University Press, 1992), 175–96, and John Kleinig, "Good Samaritanism," in *Philosophy of Law*, 5th ed., ed. Joel Feinberg and Hyman Gross (Belmont, Calif.: Wadsworth, 1995), 529–32.

28. Lyons, "Corrective Justice, Equal Opportunity, and the Legacy of Slavery and Jim Crow," 1386.

29. Lyons, "Corrective Justice, Equal Opportunity, and the Legacy of Slavery and Jim Crow," 1387.

30. Charles J. Ogletree, Jr., "The Current Reparations Debate," *U.C. Davis Law Review* 36 (2003): 1060.

31. Corlett, *Race, Racism, and Reparations*, chaps. 8–9.

32. I assume that the U.S. Constitution contains valid legal rules and principles some of which are morally valid, and that the U.S. Declaration of Independence contains valid legal and moral principles, though it fails to carry the legal authority of the U.S. Constitution. Nonetheless, my appeal to some of the content of the Declaration of Independence is one that makes use of the moral authority it may have for those who consider themselves "good American citizens."

33. Joseph Raz, *Between Authority and Interpretation* (Oxford: Oxford University Press, 2009), 370.

34. Less relevant to the matter of collective governmental identity but significant to the issue of U.S. societal identity, the familial lineages of many of the folk who lived during the eras of U.S. racist oppression against Indians and African slaves are the forebears of many current U.S. citizens. Equally important, some of the corporate institutions that profited from such evils exist today.

35. Ronald Dworkin, *Taking Rights Seriously* (Cambridge, Mass.: Harvard University Press, 1977), and Ronald Dworkin "Review of Cover, *Justice Accused*," *Times Literary Supplement*, December 5, 1975; Robert Cover, *Justice Accused* (New Haven, Conn.: Yale University Press, 1975). For other discussions of legal interpretation, see J. Angelo Corlett, "Dworkin's *Empire* Strikes Back!" *Statute Law Review* 21 (2000): 43–56; J. Angelo Corlett, *Race, Rights, and Justice*, Law and Philosophy Library 85 (Dordrecht, Netherlands: Springer, 2009), chaps. 1–2; Joel Feinberg, *Problems at the Roots of Law* (Oxford: Oxford University Press, 2003), chap. 1; *The Journal of Ethics* 5, no. 3 (2001).

36. Bernard Boxill, "A Lockean Argument for Black Reparations," *The Journal of Ethics* 7 (2003):69.

37. For a fuller description of the details of the DeWolf family's slave trading legacy and its support system, see Thomas Norman DeWolf, *Inheriting the Trade* (Boston: Beacon, 2008).

38. Boxill, "A Lockean Argument for Black Reparations," 71.

39. The core of the reparations argument seems to lie in the "principle of morally just acquisitions and transfers," which I modified from a well-known principle of justice in holdings in Robert Nozick's *Anarchy, State, and Utopia* (New York: Basic Books, 1974), 150ff.: Whatever is acquired or transferred by morally just means is itself morally just; whatever is acquired or transferred by morally unjust means is itself morally unjust. This principle is meant to capture the essential gist of Nozick's "principle of acquisition of holdings," "principle of transfer of holdings," and "principle of rectification of violations of the first two principles." It draws a great deal of its moral inspiration from Socrates' words: "Doing what is unjust is the second worst thing. Not paying what's due when one has done what's unjust is by its nature the first worst thing, the very worst of all" (Plato, *Gorgias*, 479d7–9, trans. Donald J. Zeyl, text by E. R. Dodds [1959], in *Plato: Complete Works*, ed. John M. Cooper and D. L. Hutchinson [Indianapolis: Hackett Publishing Company, 1997], 824).

40. For discussions of why reparations to blacks have yet to be paid by the United States, see Rodney C. Roberts, "Why Have the Injustices Perpetrated against Blacks in America Not Been Rectified?" *Journal of Social Philosophy* 32 (2001): 357–73; Laurence Thomas, "Morality, Consistency, and the Self: A Lesson From Rectification," *Journal of Social Philosophy* 32 (2001): 374–81; Bernard Boxill, "Power and Persuasion," *Journal of Social Philosophy* 32 (2001): 382–85; Rodney C. Roberts, "Toward a Moral Psychology of Rectification: A Reply to Thomas and Boxill," *Journal of Social Philosophy* 33 (2002): 339–43.

41. Boxill, "A Lockean Argument for Black Reparations," 71.

42. Boxill, "A Lockean Argument for Black Reparations," 76, 78.

43. See J. Angelo Corlett, *Terrorism*, Philosophical Studies Series 101 (Dordrecht, Netherlands: Kluwer, 2003), chaps. 5–7.

44. For a philosophical analysis of the nature of an apology, see chapter 8.

45. I borrow this point from Boxill.

CHAPTER 8

1. Cited in Phil Cousineau, ed., *A Seat at the Table* (Berkeley: University of California Press, 2006), 2.

2. Cited in Cousineau, *A Seat at the Table*, 55. This statement concurs with the claim of Charlotte Black Elk that respect for law requires reparations: "In the United States that means returning stolen lands to the native people" (72).

3. Cited in Cousineau, *A Seat at the Table*, 82.

4. Charles Griswold, *Forgiveness* (Cambridge: Cambridge University Press, 2007), 49–51.

5. Griswold, *Forgiveness*, 56.

6. Griswold, *Forgiveness*, 58.

7. Griswold, *Forgiveness*, 61–62.

8. Griswold, *Forgiveness*, 39.

9. Griswold, *Forgiveness*, 69–72.

10. Griswold, *Forgiveness*, 69.

11. J. Angelo Corlett, *Race, Racism, and Reparations* (Ithaca, N.Y.: Cornell University Press, 2003), chaps. 8–9.

12. J. Angelo Corlett, *Responsibility and Punishment*, 3rd ed. (Dordrecht, Netherlands: Springer, 2006), chap. 5.

13. J. Angelo Corlett, "Forgiveness, Apology, and Retributive Punishment," *American Philosophical Quarterly* 42 (2006): 33.

14. This section is taken from Corlett, "Forgiveness, Apology, and Retributive Punishment."

15. See, for instance, Zoltan Balazs, "Forgiveness and Repentance," *Public Affairs Quarterly* 14 (2000): 105–27; Joseph Beatty, "Forgiveness," *American Philosophical Quarterly* 7 (1970): 246–52; Piers Benn, "Forgiveness and Loyalty," *Philosophy* 71 (1996): 369–83; Cheshire Calhoun, "Changing One's Heart," *Ethics* 103 (1992): 76–96; Richard S. Downie, "Forgiveness," *The Philosophical Quarterly* 15 (1965): 128–34; A. C. Ewing, *The Morality of Punishment* (Montclair, N.J.: Patterson-Smith, 1970); Joel Feinberg, *Doing and Deserving* (Princeton, N.J.: Princeton University Press, 1970); Eve Garrard and David McNaughton, "In Defense of Unconditional Forgiveness," *Proceedings of the Aristotelian Society* 103 (2002): 39–60; Kathleen A. Gill, "The Moral Functions of an Apology," *The Philosophical Forum* 31 (2000): 11–27; Trudy Govier, *Forgiveness and Revenge* (London: Routledge, 2002); "Forgiveness and the Unforgivable," *American Philosophical Quarterly* 36 (1999): 59–75; Trudy Govier and Wilhelm Verwoerd, "The Promise and Pitfalls of Apology," *Journal of Social Philosophy* 33 (2002): 67–82; Joram Graf Haber, *Forgiveness* (Savage, Md.: Rowman and Littlefield, 1991); Pamela Hieronmi, "Articulating an Uncompromising Forgiveness," *Philosophy and Phenomenological Research* 62 (2001): 529–55; Margaret Holmgren, "Forgiveness and the Intrinsic Value of Persons," *American Philosophical Quarterly* 30 (1993): 341–52; "Self-Forgiveness and Responsible Moral Agency," *Journal of Value Inquiry* 32 (1998): 75–91; H. J. N. Horsbrugh, "Forgiveness," *Canadian Journal of Philosophy* 4 (1974): 269–82; Martin Hughes, "Forgiveness," *Analysis* 35 (1975), 113–17; Paul M. Hughes, "On Forgiving Oneself," *The Journal of Value Inquiry* 28 (1994): 557–60; Paul M. Hughes, "What Is Involved in Forgiving?" *Philosophia* (Israel) 25 (1997): 33–49; Aurel Kolnai, "Forgiveness," *Proceedings of the Aristotelian Society* 74 (1973–1974): 91–106; Berel Lang, "Forgiveness," *American Philosophical Quarterly* 30 (1994): 105–17; Howard McGary, "Achieving Democratic Equality," *The Journal of Ethics* 7 (2003): 93–113; Kathleen D. Moore, *Pardons* (Oxford: Oxford University Press, 1989); Herbert Morris, "Murphy on Forgiveness," *Criminal Justice Ethics* 7 (1988): 15–19; Jeffrie G. Murphy, "Forgiveness and Resentment," *Midwest Studies in Philosophy* 7 (1982): 503–16; Jeffrie G. Murphy, *Getting Even* (Oxford: Oxford University Press, 2003); Jeffrie G. Murphy, "A Rejoinder to Morris," *Criminal Justice Ethics* 7 (1988): 20–22; Jeffrie G. Murphy and Jean Hampton, *Forgiveness and Mercy* (Cambridge: Cambridge University Press, 1988); William R. Neblett, "Forgiveness and Ideals," *Mind* 83 (1974): 269–75; Joanna North, "The 'Ideal' of Forgiveness," in *Exploring Forgiveness*, ed. Robert D. Enright and Joanna North (Madison: University of Wisconsin Press, 1998), 15–34; "Wrongdoing and Forgiveness," *Philosophy* 62 (1987): 499–508; David Novitz, "Forgiveness and Self-Respect," *Philosophy and Phenomenological Research* 58 (1998): 299–315; R. J. O'Shaughnessy, "Forgiveness," *Philosophy* 42 (1967): 336–52; Norvin Richards, "Forgiveness,"

Ethics 99 (1988): 77–97; Robert Roberts, "Forgivingness," *American Philosophical Quarterly* 32 (1995): 289–306; Geoffrey Scarre, *After Evil* (Burlington, Vt.: Ashgate, 2004); Tara Smith, "Tolerance and Forgiveness" *Journal of Applied Philosophy* 1 (1997): 31–42; Nancy Snow, "Self-Forgiveness," *The Journal of Value Inquiry* 28 (1994): 75–80; I. Thalberg, "Remorse," *Mind* 72 (1963): 545–55; P. Twambley, "Mercy and Forgiveness," *Analysis* 36 (1976): 84–90; Nigel Walker, "The Quiddity of Mercy," *Philosophy* 70 (1995): 27–37; John Wilson, "Why Forgiveness Requires Repentance," *Philosophy* 63 (1988): 534–35; and Keith E. Yandell, "The Metaphysics and Morality of Forgiveness," in *Exploring Forgiveness*, ed. Robert D. Enright and Joanna North (Madison: University of Wisconsin Press, 1998), 35–45. Also see notes 12–13, above.

16. Corlett, *Responsibility and Punishment*, 66–68.

17. Murphy and Hampton, *Forgiveness and Mercy*, 159.

18. Murphy and Hampton, *Forgiveness and Mercy*, 158.

19. See note 11.

20. Peter Strawson, "Freedom and Resentment," in *Perspectives on Moral Responsibility*, ed. John Martin Fischer and Mark Ravizza (Ithaca, N.Y.: Cornell University Press, 1993), 45–66.

21. This definition is consistent with the construal of forgiveness found in Ewing, *The Morality of Punishment*, 31; Moore, *Pardons*, 184.

22. Feinberg, *Doing and Deserving*, 70–71.

23. Murphy and Hampton, *Forgiveness and Mercy*, 15, 24.

24. For an analysis of the concept of harm, see Joel Feinberg, *Harm to Others* (Oxford: Oxford University Press, 1984). For an analysis of the concept of harmful wrongdoing, see Joel Feinberg, *Harmful Wrongdoing* (Oxford: Oxford University Press, 1990).

25. Murphy and Hampton, *Forgiveness and Mercy*, 33. Also see North, "The 'Ideal' of Forgiveness," 17.

26. Haber, *Forgiveness*, 11.

27. Downie, "Forgiveness," 128.

28. Kolnai, "Forgiveness," 92.

29. North, "Wrongdoing and Forgiveness," 505.

30. North, "Wrongdoing and Forgiveness," 506.

31. Downie, "Forgiveness," 130.

32. Scarre, *After Evil*, 17.

33. Garrard and McNaughton, "In Defense of Unconditional Forgiveness."

34. Scarre, *After Evil*, 17.

35. Govier, *Forgiveness and Revenge*, 77.

36. Murphy and Hampton, *Forgiveness and Mercy*, 24.

37. Murphy, *Getting Even*, 35. However, Murphy does state that "it is not unreasonable to make forgiveness contingent on sincere repentance" (36, 39).

38. Murphy and Hampton, *Forgiveness and Mercy*, 42.

39. Murphy and Hampton, *Forgiveness and Mercy*, 42–43.

40. Murphy and Hampton, *Forgiveness and Mercy*, 52–53.

41. Corlett, *Responsibility and Punishment*, chaps. 1 and 7.

42. Murphy and Hampton, *Forgiveness and Mercy*, 55. Hampton provides a more precise account of the nature of resentment (Murphy and Hampton, *Forgiveness and Mercy*, 57). She even distinguishes, rather incisively, between resentment and malicious hatred (Murphy and Hampton, *Forgiveness and Mercy*, 70–71).

43. Roberts, "Forgivingness," 299.
44. Downie, "Forgiveness"; North, "Wrongdoing and Forgiveness."
45. Kolnai, "Forgiveness," 98.
46. Horsbrugh, "Forgiveness," 272.
47. Balazs, "Forgiveness," 118ff.
48. Govier and Verwoerd, "The Promise and Pitfalls of Apology," 67.
49. Murphy and Hampton, *Forgiveness and Mercy*, 83–84.
50. Murphy and Hampton, *Forgiveness and Mercy*, 151.
51. Murphy and Hampton, *Forgiveness and Mercy*, 148.
52. Murphy and Hampton, *Forgiveness and Mercy*, 150–52.
53. Murphy and Hampton, *Forgiveness and Mercy*, 158.
54. Robert Nozick, *Philosophical Explanations* (Cambridge, Mass.: Harvard University press, 1981), 366–68.
55. Joel Feinberg, "What, If Anything, Justifies Legal Punishment?" in *Philosophy of Law*, 5th ed., ed. Joel Feinberg and Hyman Gross (Belmont, Calif.: Wadsworth, 1995), 613–17.
56. Murphy and Hampton, *Forgiveness and Mercy*, 119.
57. Neblett, "Forgiveness and Ideals," 269.
58. A similar but independently arrived at point can be found in Scarre, *After Evil*, 83: "There is an important distinction to be drawn between forgiveness as an act and as the state brought about by that act."
59. It is possible for forgiveness to obtain without any words being spoken or written.
60. O'Shaughnessy, "Forgiveness," 350.
61. This distinction is violated in Nick Smith, "The Categorical Apology," *Journal of Social Philosophy* 36 (2005): 473–96, though the author does in general agree that a categorical apology requires "reform and reparations" (485–89). Also missing from the author's account is the notion of a victim's right(s) being violated. See also Nick Smith, *I Was Wrong* (Cambridge: Cambridge University Press, 2008), chap. 1.
62. A similar point is made in Balazs, "Forgiveness," 120, except that Balazs argues that "inasmuch as repentance is a moral duty, forgiveness is one, too" (Balazs, "Forgiveness," 126). I proffer a different notion of forgiveness, as we shall see. Rather than being a moral duty, forgiveness is morally supererogatory. However, that forgiveness requires apology (e.g., repentance) is found in Wilson, "Why Forgiveness Requires Repentance," 534: "Genuine forgiveness does require repentance on the part of the wrongdoer, and must be . . . a bilateral and not just a unilateral operation." Failure of the wrongdoer to apologize, Wilson and I concur, serves as an obstacle to that wrong-doer experiencing true forgiveness. This does not prevent, I would add, her victim from forgiving her for whatever reasons. Those who deny that forgiveness requires an apology include Benn, "Forgiveness and Loyalty," 382.
63. Martha Minow, *Between Vengeance and Forgiveness* (Boston: Beacon, 1998), 114.
64. These conditions of a genuine apology are first found in J. Angelo Corlett, *Responsibility and Punishment*, Library of Ethics and Applied Philosophy 9 (Dordrecht, Netherlands: Kluwer, 2001), 84. The rectificatory condition of an apology is also found in Claudia Card, *The Atrocity Paradigm* (Oxford: Oxford University Press, 2002), 198; Nick Smith, "The Categorical Apology," *Journal of Social Philosophy* 36 (2005): 485–89, though neither of these latter two accounts links an apology to forgiveness.

65. Combining part of text and footnote in Charles J. Ogletree, Jr., "The Current Reparations Debate," *U.C. Davis Law Review* 36 (2003): 1063.

66. Minow, *Between Vengeance and Forgiveness*, 112–17. Also see E. Barkan, *The Guilt of Nations* (New York: Norton, 2000), 324, for another example of the idea that compensation of any kind is not necessary for an apology.

67. Minow, *Between Vengeance and Forgiveness*, 115.

68. Minow, *Between Vengeance and Forgiveness*, 112.

69. Minow, *Between Vengeance and Forgiveness*, 106.

70. Aaron Lazare, *On Apology* (Oxford: Oxford University Press, 2004), 107.

71. For a philosophical analysis of the concept of remorse, see I. Thalberg, "Remorse," 545–55.

72. North, "The 'Ideal' of Forgiveness: A Philosopher's Exploration," 30–33.

73. Thalberg, "Remorse," 554.

74. Thalberg, "Remorse," 546.

75. Unless, of course, a purely utilitarian theory of punishment is assumed.

76. See Benn, "Forgiveness and Loyalty," 373. "While the ideal result of forgiveness is reconciliation, it seems plain that the reconciliation of victim and offender cannot, itself, be an essential element in the victim forgiving the offender" (Yandell, "The Metaphysics and Morality of Forgiveness," 44). I might add that it has yet to be demonstrated by independent argument that "the ideal result of forgiveness is reconciliation" of victim and offender.

77. Govier, *Forgiveness and Revenge*, 46–47.

78. Murphy and Hampton, *Forgiveness and Mercy*, 154; Richards, "Forgiveness," 87. That forgiveness is a discretionary right is noted in Hughes, "Forgiveness," 113. Also see Howard McGary and Bill E. Lawson, *Between Slavery and Freedom* (Bloomington: Indiana University Press, 1992), xxv.

79. Richards, "Forgiveness," 80.

80. Card, *The Atrocity Paradigm*, 174.

81. "Necessarily" because it is possible to not forgive one unjustifiably, particularly when the one refusing to forgive knows that her not forgiving her offender (whom the victim knows has offered a genuine apology) will result in harm experienced by the offender that far outweighs the victim's experienced harm from her offender.

82. Murphy and Hampton, *Forgiveness and Mercy*, 16–19.

83. Murphy and Hampton, *Forgiveness and Mercy*, 21.

84. J. D. Mabbott, "Punishment," *Mind* 48 (1939): 158. For a similar view, see Benn, "Forgiveness and Loyalty," 376ff.; Holmgren, "Forgiveness and the Intrinsic Value of Persons," 341. For a denial of this claim based on the assumption of third party forgiveness, see Neblett, "Forgiveness and Ideals," 270.

85. That there are unilateral cases of forgiveness is found in Margaret Urban Walker, *Moral Repair* (Oxford: Oxford University Press, 2006), 171. Again, this idea confuses forgiveness with forgiving.

86. Perhaps attitude forgiveness is what some newly freed slaves in the United States engaged in when they "forgave" their former masters (see McGary and Lawson, *Between Slavery and Freedom*). One likely reason for these instances of forgiving was for the newly freed slaves to be able to get along with others in a society that still largely denied them the full rights of citizenship, as Howard McGary and Bill Lawson so incisively explain.

87. That is, concerning the primary victim(s) of her crime.

88. Benn, "Forgiveness and Loyalty," 383.

89. For a similar view of third party forgiving, see Benn, "Forgiveness and Loyalty," 374–75.

90. Murphy and Hampton, *Forgiveness and Mercy*, 17.

91. Howard McGary, "Achieving Democratic Equality," *The Journal of Ethics* 7 (2003): 103.

92. This point is consistent with McGary's claim that forgiveness is a necessary condition of reconciliation (McGary, "Achieving Democratic Equality," 104–5).

93. Boxill, "A Lockean Argument for Black Reparations," 70–81.

94. At this point of argument, it should be pointed out that the "Scope of Responsibility Principle" states that if I am responsible for the harm caused by my act, omission, or attempt, and a reasonable person could have understood that under the circumstances my act, omission, or attempt could have in turn readily caused another harm to occur, then I am also responsible for the other harm, however indirectly (Corlett, *Responsibility and Punishment*, 17). This implies that the United States is responsible not only for the oppression of millions of Indians and blacks throughout its history, but it is also responsible for the commonsense foreseeable indirect oppression caused to subsequent generations of Indians and blacks (i.e., the victim heirs of oppression) as a result of the initial "rounds" of oppression against these groups by the U.S. government and its citizenry.

CHAPTER 9

1. August Wilson, *Gem of the Ocean* (New York: Theatre Communications Group, 2006), 75.

2. J. Angelo Corlett, *Race, Racism, and Reparations* (Ithaca, N.Y.: Cornell University Press, 2003), chaps. 8–9, as well as chapters 6 and 7, above.

3. As Boris Bittker states: "The case for black reparations, however, need not rest on the theory that damages should be paid for every species of improper official conduct. We are in the realm of legislative discretion" (Boris Bittker, *The Case for Black Reparations* [New York: Random House, 1973], 21). And the same might well be said for U.S. reparations to Indians.

4. As the ICC requests, such matters ought to first be handled by a country's federal (or other suitable) court system before advancing the case to the ICC for due consideration.

5. Bittker, *The Case for Black Reparations*, 27.

6. I borrow the point about general means of diplomacy from James W. Nickel, "Are Human Rights Mainly Implemented by Intervention?" in *Rawls's Law of Peoples*, ed. R. Martin and D. Reidy (London: Blackwell, 2006), 271–72.

7. This phrase is borrowed from E. Barkan, *The Guilt of Nations* (New York: Norton, 2000), 320.

8. This idea is borrowed from Peter A. French, *Collective and Corporate Responsibility* (New York: Columbia University Press, 1984), chap. 14.

9. Alfred Brophy, *Reparations* (Oxford: Oxford University Press, 2006), 32.

10. Brophy, *Reparations*, 49.

11. Brophy, *Reparations*, 179.

12. Each of the following possible policies of reparations is consistent with *each* of the reparations standards found in Tyler Cowan, "Discounting and Restitution," *Philosophy and Public Affairs* 26 (1997): 171–75. Also assumed is a principle of proportional compensation according to which compensation in the form of reparations must be commensurate to the harms inflicted on Indians by the U.S. government and its agencies/institutions.

13. Bittker, *The Case for Black Reparations*, 27.

14. For a discussion of these issues, see Bittker, *The Case for Black Reparations*, chap. 8.

15. J. Angelo Corlett, *Race, Racism, and Reparations* (Ithaca, N.Y.: Cornell University Press, 2003), chap. 2.

16. Bittker, *The Case for Black Reparations*, 103.

17. Bittker, *The Case for Black Reparations*, 103.

18. This concern is raised in Bittker, *The Case for Black Reparations*, 78.

19. Bittker, *The Case for Black Reparations*, 97.

20. Corlett, *Race, Racism, and Reparations*, chap. 1–3.

21. Bittker, *The Case for Black Reparations*, 98.

22. Bittker, *The Case for Black Reparations*, 100.

23. Bittker, *The Case for Black Reparations*, 89.

24. Such views are propounded by Charles J. Ogletree, Jr., "Reparations, a Fundamental Issue of Social Justice," *The Black Collegian*, 2002, 118–22; "Reparations for the Children of Slaves," *University of Memphis Law Review* 33 (2003): 245–64; "Repairing the Past," *Harvard Civil Rights—Civil Liberties Law Review* 38 (2003): 279–320.

25. Bittker, *The Case for Black Reparations*, 86.

26. Jules L. Coleman, "Corrective Justice and Property Rights," in *Injustice and Rectification*, ed. Rodney C. Roberts (New York: Peter Lang, 2002), 53.

27. Coleman, "Corrective Justice and Property Rights," 56. Of course, "this is not to say that every duty of compensation arises from a previous wrongful act—that is, that compensation must always be viewed as reparation" (Phillip Montague, "Rights and Duties of Compensation," in *Injustice and Rectification*, ed. Rodney C. Roberts [New York: Peter Lang, 2002], 80).

28. A similar claim can be found in Gerald F. Gaus, "Does Compensation Restore Equality?" in *Injustice and Rectification*, ed. Rodney C. Roberts (New York: Peter Lang, 2002), 104.

29. Several attorneys can attest to the fact that this is a rather conservative estimate of what a human life is currently worth in a wrongful death case. Some cases of singular wrongful death garner awards of more than twice the amount stipulated in my conservative estimate.

30. Bear in mind that many are raped prior to or during the killing, and several others not killed are raped, or otherwise beaten severely or enslaved.

31. David E. Stannard, *American Holocaust* (Oxford: Oxford University Press, 1992), 267–68; Francis Jennings, *The Founders of America* (New York: Norton, 1993), 395. Of course, some estimates are higher, while others are lower. For those who think that this figure is inflated because England, France, Spain, and some other countries and nations are also co-responsible for such deaths (as my own account indicates in chapter 6), I would point out that many of the "settlers" who became colonists and then founded the United States were guilty of committing genocide against Indians

also. And since the overall figure of Indians killed is far below the mean estimate, it is unreasonable to think that my estimate is inflated, though I am of course open to a thorough historical investigation that could, hopefully, resolve the matter once and for all and with great precision.

32. This issue is raised in Coleman, "Corrective Justice and Wrongful Gain," 421.

33. A restricted version of this policy is proposed in Janna Thompson, "Historical Obligations," *Australasian Journal of Philosophy* 78 (2000): 328.

34. For a detailed argument for the unjustifiedness of the U.S. secession from England, see J. Angelo Corlett, *Terrorism*, Philosophical Studies Series 101 (Dordrecht, Netherlands: Kluwer, 2003), chap. 4.

35. Note that the 5 percent figure currently amounts to only billions of dollars per year for Indians in the United States, which is far below the figure estimated for both the genocide and land theft: $100,090,000,000,000.

36. One recent example is found in Howard McGary, *Race and Social Justice* (London: Blackwell, 1999), 100–104. Another is Bernard Boxill, *Blacks and Social Justice* (Totowa, N.J.: Rowman and Allenheld, 1984), chap. 7.

37. This general line of argument can also be applied to the Indian case for reparations.

38. It is worthy of note that my approach to reparations to blacks evades the concern of Boris Bittker that "to concentrate on slavery is to understate the case for compensation" to blacks (Bittker, *The Case for Black Reparations*, 12). For reparations to blacks by the United States seek compensatory damages not only for the harmful wrongdoings of slavery of Africans, but for the harmful and wrongful treatment of blacks during Reconstruction and Jim Crow.

39. Roy L. Brooks, *Atonement and Forgiveness* (Berkeley: University of California Press, 2004), 156. This distinction is essentially the same as the one between the reconciliation and rectification models of reparations I articulated in the previous chapter.

40. Brooks, *Atonement and Forgiveness*, 141.

41. Brooks, *Atonement and Forgiveness*, 144.

42. Brooks, *Atonement and Forgiveness*, 146.

43. Brooks, *Atonement and Forgiveness*, 147.

44. Brooks, *Atonement and Forgiveness*, 157.

45. Brooks, *Atonement and Forgiveness*, 159.

46. Brooks, *Atonement and Forgiveness*, 161–62.

47. Brooks, *Atonement and Forgiveness*, 163.

48. Corlett, *Race, Racism, and Reparations*, chap. 5.

49. Brooks, *Atonement and Forgiveness*, 169.

50. Brooks, *Atonement and Forgiveness*, 168.

51. George Breitman, ed., *Malcolm X Speaks* (New York: Pathfinder, 1992), 10–12. Also see Malcolm X, *By Any Means Necessary* (New York: Pathfinder, 1970), 183–84.

52. A similar point is found in Robert A. Williams, Jr., "The Algebra of Federal Indian Law," in *Jurisprudence Classical and Contemporary*, 2nd ed., ed. Robert L. Hayman, Jr., Nancy Levit, and Richard Delgado (St. Paul, Minn.: West Group, 2002), 642.

53. Derrick Bell, "Racial Realism," in *Jurisprudence Classical and Contemporary*, 2nd ed., ed. Robert L. Hayman, Jr., Nancy Levit, and Richard Delgado (St. Paul, Minn.: West Group, 2002), 663.

54. Stannard, *American Holocaust*, 317.

55. My program for black reparations differs from that found in Charles J. Ogletree, Jr., "The Current Reparations Debate," *U.C. Davis Law Review* 36 (2003): 1071. While he states rather sketchily that reparations to blacks should focus on "establishing a trust fund to administer money received through claims and an independent commission to distribute those funds to the poorest members of the black community," and while he is correct to note that while harmful wrongdoings have been experienced by the group of blacks, not all blacks have been as badly affected as others, it is still a matter of compensatory right that each black person receive the monetary payments equitably, which means perhaps the poorest blacks in the United States will receive other benefits that wealthier blacks already enjoy due to their wealth. This is a compromise position on the distribution of reparations to blacks (and to Indians also, for that matter). It does not penalize those blacks who through hard work (and some good luck) have become successful despite the incredible odds by discounting or altogether eliminating their compensatory right to reparations based on the facts of harmful wrongdoings to their enslaved forebears. Yet it recognizes that the poorest blacks in the United States may not have experienced the good luck that more successful blacks on average have experienced, and thus award to them free and excellent health care, education, and housing which the wealthier blacks already possess.

Another difference between Ogletree's "Reparations Trust Fund" and my black reparations tax is that his trust fund makes no mention as to who controls it, while the black reparations tax is controlled completely by the committee on black reparations, ensuring blacks a maximal amount of autonomy. In so doing, my reparations plan, unlike Ogletree's, makes it possible for blacks to segregate from whites should they choose to do so and to whatever degree they choose, thereby further respecting black autonomy. Of course, most blacks would likely for a variety of reasons remain integrated with whites. But my plan ensures that it is a voluntary integration, rather than the coerced integration implied in the presumptuous reasoning of utilitarian-based reparations approaches.

56. Brooks, *Atonement and Forgiveness.*

57. I urge court-ordered (ICC) remedies only should the United States continue to refuse to legislate on its own the reparations in question and if a federal court refuses to award them. But even should an ICC order be required, the United States would still need to legislate the reparations taxes required for compensatory justice in these cases as a matter of court-ordered policy of distributing reparations to the committee on Indian reparations and the committee on black reparations.

58. Anthony G. Amsterdam and Jerome Bruner, *Minding the Law* (Cambridge, Mass.: Harvard University Press, 2000), 225.

59. McGary, *Race and Social Justice*, 115. These points are echoed by George Sher, who writes: "There is no reason to believe that the psychological effects of a wrong act are any less long-lived, or any less likely to be transmitted from generation to generation, than their economic counterparts" (George Sher, "Ancient Wrongs and Modern Rights," *Philosophy and Public Affairs* 10 [1981]: 10).

60. W. E. B. Du Bois, *The Souls of Black Folk* (Greenwich, Conn.: Fawcett, 1961), 149.

61. W. E. B. Du Bois, *An ABC of Color* (New York: International Publishers, 1971), 164.

62. Peter Strawson, "Freedom and Resentment," in *Perspectives on Moral Responsibility,* ed. John Martin Fischer and Mark Ravizza (Ithaca, N.Y.: Cornell University Press, 1986), 45–66.

63. John Rawls, *Collected Papers*, ed. Samuel Freeman (Cambridge, Mass.: Harvard University Press, 1999), chap. 5.

64. Joel Feinberg, *Rights, Justice, and the Bounds of Liberty* (Princeton, N.J.: Princeton University Press, 1980), chap. 7.

65. This claim is to be understood with an extremely sarcastic tone.

66. Barkan, *The Guilt of Nations*, 171.

67. Barkan, *The Guilt of Nations*, 191.

68. Barkan, *The Guilt of Nations*, 188.

69. Barkan, *The Guilt of Nations*, 190–201.

70. Feinberg, *Rights, Justice, and the Bounds of Liberty*, 173.

71. Feinberg, *Rights, Justice, and the Bounds of Liberty*, 174.

72. Feinberg, *Rights, Justice, and the Bounds of Liberty*, 174.

73. Feinberg, *Rights, Justice, and the Bounds of Liberty*, 174.

74. Feinberg, *Rights, Justice, and the Bounds of Liberty*, 174.

75. Brophy, *Reparations*, 29. Let us not forget that lynchings of many blacks occurred after this period, such as in the case of James Byrd, Jr., in Jasper, Texas, in 1998.

76. Margaret Urban Walker, *Moral Repair* (Oxford: Oxford University Press, 2006), 225.

77. Feinberg, *Rights, Justice, and the Bounds of Liberty*.

CHAPTER 10

1. George Sher, "Ancient Wrongs and Modern Rights," *Philosophy and Public Affairs* 10 (1981): 13.

2. Sher, "Ancient Wrongs and Modern Rights," 14.

3. This issue is raised in relation to reparations to blacks. See Boris Bittker, "Identifying the Beneficiaries," in *Reverse Discrimination*, ed. Barry R. Gross (New York: Prometheus, 1977), 279ff. A philosophical analysis of the conditions of ethnic group membership is found in J. Angelo Corlett, *Race, Racism, and Reparations* (Ithaca, N.Y.: Cornell University Press, 2003), chaps. 2–3.

4. Quoted in Alcides Arguedas, "The Sick People," in *Nineteenth-Century Nation Building and the Latin American Intellectual Tradition*, trans. and ed. J. Burke and T. Humphrey (Indianapolis: Hackett, 2007), 344.

5. Anthony Appiah, "'But Would That Still Be Me?'" in *Race/Sex*, ed. Naomi Zack (Philadelphia: Temple University Press, 1997), 75–82; Corlett, *Race, Racism, and Reparations*, chaps. 1–3; Jorge Gracia, *Hispanic/Latino Identity* (London: Blackwell, 2000); Jorge Gracia, *Surviving Race, Ethnicity, and Nationality* (Lanham, Md.: Rowman and Littlefield, 2005); Naomi Zack, *Thinking about Race* (Belmont, Calif.: Wadsworth, 2005).

6. Arguedas, "The Sick People," 344.

7. José Martí, "Our America," in *Nineteenth-Century Nation Building and the Latin American Intellectual Tradition*, trans. and ed. J. Burke and T. Humphrey (Indianapolis: Hackett, 2007), 266.

8. Corlett, *Race, Racism, and Reparations*, chap. 1.

9. Appiah, "But Would That Still Be Me?" 75–82; Gracia, *Hispanic/Latino Identity*; Zack, *Thinking about Race*.

10. Corlett, *Race, Racism, and Reparations*, 130. This analysis is quite misunderstood as being nonhistorical in Joshua Glasgow, "On the Methodology of the Race Debate," *Philosophy and Phenomenological Research* 76 (March 2008): 333–58.

11. E. Barkan, *The Guilt of Nations* (New York: Norton, 2000), 174.

12. One must be ever mindful that my normative account of ethnic identity is meant to serve as a corrective to the abuses of the U.S. government to classify Indians: "The federal government had taken the original rolls of the allotment period and insisted that the descendants of those original allottees be considered members of the tribe whether they had sufficient Indian blood to qualify for membership or whether they lived in the communities on the reservation. The internal social mechanisms that ordinarily would have operated to define community membership were forbidden by federal law" (Vine Deloria Jr., *God Is Red* [Golden, Colo.: Fulcrum, 1994], 245).

13. Corlett, *Race, Racism, and Reparations,* 139.

14. Gracia, *Hispanic/Latino Identity;* Gracia *Surviving Race, Ethnicity, and Nationality,* chap. 3.

15. Alvin Goldman, *Knowledge in a Social World* (Oxford: Oxford University Press, 1999), 84.

16. For a philosophical discussion of the nature of Latinohood along these lines, see Jorge Gracia, *Hispanic/Latino Identity* (London: Blackwell, 1999).

17. See Corlett, *Race, Racism, and Reparations,* chap. 1.

18. Gracia, *Surviving Race, Ethnicity, and Nationality,* 40.

19. Gracia, *Surviving Race, Ethnicity, and Nationality,* 40.

20. Admittedly, there is no sure way to set such a standard nonarbitrarily, wherein no one who ought to be a member of the nation or group is excluded or slighted. But there appears to be no better alternative means by which to deal with such matters of group or national identification for purposes of positive public policy administration.

21. One ethical concern is that such testing companies sometimes use DNA results to form the basis of their "gene bases" in ethically problematic ways. For example, some indigenous peoples' DNA tests that were conducted for purposes of testing for diabetes were then used for DNA testing for purposes of forming a genetic database for ethnic ancestry without the permission of those tested for diabetes. Furthermore, a scientific concern about such ancestry testing is that most if not all current means of such testing fail to take into account more than a small fraction of the genetic markers that would adequately identify a person's ancestry.

While these concerns are certainly legitimate and must be dealt with if DNA testing is to serve as an adequate means of ethnic identification, there is no reason to suppose that they cannot be overcome as the science of DNA testing becomes less concerned about business profitability and more concerned about ethical and scientific excellence.

22. Gracia, *Surviving Race, Ethnicity, and Nationality,* 41.

23. Gracia, *Surviving Race, Ethnicity, and Nationality,* 41.

24. Gracia, *Surviving Race, Ethnicity, and Nationality,* 41.

25. Corlett, *Race, Racism, and Reparations,* chap. 1.

26. Gracia, *Surviving Race, Ethnicity, and Nationality,* 41.

27. Subject to the concerns noted in note 21, above.

28. Corlett, *Race, Racism, and Reparations,* chaps. 2–3.

29. Jorge Gracia, "The Nature of Ethnicity with Special Reference to Hispanic/ Latino Identity," *Public Affairs Quarterly* 13 (1999): 25–42.

30. Gracia, *Surviving Race, Ethnicity, and Nationality,* 47.

31. Gracia, *Surviving Race, Ethnicity, and Nationality,* 48.

32. Ludwig Wittgenstein, *Philosophical Investigations,* 3rd ed., trans. G. E. M. Anscombe (New York: Macmillan, 1958), 31ff.

33. The family resemblance idea is also presented and explored in the "Preliminary Studies for the *Philosophical Investigations,*" commonly known as Ludwig Wittgenstein, *The Blue and Brown Books,* 2nd ed. (New York: Harper Torchbooks, 1960), 17.

34. Wittgenstein, *Philosophical Investigations,* 31.

35. Gracia, *Surviving Race, Ethnicity, and Nationality,* 48.

36. Gracia, *Surviving Race, Ethnicity, and Nationality,* 48.

37. Gracia, *Surviving Race, Ethnicity, and Nationality,* 49.

38. Gracia, *Surviving Race, Ethnicity, and Nationality,* 49.

39. Gracia, *Surviving Race, Ethnicity, and Nationality,* 50.

40. Gracia, *Surviving Race, Ethnicity, and Nationality,* 58.

41. Gracia, *Surviving Race, Ethnicity, and Nationality,* 63.

42. See Corlett, *Race, Racism, and Reparations,* chap. 2.

43. Subject to the conditions mentioned in note 21, above.

44. Charles W. Mills, "Reconceptualizing Race and Racism? A Critique of J. Angelo Corlett," *Journal of Social Philosophy* 36 (2005): 546–52.

45. Linda Alcoff, "Latino Oppression," *Journal of Social Philosophy* 36 (2005): 538.

46. As in *Race, Racism, and Reparations,* I refrain from stipulating what that minimal percentage should be, as there seems to be no nonarbitrary way of deciding that question. That appears to be a question of morally informed public policy.

47. Bernard Boxill, *Blacks and Social Justice* (Totowa, N.J.: Rowman and Allenheld, 1984), chap. 7.

48. This view is clearly the one that has been employed throughout the past few decades in which affirmative action has been at work in the United States, and is assumed in such writings as Barbara R. Bergmann, *In Defense of Affirmative Action* (New York: Basic Books, 1996).

49. As one commentator puts it: "Not all oppressive structures are equally harmful, and they should not all be regarded with the same degree of concern" (Sally Haslanger, "Oppressions: Racial and Other," in *Racism in Mind,* ed. Michael P. Levine and Tamas Pataki [Ithaca, N.Y.: Cornell University Press, 2004], 120); and as another states: "We need to think clearly about oppression" and "it is perfectly consistent to deny that a person or group is oppressed without denying that they have feelings or that they suffer" (Marilyn Frye, "Oppression," in *Race, Class, and Gender in the United States,* 2nd ed., ed. Paula S. Rothenberg [New York: St. Martin's Press, 1992], 54).

50. Some of the many respected sources along the lines of documenting the racist oppression of blacks includes Randall Kennedy, *Race, Crime, and the Law* (New York: Vintage, 1997), chaps. 1–3. Of the numerous trustworthy sources documenting the racist oppression of Indians, see sources cited in Corlett, *Race, Racism, and Reparations,* chap. 8. Also see chapters 6 and 7, above.

51. However, on the assumption that substantial reparations policies are enacted for Indians and blacks, it would seem that Indians and blacks ought to be dropped as targets of affirmative action for the obvious reason that they would then receive significant and reasonable measures of justice from the reparations policies targeting them. However, there might still be sufficient reason to retain affirmative action programs instead for various other groups, including various U.S. blacks, for instance, whose genealogy does not trace back to U.S. slavery but who nonetheless belong to

groups that have experienced significant discrimination in the United States, and various indigenous group members whose groups were not historically oppressed by the United States but who suffer discrimination in the United States, and various other groups (including Latinos/as and Asian groups) that have been discriminated against in the United States in significant ways.

52. Joel Feinberg, *Doing and Deserving* (Princeton, N.J.: Princeton University Press, 1970), 74.

53. That the majority of recent full-time faculty appointees in the humanities in the United States have been women is noted in Jack H. Schuster and Martin J. Finkelstein, "On the Brink," *Thought and Action* 22 (2006): 56. For documentation of this point, see Jack H. Schuster and Martin J. Finkelstein, *The American Faculty* (Baltimore: Johns Hopkins University Press, 2006), chap. 3. Of course, the majority of these women are white women. And it is a known fact that they count as affirmative action hires, thus supporting my point that white women have benefited the most from affirmative action programs.

54. Margaret Urban Walker, *Moral Repair* (Oxford: Oxford University Press, 2006), 7. Furthermore, Walker notes that "in those cases where wrongs are done mutually or all around, however, the same person may be a victim and a perpetrator (or a complicit or negligent bystander), but that person is a victim of some *particular* wrong and a perpetrator of *another* distinct one" (Walker, *Moral Repair,* 7).

55. Alcoff, "Latino Oppression," 544.

56. For an account of white privilege, see Stephanie M. Wildman et al., *Privilege Revealed* (New York: New York University Press, 1996).

57. Alcoff, "Latino Oppression," 545.

58. We must become and remain ever mindful that it is one thing to be poor and white in the United States; it is quite another to be, say, an Indian or black and all that typically accompanies their experiences, both historically and (to a lesser extent) today.

59. J. Angelo Corlett, "The Whitewashing of Affirmative Action," in *Race and Human Rights,* ed. Curtis Stokes (East Lansing: Michigan State University Press, 2008), 255–63.

60. See bell hooks, *Ain't I a Woman* (Boston: South End Press, 1981), 119–58. Also see J. Angelo Corlett, "Race, Ethnicity, and Public Policy," in *Black Ethnicity/Latino Race?* ed. Jorge Gracia (forthcoming); Corlett, *Race, Racism, and Reparations,* 147–48n2; Corlett, "The Whitewashing of Affirmative Action"; John Hope Franklin, *From Slavery to Freedom,* 3rd ed. (New York: Knopf, 1967); Kennedy, *Race, Crime, and the Law,* chap. 2; Howard McGary and Bill E. Lawson, *Between Slavery and Freedom* (Bloomington: Indiana University Press, 1992), chap. 1, among several other worthy sources on the U.S. history of Indians and blacks.

61. Akhil Reed Amar, *The Bill of Rights* (New Haven, Conn.: Yale University Press, 1998), 48.

62. Kimberlé Crenshaw, "Demarginalizing the Intersection of Race and Sex," in *Feminist Legal Theory,* ed. Katherine T. Bartlett and Rosanne Kennedy (Boulder, Colo.: Westview, 1991), 63.

63. Crenshaw, "Demarginalizing the Intersection of Race and Sex," 67.

64. For philosophical analyses of responsibility for failures to act, see Joel Feinberg, *Freedom and Fulfillment* (Princeton, N.J.: Princeton University Press, 1992), chap. 7; John Kleinig, "Good Samaritanism," in *Philosophy of Law,* 5th ed., ed. Joel Feinberg and Hyman Gross (Belmont, Calif.: Wadsworth, 1995), 529–32.

65. Clarence Darrow, *Verdicts Out of Court* (Chicago: Quadrangle Books, 1963), 70.

66. For philosophical analyses of rights, see J. Angelo Corlett, *Race, Rights, and Justice*, Law and Philosophy Library 85 (Dordrecht, Netherlands: Springer, 2009); Ronald Dworkin, *Taking Rights Seriously* (Cambridge, Mass.: Harvard University Press, 1978); Joel Feinberg, *Rights, Justice, and the Bounds of Liberty* (Princeton, N.J.: Princeton University Press, 1980); Feinberg, *Freedom and Fulfillment*, chaps. 8–10; Wesley Hohfeld, *Fundamental Legal Conceptions* (New Haven, Conn.: Yale University Press, 1921).

67. See J. Angelo Corlett, *Responsibility and Punishment*, 3rd ed. (Dordrecht, Netherlands: Springer, 2006), chap. 7; Feinberg, *Doing and Deserving*, chap. 8; and Howard McGary, *Race and Social Justice* (London: Blackwell, 1999), chap. 5, for philosophical analyses of collective liability responsibility for past harmful wrongdoings.

68. See note 49.

69. By this I mean that those whites whose significant others are white women and who thereby benefit economically from the affirmative action employment of white women indeed benefit from the whitewashing of affirmative action. Also, insofar as white women benefit from affirmative action in education, white men and women close to them benefit also, and so on.

70. hooks, *Ain't I a Woman*, 121.

71. Gerda Lerner, "Reconceptualizing Differences among Women," in *Feminist Frameworks*, ed. Alison M. Jaggar and Paula S. Rothenberg (New York: McGraw-Hill, 1993), 237–38.

72. "Despite the predominance of patriarchal rule in American society, America was colonized on a racially imperialistic base and not on a sexually imperialistic base. . . . Racism took precedence over sexual alliances in both the white world's interaction with Indians and Blacks, just as racism overshadowed any bonding between black women and white women on the basis of sex" (hooks, *Ain't I a Woman*, 122). "In America, the social status of black and white women has never been the same. . . . Although they were both subject to sexist victimization, as victims of racism black women were subject to oppressions no white woman was forced to endure. In fact, white racial imperialism granted all white women, however victimized by sexist oppression they might be, the right to assume the role of oppressor in relationship to black women and black men" (122–23). "To black women the issue is not whether white women are more or less racist than white men, but that they are racist. . . . That means confronting the reality of white female racism. Sexist discrimination has prevented white women from assuming the dominant role in the perpetuation of white racial imperialism, but it has not prevented white women from absorbing, supporting, and advocating racist ideology or acting individually as racist oppressors in various spheres of American life" (124). Also see Angela Y. Davis, *Women, Race, and Class* (New York: Random House, 1981), 85, 121, for an account of how some leaders of the early (white) women's movement in the United States explicitly and in racist tones rejected black progress in favor of white women's progress.

73. Recall the above-cited claims to the effect that not all oppressive structures are equally harmful and ought not to be treated with equal concern.

74. Corlett, *Race, Racism, and Reparations*, chap. 7.

75. "Every women's movement in America from its earliest origin to the present day has been built on a racist foundation. . . . The first white women's rights advocates were never seeking social equality for all women; they were seeking social equality for

white women. . . . In contemporary times there is a general tendency to equate aboli-
tionism with a repudiation of racism. In actuality, most white abolitionists, male and
female, though vehement in their anti-slavery protest, were totally opposed to granting
social equality to black people" (hooks, *Ain't I a Woman*, 124). "While they strongly
advocated an end to slavery, they never advocated a change in the racial hierarchy that
allowed their caste status to be higher than that of black women or men" (hooks, *Ain't
I a Woman*, 125). "And it was in the context of endless comparisons of the plight of
'women' and 'blacks' that they revealed their racism. In most cases, this racism was an
unconscious, unacknowledged aspect of their thought, suppressed by their narcissism—a narcissism which so blinded them that they would not admit two obvious
facts: one, that in a capitalist, racist, imperialist state there is no one social status
women share as a collective group; and second, that the social status of white women
in America has never been like that of black women or men" (hooks, *Ain't I a Woman*,
136).

76. Consider the words of bell hooks:

> White feminists did not challenge the racist-sexist tendency to use the term "woman" to refer
> solely to white women; they supported it. For them it served two purposes. First, it allowed
> them to proclaim white men world oppressors while making it appear linguistically that no
> alliance existed between white women and white men based on shared racial imperialism.
> Second, it made it possible for white women to act as if alliances did exist between them-
> selves and non-white women in our society, and by doing so they could deflect attention
> away from their classism and racism. Had feminists chosen to make explicit comparisons
> between the status of white women and that of black people, or more specifically the status
> of black women and white women, it would have been more than obvious that the two
> groups do not share an identical oppression. (hooks, *Ain't I a Woman*, 140–41)

> This constant comparison of the plight of "women" and "blacks" deflected attention away
> from the fact that black women were extremely victimized by both racism and sexism—a
> fact which, had it been emphasized, might have diverted public attention away from the
> complaints of middle and upper class white feminists. (hooks, *Ain't I a Woman*, 141)

77. Patricia Williams, *The Alchemy of Race and Rights* (Cambridge, Mass.: Harvard
University Press, 1991), 174.

78. In 1901 alone, over 100 black men were mob-lynched for a wide range of "reasons." See Clarence Darrow, *Verdicts Out of Court*, 65.

79. Darrow, *Verdicts Out of Court*, 72.

80. John Rawls, *Collected Papers*, ed. S. Freeman (Cambridge, Mass.: Harvard University Press, 1999), chap. 2.

81. Lerner, "Reconceptualizing Differences Among Women," 242. Also see Crenshaw, "Demarginalizing the Intersection of Race and Sex," 69.

82. Crenshaw, "Demarginalizing the Intersection of Race and Sex," 68.

83. Crenshaw, "Demarginalizing the Intersection of Race and Sex," 68–69. The
white feminist refusal to take seriously the rights of black women is illustrated well by
a women's studies major in my ethics course who, in an emotive response to my pointing out how white women were not oppressed in nearly the same ways and degrees of
enslaved women of the U.S. South and how it was part and parcel of the enslaved
women's life to be raped often by her white male master, replied: "Well, think of how
the poor wife of the master felt, having her husband cheat on her like that!" This sort

of narcissistic attitude tends to distort U.S. history, conveniently in favor of white women's experience.

84. Lerner, "Reconceptualizing Differences among Women," 242.

85. When I refer to the United States as "evil," I am making an on balance moral judgment based on the fact that unrectified evil is evil still, along with other claims and arguments made in Corlett, *Race, Racism, and Reparations,* chaps. 8–9.

86. Lerner, "Reconceptualizing Differences among Women," 244.

87. The notion that black women are theoretically "erased" from racist white-oriented feminist frameworks is argued most eloquently in Crenshaw, "Demarginalizing the Intersection of Race and Sex," 57–80.

88. I owe this point to Howard McGary.

89. Also see Davis, *Women, Race, and Class.*

90. Robert Fullinwider, "The Case for Reparations," in *Redress for Historical Injustices in the United States,* ed. Michael T. Martin and Marilyn Yaquinto (Durham, N.C.: Duke University Press, 2007), 127.

91. Alfred L. Brophy, *Reparations* (Oxford: Oxford University Press, 2006), 35.

92. Brophy, *Reparations,* 35.

93. Derrick Bell, *And We Are Not Saved* (New York: Basic Books, 1984), pt. 1; David Lyons, "Racial Injustices in the U.S. and Their Legacy," in *Redress for Historical Injustices in the United States,* ed. Michael T. Martin and Marilyn Yaquinto (Durham, N.C.: Duke University Press, 2007), 33–54.

94. W. E. B. Du Bois, *The Souls of Black Folk* (Greenwich, N.Y.: Fawcett, 1961), 86.

95. Eric J. Miller, "Reconceiving Reparations," *Boston College Third World Law Journal* 24 (2004): 45–79.

CONCLUSION

1. Joel Feinberg, *Doing and Deserving* (Princeton, N.J.: Princeton University Press, 1970), 231.

2. Feinberg, *Doing and Deserving,* 233.

3. Feinberg, *Doing and Deserving,* 234.

4. Feinberg, *Doing and Deserving,* 236.

5. Feinberg, *Doing and Deserving,* 248.

6. Feinberg, *Doing and Deserving,* 249.

7. Feinberg's condition of "prior notice" relates to the idea of acting knowingly, and it is unclear whether this ought to stand in the way of my argument for reparations based on U.S. collective responsibility for the oppressions in question. For it might be asked how anyone can *not* be expected to know right from wrong on such matters, that Indians and blacks are just as human as everyone else and ought to be accorded the same rights as all others and treated accordingly, etc. And here it is also relevant that at virtually any period of U.S. history there were dissenting voices, however few. Thus there is no excuse that ignorance can countenance here.

8. E. Barkan, *The Guilt of Nations* (New York: Norton, 2000), 317.

Selected Bibliography

Adams, E. M. "The Ground of Human Rights." *American Philosophical Quarterly* 19 (1982): 191–95.

Adams, M. M. *Horrendous Evils and the Goodness of God.* Ithaca, N.Y.: Cornell University Press, 1999.

Adler, Mortimer, ed. *The Negro in American History.* 3 vols. Chicago: Encyclopedia Britannica Educational Corporation, 1969.

Ahlstrom, Sydney. *A Religious History of the American People.* Vols. 1–2. New York: Image Books, 1975.

Alcoff, Linda Martín. "Latino Oppression." *Journal of Social Philosophy* 36 (2005): 536–45.

Alexander, Larry. *Is There a Right of Freedom of Expression?* Cambridge: Cambridge University Press, 2005.

Alford, C. Fred. *Psychology and the Natural Law of Reparation.* Cambridge: Cambridge University Press, 2006.

Alston, Philip. "Conjuring Up Human Rights." *The American Journal of International Law* 78 (1984): 607–21.

Amar, Akhil Reed. *The Bill of Rights.* New Haven, Conn.: Yale University Press, 1998.

Amsterdam, Anthony G., and Jerome Bruner. *Minding the Law.* Cambridge, Mass.: Harvard University Press, 2000.

Anderson, William L., ed. *Cherokee Removal.* Athens: University of Georgia Press, 1991.

Anscombe, G. E. M. *Intention.* 2nd ed. Ithaca, N.Y.: Cornell University Press, 1969.

Appiah, Anthony. "'But Would That Still Be Me?'" In *Race/Sex,* edited by Naomi Zack, 75–82. Philadelphia: Temple University Press, 1997.

Arguedas, Alcides. "The Sick People." In *Nineteenth-Century Nation Building and the Latin American Intellectual Tradition,* edited and translated by Janet Burke and Ted Humphrey, 342–64. Indianapolis: Hackett, 2007.

Arneson, Richard J. "Egalitarian Justice versus the Right to Privacy." *Social Philosophy and Policy* 17 (2000): 91–119.

———. "Equality and Responsibility." *The Journal of Ethics* 3 (1999): 225–47.

———. "Luck and Equality." *Proceedings of the Aristotelian Society* 75, supp. vol. (2001): 73–90.

Bacharach, Michael. *Beyond Individual Choice.* Edited by Natalie Gold and Robert Sugden. Princeton, N.J.: Princeton University Press, 2006.

Bailey, Garrick, and Roberta Glenn Bailey. *A History of the Navajos.* Santa Fe, N.M.: School of American Research Press, 1986.

Balazs, Zoltan. "Forgiveness and Repentance." *Public Affairs Quarterly* 14 (2000): 105–27.

Barkan, E. *The Guilt of Nations.* New York: Norton, 2000.

Barkan, E., and A. Karn, eds. *Taking Wrongs Seriously.* Stanford, Calif.: Stanford University Press, 2006.

Barry, Brian M. *Liberty and Justice.* Oxford: Oxford University Press, 1989.

Beckwith, Martha. *Hawaiian Mythology.* Honolulu: University of Hawaii Press, 1976.

Beitz, Charles R. "Human Rights and the Law of Peoples." In *The Ethics of Assistance,* edited by Deen K. Chatterjee, 193–216. Cambridge: Cambridge University Press, 2004.

———. *Political Equality.* Princeton, N.J.: Princeton University Press, 1989.

———. *Political Theory and International Relations.* Princeton, N.J.: Princeton University Press, 1979.

Bell, Derrick. *And We Are Not Saved.* New York: Basic Books, 1987.

———. "Racial Realism." In *Jurisprudence,* 2nd ed., edited by Robert L. Hayman, Jr., Nancy Levit, and Richard Delgado, 660–66. St. Paul, Minn.: West Group, 2002.

Benn, E. Stanley. "An Approach to the Problems of Punishment." *Philosophy* 33 (1958): 325–41.

Benn, Piers. "Forgiveness and Loyalty." *Philosophy* 71 (1996): 369–83.

Bergmann, Barbara R. *In Defense of Affirmative Action.* New York: Basic Books, 1996.

Berkhofer, Robert F., Jr. *Salvation and the Savage.* New York: Atheneum, 1965.

Berlin, Ira, Marc Favreau, and Steven F. Miller, eds. *Remembering Slavery.* New York: New Press, 1998.

Bigelowab, John, Robert Pargetter, and Robert Young. "Land, Well-Being and Compensation." *Australasian Journal of Philosophy* 68 (1990): 330–46.

Bishop, John. "Locke's Theory of Original Appropriation and the Right of Settlement in Iroquois Territory." *Canadian Journal of Philosophy* 27 (1997): 311–38.

Bittker, Boris L. *The Case for Black Reparations.* New York: Random House, 1973.

Bittker, Boris L., and Roy L Brooks. "The Constitutionality of Black Reparations." In *Redress for Historical Injustices in the United States,* edited by Michael T. Martin and Marilyn Yaquinto, 143–59. Durham, N.C.: Duke University Press, 2007.

———. "Identifying the Beneficiaries." In *Reverse Discrimination,* edited by Barry R. Gross, 329–87. New York: Prometheus Books, 1977.

Boxill, Bernard R. *Blacks and Social Justice.* Totowa, N.J.: Rowman and Allanheld, 1984.

———. "Global Equality of Opportunity and National Integrity." *Social Philosophy and Policy* 5 (1987): 143–68.

———. "A Lockean Argument for Black Reparations." *The Journal of Ethics* 7 (2003): 63–91.

———. "The Morality of Reparation." *Social Theory and Practice* 2 (1972): 113–22.

———. "The Morality of Reparation." In *Reverse Discrimination,* edited by Barry R. Gross, 270–78. Buffalo, N.Y.: Prometheus, 1977.

———. "The Morality of Reparations II." In *A Companion to African-American Philosophy,* edited by Tommy Lee Lott and John P. Pittman, 134–47. Malden, Mass.: Blackwell, 2003.

———. "Power and Persuasion." *Journal of Social Philosophy* 32 (2001): 382–85.

Bradford, William C. "Beyond Reparations." *Human Rights Review* 6 (2005): 5–79.

Brandt, Richard B. "The Concept of a Moral Right and Its Function." *The Journal of Philosophy* 80 (1983): 29–45.

Bratman, Michael E. "Responsibility and Planning." *The Journal of Ethics* 1 (1997): 27–43.

———. "Shared Cooperative Activity." *The Philosophical Review* 101 (1992): 327–41.

———. "Shared Intention." *Ethics* 104 (1993): 97–113.

Braybrooke, David. "The Firm but Untidy Correlativity of Rights and Obligations." *Canadian Journal of Philosophy* 1 (1972): 351–63.

Brietman, George, ed. *Malcolm X Speaks*. New York: Pathfinder, 1992.

Brooks, Roy L. *Atonement and Forgiveness*. Berkeley: University of California Press, 2004.

Broome, John. *Weighing Goods*. Oxford: Oxford University Press, 1991.

———. *Weighing Lives*. Oxford: Oxford University Press, 2004.

Brophy, Alfred L. *Reparations*. Oxford: Oxford University Press, 2006.

Brown, Dee. *Bury My Heart at Wounded Knee*. New York: Henry Holt, 1970.

Buchanan, Allen E. *Justice, Legitimacy, and Self-Determination*. Oxford: Oxford University Press, 2005.

———. *Secession*. Boulder, Colo.: Westview, 1991.

Calhoun, Cheshire. "Changing One's Heart." *Ethics* 103 (1992): 76–96.

Cane, Peter. *Responsibility in Law and Morality*. Oxford: Hart, 2002.

Card, Claudia. *The Atrocity Paradigm*. Oxford: Oxford University Press, 2002.

Carson, Clayborne, consultant. *Civil Rights Chronicle*. Lincolnwood, Ill.: Legacy, 2003.

Cavanaugh, Matt. *Against Equality of Opportunity*. Oxford: Oxford University Press, 2002.

Chisholm, Roderick M. *Theory of Knowledge*. 3rd ed. Englewood Cliffs, N.J.: Prentice Hall, 1989.

Clark, Austen. "Beliefs and Desires Incorporated." *The Journal of Philosophy* 91 (1994): 404–25.

Cleveland, Catherine C. *The Great Revival in the West*. Gloucester, Mass.: Peter Smith, 1959.

Cobb, John, Jr. "Imperialism in American Economic Policy." In *The American Empire and the Commonwealth of God*, edited by David Ray Griffin, John Cobb Jr., Richard Faulk, and Catherine Keller, 23–43. Louisville, Ky.: Westminster John Knox Press, 2006.

Cohen, Felix. *The Legal Conscience, Selected Papers*. Edited by Lucy Kramer Cohen. New Haven, Conn.: Yale University Press, 1960.

Cohen, G. A. *If You're an Egalitarian, How Come You're So Rich?* Cambridge, Mass.: Harvard University Press, 2000.

———. *History, Labour, and Freedom*. Oxford: Oxford University Press, 1988.

———. *Self-Ownership, Freedom, and Equality*. Cambridge: Cambridge University Press, 1995.

Coleman, Jules L. "Corrective Justice and Property Rights." *Social Philosophy and Policy* 11 (1994): 124–38. Also in Roberts, Rodney C., ed. *Injustice and Rectification*. New York: Peter Lang, 2002, 53–65.

———. "Corrective Justice and Wrongful Gains." *Journal of Legal Studies* 11 (1982): 421–40.

Constable, Marianne. *Just Silences*. Princeton, N.J.: Princeton University Press, 2005.

Copp, David. "Collective Actions and Secondary Actions." *American Philosophical Quarterly* 16 (1979): 177–86.

———. "Responsibility for Collective Inaction." *American Philosophical Association* (Central Division), Chicago, IL, 1990.

———. "What Collectives Are: Agency, Individualism and Legal Theory." *Dialogue* 23 (1984): 249–70.

Corlett, J. Angelo. *Analyzing Social Knowledge.* Lanham, Md.: Rowman and Littlefield, 1996.

———. "Collective Punishment." In *The Blackwell Encyclopedic Dictionary of Business Ethics*, edited by Patricia Hogue Werhane and R. Edward Freeman, 117–20. London: Blackwell, 1997.

———. "Collective Punishment and Public Policy." *Journal of Business Ethics* 11 (1992): 207–16.

———. "Corporate Punishment and Responsibility." *Journal of Social Philosophy* 28 (1997): 96–100.

———. "Collective Moral Responsibility." *Journal of Social Philosophy* 32 (2001): 573–84.

———. "Collective Responsibility." In *The Blackwell Encyclopedic Dictionary of Business Ethics*, edited by Patricia Hogue Werhane and R. Edward Freeman, 120–25. London: Blackwell, 1997.

———. "Corporate Responsibility for Environmental Damage." *Environmental Ethics* 18 (1996): 195–207.

———. "Corporate Responsibility and Punishment." *Public Affairs Quarterly* 2 (1988): 1–16.

———. "Dworkin's *Empire* Strikes Back!" *Statute Law Review* 21 (2000): 43–56.

———. "Forgiveness, Apology and Retributive Punishment." *American Philosophical Quarterly* 43 (2006): 25–42.

———. "Moral Compatibilism: Rights, Responsibility, Punishment and Compensation." Ph.D. diss., Department of Philosophy, University of Arizona, 1992.

———. "On Evil." *Analysis* 64 (2004): 81–84.

———. "Race, Ethnicity, and Public Policy." In *Race or Ethnicity?* edited by Jorge Gracia, 248–66. Ithaca, N.Y.: Cornell University Press (forthcoming).

———. *Race, Racism, and Reparations.* Ithaca, N.Y.: Cornell University Press, 2003.

———. *Race, Rights, and Justice.* Law and Philosophy Library 85. Dordrecht, Netherlands: Springer, 2009.

———. "Reparations to Native Americans?" In *War Crimes and Collective Wrongdoing*, edited by Aleksander Jokic, 236–69. Malden, Mass.: Blackwell, 2001.

———. *Responsibility and Punishment.* Library of Ethics and Applied Philosophy. Dordrecht, Netherlands: Kluwer Academic Publishing, 2001.

———. *Responsibility and Punishment.* 3rd ed. Library of Ethics and Applied Philosophy 9. Dordrecht, Netherlands: Springer, 2006.

———. "The Problem of Collective Moral Rights." *Canadian Journal of Law and Jurisprudence* 7 (1994): 237–59.

———. "The Philosophy of Joel Feinberg." *The Journal of Ethics* 10 (2006): 131–91.

———. *Terrorism.* Philosophical Studies Series 101. Dordrecht, Netherlands: Kluwer Academic Publishers, 2003.

———. "U.S. Reparations to Iraq" (forthcoming).

———. "Was 9/11 Morally Justified?" *The Journal of Global Ethics* 3 (2007): 107–23.

————. "The Whitewashing of Affirmative Action." In *Race and Human Rights*, edited by Curtis Stokes, 255–64. East Lansing: Michigan State University Press, 2007.

Cousineau, Phil, ed. *A Seat at the Table*. Berkeley: University of California Press, 2006.

Cover, Robert. *Justice Accused*. New Haven, Conn.: Yale University Press, 1975.

Cowan, Tyler. "Discounting and Restitution." *Philosophy and Public Affairs* 26 (1997): 168–85.

Cranston, Maurice. "Human Rights, Real and Supposed." In *Political Theory and the Rights of Man*, edited by D. D. Raphael, 43–53. Bloomington: Indiana University Press, 1967.

Crenshaw, Kimberlé. "Demarginalizing the Intersection of Race and Sex." In *Feminist Legal Theory*, edited by Katherine T. Bartlett and Rosanne Kennedy, 57–80. Boulder, Colo.: Westview, 1991.

Cudd, Ann E. *Analyzing Oppression*. Oxford: Oxford University Press, 2006.

Cullity, Garrett. *The Moral Demands of Affluence*. Oxford: Oxford University Press, 2004.

Daniels, Norman. *Am I My Brother's Keeper?* Oxford: Oxford University Press, 1988.

Danley, John R. "Liberalism, Aboriginal Rights, and Cultural Minorities." *Philosophy and Public Affairs* 20 (1991): 168–85.

Darrow, Clarence. *Verdicts Out of Court*. Chicago: Quadrangle Books, 1963.

Davis, Angela Y. *Women, Race, and Class*. New York: Random House, 1981.

Debo, Angie. *And Still the Waters Run*. Norman: University of Oklahoma Press, 1989.

————. *A History of the Indians of the United States*. Norman: University of Oklahoma Press, 1970.

Deloria, Vine, Jr. *God Is Red*. Golden, Colo.: Fulcrum Publishing, 1994.

Devlin, Patrick. *The Enforcement of Morals*. Oxford: Oxford University Press, 1965.

DeWolf, Thomas Norman. *Inheriting the Trade*. Boston: Beacon, 2008.

Diamond, Cora, and Jenny Teichman, eds. *Intention and Intentionality*. Ithaca, N.Y.: Cornell University Press, 1979.

Dieterlen, Paulette. *Poverty*. Amsterdam: Rodopi, 2005.

Dobzhansky, Theodosius. *Genetic Diversity and Human Equality*. New York: Basic Books, 1973.

Dougherty, Michael. *To Steal a Kingdom*. Waimanalo, Hawaii: Island Style Press, 1992.

Douglas, William O. *An Almanac of Liberty*. Garden City, N.Y.: Doubleday, 1964.

Downie, Richard S. "Forgiveness." *The Philosophical Quarterly* 15 (1965): 128–34.

————. "Responsibility and Social Roles." In *Individual and Collective Responsibility*, edited by Peter French, 65–80. New York: Schenkman, 1972.

Du Bois, W. E. B. *An ABC of Color*. New York: International Publishers, 1963.

————. *The Souls of Black Folk*. Greenwich: Fawcett, 1961.

Dworkin, Gerald. "Paternalism." In *Philosophy of Law*, 5th ed., edited by Joel Feinberg and Hyman Gross, 208–19. Belmont, Calif.: Wadsworth, 1995.

————. "Paternalism: Some Second Thoughts." In *Philosophy of Law*, 5th ed., edited by Joel Feinberg and Hyman Gross, 219–23. Belmont, Calif.: Wadsworth, 1995.

Dworkin, Ronald. "What Is Equality? Part 1." *Philosophy and Public Affairs* 10 (1981): 185–246.

————. "What Is Equality? Part 2." *Philosophy and Public Affairs* 10 (1981): 283–345.

————. "What Is Equality? Part 3." *Iowa Law Review* 73 (1987): 1–54.

————. "What Is Equality? Part 4." In *Philosophy and Democracy*, edited by Thomas Christiano, 116–37. Oxford: Oxford University Press, 2003.

————. "Review of Robert Cover, *Justice Accused.*" *Times Literary Supplement*, December 5, 1975.

————. *Taking Rights Seriously.* Cambridge, Mass.: Harvard University Press, 1978.

Ehle, John. *Trail of Tears.* New York: Anchor Books, 1988.

Elkins, Stanley M. *Slavery.* Chicago: University of Chicago Press, 1968.

Ewing, A. C. *The Morality of Punishment.* Montclair, N.J.: Patterson-Smith, 1970.

Falk, Richard. "Revisioning Cosmopolitanism." In *For Love of County*, edited by Joshua Cohen and Martha Nussbaum, 53–60. Boston: Beacon, 1996.

Feinberg, Joel. *Doing and Deserving.* Princeton, N.J.: Princeton University Press, 1970.

————. *Freedom and Fulfillment.* Princeton, N.J.: Princeton University Press, 1992.

————. *Harm to Others.* Oxford: Oxford University Press, 1984.

————. *Harm to Self.* Oxford: Oxford University Press, 1986.

————. *Harmful Wrongdoing.* Oxford: Oxford University Press, 1990.

————. "The Moral and Legal Responsibility of the Bad Samaritan." In *Freedom and Fulfillment*, edited by Joel Feinberg, 175–96. Princeton, N.J.: Princeton University Press, 1992.

————. "The Nature and Value of Rights." *Journal of Value Inquiry* 4 (1970): 243–57.

————. *Problems at the Roots of Law.* Oxford: Oxford University Press, 2003.

————. "Responsibility for the Future." *Philosophy Research Archives* 14 (1988–1989): 93–113.

————. "Responsibility *Tout Court.*" *Philosophy Research Archives* 14 (1988–1989): 73–92.

————. *Rights, Justice, and the Bounds of Liberty.* Princeton, N.J.: Princeton University Press, 1980.

————. *Social Philosophy.* Englewood Cliffs, N.J.: Prentice-Hall, 1973.

————. "What, If Anything, Justifies Legal Punishment?" In *Philosophy of Law*, 5th ed., edited by Joel Feinberg and Hyman Gross, 613–17. Belmont, Calif.: Wadsworth, 1995.

Fischer, John Martin. *The Metaphysics of Free Will.* London: Blackwell, 1994.

————. *Moral Responsibility.* Ithaca, N.Y.: Cornell University Press, 1986.

————. *My Way.* Oxford: Oxford University Press, 2006.

————. "Responsibility, Control, and Omissions." *The Journal of Ethics* 1 (1997): 45–67.

Fischer, John Martin, and Mark Ravizza, eds. *Perspective on Moral Responsibility.* Ithaca, N.Y.: Cornell University Press, 1993.

————, eds. *Responsibility and Control.* Cambridge: Cambridge University Press, 1998.

Fishel, Leslie H., and Benjamin Quarles, eds. *The Black American.* Glenview, Ill.: Scott Foresman, 1970.

Foreman, Grant. *Indian Removal.* Norman: University of Oklahoma Press, 1932.

Frankfurt, Harry. *The Importance of What We Care About.* Cambridge: Cambridge University Press, 1988.

Franklin, John Hope. *From Slavery to Freedom.* 3rd ed. New York: Knopf, 1967.

————. *Reconstruction.* Chicago: University of Chicago Press, 1961.

French, Peter. *Collective and Corporate Responsibility.* New York: Columbia University Press, 1984.

Frey, R. G. Editor. *Utility and Rights.* Minneapolis: University of Minnesota Press, 1984.

Friedman, Richard. "The Basics of Human Rights: A Criticism of Gewirth's Theory." In *Human Rights*, edited by J. R. Pennock and J. W. Chapman, 148–57. New York: New York University Press, 1981.

Frye, Marilyn. "Oppression." In *Race, Class, and Gender in the United States*, 2nd ed., edited by Paula S. Rothenberg, 54–57. New York: St. Martin's Press, 1992.

Fullinwider, Robert. "The Case for Reparations." *Institute for Philosophy and Public Policy* 20 (2000): 1–11.

———. "The Case for Reparations." In *Redress for Historical Injustices in the United States*, edited by Michael T. Martin and Marilyn Yaquinto, 121–33. Durham, N.C.: Duke University Press, 2007.

Garrard, Eve, and David McNaughton. "In Defense of Unconditional Forgiveness." *Proceedings of the Aristotelian Society* 103 (2002): 39–60.

Gaus, Gerald F. "Does Compensation Restore Equality?" In *Injustice and Rectification*, edited by Rodney C. Roberts, 83–104. New York: Peter Lang, 2002.

Gewirth, Alan. *The Community of Rights*. Chicago: University of Chicago Press, 1995.

Gilbert, Margaret. "Collective Remorse." In *War Crimes and Collective Wrongdoing*, edited by Aleksandar Jokic, 216–35. Malden, Mass.: Blackwell, 2001.

———. "Group Wrongs and Guilt Feelings." *The Journal of Ethics* 1 (1997): 65–84.

———. "Modeling Collective Belief." *Synthese* 73 (1987): 185–204.

———. *On Social Facts*. Princeton, N.J.: Princeton University Press, 1989.

———. *Sociality and Responsibility*. Lanham, Md.: Rowman and Littlefield, 2000.

Gill, Kathleen, A. "The Moral Functions of an Apology." *The Philosophical Forum* 31 (2000): 11–27.

Glasgow, Joshua. "On the Methodology of the Race Debate: Conceptual Analyses and Racial Discourse." *Philosophy and Phenomenological Research* 76 (2008): 333–58.

Goldman, Alvin. *Epistemology and Cognition*. Cambridge, Mass.: Harvard University Press, 1986.

———. *Knowledge in a Social World*. Oxford: Oxford University Press, 1999.

———. *A Theory of Human Action*. Princeton, N.J.: Princeton University Press, 1970.

Goodin, Robert. "Waitangi Tales." *Australasian Journal of Philosophy* 78 (2000): 309–33.

Govier, Trudy. *Forgiveness and Revenge*. London: Routledge, 2002.

———. "Forgiveness and the Unforgivable." *American Philosophical Quarterly* 36 (1999): 59–75.

Govier, Trudy, and Wilhelm Verwoerd. "The Promise and Pitfalls of Apology." *Journal of Social Philosophy* 33 (2002): 67–82.

Gracia, Jorge. *Hispanic/Latino Identity*. London: Blackwell Publishers, 2000.

———. *Surviving Race, Ethnicity, and Nationality*. Lanham, Md.: Rowman and Littlefield, 2005.

———. "The Nature of Ethnicity with Special Reference to Hispanic/Latino Identity." *Public Affairs Quarterly* 13 (1999): 25–42.

Green, Michael D. *The Politics of Indian Removal*. Lincoln: University of Nebraska Press, 1982.

Griffin, David Ray. "America's Non-accidental, Non-benign Empire." In *The American Empire and the Commonwealth of God*, edited by David Ray Griffin, John Cobb, Jr., Richard Faulk, and Catherine Keller, 3–22. Louisville, Ky.: Westminster John Knox Press, 2006.

Griffin, James. "First Steps in an Account of Human Rights." *European Journal of Philosophy* 9 (2001): 306–27.

———. *On Human Rights*. Oxford: Oxford University Press, 2008.

Griswold, Charles. *Forgiveness*. Cambridge: Cambridge University Press, 2007.

Haber, Joram Graf. *Forgiveness*. Savage, Md.: Rowman and Littlefield, 1991.

Habermas, Jürgen. "Private and Public Autonomy, Human Rights and Popular Sovereignty." In *The Politics of Human Rights*, edited by Obrad Savić, 50–66. London: Verso, 1999.

Handlin, Oscar. *Race and Nationality in American Life*. Garden City, N.Y.: Doubleday Anchor, 1957.

Hardimon, Michael O. "The Ordinary Concept of Race." *The Journal of Philosophy* 100 (2003): 437–55.

Harvey, J. *Civilized Oppression*. Lanham, Md.: Rowman and Littlefield, 1999.

Haslanger, Sally. "Oppressions." In *Racism in Mind*, edited by Michael P. Levine and Tamas Pataki, 97–123. Ithaca, N.Y.: Cornell University Press, 2004.

Hawkins, Hugh, ed. *The Abolitionists*. 2nd ed. London: D. C. Heath and Company, 1972.

Hechter, Michael. *Principles of Group Solidarity*. Berkeley: University of California Press, 1987.

Held, Virginia. "Can a Random Collection of Individuals Be Morally Responsible?" *The Journal of Philosophy* 67 (1970): 471–81.

———. "Corporations, Persons, and Responsibility." In *Shame, Responsibility and the Corporation*, edited by Hugh Cutler, 161–81. New York: Haven, 1986.

———. "Moral Responsibility and Collective Action." In *Individual and Collective Responsibility*, edited by Peter A. French, 101–18. New York: Schenkman, 1972.

Henkin, Louis. "International Human Rights as 'Rights.'" In *Human Rights*, edited by J. R. Pennock and J. W. Chapman. New York: New York University Press, 1981.

Herbert, Gary B. *A Philosophical History of Rights*. New Brunswick, N.J.: Transaction, 2002.

———. "Postscript to *A Philosophical History of Rights*." *Human Rights Review*, 2002, 3–29.

Hieronmi, Pamela. "Articulating an Uncompromising Forgiveness." *Philosophy and Phenomenological Research* 62 (2001): 529–55.

Hohfeld, Wesley. *Fundamental Legal Conceptions*. New Haven, Conn.: Yale University Press, 1921.

Holmgren, Margaret. "Forgiveness and the Intrinsic Value of Persons." *American Philosophical Quarterly* 30 (1993): 341–52.

———. "Self-Forgiveness and Responsible Moral Agency." *Journal of Value Inquiry* 32 (1998): 75–91.

Holt, Thomas. *Black Over White*. Urbana: University of Illinois Press, 1977.

———. *The Problem of Race in the 21st Century*. Cambridge, Mass.: Harvard University Press, 2000.

hooks, bell. *Ain't I a Woman*. Boston: South End Press, 1981.

Horsbrugh, H. J. N. "Forgiveness." *Canadian Journal of Philosophy* 4 (1974): 269–82.

Hughes, Martin. "Forgiveness." *Analysis* 35 (1975): 113–17.

Hughes, Paul. "On Forgiving Oneself." *The Journal of Value Inquiry* 28 (1994): 557–60.

———. "What Is Involved in Forgiving?" *Philosophia* (Israel) 25 (1997): 33–49.

Isasi-Diaz, Maria. *Mujerista Theology*. Maryknoll, N.Y.: Orbis Books, 2002.

Jacobs, Harriet. *Incidents in the Life of a Slave Girl*. Edited by J. F. Yellin. Cambridge, Mass.: Harvard University Press, 2000.

Jennings, Francis. *The Founders of America*. New York: Norton, 1993.

Johnson, E. Pauline. *Flint and Feather*. Ontario: PaperJacks, 1972.

Jordan, Winthrop. *White Over Black*. Baltimore: Penguin, 1968.

Kamm, F. M. *Intricate Ethics*. Oxford: Oxford University Press, 2007.

Kant, Immanuel. *The Metaphysical Elements of Justice*. Translated by John Ladd. London: Macmillan, 1965.

———. *The Metaphysical Elements of Justice*. In *The Metaphysics of Morals*, translated and edited by Mary Gregor. Cambridge: Cambridge University Press, 1996.

Kennedy, Randall. *Race, Crime, and the Law*. New York: Vintage, 1997.

King, Martin Luther, Jr. *Stride Toward Freedom*. New York: Ballantine, 1958.

Kitcher, P. "Does 'Race' Have a Future?" *Philosophy and Public Affairs* 35 (2007): 293–317.

———. "Race, Ethnicity, Biology, Culture." In *Racism*, edited by Leonard Harris, 87–117. Amherst, N.Y.: Humanity Books, 1999.

Kleinig, John. "Good Samaritanism." *Philosophy and Public Affairs* 5 (1975): 382–407.

———. "Good Samaritanism." In *Philosophy of Law*, 5th ed., edited by Joel Feinberg and Hyman Gross, 529–32. Belmont, Calif.: Wadsworth, 1995.

———. *Punishment and Desert*. The Hague: Martinus Nijhoff, 1973.

———. "Punishment and Moral Seriousness." *Israel Law Review* 25 (1991): 401–21.

Kohen, Ari. "The Possibility of Secular Human Rights." *Human Rights Review* 7 (2005): 49–75.

Kolnai, Aurel. "Forgiveness." *Proceedings of the Aristotelian Society* 74 (1973–1974): 91–106.

Korsgaard, Christine M. "Taking the Law into Our Own Hands." In *Reclaiming the History of Ethics*, edited by Andrews Reath, Barbara Herman, and Christine M. Korsgaard, 297–328. Cambridge: Cambridge University Press, 1997.

Kymlicka, Will. *Liberalism, Community, and Culture*. Oxford: Oxford University Press, 1989.

———, ed. *The Rights of Minority Cultures*. Oxford: Oxford University Press, 1995.

Ladd, John. "Morality and the Ideal of Rationality in Formal Organizations." *Monist* 54 (1970): 488–516.

Lake, Christopher. *Equality and Responsibility*. Oxford: Oxford University Press, 2001.

Lang, Berel. "Forgiveness." *American Philosophical Quarterly* 30 (1994): 105–17.

Lauterpacht, H. *International Law and Human Rights*. Hamden, Conn.: Archon, 1968.

Lawson, Gary. "Providing Ownership." *Social Philosophy and Policy* 11 (1994): 139–52.

Lazare, Aaron. *On Apology*. Oxford: Oxford University Press, 2004.

Lehrer, Keith. "Freedom, Preference, and Autonomy." *The Journal of Ethics* 1 (1997): 3–25.

———. *Metamind*. Oxford: Oxford University Press, 1990.

———. *Theory of Knowledge*. Boulder, Colo.: Westview, 1990.

———. *Theory of Knowledge*. 2nd ed. Boulder, Colo.: Westview, 2000.

Lerner, Gerda. "Reconceptualizing Differences among Women." In *Feminist Frameworks*, 3rd ed., edited by Alison M. Jaggar and Paul S. Rothenberg, 237–48. New York: McGraw-Hill, 1993.

Levine, Andrew. *Rethinking Liberal Equality*. Ithaca, N.Y.: Cornell University Press, 1998.

Levinson, Sanford. "Responsibility for Crimes of War." *Philosophy and Public Affairs* 2 (1973): 244–73

———, ed. *Torture*. Oxford: Oxford University Press, 2004.

Litwack, Leon F. *North of Slavery*. Chicago: University of Chicago Press, 1961.

Locke, John. *The Second Treatise of Government*. Indianapolis: Bobbs-Merrill, 1952.

Lomasky, Loren. *Persons, Rights, and the Moral Community.* Oxford: Oxford University Press, 1987.

Lyons, David. "Corrective Justice, Equal Opportunity, and the Legacy of Slavery and Jim Crow." *Boston University Law Review* 84 (2004): 1375–1404.

———. "The Correlativity of Rights and Duties." *Nous* 4 (1970): 45–55.

———. "The New Indian Claims and Original Rights to Land." *Social Theory and Practice* 6 (1977): 249–77.

———. "Human Rights and the General Welfare." In *Rights*, edited by David Lyons, 174–86. Belmont, Calif.: Wadsworth, 1979.

———. "Racial Injustices in the U.S. and Their Legacy." In *Redress for Historical Injustices in the United States*, edited by Michael T. Martin and Marilyn Yaquinto, 33–54. Durham, N.C.: Duke University Press, 2007.

———. *Rights, Welfare, and Mill's Moral Theory.* Oxford: Oxford University Press, 1994.

Mabbott, J. D. "Punishment." *Mind* 48 (1939): 152–67.

MacCormick, D. N. "The Obligation of Reparations." *Proceedings of the Aristotelian Society* 78 (1977–1978): 175–93.

Malcolm X. *By Any Means Necessary.* New York: Pathfinder, 1970.

Martí, José. "Our America." In *Nineteenth-Century Nation Building and the Latin American Intellectual Tradition*, translated and edited by J. Burke and T. Humphrey, 260–68. Indianapolis: Hackett, 2007.

Matsuda, Mari. "Looking to the Bottom." In *Critical Race Theory*, edited by Kimberlé Crenshaw, Neil Gotanda, Gary Peller, and Kendall Thomas, 63–79. New York: New Press, 1995.

May, Larry. "Collective Inaction and Shared Responsibility." *Nous* 24 (1990): 269–78.

———. *The Morality of Groups.* Notre Dame, Ind.: University of Notre Dame Press, 1987.

———. *Sharing Responsibility.* Chicago: University of Chicago Press, 1992.

Mayo, Bernard. "What Are Human Rights?" In *Political Theory and the Rights of Man*, edited by D. D. Raphael, 68–80. Bloomington: Indiana University Press, 1967.

McCloskey, H. J. "Respect for Human Moral Rights versus Maximizing Good." In *Utility and Rights*, edited by R. G. Frey, 121–36. Minneapolis: University of Minnesota Press, 1984.

McGary, Howard. "Achieving Democratic Equality." *The Journal of Ethics* 7 (2003): 93–113.

———. "Justice and Reparations." *The Philosophical Forum* 9 (1978): 250–63.

———. "Morality and Collective Liability." *The Journal of Value Inquiry* 20 (1986): 157–68.

———. *Race and Social Justice.* London: Blackwell Publishers, 1999.

McGary, Howard, and Bill E. Lawson. *Between Slavery and Freedom.* Bloomington: Indiana University Press, 1992.

Meier, August, and Elliot M. Rudwick, eds. *From Plantation to Ghetto.* New York: Hill and Wang, 1966.

———. *The Making of Black America.* New York: Atheneum, 1969.

Melden, A. I. *Rights and Right Conduct.* Oxford: Basil Blackwell, 1959.

Mellema, Gregory. "Shared Responsibility and Ethical Dilutionism." *Australasian Journal of Philosophy* 63 (1985): 177–87.

Mill, John Stuart. *On Liberty.* Indianapolis: Hackett, 1978.

Miller, David. "Against Global Egalitarianism." *The Journal of Ethics* 9 (2005): 55–79.

————. "Distributing Responsibilities." In *Global Responsibilities*, edited by Andrew Kuper. London: Routledge, 2005.

————. *National Responsibility and Global Justice*. Oxford: Oxford University Press, 2007.

————. "National Responsibility and International Justice." In *The Ethics of Assistance*, edited by Deen Chatterjee. Cambridge: Cambridge University Press, 2004.

Miller, Eric J. "Reconceiving Reparations." *Boston College Third World Law Journal* 24 (2004): 45–79.

Mills, Charles. "Contract of Breach." In *Reparations for African Americans*, edited by Howard McGary. Lanham, Md.: Rowman and Littlefield, forthcoming.

————. "Reconceptualizing Race and Racism?" *Journal of Social Philosophy* 36 (2005): 546–52.

Minow, Martha. *Between Vengeance and Forgiveness*. Boston: Beacon, 1998.

Moellendorf, D. *Cosmopolitan Justice*. Boulder, Colo.: Westview, 2002.

Montague, Phillip. "Rights and Duties of Compensation." In *Injustice and Rectification*, edited by Rodney C. Roberts, 76–82. New York: Peter Lang, 2002.

Moore, Kathleen D. *Pardons*. Oxford: Oxford University Press, 1989.

Morgan, H. Wayne. *America's Road to Empire*. New York: Wiley, 1965.

Morris, Herbert. "Murphy on Forgiveness." *Criminal Justice Ethics* 7 (1988): 15–19.

Mosley, Albert. "Affirmative Action as a Form of Reparations." *University of Memphis Law Review* 33 (2003): 353–65.

Mouffe, Chantel. *On the Political*. London: Routledge, 2005.

Mullin, Gerald W. *Flight and Rebellion*. Oxford: Oxford University Press, 1972.

Murphy, Jeffrie G. "Forgiveness and Resentment." *Midwest Studies in Philosophy* 7 (1982): 503–16.

————. *Getting Even*. Oxford: Oxford University Press, 2003.

————. "A Rejoinder to Morris." *Criminal Justice Ethics* 7 (1988): 20–22.

Murphy, Jeffrie G., and Jean Hampton. *Forgiveness and Mercy*. Cambridge: Cambridge University Press, 1988.

Murray, Robert. "Liberalism, Culture, Aboriginal Rights." *Canadian Journal of Philosophy* 29 (1999): 109–38.

Neblett, William. "Forgiveness and Ideals." *Mind* 83 (1974): 269–75.

Nickel, James. "Are Human Rights Mainly Implemented by Intervention?" In *Rawls's Law of Peoples*, edited by R. Martin and David Reidy, 263–77. London: Blackwell, 2006.

————. *Making Sense of Human Rights*. Berkeley: University of California Press, 1987.

————. "Poverty and Rights." *The Philosophical Quarterly* 55 (2005): 385–402.

————. "Should Reparations Be to Individuals or to Groups?" *Analysis* 34 (1974): 154–60.

North, Joanna. "The 'Ideal' of Forgiveness." In *Exploring Forgiveness*, edited by Robert D. Enright and Joanna North, 19–34. Madison: University of Wisconsin Press, 1998.

————. "Wrongdoing and Forgiveness." *Philosophy* 62 (1987): 499–508.

Novitz, David. "Forgiveness and Self-Respect." *Philosophy and Phenomenological Research* 58 (1998): 299–315.

Nozick, Robert. *Anarchy, State, and Utopia*. New York: Basic Books, 1974.

————. "Distributive Justice." *Philosophy and Public Affairs* 3 (1973): 45–126.

————. *Philosophical Explanations*. Cambridge, Mass.: Harvard University Press, 1981.

Nussbaum, Martha. "Capabilities and Human Rights." In *Global Justice and Transnational Politics*, edited by Pablo De Greiff and Ciaran Cronin, 117–49. Cambridge: MIT Press, 2002.

————. "Reply." In *For Love of Country*, edited by Joshua Cohen, 131–44. Boston: Beacon, 1996.

Ogletree, Charles J, Jr. "The Current Reparations Debate." *U.C. Davis Law Review* 36 (2003): 1051–72.

————. "Repairing the Past." *Harvard Civil Rights—Civil Liberties Law Review* 38 (2003): 279–320.

————. "Reparations for the Children of Slaves." *University of Memphis Law Review* 33 (2003): 245–64.

————. "Reparations, a Fundamental Issue of Social Justice." *The Black Collegian*, 2002, 118–22.

O'Neill, Onora. "Agents of Justice." In *Global Responsibilities*, edited by Andrew Kuper, 37–52. London: Routledge, 2005.

————. "Global Justice." In *The Ethics of Assistance*, edited by Deen Chatterjee, 242–59. Cambridge: Cambridge University Press, 2004.

————. *Towards Justice and Virtue*. Cambridge: Cambridge University Press, 1996.

O'Shaughnessy, R. J. "Forgiveness." *Philosophy* 42 (1967): 336–52.

Otsuka, Michael. *Libertarianism Without Inequality*. Oxford: Oxford University Press, 2003.

Panikkar, R. "Is the Notion of Human Rights a Western Concept?" *Diogenes* 120 (1982): 75–120.

Perrett, Roy. "Indigenous Language Rights and Political Theory." *Australasian Journal of Philosophy* 78 (2000): 405–17.

Perry, Bruce, ed. *Malcolm X: The Last Speeches*. New York: Pathfinder, 1989.

Peskin, Allan, ed. *North into Freedom*. Kent, Ohio: Kent State University Press, 1988.

Pinkney, Alphonso. *Black Americans*. Englewood Cliffs: Prentice-Hall, 1969.

Plato. *Gorgias*. Translated by Donald J. Zeyl. In *Plato: Complete Works*, edited by John M. Cooper and D. L. Hutchinson. Indianapolis: Hackett, 1997.

Pleas, William H., and Jane H. Pleas, eds. *The Antislavery Argument*. Indianapolis: Bobbs-Merrill, 1965.

Pogge, Thomas. "Human Rights and Human Responsibilities." In *Global Responsibilities*, edited by Andrew Kuper, 3–36. London: Routledge, 2005.

————. "The International Significance of Human Rights." *The Journal of Ethics* 4 (2000): 29–53.

————. *World Poverty and Human Rights*. London: Polity, 2002.

Pojman, Louis P. "The Moral Response to Terrorism and Cosmopolitanism." In *Terrorism and International Justice*, edited by James Sterba, 135–57. Oxford: Oxford University Press, 2003.

Pole, J. R. *The Pursuit of Equality in American History*. Berkeley: University of California Press, 1978.

Pollock, John. *Contemporary Theories of Knowledge*. Totowa, N.J.: Rowman and Allenheld, 1986.

Primoratz, Igor. *Justifying Legal Punishment*. London: Humanities Press International, 1989.

————. "Utilitarianism, Justice and Punishment." *Israel Law Review* 25 (1991): 388–97.

Quarles, Benjamin. *Black Abolitionists*. Oxford: Oxford University Press, 1969.

————. *The Negro in the Making of America*. New York: Collier Books, 1964.

Quinton, Anthony M. "Punishment." *Analysis* 14 (1954): 133–42.

Raphael, D. D. "Human Rights, Old and New." In *Political Theory and the Rights of Man*, edited by D. D. Raphael, 54–67. Bloomington: Indiana University Press, 1967.

Rawls, John. *Collected Papers*. Edited by Samuel Freeman. Cambridge, Mass.: Harvard University Press, 1999.

———. *Political Liberalism*. New York: Columbia University Press, 1993.

———. *The Law of Peoples*. Cambridge, Mass.: Harvard University Press, 1999.

———. *A Theory of Justice*. Cambridge, Mass.: Harvard University Press, 1971.

———. *A Theory of Justice*. Rev. ed. Cambridge, Mass.: Harvard University Press, 1999.

———. "Two Concepts of Rules." *The Philosophical Review* 64 (1955): 3–32.

Raz, Joseph. *Between Authority and Interpretation*. Oxford: Oxford University Press, 2009.

Redding, Saunders. *On Being Negro in America*. New York: Bantam, 1951.

Remini, Robert. *The Legacy of Andrew Jackson*. Baton Rouge: Louisiana State University Press, 1988.

Richards, Norvin. "Forgivingness." *Ethics* 99 (1988): 77–97.

Roberts, Robert. "Forgiveness." *American Philosophical Quarterly* 32 (1995): 289–306.

Roberts, Rodney C., ed. *Injustice and Rectification*. New York: Peter Lang, 2002.

———. "The Morality of a Moral Statue of Limitations on Injustice." *The Journal of Ethics* 7 (2003): 115–38.

———. "More on the Morality of a Moral Statue of Limitations on Injustice." *The Journal of Ethics* 11 (2007): 177–92.

———. "Toward a Moral Psychology of Rectification." *Journal of Social Philosophy* 33 (2002): 339–43.

———. "Why Have the Injustices Perpetrated against Blacks in America Not Been Rectified?" *Journal of Social Philosophy* 32 (2001): 357–73.

Robinson, Randall. *Equality of Opportunity*. Cambridge, Mass.: Harvard University Press, 1998.

———. *Theories of Distributive Justice*. Cambridge, Mass.: Harvard University Press, 1996.

Ryberg, Jesper. *The Ethics of Proportionate Punishment*. Library of Ethics and Applied Philosophy 16. Dordrecht, Netherlands: Kluwer Academic Publishing, 2004.

Sadurski, W. "Social Justice and the Problem of Punishment." *Israel Law Review* 25 (1991): 302–31.

Scarre, Geoffrey. *After Evil*. Burlington, Vt.: Ashgate, 2004.

Scheffler, Samuel. *Boundaries and Allegiances*. Oxford: Oxford University Press, 2001.

———. "Conceptions of Cosmopolitanism." *Utilitas* 11 (1999): 255–76.

———, ed. *Consequentialism and Its Critics*. Oxford: Oxford University Press, 1988.

———. *The Rejection of Consequentialism*. Oxford: Clarendon Press, 1982.

———. "What Is Egalitarianism?" *Philosophy and Public Affairs* 31 (2003): 5–39.

Schuster, Jack H., and Martin J. Finkelstein. *The American Faculty*. Baltimore: Johns Hopkins University Press, 2006.

Sellars, Wilfred. *Science and Metaphysics*. London: Routledge and Kegan Paul, 1968.

Sen, Amartya. "Elements of a Theory of Human Rights." *Philosophy and Public Affairs* 32 (2004): 315–57.

———. *Inequality Reexamined*. Cambridge, Mass.: Harvard University Press, 1992.

———. *On Economic Inequality*. Exp. ed. Oxford: Oxford University Press, 1978.

Sher, George. "Ancient Wrongs and Modern Rights." *Philosophy and Public Affairs* 10 (1981): 3–17.

———. *Approximate Justice*. Lanham, Md.: Rowman and Littlefield, 1997.

———. *Desert*. Princeton, N.J.: Princeton University Press, 1987.

Simmons, A. John. *The Edge of Anarchy*. Princeton, N.J.: Princeton University Press, 1993.

———. "Historical Rights and Fair Shares." *Law and Philosophy* 14 (1995): 149–84.

———. *Justification and Legitimacy*. Cambridge: Cambridge University Press, 2001.

———. *The Lockean Theory of Rights*. Princeton, N.J.: Princeton University Press, 1992.

———. "Maker's Rights." *The Journal of Ethics* 2 (1998): 197–218.

———. "Original Acquisition Justifications of Private Property." *Social Philosophy and Policy* 11 (1994): 63–84.

Simons, Lewis M. "Genocide and the Science of Proof." *National Geographic*, January 2006, 28–35.

Singer, Peter. "Famine, Affluence, and Morality." *Philosophy and Public Affairs* 1 (1972): 229–43.

Smith, Holly. "Culpable Ignorance." *The Philosophical Review* 92 (1983): 543–71.

Smith, Nick. "The Categorical Apology." *Journal of Social Philosophy* 36 (2005): 473–96.

———. *I Was Wrong*. Cambridge: Cambridge University Press, 2008.

Smith, Tara. "Tolerance and Forgiveness." *Journal of Applied Philosophy* 1 (1997): 31–42.

Snow, Nancy. "Self-Forgiveness." *Journal of Value Inquiry* 28 (1994): 75–80.

———. "Virtue and the Oppression of African Americans." *Public Affairs Quarterly* 18 (2004): 57–74.

Sparrow, Robert. "History and Collective Responsibility." *Australasian Journal of Philosophy* 78 (2000): 346–59.

Stannard, David E. *American Holocaust*. Oxford: Oxford University Press, 1992.

Steele, Ian. *Warpaths*. Oxford: Oxford University Press, 1982.

Steiner, Hillel. "How Equality Matters." *Social Philosophy and Policy* 19 (2002): 342–56.

Sterba, James P. "Global Justice for Humans or for All Living Beings and What Difference It Makes." *The Journal of Ethics* 9 (2005): 283–300.

———. "Review of Corlett, *Race, Racism and Reparations*." *Mind* 114 (2005): 407–9.

———. "Understanding Evil." *Ethics* 106 (1996): 424–48.

Strawson, Peter. "Freedom and Resentment." In *Perspectives on Moral Responsibility*, edited by John Martin Fischer and Mark Ravizza, 45–66. Ithaca, N.Y.: Cornell University Press, 1993.

Sumner, L. W. *The Moral Foundations of Rights*. Oxford: Oxford University Press, 1987.

Taylor, Charles. "Conditions on an Unforced Consensus on Human Rights." In *The Politics of Human Rights*, edited by Obrad Savić, 101–19. London: Verso, 1999.

Taylor, Gabrielle. *Pride, Shame, and Guilt*. Oxford: Oxford University Press, 1985.

Temkin, Larry S. *Inequality*. Oxford: Oxford University Press, 1993.

———. "Thinking about the Needy." *The Journal of Ethics* 8 (2004): 409–58.

Tesón, Fernando. *A Philosophy of International Law*. Boulder, Colo.: Westview, 1998.

Thalberg, I. "Remorse." *Mind* 72 (1963): 545–55.

Thomas, Laurence. "Morality, Consistency and the Self." *Journal of Social Philosophy* 32 (2001): 374–81.

Thompson, Janna. "Historical Injustice and Reparation." *Ethics* 112 (2001): 114–35.

———. "Historical Obligations." *Australasian Journal of Philosophy* 78 (2000): 334–45.

———. "Land Rights and Aboriginal Sovereignty." *Australasian Journal of Philosophy* 68 (1990): 313–29.

———. *Taking Responsibility for the Past*. Cambridge: Polity, 2002.

Thomson, Judith. *The Realm of Rights*. Cambridge, Mass.: Harvard University Press, 1990.

Tomasi, John. "Kymlicka, Liberalism, and Respect for Cultural Minorities." *Ethics* 105 (1995): 580–603.

Trafzer, Clifford. *The Kit Carsen Campaign*. Norman: University of Oklahoma Press, 1982.

Tully, James. "Aboriginal Property and Western Theory." *Social Philosophy and Policy* 11 (1994): 153–80.

Tuomela, Raimo. "Actions by Collectives." *Philosophical Perspectives* 3 (1989): 471–96.

———. "Collective Action, Supervenience, and Constitution." *Synthese* 80 (1989): 243–66.

———. "Intentional Single and Joint Action." *Philosophical Studies* 62 (1991): 235–62.

———. "We Will Do It." *Philosophy and Phenomenological Research* 60 (1991): 249–77.

Twambley, P. "Mercy and Forgiveness." *Analysis* 36 (1976): 84–90.

Unger, Peter. *Living High and Letting Die*. Oxford: Oxford University Press, 1996.

Von Hirsch, Andrew. *Censure and Sanctions*. Oxford: Clarendon, 1993.

———. *Doing Justice*. Boston: Northeastern University Press, 1986.

———. *Past or Future Crimes*. New Brunswick, N.J.: Rutgers University Press, 1987.

Von Hirsch, Andrew, and Andrew Ashworth, eds. *Principled Sentencing*. Boston: Northeastern University Press, 1992.

———. *Proportionate Sentencing*. Oxford: Oxford University Press, 2005.

Wade, Richard C. *Slavery in the Cities*. Oxford: Oxford University Press, 1964.

Waldron, Jeremy, ed. *Nonsense Upon Stilts*. London: Methuen, 1987.

———. *The Right to Private Property*. Oxford: Oxford University Press, 1988.

———. "Superseding Historic Injustice." *Ethics* 103 (1992): 4–28.

———. "Two Worries about Mixing One's Labor." *The Philosophical Quarterly* 33 (1983): 37–44.

Walker, Margaret Urban. *Moral Repair*. Oxford: Oxford University Press, 2006.

Walker, Nigel. "The Quiddity of Mercy." *Philosophy* 70 (1995): 27–37.

Walzer, Michael. *Just and Unjust Wars*. 3rd ed. New York: Basic Books, 2000.

Washington, Booker T. *Up from Slavery*. Garden City, N.Y.: Doubleday Page, 1924.

Wasserstrom, Richard. "Rights, Human Rights, and Racial Discrimination." In *Rights*, edited by David Lyons, 46–57. Belmont, Calif.: Wadsworth, 1979.

Weber, Max. *The Theory of Social and Economic Organizations*. Translated by A. M. Henderson and Talcott Parsons. New York: Free Press, 1947.

Wellman, Carl. *The Proliferation of Rights*. Boulder, Colo.: Westview, 1999.

———. *A Theory of Rights*. Totowa, N.J.: Rowman and Allenheld, 1985.

Wildman, Stephanie M., et al. *Privilege Revealed*. New York: New York University Press, 1996.

Wilkins, Burleigh. "Principles for the Law of Peoples." *The Journal of Ethics* 11 (2007): 161–75.

———. *Terrorism and Collective Responsibility*. London: Routledge, 1992.

Williams, Bernard. *In the Beginning Was the Deed*. Edited by Geoffrey Hawthorn. Princeton, N.J.: Princeton University Press, 2005.

Williams, Patricia J. *The Alchemy of Race and Rights*. Cambridge, Mass.: Harvard University Press, 1991.

Williams, Robert. "The Algebra of Federal Indian Law." In *Jurisprudence Classical and Contemporary*, 2nd ed., edited by Robert L. Hayman, Jr., Nancy Levit, and Richard Delgado, 638–44. St. Paul, Minn.: West Group, 2002.

Wilson, August. *Gem of the Ocean*. New York: Theatre Communications Group, 2006.

Wilson, John. "Why Forgiveness Requires Repentance." *Philosophy* 63 (1988): 534–45.

Wittgenstein, Ludwig. *Philosophical Investigations*. 2nd ed. New York: Harper Torch Books, 1960.

———. *Philosophical Investigations*. 3rd ed. Translated by G. E. M. Anscombe. New York: Macmillan, 1958.

Wood, Peter H., Gregory Waselkov, and M. Thomas Hatley, eds. *Powhatan's Mantle*. Lincoln: University of Nebraska Press, 1989.

Woodward, C. Vann. *The Strange Career of Jim Crow*. 2nd rev. ed. Oxford: Oxford University Press, 1966.

Woodward, Grace Steele. *The Cherokees*. Norman: University of Oklahoma Press, 1963.

Yamamoto, Eric. "Race Theory and Political Lawyering in Post–Civil Rights America." *Michigan Law Review* 95 (1997): 821–900.

Yandell, Keith E. "The Metaphysics and Morality of Forgiveness." In *Exploring Forgiveness*, edited by Robert D. Enright and Joanna North, 35–45. Madison: University of Wisconsin Press, 1998.

Zack, Naomi. "Lockean Money, Indigenism, and Globalism." *Canadian Journal of Philosophy*, Suppl. Vol. 25 (1999): 31–53.

———. *Thinking about Race*. Belmont, Calif.: Wadsworth, 2005.

Index

affirmative action, 6–7, 26, 30–31, 45, 62, 64, 76, 168, 176, 214, 228, 243, 256, 259, 263–64, 267–87; whitewashing of, 270–87

Alien and Sedition Acts, 21, 271

Alston, William P., 254–55

apology, xiv, 23, 32, 61, 68–71, 95, 110, 114, 177, 188–94, 196–212, 217, 226, 231, 233–34, 240–46, 291, 293, 296

Appiah, Anthony, 252

Aquinas, Thomas, 145

Arguedas, Alcides, 251

Aristotle, 22; Aristotelian view, 2, 195, 273

Arneson, Richard, 45

autonomy, xi, xiii, 20, 36, 41, 45, 55–56, 66–71, 74, 77, 110, 164, 212, 217, 220, 224, 232–33, 242, 258, 272, 296

Baker, Josephine, 281

Beitz, Charles, R., 46, 86

Bell, Derrick, xv, 236

Bittker, Boris L., xv, 213, 217–21

Boxill, Bernard R., xiv–xv, 11, 25, 27, 36, 40, 47–48, 55, 60, 72, 110, 113, 168, 170–72, 177, 178–83, 240, 269, 297

Bradford, William C., 141

Brooks, Roy L., 231–36, 240. *See also* reparations, arguments

Broome, John, 45

Buchanan, Allen E., 51–54

Card, Claudia, 74, 206

Civil Rights Act, 13, 164

civil rights legislation and reform, 22–23, 167, 173–74

Cohen, Felix, 131–32, 135

Cohen, G. A., 11, 38–39, 45

compensation. *See* justice

cosmopolitanism, xiii, 35–57, 59, 74–77, 85, 90, 110, 233

cosmopolitan liberalism. *See* cosmopolitanism

Crenshaw, Kimberlé, 275, 282, 285

Cudd, Ann, 3–8

Darrow, Clarence, 276, 282

Dawes Act, 275. *See also* oppression

Delgado, Richard, xv

Deloria, Vine, Jr., 131

desert, xiii, 25, 28, 63–65, 72, 92, 134, 156, 192, 194, 220, 227, 241, 274

DeWolf family, 178–79

Du Bois, W. E. B., 239, 241–42, 290

duty, 27–28, 37–38, 42, 46–49, 53, 55, 59, 61, 69, 79, 85, 89–90, 93, 95, 101–5, 107, 110, 113, 133–34, 154, 175, 180, 222, 239

Dworkin, Gerald, 36

Dworkin, Ronald, 11, 96, 176

egalitarianism, 11, 31, 39, 45, 48, 49, 55, 270

ethnic identity. *See* ethnicity
ethnicity, 21, 37, 94, 250–68; DNA analysis of, 219–20, 257–60, 264–66; family-historical model of, 260–62; family-resemblance model of, 260–62; genealogical conception of, 10–11, 30, 218–20, 251–68; social construction of, 30, 251, 254–67. *See also* race; Wittgenstein, Ludwig
Evers, Medger, 13
evil(s), xi–xii, xiv, 1–3, 5, 9, 12–17, 23, 46, 60, 62, 90, 92, 94, 113, 129, 131, 135, 137, 142, 144, 148, 153, 156, 159, 162, 168, 170, 173, 176–77, 179–80, 182–86, 188–90, 209–11, 222, 226, 228–30, 232, 234, 240, 246, 264, 267–68, 271, 273, 277, 279–82, 284, 290, 292–96; problem of, 2; unrectified, ix, 2–3, 9, 92, 138, 184, 186, 210–11, 250

Feinberg, Joel, xv, 12, 22–24, 29, 36, 48, 62, 67, 74, 84–86, 88, 93–94, 99, 105, 109, 118, 124, 157, 164, 170, 193, 199, 242, 244, 271, 294–95; Feinbergian, 10, 53, 85, 87, 89, 93, 96, 98–99, 106, 109
forgiveness, xiv, 23, 32, 60–61, 65, 67–71, 74, 78, 95, 110, 113–14, 187, 191, 193–204, 206–12, 224, 233–34, 240, 249, 291, 293, 296; as moral, virtue, duty or obligation, 60, 64–71, 74, 195; as a moral prerogative or right, 61, 190, 192–93, 196, 198–99, 205–6, 211–12; offender-centered, 202; reconciliation model of, xii, 65–71, 142, 188–89, 205; rectification model of, xii, 95, 110, 188, 190–91, 208; victim-centered, 196–97. *See also* forgiving
forgiving, xiv, 68, 71, 187, 189, 191, 193, 195–98, 200, 202–8, 211; action forgiving, 193–94; attitude forgiving, 193–94; third party, 207. *See also* forgiveness
Fugitive Slave Laws, 8, 15, 173–74, 176, 275, 280. *See also* oppression

Gates, Henry Louis, Jr., 259
genocide, ix, xi, xiv, 1–2, 11, 13–15, 21, 27, 30–31, 43, 46, 68–69, 90, 92, 94, 96, 103, 107–8, 131, 133, 141–42, 147, 149, 151, 162, 169, 184, 221–26, 230, 271, 275, 279–81
Geronimo, 149, 271
Gewirth, Alan, 89
Gilbert, Margaret, 127–28
Goldman, Alvin I., 122, 254–55
Gracia, Jorge J. E., xv, 252, 254, 256–65
Griswold, Charles, 188–89

Hampton, Jean, 197–99
Held, Virginia, 117–21
holocaust: American, x–xi, 14–15, 92, 133, 150–51, 156, 216, 221, 226, 267, 271, 274, 275; Jewish, 180, 183
hooks, bell. *See* Watkins, Gloria
Horsbrugh, H. J. N., 198

ICC. *See* International Criminal Court
imperialism, 15–16, 36, 40, 46–47, 49, 55, 84, 91–92, 142
Indian Appropriations Act of 1871, 275. *See also* land theft
Indian Boarding Schools, 15, 131, 141–42, 162, 280. *See also* oppression
integrationism, xi, 26, 31, 46, 50–51, 67, 69–70, 73–74, 142, 190, 227, 228, 232, 236, 241–42, 246, 258, 271–72, 296. *See also* reconciliation
International Criminal Court (ICC), 135, 213, 215, 225, 240, 293, 297

Jackson, Andrew, 63, 93, 131, 137, 143–44, 151, 240
Jefferson, Thomas, 21, 143, 178
Jim Crow, x–xi, xiv, 8, 10–11, 13, 30, 68–69, 92, 108, 163–64, 166–67, 171–73, 175, 179–85, 219, 229–34, 237–38, 240, 244, 264, 267, 271, 273–74, 280–82, 289, 295. *See also* segregation
Johnson, E. Pauline, 153
Joseph, Chief, 148–49, 271
justice: compensatory, 26, 59–60, 72–73, 84, 213–14, 217, 221, 223, 269, 288; criminal, x, xii, 13–14, 28–29, 97, 128,

133, 152, 190–92, 195, 197–99, 201–2, 204, 207–9, 243–45, 271; distributive, 3, 26, 37, 39, 44–46, 49–51, 55–56, 63, 75, 268, 276; global, xiii, 3, 35–48, 55–56, 75–77, 100–104, 108–11, 215, 296; rectificatory, xiii, 19, 67, 93, 103, 110, 151, 208, 291; reparative, xii–xiii, 12, 14, 22, 32, 43, 59–65, 69–74, 76–78, 108, 134, 137, 139, 161, 175, 185, 212, 222, 230, 241, 245–46; retributive, 63, 65–66, 73, 183. *See also* desert; punishment; rectification; reparations, arguments; responsibility; retributivism; rights

Kant, Immanuel, xiii, 12, 27, 65, 192, 207; Kantian, xii, 192
King, Martin Luther, Jr., 13, 281
Korsgaard, Christine M., 157
Kymlicka, Will, 134

labor value theft, 15, 163–72, 179, 184, 228, 230, 238, 250, 283, 289. *See also* oppression
Laches doctrine, 63, 158. *See also* land theft
LaDuke, Winona, 187
land theft, ix, xi, xiv, 9–10, 14–16, 19, 27, 31, 46, 60, 94, 108, 132, 141, 149–52, 157, 162–64, 179, 221–22, 224, 230, 240, 275, 279–81. *See also* Dawes Act; Indian Appropriations Act of 1871; *Laches* doctrine; principle of morally just acquisitions and transfers
Latino/a identity, 251–70, 277–78
Law of Peoples, 35, 51–54, 88, 100, 102–3, 214. *See also* Rawls, John
Lerner, Gerda, 278, 283–85
liability. *See* duty; responsibility; responsibility, collective
Lincoln, Abraham, 44, 147, 167, 289
Locke, John, 139, 153, 155–59, 181–83. *See also* Lockean Proviso
Lockean Proviso, 139, 158–59, 250. *See also* Locke, John
Lyon, Matthew, 21, 272. *See also* Alien and Sedition Acts

Lyons, David, 28, 134, 157, 174
Lyons, Chief Oren, 187

Mabbott, J. D., 207
Malcolm X, 13, 164, 235–36, 268
Mandela, Nelson, 187
manifest destiny, 15, 44, 133, 141, 145, 150, 162, 221, 223
Mann Act, 275, 282. *See also* oppression
Marable, Manning, xv
Martí, José, 251
Marx, Karl, 39; Marxism, 38–39, 136, 166
Matsuda, Mari, xv
McCloskey, H. J., 77
McGary, Howard, v, xiv–xv, 11, 23, 27, 31–32, 63, 68, 72, 110, 114, 120, 138, 168–70, 174–75, 209–11, 240–42, 265, 297
mercy. *See* forgiveness
Mill, John Stuart, 36
Miller, David, 45, 48, 113
Murphy, Jeffrie G., 193, 196, 206–8

Nickel, James W., 98, 99–100, 104–11
nongovernmental organizations (NGOs), xiii–xiv, 9, 37, 76, 85, 94, 107, 165–66, 184, 216
Nozick, Robert, 61, 199. *See also* rights

Ogletree, Charles J., Jr., xv, 24, 201
oppression, ix–xiii, xv, 3–10, 14–17, 23–24, 29–31, 43, 55, 61–64, 66–72, 75–78, 90, 92, 108, 114–16, 119, 128, 131, 181–85, 187, 189, 199, 210–12, 220, 222, 230–35, 236, 240–42, 245–51, 273–88, 290; of Africans (blacks), x, 5–6, 10, 12, 77, 129, 162–86, 190, 209, 211, 213–16, 219, 230, 237, 239, 242–44, 246, 249–50, 270, 272, 279–84, 289–90, 296; of American Indians (Indians), x, 5–6, 10, 12, 77, 129, 134, 138–52, 159, 177, 180, 190, 203, 209, 211, 213–17, 219, 242, 244, 246, 249–50, 270, 272, 283–84, 290, 296; socio/psychological dimension of, 8, 65, 166, 193, 230, 236, 240–46, 280, 284, 291. *See also* evil; Fugitive Slave Laws; Indian Boarding Schools; Mann

Act; oppressor heirs; *Plessy vs. Ferguson*;
Slave Powers Act; victim heirs
oppressor heirs, xiii, 9, 134, 172, 177,
179, 187, 203, 209, 227, 233
oppressors. *See* oppression; oppressor
heirs

paternalism, xii–xiii, 36, 46, 50–51, 54,
56, 74, 76, 242, 290, 296
Plessy vs. Ferguson, 275. *See also* oppression
Pogge, Thomas, 37, 43–44, 46–48
poverty, 7, 11, 26, 37–38, 40–45, 48, 50,
55–56, 72–73, 90, 101, 104, 108–9,
149–50, 224, 226, 238
principle of morally just acquisitions and
transfers, 10, 27–28, 61, 133, 136,
144, 152, 156–60, 165, 171, 179, 184,
250, 294. *See also* land theft; oppression; rights
principles of proportionality, 23, 25–26,
28–29, 31, 43, 51, 63–64, 78, 86, 92,
119, 133, 159, 162, 180, 185, 192,
214, 219, 222, 233–34, 236, 268, 269,
274, 279. *See also* rectification
punishment, x, xiii, 13, 19–21, 23, 25–
26, 64, 67, 86, 92, 97, 119, 150, 180,
191–94, 205, 207–11, 214, 242–46,
271, 282; utilitarian model of, 26,
199, 208. *See also* cosmopolitanism;
justice; reparations, arguments;
responsibility; retributivism; utilitarianism

race, 21, 35, 49, 72, 77, 153, 241, 273,
275, 278, 287; classical or primitive
race theories, 253, 255–56, 266–77;
social constructivist accounts of, 30,
251, 282–83. *See also* ethnicity
racism, 12–14, 30, 77, 115, 144, 155,
163, 166, 171, 180, 184–85, 232–33,
238, 251–53, 259, 264, 266, 273–74,
276, 278, 280, 283–84
Rawls, John, xv, 1, 35–37, 41, 44–46, 50–
57, 75, 79, 81, 89, 90–92, 99, 100–
104, 108, 111, 171, 183, 214, 242,
282, 296; Rawlsian, 36, 75, 88, 90, 93,

94, 96, 104, 111, 134, 276. *See also*
Law of Peoples; Society of Peoples
Raz, Joseph, 176
reconciliation, xii–xiv, 23, 25, 31–32, 51,
57, 59–79, 94–95, 110, 113–14, 142,
183, 187–212, 217, 227, 231–34,
240–41, 243, 249, 291–93, 296. *See
also* integrationism
rectification, ix–x, xii, xiv, 9, 11, 20, 23,
32, 63, 71, 92, 95–96, 103, 107, 110,
134, 151, 183–84, 188–90, 201–3,
217, 219, 226, 239, 246, 291. *See also*
justice; principles of proportionality;
reparations, arguments; rights
Red Cloud, 271
reparations, arguments: atonement
model of, 231–34, 240; compensatory
model of, xiii–xiv, 1, 6–7, 9–11, 17,
19–32, 59–64, 66–67, 70–79, 220,
226, 231–33, 236, 239, 256, 268, 271,
288, 291–93, 296; rights-based theories of, 10–11, 25–26, 32, 61, 64, 66,
78–79, 81, 90, 184, 242–43, 296–97;
utilitarian theories of, 26, 33, 61–62,
111, 212, 233, 242, 271. *See also* cosmopolitanism; justice; rectification;
responsibility; rights; utilitarianism
reparations for blacks, policies of: black
reparations and collective moral
responsibility, 168–86; black reparations tax, 227–39
reparations for Indians, policies of:
Indian reparations tax, 221–27
reparations to blacks, objections to/from:
historical reparations objection to
black reparations, 166–68
reparations to blacks and Indians, objections to/from: affirmative action
objection, 268–70; decreasing value of
the transferability of entitlements
objection, 249–50; indeterminacy of
ethnicity objection, 250–51; objection
from immigration, 288; objection
from nonresponsibility, 290–91;
objection that reparations are confrontational, 291–92; objection that the
U.S. Civil War has already paid the

"blood sacrifice" for slavery, 289–90. *See also* affirmative action; ethnicity

reparations to Indians, objections to/from: acquired rights trumping original land rights objection, 156–60; historical reparations objection, 155–66; no Indian concept of moral rights objection, 153–55; objection from historical complexity, 135–57; objection to collective responsibility, 137–52. *See also* responsibility, collective

responsibility, xv, 5–10, 13–14, 25, 27, 42–45, 48, 55–56, 62, 64–65, 69, 72, 86, 92, 156–57, 188, 192–93, 198–99, 201, 205, 274. *See also* desert; duty; justice; reparations, arguments; responsibility, collective; retributivism

responsibility, collective, ix, 9–10, 15, 29, 41, 60, 63, 72, 113–29, 134–35, 157–59, 168–86, 210, 217, 219, 224–25, 245, 276, 294–95; nonsummativist model of, 114; summativist model of, 114. *See also* DeWolf Family; reparations to Indians, objections to/from

restitution. *See* reparations, arguments; justice

retributivism, 64, 71, 78, 134, 151, 182, 190–93, 208–9, 242, 245. *See also* desert; justice; punishment; reparations, arguments; responsibility, collective

rights: compensatory, xiii–iv, 20, 24, 26–27, 41, 43–45, 50–51, 56–57, 62, 67, 71, 73–77, 89–90, 93, 95, 101–4, 107, 109, 111, 183–84, 211, 232–33, 243, 246, 271–72, 276–78, 288; entitlement-based theory of, 61, 77, 136, 153–54, 249–50; human, x–xi, xiv, 24, 46–49, 51, 53–54, 56–57, 77, 81, 83–111, 144, 168; moral, xi, xiv, 15, 20, 23, 27, 47, 66–67, 76–77, 81, 133–36, 144, 152–60, 162, 168, 171–77, 181, 183–84, 203, 239, 243–44, 250, 271, 276, 290–91; obligation-based approach, 41, 47, 60–61, 75, 85; rights-based approach, 10, 25–26, 32, 66, 78, 90, 268–70; violations of, x, xiv, 26–27, 60–61, 88, 110, 134–35,

156, 162, 165, 168, 173, 177, 184, 223, 225, 228, 246, 272. *See also* genocide; justice; oppression; principle of morally just acquisitions and transfers; slavery

Roemer, John, 45

Santayana, George, 23, 227, 236

Scheffler, Samuel, 37, 45, 56

segregation, 166, 173, 175, 184–85, 227, 230, 236. *See also* Jim Crow

Sen, Amartya, 45

Sher, George G., 159, 249–50

Simmons, A. John, 27

Singer, Peter, 45

Sitting Bull, 148, 154, 271

Slave Powers Act, 275. *See also* oppression

slavery, ix–xi, xiv, 8–15, 19, 27, 30–31, 43–46, 55, 60, 62, 67–69, 92, 94, 96–97, 103, 105–9, 113, 131, 139–40, 146, 148–50, 162–86, 215–19, 223–24, 228, 230–38, 240, 244, 249–52, 265, 267–68, 274–75, 279–80, 288–90, 296. *See also* oppression

social utility. *See* utilitarianism

Society of Peoples, 52, 56, 88, 96, 100, 102, 111. *See also* Rawls, John

Socrates, 19, 33

sovereignty, x–xi, xiii, xv, 22, 31, 45, 56, 68–69, 71, 74, 83, 110, 136, 142, 150, 154, 165, 212, 217, 220, 224, 227, 233, 242, 258, 272, 296. *See also* rights

Sterba, James P., xv, 75–76

Strawson, Peter, 193, 242

Temkin, Larry, 11, 37, 41, 45–46, 49

terrorism, xii, 96, 174, 184, 186, 271, 281, 282

Thalberg, I., 204

Thompson, Janna, 59–63, 78, 211, 233

Truth, Sojouner, 13, 271

Tully, James, 155

Unger, Peter, 46

utilitarianism, xii–xiii, 11, 12, 25–26, 31–32, 62, 89, 107, 142, 145, 183, 199, 208, 212, 231, 291, 296

victim heirs, xii, 9, 177, 179, 203, 209,
    217, 219–20, 291, 293, 296
von Hirsch, Andrew, 77

Waldron, Jeremy, 23, 157
Walker, Margaret Urban, 64–75, 78, 211,
    233, 240, 273
Washington, George, 132, 140, 240

Wasserstrom, Richard, 85
Watkins, Gloria (bell hooks), 278,
    284–85
Wilkins, Burleigh T., xv, 115, 118–19
Williams, Bernard, 46
Williams, Patricia, xv, 24, 281
Wittgenstein, Ludwig, 261; Wittgenstei-
    nian, 260–62, 264. *See also* ethnicity

About the Author

J. Angelo Corlett is professor of philosophy and ethics at San Diego State University.